Sybex's Quick Tour of Windows 95

P9-AOV-471

Minimize Maximize Close

Start button Documents A folder Taskbar Shortcuts Speaker volume Time & date

The Desktop *is where your programs, files, and shortcuts reside.*

My Computer *allows you to browse the contents of your computer, open folders, open documents, and run programs.*

Network Neighborhood *gives you direct access to other computers (and shared resources, such as printers).*

The Microsoft Network *dials up your connection to Microsoft's online service.*

The Internet *starts up the Internet Explorer, a World Wide Web browser (available only with Plus!).*

Inbox *starts Microsoft Exchange and opens your inbox, so you can see if you have any new mail.*

My Briefcase *is a new feature for keeping documents consistent as you move them between computers.*

Recycle Bin *makes it easy to delete and undelete files.*

The Start button *pops up the Start menu, from which you can run just about every program.*

The Taskbar *displays a button for every running program.*

Create **shortcuts** *on your Desktop for frequently used programs and documents.*

Every window has a **Minimize**, **Maximize** *(alternating with Restore), and* **Close** *button. The Close button is new; the others just look different.*

One of the best new features of Windows 95 is shortcuts. Each shortcut you create takes up only a small amount of disk space, but can save you time and energy by opening a program or document that you'd otherwise have to hunt around for. You can recognize a shortcut by the little doubling-back arrow in the bottom-left corner of its icon.

Putting a Shortcut on the Desktop

There are many ways to do this. If you have a document or program already visible on the screen and want to create a shortcut to it on the desktop, right-click on the icon, drag it onto the Desktop, and then choose Create Shortcut(s) Here. You can also start from the Desktop when the "target" of your shortcut-to-be is not readily available.

Right-click on the Desktop, select New, and then Shortcut.

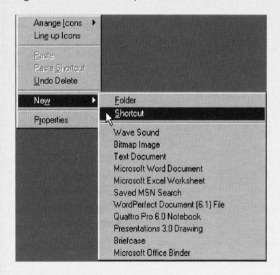

This brings up the Create Shortcut wizard. If you don't know the command line for the program you want, click the Browse button. This brings up an Open-style dialog box; work your way through various folders until you find the program you want to make a shortcut to. Then click the Open button, click Next (or type a different name for the shortcut and click Next), and click Finish when you're done. Voila! Your shortcut appears on the Desktop.

Making a Keyboard Shortcut

Once you've created a shortcut icon, you can also set up a keyboard shortcut to launch the program (or open the document) automatically.

Right-click the shortcut icon and choose Properties. Click the Shortcut tab in the Properties dialog box, click inside the Shortcut Key box, and then press the keyboard shortcut you want. It will appear in the box as you press it.

Shows the default folder for the program

Controls how the program's window appears when you first run it (other choices are Minimized and Maximized)

Mastering Word
for Windows 95

Mastering Word for Windows® 95

Third Edition

Ron Mansfield

SYBEX

San Francisco • Paris • Düsseldorf • Soest

Acquisitions Manager: Kristine Plachy
Developmental Editor: James Sumser
Editor: James A. Compton
Technical Editor: Elizabeth Shannon
Book Design: Helen Bruno; adapted by London Road Design
Desktop Publisher: Dina F Quan
Proofreader/Production Assistant: Ron Jost
Indexer: Matthew Spence
Cover Designer: DesignSite
Cover Photographer: Mark Johann

Screen reproductions produced with Collage Plus.

Collage Plus is a trademark of Inner Media Inc.

SYBEX is a registered trademark of SYBEX Inc.

TRADEMARKS: SYBEX has attempted throughout this book to distinguish proprietary trademarks from descriptive terms by following the capitalization style used by the manufacturer.

Every effort has been made to supply complete and accurate information. However, SYBEX assumes no responsibility for its use, nor for any infringement of the intellectual property rights of third parties which would result from such use.

First edition copyright ©1994 SYBEX Inc.

Second edition copyright ©1995 SYBEX Inc.

Library of Congress Card Number: 95-70850
ISBN: 0-7821-1767-8

Manufactured in the United States of America
10 9 8 7 6 5 4 3 2 1

To both of my wonderful sons, Adam and Scott

Acknowledgments

You are holding a miracle of cooperation and the product of one of the hardest-working book crews on earth. Hats off to the *entire* Sybex crew. You put this on the shelves in record time!

Jim Compton deserves a special attaperson for efforts above and beyond any editor's job description. Elizabeth "the Whirlwind" Shannon did an outstanding job of technical editing with incredible speed and accuracy.

I'd also like to thank author/editor/juggler David Krassner for his heroic efforts while preparing this edition.

Contents at a Glance

Contents

Introduction

Word for Windows 95 (also called Word 95) is a significant upgrade to an already full-featured program. More and better templates have been added, along with features such as automatic symbol replacement and on-the-fly spell checking. Some of the most significant changes to Word 95 are the changes to Windows 95. These allow for long file names and easier document retrieval and management. Be sure you have some sense of the new features of Windows 95 to take full advantage of Word 95's power and flexibility.

Whether you are a seasoned Word user or a first-timer, this book is for you. If you're already familiar with Word's functionality, you'll find plenty of tips to help you streamline your work. We've highlighted features new to Word 95 so you can quickly find the information you need to see what has changed and how. New Word users will appreciate the many tutorials, each carefully designed to illustrate a particular feature or skill in Word. In addition, there are tips to turn you into a competent Word wonk quickly and warnings to keep you from making "rookie" mistakes.

Any product with so many features can be a little intimidating at first. But mastering Word is a bit like playing chess or the piano—you can spend the rest of your life learning new tricks and techniques every day.

What You Need for the Practice Exercises

If you haven't already installed Word for Windows 95, see Appendix A of this book.

This book assumes that you have used Windows at least briefly and that you know how to click, drag, select text, and make menu choices. The first part of the book *reviews* these concepts, but you might want to keep your Windows manuals within reach if you are just getting started—or see the *Quick Tour of Windows 95* in the front of this book.

If you want to practice saving work to floppies, find a spare diskette before you settle down to work. Let's do it!

Where to Go from Here

The book's organization is fairly straightforward, except for a detour to Appendix A if you need to install Microsoft Word. Here's an overview of each section.

Part One: Up and Running

Part One helps you dive right in. Sit at a computer when you read it. You'll soon be creating, saving, and printing impressive documents, beginner or not. Word offers a number of different ways to view and move through your documents. Part One will introduce you to these time-saving techniques. Chapter 1 gives a comprehensive overview of all the new features in Word for Windows 95; you may wish to use Chapter 1 as a jumping-off point to other sections of the book for topics that interest you.

Part One also covers Word's graphics features, both new and old. You'll learn to create, import, position, and size graphic elements. The process of flowing text around graphics is illustrated. We'll also try to make some sense out of the growing collection of graphics and font standards (TIFF, PICT, EPS, TrueType, etc.) and show how they relate to Word for Windows 95.

You'll explore printing issues and see how your choice of printers and printing options affects the final look of your documents.

Word for Windows 95's robust Find File command and Properties features are also demonstrated in Part One. You'll see how they work together to help you organize your hard disk and find misplaced files.

Part Two: Formatting Fundamentals

Part Two shows you how to look great in print. It is organized to help you quickly find illustrated answers to specific questions. You'll learn the fundamentals of formatting characters, lines, paragraphs, and sections. Tabs, tables, styles, style sheets, headers, footers, hyphenation, and page numbering are also covered here. Those of you who need to create footnotes will find out how in Part Two.

There are numerous step-by-step "recipes" for getting the results you desire. You'll also see plenty of illustrations of the techniques at work.

Part Three: Time Savers

As you might expect, Part Three is filled with tips and techniques. Here you will learn how Word makes envelope and label printing a snap, and you'll learn to find and replace text or styles. Word for Windows 95 offers an incredible variety of templates and Wizards. You'll see how to use them to create:

Agendas

Awards

Brochures

Calendars

Directories

Faxes

Invoices

Letters

Manuals

Memos

Newsletters

Pleadings

Press Releases

Purchase Orders

Reports

Resumes

Tables

Theses

Weekly Time Sheets

We'll also demystify Word's AutoText features and show how to create templates for repetitive tasks. Then you'll learn how to improve your documents' contents with Word's built-in thesaurus and its Spelling and Grammar checkers. If you write or work on long, complex documents, be sure to read about Word's outlining features in Part Three, as well.

Part Four: Desktop Publishing

Because some desktop publishing projects can be quite complex, you'll see how to work with Word's Master Documents feature. Word's table-of-contents and indexing features are explored here as well. If you and others collaborate on big jobs, Part Four will show you how to give documents a uniform look and feel, even when they have multiple authors.

There's a chapter on how to print documents on specialty paper stock, and then there's the Document Shop, which provides step-by-step instructions on how to prepare all kinds of useful documents.

Part Five: Power Tools

Finally, Part Five deals with topics of interest to advanced users of Word. Few other programs offer as much opportunity for customization. Word lets you rearrange menus and toolbars, change default settings, modify dictionaries and grammar rules, and much, much more.

Part Five also contains chapters describing Word's text- and voice-annotation features, and the print-merge feature for personalized mailings and similar documents. In Chapter 28 you'll actually set up a simple, personalized mailing project and create some mailing labels, envelopes, and postcards.

Chapter 29 presents Microsoft Graph, which can be used to create charts in a variety of formats from data in your Word documents.

And don't miss Chapter 30. It details ways to use Object Linking and Embedding (OLE) to automatically update documents when things change elsewhere.

If your computer is on a network with others, read about Word's e-mail and other network tools in Chapter 31.

Chapters 32, 33, and 34 are packed with information about field codes, forms, and macros (including some helpful WordBasic advice).

Chapter 35 covers the ins and outs of exchanging documents between Word and other programs; and Chapter 36 shows how you can customize Word to meet your particular needs.

Appendices

To top it all off, the appendices function as a handy reference section. You'll find installation instructions, a list of keyboard shortcuts to Word commands, complete field code and switch information, and an alphabetical glossary of Word's menu commands.

Book Conventions

We've used some standard conventions and typographer's tricks to make the book easier to read. While most of them will be obvious, scan the next few paragraphs just in case.

About the Examples and Exercises

The book contains a number of exercises and lists of steps that you may want to try as you read along. Whenever you need to hold down one key and then press another, you'll see the keys separated by a plus sign. For instance, *Ctrl+S* tells you to hold down the Ctrl key while pressing the S key. Boldface text indicates things you are expected to type. Also, some keys (such as the arrow keys and the Enter key) are indicated by icons. The icon for the Enter key is ↵. So, if you are being asked to type Mark Twain's name and then press the Enter key in an exercise, you'll read something like "Type **Mark Twain** and press ↵."

Menu Commands

As a shortcut and an eye-catcher, we've used a special convention to indicate menu commands. When we want you to choose a menu command, it will follow this pattern: *menu name* ➤ *command*. Also, to help you out, we have underlined the *hot key* for the menu and the command. Pressing the hot key letter is the same as choosing the command. For example, if we want to choose the Save command from the File menu, we will say "Choose <u>F</u>ile ➤ <u>S</u>ave." In this case, if you were to hit the Alt key to highlight the menu bar, and then press the *F* and *S* keys, it would be the same as choosing the command from the menu with the mouse.

Tips, Warnings, Notes, and New

Throughout the book you'll find notes, tips, warnings, and discussions of new features. They are marked so they're easy to spot.

 Because there is so much neat new stuff in Word 95 that we don't want you to miss, we've added this "New" icon in the margin to help experienced Word users spot differences. If you are a longtime Word user, it might be a good idea to skim each chapter looking for these easy-to-spot items.

Fast Tracks

Fast Tracks summarize the important steps, keystrokes, and menu commands for major Word features. You'll find them at the beginning of each chapter. Think of them as bite-sized how-to instructions that can often save you a trip through the entire chapter.

Up and
Running

Chapter 1

What's New in Word for Windows 95

Word for Windows 95 is a significant upgrade to the Word software. There are fewer changes than there were from Word 2 to Word 6, so if you're dreading the upgrade because you had a bad experience last time, you're in for a pleasant surprise. All of the changes improve upon the already slick interface and functionality of Word for Windows, and some of the new features are so terrific, they might just be best-of-breed for this year's crop of new Windows word processors.

NEW   By the way… see that icon in the margin? You'll see it throughout the book. That's your signal that what's being discussed in the paragraph next to it is *new* to Word for Windows 95.

AnswerWizard

Have you ever been working on a document and gotten stuck because you didn't know how to do what you wanted to do? Wouldn't it have been nice if you could have asked your *computer* (which is supposedly so clever) to tell you what to do? Well, AnswerWizard has the answers to all your problems. This feature allows you to ask questions in *real English,* that's right, real everyday you-'n'-me-speak. Wanna know how to delete a bookmark? You just type "How do I delete a bookmark?" and, *whizbang!* the topic appears for you to peruse, as shown in Figure 1.1. See Chapter 16 for more info.

TipWizard

TipWizard is Big Brother and Donna Reed rolled into one. It watches *every* move you make and then sweetly suggests how you could perform your tasks more efficiently, as illustrated in Figure 1.2. TipWizard can be positively scary at times in its omniscience, but it will be a boon to new Word users and veterans alike. Just keep repeating to yourself "I really am smarter than this computer…" You can also click on the Show Me button to see how changes will look. See Chapter 16 for more details.

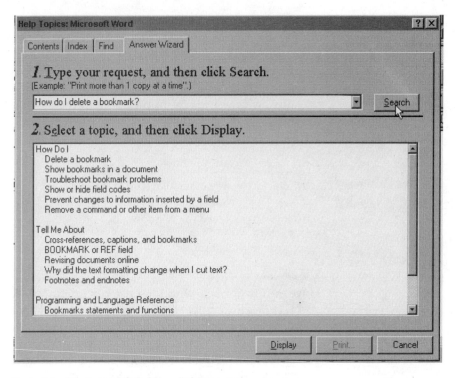

Figure 1.1   **The AnswerWizard has all the answers!**

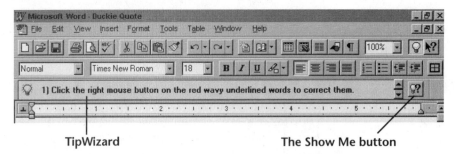

TipWizard   **The Show Me button**

Figure 1.2   *TipWizard knows all.... In your first hour of using Word for Windows 95, you'll probably learn more shortcuts and tricks than you learned in the last year.*

IntelliSense

Microsoft is trying to make software kinder and gentler for all of us; one way they're doing this is via IntelliSense, a catch-all term for many new features in Word and in Windows. These features are endowed with a form of artificial intelligence known as fuzzy logic; that is, they can *learn* from you how you like to work. For instance, if Word corrects what it perceives to be a spelling mistake and you change the "mistake" back to what you had originally, Word will not make the same change again. Pretty slick, eh? This means that, with all the power and automation the program boasts, you never have to worry about Word taking over your life. This feature is discussed in Chapter 17.

More and Better Word Templates

Microsoft has expanded upon the number of "canned" documents that come with Word. The number of different *kinds* of documents is almost as amazing as the number of different *styles* of each kind of document! Check out Figure 1.3. You'll find everything from resumes to memos to

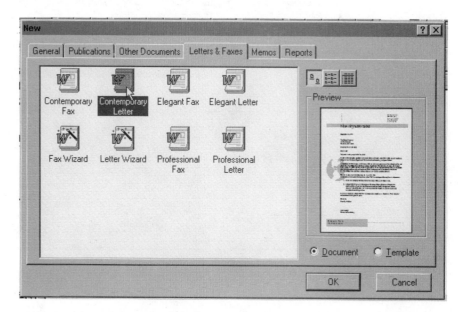

Figure 1.3 Word offers you many kinds of letters and faxes, and it will even guide you through the steps of creating one with its Wizards.

invoices to letters to, no kidding, a *thesis* format. Seldom are you limited to just one style for your document. You can choose between professional, contemporary, or elegant, at the very least. Look in Chapter 16 for the skinny on this feature.

The Improved Edit ➤ Find Command

One very handy new feature of Word for Windows 95 is its ability to search for different forms of words. Before, if you wanted to change all occurrences of a word, you had to search for it in each different form in which it appeared. For example, you might have wanted to change *talk* to *chat*. Unfortunately, that meant you had to also search and replace *talked* with *chatted*, *talks* with *chats*, *talking* with *chatting*, and so on. Now, you can just search for *talk* and replace all forms of it with the correct forms of *chat*. Figure 1.4 shows this option selected in the Replace dialog box. The power of this feature is brought home most convincingly when you use it. See Chapter 20.

Figure 1.4   You can now search for forms of words, greatly simplifying replace operations.

Finding Files with the Improved Open Command

The old File ➤ Find File command has now been incorporated into the File ➤ Open command, which makes more sense anyway. This command has some really useful features and it is *very* fast. For example, you can find files by particular phrases or text strings, designate files as "favorites," and even preview documents without opening them. For more on this feature, turn to Chapter 7.

Superior Document Tracking with the Properties Command

The old Summary Info dialog box has been replaced by the Properties dialog box (choose File ➤ Properties), shown in Figure 1.5. Here you'll find an extraordinary amount of information about your documents, including the stuff that used to be in the Summary Info dialog box, along with statistics and contents. See Chapter 7 for more info.

New E-Mail Features

You can now do your e-mailing in Word with WordMail. This works with Microsoft Exchange (from the Windows 95 package) to make e-mail a snap. What's more, your messages will look more like documents, because you have all of Word's features at your fingertips, as shown in Figure 1.6. See Chapter 31 for more details.

Automatic Borders

This is a really cool new feature. You can easily create borders with a few simple keystrokes. Just type three consecutive hyphens and press Enter, and Word automatically runs a border across the page! If you type equal signs instead, you get a double border, as shown in Figure 1.7. This feature is discussed in Chapter 10.

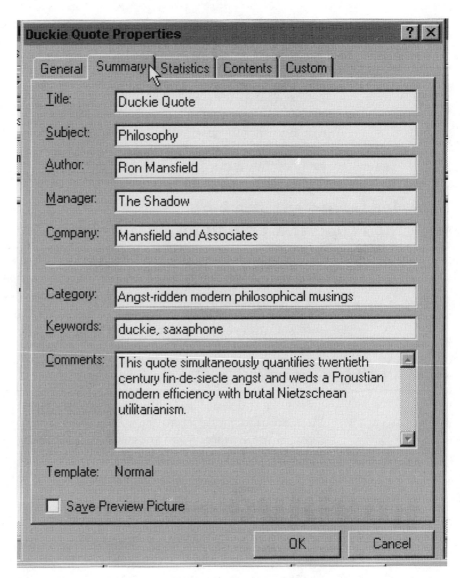

Figure 1.5   The File ➤ Properties dialog box gives you an abundance of information about your documents.

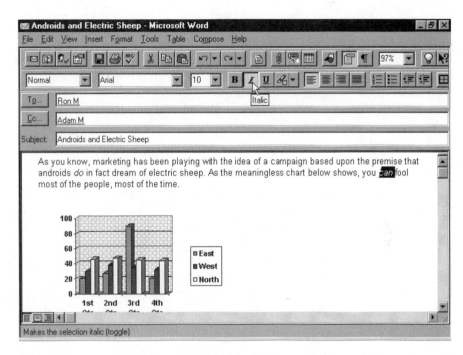

Figure 1.6   Use Word's new WordMail feature to make great looking and informative e-mail messages.

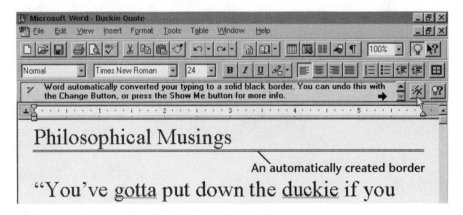

Figure 1.7   Word creates borders like this one automatically.

Improved Automatic Correction

Word 6 introduced a terrific automated feature that corrected misspellings and typos as you worked. It could even replace simple abbreviations with long or complicated words, thus saving you time. Word for Windows 95 takes the automation one step further with CAPS LOCK and plural or possessive autocorrection.

CAPS LOCK ERRORS...Oops! I Mean Errors

How many times have you typed a word or sentence only to realize that you had accidentally hit CAPS LOCK before you began typing? It's a nuisance to correct, even with Word's Format ➤ Change Case... command. Now, Word automatically corrects such errors, lowercasing all but the first letter of uppercased words, as shown in Figure 1.8. Again, though, you only have to change a correction back once for Word to get the message; it will not make the same change again after you have overridden it. Look in Chapter 17 for the lowdown on this feature.

"YOu've gotta put down the duckie if you wanna play the saxaphone..."

—Ernie, 1992

"You've gotta put down the duckie if you wanna play the saxaphone..."

—Ernie, 1992

Figure 1.8   **The top image shows how the text was typed. The bottom image shows how Word corrected the error, all by itself!**

Up and Running

Plural and Possessive Corrections

Like the CAPS LOCK corrector, the plural and possessive feature is fully automated. You can insert AutoCorrect entries with plurals or possessives and Word will automatically amend the entry to its proper plural or possessive form, as shown in Figure 1.9. This is really handy, because it means you don't have to have multiple entries. See Chapter 17 for more details.

so I turned to Dr. BF, not knowing how he or the swarthy gentleman from Kuala Lumpur would react to the disappearance of the solid tungsten bidet, failing to notice BF's eyes narrowing in anger. Suddenly, the mysterious gypsy seized BF by the wrist and pointed to the glowing walrus shouting in broken Swahili that the battle of Waterloo was won on the playing fields of Eton. I didn't wait to hear more, but crashed headlong through the window of the tiny Himalayan hut where we'd been bivouacked for more than three

so I turned to Dr. Blumenfeldt, not knowing how he or the swarthy gentleman from Kuala Lumpur would react to the disappearance of the solid tungsten bidet, failing to notice Blumenfeldt's eyes narrowing in anger. Suddenly, the mysterious gypsy seized Blumenfeldt by the wrist and pointed to the glowing walrus shouting in broken Swahili that the battle of Waterloo was won on the playing fields of Eton. I didn't wait to hear more, but crashed headlong through the window of the tiny Himalayan hut where

Figure 1.9   The top image shows how the text was typed. In AutoCorrect, I specified BF as the Replace entry and Blumenfeldt as the With entry. The bottom image shows how Word corrected the typing, replacing the possessive as well as the ordinary form of the entry.

Automatic Updating of the Exception List

Automation can be great—or awful. Many of Word's AutoCorrect features are real time-savers, because they free you from the mundane task of checking through your documents for mistakes the spellchecker might not catch. However, this AutoCorrect has a potential downside. Imagine that you often refer to something with an odd capitalization scheme (such as *GEnie*); it would be a nightmare if Word "helpfully" corrected it each time. Fortunately, AutoCorrect is smart enough to know when it shouldn't push you. Once you've reversed one of Word's decisions, it will not make the same change again. See Chapter 17 for more info.

Automatic Headings

This very nice new feature can make reports a snap. Simply type the text you want in your main head and hit the Enter key twice. Word will automatically make the line a first-level head! See Figure 1.10. If you hit the Tab key before typing the next lines of text, these will become subheads. Pretty slick, eh? As with all of Word's automated helpers, automatic headings can be turned on and off. This feature is discussed in Chapter 14.

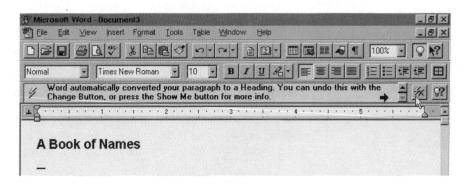

Figure 1.10 **Word changed this ordinary text into a head—automatically!**

Automatic Numbered and Bulleted Lists

You can now make numbered and bulleted lists automatically. All you have to do is start your list with a number or asterisk. Word then adds the succeeding numbers or more bullets for each item in the list. This is remarkable to see in action and it works more or less invisibly, as shown in Figure 1.11. Like all of Word's automated helpers, automatic lists can be turned on and off. For more on this feature, turn to Chapter 9.

Figure 1.11 *By typing an asterisk before the word* **Humorous**, *I told Word to create a bulleted list.*

Automatic Numbering

Somewhat different from automatic numbered lists are Word's two new features for automatic ordinals and fractions.

Ordinals

The automatic ordinals feature is one that you'll wonder how you ever lived without, even if you've never before wanted to do what it does! Most of us like to make our documents look as spiffy and professional as possible (read, *typeset*). Well, you'd never see the following in a typeset book: *1st*. You'd always see it written as 1st. Word now does this lovely little bit of typesetting without your having to lift a finger or mess around with superscripting. It's these little details that can make a document seem "professional" to prospective clients, your boss, or whomever you are trying to impress, as illustrated in Figure 1.12. See Chapter 17 for more info.

Some scholars believe that the oeuvre normally attributed to Shakespeare might actually have been written by the 20th Earl of Oxford. In a recent

Figure 1.12 *Details like the* **20th** *shown here can really make a document look professional.*

Fractions

The automatic fractions feature is one that you probably *have* thought about before and wished there were an easy way. It always looks so cheesy to have 1/2 in the middle of nicely typeset text. Doesn't it look bad here? Word now automatically turns such unsightly and unprofessional fractions into genuine typeset fractions: $\frac{1}{2}$. Isn't that nicer? See Figure 1.13 if you're not convinced. This feature is discussed in Chapter 17.

> Sales of 1996½ floppy disks are up 23% over last year's projections. The 3½-inch disk, normally a slow starter, has surprised even optimists in its

Figure 1.13   **The ½ shown here looks very nice. It was done automatically, too.**

Automatic Symbol Replacement

For all those times you've had to browse through those impossibly small icons or endless lists in the Symbol dialog box, Word finally comes to the rescue. A number of commonly used symbols will now appear automatically when you press certain simple key combinations. For example, the equal sign and the greater-than symbol turn into an arrow ($\rightarrow$). And that indispensable symbol for e-mail users, the happy face (☺), shown in Figure 1.14, is created with the colon and the closing parenthesis. For more on this feature, turn to Chapter 9.

> So I guess I'll see you in Rochester over the summer. Take care! ☺

Figure 1.14   **This happy face was brought to you courtesy of Word, automatically.**

Help Is At the Corner

Reasoning that most people want help NOW!!!, Microsoft has added a nice option to every dialog box in Word called ScreenTips. To access ScreenTips, you simply click on the icon in the top-right corner, as shown in Figure 1.15, and then click on the dialog box item you wish to know more about. Word will display a brief explanation for you to read

Figure 1.15 *Just click on the ScreenTips icon and click on any dialog box item you wish to know more about.*

before continuing with your work. It's a great way to get help on the fly. Look in Chapter 2 for details on this feature.

On-the-Fly Spellchecking

Another of Word's slick new automatic features is on-the-fly spellchecking. As Word comes across words that it believes to be misspelled (i.e., that are not in the dictionary), it calls your attention to them with a squiggly red line, as shown in Figure 1.16. To correct the misspelling, all you have to do is point to the word and click the right mouse button. A pop-up menu will appear, offering you several choices, including the option to go to the regular spellcheck dialog box. See Chapter 19 for more information about spellchecking.

Highlighting and Addresses Right from the Toolbar

When you really want to draw attention to text on screen, you'll appreciate Word's new highlighter. Simply select the text you want highlighted, and click the highlighter button on the Formatting toolbar, as shown in Figure 1.17. (Chapter 17 has more about highlighting.)

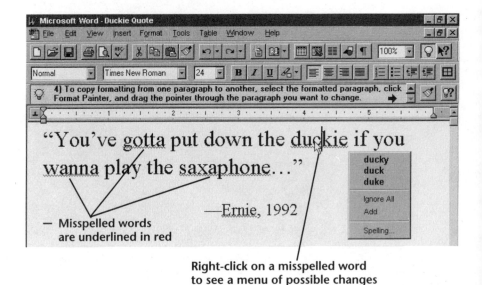

Figure 1.16   *You can change spelling mistakes on-the-fly with Word's new auto spellchecker.*

Figure 1.17   *You can emphasize text on screen with the highlighting feature or insert an address directly into your document.*

Note also that the Standard toolbar now has an address book button. When you click this, a list of addresses appears. (See Chapter 15 for the details.)

New Windows-Related Features

Windows 95 is a major upgrade to Windows 3.1. In fact, the new Windows will probably take more getting used to than the new Word will. Since Word is a Windows program, though, changes in Windows affect how you will work in Word—whether you like it or not. Most of the changes in Windows truly enhance the interface, making it even more graphical and intuitive. For example, you can much more easily copy and move files from one disk or directory to another with a simple drag-and-drop (see Figure 1.18). Needless to say, such changes will improve your file management of Word documents along with those of all your other Windows programs.

Figure 1.18   You can easily move files around now just by dragging them from one folder or disk to another.

Several new aspects of Windows deserve special mention...

Longer Document Names—Hurrah!

Finally recognizing that even computer users have enough imagination to think up file names of more than eight characters, Microsoft has made names of up to 255 characters legal. This means you will no longer have to decipher names such as mslfgl42.doc. You'll know immediately that this document is Microsoft Long Filename Gripe Letter Number 42, because that's what you will have named your file. (See Figure 1.19.) 'Nuff said. See Chapter 2 for more info.

Figure 1.19 *You can now give your documents real names, making them seem more human (sort of).*

Document Scraps

Document scraps are another very clever new Windows feature. A scrap is any bit of text, image, table, etc. that you drag out onto the desktop. That's right, onto the desktop—you don't have to use the Clipboard to save scraps anymore. See Figure 1.20. This will be somewhat reminiscent of the Spike feature of Word 6, but scraps are more useful because they are general to Windows. This means you can write something up in Word and then paste it into Excel. Or Access. Or PowerPoint. You get the idea. This feature is discussed in Chapter 2.

File Management

As you can see in Figure 1.21, the whole way you view files, folders, and applications in Windows has changed, and for the better. There's even a Recycle Bin! Assiduous file management is a must for the organized office. It will be worth your while to learn the new techniques of file management. You'll find them quicker, more intuitive, and easier than before. For more on these Windows features, please see one of the new SYBEX crop of Windows 95 books, such as *Mastering Windows 95*, by Bob Cowart.

Up and Running

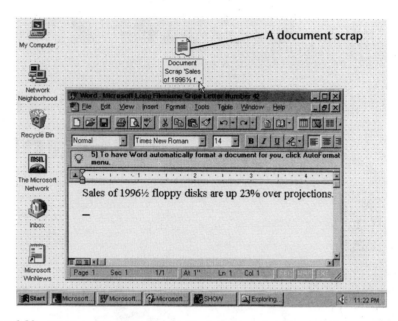

Figure 1.20   *Here is a document scrap on the desktop, ready to be pasted into any Windows application.*

Figure 1.21   *A lot of things have changed in Windows 95, mostly for the better. Learning how to get around in Windows will improve your facility and efficiency in Word.*

Chapter 2

Creating Your First Document

FAST TRACK

In this chapter we'll explore Word's basic text-editing features, using default settings and a Mark Twain quote. You'll type, edit, save, close, and reopen your first Word for Windows project. It's a long chapter, but worth the effort. Chapter 2, along with the two chapters that follow it, will give you the essential foundation you need to master Word for Windows.

Document Setup

Although we'll use Word's standard settings for this first exercise, it is worth noting that many experienced users start each new project by thinking about the document's overall design and final appearance. Word for Windows gives you on-screen clues about how your document will look on paper. It can show you line endings, page endings, the relative size and placement of text, graphics, margins, and so on. In order to do this, Word needs some information from you—like the paper size you plan to use and the kind of printer you will be using. You may also have strong feelings about how much white space you want around the edges of your pages. Once you tell Word these things, it changes the on-screen appearance of margins, the ruler, and other settings to accommodate and reflect your design.

Thus, it is always a good idea to input (at least preliminary) printer, paper, margin, and other document-design decisions before you start typing. In Part Two, you will learn how to do this by using Page Setup and other tools. Word for Windows 95 also provides *templates* that contain settings for particular kinds of jobs, making setup quick and easy.

If you are lucky enough to have a simple life with only one printer, one paper size, and similar projects, you may be able to make your setup decisions once and forget about them or even use Microsoft's default factory settings and perhaps a few standard templates for every project. If you do complex tasks, a variety of projects, or you're a perfectionist, though, you'll frequently change specialized printer and document settings.

 TIP Get in the habit of thinking about which printer and paper size you plan to use, the orientation of pages, and other design elements right when you start a new project. Visit Page Setup before you start typing.

Typing Habits to Break

If you learned to type on a typewriter or even an old word processor, chances are you have established habits that will be counterproductive in your use of Word for Windows. Here are a few habits you should try to break:

▶ Do not use the Tab key or the spacebar to indent paragraphs. Instead, use the indent control in Word's ruler (the top "handle" at the left side of the ruler). You'll learn more about this in Chapter 10.

▶ Never use the spacebar to center or otherwise position text. Use the center-alignment button on the Formatting toolbar instead. You'll learn about toolbars later in this chapter.

▶ Don't use the spacebar to make columns. Instead use tabs, Word's multicolumn features, or tables. See Chapter 11.

▶ Do not manually space paragraphs with carriage returns. Use Word's paragraph spacing instead, as explained in Chapter 10.

▶ Do not hit ↵ repeatedly to start a new page. Instead, use Word's Insert Page Break command.

Your First Word for Windows Project

With those preliminaries out of the way, you're ready to roll. We'll use Word's default settings for this first example in order to simplify things.

Starting Word from within Windows

The best way to start Word for Windows is by placing the program on your Start menu. To do so, choose Start ➤ Settings ➤ Taskbar, go to the Start Menu Programs tab, click Add, and follow the prompts. Be sure to choose the Start menu when the Select Program Folder screen appears. This way, you can launch Word right from the Start menu. An equally handy way to start Word is to double-click on a Word for Windows *document* icon. This will launch Word and immediately open the document itself so that you can get right to work on it. Or, you can start

Word from the DOS prompt along with Windows. For now, let's use the Start menu:

1. Click Start (in the lower-left corner of your screen) to bring up the Start menu.

2. Slide the highlight to Microsoft Word, as shown in Figure 2.1, and click once. Alternately, if you are running Microsoft Office, you can start Word from the Microsoft Office Shortcut Bar, also shown in Figure 2.1. By the way, unless you've reconfigured your mouse, whenever you are clicking, you want to use the *left* mouse button, sometimes referred to as the *primary* mouse button.

3. Unless someone has turned off this feature, you'll see a "tip of the day" each time you start Word, found in the TipWizard box just below the Formatting toolbar. Take a moment to read these tips; often they are helpful and entertaining. Sometimes, as shown in Figure 2.2, they are whimsical. Figure 2.2 also notes useful parts of the Word window.

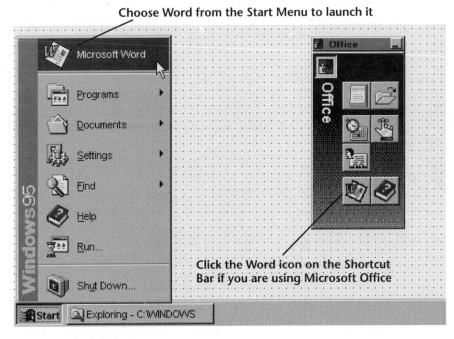

Figure 2.1   The fastest way to start Word is from the Start menu. If you have Microsoft Office, you can start Word from the Microsoft Office Shortcut Bar.

Part
1

Up and Running

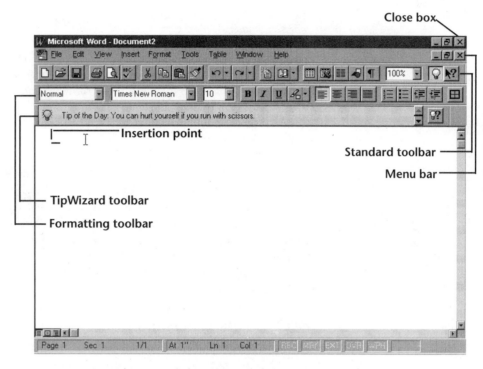

Figure 2.2 *A new document window appears each time you start Word.*

 TIP There is a great shortcut for adding programs, folders, documents, or whatever to the Start menu. Just drag the icon of what you want to add (or a shortcut of it) to the Start button, and it will be automatically added to the Start menu.

The Parts of a Word Window

An active Word window has standard Windows scroll bars, a title bar, zoom boxes, a menu bar, and so on. (If you are unfamiliar with these terms and concepts, take a moment to review your Windows manuals.)

NOTE It is good to distinguish between the *document* window and the *application* window. The document window is where individual Word files appear, while the application window will be open even if there are no files open, as long as Word for Windows is running. Some of the items we talk about below are specific to the document or application window, but it is not crucial to know what belongs where. The important thing is to know which items are which.

In addition to the usual Windows tools, you should see a ruler, toolbars, a flashing insertion point, and possibly a few other things. Word for Windows now has many toolbars, and you may see up to eight at one time on-screen (although two is more common). You may see more or fewer buttons on the toolbar than those illustrated in Figure 2.2. This is normal. The exact size and shape of your Word for Windows workspace will vary with your screen size and other factors. Let's look at a few of Word's window parts in a little more detail.

The Menu Bar and Commands

Normally, the top of your screen will contain traditional Windows-style menus in a menu bar. When you point to a menu title with the mouse pointer and click once, the menu will drop. Clicking on the desired command in a menu tells Word to execute that command. Commands with ellipses (…) after their names will ask you for additional information before they go to work. Dimmed commands are not currently available and require you to do something else first.

TIP If you highlight a command and then change your mind before releasing the mouse button, simply slide the pointer off the menu to make the command list disappear; alternately, slide the highlight up or down the menu list without releasing the mouse button to select a different command.

Many commands can also be executed by holding down specific key combinations (often called *hot keys*). These keyboard shortcuts are usually listed next to command names in menus. For instance, holding down the Ctrl key and pressing the P key is the same as choosing File ➤ Print. You'll learn more about this later.

The Mouse Pointer

Your mouse pointer should look like an I-beam and move freely about the screen. The pointer will change shapes when it passes over certain parts of the Word for Windows workplace. For instance, it turns into a large arrow at the edges of Word windows. You'll soon learn how these changes in the pointer's appearance tell you what you can do next.

The Insertion Point

The *insertion point* or cursor denotes where text, graphics, and other things will be placed when you type or insert them. The insertion point is a tall, skinny, blinking vertical stick. Don't confuse it with the mouse pointer. The I-beam mouse pointer and insertion point are two very different devices. Take a moment to locate them both in Figure 2.2 and on your own screen.

 NEW   Word now provides a TipWizard toolbar, just below the Formatting toolbar. This feature is extremely valuable, since it watches your every move and suggests better ways of accomplishing tasks.

Toolbars

Word for Windows provides nine different toolbars, although you'll normally display only two or three at any one time. Microsoft's "factory settings" display only the Standard, Formatting, and TipWizard toolbars. Here are the names of all nine:

- Standard
- Formatting
- Borders
- Database
- Drawing
- Forms
- Microsoft
- Word for Windows 6.0
- TipWizard

Toolbars contain buttons, drop-down menus, and other controls that help you quickly alter the appearance and arrangement of documents by executing a variety of Word for Windows commands.

For example, you can use the Formatting toolbar's Bold button to make text bold, or its drop-down font menus to pick a font and size. Point to the buttons containing arrows (next to the font and type-size menus) to see drop-down lists of choices. You can also type font names or sizes directly into the font and size boxes.

The button containing the paragraph mark (¶) alternately shows and hides paragraph marks, tab marks, space marks (the little dots), and other nonprinting items.

We'll explore toolbar buttons in depth throughout the book. To display or hide toolbars, choose View ➤ Toolbars.

NEW   Word's new TipWizard does a lot more than just offer advice. When Word makes an automatic change to your document, it explains itself in the TipWizard box; by clicking the Change box, you can undo what it has done. Furthermore, if Word offers to make changes, you can often preview the changes by clicking the Show Me button, also found on the TipWizard toolbar.

The Ruler

The ruler lets you quickly change margins and indents. It serves additional roles when working in columns and tables. The ruler lets you alter the appearance of multiple paragraphs or just the paragraph containing the insertion point. You'll learn more about the ruler later in this chapter.

To display or hide the ruler, choose View ➤ Ruler.

TIP   Word for Windows offers many formatting capabilities not found on the ruler or any of the toolbars. For instance, while there is only one underline choice on the toolbar, you can specify four types (single, words only, double, and dotted) by choosing Format ➤ Font. Think of the toolbars and ruler as mini-formatting features. If you want to master Word, you should get to know the more powerful menu commands, as well.

Status Area

The bottom of your Word window gives additional information about your work in a place called the *status area*. It's always present unless you choose the Full Screen view (or unless you've turned it off using ⊤ools ➤ ⊙ptions ➤ View).

> **NEW** As you work on your documents, you might notice a new animated icon in the status area (it looks like a book whose leaves are turning over). This is the automatic spellchecker, which checks your spelling as you write! You'll learn more about this feature in Chapter 19.

As you'll read later, there are occasions when you might be asked to type things or click in the status area. Right now, let's start a document and put some of this horsepower to work. If it's not already running, start Word for Windows now.

Typing Text

Type the following quotation (intentionally type **The the** rather than simply *The* at the beginning). Don't worry if you also make other typing mistakes; you'll learn how to fix them in a moment.

```
The the difference between the right word and the almost
right word is the difference between lightning and the
lightning bug.
```

Watch the screen as you type. Notice that Word for Windows automatically moves text down to the next line when it runs out of room near the right edge of the screen. This is called automatic word wrap, a common and useful word processing feature. For this exercise, do not press ⏎ until you've typed the period after the word *bug*.

> **NEW** You might notice that Word has marked the second *the* in your document with a red underscore. This marking indicates that Word believes the second *the* to be redundant, part of Word's new automatic spellchecker.

Finish by typing Mark Twain's name, then press ⏎ again. When you are done, your screen should look something like Figure 2.3.

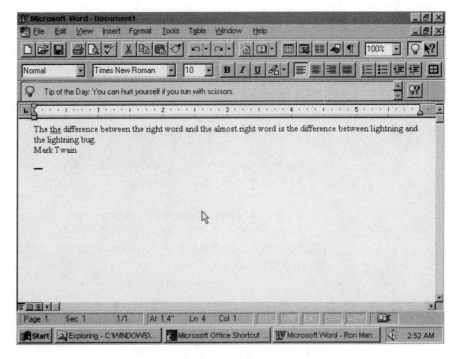

Figure 2.3   Type in Mark Twain's unembellished quote.

Selecting Text

Word lets you do a lot with text after you've typed it. You can change its appearance, move it around, delete it, and copy it. The first step is *always* to tell Word which text you want to work with. This is done by *selecting* it. Word has many, many ways to select text. For instance, you can drag your mouse pointer over the text while holding down the primary mouse button. There are shortcuts for selecting individual words, lines, sentences, and paragraphs, which you will read about in a moment.

Depending on your system configuration, selected text will either change color or be surrounded by a gray or black background. That's how you know what you have selected, as you can see here.

The the difference between
and the lightning bug.¶

TIP If you have selected text and changed your mind, click anywhere outside of the selected area or press an arrow key to cancel the selection.

Selecting Specific Blocks of Text with a Mouse

Here is a summary of text selection shortcuts for specific units of text, such as words, sentences, and graphics. Practice them all until they become second nature.

NOTE   For purposes of selecting, graphics are treated the same as text.

Selecting Entire Words

Double-click anywhere on a word to select the entire word and the space that follows it. To select adjacent words, drag after double-clicking on the first word of interest. Entire words will be selected when you drag this way. (With the default Automatic Word Selection turned on, you can single-click and drag to get this effect.)

Selecting Entire Lines

To select entire lines, follow these steps:

1. Move the mouse pointer to the *selection bar* (an invisible strip running down the extreme left edge of the document window). The mouse pointer will change from the I-beam to an arrow.

2. Click the primary mouse button only once. The entire *line* to the right of where you've clicked will be selected.

Continue dragging down to select additional lines.

Selecting Entire Sentences

Hold down the Ctrl key while you click anywhere in the sentence of interest. This also selects the sentence's punctuation mark (period, question mark, etc.) and the space following the sentence, if there is one. Dragging after you click this way selects additional sentences.

Selecting Entire Paragraphs

The quickest way to select a paragraph with your mouse is to *triple-click* anywhere in a paragraph. That is to say, point anywhere in the paragraph and quickly press and release the mouse button three times in succession. You can also select paragraphs using the selection bar by following these steps:

1. Move the mouse pointer to the selection bar (the invisible strip running down the extreme left edge of the document window). The pointer will become an arrow.

2. Double-click. The adjacent paragraph will be selected.

Selecting Your Entire Document

To select the entire document, follow these steps:

1. Move the mouse pointer to the selection bar at the left edge of the document and the pointer will become an arrow.

2. Hold down the Ctrl key and click. The entire document will be selected. Alternately, you can triple-click to select the whole document.

Selecting Graphics and Other Objects

Click anywhere within the graphic or other object. You'll see a border— usually with *handles* (small black boxes) surrounding the selected object.

Selecting Variable Units of Text

Sometimes you'll want to select just a single character or parts of a text string. Here are some techniques to use.

Automatic Word Select

Word for Windows features an option called Automatic Word Select to help in selecting text. You select as many or as few characters of the first word you want to change. Then when you drag over to the next word, the *entire* second word is selected. You must hold down Alt to select partial words when Automatic Word Select is on (as it is by default). You can turn this option off in the Edit tab in the Options dialog box.

Dragging to Select

To select adjacent bits of text, follow these steps:

1. Point to the place where you want selection to begin.

2. Hold down the primary mouse button and drag in any direction.

3. When the pointer hits a screen boundary (top, bottom, or side) the document will scroll as highlighting continues.

4. Release the mouse button when you've selected the desired area.

Shift-Clicking to Select Large Areas

To select large blocks of continuous text, follow these steps:

1. Point to the place where you want selection to begin.

2. Click to place the insertion point there.

3. Point to the end of the desired area (scroll if necessary) and hold down the Shift key while you click.

4. Release the mouse button.

Selecting Rectangular Areas

To select rectangular areas (like columns in a tabbed list), hold down the Alt key while you drag the mouse.

Selecting in Tables

There are many specific tools you can use to select items in tables. See Chapter 11 for details.

Deleting Text

There are several ways to delete unwanted text like that extra *the* you typed in the sample Twain quote. If you had spotted your mistake right after typing it, pressing the backspace key four times would have removed the unwanted characters and space.

Even if you did not make the correction earlier, it is easy to go back now, select the undesired text, and remove it. Follow these steps:

1. Double-click on the word to be deleted (*the* in this example).

2.   The entire word and the space following it become highlighted.

3.   Press the Delete key once.

4.   You can use "Undo Clear" (discussed in a moment) if you accidentally delete something of value.

NEW   In this case, since the unwanted text is also a spelling mistake (redundancy is considered a spelling error by Word), you can delete it by *right*-clicking on the word with the red underline and choosing Delete Repeated Word from the pop-up menu that appears.

Later, you will learn other ways to delete text and numerous strategies to reuse deleted text (move it) elsewhere. If you haven't already done so, delete that unwanted *the*.

Undo, Redo, and Repeat

Do you know what a damnosecond is? It's that fleeting instant when you realize you've done something really stupid on your computer—like accidentally deleting or reformatting twenty pages of text.

Everyone makes choices they wish they could undo. Like few other things in life, Word often lets you rewrite history. You can even undo an Undo by *redoing* it.

And, for tasks that are repetitive and complex, it is nice to have your computer handle some of the drudgery. That's where Word's Repeat command can help. The combination of Undo, Redo, and Repeat can be both powerful and perplexing. Let's begin by looking at Undo.

Undo

Word watches as you work. With surprising attention to detail, it remembers which steps you last took. When asked, it can frequently undo your errors. The exact name of the Undo choice on the Edit menu changes as you work. Sometimes it says Undo Typing. At other times it says Undo Formatting or Undo Sort, or some such.

Here are some examples of things Word can undo if you ask soon after you discover a problem:

▶ Editing changes (typing, cutting, pasting, etc.)

▶ Most formatting actions (changing styles, fonts, etc.)

▶ Most projects done with tools (for example, replacing Bill with Bob, etc.)

▶ Most drawing actions (dragging, filling, etc.)

There are three ways to undo:

▶ Edit ➤ Undo reverses just your last action.

▶ If you press Ctrl+Z repeatedly, it will reverse previous actions.

▶ The Undo toolbar button and its associated drop-down list menu let you undo multiple actions in sequence.

TIP Word for Windows lets you undo more than one previous action. To see a list of your prior actions, click on the arrow next to the Standard toolbar's Undo button. You can undo one or more selected actions by picking them from the list.

Using Undo

To undo your last action only, choose Edit ➤ Undo. The Ctrl+Z keyboard shortcut will reverse previous actions. Clicking the Undo button on the toolbar will also work.

To undo multiple actions or selected actions, use the drop-down list reached with the arrow button next to the toolbar's Undo button.

1. Reveal the list by pointing to the Undo list arrow. The last thing you've done will be on the top of the list.

2. Click on an item to undo it and any subsequent actions.

3. If you accidentally undo the wrong things, use the Redo list to the right of the Undo list to "undo your Undo."

Redo

Yes, it *is* possible to undo an Undo. To redo just your last action, choose Edit ➤ Redo, press the keyboard shortcut (F4), or click the new Redo button on the Standard toolbar.

To redo multiple actions or selected actions, use the drop-down list reached with the arrow button next to the toolbar's Redo button.

1. Reveal the list by pointing to the Redo list arrow. The last thing you've undone will be on the top of the list.

2. Click on an item to redo (undo the Undo) it and any subsequent actions.

3. If you accidentally redo the wrong things, use the Undo list to the right of the Redo list to "undo your Redo."

Whaddaya Mean I Can't Undo?

Occasionally, you will see a "Can't Undo" message indicating that your most recent action cannot be undone. That's why it is a good idea to save your work early and often. Then, when such a message appears, you can either close the messed-up document by saving it under a different name (with File ➤ Save As) or close it without saving the changes (i.e., without saving your mistakes). Then open the earlier version that is (we hope!) in better shape. Sometimes you can save time by cutting and pasting between the earlier version and portions of the new (messed-up) work if you've saved it under a different file name.

TIP   The best approach is to stop and think immediately after you notice a big, potentially time-consuming mistake. Get help. Sometimes more experienced Word for Windows users or Microsoft's telephone support staff can talk you through time-saving repair techniques. The less you fiddle after noticing a big mistake, the better your chances of salvation. If you are a new user, don't be embarrassed to ask for help right away when you notice a problem!

Repeat

Sometimes, after you've done something repeatable (like formatting or typing) you will find a *Repeat* command on Word's Edit menu. The shortcut is the F4 function key. Repeat watches you work and attempts to remember and recreate your actions on demand. Suppose, for instance, you change the width of a paragraph. If you have several other paragraphs scattered around your document that also need to be reformatted the same way, you could select each paragraph and use the Repeat feature to reformat them.

Like Undo, Repeat's name changes based on what you have last done, and it works with most Word for Windows actions immediately after you take them. Experiment.

Incidentally, there are often better ways to repeat actions. For instance, Word provides a format "paintbrush" you'll learn about in Chapter 14 that you may find easier to use when repeating format changes.

Inserting Text

Word offers several ways to insert new text into an existing document. The most straightforward approach is to move the insertion point to the desired location, then start typing. Word accommodates the new text by pushing the existing text to the right and down as necessary.

Suppose you wanted to add the word *obviously* between *the* and *right* in the first line of Mark Twain's quote. You would start by placing the mouse pointer (the I-beam) where you want to begin inserting text—between the space and the *r* in *right* for this example. Next, you'd press and release the mouse button to move the insertion point to the desired position.

WARNING   Beginners sometimes forget to press the mouse button after pointing with the I-beam. Don't confuse the I-beam with the insertion point! First you use the I-beam to point to where you want the insertion point placed. Then you must press and release the mouse button to move the insertion point.

Try it. Position the insertion point and type the word **obviously**, including the space that follows it. Your screen should look something like Figure 2.4.

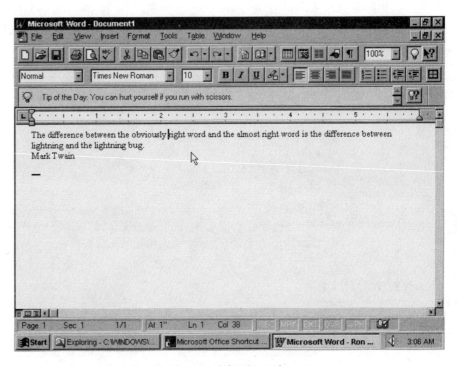

Figure 2.4   **You must position the I-beam and then insert the text.**

Replacing Text

Word also makes it easy to replace text. It combines the steps of deleting unwanted text, positioning the insertion point, and inserting replacement text. Simply highlight the unwanted text and start typing. The old text disappears and the new text snakes across the screen as you type it.

For example, watch the screen while you highlight the word *almost* (double-click on it) and type **nearly**. See how easily you can turn great prose into drivel? Because we'll be using this text for some future exercises, take a moment now to restore Mark Twain's actual words using the text-editing tricks you've learned so far.

Simple Formatting Tricks

Let's take a quick look at a few of Word's most often used ways to modify the appearance of text. They include toolbars, menus, and keyboard shortcuts.

Toolbars

Word's *Formatting toolbar* is shown here.

There are other toolbars containing formatting buttons, as you'll see later. Among other things, toolbars let you make style changes by clicking buttons or pulling down single-level menus, rather than going to the more crowded menu bar.

As always, you must select text before working with it. For this exercise, select all the text either by dragging, choosing <u>E</u>dit ➤ Select <u>A</u>ll, or by using the keyboard shortcut Ctrl+A.

> **TIP** Get in the habit of using the Ctrl+A shortcut (or triple-clicking in the style area) when you want to select your entire document. These shortcuts can save you a lot of scrolling in large documents.

Let's start by increasing all of the type from 12 to 24 points. The third arrow in the upper-left corner of the toolbar reveals a list of type sizes, as shown here.

To reveal the type sizes, point at the triangle, then press and hold the mouse button. Slide the pointer down to highlight *24* and release the mouse button. Your screen should look something like Figure 2.5.

> The difference between the right word and the almost right word is the difference between lightning and the lightning bug. Mark Twain

Figure 2.5   **The type size has been enlarged to 24 points.**

TIP   You can also *type* font names or sizes directly into their respective Toolbar boxes. Simply click in the box to highlight the old size (10 in our example) and type the desired size (24 in our exercise). When you're finished typing, press ↵ to change the size.

Regardless of which technique you use to change the size of text, you can change as much or as little as you like. For instance, you could highlight just the first letter *T* in the quote and make it 48-point type, creating a large initial cap effect.

TIP   You can accomplish better-looking versions of this and other "drop cap" effects automatically using Word's Drop Caps feature. Read about it in Chapter 9.

To change the appearance of characters (making them bold or italicized, for instance), first select them, then click the appropriate button on the Formatting toolbar. Try italicizing the word *almost* in your Twain quote now:

1. Point and click to select the word *almost*.

2. Click on the Italic button in the toolbar, as illustrated in Figure 2.6. Word will italicize the selected text.

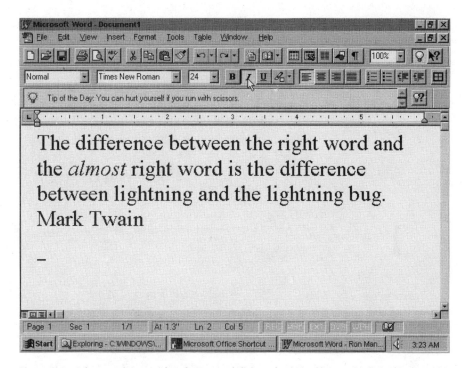

Figure 2.6 **Select words you wish to format and click on the desired button (Italic in this example).**

Next, use the same basic techniques to make Mark Twain's name appear in boldface. Start by selecting his first and last names by double-clicking or dragging. Then press the Bold button on the Formatting toolbar (the uppercase B).

As you know, the button to the right of the Bold button italicizes text. The Underscore button is next to the Italic button.

Aligning Text with the Formatting Toolbar

Notice the group of four buttons to the right of the Underline button in the Formatting toolbar. They contain horizontal lines. These let you specify left-aligned, centered, right-aligned, or fully justified text.

These "paragraph formatting" buttons and similar formatting tools work on entire paragraphs. They can be used on a single paragraph by simply placing the insertion point in the paragraph to be affected before using the button. For instance, to right-align Mark Twain's name:

1. Place the insertion point anywhere in Mark Twain's name (point and click), as shown in Figure 2.7.

2. Click on the Right-align button. The text will move to the right, as illustrated in Figure 2.8.

The difference between the right word and the *almost* right word is the difference between lightning and the lightning bug. Mark Twain

Figure 2.7   **Click anywhere on text to be right-aligned.**

The difference between the right word and the *almost* right word is the difference between lightning and the lightning bug.

Mark Twain

Figure 2.8   **The finished Twain quote.**

To change multiple paragraphs simultaneously, select them first. Remember how plain the initial document looked? With a few mouse clicks you've changed its appearance considerably.

There's much more to learn about formatting, as you'll see throughout this book. You are probably itching to print by now, and you will in a moment, but it would be a good idea to save your work first. That way if you have a printer or system problem, you won't need to redo the entire exercise.

Saving Documents the First Time

The words that you have typed and stylized so far exist only on your screen and in your computer's volatile RAM (random-access memory). If you were to switch off the computer or experience a power failure or other malfunction, your work would be forever lost. By saving your work to disk as you go, you can pick up where you have left off without losing your changes.

TIP Many experienced computer users save every fifteen minutes or whenever they are interrupted by phone calls or visitors. That's a good habit to establish. Word for Windows will even do the saving for you automatically, if you wish, as described in Chapter 7.

Once you are happy with the appearance of the Mark Twain quote, select File ➤ Save. You will see the Save As dialog box, illustrated in Figure 2.9.

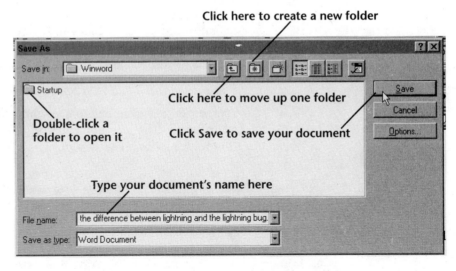

Figure 2.9   You see the Save As dialog box the first time you save a file.

TIP The Ctrl+S keyboard shortcut is a convenient way to save without visiting the File menu. Some folks use it exclusively. The Standard toolbar includes a button that looks like a floppy disk, which will also start the Save process.

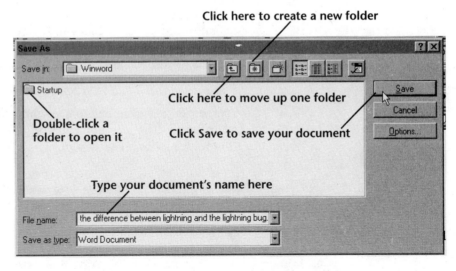 *(labels within figure:)*

Click here to create a new folder

Click here to move up one folder

Double-click a folder to open it

Click Save to save your document

Type your document's name here

Up and Running

The Save dialog box tells you where Word for Windows plans to store your work and requests a name for the file. It also gives you many other Save options, which are discussed in Chapter 7.

Let's keep things simple for now and use Word's default save options. Start by noticing where Word proposes to put your document. This is a very important habit to establish.

> **WARNING**   If you do not get in the habit of thinking about where you and Word for Windows save documents, you will misplace them. When saving to a floppy disk or your own small, uncluttered hard disk, this can be a minor annoyance. If you work on a far-flung network with multiple servers and gigabytes of storage space, it can take hours or days to locate lost files.

In Figure 2.9, Word for Windows is proposing to store our new document in the directory containing Word itself—called Winword. You can tell this from the picture of a folder next to its name (Winword) near the top of the dialog box.

> **TIP**   It's not a good idea to clutter up your Word for Windows directory with a lot of documents, so in Chapter 7 we'll create some directories specifically for Word documents. If you are an experienced Windows user, you might want to do that now.

Look at your screen. Take a moment to see where Word for Windows plans to save your work. Chances are you will see something slightly different from the folder location shown in Figure 2.9.

Telling Word Where to Save Your Document

Word allows you to specify save locations. You do this by double-clicking folders and disks to open them. You can also click the Up One Level or Create New Folder icons (noted in Figure 2.9) to help you get around and get organized. See your Windows documentation for tips on maneuvering through your disk's or network's drives and folders. (For more information, see Chapter 7.)

Naming Word Documents

Type a name for your document in the File Name box and then click the Save button. Names can be any length up to 255 characters. This allows you to be very specific about names, dates, and subjects; you'll find that this new flexibility will greatly enhance the organization of your iles. Note that if you want to use older Word documents, Word for Windows 95 still supports them and their eight-character names. In fact, Windows 95 keeps track of all files by means of long and short names, so you never have to worry about backward-compatibility.

> **TIP** Instead of clicking on the Save button, tap ⏎. This will have the same effect as clicking Save. With Word, like most Windows programs, pressing ⏎ will execute the button with the bold border in the active dialog box.

One way or the other, Word for Windows will save your document and, if the Properties feature is turned on (see Chapters 7 and 36), you will see a Properties dialog box similar to the one shown here,

with blanks in many places. Don't be alarmed if you don't see the Properties dialog box right now. The information it collects is optional and can be added later, if you like.

Properties

You needn't type anything in the Properties dialog box, and by default it will not appear when you save documents. But if you plan to keep many documents on your hard disk, and particularly if you will be storing things on a crowded network server, it is a good idea to use this handy feature. As you'll see in Chapter 7, it will help you quickly locate projects with the File ➤ Open command when you want to round them up for later use.

Because we'll be using this document to explore the File ➤ Open feature later, take a moment to enter the information.

1. If you didn't see the Properties dialog box when you saved the Twain Quote, open it now by choosing File ➤ Properties.

2. Type **Twain Quote** as the title. Do not press ↵ yet, though.

3. Press the Tab key or point with the I-beam and click to move the insertion point to the next blank.

4. Type **Writing** as the subject.

5. Tab or point and click again and enter your name if it is not already in the Author: box.

6. Tab again and fill in the Manager:, Company:, and Category: fields as you choose. You may leave fields blank.

7. Tab once more and enter some keywords (such as *Twain* or *lightning*).

8. Tab again and type **Draft**.

9. If you would like to be able to preview this document when you are scrolling in the Open dialog box, click to place a check in the Save Preview Picture box.

10. When you are satisfied with your entries, click OK or press ↵, the shortcut!

Once you have saved a document's Properties information, you will not be asked for it again when you save your work. You can modify the entries by simply following the above steps. Other aspects of the Properties dialog box will be covered in Chapter 7.

TIP To prevent the Properties dialog box from appearing when you initially save a new document, turn it off via the Save category of the dialog box brought up by choosing <u>T</u>ools ➤ <u>O</u>ptions (Chapter 36).

Saving as You Work

Once you've named a document and specified a place to save it, you won't see the Save As dialog box when you save unless you request it. A quick trip to <u>F</u>ile ➤ <u>S</u>ave or better still, the key combination Ctrl+S, will save your work whenever you desire. So will clicking the Save button on the Standard toolbar. Save early, save often, and *always* save before you print or make major changes.

If you need help remembering to save regularly, Word can even save automatically at time intervals you specify. This feature is described in Chapter 7.

Quitting and Restarting Word

There are several ways to completely quit Word. You can choose <u>F</u>ile ➤ E<u>x</u>it or click on the close box in the upper-right corner of the main Word window, both of which are shown in Figure 2.10. Try one or the other method now.

Click the close box to quit Word

Figure 2.10 *Quit by choosing <u>F</u>ile ➤ E<u>x</u>it or by double-clicking the close box in the Word for Windows application window.*

If you have made any changes since the last time you saved, Word will ask if you want them saved. Select Yes to save changes, No to ignore the most recent changes, or Cancel to abort your exit request and return to word processing.

After you have satisfied Word that you have saved everything of value, Word will quit.

WARNING Word needs to do some housekeeping when you exit. For instance, Word updates its settings files and asks if you want to save last-minute changes to your documents. When you use Word's Exit command, or attempt to quit Windows, this housekeeping will proceed smoothly. But if you use the power switch on your computer (or simply unplug it) without first executing a Word Exit or Windows Shut Down command, you may damage a document file or lose valuable changes to your Word settings (described in Chapter 34).

Minimizing Instead of Quitting

Like other Windows programs, Word can run *minimized*, which lets you get the program "out of the way" without actually exiting it. See your Windows documentation for information about multitasking between Word and other applications.

Launching Word by Double-Clicking on a Document

Once you've quit (exited) Word, you will need to restart the program before you can use it again. You could launch Word from the Start menu as you did before, then tell Word to load the document that you want to revise. But there is a shortcut. It is possible to load Word for Windows by double-clicking on a Word document icon. Try this by double-clicking on your Twain Quote document icon in Windows Explorer.

1. Click Start in the lower-left corner of your screen and slide up to Programs. From the cascading list, choose Windows Explorer.

2. Find your Twain Quote (in your Winword folder), as shown in Figure 2.11.

3. Double-click the Twain Quote document icon.

4. After a moment, Word will appear on your screen, along with the Twain document, ready for you to edit.

Figure 2.11 **Locate the Twain document.**

It is even possible to launch Word for Windows, version 7, by double-clicking on documents created with earlier Word versions. Word 7 will convert them for you automatically. See Chapter 35 before doing this.

Quick Access to Recent Projects

Once you have saved some Word for Windows documents, Word remembers their names and locations and lists them at the bottom of your File menu, as shown in Figure 2.12.

Choose the file of interest and Word will attempt to locate and load it. If you have changed the document's name or moved it since your last Word session, Word may ask for help locating it.

By default, Word lists your last four documents. You can specify longer or shorter lists in the General category of the dialog box reached with the Tools ➤ Options command (discussed in Chapter 36).

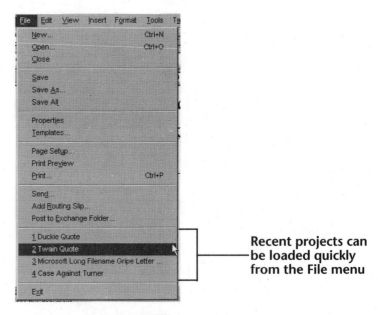

Recent projects can be loaded quickly from the File menu

Figure 2.12   *Word lists your four most recent projects at the bottom of the File menu.*

Copying and Moving

Word for Windows supports all of the usual Windows techniques for copying and moving information. It also provides a feature called *drag-and-drop*, a handy one-step, mouse-assisted mover.

Cut, Copy, and Paste

The traditional way to move or duplicate things in Windows programs is to select the item of interest, cut or copy it to the Clipboard, move the insertion point to the new position, and paste the item in. For example, suppose you wanted to move the word *almost* so that it came before the first *right* in the Twain quotation.

1. Start by selecting the desired text (you could simply double-click on *almost*, as shown in Figure 2.13).

The difference between the right word and the *almost* right word is the difference between lightning and the lightning bug.

Mark Twain

Figure 2.13   **First, select the item(s) you wish to move.**

2. Choose <u>E</u>dit ➤ <u>C</u>ut or press the Ctrl+X shortcut. You can also click the Cut button on the toolbar.

3. The selected text will disappear from the screen and will be placed on the Clipboard.

4. Now place the insertion point at the desired location (point and click). In this example, place it to the left of the first occurrence of the word *right*, as illustrated in Figure 2.14.

5. Paste, using <u>E</u>dit ➤ <u>P</u>aste, the Ctrl+V shortcut, or the toolbar's Paste button. Text will flow to the right and down as the Clipboard's contents move into place. In our example, the resulting move would look like Figure 2.15.

> The difference between the right word and the right word is the difference between lightning and the lightning bug.
>
> **Mark Twain**

Figure 2.14   **You must position the insertion point before pasting.**

> The difference between the *almost* right word and the right word is the difference between lightning and the lightning bug.
>
> **Mark Twain**

Figure 2.15   **The pasted (inserted) material forces the other material to the right and down.**

Copying from One Word Document to Another

Because you can open and work on multiple Word documents at the same time, it is easy to move things from one document to another. For example, there are two legal documents open in Figure 2.16.

With a large screen, it is easy to size and position multiple windows in plain sight and quickly move back and forth simply by clicking in the window of interest. You can arrange your workspace by clicking and dragging the size boxes in the lower-right corners of windows to adjust their size and shape. You can move windows around by pointing to their title bars and dragging them.

While it is possible to have many windows in view at the same time, you can have only one active window. It is easy to tell which is the active window—it's the top one with the highlighted title bar in Figure 2.16.

There are several ways to activate a window. The easiest is simply to click in it. Even if only a small portion of an inactive window is showing, clicking on it will activate it and bring it forward.

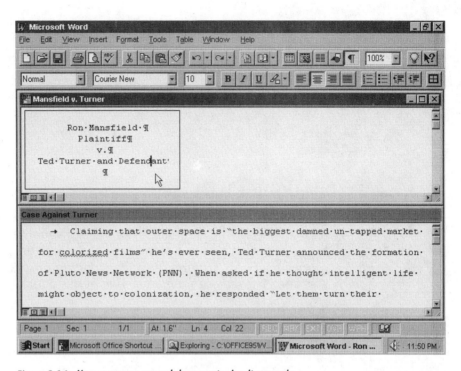

Figure 2.16 **You can open several documents simultaneously.**

1. Locate any portion of the desired window.
2. Click in it.
3. Resize and/or move windows if necessary to make it easier to work.

Word's Window Menu

Sometimes your screen may not be big enough to display multiple Word documents in useful sizes. Word provides the Window menu for these instances. As you can see in Figure 2.17, the Window menu lists the open documents and lets you switch between them. A check mark indicates the active window. Using this menu, you can activate one window to copy information, go back to the Window menu to activate and display another window, and then paste.

**This command neatly
arranges multiple windows**

Figure 2.17   The Window menu allows you to switch between documents.

What Formatting Gets Pasted?

When pasting from one document to another, sometimes you want the text being pasted to look as it did in its document of origin. At other times you want the text to take on the appearance of the document receiving it. This requires an understanding of styles, section formats, and other topics covered in Part Two of this book.

Some Reminders about the Clipboard

It is important to remember that when you cut or copy to the Clipboard, you replace whatever is stored there. If you do this by accident and spot your error immediately, Word's Undo command will restore the Clipboard's contents.

The Clipboard can store text, graphics, even sound and animation. While you normally don't need to see the Clipboard to use it, you can view its contents with the Windows Clipboard Viewer.

 Similar to the Clipboard is the new Document Scraps feature of Windows 95. Like the Clipboard, a scrap can store text, graphics, sound, or animation; the difference, though, is that you can have multiple scraps, and when you create one scrap it doesn't overwrite others. For purposes of comparison, here are the Clipboard Viewer and a document scrap.

WARNING The contents of the Clipboard disappear when you turn off your computer. If you want to save something permanently, save it in a Word document.

In a sense, a scrap is like a little document, and as such can be stored on disk. So it is safe, even when your computer is off. To make a scrap, you simply highlight what you want to place in the scrap file and drag it onto the desktop. To use a scrap, you just drag it into another document or application. Note that a *copy* of what you've highlighted is placed in the scrap file; the original document is not altered, so you don't damage the original. Double-click on a scrap to view its contents.

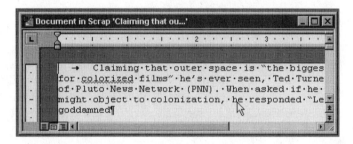

The contents of your Clipboard usually stay the same when you switch from document to document or from program to program, so if you're only moving small bits of text or graphics, it may be more efficient to use the Clipboard. You'll find that much of what you formerly used the Clipboard for, though, has been replaced by new features in Word.

TIP The Clipboard is probably best used now just for operations between Word documents. New Windows 95 features such as document scraps and the Insert Address button on the Formatting toolbar offer easier ways to copy or move material between Windows applications.

If you are running several programs at once, you may find your computer will respond more quickly if you minimize one of the programs while working with the other. For instance, when copying from a spreadsheet, run Word minimized, then minimize the spreadsheet and reactivate Word. If you are unfamiliar with this concept, consult your Windows documentation.

> **TIP** Advanced users will also want to explore other pasting options, including Linking and Embedding (described in Chapter 30). These advanced techniques make it possible to keep multiple documents up-to-date when things change.

Collecting Information with the Spike

A Word tool called the *Spike* lets you collect multiple items from within the same document, then paste them all at once. See Chapter 17 for details.

Drag-and-Drop

Word's drag-and-drop move feature lets you highlight text or other movable objects and drag them to a new location. For instance, in Figure 2.18 the word *almost* has been highlighted with drag-and-drop enabled. With the primary mouse button depressed, the mouse pointer changes appearance slightly. Notice the small rectangle near the arrow. Notice also the pointer. The arrow, box, and pointer move as one when you move the mouse with the button held down. Once you release the mouse button, the selected items will be moved to the drag-and-drop insertion point. In Figure 2.18, the word *almost* would be inserted between *the* and *right*. If you use drag-and-drop while holding down the Ctrl key, you will move a copy of the highlighted text, leaving the original untouched.

The selected word will be moved to the insertion point

The difference between the right word and the █almost█ right word is the difference between lightning and the lightning bug.

Mark Twain

Figure 2.18   *The pointer and insertion point change when drag-and-drop is enabled.*

NOTE If you've held down your primary mouse button while selecting things (while dragging or double-clicking, for instance), you'll need to release the mouse button and press it again before you'll see the drag-and-drop pointer. Practice will make this second nature. Start by dragging and dropping the word *almost* to restore the Twain quote.

Steps for Moving with Drag-and-Drop

To move text with drag-and-drop, follow these steps:

1. Select the desired text or other item(s).

2. Release the mouse button, if necessary; then point to the selected item(s), and press and hold down the mouse button. Watch the mouse pointer.

3. When you see the pointer change to its drag-and-drop shape, drag the pointer while holding down the mouse button until the insertion point is at the desired new location.

4. Release the mouse button. The selected item(s) should move.

5. Undo immediately (Ctrl+Z) if things didn't go right.

Steps for Copying with Drag-and-Drop

Drag-and-drop copying works just like drag-and-drop moving, with one exception. You hold down the Ctrl key while you work.

1. Select the desired text or other item(s).

2. Press and hold down the Ctrl button.

3. Release the mouse button, if necessary (while still holding down the Ctrl key), then point to the selected item(s) and press and hold down the mouse button. Watch the mouse pointer.

4. When you see the drag-and-drop pointer, drag the pointer while holding down the mouse button until the insertion point is at the desired new location.

5. Release the mouse button and the Ctrl key. The selected item(s) should be copied.

6. Undo immediately (Ctrl+Z) if you had a problem copying.

TIP   From time to time, you might accidentally drag and drop something when you intend to simply select by dragging. An immediate Undo (Ctrl+Z) will make things right. If you really hate drag-and-drop (and some people do), you can shut it off. Chapter 36 has details.

Creating New Documents if Word is Running

Whenever you start Word for Windows, it opens a new, untitled document so you can begin a new project from scratch. If you want to start a new project with Word already running, simply click the New button on the Standard toolbar or use the Ctrl+N keyboard shortcut. Word will open a new, untitled document window. Each new window opened this way in a session is sequentially numbered (Document1, Document2, and so on). You'll be given a chance to use templates and Wizards (described in Part Two) when opening new document windows with the File ➤ New command. When in doubt, start with Word's default—the Normal template, shown here.

TIP   You can open a new, untitled document window by clicking on the dog-eared document icon located on the Standard toolbar.

Keyboards and Word

The first computers were like Ford's Model T—simple and utilitarian. You had no choice of keyboards. Today, manufacturers provide keyboards with a variety of layouts and features. For instance, there are international keyboards labeled with accent marks and configured with special characters for a variety of languages. Some portable computers have unique space-saving keyboard layouts and keys.

Fortunately, Word accommodates most of these differences. To use international keyboard layouts, visit the Keyboard control panel. Click on the Language tab. See your Windows documentation for details.

Keyboard Shortcuts

Touch-typists often dislike taking their hands off of the keyboard, so, as you've already seen, Word for Windows offers a variety of keyboard shortcuts, such as Ctrl+X for Cut. These shortcuts make it unnecessary to reach for the mouse. Keyboard shortcuts are mentioned throughout this book, and many are shown on Word's menus. The Customize dialog box (Tools ➤ Customize) will help you explore all of Word's keyboard shortcuts. It is possible to change or delete shortcuts or add your own new ones, as you will learn in Chapter 36.

Key Combinations for Special Characters

Your computer and Word for Windows can work together to display and print special characters that aren't shown on your keyboard. Examples include the copyright symbol and international characters with diacritical marks (umlauted letters, for instance). In general, you either specify these characters by using key combinations or with the Insert ➤ Symbol command. For instance, you can type the copyright symbol (©) by holding down the Alt key and pressing the Ctrl and c keys simultaneously.

new A few symbols that you're likely to use fairly often have now been made easily accessible. For instance, to obtain a right-pointing arrow, just type an equal sign and the greater-than sign (=>) and Word will automatically change the characters to an arrow (→). You can even make a happy face (☺) by typing a colon and a closing parenthesis!

The available special characters and the procedures used to create them vary depending on which fonts you are using. That's why it's often easier to use the Insert ➤ Symbol command. Chapter 9 shows you how to get the characters you need. Figure 2.19 gives you a glimpse of this feature.

Click on tabs to see new choices

Figure 2.19   *The **Insert** ➤ **Symbol** command lets you see and type special characters.*

Numeric Keypads and Word

Most newer keyboards have numeric keypads and cursor-movement keys (Home, Page Up, and so on). Word for Windows uses many of these keys if you have them.

Numeric keypads serve two functions in Word. With the Num Lock feature enabled, you can use the keypad to enter numbers. With Num Lock off (the default) you can use the numeric pad to navigate through your documents. Pressing 9 (Page Up) on the numeric pad scrolls the screen up, 3 (Page Down) scrolls down, and so on. If you have a separate cursor-movement keypad, it's generally best to use that instead of the numeric keypad for navigating.

The key in the upper-left corner of the numeric keypad toggles Num Lock on and off. Some newer keyboards contain both the word *Clear* and the abbreviation *Num Lock*. On some, it is labeled just *Clear*.

Most keyboards have a light that tells you when Num Lock is enabled; others do not.

Up and Running

A few keyboard shortcuts are unavailable to users without numeric keypads. For example, the Unassign Keystroke command shortcut is unavailable without a numeric keypad. If you don't have a numeric keypad, and you want to assign your own keyboard shortcuts to replace the ones you are missing, that is possible. Appendix B lists all of Word's standard shortcuts and numeric-keypad shortcuts.

Repeating Keys

Most of the character keys and many of the navigational keys (like arrows) will repeat if you hold them down. This is an easy way to type a series of keystrokes.

You can change the speed of this feature in the Speed tab of the Windows Keyboard Control Panel. The speed at which identical keystrokes are issued is called the Repeat rate. A slider lets you pick anything from Slow to Fast. The length of time your computer waits between your first key depression and the rapid-fire insertion of identical keystrokes is called the *Repeat delay* setting. See your Windows documentation for details.

Using Word's Menus without a Mouse

Beginners may want to skip this topic and revisit it at a later time. If you really hate to reach for your mouse when typing, or if your mouse dies in the middle of a project, you can use Word's Keyboard Menus feature. It lets you use → and ← to flip from menu to menu and ↑ and ↓ to make menu choices. Beginners—give yourself a week or two to get your eyes, hands, and brain working together before abandoning the mouse or trackball. If you must work sans mouse, here's how:

1. Activate the Keyboard Menu feature by pressing the Alt key.

2. Press the underlined letter of the desired menu, usually the first letter (*V* for <u>V</u>iew, *W* for <u>W</u>indow, etc.) or you can use ← and → to display the desired menu. Menus drop down and stay down as you pick them.

3. Because two of Word's menu choices start with the letter *F* (<u>F</u>ile and F<u>o</u>rmat), you must remember that the shortcut for the F<u>o</u>rmat menu is *O*.

4. Pressing ↵ is equivalent to releasing the mouse button. Your choice will be carried out. To cancel the Keyboard Menu feature without taking any action, press the Esc (escape) key.

Keyboard Tricks in Dialog Boxes

Word supports the usual Windows navigating tricks in dialog boxes. For instance, in dialog boxes where you are asked to type text or dimensions, you can tab from box to box. Holding down the Shift key will move you backwards when you press Tab. Anytime you see a button with a dark border, pressing ↵ will work in place of clicking on the button. If you are unfamiliar with tricks like these, consult your Windows manuals or try the tutorial programs that came with Windows.

Hotspots

Even experienced users are sometimes unaware that you can bring up dialog boxes, windows, and other tools of interest by double-clicking at appropriate areas (called *hotspots*) in Word for Windows. There may even be some undocumented hotspots you can discover on your own.

Beginners may want to just skim this topic for now. As you gain experience with Word, you'll want to try some of these hotspot tricks and explore to find others.

Paragraph Dialog Box   Double-click on any indent marker.

Page Setup Dialog Box Hotspot   If you double-click on the small square box at the right end of the Ruler, you'll see the Page Setup dialog box used to control header, footer, and other measurements precisely.

When in Page Layout view, if you double-click in the margins at the corners of your document, you will also see the Document dialog box.

Footnote Window Hotspots   To reveal a footnote window, simply double-click on a footnote reference mark.

The Go To Dialog Box Hotspot   To bring up the Go To dialog box, useful for navigating in big documents, double-click on a page or section number in the status area at the lower-left portion of the document window.

Cell Height and Width Dialog Box   The space on the ruler that separates cells.

Section Hotspot   Double-click on section break marks to reveal the Page Setup dialog box. It contains section break information.

Mouse Command Shortcuts

Word for Windows also offers a nifty mouse feature that employs the nonprimary (usually the right) mouse button. Frequently, when you point to items on the screen and press the nonprimary mouse button, you'll see a list of commands that you can issue with your mouse. For instance, in Figure 2.20, Word is telling you that you can cut, paste, change fonts, change paragraph settings, and more, simply by dragging to pick a choice from the list.

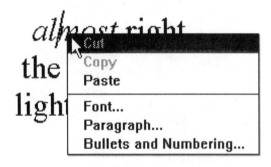

Figure 2.20 *Use the nonprimary mouse button to view and pick commands without visiting menus or toolbars.*

Getting Help with Word

It's a little ironic that Word for Windows has so many online help features that it takes several pages of a book to describe them. Word has four kinds of online help—topic-specific help, Answer Wizard, screen-element help, and (for WordPerfect users) WordPerfect help. In addition, Microsoft offers product support over the telephone, via fax, and through CompuServe and other bulletin board services (BBS). There is also TTY assistance for the hearing impaired.

Because Word's Help feature does a good job of explaining itself, we'll just touch on it here.

Searching for Specific Words of Wisdom

The <u>H</u>elp ➤ Answer <u>W</u>izard command lets you enter specific words and phrases that Word uses to pull up help information. For instance, to find out more about printing, you might:

1. Choose <u>H</u>elp ➤ Answer <u>W</u>izard.

2. Type the search word or phrase of interest (*print*, for example). Word will show you a list of possible topics, as illustrated in Figure 2.21.

3. Select a topic and click the Display button to list other subtopics, from which you can explore points of interest.

4. If you get a slew of possible topics, Word may advise you to rephrase your question, making it more specific, to help narrow down your range of choices.

Figure 2.21   *Searching Help files for specific words or phrases.*

The Help Contents Window

To see an overview of Word's online help, choose the <u>H</u>elp ➤ Microsoft Word Help Topics command and choose the Contents tab. You'll see a scrolling list, as shown in Figure 2.22.

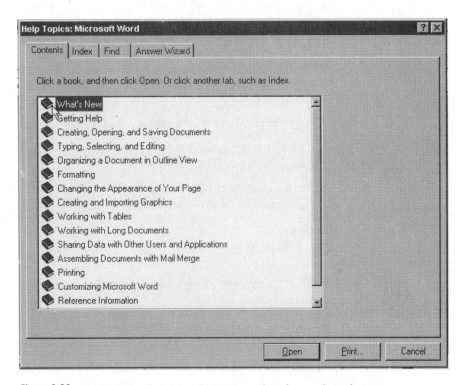

Figure 2.22   Use this Help window to select topics and read more about them.

Getting Different Kinds of Help

Double-click on an icon to see a list of subtopics. Then double-click on topics of interest to find out more about them. For example, if you double-click What's New, you'll see a handy list of new Word features. You can then choose to find out more about TipWizard, for instance.

Pointing to Get Online Help

You can often use your mouse to point to things on your screen and get help. For instance, pointing to a button on the toolbar will reveal its function.

You can also use Word's Help button on the Standard toolbar. It changes the pointer into an arrow with a question mark. When you point and click with that pointer, you get online help. Here's an example:

1. Press the Help button on the Standard toolbar. Your mouse pointer will become a giant question mark with an arrow. (Press Esc if this happens by mistake.)

2. Using your mouse, point to the item of interest. (The ruler, for instance.)

3. Click on the desired item (the ruler in this case). The topic of interest will appear in the Help window.

4. Read the Help text or click the Help window's buttons to narrow in on the information of interest. Scroll, if necessary, to read the entire text.

5. Click the Contents button, press C to see the topics list again, or choose File ➤ Exit to quit Help.

To Get Online Help in Open Dialog Boxes

Many dialog boxes contain Help buttons. Use them when you get stumped or when you want to learn more about a dialog box's capabilities.

WordPerfect Help

WordPerfect Help is available for reformed WordPerfect users. With Word-Perfect Help enabled, you'll see brief descriptions of items and their functions as you point to them with your mouse pointer. Figure 2.23 illustrates this.

To access WordPerfect Help, follow these steps:

1. Make sure WordPerfect Help has been installed and enabled.

2. Choose Help ➤ WordPerfect Help.

3. Pick the topic of interest from the scrolling list, as illustrated in Figure 2.23.

Figure 2.23   WordPerfect Help in action.

4.   Point and click on a topic to read about it.

5.   Use the buttons at the bottom of the window to see demos and explore other Help options.

6.   Press Esc or use the Close button to quit.

> **TIP**   Double-click on the WPH button in the status area for WordPerfect Help.

Printing Online Help

You can often print online help topics by using the Print button in a Help window. Be sure your printer is set up and ready first. For more information on printing, see Chapter 3.

Quitting Online Help

Pressing Esc closes the Help window. So does clicking in the Help window's close box, found in the upper-right corner of the window.

Microsoft Product Support Services

When you really get stuck, Microsoft's huge technical support staff can be a big help. They provide technical note downloading services, CompuServe forums, prerecorded support messages, and even real live people to answer your questions.

The first step, as they say in tech-support circles, is to "Read Your Friggin' Manuals." People who don't read are referred to as RYFMs. If you can't find the answers you need in Word's online help, or your manuals, or books like this one, it is time to call out the big guns.

To Find Out More about Tech Support Options

Microsoft is changing the way it supports users, and things that were once free are now often quite expensive. To read more about available support options, use the About Microsoft Word command on Word's Help menu and click the Tech Support button. It will show you a list of topics something like the one in Figure 2.24. Click on topics to learn more.

WARNING   Microsoft technical support is not always free. Be sure you understand the costs before obtaining support.

Figure 2.24   **Click on a topic to read more about Microsoft technical support operations.**

Chapter 3
Viewing and Navigating

Fast Track

To go quickly to a specific page (or a specific page in a section) 76

use the Go To dialog box, reached by choosing _Edit_ ➤ _G_o To or by pressing F5. Type the page number you want to find and press ↵. If you want to find a page in a particular section, preface the page with a P and the section with an S.

To return to the last three places you've edited 78

use the Go Back command (Shift+F5 or Ctrl+Alt+Z).

To locate text quickly 79

use the _Edit_ ➤ _F_ind command (Ctrl+F—see Chapter 20 for details).

To switch quickly from one view to another 81

use the view buttons in the lower-left corner of the status area.

To see text as it will print (almost!) 82

use Print Preview (fairly accurate) or Page Layout view (very accurate).

To see widely separated parts of a document 85

use the split-screen feature. You can split the screen by double-clicking the Split-bar rectangle in the upper-right corner of the document window. Alternately, you can drag the Split-bar pointer down to show Word how to size the panes. To unsplit the document window, double-click the Split-bar rectangle or use the Alt+Ctrl+S shortcut.

To clear the screen of everything but text 90

choose _V_iew ➤ F_u_ll Screen. To return to the prior view, click on the little Full button.

Y̶ou do your work in Word for Windows in *document windows*, which you can position and resize for your convenience. Word for Windows offers navigational tools that let you move quickly to the desired part of even huge documents. Several views make it easy to see what your document will look like without printing it. Other views are available to simplify and speed up the creation of rough drafts and outlines. In addition, you can hide and show elements such as paragraph marks (¶) and the little dots between words that denote spaces. Let's take a look.

Scrolling in a Window

Most documents are too big to be displayed in their entirety on your screen. You reveal unseen portions of your document by scrolling to bring parts of the document into view while temporarily hiding other parts. Usually, you'll scroll up and down to see long documents, but you will sometimes need to scroll left and right to see different parts of wide documents. There are many ways to scroll.

Scrolling with the Scroll Arrows

When you click on a scroll arrow you will see a different part of your document. For instance, suppose you are looking at page 2 of a three-page document. If you click on the up scroll arrow (located near the top-right of the active window), you will move a little nearer to the beginning of the document. Clicking on the down-pointing arrow will take you closer to the end of the document. (Typically, one click moves you up or down about one line.) The right- and left-pointing arrows let you see corresponding portions of wide documents.

TIP   If you click and hold down the mouse button while pointing to any of the four scrolling arrows, your document will scroll continuously until you reach the end of the document or release the mouse button. But there are better ways to scroll long distances. Read on.

Scrolling by Clicking in the Scroll Bars

Clicking in the shaded areas of scroll bars (as opposed to clicking on the scroll arrows themselves) scrolls approximately one screen's worth. The

Part
1

Up and Running

exact scroll distance will vary with your screen and document window size. Experiment.

Scrolling with the Scroll Boxes

The square boxes in the horizontal and vertical scroll bars can be used to move great distances quickly. For instance, if you are looking at page 1 of a 100-page document, the scroll box will be at the top of the vertical scroll bar. Dragging it with your mouse exactly half way down the scroll bar will bring page 50 into view; dragging it three-quarters of the way will take you to page 75; and so forth. Horizontal scroll boxes can be used the same way to scroll wide documents quickly.

Obviously, it is difficult to drag to the exact middle or three-quarters position on the scroll bar. Use the scroll boxes to get you in the neighborhood, then use other scrolling tools to fine-tune, as shown in Figure 3.1.

WARNING   It's easy to forget to move the insertion point when you bounce from place to place in a document by scrolling or using the navigational tricks discussed in this chapter. Get into the habit of repositioning and then looking for the insertion point before you type, paste, or do other potentially destructive things!

Figure 3.1   Use the scroll tools and your mouse to see different parts of your document.

Navigating with Your Keyboard

Word for Windows offers many, many keyboard shortcuts for navigating. You can just scroll using keyboard commands, or you can scroll and move the insertion point at the same time. Be sure you understand the difference!

Moreover, frequently if you hold the Shift key down while using keyboard shortcuts, you will select text in addition to scrolling and moving the insertion point. For example, pressing the Ctrl+→ key combination moves the insertion point to the beginning of the next word; while Ctrl+Shift+→ selects the current word starting at the insertion point and the space following it.

There should be a keyboard shortcut that lists all of Word's keyboard-navigation shortcuts, but there isn't. Table 3.1 is the next-best thing.

Scrolling	
To move to...	**Press**...
Up	↑ or 8 (keypad)
Down	↓ or 2 (keypad)
Left	← or 4 (keypad)
Right	→ or 6 (keypad)
Previous Word	Ctrl+← or Ctrl+4 (keypad)
Next Word	Ctrl+→ or Ctrl+6 (keypad)
Beginning of line	Home or 7 (keypad)
End of line	End or 1 (keypad)
One paragraph up	Ctrl+↑ or Ctrl+8 (keypad)
One paragraph down	Ctrl+↓ or Ctrl+2 (keypad)
Next page	Ctrl+Alt+Page Down
Previous page	Ctrl+Alt+Page Up

Table 3.1 **Keyboard Shortcuts for Navigating and Editing**

To move to...	Press...
Top of window	Ctrl+Page Up
Bottom of window	Ctrl+Page Down
Start of document	Ctrl+Home
End of document	Ctrl+End
Scroll up one screen	Page Up or 9 (keypad)
Scroll down one screen	Page Down or 3 (keypad)

In tables or page layout view

To move to...	Press...
Next cell in table	Tab
Previous cell in table	Shift+Tab
Next page element	Ctrl+Alt+Page Down or 3
First cell in row	Alt+Home
Top cell in column	Alt+Page Up
Last cell in row	Alt+End
Last cell in column	Alt+Page Down
Up or down in row	$\uparrow, \downarrow, \leftarrow, \rightarrow$

Editing

To...	Press...
Select the entire document	Ctrl+A
Delete character to left of cursor or selected text	Delete (Backspace)
Delete character after cursor or selected text	Ctrl+Alt+F or Del
Delete previous word	Ctrl+Backspace

Table 3.1 **Keyboard Shortcuts for Navigating and Editing (continued)**

To...	Press...
Delete next word	Ctrl+Delete
Copy text	Ctrl+C
Copy formats	Ctrl+Shift+C
Paste formats	Ctrl+Shift+V
Add selection to Spike	Ctrl+F3
Insert Spike contents	Ctrl+Shift+F3

Table 3.1   Keyboard Shortcuts for Navigating and Editing (continued)

If your keyboard has no cursor-movement keys, use the numbers on the numeric keypad (with Num Lock off) for the tasks listed in Table 3.1. Home, End, Page Up, and Page Down keys are not available on all keyboards. If you ever memorize all of Word's keyboard shortcuts, you are spending too much time with Word for Windows. Take a very long vacation.

WARNING   Be careful when using the numeric keypad to navigate. For instance, if you select some text, then press the asterisk key (*) by accident when you meant to hit the Page Up key on the keypad, your text will be replaced with an asterisk! Or, if Num Lock is accidentally turned on, when you press the ↑ key (or any other arrow key), the selected text will be replaced with the number corresponding to the key you've pressed. Some users avoid the numeric pad navigation shortcuts for these reasons.

The Go To Command

When editing big documents, particularly when you have a marked-up paper copy in your hand, it is useful to be able to scoot quickly to a particular page or to a specific page within a certain section. If you know page (and section) numbers, Word for Windows makes this easy. Word can also take you to specified lines, bookmarks, annotations, footnotes, endnotes, fields, tables, graphics equations, and objects. This is all accomplished in the Go To dialog box (see Figure 3.2), reached with the Edit ➤ Go To command or the F5 function key.

1. Pick the defined item   **3. Click here or press Enter**

2. Type your choice

Figure 3.2   The Go To dialog box

In single-section documents or documents where page numbers do not restart in each section, just type the desired page number and press ↵ or click the Go To button. Quicker than you can say *amen*, Word will take you to the requested page and place the insertion point at the beginning of the first line on the page. Here are the steps:

1.   Press the F5 function key or choose <u>E</u>dit ➤ <u>G</u>o To.

2.   Type the desired page number when you see the dialog box.

3.   Press ↵. Word will take you to the requested page.

4.   Close the Go To dialog box with the Close button or close box or press Esc.

5.   Get back to work.

Section Numbers and the Go To Command

If your document is broken into sections with page numbers that restart in new sections, you must specify section numbers in the Go To dialog box. (See Chapter 13 for more about sections.) To specify a section number in the Go To dialog box, type an **S**. For instance, typing **S4** would take you to the beginning of Section 4, (assuming your document has a Section 4).

To specify a particular page and section, type **P**, the page number, **S**, and the section number. Thus, **P3S5** would take you to the third page in the fifth section. **S5P3** will do the same thing.

You can also go to a particular section by selecting Section in the scrolling list and then typing the desired section number. Once in the desired section, you can use Go To again to get to the appropriate page within the section.

Many Ways to Use the Go To Command

You can also use the Go To command to move forward or backward a specific number of pages. And you can use it to go to the end of a document, even if you don't know the last page number. Here's a list of some of the things you can do with the Go To dialog box and samples of typical entries:

▶ Move to the beginning of the document (0)

▶ Move to the next page (+ or leave blank)

▶ Move to the last page (enter any number greater than the number of pages in the document)

▶ Move to a specific page number (4 or P4)

▶ Move to a specific page within a specific section (P4S3)

▶ Move to the first page of a specific section (S3)

▶ Move forward a specified number of pages—3 for example (+3)

▶ Move back a specific number of pages—5 for instance (–5)

▶ Move to other specific document elements like graphics, tables, bookmarks, annotations, etc.

TIP Double-clicking on the Page Number portion of the status area will bring up the Go To dialog box.

Go Back

Here's a handy but often confusing gizmo. When you are editing, it is sometimes necessary to bounce from one part of a document to another part of the same document. Or, if you have two different documents open, you may find yourself repeatedly moving from one document to the other.

Word for Windows remembers the last three places you have edited plus the current insertion-point location. The Go Back feature lets you quickly move to those edit points. Simply press Shift+F5 (or Ctrl+Alt+Z) repeatedly to cycle you through the last three insertion-point locations. The Go Back command is not on Word's standard menus, but you can add it or even create a toolbar button for it. See Chapter 36.

Incidentally, simply moving the insertion point somewhere in a document does not necessarily add that point to the places in the Go Back list. Generally, you need to edit something there.

Using Find to Navigate

Word's Find command is a great way to move to an area needing work. For instance, if you are looking at a printout containing a typo you want to fix, use the Find command to get to the corresponding spot on your screen. Here are the basics (Chapter 20 has the details):

1. Press Ctrl+F or choose <u>E</u>dit ➤ <u>F</u>ind to bring up the Find dialog box.

2. Enter the text you wish to find, then press ↵. Word will search (usually down from the insertion point) and show you the first occurrence of the specified text.

NEW Word now has a new feature in Find called Find All Word Forms, which lets you broaden the scope of your searches. See Chapter 20 for more details.

3. Click on Next or press ↵ to move to the next occurrence, if that's not the occurrence you want.

4. If necessary, answer Yes (press ↵) when Word asks if it should search from the beginning of the document.

5. When you find what you need, close the Find dialog box or click in the document window to activate it.

6. Edit away.

There is much, much more to know about Find and its companion, the Replace command. Be sure to read Chapter 20.

Views

Word for Windows can show your document with varying levels of detail to make things easier to visualize or quicker to work with. These different display options are called *views*. Word provides six different views:

▶ Normal view

▶ Page Layout view

▶ Outline view

▶ Print Preview

▶ Split screen

▶ Master Document

Normal View

Unless you are very patient, or have a very fast computer with a large screen, use Normal view for most of your heavy-duty text entry and editing. Word's other views respond noticeably slower to typing, editing, and scrolling.

Normal view (illustrated in Figure 3.3) keeps repagination and screen redraw delays to a minimum. It shows your text as you have typed it and displays graphics where you've inserted them (which is not necessarily where they'll print).

Normal view (the default) depicts things like type sizes, line spacing, indents, and so on with reasonable accuracy. It does not show side-by-side column positioning, footers, headers, nor the printing position of framed items. Columns are shown at their actual width, but not side-by-side. Automatic page breaks are shown as dotted lines. Manual page breaks, if you've defined any, are shown as darker lines containing the words *Page Break*, while section breaks are double dark lines with the words *End of Section*, and so on.

NOTE If you have instructed Word for Windows to number lines, the numbers will not appear in Normal view. Use Page Layout view or Print Preview to see line numbers.

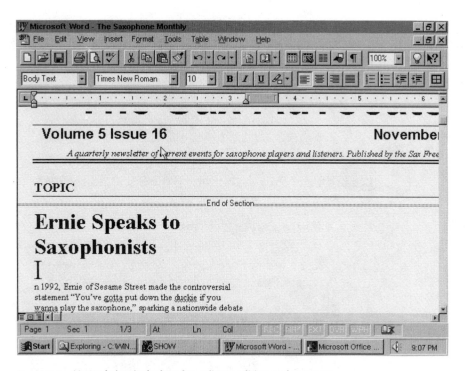

Figure 3.3   *Normal view is the best for ordinary editing and text entry.*

Editing in Normal View

You can create and edit text, columns, and graphics as usual in Normal view. To work on headers or footers, though, you must open Header or Footer windows from the <u>V</u>iew menu. For more detail, see Chapter 12.

Switching Views

Word for Windows has a <u>V</u>iew menu that you can use to select <u>N</u>ormal, <u>O</u>utline, or <u>P</u>age Layout views.

Three buttons in the bottom-left corner of Word's status area let you quickly switch views. They are (from left to right) Normal view, Page Layout view, and Outline view.

Switch to Print Preview by choosing File ➤ Print Preview or clicking the Print Preview button on the Standard toolbar.

Page Layout View

Figure 3.4 shows what happens to the text from Figure 3.3 when it is displayed in Page Layout view. In this view, the screen resembles a white sheet of paper, or at least a portion of a sheet.

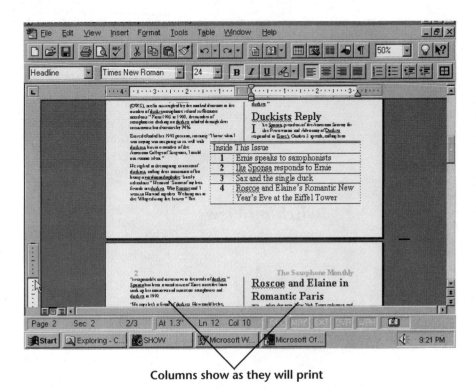

Columns show as they will print

Figure 3.4   *In Page Layout view, you can see text as it will print.*

Look closely at the top and left edges of the screen in Figure 3.4. You will see a dark background that Word for Windows places behind the "paper." With the Zoom Control set to Whole Page View (or on a large enough screen), you will see the whole page. On smaller screens, with Zoom Control magnified, or when using a large paper setting in Page Setup, you may need to scroll to see these representations of the paper's edges.

Editing in Page Layout View

Generally, you edit as usual in Page Layout view. Text and graphics are positioned where they will print. Headers and footers can be both seen and edited. Click in a header, footer, or body text to position the insertion point. Page breaks, be they automatic or forced, are represented by new pages on the screen rather than by dashed lines in the text. You can scroll from page to page, as you'd expect.

Hidden Text in Page Layout View

If you have hidden text in your document and you reveal it, Page Layout view will display line and page endings adjusted to include the hidden text. This may not correspond to pages that you print if the Print dialog box's Print Hidden Text box is unchecked. In order to see what your pages will look like without the hidden text, you must hide the text by unchecking the Show Hidden Text box in the Preferences dialog box. (See Chapters 9 and 28 for information about hidden text.)

Headers and Footers in Page Layout View

You can see headers and footers in Page Layout view. To edit, click anywhere in a header or footer. It will "undim" and be surrounded by a dashed line, as shown in Figure 3.5. The Header and Footer toolbar will also appear if it's not already on your screen.

To add date or time entries and page numbering to headers and footers, use the buttons on the Header and Footer toolbar. You can format text in headers just as you would anywhere else in a Word for Windows document. For instance, to right-align header text, place the insertion point in the text (or select multiple lines in the header) and use the Formatting toolbar's Right-align button.

Double-click to activate a header or footer

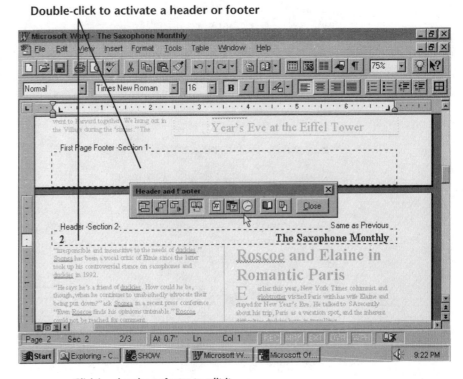

Figure 3.5   *Click in a header or footer to edit it.*

Even Line Numbers Show in Page Layout View

If you have requested numbered lines, the numbers will appear in Page
Layout view as shown here:

```
0


1
      Harvy Herzmycard
2     Herzmycard, Soreneck and Numb
      425 Hurtz Drive
3     Teaneck on the Hudson, NY  12345
      Telephone: (800) 555-4321
4     Fax: (123) 456-9876


5
      Attorney For: Ron Mansfield
```

Split Screen View

Regardless of which view you prefer, you can profit from using Word's split-screen feature. You can use the split-screen to keep two widely separated portions of a document in view at the same time. To split the screen, simply point to the small horizontal bar above the top scroll bar arrow. The pointer will change to the Split-bar pointer, as shown in Figure 3.6. Drag the Split-bar pointer down to divide the screen.

When the pointer changes shape, drag the black bar to split the window

Figure 3.6 *The pointer will change shape.*

When you release the mouse button, your screen will split into two independent windows, each with its own scroll bar. To return to a single screen, double-click the Split bar or drag it to just below the title bar. This takes some practice. Alternately, you can use the keyboard shortcut Alt+Ctrl+S.

TIP   When you unsplit the screen, the portion that the insertion point was in becomes the only screen. This can be a nuisance if you actually wanted to be in the other portion of text! So be sure that the insertion point is in the correct pane before you unsplit.

Why Split Screens?

With the screen split you can see two parts of your document at once. Use this feature to refer to different portions of a document as you write or to speed copying, cutting, and pasting. But there's another powerful reason to use split screens.

Split Screen and Different Views

You can use a different view in each portion of the split screen. For instance, you might want to speed scrolling and editing by working in a window pane set to Normal view while watching the effects of your changes in a Page Layout view pane, as shown in Figure 3.7.

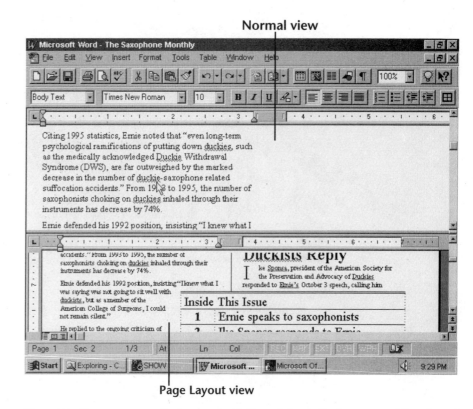

Figure 3.7 You can arrange the document with Normal view in the top pane and Page Layout view in the bottom.

Print Preview

Print Preview is more than just another way to view documents. Choose File ➤ Print Preview or use Ctrl+Alt+I, Ctrl+F2, or the Print Preview button.

Depending on your screen size and settings, you will see either an unreadable bird's-eye view of a page or two (like the one in Figure 3.8), or a full, readable page. You can even click on your document to see a close-up view when the cursor looks like a magnifying glass.

In either case, you will be able to reposition margins in Print Preview. Notice that line numbers are displayed in Print Preview. You cannot edit text or headers and footers in Print Preview. You also will not be able to see certain Page Setup printer tricks, such as image flips.

Prints
Lets you zoom in and out
Shows a single page
Shrinks pages to fit screen
Determines the number
of pages on screen
Full screen
Takes you back to the
view you were last using
Toggles rulers

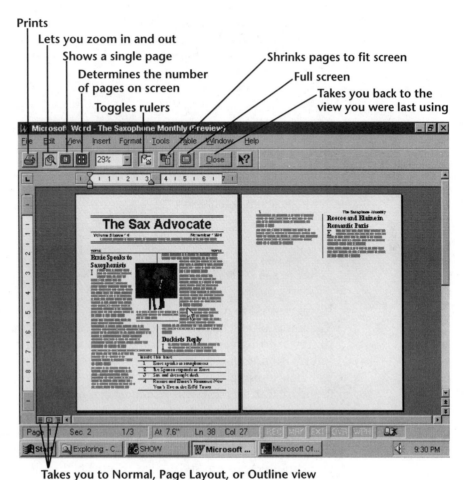

Takes you to Normal, Page Layout, or Outline view

Figure 3.8 *Print Preview gives you a bird's-eye view of one or two pages at once.*

 TIP Use the Close button in Print Preview to bring you back to whatever view you were in previously.

Outline View

A complete description of Word's Outline feature can be found in Chapter 21. For now it is enough to know that if your document is properly formatted, switching to Outline view lets you quickly navigate and reorganize even large, complex documents. Outline view allows you to see the entire contents of the document, just chapter headings, just section headings, and so on. For instance, Figure 3.9 shows part of a book outline down to paragraph headings, but does not include the text of the book itself.

Dragging in Outline view moves headings and all associated text

Figure 3.9   Part of a book outline view at paragraph-heading level.

If you wanted to move all of the Landing Gear information to before the Tail information, you might ordinarily use Normal or Page Layout view to scroll through and select the complete text of all of the Landing Gear information; then you would cut and paste it into the new position. But by using Outline view, you could simply "collapse" the view, as shown in Figure 3.9, and drag the *+Landing gear* heading up. All of its associated text would follow.

You need not begin projects by creating an in-depth outline, as you will see later when you read about styles and outlines. But by creating and applying appropriate styles for various heading levels, you can quickly create a document that can be expanded or compressed for viewing and editing with Outline tools. And of course, creating an outline is a good way to organize your thoughts before you begin writing.

Document View

This view is used when working on large documents. See Chapter 24.

View Defaults

Normal view is the default for new documents. Word for Windows will, however, remember the view you were using when you last saved a document and open the document in that view. If you opened a new document in Normal view, did some work, switched to Page Layout view, saved, and exited, the next time you opened the document it would appear in Page Layout view.

Showing Paragraph Marks, Spaces, Etc.

Word for Windows can display helpful nonprinting characters to let you see what's going on. Examples include:

▶ Paragraph marks (¶)

▶ Dots denoting spaces

▶ Arrows denoting tab characters

▶ Dashed lines for page, section, and column breaks

▶ Text and graphic boundaries

 I like to leave these on, although turning them off can sometimes help you better visualize the final appearance of a document. To toggle the display of these items, use the Show/Hide ¶ button on the Standard toolbar.

Zooming

The little drop-down list near the right end of the Formatting toolbar is called the Zoom Control. It lets you zoom in and out to see bigger or smaller on-screen representations. It does not affect printing size. Figure 3.10 shows it in use, magnifying the text 200 percent.

The View ➤ Zoom command gives you even more control over on-screen character size.

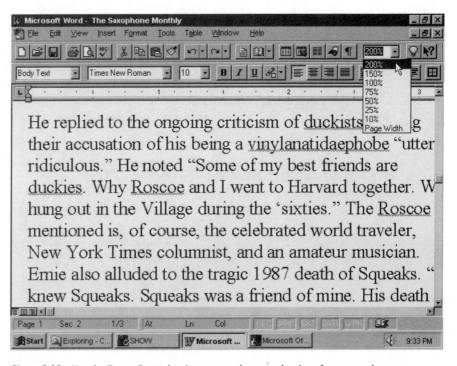

Figure 3.10 *Use the Zoom Control to increase or decrease the size of on-screen images.*

Full Screen—Seeing Just Your Work

The <u>V</u>iew ➤ F<u>u</u>ll Screen command, or the corresponding button that you'll find in Print Preview, removes all the usual workspace clutter and fills your screen with your current document. You'll also see a very small window containing a button, as shown in Figure 3.11.

Edit as usual. Navigate with Page Up, Page Down, and the rest of the keyboard tools. To return to the prior view, click on the little Full button or use the Alt+V+U keyboard shortcut. Incidentally, the Full button's window can be dragged out of the way.

TIP If you accidentally close the Full button's window, don't panic. Just press the Esc button to restore all of your toolbars, menus, and other controls.

He replied to the ongoing criticism of duckists, calling
their accusation of his being a vinylanatidaephobe "utterly
ridiculous." He noted "Some of my best friends are
duckies. Why Roscoe and I went to Harvard together. We
hung out in the Village during the 'sixties." The Roscoe
mentioned is, of course, the celebrated world traveler,
New York Times columnist, and an amateur musician.
Ernie also alluded to the tragic 1987 death of Squeaks. "I
knew Squeaks. Squeaks was a friend of mine. His death
was a very personal issue."

Squeaks, noted jazz pianist and outspoken duckie was
playing with Branford Marsalis at a charity to benefit
unwed duckies when the saxophonist accidentally inhaled
him during an unusually lively rendition of Cannonball
Adderly's *Yakkity Sax*. Marsalis survived, but doctors
were not able to resuscitate Squeaks. His death has often
been cited by Ernie's supporters.

With remarkable prescience, Ernie anticipated a response
from duckists, saying "I know the fusillade will continue.
Every time I open the paper, I expect another broadside.

Figure 3.11   Full Screen removes everything but your work and a small button window.

Speeding Up Screen Scrolling

If you find scrolling and other screen actions somewhat sluggish, here
are some suggestions:

▶ Add more RAM and try the other usual Windows speed-up tricks
well-documented elsewhere. Word for Windows runs best in 8 MB or
more.

▶ Work in Normal view whenever possible.

▶ Close unwanted windows and applications that you are not using.

▶ Consider breaking one very large document into several smaller ones
(books into chapters, for instance).

Chapter 4

Previewing and Printing

FAST TRACK

Printing can be quite simple or relatively involved, depending on what you're trying to do. First, be certain that: the printer is cabled properly; you have set up your printer in Windows (see your Windows documentation for details); your printer is turned on and loaded with supplies (paper, toner, etc.); it is warmed up, if necessary, and the ready light is on.

TIP It is always a good idea to *save before you print!* Occasionally, printing problems can lock up your computer, and you might lose any unsaved changes if you are forced to reboot or power-down. Get in the habit of clicking the Save button on the Standard toolbar or using the Ctrl+S keyboard shortcut before you print.

Simple Printing

If you just want to print a single copy of the current document, and your one printer is properly installed and ready to go, just click the Print button on the Standard toolbar. Try this now with your Twain Quote.

The status area will chart Word's progress as it prints. Page numbers and a little animated printer icon will tell you how many pages have been sent to the printer or to the Windows background printing feature.

Printing as an Interactive Process

While printing can be as simple as previously described, it is a good idea to get into the habit of visiting the Page Setup dialog box, and possibly the Print dialog box, whenever you begin to create a new document—particularly if you work with a variety of printers, paper sizes, and document designs. If you wait until you have finished working on your document before choosing a printer, your page and line endings may change considerably from those you initially saw on your screen. This can be a minor annoyance or a major disaster.

For example, if you write a long document, create a table of contents, and then change printer models or choose different printing features, you will find that line and page endings may change. You'll need to redo the table of contents, or it will not agree with the printed pages. The following printer decisions affect pagination and should be selected or determined when you begin a project:

▶ Page Setup options (like paper source)

▶ Printer model

▶ Paper size

▶ Reduction/enlargement (scaling)

▶ Page orientation

▶ Margins (Chapter 8)

▶ Gutters (Chapter 8)

▶ Larger print area

▶ Printing/not printing hidden text

▶ Printing/not printing footnotes and endnotes

▶ Font substitution options (Chapter 9)

> **NOTE** Except as noted, these options and decisions are all discussed in depth later in this chapter.

Other changes affect the appearance of printed pages but have little impact on pagination.

If you have only one printer and it works properly, you can skip ahead to the section *Choosing Print Dialog Box Options* later in this chapter.

Choosing a Printer

To choose a printer:

1. Choose File ➤ Print or use the Ctrl+P shortcut. You will see a dialog box like the one in Figure 4.1.

2. Notice the scroll box of printers in the Printer region. Click the triangle to see a list of printers, and choose the one you wish to use, as illustrated in Figure 4.2.

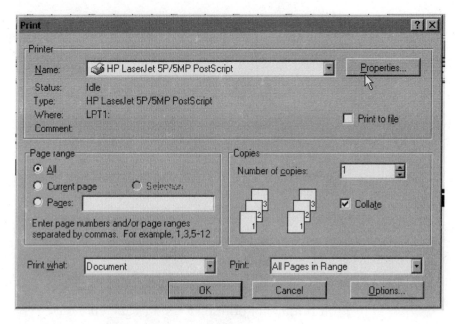

Figure 4.1   *The Print dialog box.*

Figure 4.2   *Use the Printers scroll list to pick a printer.*

3. If the printer you've chosen has options (letter quality vs. draft, lighter/darker, etc.) you can usually reach these by clicking the Properties button.

4. When you are finished checking the printer's settings, click OK (↵). You may have to click OK more than once to get back to the Print dialog box. If you click OK there, your document will print.

Choosing Print Dialog Box Options

The Print dialog box will show you which printer is selected. Use this dialog box to make decisions, such as how many copies of which pages you need.

What to Print

Normally, you'll want to print all or part of your document. But sometimes you'll want to print other things, such as the document's annotations or other settings information. Use the drop-down list to pick any of the following options:

▶ Document

▶ Summary Info

▶ Annotations

▶ Styles

▶ AutoText entries (typing shortcuts)

▶ Key assignments (keyboard shortcuts)

Copies

To specify more than one copy of whatever you intend to print, either type a number in the Copies box or click the up or down arrows next to the box to scroll and choose a number.

Page Range

To print the entire page range, make sure the All button is darkened (the default). Click on the little button next to All, if necessary.

To print just the page in your document currently containing the insertion point, click on the Current Page button.

To print selected text, first select it, then bring up the Print dialog box and use the Selection button in the Page Range area. This choice will be dimmed unless you've selected something in your document.

To print a range of pages (pages 6–10 in a 50-page document, for instance), type the first and last desired page number in the Pages text box. Separate the numbers with hyphens (*6-10*, for instance).

To print specific pages, list them separated by commas (*3,5,8* for example). Ranges and single pages can be combined, so *6-10,13,19,83* will work as well.

Print All, Odd, or Even

Normally, Word prints all pages in order, but if you are planning to do "manual" two-sided printing, or you have other reasons to separate odd and even pages, use the drop-down Print list at the bottom of the Print dialog box to specify Odd Pages or Even Pages. For example, you might first print all odd-numbered pages, then put those pages back in the printer to print the even-numbered pages on the other side.

Print to File

It's possible to print to disk files instead of to a printer. This technique is sometimes used when you want to take a document to a service bureau for typesetting or other special services. A print file contains all the information needed to allow printing even if the other computer does not have exactly the same fonts used in creating the file. It is a very good idea to do a test run before trying this technique for rush work, as there are many land mines. Consider providing your service bureau copies of the actual Word document files instead of (or in addition to) print files and a hard copy. Here are the steps for printing to a file:

1. Edit and polish your document as usual.

2. Consider creating a paper copy by printing normally.

3. Open the Print dialog box with File ➤ Print or Ctrl+P.

4. Place a check in the Print to File box in the Print dialog box.

5. Click OK. You'll see the Print to File dialog box, illustrated in Figure 4.3.

6. Use any of the Windows 95 techniques to specify where you want to save the file.

Part
1

Up and Running

Figure 4.3   *Enter a file name for your print file.*

 TIP Print files can get pretty big, particularly if they contain graphics. Consider printing small ranges of pages to multiple files if you need to transport print files on floppies. You'll need to experiment, since the actual number of bytes per page can vary widely, even between several pages in the same document.

Collate Copies

If you request multiple copies (five copies of a ten-page document, for instance) and don't choose the Collate Copies option, Word will print all five page 1's, then all five page 2's, and so on. You'll need to hand-collate them to make orderly sets.

The Collate Copies option prints five "books," each one complete and in order. This may or may not increase overall printing time depending on your printer and a number of other factors. Experiment.

Letterheads, Second Sheets, and Two-Tray Printers

If your printer has two paper sources (two trays or a tray and a "pass-through," for instance), Word can switch sources as needed. Use the *First Page*, *Other Pages*, and perhaps *Apply To* choices found under the Paper Source tab in the Page Setup dialog box, as shown in Figure 4.4.

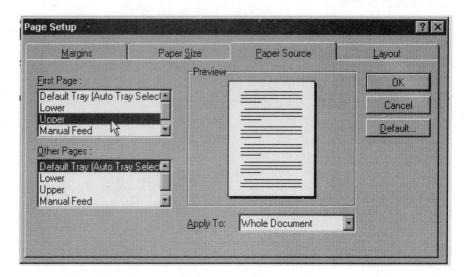

Figure 4.4 **The Page Setup dialog box.**

Other Printing Options

There are other printer options available. They can be reached by choosing the Print tab in Word's Options dialog box, shown in Figure 4.5, and are discussed in the following section.

You can display the Options dialog box either by choosing Tools ▶ Options or by pressing the Options button in the Print dialog box. Most of these settings remain in place once you choose them and are used for each new printing job until you change them.

Draft Output

This option can speed up printing. Its effect varies from printer to printer. Usually everything is printed in a single font, as efficiently as possible, and at the expense of appearance.

Reverse Print Order

Use Reverse Print Order when you want pages to come out last-to-first. This is handy for printers that "stack" pages in the wrong order.

Figure 4.5   *The Print Options tab.*

Update Field and Update Links

As you'll see when you learn about linking and fields in Part Three, this is how you determine when and if things get updated before printing.

Background Printing

A check in this option box causes Word to use the Windows Background printing feature. Theoretically, it lets you work on other things while your document prints in the background. In real life, it often makes your computer so sluggish that you'll end up taking a break anyway. If you keep getting printing errors or low memory messages while printing, try turning off background printing.

Include with Document

The Include with Document choices in the Print tab of the Options dialog box are pretty self-explanatory. A check causes the item (summary info, annotations, etc.) to be delivered with the printed pages. Click on a check mark to remove it and prevent the item from printing. It's a good idea to keep the update options enabled.

Current Document Options

The options that will appear here vary with the contents of your document. For instance, you may be given the option to print data without printing forms. See Chapter 33 for more about forms.

Tray Choice

Use this choice to force something other than the standard tray choice for special printing jobs (for example, a cover letter on your business letterhead). Obviously the selected printer must have more than one paper source for this to be useful.

Print Preview

You can bypass Print Preview and print immediately to hard copy, but previewing is advised. It lets you see a screen representation of one or more entire pages before you print them, often saving paper and time.

If you didn't try Print Preview on the Twain quote when you read about it earlier, this would be a good time to experiment. Choose File ➤ Print Preview (or use the keyboard shortcut Ctrl+Alt+I or Ctrl+F2).

This will give you an excellent idea of where the text will print on the paper. You can also edit this text. You will be able to see margins as well. If your document contains headers, footers, line numbers, and other embellishments, you will see them, too, as illustrated in Figure 4.6.

Notice the buttons along the top of the screen. They let you control many of Print Preview's functions. As always, if you forget a button's function, simply pointing to it without clicking will reveal button help. Here is a general description of each button.

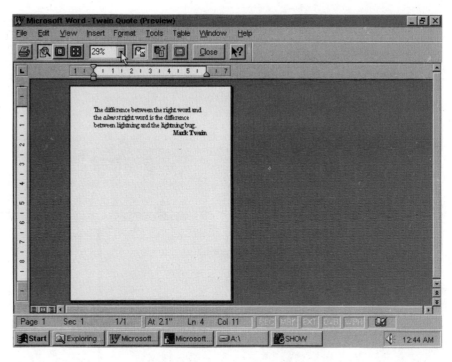

Figure 4.6 Use Print Preview to get an overview, adjust margins, and even edit before printing.

Print Preview's Print Button

The leftmost button prints a single copy of the document without taking you to the Print dialog box. (If you really want to visit the Print dialog box, choose File ➤ Print or use the Ctrl+P shortcut.)

Magnifier

The Magnifier button lets you zoom in to better read small portions of the page and zoom out to get a bird's-eye view of one or more pages. It also toggles you in and out of the edit mode, as you will see momentarily.

One Page

The next button (called One Page) displays a single page even if you are working with a multiple-page document.

Multiple Pages

The Multiple Pages button looks like four little pages. It lets you specify the number of miniaturized pages you'll see on-screen. Pressing this button reveals a matrix that you drag across to design your screen display. Choices range from a single page to 3×6 (18) pages, as shown in Figure 4.7.

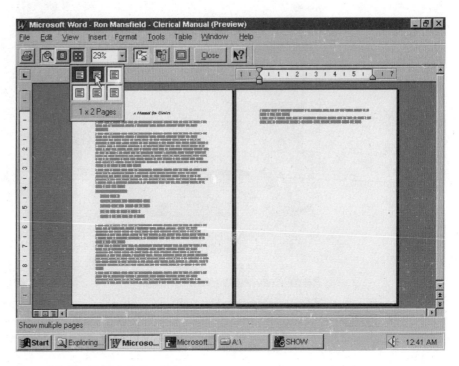

*Figure 4.7   **The Multiple Pages choices.***

Zoom Control

The Percentage text box and related zoom list are called the *Zoom controls*. They tell you the current zoom percentage and let you pick a variety of zoom options from a drop-down list.

View Rulers

Next you'll see a View Rulers button. It is used to toggle the rulers that you use to see and change margin settings.

Shrink to Fit

When you press the Shrink to Fit button (to the right of the View Rulers button), Word attempts to tighten up documents that end with a mostly white page. For example, Figure 4.8 shows how Word proposes to tighten up the two pages shown in Figure 4.7.

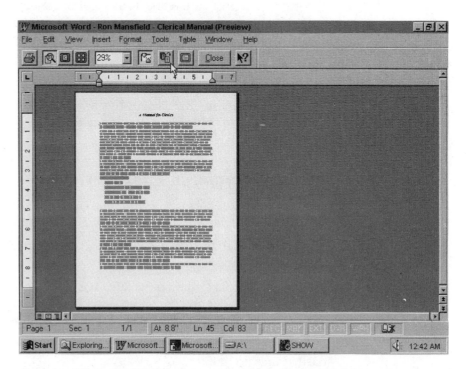

Figure 4.8 Word's Shrink to Fit button can often remove those ugly short last pages.

To undo proposed changes, use the Ctrl+Z shortcut or Edit ➤ Undo Shrink to Fit. Occasionally, Word can't shrink your document and will tell you so.

Full Screen

The Full Screen button removes most of the Print Preview clutter (menu bar, status line, etc.) so that you can see a bigger version of your document. Pressing the Full Screen button a second time returns the hidden controls.

Close Button

The Close button takes you back to the previous view.

Help Button

The Help button will turn your pointer into a question mark. Point to the item of interest (the vertical ruler, for instance) to read any available help. Double-click on the Help window's Close box to quit help.

Leaving Print Preview

Use the Close button to leave Print Preview and return to your previous view. The three standard view buttons (Normal, Page Layout, and Outline) are also available in the lower-left corner of the status area of Print Preview.

Moving Margins in Print Preview

While a complete explanation of margins will have to wait until Chapter 8, here is a quick trick you can try on your Twain quote in Print Preview:

1. Display the rulers if they are not already on-screen by clicking on the View Rulers button.

2. Point to the vertical ruler on the left edge of your screen. Notice how the pointer gets smaller and has an up-and-down-pointing head if you point to the exact line where the margin setting is, as shown in Figure 4.9.

3. Hold down the primary (usually the left) mouse button and notice the dashed margin line.

4. While holding down the mouse button, drag down to specify a new top margin while watching the dashed line.

5. Release the mouse button and Word will adjust the margin, moving the text down, as illustrated in Figure 4.10.

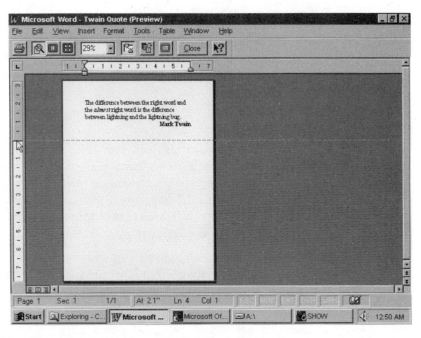

Figure 4.9   **Drag the margin handle to adjust the margins.**

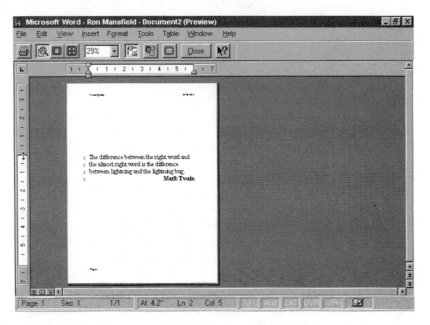

Figure 4.10   **The Twain quote after dragging to increase the top margin.**

Printing Labels and Envelopes

See Chapters 15 and 28 for envelope and label-printing tricks. Be sure to check out the envelope printing feature discussed in Chapter 15!

Background Printing

Because some printing jobs can take many minutes or even hours, background printing can be a real productivity booster—at least in theory—as it supposedly lets you do other things while the printer prints "in the background." Moreover, you can use the Windows task bar to check and control the status of multiple print jobs. Just double-click your printer's icon in the task bar.

Your system does all of this by quickly sending print jobs to a file on your hard disk rather than directly to the printer. It then spools the work to your printer in the background.

Enabling Background Printing

Turn on background printing from the Print tab in the Options dialog box:

1. Choose Tools ➤ Options.

2. Click the Print tab, if necessary, to reveal printing options.

3. Make sure there is a check in the Background Printing box (click if necessary).

4. Click OK and print as usual. Your documents will print in the background while you're working on other things.

TIP A great Windows shortcut to know is Alt+Tab. If you hit this key combination, Windows brings up a dialog box with icons of all open applications. There will be a box around the active application. Repeatedly pressing Alt+Tab cycles through the icons; when you release Alt+Tab, you will switch to the selected application.

Checking the Status of a Print Job

With background printing at work, you can check and change the status of multiple print jobs. Follow these steps:

1. Double-click the printer's icon in the Windows task bar.

2. Click to select the job or jobs you wish to cancel or reschedule.

3. Click on the appropriate button (Pause, Resume, or Delete).

4. Use the menus for other options.

5. To return to Word for Windows, hold down the Alt key and press Tab as many times as necessary.

For more information about background printing with Windows, use the online help and see your Windows documentation.

Aborting Printing

To stop a print job before it's finished, try pressing the Esc key repeatedly until the printing-status information disappears from your screen. Even after the print-status information disappears, your printer may print a few pages that were sent before print cancellation, as many printers contain their own memory (called a *buffer*). Check your printer manual for ways to quickly clear the printer's memory if this annoys you.

If you are using background printing, you will need to double-click the printer's icon in the task bar and cancel the job from there.

Chapter 5

Working with Graphics

FAST TRACKS

Word for Windows lets you draw, place, resize, reposition, and embellish graphics. You can work with your own drawings, charts from spreadsheet packages, photos from scanners, and just about any other computer-compatible art form. In fact, Word for Windows even comes with some clip art you can use to get your graphics library started.

You can simply *paste* graphics or place them in *frames*. As you'll see in Chapter 6, using frames makes it easier to reposition and work with graphics.

There are plenty of graphics-related buzzwords and standards to know. In fact, another book the size of this one could be written just on those subjects. But this chapter contains all you'll need to start creating your own art and using free or low-cost clip art.

Importing Graphics

Like text, computer art can be stored in disk files. Unfortunately, different drawing packages, scanners, and other graphic tools create files in their own unique formats. Word for Windows can use some graphic formats as-is; the program comes with a number of built-in translation utilities (called *filters*) that can convert graphics from many sources, allowing you to insert them into Word for Windows documents. At a minimum, you will be able to work with the following graphic formats (their usual file extensions are listed after their names):

AutoCAD 2-D (DXF)

Computer Graphics Metafile (CGM)

CompuServe GIF (GIF)

CorelDRAW (CDR)

DrawPerfect (WPG)

Encapsulated PostScript (EPS)

HP Graphic Language (HGL)

Kodak Photo CD (PCD)

Lotus 1-2-3 (PIC)

Macintosh PICT (PCT)

Micrografx Designer 3/Draw Plus (DRW)

PC Paintbrush (PCX)

Targa (TGA)

TIFF (Tagged Image File Format—TIF)

Windows Bitmap (BMP)

Windows Metafile (WMF)

If you don't see the format you need here, contact Microsoft technical support. They may be able to provide you with new filters, give you some workaround tips, or they can refer you to makers of graphics-conversion programs.

Other Sources of Clip Art

If you don't have the time or inclination to draw your own art, you can purchase compatible clip art disks from mail-order firms and retail software dealers like Egghead. Many companies and nonprofit groups also distribute low-cost or free shareware and public domain clip art. Check local computer user groups and online art libraries like the ones provided by America Online and CompuServe. If you have a scanner, you can convert printed images to Word-compatible art. Be sure you understand and honor any copyright restrictions when you use other people's art.

Using the Insert Picture Command

The easiest way to get hooked on graphics is to import a picture or two. Let's try it.

1. Start by opening your Twain document.

2. Place the insertion point where you want the picture to appear (on a new line after Mark's name, perhaps).

3. Choose Insert ➤ Picture as shown in Figure 5.1.

4. You'll see a dialog box something like Figure 5.2. Click the Preview button to enable the preview option.

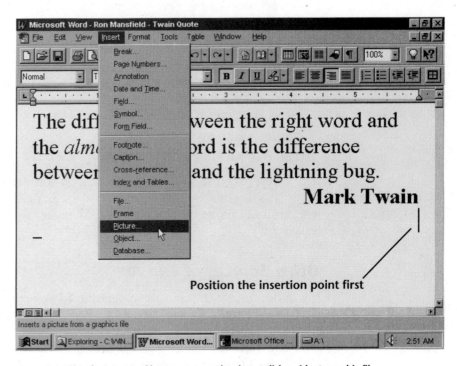

Figure 5.1   *Use the Insert ➤ Picture command to insert disk-resident graphic files.*

5. Browse by clicking on directories and files until you see something you like.

6. When you find your favorite graphic, click OK to insert it. (Figure 5.3 shows books.wmf, which comes with Word.)

7. Reposition and perhaps resize or otherwise embellish the image as described later in this chapter.

    In addition to the Word for Windows clip art folder, chances are you have other graphic images on your hard disk. For instance, your Windows directory probably has a dozen or so bitmap files (files ending in BMP). Use the scrollable lists to find files of interest. When you see one, click on the name to highlight it, then click the Preview button to get an idea of what it will look like, as before.

**Click the Preview button to see
graphics before inserting them**

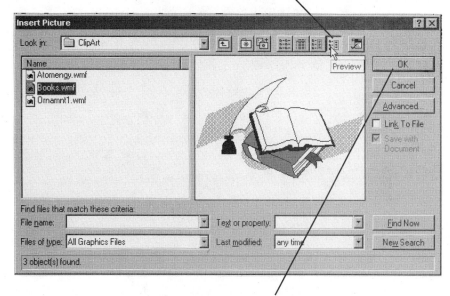

**Click to insert the selected graphic
into your Word document**

Figure 5.2   Enable the Preview Picture feature to browse.

The difference between the right word and
the *almost* right word is the difference
between lightning and the lightning bug.

Mark Twain

Figure 5.3   Graphics are placed at the insertion point.

Using Your Clipboard to Insert Art

If you already have a drawing program that you use to create and edit artwork, it is possible to copy your work to the Clipboard, and then paste it into a Word for Windows document:

1. Switch to or run the drawing program.

2. Select the art of interest.

3. Copy it to the Clipboard (Ctrl+C).

4. Switch to or start Word (quit or minimize the drawing program if you like—this may be necessary to run Word for Windows).

5. Move the insertion point to the desired location in your Word document.

6. Paste the graphic with Edit ➤ Paste command or Ctrl+V.

NEW   Another way of getting graphics to Word from other applications is to use the new document scraps feature of Windows 95. Just drag the image out onto the desktop and it will form a new file—a scrap—leaving your original untouched. Then just drag it into Word. The advantage of this is that you can drag it into other documents as well, and it won't be replaced the next time you copy something, as it would with the Clipboard. The disadvantage is that when you no longer need it, you have to drag it to the recycle bin, or it just sits on your desktop like a wedge of week-old camembert.

Resizing Graphics with Your Mouse

When you click on a graphic in a Word for Windows document to select it, the picture will be surrounded by a box containing eight handles—one in each corner and one on each side of the outline box. When you position the mouse pointer on a handle it turns into a two-headed arrow.

To increase or decrease the size of the entire graphic *proportionally*, drag a *corner* handle diagonally, releasing it when you are happy with the proposed size.

NOTE   Sizing something (a graphic, for example) *proportionally* means that as the size changes, the width and height retain the same proportions, relative to each other. That is, if the height gets three times larger, the width will get three times larger as well.

To distort a dimension, use the handles on the *edges* of the graphic outline to stretch or condense the graphic, as shown in Figure 5.4. Undo works if you act promptly.

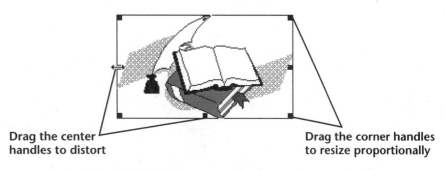

**Drag the center
handles to distort**

**Drag the corner handles
to resize proportionally**

Figure 5.4   *Drag center handles to distort, corner handles to resize proportionally.*

Cropping Graphics with Your Mouse

To crop a graphic (hide part of it), hold down the Shift key while you drag any of the handles to create the desired effect (see Figure 5.5). The mouse pointer will turn into a square with a line through it.

**Hold down Shift and
drag to crop (notice
different pointer shape)**

Figure 5.5   *Hold down the Shift key when dragging to crop (hide) part of a graphic.*

Adding White Space around Graphics

To add white space around a graphic, hold down the Shift key and drag handles away from the graphic (see Figure 5.6). Undo can restore the original size.

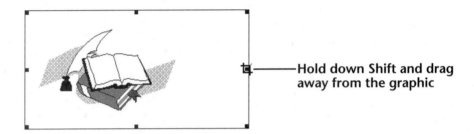

Hold down Shift and drag away from the graphic

Figure 5.6   Hold the Shift key and drag handles away from the graphic to add white space.

Sizing and Cropping Graphics with the Picture Command

The Format ➤ Picture command reveals the Picture dialog box, shown in Figure 5.7. It contains information about a selected picture's original size and any cropping or resizing that's been done.

Use Reset to return the graphic to its original size and eliminate any cropping

Picture		? X
Crop From	**Scaling**	OK
Left: -0.05"	Width: 75.9%	Cancel
Right: 0.05"	Height: 91.5%	Reset
Top: -0.27"	**Size**	Frame...
Bottom: -0.26"	Width: 1.58"	
	Height: 1.26"	
Original Size		
Width: 1.66"	Height: 0.85"	

Click to select the graphic of interest

Figure 5.7   Use the Picture dialog box to see what you've done; you can modify or undo resizing and cropping settings here.

You can also use this box to specify new size and cropping dimensions. The Reset button returns a graphic to its original size and uncrops it.

Using Word's Drawing Features

To create a new drawing using the Word for Windows drawing features:

1. Open a new or existing Word document.

2. Place the insertion point where you want your new art to be inserted.

3. Click on the Standard toolbar's Draw button. (Or, if you have a Word document containing a graphic you want to modify, double-click on the graphic.)

4. You'll see the Drawing toolbar, illustrated in Figure 5.8.

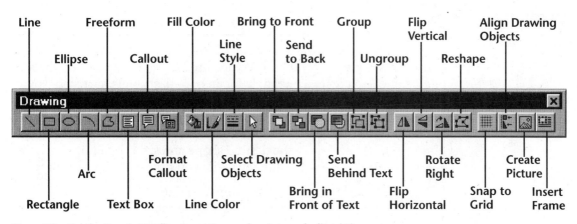

Figure 5.8 *Use the Drawing toolbar to create new drawings and edit existing ones.*

You'll use a series of buttons, menu commands, and your mouse to draw, resize, and rearrange shapes, lines, and text.

TIP You might want to reshape the Drawing toolbar to make it easier to move around and keep out of the way. Drag an edge of the toolbar to change its shape from wide and short to tall and skinny, for instance, as shown in Figure 5.9.

Drag to reshape

Figure 5.9   Change the shape of the toolbar if you like, by dragging any side.

Drawing Things

First click on a shape button or line button (line, ellipse, rectangle, etc.) in the Drawing toolbar, then use your mouse to create lines or shapes. For instance, to create a rectangle for an organizational chart, you would click on the rectangle button, click on the page to set the rectangle's upper-left corner, and drag with your mouse to create a rectangle of the desired shape and size. (Holding down the Shift key while you do this creates squares.)

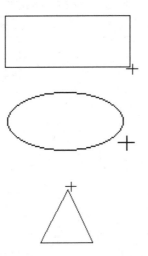

Use the ellipse tool for ovals and circles. (The Shift key helps you make precise circles.)

To create polygons, choose the free-form tool, then click and drag repeatedly until you are done. For example, to make a triangle, you would click once to anchor the first point and drag for the first side. Click again to anchor the second point and drag again. Click to anchor the third point, then drag back to the starting point and click one last time to complete the triangle.

TIP To change the shape of a polygon, select it using the techniques described next, then click the Reshape tool on the Drawing toolbar. Handles will appear at each intersection of the shape. Drag them as necessary to create the desired shape.

Selecting Objects

To select rectangles or other drawing elements (lines, text, etc.), click on the arrow button in the center of the Drawing toolbar, then point to the item you want to move. This selects it.

Holding down the Shift key lets you select multiple objects. The Edit ➤ Select All command selects all text and clip art, but not drawing objects. Selected objects are surrounded by small handles. Click outside of any selected object to deselect all selected objects.

Text in Drawings

You can create text for drawings either in *text boxes* or in *frames* (covered in Chapter 6). To create a text box, use the Drawing toolbar's Text Box button. Text in boxes is automatically surrounded by black lines unless you eliminate them.

1. Click on the toolbar's Text Box button.

2. Drag the text box to its desired size and shape. Make it big if in doubt.

3. Type the word **Marketing** (the insertion point's already in the box, so there's no need to position it).

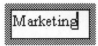

4. If necessary, you can increase the size of a text box by dragging, just as if it were any other graphic object.

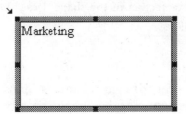

Embellishing Text in Drawings

You can embellish text (make it bold, center it, change type styles, and so on), and you can combine the effects using most of Word's formatting tools. For example, here's a box with two typefaces, some bold characters, and a bulleted list, created with the Bullets tool on the Format toolbar.

Marketing Department
- Sandra Lexington
- William Johnson
- Karin Danialson
- Bobbi Wrightwood

NEW   You can have Word automatically create the bulleted list shown here. When you type the first name, instead of trying to remember the keyboard combination for the bullet symbol, just type an asterisk (*) and a space. Then type the name and hit Enter (↵). Word will change the asterisk into a bullet (•) and place bullets in front of all other entries you make in the list. When you reach the end of your list, hit the backspace key to return to the normal style.

More or Less Space between Text and Box Lines

To increase or decrease the white space between the text and text box lines:

1. Select the text box.

2. Choose Format ➤ Drawing Object.

3. Select the Size and Position tab. You'll see the choices illustrated in Figure 5.10.

4. Specify a new internal margin by typing a new setting in the appropriate box or using the up and down arrow buttons. For instance, here's the marketing text box with 6 points (6pt) of internal margin:

Marketing Department
- Sandra Lexington
- William Johnson
- Karin Danialson

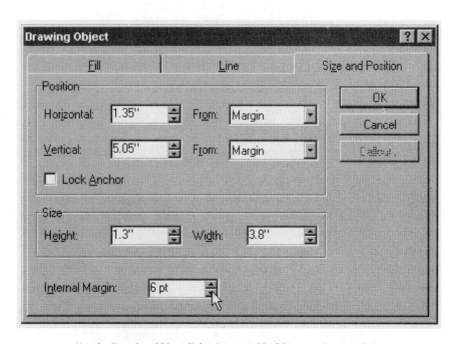

Figure 5.10   *Use the Drawing Object dialog box to add white space in a text box.*

Eliminating Text Box Lines

To eliminate the lines surrounding the text box, follow these steps:

1. Select the box or boxes by clicking or shift-clicking.

2. Use the Drawing toolbar's Line Color button to reveal the line color palette.

3. Click on the None choice (at the top), as shown here:

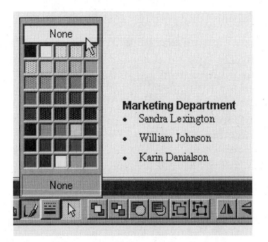

Moving Objects

To move objects, follow these steps:

1. Select the item or items to be moved.

2. Point to one of the selected items with your mouse pointer, avoiding the object's handles.

3. The pointer will change, now looking like an arrow with four heads:

Marketing Department
- Sandra Lexington
- William Johnson
- Karin Danialson

4. While the pointer has this shape, drag with your mouse and watch as an outline of the object(s) proposes a new location.

5. Releasing the mouse button completes the move.

Grid Lines

Word's drawing feature has optional *invisible gridlines* that make it easy to align things. This makes dragging a little jerky when the Snap To Grid feature is enabled. The gridlines act like magnets, and moved objects migrate to them no matter how hard you try to prevent this. For precise, smooth moves, turn the Snap to Grid feature off. You can also change the spacing and origin of grids. Do all of this with the Snap to Grid dialog box. Reach it with the Snap to Grid button near the right end of the Drawing toolbar.

The button reveals the Snap to Grid dialog box, shown in Figure 5.11.

To turn off the snap feature, remove the check mark from the Snap to Grid box by clicking, as shown in Figure 5.11. Even if the grid is turned off, you can still use it whenever you wish by holding down the Alt key while you drag.

Use the other tools in the dialog box to change the grid's dimensions and starting point with respect to the upper-left corner of the window.

Figure 5.11   **Use the Snap to Grid dialog box to change the spacing and origin of grids.**

Layers

You can construct objects from multiple elements placed near, on top of, or beneath each other. For instance, the illustration in your Twain quote contains a number of separate elements.

Things piled on top of each other are said to be *layered*. You can select items and use the Bring to Front or Send to Back buttons on the Drawing toolbar to arrange layers to your liking.

Grouping and Ungrouping

Sometimes you'll want to turn multiple drawing parts into a single object. This makes it easier to move and resize complex elements (see Figure 5.12). Simply select all of the elements of interest by Shift-clicking, then use the Group button on the Drawing toolbar.

Henceforth, all of the items will act as a single item, as you can see here,

until you select the group and choose Draw ➤ Ungroup.

Select all the items you wish to group...

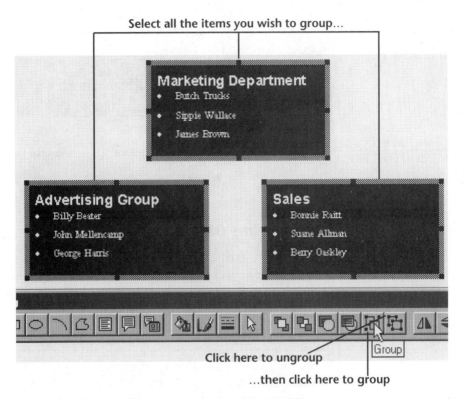

Click here to ungroup

...then click here to group

Figure 5.12   Grouping objects makes them easy to keep together.

TIP If you select multiple objects, they will move together as if grouped, but if you click only one object, you can move it independently.

Rotating and Flipping Objects

To rotate or flip objects, select them and use the Flip Horizontal, Flip Vertical, and Rotate Right buttons on the Drawing toolbar, shown in Figure 5.13.

NOTE These buttons won't work on Text boxes. Use WordArt, described in Chapter 6, to manipulate the orientation of text.

Flip Horizontal   Flip Vertical   Rotate Right

Figure 5.13   Use these buttons to rotate and flip objects.

Duplicating Objects

Once you've created an object (an "org chart" box, for instance), you can select, copy, and paste it to save time. Consider grouping complex collections of lines and shapes and text before duplicating them.

Pictures vs. Drawing Objects

There are two general types of graphic images—drawings like the ones created and discussed in this chapter, and "pictures" or "painted" images created with paint programs. Drawings are made up of individual elements—lines, circles, etc.(These elements are sometimes known as *vectors*.) Paint images are generally treated as one large collection of dots. Files that end with the extension .BMP are bitmap "paintings." So are many Windows Metafiles (.WMF). Word for Windows can use both drawings and bitmaps, but if you want to edit them, you must do so in a special window. Suppose, for instance, you want to change the color and shading of the ornamnt1.wmf file. Here are the required steps:

1. Position the insertion point where you want the graphic to appear in your Word document.

2. Choose Insert ➤ Picture and locate the desired file (ornamnt1.wmf) as shown in Figure 5.14.

3. Click OK to insert the graphic. It will appear in the Word document, but most of the Drawing toolbar buttons won't work. You can confirm this by watching the Status area as you point to the various buttons.

Figure 5.14 **Find the graphic file you wish to edit.**

4. Double-click on the graphic to open a picture window. You'll see the graphic, a *picture boundary,* and a small dialog box:

5. Click on the Reset Picture Boundary button to move the picture into the boundary as shown here:

6. Edit the picture (Shift-click to select all elements and use the Fill Color button on the Drawing toolbar to choose a 20 percent gray, as illustrated here):

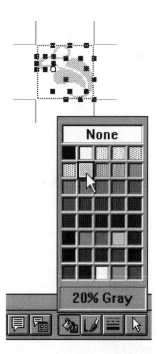

7. When done editing, click the Close Picture button in the little Picture window. The edited graphic will be placed in your Word for Windows document at the insertion point.

Callouts

You can use callouts to label graphics in Word for Windows documents. Here are the steps:

1. Create or import a graphic.

2. Click the Callout button on the Drawing toolbar.

3. Click where you want the callout arrow to point.

4. Drag to where you want to position the text, then release the mouse button. The callout will appear:

5. Type any text you want to show in the callout, then select the text and change its appearance if you like.

6. Select the callout box and resize it if you wish.

7. Drag the box and line as desired to reposition them.

 8. To change the design of the callout box, use the Callout Defaults dialog box shown in Figure 5.15. Reach it with the Format Callout button (to the right of the Callout button).

 NOTE If you select a callout and then click on Format Callout, changes you make will affect that callout and the defaults, but not any other existing callouts.

Filling

To fill drawn items with different colors or shades of gray, follow these steps:

1. Select the desired item(s).

 2. Use the Fill Color button on the Drawing toolbar to bring up the fill palette.

3. Click to select the desired fill color.

Figure 5.15   **Use the Callout Defaults dialog box to change the design of the callout box.**

Line Colors and Shades of Gray

To change the color or shade of lines:

1. Select the desired item(s).

2. Use the Line Color button on the Drawing toolbar to bring up the line color palette.

3. Click to select the desired line color.

Line Sizes and Arrowheads

To change the types of lines and any arrowheads:

1. Select the desired line(s).

2. Use the Line Style button on the Drawing toolbar to bring up the line style palette.

3. Click to select the desired line type.

4. Choosing More brings up the Line tab in the Drawing Object dialog box, illustrated in Figure 5.16.

Figure 5.16   **The Drawing Defaults dialog box gives you more control over line appearance.**

Time to Practice

If you have some free time, this would be a good place to stop and try some of your newfound skills. Type, edit, save, draw, print, and so on. At this point you know all the basics.

But don't put away the book just yet. There's lots more to know if you plan to *master* Word for Windows.

Chapter 6

Using Frames to Position and Anchor Things

FAST TRACK

Frames are a sure source of confusion. Push on, though. It is worthwhile to understand them! Part of the confusion comes from the fact that the word *Frame* appears twice in the Word for Windows workplace—there's the Insert ➤ Frame command and the Format ➤ Frame command. They do different things, so try to keep them straight.

If you simply paste a graphic into a Word for Windows document (without framing it), it is treated like a character. You can place the graphic between characters, move it from one line to another, copy it, delete it, and so on. But it is a slave to things like line and paragraph specifications, margins, indents, and such. To have maximum control over graphics and other document elements, you should place them in *frames*.

Frames can contain either graphics, text, or both. Frames let you precisely position objects virtually anywhere in your document. And, as illustrated in Figure 6.1, you can tell Word for Windows to flow your unframed text around frames if you like. Frames can contain graphics, Excel charts, Word text, or any combination thereof. In fact, it may be helpful to think of frames as pages within a page that you can move, resize, and embellish.

To use frames, you create them, insert things into them, then size and position them either with your mouse or with the Frame dialog box. Normally, you'll want to work with framed items in Page Layout view or Print Preview so that you can easily see and move them.

TIP It's a good idea to turn on hidden paragraph marks when working with frames. If they are not visible, click on the Show/Hide ¶ button in the Standard toolbar. It looks like a ¶ mark.

Inserting Frames and Framing Things

You can either insert an empty frame and then place something in it, or select something and then frame it. In either case, you use the Insert ➤ Frame command *or* the Insert Frame button on the Drawing toolbar.

Up and Running

Frame graphics, and text will wrap around them

Frame text, and it will span columns

A Business Lesson at 2,000 Feet

Ron Mansfield

 I recently started learning how to fly gliders, a long-time ambition of mine. In the process, I've learned something that is very relevant to the art of small business computing.

While Hal, my flight instructor and I walked to the plane last week the talk turned to emergency procedures. "What's the first thing to do if you are solo and discover a rattlesnake in your glider at 2,000

matically. But, consider this. There have been several disastrous commercial jet crashes apparently because entire crews have focused on relativity small distractions while their *planes* flew *themselves* straight into the ground.

In one case, three seasoned pilots appear to have simultaneously wrestled with the same burned-out indicator lamp. They were all completely oblivious to audible low altitude warnings from their cockpit

try program from one software vendor with a general ledger program from another maker. It would save his company about $3000 since they could avoid buying the complete set of accounting modules that included his favorite order entry program. He wanted to know if he should keep trying to force the two dissimilar products to work together. He also talked about using a complex database management package to personally program a new order entry pro-

---

> That busy CEO had no business spending three *hours*, much less three
> *days* on programming a computer, but that's what he had done.

---

feet?" He asked.

I blurted out something about avoiding quick leg movements and making a radio request for a precautionary ambulance. Hal ticked-off three or four more nightmares that had occurred at or near our desert airport. "What if you hear a loud clunk in the tail section? What if the rear canopy blows off?" And so-on.

Each time I had a different opinion–a reaction, I suppose, to the stated problem. Each time I was wrong.

"You should do the same thing immediately and continuously in each situation.", Hal said more firmly than I'd ever heard him before.

"Fly the plane, Ron Fly the plane."

The answer sounds too obvious at first, since "flying the plane" is something that you would expect pilots to do auto-

instruments; and ignored inquiries from puzzled air traffic controllers. Investigators believe that none of the flight crew members even looked outside!

We do the same thing in business. Just today I got a call from the CEO of a nine-month old, multi-million dollar startup manufacturing company. We talked for ten minutes about the rapid growth of his business, the challenges of managing far-flung offices, and so on. Then he got to the real purpose of the call–what he thought was the rattlesnake in his cockpit. He had personally spent three days trying to integrate an order en-

gram from scratch. He never once mentioned spending the extra $3000 for a complete set of compatible accounting modules, or hiring someone else to do the programming.

You see, executives, like pilots are problem solvers at heart. We enjoy mental challenges, and computers provide them. They appear seductively easy to use, and their problems draw us in as they unfold. Solutions that seem moments away often elude us for days.

So, next time you find yourself caught-up in an intriguing computer challenge–somewhere between the second and third cup of coffee, ask yourself "Who's flying the plane?" Maybe someone else should change the light bulbs while you get back to the controls. Thanks, Hal for reminding me of that.

Place frames in headers and footers, and they'll print on each page

Figure 6.1   Use frames to contain and position both text and graphics. Notice how frames "make room for themselves" in text.

Inserting Empty Frames

Here are the steps for creating a new, empty frame:

1. Start by switching to Page Layout view, if you are not already in it. (If you forget to do this, Word for Windows will ask if it can switch views for you.)

2. Click the Drawing toolbar's Insert Frame button or choose Insert ➤ Frame.

3. Your pointer will change to a crosshair. Drag to create a frame of the approximate size and shape you desire, located about where you want it to be placed.

4. Shortly after you release the mouse button, you'll see a frame surrounded by a border. If you have the Show/Hide Paragraph feature enabled, you will see a paragraph mark within the frame and an anchor outside it, as shown in Figure 6.2.

5. You can either type text in the resulting frame (you'll learn how in a moment), paste things from the Clipboard, or use one of the Insert menu commands, such as the Picture and Object commands.

The frame's anchor

The frame looks like cross-hatched lines

Figure 6.2   The new frame will appear, surrounded by a cross-hatched border, along with a little anchor.

Framing Existing Objects

If you already have something in your document that needs framing, you can frame it by following these steps:

1. Switch to Page Layout view if you are not there already.

2. Select the item or items to be framed.

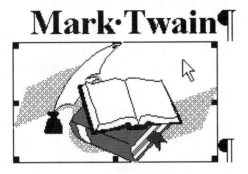

3. Either click the Frame button on the Drawing toolbar or choose <u>I</u>nsert ➤ <u>F</u>rame.

4. Your selected item(s) will be surrounded by a frame, and you'll see a paragraph mark and an anchor, as illustrated here, if you have clicked the Show/Hide ¶ button.

the·*almost*·right·word·is·the·difference·
between·lightning·and·the·lightning·bug.¶

Framed items and their frames can be resized just as you resize graphics. Drag their handles. If you accidentally frame the wrong thing or too many or too few things, or accidentally distort the size or shape of a graphic, Undo should work.

 TIP If you start the framing process (choose <u>I</u>nsert ➤ <u>F</u>rame) and change your mind, cancel it by pressing Esc.

Try It

Try framing the picture in your Twain quote. Follow these steps:

1. Load the Twain Quote document.

2. If you don't have a picture in your Twain document, use the Insert ➤ Picture command to add one. (The books.wmf picture is shown here.)

3. Switch to Page Layout View if you are not already there.

4. Select the picture by clicking on it.

5. Choose Insert ➤ Frame.

6. Shrink the graphic to 50 percent of its original size by dragging the lower-right corner of the frame while watching the statistics in the status area:

Positioning Framed Items with a Mouse

The dirt-simple way to position frames is to drag them with your mouse while in Page Layout view or Print Preview. Follow these steps:

1. Place the pointer anywhere within the frame and watch the pointer.

2. The pointer will change to include a four-headed arrow.

3. Press down on the primary mouse button and drag the frame to the upper-left corner of the text.

4. Release the mouse button.

5. Soon after you release the mouse button, the frame will take up residence in its new location. Text will move out of the way for the frame; and the little anchor icon will move as well.

You can continue to drag the framed graphic around to suit yourself. Switch to Print Preview and try moving it there too. Remember—you'll need to click on the Magnifier button in Print Preview before you can edit the document.

A frame is always anchored to a paragraph. When you position a frame by dragging it, it is initially anchored to its closest paragraph. When you move it, the anchor moves to the next nearest paragraph. To see where a frame's anchor is, select the frame. A little anchor icon like the one in Figure 6.3 will appear.

Figure 6.3 *Normally, frames are anchored to nearby paragraphs.*

As you add or delete text in your document, the framed item stays with its paragraph. A frame always appears on the same page with its paragraph.

This is often the desired effect. But what if you want to keep a framed item on a particular page, or a specific distance from a particular paragraph?

Positioning Framed Items with the Frame Dialog Box

When you want to position frames precisely or force a frame to position itself relative to other things that might move, use the Frame dialog box (reached by choosing Format ➤ Frame); it's shown in Figure 6.4.

When you select a frame and open this dialog box, you will see the current size and position of the frame. You can specify new size and position settings for the frame in inches (in), centimeters (cm), points (pt), or picas (pi). You change the units of measurement by using the General tab in the Options dialog box (reached by choosing Tools ➤ Options).

*Figure 6.4　**Use the Frame dialog box for precise frame sizing and positioning.***

Aligning Frames with Reference Points

The Frame dialog box also provides a mind-boggling array of positioning and reference options. For instance, you can force a frame to remain in the exact horizontal and vertical center of a page, even when you change margins or page sizes. Or, you can tell Word for Windows to keep a frame a specified distance from margins or columns. Finally, you can anchor a frame to text, so when the text moves, the frame accompanies it. Place a check mark in the Move with Text box to accomplish this.

Text and Frames

Frames and text can be used together several ways. Besides framing text, you can position frames relative to text or have text flow around frames. Here are a few ways to work with frames and text.

Placing Text in Frames

You can use frames as small text windows that can be moved anywhere in your document. For instance, in Figure 6.5, Adam's paragraph headings are being framed and moved into his document's margin. (You may want to remove the frame borders when you do this.)

By checking the Move with Text option in the Frame dialog box, you can make sure the headings will stay with their paragraphs when you edit the document.

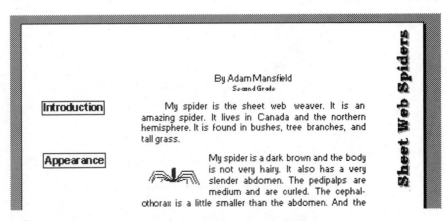

Figure 6.5 *Frame text can be used to place headings in margins, among other things.*

A quick way to create a lot of marginal headings like Adam's is to create one, and then *redefine the document's heading style(s)* based on the example. All of your headings will be framed and placed in the margin quicker than you can say "arachnid." (Chapter 14 shows how to work with styles.)

When framing existing *text*, Word for Windows will make the frame big enough to accommodate all of the text you've selected. But if you paste text into an existing *frame*, make sure the frame is big enough to prevent "weird word wrap," a problem that arises when you specify large line indents or place long words in narrow frames. If the text you insert changes into a long vertical string of characters, try resizing the frame to make the text legible. Feel free to use all of Word's text formatting tools in frames. You can have multiple paragraphs in frames.

Word's Formatting toolbar and ruler work in frames. You can change type sizes and styles, center, justify, and otherwise fool with text in frames. Even Word's spelling checker peeks into them.

Inserting Text in Framed Graphics (Captioning)

If you want to add a caption to a framed graphic, select the frame and press ↵. You'll see a new paragraph mark in the frame. Type the caption. Stylize the text, if you like. The caption will stay with the frame when you move it.

How Framed Items Appear in Different Views

You can see where framed items will print by displaying them in Print Preview or Page Layout view. When you switch to Normal or Outline view, framed items will appear within the page boundaries where they will print but not necessarily in their printing positions. You can easily spot framed items in Normal and Outline views.

Selecting and Deleting Framed Items

It's possible to delete frames *and their contents* by simply selecting the frame and then cutting it (Ctrl+X) or pressing the Delete key. (Select a frame by pointing and clicking with your mouse. Eight dark black

Up and Running

handles and a black line will appear around the frame when you've selected it.)

To remove a frame, but not its contents, select the frame and then use the Remove Frame button in the Frame dialog box (reached by choosing Format ➤ Frame). If you use this method to remove a frame that has a printing border, the frame's *border* will remain along with the contents. Delete it or change it as described next.

Deleting or Changing Frame Borders

Frames are created without printing borders, but these can be added and altered.

1. Select a framed object in Page Layout view by clicking on the object.

2. Use the Format ➤ Borders and Shading command to add, change, or remove the border. For instance, clicking on the None icon in the Presets area on the Borders tab removes a frame's border.

See Chapter 10 for more information about borders and shading.

TIP There is also a border button on the Standard toolbar. It's on the right end and looks like a four-pane window.

Special Effects with WordArt

There's an intriguing little program installed with Word for Windows called WordArt. You can use it to create unusual-looking text objects. Choose Insert ➤ Object, then scroll to Microsoft WordArt 2.0 and double-click on it. You'll see a dialog box like the one in Figure 6.6.

Figure 6.6   Use WordArt to create text containing special effects, then paste it into your Word for Windows document and move your masterpiece into position...

Try it out on your Twain quote. Here's how:

1. Open the Twain Quote in Page Layout view.

2. Place the insertion point on a new line after Mark's name.

3. Choose Insert ➤ Object.

4. Pick MS WordArt from the scrolling list in the Create New tab by double-clicking, as shown here:

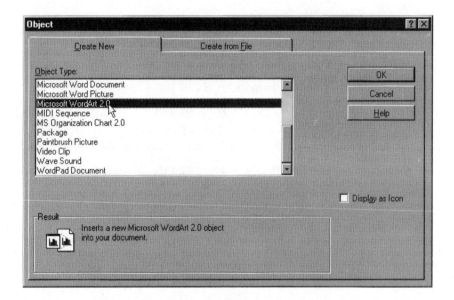

5. In the resulting dialog box, either type new text or paste text from your Clipboard. Then click Update Display to insert it into your document.

6. Notice that the menu bar has changed. It has a drop-down list of special effects. Experiment with the fonts, sizes, styles, alignment, and other options. You'll see a preview as you work, but it will take a moment for the screen to update fully. Don't panic if you see gnarly-looking "interim" images. The fonts supplied with WordArt are bitmap and may be hard to read in small sizes or appear jagged if they get too big. Figure 6.7 shows Footlight MT Light and the Arch Up effect.

7. When you are happy with your concoction, click on Update Display, and WordArt will paste it into your active Word for Windows document at the insertion point.

Figure 6.7 **Experiment with WordArt to create special text effects.**

8. Click in the document to close WordArt.

9. Frame the finished object to make it easier to move.

10. Reposition it like any other framed item.

11. Go show someone!

Creating Vertical Text

WordArt is the tool to use if you want to run an occasional piece of vertical text. Follow these steps:

1. Open the Twain quote in Page Layout view.

2. Place the insertion point on a new line after Mark's name.

3. Choose Insert ➤ Object.

4. Pick MS WordArt from the scrolling list in the Create New tab, as before.

5. Either type new text or paste text from your Clipboard in the resulting dialog box, then click Update Display to insert it into your document.

6. Choose a font (Arial in this example).

7. Click the Rotate tool. In the resulting dialog box, rotate the text 90 degrees by using ↑.

8. Click in the Word for Windows document itself to close WordArt.

9. Select the rotated text by dragging.

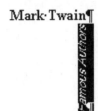

10. Frame the selected object by using <u>I</u>nsert ➤ <u>F</u>rame. The frame will move to the left of your screen:

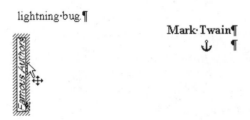

11. Reposition your rotated text like any other framed item—in the upper-right corner of the page, for instance. Remember that if you drag it too close to the edge of a page, your printer may not be able to print it.

Repeating Framed Items on Multiple Pages

To repeat the same framed object on multiple pages, create or anchor it in headers or footers. You'll learn more about headers and footers in Chapter 12.

Experiment

It's time to put down the book and grab your mouse. Try a few of the techniques in this chapter. When you're done frittering—err, I mean *learning,* check out the next chapter, where you'll see how Word for Windows can help you organize your documents.

Chapter 7

Managing Your Files

FAST TRACK

Your hard disk can contain hundreds or even thousands of files. If you work in a large, networked organization, you may have access to ten times this many documents. If you've ever misplaced a file, you know how frustrating and time-consuming trying to find it can be.

Word for Windows provides two features to help you organize and locate files. They are the Search utility of the Open command and the Summary tab of the Properties command, both found on the File menu. For those of you new to Windows 95, we'll start with a quick review of the new methods for managing files and directories, and for navigating paths.

Files, Directories, and Paths

Your computer lets you arrange your files in a hierarchical structure. Files (Word for Windows documents, for instance) can be stored in *directories*, also called *folders*. Directories, or folders, can also be stored within directories. Figure 7.1 shows an example of this.

In the example, there is a directory called Clients. It contains all of the client-related directories and files for this computer. Within the Clients directory there are three client subdirectories, one for each client (B&N, CNN, and Xerox). Each of these client directories contains additional

Figure 7.1 *A hierarchical directory arrangement contains directories within directories.*

subdirectories and files relating to the particular client. For instance, the B&N directory contains the B&N Progress directory, in which project-related memos, lists, and reports are stored. The B&N subdirectory also contains other directories with billing and contract information, hardware information, etc. If you were to open the Xerox subdirectory, you might find a similar arrangement of Xerox-specific files.

This hierarchy makes it easy to store and find things. It also provides good hiding places for lost files. For instance, you'd need to open three directories to find the Projects file.

The steps that you take to find a file form a *path*. To get to the Projects document or the Task List Memo, for example, you would start by choosing the hard disk containing the directories, and then open the Clients directory. Next you would open the B&N directory, and finally the B&N Progress subdirectory. You can do this from the Windows Explorer by double-clicking on directories, or you can do it from within Word for Windows itself by using File ➤ Open (Ctrl+O).

new You might have noticed that, both in Windows Explorer and in Word, you no longer see file extensions (.exe, .doc, and so on). Extensions are now hidden from you unless you specifically ask for them to be shown. (See your Windows manuals for details.) This can be a bit disconcerting, especially if you've just saved a document as *Memo.doc*, and it now appears as just *Memo*. What this means practically is that you should *not* try to type extensions for your documents once you've saved them. The first time, it's okay. You type **.doc**, it disappears, and everybody's happy. If you later explicitly add the extension, though, either in Explorer or in some other fashion, your document's real name is now *Memo.doc.doc*! Oops.

If you are worried about sharing files with people using older versions of Word or other word processors, your concerns are justified. Windows keeps track of both long and short (DOS-compatible) names, but its methods are by no means perfect. For instance, if you are a lawyer and you have 400 files that all begin *Motion to...* or some such, you're okay as long as you work in a Windows 95 environment. If you go to a pre-95 machine, though, it's gonna be an absolute nightmare trying to figure out which file is *Motion to Desist, ABC Trucking* and *Motion to Desist, ABC Bakery*. There is no single best solution to this dilemma; if you know you will often be working in non–Windows 95 environments, you may wish to limit yourself to the old eight-character DOS constraints or work out a formalized folder scheme.

Opening Previously Saved Documents

When you pick File ➤ Open, you will be presented with a dialog box that looks something like the one in Figure 7.2.

You show Word for Windows the path to your document by opening successive directories until the file you want is visible in the scrollable document list. To open directories, scroll through the drop-down Directories list, double-clicking to open directories. In cases where you have directories within directories, you will need to double-click on more than one folder.

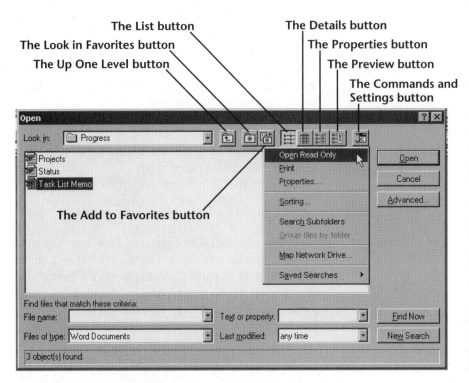

Figure 7.2   From the Open dialog box, use the Look In drop-down menu to open the drive containing the document you need, then choose subdirectories and files from scrolling lists.

If you open one directory too many, click the Up One Level button.

When you see the file (the document) that you want to work with, double-click on the document's name or just click on it and press ↵. Your Windows manuals and online tutorials contain more information on this subject and practice exercises if you need additional help. If you choose the Open Read Only option from the Commands and Settings dropdown menu, you will not be able to save any changes to the file; rather, you will be asked to save edits to a new file.

TIP If you are looking for non-Word documents, don't be surprised if they don't appear in the list. By default, Word shows only Word files. To see other kinds of files, pick the appropriate type from the Files of Type drop-down list. If you choose All Files, Word will display any non-hidden files.

Word's Open dialog box has several new buttons to help you get around and organize your files (these are noted in Figure 7.2). First, there is the Up One Level button. Clicking this button lets you see what's in the folder that contains the folder listed in the Look In box. Next to that is the Look In Favorites button. Clicking this takes you to a folder called Favorites, found in the Windows directory. Put commonly used files in here to find them quickly. The Add To Favorites button automatically adds to the Favorites folder a *shortcut* to the selected document.

NEW Windows 95 has a nifty new feature called *shortcuts*. A shortcut is a shadow file that points to a file, folder, or application, but does not contain any of its data. What makes shortcuts useful is that you can place them anywhere, usually in easy-to-find places (such as the Favorites folder), while leaving your original file, folder, or application in whatever place makes the most sense for your file organization.

The next four buttons let you specify how you want to view files. The List button just shows a list. The Details button shows each document's name, size, type, and when it was last modified. The Properties button shows a window that tells you what revision of the document you are looking at, how many pages, words, and characters it contains, and so on. This is more or less the same information you see in the Summary and Statistics tabs of the Properties dialog box. The Preview button lets you see the contents of the file without actually opening it. Finally, the Commands and Settings button drops down a menu where you can make a variety of selections, including to open the document as read-only or to print it.

In addition, Word lets you restrict the types of files you will see. For instance, you can ask to see only document templates or only Rich Text Format files. You make your choice in the Files of Type drop-down list. Word also has a search utility built right into the Open dialog box.

Steps for Opening Documents from within Word

Here are the general steps for opening Word documents with Word for Windows running:

1. From within Word, choose File ➤ Open, press Ctrl+O, or click the Open button on the Standard toolbar.

2. Use the Look In list to open the appropriate disk or scroll through the directory list.

3. Double-click on the desired file name to load the document.

Opening Non-Word Documents

Each different word-processing program (Ami Pro, WordPerfect, etc.) creates document files containing unique control codes for things like character attributes, margins, and so forth. Frequently, if you use one word-processing program to open a document created by a different program, you will see these codes that look like unintelligible gibberish intermixed with the document's text. Margins may be different. Fonts and line spacing will often change.

There are third-party file-conversion programs that can minimize these problems (such as Word for Word, by Mastersoft). Word also has some file-conversion capabilities of its own. See Chapter 35.

Don't expect perfection when moving documents from one program or computer to another. You will probably need to make some formatting changes, deal with line-ending differences, and so on. Here are the general steps for loading non-Word documents:

1. From within Word, choose File ➤ Open or Ctrl+O.

2. Point to the Files of Type drop-down list to pick the kind of files you wish to view and open, or choose All Files to see a list of all files.

3. Use the Look In drop-down list to open the appropriate disk and directory (by double-clicking).

4. Double-click on the desired file name in the scrollable list.

5. Word will convert and load the document or alert you to the fact that it cannot do the necessary conversion.

> **TIP** If you want Word to notify you of successful conversions, visit the General tab of the Tools ➤ Options dialog box and activate the Confirm Conversions at Open option.

6. Inspect and clean up the document.

7. Save it as a Word for Windows document if you plan to use it with Word in the future, or use the Save As command to save it in the originating program's format, if that's where you will be working on the document in the future.

Opening Documents as Read-Only

If you wish to open a document as read-only to prevent yourself from accidentally making changes to the disk file, choose the Open Read Only option from the Open dialog box.

Template documents, when opened as templates, are always opened as read-only. When you open a template document and then make changes and save them, you will be automatically prompted for a different file name. Templates are discussed in more detail in Chapter 16.

Finding Files

Word's file-finding utility, found in the Open dialog box, is a powerful tool that helps you locate, list, sort, examine, open, and print documents based on simple or complex search criteria. You can examine your computer's hard disk(s) or even search a server or shared drive over a network. Both Word and non-Word files can be located using this feature. You can find files by file name, creation date, and much more. For instance, if you enter document Properties when saving Word for

Windows documents, you can round up files based on their authors, keywords, and so on.

Let's start with a simple search. Suppose, for instance, that you've lost your Twain Quote document. Start by choosing File ➤ Open or by clicking the Open button in the Standard toolbar.

Use the four drop-down menus at the bottom of the screen, along with the Look In box, to specify where you want Word to search. In general, you need to tell Word the following:

▶ Which directory or directories to search

▶ What to look for

▶ Optional, advanced criteria to narrow the search (Summary info entries, for example)

Searching by File Names

Continuing with the case of the missing Twain Quote, let's assume you forgot where you had saved it and you are at the root directory of your hard disk. It would be a real nuisance to open Windows Explorer and navigate through all your directory folders to find the missing document. Instead, let Word do the work for you! Follow these steps.

> **TIP** You can still use those old-fashioned DOS wildcards (*, ?, etc.) in your searches, if you wish. For example, typing *.DOC in the File Name box will find all files that have the extension *doc*. While this might be handy at times (for finding graphics files of a particular kind, for example), it is a bit outdated. Now that you can use longer, more meaningful file names, searches will probably be quickest if you search for files by their names.

1. If it is not still open, bring up the Open dialog box by choosing File ➤ Open, pressing Ctrl+O, or clicking the Open button on the Standard toolbar.

2. Type **Twain Quote** in the File name: box.

3. Click the Commands and Settings button and choose the Search Sub-folders option from the drop-down menu, as shown in Figure 7.3. This is a very important step; if you omit it, Word will search only the selected folder. Worse yet, if no folder is selected, Word will do nothing. (Well, at least nothing useful.)

Up and Running

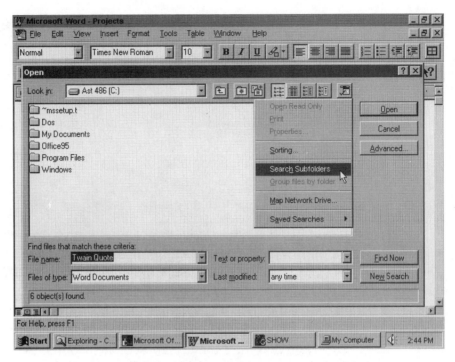

Figure 7.3   Choose the Search Subfolders option from the Commands and Settings menu.

4.   Word will start searching for the Twain Quote file. If you want to stop the search, click Stop. Word will then show you the results of its search, as shown in Figure 7.4. You can then do one of several things to see which file is the one you want. Click the Details button to see where these files are on your disk, as in Figure 7.4. Alternately, click the Preview button to get a peek at the selected file's contents.

5.   In Figure 7.4, two of the three Twain Quote files are shortcuts (Word helpfully tells us this), but we want the real thing. Double-click on the correct file or preview it first if you wish, and Word will open the Twain Quote file.

TIP   With the Search Subfolders option selected, the file-finding utility is an active function; that is, you don't have to tell it to start running. It will begin searching as soon as you choose a folder in the Open dialog box or from the Look In box. This is tricky and takes some getting used to, but it is quite slick.

Figure 7.4 Word makes a list of files that match the file name you have specified. By clicking the Details button, you can see which is the one you want, as shown here.

6. If you don't use the Searc̲h Subfolders option, you can always initiate searches by clicking the F̲ind Now button in the Open dialog box. Be sure that you have selected a folder to be searched, though; otherwise nothing will happen.

7. Once Word has found the files you've requested, if you wish to clear the list and begin a new search, click the Ne̲w Search button in the Open dialog box.

Dealing with Large Lists

Long lists of found files can be handled in a number of ways. You can use the Sort̲ing option on the Commands and Settings menu in the Open window to bring up the Sort By dialog box, which lets you sort your list (see Figure 7.5).

If you know the approximate time frame of a project, date sorts will help you narrow down the list to examine. If you knew this was a big document, a sort by file size might help. Choose the appropriate setting. When you are satisfied with your criteria, click OK or press ↵.

Figure 7.5   *The Sort By dialog box lets you arrange lists of files in different ways.*

Another alternative is to redo the search with more specific criteria. Click on the Advanced button in the Open dialog box to reach the Advanced Find dialog box, shown in Figure 7.6.

There are three drop-down lists in this dialog box designed to let you specify different kinds of information and limitations on your searches. Here is where you can use the information entered in the Summary tab of the Properties dialog box (discussed under the section *Finding Files with Document Properties*). You can even save search specifications for reuse.

Figure 7.6   *Advanced search options can help shorten your hit list.*

Searching Inside Documents

Searches on file names alone are the quickest and are recommended as the starting point for searches of any but the smallest disk drives. But if you cannot find a file with a file-name search, or if you find too many files containing the search word, it is possible to ask Word for Windows to look *inside* each file on the disk being searched and list only those files containing the word or words meeting your criteria. The file-finding utility searches entire Word documents including headers, footers, and hidden text.

 First, choose the appropriate setting from the Condition drop-down menu. You might choose "includes" for this particular search. Then, in the Value box, you type what you want Word to look for. For example, you might type **Twain**. Finally, click the Add to List button to add this criterion to the window at the top of the Advanced Find dialog box. You need to use the same care when specifying search text that you use with Word's Find and Replace commands. If you are too specific, you may miss the file you are looking for. Use too vague a search string, and you will get excessively long file lists.

Suppose, for instance, you want to round up everything you've written about DAT (Digital Audio Tape). If you use *DAT* as your search text, Word for Windows will also list files containing the words *database*, *date*, and *Datsun*. Placing a space after *DAT* in the search string or enabling the Match Case option solves that problem.

Several wild cards work here. You will type them from the keyboard. For example, *Sm?th* will find both *Smith* and *Smyth*. The wild card ^W searches for white space. See Chapter 20 for more about Find and Replace wild cards that can be used here too.

Once you've entered search criteria in the Advanced Find dialog box and started the search by clicking Find Now or pressing ↵, Word for Windows will start examining the contents of your disk. This can take a while.

Eventually a list will appear and you can preview the hits or use the other buttons to open, sort, and so on.

Finding Files with Document Properties

If you and your colleagues have been religious about entering consistent information in the Summary tab of the Properties dialog box, you can use the file-finding feature to search for those entries. If you open the Advanced Find dialog box (from the Open dialog box), you'll notice the Property box in the lower-left corner. This drop-down menu contains dozens of criteria you can use in your file searches. These properties are keyed to the entries you've made in the Properties dialog box, however; so the usefulness of this feature will depend upon how assiduous you've been in recording this information.

Just remember that if you've created documents and failed to put your name in the author box when creating Summary info, or if you sometimes type your whole name and at other times use your initials, you run the risk of missing documents when your search criteria include Summary info search restrictions.

Naturally, documents created with programs that do not collect Summary info (such as WordPerfect) will be ignored.

TIP   Written policies and procedures regarding file naming and Summary information entries can be a big help in law firms, publishing houses, and other organizations with networks and thousands of files.

Try It, You'll Like It

If you haven't already done so, search for your Twain Quote using some of the Summary info you entered via the Properties dialog box when you initially saved the document.

Multiple Searches

There are times when you will want to do multiple searches. For instance, in our earlier example, you may discover that sometimes you referred to DAT in documents by the complete name and not the acronym. You might think you would need to search once for *DAT* and a second time for *Digital Audio Tape* to find each relevant document. Similarly, you might think that if you use multiple disk drives you will need to perform multiple searches. Fortunately, you can *combine* search criteria. This means you can do all of the above in a *single* search. Read on....

Combining Searches

The classic combined search works like this. Search for the first criterion of interest (Value: = DAT for instance). Review the list.

Return to the Advanced Find dialog box and add additional search criteria. You might, for instance, type **Digital Audio Tape** in the Value box. Each time you add another limitation, click the Add to List button to add it to the criteria list at the top of the dialog box. Then run another search by clicking the Find Now button. The resulting list will now contain documents meeting either criterion.

You can combine the results of different types of searches. For example, you can search first by file name, then by author, and so on.

Searching Multiple Disks

If you have more than one disk drive on your computer, or if you want to search both your computer's disk and other drives on a network, you can instruct Word to look in more than one place. Do this in the Look In box of the Advanced Find dialog box, as illustrated in Figure 7.7.

Saving Initially—a Review

You've already learned the basic steps for saving in Chapter 2. Here's a review and some additional information and advice about saving.

▶ Until you save your document for the first time, it resides only in RAM (random-access memory) and will be lost if there is a power failure or other malfunction.

▶ Save about every fifteen minutes or whenever you are interrupted.

▶ Turn on Word's automatic save feature if you have trouble remembering to save. (Use the Save tab in the Options dialog box to enable automatic saves.)

▶ Always save before printing.

▶ Save before you do complex tasks that might drastically alter your document, such as replacing or hyphenating.

Figure 7.7   *The Look In box of the Advanced Find dialog box.*

▶ To save initially, select <u>F</u>ile ➤ <u>S</u>ave, use the Ctrl+S keyboard shortcut, or click the toolbar's Save button.

▶ Pay attention to the part of the Save dialog box that tells you *where* Word plans to store your work.

▶ To specify a different drive, use the Save In drop-down list.

▶ Type a name for your document in the File Name box, then click the OK button or press ↵. File names may now be as long as 255 characters. Do not include colons (:) in your file names.

▶ You needn't type anything in the Properties dialog box, and you can prevent it from even appearing. But if you plan to keep many documents on your hard disk, and particularly if you will be storing things on a crowded network server, it is a good idea to use this feature.

▶ Once you have saved a document's Summary information, you will not be asked for it again when you save your work. Summary information can be viewed and modified by picking <u>F</u>ile ➤ Proper<u>t</u>ies.

A quick trip to File ➤ Save, or better still the key combination Ctrl+S, will save your work whenever you desire. So will clicking the Save button on the Toolbar. Save often.

TIP As you learned in Chapter 2, to prevent the Properties dialog box from appearing when you initially save a new document, turn it off via the Save tab in the dialog box brought up by the Tools ➤ Options command. For more information on this subject see Chapter 36.

Save Options

It's worth exploring Word's save options, even though the default choices will work well for most people. Reach the save options with the Options button in the Save As dialog box or via the Save tab in the Tools ➤ Options command. It looks like Figure 7.8.

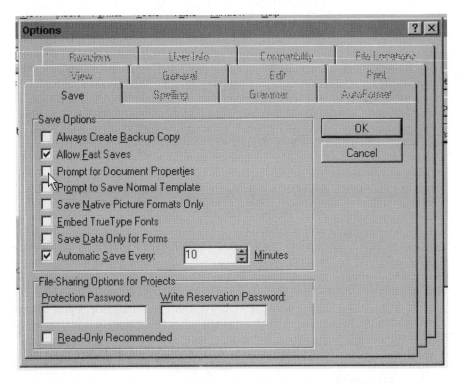

Figure 7.8 *Word's save options can be found in the Save tab of the Options dialog box (Tools ➤ Options).*

Here is a list of the options you'll see in the Save As dialog box and some information about their use, followed by examples of typical save operations.

Always Create Backup Copy

Beware the Create Backup Copy option! With this option selected, Word for Windows makes a copy of the most recent disk-resident version of your file (giving it the extension .BAK) before saving your current changes to the original file. This is *not* a true backup, for reasons described later in this chapter.

Allow Fast Saves

The Allow Fast Saves option instructs Word for Windows to save just your changes most of the time rather than making you wait while it rewrites your entire document to disk each time you save. While this option can let you get back to typing and editing more quickly, it consumes extra RAM, uses more disk space, and can create real recovery problems if you have trouble with your disk while working on a big project.

> **TIP** Many experienced Word for Windows users leave Allow Fast Saves off. Always Create Backup Copies and Allow Fast Saves are mutually exclusive options; you can't select both at the same time.

Prompt for Document Properties

With this option checked, Word interrupts you the first time you save a new document and prompts for author name, document title, keywords, and other information.

Save Native Picture Formats Only

This option saves only the Windows versions of graphics, thereby reducing file sizes when you've imported a graphic from another platform (a Macintosh, for instance). Leave it off if you plan to swap Word for Windows documents between platforms.

Prompt to Save Normal Template

This choice displays a message when you exit Word (File ▸ Exit), asking whether you want to save changes made to default settings in the Normal

Template file. If you don't display this prompt, Word automatically saves such changes, including words added to the dictionary and new macros.

Embed TrueType Fonts

This option instructs Word for Windows to save any TrueType fonts you've used with the document file so that other users can read your documents, even if they don't have the same TrueType files installed on their machines. Leave this feature off unless *all* of the following are true:

▶ You exchange files with others

▶ You use TrueType fonts

▶ The users you share with do not have the fonts installed

Save Data Only for Forms

When creating forms and collecting data on forms, Word for Windows can be instructed to save the data to disk without saving the forms. See Chapter 34 for details.

Automatic Save Every N Minutes

This can be a blessing or a curse. If you are one of those people who never remembers to save early and often, Word for Windows can do it for you. Place a check in the appropriate box and tell Word the desired save interval (10 minutes is the default). Thereafter Word will save every 10 minutes or whatever without even asking.

On the other hand, if you have a slow machine, this automatic save feature can be a problem.

The File-Sharing Options

These options let you protect documents that are shared with others. If you password protect a document, you and others must use the password each time you reopen the document. Document passwords can be up to 30 characters long. Upper- and lowercase matters, so use care when assigning and entering passwords.

Protection Passwords   This type of password prevents opening a document without knowing its password. If you use protection passwords, don't forget them.

Write Reservation Passwords Documents saved with only write reservation passwords let users open them without knowing the password. Only users who know the write reservation password can save changes, though.

Read-Only Recommended A check in this option box instructs Word to recommend that users open the document as read-only. It will *not*, however, prevent modification or deletion.

Saving under a Different File Name

Normally, once you've named a document, Word for Windows will keep saving the document under the same name. Use the File ➤ Save As command to save a document under a different file name. Follow these steps:

1. If necessary, make the document you wish to save the active document, then choose File ➤ Save As or use the F12 shortcut.

2. Type a new file name in the File name area of the dialog box. Because the cursor goes there by default, you can just start typing.

3. Specify a new directory and disk location if you wish, then click the Save button or simply press ↵.

4. Future saves will use this new name and location.

Saving to Floppy and Other Disk Drives

Normally, once you've saved a document, Word will keep saving the document to the same disk and into the same directory you initially specified. Again, you use the File ➤ Save As command (or F12) to save a document to a different disk or directory. Follow these steps:

1. If you plan to save to a floppy, insert it into your computer's floppy drive. If you plan to save to a different hard drive, be sure it is turned on and available. If you plan to save on a server, be sure your network connection has been established and that the desired server drive is mounted. (See your computer manuals or contact your network manager for assistance.)

2. If necessary, make the document you wish to save the active document; then choose File ➤ Save As or use the F12 shortcut.

3. Specify the desired disk drive in the Save As dialog box by selecting a drive from the Save In drop-down list. When you've chosen the appropriate disk (or a directory on that disk), click the OK button or press ↵.

4. Future saves will use this new location.

> **TIP**   Floppy disks are best used as a medium for transporting and archiving files. Do all of your work in Word on files located on your hard disk or a network drive and save them there; then copy the finished files to a floppy disk as needed.

Saving in Non-Word Formats

Just as you can open non-Word files with Word for Windows, you can save your work in non-Word formats. Use the drop-down Save as Type list in Word's Save As dialog box to specify the desired file format.

When Your Disk Gets Full

Occasionally, when you attempt to save, Word will tell you that there is not enough room for your project on the current disk. You may even get an "insufficient disk space" message seemingly out of the blue. This is because Word for Windows sometimes creates temporary files that need disk space of their own. There are several things you can do in this situation.

▶   Use the Save As command to save to a different hard drive on your computer or perhaps to a different hard drive elsewhere on your network.

▶   Use the Save As command to save to a floppy disk.

▶   Switch to the Explorer, delete old unwanted files, and then switch back to Word and attempt to save again.

Making Backup Files for Safekeeping

It's a fact of life: Hard disks fail. Floppy disks are easily damaged. Fires, floods, winds, and earthquakes destroy computers and the files stored on their disks. Punks walk off with them. Nice people like you and me accidentally delete important files. Computers and software have a mean-spirited habit of trashing your important work-in-progress, usually when you are in a big hurry.

You need to make regular backup copies of your important Word for Windows documents, and you need to store those files far enough away from your computer so that they will survive a neighborhood disaster.

The easy way to save small, simple files is to copy them to floppies. Use File ➤ Save As (F12) to place copies of important documents on separate disks, which should be stored away from your computer. Or you can save entire directories to floppies with the Windows Backup program.

For big Word files and large collections of documents, consider backing up to removable portable hard disks or look into tape-backup systems.

Whatever you do, don't rely upon Word's automatic-backup feature as your only backup method! Backup files created with this automatic feature will almost never contain the most recent changes you've made. Many experienced users leave this automatic backup feature turned off and take active responsibility for backups themselves. (Turn it off in the Save tab of the Options dialog box, reached by choosing Tools ➤ Options. See Chapter 36 for details.) If your organization has a computer support person or network manager, ask about backup policies and procedures.

Recovering Damaged Files

If, while you're working in Word for Windows, there is a power failure or other gremlin that causes your computer to lock up or otherwise misbehave, you may find yourself with a damaged document that will either refuse to load when you're back in business or be missing information. Word may be able to recover most of your recent work by loading the appropriate temporary file that Word has probably created. Restart Word.

WARNING　Never delete or rename temporary files when Word is running. Exit Word first.

Formatting Fundamentals

2

Chapter 8

Margins and Page Breaks

FAST TRACK

The amount of white space around the edges of a Word for Windows page is determined primarily by margin and optional gutter settings. (Gutters add extra white space for bound documents.) One set of margin and gutter settings can be used for an entire document, or you can define different settings for different pages in your document. The paper size, paper orientation (portrait vs. landscape), margin, and gutter settings you choose work together to determine the size and shape of the text area of pages.

Larger margins and gutter settings decrease the available text area while increasing the surrounding white space on each page. Figure 8.1 shows the Word default margin and text-area dimensions for both portrait and landscape orientations when creating U.S. letter-size documents without gutters.

Get Off to a Good Start

Because margin settings (and Page Setup information) all affect pagination, it is a good idea to define these dimensions right when you begin a new project. This will give you a better grasp of the page count and overall look of the document as you work. You can always fine-tune margin settings just before final printing.

Margins need not all be the same width. It is possible, for instance, to have a $1\frac{1}{2}''$ left margin and a 1.0″ right margin, a $\frac{1}{2}''$ bottom margin and a $\frac{3}{4}''$ top margin, or just about any combination you desire.

When printing two-sided documents, you may want to use Word's Mirror Even/Odd margin feature and possibly add gutters to place extra white space near the center of your book. (Note that it is conventional to have odd-numbered pages on the right and even on the left—just look at any book!) If you plan to have different left and right margins in a two-sided document (a wide left and narrow right, for instance), it is useful to think of these as *inside* and *outside* margins rather than left and right margins, as the wide margin will be on the left side of odd-numbered pages but on the right of even-numbered pages. In this chapter you'll learn how to create such margins.

If you use headers and footers, you will want to know how they interact with margin settings. Word makes this all fairly painless.

Part
2

Formatting
Fundamentals

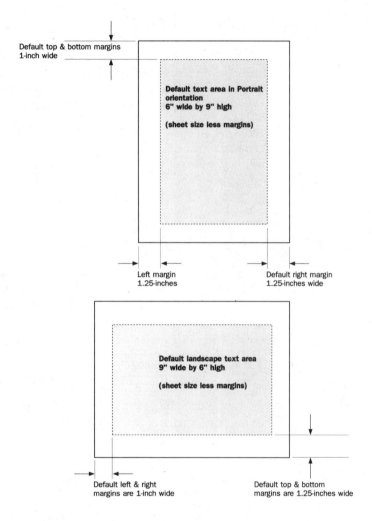

Figure 8.1 Margin settings, paper size, and orientation are three of the many factors that affect the available text area.

 NOTE   Some printers cannot print at the extreme edges of a page. This can be a consideration when setting margins.

Document Margins vs. Indents

Don't confuse Word's margin settings with its paragraph-indentation feature. A Word *page* can have only one user-specified left *margin* setting and only one user-specified right margin setting, but each *paragraph* on the page can have a different left and right *indentation* setting.

Indents are *added* to margin settings. That is to say, if you specify a 1.0″ left margin and a $\frac{1}{2}$″ left indent, your text will print $1\frac{1}{2}$″ from the left margin. If you set a 1.0″ right margin and indent the right edge of a paragraph 1.0″, the text will stop 2.0″ from the right edge of the page. See Chapter 11 to learn more about indenting.

Changing Document Margins

There are three ways to set margins. The most straightforward method is to use the Margins portion of the Page Setup dialog box, reached with the File ➤ Page Setup command. Curiously, there is neither a standard keyboard shortcut nor a toolbar button for this oft-visited dialog box. You can add your own as described in Chapter 36.

It is also possible to drag margins using the rulers in Print Preview. This lets you see the results of margin changes after a slight repagination delay.

Finally, you can drag new margins with the rulers in Page Layout view. The margin brackets are located on the ruler. Let's look at all three techniques, starting with the dialog box.

TIP   Document margins are affected by your printer choice, page orientation, and other decisions made in the four tabs in the Page Setup dialog box (Layout, Paper Source, Paper Size, and Margins). Therefore, you should choose your printer, if you have more than one, *then* use the other tabs in the File ➤ Page Setup command to make any necessary changes before adjusting margins. Double-clicking on a dark-gray part of the ruler will bring up the Page Setup dialog box.

The Page Setup Dialog Box Margin Settings

Figure 8.2 shows the Margins tab in the Page Setup dialog box (File ➤ Page Setup). You are invited to enter new Top, Bottom, Left, Right, and Gutter margins.

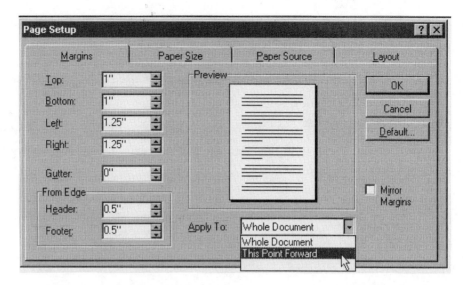

Figure 8.2 **You have complete control over margins in the Margin tab of the Page Setup dialog box, reached by choosing *File* ➤ *Page Setup*.**

The From Edge settings tell Word how close to the edges of the page you want headers and footers to print. For instance, a Header setting of 0.5″ means that the top of a header will be 0.5″ from the top edge of the paper, while the same setting for a footer means the bottom of a footer will be 0.5″ from the paper's bottom edge.

It is important to note that settings can be uniform document-wide, or different on any and all pages. Be sure to check the setting in the Apply To box. Choices are Whole Document, this Point Forward, or (if there are section breaks) This Section. This Point Forward means from (and including) the page containing the insertion point. This section sets new margins for the section containing the insertion point, even if this occurs in the middle of a page. If you have section breaks, This Section is the default, which requires a bit of extra attention if you want to change the margins for the whole document.

The Preview will change to show you a miniature representation of the new settings as you adjust them. After you type in each new setting, press Tab to move to the next box. As with other Word dialog boxes, enter fractions as decimals; $\frac{1}{4}$″ would be 0.25, and so on).

Follow these general steps to change margins from within the Document dialog box:

1. Place the insertion point on the page where you want margin settings to be changed (unless you plan to use the Whole Document choice).

2. Choose File ➤ Page Setup.

3. Change paper size and orientation, if required, by using the Paper Size tab.

4. Switch to the Margins tab if it is not already displayed.

5. Current settings are shown in the various margin dimension boxes.

6. Type the dimensions you desire, or click in the little triangles to increase and decrease settings. The Preview will change as you work.

7. When satisfied, click OK.

TIP   Dimensional settings in most Word dialog boxes can be expressed in inches (in), points (pt), centimeters (cm), picas (pi), and, frequently, lines (li). For instance, to set a top margin's height to 12 points, you would type 12pt in the Top margin box. A 1½-line top margin would be 1.5li, etc. It is worth noting that while you can type dimensions in any of these units of measure, Word will convert them to the default unit of measure when you close the dialog box. You change the default measurement unit in the General tab of the Options dialog box.

Dragging Margins in Print Preview

It's easy to change a document's margins while in Print Preview. Drag on the ruler ends, as shown in Figure 8.3; then wait a moment for your computer to redisplay the page with your new margin settings. Watch the ruler markings as you work. They will give you a good idea of the dimensions. For more precise settings, however, use the dialog box.

TIP   If you don't see the rulers in Print Preview, click the fifth button from the *right* at the top of the Print Preview window as shown in Figure 8.4. This will display the rulers.

When displaying multiple pages in Print Preview, you will need to click in a page before adjusting margins. The ruler(s) and guidelines will move to the page where you click. This lets you work with different left, right

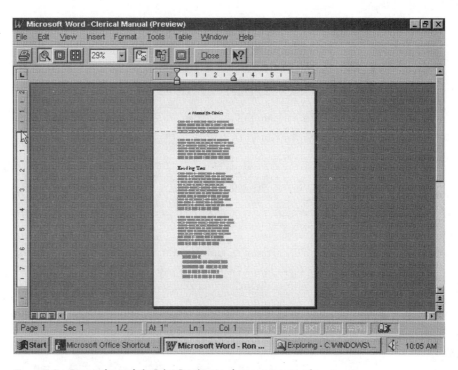

Figure 8.3   Drag ruler ends in Print Preview to change your margins.

Figure 8.4   Click here if necessary to reveal margin guidelines and handles.

(or inside/outside), top, and bottom margin combinations. The general steps for changing margins in Print Preview are:

1. Choose File ➤ Print Preview.

2. If the rulers are not visible, click on the ruler icon.

3. If necessary, click in a page.

4. Point to a ruler's edge. The pointer will change to a two-headed arrow.

5. Drag. Watch the ruler's marks as you drag.

6. Release the mouse button to see the effect of the margin changes.

7. Repeat steps 3 through 6 to fine-tune, if necessary.

TIP If you've chosen Mirror margins in the Margins tab of the Page Setup dialog box, be sure to display at least two pages in Print Preview to see the effect on facing margins as you drag. Odd pages (pages 1, 3, etc.) are always displayed on the right.

Dragging Margin Brackets on the Ruler

Word's rulers display margins as dark gray areas (this may vary, depending on your color scheme). These can be dragged to change the document's margins. Don't confuse margin dragging techniques with indent dragging techniques, which are similar, but have a very different effect. Follow these steps:

1. Change to Page Layout view if you're not there already.

2. If the ruler is not displayed, choose View ➤ Ruler.

3. Point to the transition area on the ruler where its color changes, as shown in Figure 8.5.

4. The mouse pointer will become a two-headed arrow.

5. Drag the margin to the desired position with your mouse. Watch the ruler's dimensions change as you drag.

Drag the ruler's edges (not the handles) to change the margins

connection·between·the·burden·on·society·created·by·

Don't accidentally drag the indent handles if you want to change margins

Figure 8.5   *Drag the edges where the ruler's color changes to move margins.*

Alternate Facing (Mirror) Margins

Select the Mirror Margins feature in the Margins tab of the Page Setup dialog box (File ➤ Page Setup) when you want different left and right margin widths and your final output will be two-sided. Word makes inside margins of odd- and even-numbered pages the same size and does the same with the outside margins of odd and even pages, as illustrated in Figure 8.6. This is how you get white space on the appropriate side of even and odd two-sided pages.

Inside Margins Same

Outside Margins Same

Figure 8.6   *Mirror Margins compensates for two-sided documents with dissimilar left and right margins.*

When adjusting margins in Print Preview, if you've chosen the Mirror Odd/Even feature, be sure you display two pages in Print Preview. Otherwise you won't know if you're working with an odd or even page.

Gutters Facilitate Binding

Here's a feature that apparently exists simply because other products have it. Gutter margins compensate for the paper tucked away in the binding of a two-sided book that would be unreadable. Gutters are additional white space in the inside margins. The gutter width, which you specify in the Margin tab of the Page Setup dialog box, reduces the text area, as shown in Figure 8.7.

In Print Preview, you can see the effect of gutter margins, but you cannot adjust them. To adjust the gutter, leave Print Preview and visit the Margin tab in the Page Setup dialog box (File ➤ Page Setup).

Figure 8.7   **Gutter space compensates for paper used in the binding process by adding space to inside margins in two-sided documents.**

TIP Instead of using gutters, simply increase the size of the inside margins to accommodate binding.

Printer Capabilities Limit Margins

Many printers, including most laser printers, are incapable of printing all the way to the edge of the paper. Keep this in mind when setting margins. If, for instance, your printer cannot print past the last half-inch of a page, any margin of less than $1/2''$ will result in cropped (chopped-off) text.

Some printers offer ways to increase printing area. For instance, some laser printers let you trade font memory for larger printing areas. See your printer manual for details.

Printing in the Margins

As you can see from Figure 8.8, it is possible to place text, graphics, and page numbers in margins by using indent markers. You can drag indent markers into margins, and text or graphics will follow. You can also use the Insert ➤ Frame command to place things in margins, as described in Chapter 6. Page numbers can also be positioned in margins, as you will learn in Chapter 12.

How Headers and Footers Affect Margins

Headers and footers print in the top and bottom margins. The inclusion of headers and footers causes Word to automatically adjust top and bottom margins when necessary. For instance, if you use the Margin tab of the Page Setup dialog box to specify a minimum top margin of $1/2''$, and then create a header that is 1.0″ high, Word will increase the top margin size to make room for the big header. You can override this feature by specifying exact top or bottom margins in the Margins tab of the Page Setup dialog box. This will force Word to limit top and bottom margins, unless this would encroach upon headers and footers. This can create some interesting effects, desired and otherwise. Read about headers and footers in Chapter 12.

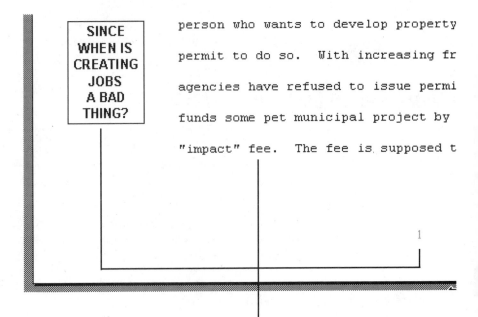

Page numbers, text, and graphics can all be printed in margins

Figure 8.8   It's easy to print in the margins.

Page Breaks

Page breaks are the places in your document where one page ends and a new page begins. Many things affect where page breaks will occur. Factors include the size of your paper, margin settings, paragraph formats, and section breaks. Word automatically computes and displays page breaks as you add and delete information. Breaks appear as dotted lines in Normal and Outline views. Because both Page Layout view and Print Preview simulate sheets of paper, page breaks are easy to see in those views as well.

You can force your own page breaks. For instance, if you always want new chapters to start on a new page, you can force this by inserting manual page breaks at the beginning of each chapter.

Repagination

In order to display and print page breaks properly, Word must recalculate page endings after you've made changes. Normally this is done automatically in the background whenever Word can steal some otherwise unused computer time. This process is called *automatic repagination*. Because page endings affect certain other features, Word always repaginates when:

▶ You ask it to print

▶ You are in Print Preview or Page Layout view

▶ You compile a Table of Contents or Index

To turn off automatic repagination (and speed up slower computers when working on large documents), follow these steps:

1. Choose Tools ➤ Options.

2. Click on the General tab if it's not already in view.

3. Clear the Background Repagination check box. (You won't be able to do this if you are in Page Layout view.)

4. Close the Options dialog box.

5. Word will repaginate only when you are in a view that requires it. To force repagination, switch to Page Layout, Print Preview, or issue a Print request.

TIP Word 95 does not have a Repaginate Now command like its predecessors.

Forcing Page Breaks

When you want to force a page break, you can insert manual page breaks. In Normal and Outline views they look thicker than Word's automatic page breaks and contain the words *Page Break*.

TIP Generally speaking, forcing a page break is not a great idea. If you must do it, wait until you have done all of your other formatting, spellchecking, and so forth.

To insert a manual page break:

1. Move the insertion point to where you want to place the break.

2. Choose Insert ➤ Break. You'll see this dialog box:

3. Make sure the Page Break button is selected (the default).

4. Click OK or tap the ↵ key.

5. The dialog box will disappear and you'll see a thick manual page break line on your screen. Text or graphics below the manual page break will appear on the next page of your document.

TIP   Press Ctrl+↵ to insert a manual page break without going through the dialog box.

Moving and Deleting Page Breaks

Manual breaks can be highlighted and deleted like text in Normal and Outline views. (You cannot delete automatic breaks placed by Word.) Select a manual break line and press Delete.

The Replace command will also let you search for and delete manual breaks. You do this by searching for manual breaks and replacing them with nothing. See Chapter 20 to learn more about replacing.

Keeping Things Together on a Page

Sometimes automatic page breaks occur where they shouldn't, such as just after paragraph headings or in the middle of lists or tables. Word offers several ways to keep things together.

Keeping Lines Together

To keep lines together and prevent a page break from separating them, do the following:

1. Select the lines you wish to keep together (this is often easiest in Normal view).

2. Choose F<u>o</u>rmat ➤ <u>P</u>aragraph.

3. If necessary, click on the Text Flow tab to reveal the options shown here:

4. Enable the Keep Lines Together option by clicking to place a check in the appropriate box.

5. Click OK.

6. Small, black, nonprinting blocks will appear next to the lines, indicating that these lines have special formatting that may not be obvious in some views.

7. The lines will stay together on the same page with each other (sometimes causing very early page breaks).

Keeping Paragraphs or Graphics and Labels Together

To keep paragraphs together, or to keep graphics and related text together on the same page, do the following:

1. Select the paragraphs (possibly including graphics) you wish to keep together.

2. Choose Format ➤ Paragraph and reveal the Text Flow tab's options, if they are not already visible.

3. Enable the Keep with Next option by clicking to place a check in the appropriate box.

4. Click OK.

5. Small, black, nonprinting blocks will appear next to the lines, indicating that these lines have special formatting that may not be obvious in some views.

6. The designated items will stay together on the same page with each other (sometimes causing very early page breaks).

Keeping Parts of Tables Together

As you will learn when you read more about tables in Chapter 11, Word treats each row in a table as a separate paragraph. Select all the rows of a table and use the Keep with Next paragraph option to keep a table intact.

Forcing Paragraphs to Start on a New Page

To force a paragraph to start on a new page (a chapter heading, for instance), do the following:

1. Select the paragraph you want to place at the top of a new page.

2. Choose Format ➤ Paragraph and reveal the Text Flow tab's options.

3. Select the Page Break Before option.

4. Click OK.

Removing Keep with Next and Similar Paragraph Options

To remove special paragraph and line options like Keep with Next, Keep Lines Together, and Page Break Before, follow these steps:

1. Select the paragraph(s) you want to change.

2. Choose Format ➤ Paragraph and switch to the Text Flow tab if it's not already visible.

3. Click to remove check marks from unwanted options.

4. Click OK.

Controlling Widows and Orphans

Widows are short lines (typically a single word) at the end of paragraphs. Orphans are the first lines of paragraphs that print by themselves at the bottom of a page. While both can be distracting to readers, some editors will tell you to eliminate orphans and live with widows (pun intended). The choice is yours, unless you work somewhere with policies about such style issues.

Word automatically eliminates both widows and orphans unless you tell it to do otherwise. You may find it helpful to turn off this feature if you are having trouble making things fit, particularly in multicolumn documents. Here's how to turn off automated widow and orphan suppression:

1. Choose Format ➤ Paragraph.

2. Remove the check from the Widow/Orphan Control option box in the Text Flow tab.

3. Click OK.

4. Widows and orphans may occur, and you can deal with them manually or choose to ignore them.

 TIP   Sometimes Print Preview's Shrink to Fit can help with widows, too.

Chapter 9

Characters and Fonts

FAST TRACK

size by the standard increments listed in Word's various Font size lists).

To boldface selected text 207

click the Bold button on the Formatting toolbar, use one of the keyboard shortcuts Ctrl+B or Ctrl+Shift+B, or enable Bold in the Font Style list in Word's Font dialog box.

To italicize selected text 207

click the Italic button on the Formatting toolbar, use one of the keyboard shortcuts Ctrl+I or Ctrl+Shift+I, or enable Italic in the Font Style list in Word's Font dialog box.

To underscore the selected text 208

click the Underline button on the Formatting toolbar (for single, continuous underline), use the keyboard shortcut Ctrl+U, or choose one of the options in the Underline list in Word's Font dialog box.

To make the selected text super- or subscript 211

either use the shortcuts Ctrl+= and Ctrl+Shift+=, click the Superscript or Subscript buttons on the Formatting toolbar, or bring up the Character Spacing tab of the Font dialog box (Format ➤ Font...) and choose either Raised or Lowered.

To change the case of the selected text 214

use the Format ➤ Change Case command.

To copy character formatting from the selected text to other text 218

double-click on the Format Painter button in the Standard toolbar and drag across the text you want to format. Release the mouse button and the text should reformat.

To make the selected text into a bulleted list 224

click the Bulleted List button on the Standard toolbar. To have greater control over the bullets, use the Format ➤ Bullets and Numbering command.

Specialists called typographers spend their whole lives studying and improving the appearance of printed words. It is a complex profession steeped in tradition and romance. Computers have added to the trivia and mystique surrounding typography. Word for Windows provides considerable typographic prowess. For instance, you can:

- ▶ Specify fonts (type designs)
- ▶ Specify character size (in points)
- ▶ Embellish text (bold, italics, and underline)
- ▶ Adjust spacing between characters (kerning)
- ▶ Specify colors for characters
- ▶ Change the case of text (e.g., lowercase to uppercase)
- ▶ Super- or subscript characters
- ▶ Copy and repeat character formatting
- ▶ Insert international accent marks and special symbols
- ▶ Hide and reveal text selectively (annotations)
- ▶ Use Word's typesetting commands for equation and technical typing

For many, it may be enough to know how to print desired characters in appropriate sizes and styles. Other readers will want to know how to get just the right look. Some will need to know about various font technologies. You may need to be aware of compatibility issues when moving documents from one computer or printer to another.

This chapter progresses from simple, nontechnical techniques to fairly complex issues. Feel free to jump from topic to topic as the need arises.

 TIP If you always use the same computer and a single printer, and you are happy with your choice of fonts and effects, you may be able to completely ignore the technology and typesetting information found near the end of this chapter.

There are very few hard-and-fast rules where the art of typography is concerned. But there are plenty of rules where the technology of computer fonts is concerned. The best way to learn is to experiment.

Terminology

People often use the terms *font* and *typeface* synonymously. The terms are not really synonyms, but because the world seems to be treating them that way these days, we will too. With apologies to professional typographers, let's start with some slightly oversimplified definitions.

Characters, Fonts, and Typefaces

Characters are the letters, numbers, punctuation marks, and special symbols that you type from the keyboard. For our purposes, we'll define a font or typeface as a collection of characters and symbols with a common appearance, or design. Courier is an example of a font. It will remind you of old electric typewriters. Times is a different font (or typeface) that will remind you of newspaper and magazine copy.

Different fonts contain different collections of characters and symbols. Some fonts are designed to be used for specific purposes like headings or drop caps. Sometimes these have only uppercase letters and may not even contain punctuation. There are scientific and math fonts that contain the necessary Greek and other symbols for technical typing. Other fonts are used for adding decorations to your document. Wingdings is an example. Instead of numbers and letters, it contains tiny pictures of airplanes, boxes, check marks, and so on.

Font Families

A collection of all of the variations of a font is called a family. For instance, you can purchase a font family from Adobe called Lucida. This family includes Lucida Roman, Lucida Italic, Lucida Bold, and Lucida Bold Italic.

One way to add emphasis to a document is to use different fonts for headlines, paragraph headings, and body copy. Sometimes you'll decide to pick different fonts from the same family, other times you'll mix fonts from different families. The headings and body type used in this book illustrate both techniques.

Character Formatting

When you use Word for Windows, you need not purchase entire font families to use effects like bold and italics. Word has features that can often embellish the appearance of single plain fonts to create boldface, italics, shadow, and other effects. The techniques used to do this are usually referred to as character formatting. Figure 9.1 shows many of the character formatting variations possible when using Word's character format tricks on the NewCenturySchlbk (schoolbook) font.

Don't confuse the character formatting tricks shown in Figure 9.1 with true bold, italics, and other fonts. Purists often prefer the real thing, and these character formatting effects can sometimes look downright awful when applied to certain fonts—including many of the low-cost shareware typefaces in common use.

Incidentally, not all font vendors provide identical-looking fonts, even when the font names are the same. The Courier installed in Windows looks slightly different from the Courier in Pacific Data's PostScript products, for instance. Occasionally (but rarely) this can cause differences in line endings. And, once in a while, you'll find different special characters in fonts from various manufacturers.

Normal (a.k.a. Plain text), **Bold,** *Italic*
Standard underline Word Underline
double underline Dotted underline
Strike-thru
all caps off, ALL CAPS ON
Small Caps Off, SMALL CAPS ON
Super Normal Subscript
Condensed character spacing Off
Condensed character Spacing On
Expanded character spacing Off
Expanded character spacing On
Black Blue Cyan Green Magenta Red Yellow
Bold + ***Italic*** + *Outline* + *Shadow* + *Condensed*

Figure 9.1   With Word's formatting capabilities, you can enhance a font in many ways.

Monospaced vs. Proportionally Spaced

Some fonts are said to be monospaced or fixed-pitch; others proportionally spaced or variable-pitch. Monospaced fonts like Courier use the same amount of horizontal space (*pitch*) on a line for each character, regardless of the width of a character. With a monospaced font like Courier a letter *i* takes the same amount of horizontal space as the letter *W*. Thus, if you can fit seventy *W*'s on a line in Courier, you can only fit seventy *i*'s in the same space. Obviously, this is an inefficient use of space and sometimes causes sloppy-looking words. Since people like lawyers, art directors, and publishers usually want to fit as many words as possible on a page, they turn to proportionally spaced fonts that tuck narrow letters in closer to their neighbors.

In Figure 9.2 the same word is printed first in 72-point Courier, a monospaced font, and then in 72-point Times and Helvetica, both proportionally spaced fonts. Notice the ocean of white space on either side of the letter *i* in the Courier example. A long base has been added to the bottom of the *i* in an attempt to distract you from this untidiness. Compare the white space on either side of all three *i*'s in Figure 9.2.

Wimp
Wimp
Wimp

Figure 9.2 **Notice that Courier's spacing (top) is much less elegant than in Times (middle) or Helvetica (bottom).**

Ironically, the monospaced Courier font uses less horizontal space on the line than either of the proportionally spaced fonts, due mainly to the much wider *W*'s and *m*'s in the proportional faces. Generally, though, proportionally spaced fonts will be more economical with space than their monospaced brethren and sistren.

Point Sizes

The various sizes of type are measured in points. There are 72 points to an inch. Thus, 72-point type will take 1 vertical inch of space, 36-point type will require $\frac{1}{2}$ inch of vertical space, and so on.

Point size is measured from the lowest descender to the highest ascender in the font. For instance, in Figure 9.2 you would measure from the bottom of the *p* to the top of the *W*. Sometimes different fonts of the same point size appear to be taller or shorter than each other, because of the amount of space the designer has allowed for the parts of characters that go below the baseline and above the tops of caps (called ascenders and descenders) and for white space above and below the characters (called leading). Notice how the 72-point Courier looks shorter than the 72-point Helvetica in Figure 9.2.

Your choice of point size affects the amount of space between lines (the leading), as well as the height of the characters. You can have more than one point size on a line, but Word for Windows will adjust the line spacing to accommodate the largest character on the line. You can override this feature, as you will see in the next chapter.

Serif vs. Sans Serif Fonts

The horizontal cross lines on the *W*, *i*, and *p* in Figure 9.2's Courier and Times examples are called *serifs*. (The fonts themselves are called serif fonts.) Popular computer fonts with serifs include Courier, Bookman, Palatino, and Times. Fonts without these embellishments are said to be *sans serif*. Avant Garde, Modern, Arial, and Helvetica are examples of sans serif fonts.

TIP   Serif fonts, which guide the eye across the page, are traditionally used for body text. Sans-serif fonts, although harder to read, are more eye-catching and so are typically used for headings, captions, and isolated bits of text.

Character Formatting Tools—An Overview

There are many ways to tell Word for Windows to make characters bold, italicized, bigger, or smaller. Tools for character formatting include the toolbar, menu choices, dialog boxes, and keyboard shortcuts. You can change the formatting of single characters, entire words, or whole documents. Let's start with an overview of the tools Word for Windows provides for character formatting, then we'll look at typical examples of the tools in use.

 TIP You can either specify the desired appearance of characters before you type them, or you can type first, then select text and change its appearance. Virtually all of the character formatting techniques described in this chapter can be accomplished either before or after you enter text.

Character Formatting Choices on Word's Menus

Word's various menus contain a number of character-related formatting choices. These let you:

▶ Pick fonts

▶ Pick font sizes

▶ Pick underline styles

▶ Highlight important text

▶ Add effects like superscript, subscript, etc.

▶ Change the color of displayed or printed characters

▶ Change default characters

▶ Preview changes in a preview window

▶ Change character spacing

▶ Insert special characters and symbols

▶ Change case (make words all uppercase, all lowercase, etc.)

▶ Create drop caps and similar effects

Part 2

Formatting Fundamentals

The Font Command

Word's Format ➤ Font command opens a two-tab dialog box. The Font tab lists all of the fonts installed on your computer and their standard sizes, as illustrated in Figure 9.3. (Yours may list different fonts.)

Figure 9.3. *The Font dialog box lists and demonstrates all fonts installed on your computer.*

TIP No, you are not seeing double. Word for Windows places the names of your most recently used fonts at the top of the font list in the toolbar for quick access. The font names are also available in their normal locations.

The Font tab also offers some choices for underlining and special effects and a preview area that lets you see the results of your selections. An information line at the bottom of the screen often provides other clues about how the font will look on your screen and how it will print.

Text boxes display the current font, size, and font style. The up and down arrows scroll through the standard sizes available for the selected font. You can type in the Size box to specify nonstandard font sizes not found in the list.

Changing Word's Default Character Formatting The Default button in the Font tab of the Font dialog box gives you the opportunity to make the current selections the new default settings used by Word.

Character Formatting with the Formatting Toolbar

The most immediately visible way to modify character appearance is to use the buttons and font menus on the Formatting toolbar, illustrated in Figure 9.4.

The new Highlight button

Figure 9.4 **You can format characters right from the Formatting toolbar.**

If the Formatting toolbar is not in view, choose the <u>V</u>iew ➤ <u>T</u>oolbars command. Choose the Formatting toolbar by placing a check in the appropriate box, as illustrated in Figure 9.5. Then click OK.

From the Formatting toolbar you can pick a font, change to a different point size, and toggle bold, italic, and simple underline. Just click on the appropriate toolbar button or pick the desired menu item from the toolbar's drop-down lists. Clicking a second time on a toolbar button removes or toggles the effect.

The Formatting toolbar has a new button called Highlight, which you can use to highlight text in your documents. You'll learn about highlighting later in this chapter.

Part 2

Formatting Fundamentals

Figure 9.5 Use the *View* ➤ *Toolbars* command to bring up the Toolbars dialog box.

Seeing Which Character Formats Are at Work

You can see most of the information regarding character formatting by selecting one or more characters and looking carefully at the Formatting toolbar. It will tell you the font name and size, and buttons will reflect the current formatting. If text is bold, for example, the toolbar's bold button will be depressed.

TIP If all of the characters you select are not identically formatted, some or all of the information areas in the toolbar will be blank or incomplete. For instance, if you select text where some of the characters are different sizes, the Font size area of the toolbar will be blank. If some of your selected text is bold and some not, the Bold button will not be depressed.

Here's a great feature. Use the Help button on the Standard toolbar along with your mouse to see which character-formatting tools have been used on characters of interest. Follow these steps:

1. Click once on the Help button in the Standard toolbar. The pointer changes shape.

2. Point to the character of interest. A balloon-like box appears, containing information about the paragraph and character styling at work, as shown in Figure 9.6.

3. Press Esc when you are done reading.

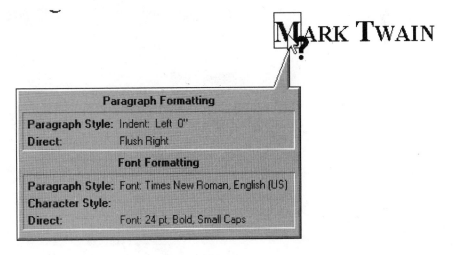

Figure 9.6 *The Standard toolbar's Help button will reveal character- and paragraph-formatting information when you point to text.*

Because this feature will tell you about one character at a time, it solves the mixed formatting problems mentioned earlier. Just move your mouse pointer from character to character to learn about each one.

The Font Dialog Box

The Font dialog box is reached with the Format ➤ Font command. It contains the most comprehensive collection of character-formatting options available in Word for Windows.

The Font dialog box lets you specify and combine a potentially gaudy array of character effects. It also presents yet another way to pick fonts, and it lets you fiddle with inter-character spacing. Drop-down menus provide you with underline and color choices. You can even enter nonstandard font sizes in the Size box. It also shows which character-formatting options have been enabled from the toolbar, menu, and keyboard shortcuts. This is one busy box! Take a good look at Figure 9.7.

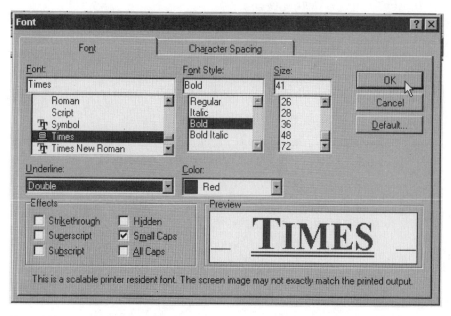

Figure 9.7   *The Font dialog box gives considerable control over character-formatting options.*

Using the Font Dialog Box

Notice the Font Style section of the Font dialog box. It contains four choices—Regular, Italic, Bold, and Bold Italic. Other fonts offer more or fewer choices. For example, Monotype Cursive offers only Regular and Bold Italic:

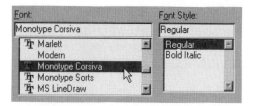

You can apply one or more of these choices to selected characters and to subsequently typed text. Simply click on the desired style. You can remove effects by clicking on Regular.

Effects can often be combined. For instance, it is usually possible to have text that is bold, italicized, and underscored. (Not all fonts accept all formatting options though, and occasionally you will see combinations on screen that will not print.) Click OK when you have selected the desired effects.

In Figure 9.7, the chosen options are Times, Bold, 41 points, Underline: Double, Small Caps, and Red.

About Effects Boxes

If the Effects box in the Font dialog box shows gray check marks next to the formatting options, it simply means that you have selected text with a variety of character-formatting options. For instance, some of your selected text may be Small Caps, other parts not:

This is an important concept, as you will learn when you work with the Replace dialog box in Chapter 20. A black check in a character format box means that all the selected text exhibits that particular attribute. A completely clear box means that the selected text does not have the specific attribute anywhere within it. A checked gray box means that some of the text may or may not exhibit the character-formatting option. (This third condition must have been invented by a politician.)

Keyboard Shortcuts for Character Formatting

Many of Word's character-formatting tools have keyboard shortcuts. They are mentioned throughout this chapter and summarized in Appendix B.

How to Specify Everyday Character Formatting

Now that you've seen an overview of the formatting tools, let's look at some specific everyday tasks.

Choosing Fonts and Sizes

Word for Windows can use any font installed in your system. Theoretically at least, you can print any font in any size from 1 point to a whopping 1638 points. This corresponds to character heights ranging from approximately $1/72^{nd}$ of an inch to about 22 inches! In reality, you'll probably work with type sizes ranging from about 7 to 72 points most of the time, as they are easy to read and look good on traditional page sizes. For most body text, the 10–12 point range is considered the most readable.

> **WARNING**   The type of printer you use, the fonts you've chosen, and other factors affect the final printed appearance of fonts at various sizes. There is more information about this at the end of the chapter.

Word for Windows offers almost too many ways to pick fonts and sizes. Here's a summary of the various techniques (as usual, changes you make apply to currently selected text and to any following text you type):

▶ Use the drop-down Font and Size lists on the Formatting toolbar.

▶ Type the name and size of the desired font directly into the font name and size boxes on the toolbar, then press ↵. For instance, click in the font name on the toolbar; then type all or part of a font name like Av for AvanteGarde. (You need type only enough letters to differentiate the desired font from other installed fonts.) Next click in the size box, if necessary, and type a new point size from 1 to 1638. Press ↵.

▶ Select fonts from within the Font dialog box, reached with the Format ▶ Font command.

▶ To increase or decrease the font size one point at a time (from 10 to 11, for instance), use the keyboard shortcuts Ctrl+] and Ctrl+[.

▶ To increase or decrease font sizes by the standard increments listed in Word's various Font size lists (10 point, 12 point, 14 point, etc.), use the keyboard shortcuts Ctrl+Shift->> and Ctrl+Shift-<<.

▶ Assign fonts and sizes as part of styles. (See Chapter 14 for details.)

Creating Bold Characters

There are a number of ways to add bold character formatting to characters you've selected or to characters you are about to type. Here are four choices:

▶ Click the Bold button on the Formatting toolbar. It looks like a bold B. (A "depressed" button indicates that bold character formatting is enabled.)

▶ Use either of the two keyboard shortcuts for bold character formatting—Ctrl+B or Ctrl+Shift+B.

▶ Enable the Bold option in the Font Style list in Word's Font dialog box.

▶ Assign bold formatting as part of styles. (See Chapter 14 for details.)

Creating Italicized Characters

Create italicized characters in much the same way you create bold ones:

▶ Click the Italic button on the toolbar. It looks like an italicized letter I. (A "depressed" I button indicates that italic character formatting is enabled.)

▶ Use either of the two keyboard shortcuts for italic character formatting—Ctrl+I or Ctrl+Shift+I.

▶ Enable the Italic style in the Font dialog box's Font Style menu.

▶ Assign italic formatting as part of styles. (See Chapter 14 for details.)

Highlighting Words and Passages

Word has a new feature that lets you highlight text, both on the screen and on paper. You can either highlight selected words or use the highlighter as a "pen" of sorts. Here are the four ways it works:

▶ If you have text selected when you click the Highlight button on the Formatting toolbar, it will become highlighted.

▶ If nothing is selected when you click the Highlight button, your cursor will turn into a pen, which you can use to highlight anything you wish. This tool works fairly intuitively. For instance, if you double-click a word, the whole word is highlighted; if you triple-click a paragraph, the whole paragraph is highlighted. To turn off highlighting, just click the Highlight button again. You can also use it like its neighbors on the toolbar, Bold and so on. Select the text you want to highlight, and click the highlight button. In this case, it turns itself off after use.

▶ If you click the arrow part of the Highlight button, a list will drop down, allowing you to choose the color of your highlight, as shown here:

Your four choices are bright yellow, bright lime, bright aquamarine, and bright magenta. Has somebody at Microsoft been watching too many old Miami Vice reruns? Once you choose your color, the highlight feature works as described above, doing slightly different things, depending upon whether you have text selected.

▶ To remove highlighting, you must first select the text; then click the Highlight button again.

Underlining

You can apply simple, single, continuous underlining with the Underline button on the Formatting toolbar or with the Ctrl+U or Ctrl+Shift+U keyboard shortcuts. If you want different underline formats, you'll need to use the Font dialog box.

There are five choices on the Underline drop-down menu in the Font dialog box: (none), Single, Words Only, Double, and Dotted. The effects of these choices are self-evident and illustrated in Figure 9.1. Unfortunately, underline choices cannot be combined in this dialog box.

> **TIP** If you routinely use different underline styles like Double or Word, you can add commands for them to your Word for Windows menus or toolbars. See Chapter 36 to learn how. There are keyboard shortcuts for various underline styles. They are listed in Appendix C.

Strikethrough

If you write contract drafts or work with other important documents, you may wish to use Word's Strikethrough feature. It is a way to indicate proposed deletions. Choose the Strikethrough option in the Font dialog box to overlay text with a horizontal line.

> **TIP** Use the Strikethrough feature to format both the text and the spaces that you plan to delete in the final copy. When it comes time to delete, you can use Word's Replace command to find text containing Strikethrough text and replace it with nothing, thereby deleting the text. See Chapter 20 for more about the Replace command.

Expanding and Condensing Character Spacing

Word for Windows lets you override the standard spacing between characters defined by their designers. You can move characters closer together with the Condensed character-formatting option, or move them farther apart with the Expanded option. The default for expanding and condensing is 1 point.

> **NOTE** *Kerning* is a typesetter's term meaning to adjust (increase or decrease) the horizontal space between two letters. Usually this is done for reasons of aesthetics, but sometimes it is necessary simply to make a word fit in the space allotted it.

Condensing can help you fit extra words on a line while Expanding can create interesting effects for headlines in newsletters, flyers, and the like. You'll see many examples of this in Chapter 23. To expand or condense, follow these steps:

1. Select the text of interest.

2. Choose Format ➤ Font.

3. Open the Character Spacing tab (click on it).

4. Choose Expanded (or Condensed) from the Spacing list, as shown in Figure 9.8.

5. Choose a new setting by typing in the By box or clicking on the increase and decrease triangles. The Preview will change as you work.

6. Click OK to save your changes or Cancel to revert to the original size.

You can condense or expand characters a maximum of 1584 points. Let common sense and aesthetics be your guides in using this feature.

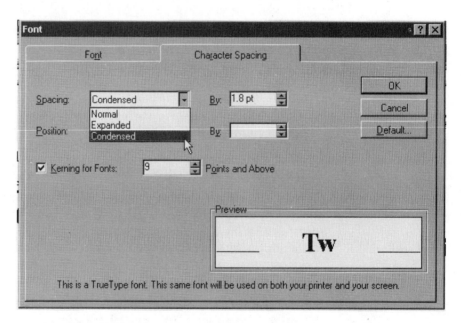

Figure 9.8   **Expand and compress text in the Character Spacing tab of the Font dialog box.**

Automatic Kerning and Manual Character Spacing

You can use the Condensed option to tuck pairs of letters closer to each other to tighten them up and improve the appearance of some awkward-looking combinations of wide and narrow letters. Simply select the letters you want to cozy up, then use the Condensed option in the Character Spacing tab of the Font dialog box. Or you can ask Word for Windows to automatically kern by enabling the Kerning option. Frequently you'll want tighter spacing than the automatic feature offers and you'll have to do it yourself.

For instance, here's how to tighten up the T and W in Twain.

1. Select just the characters T and W.

2. Open the Character Spacing tab of the Font dialog box (choose F<u>o</u>rmat ➤ <u>F</u>ont).

3. Choose Condensed spacing.

4. Choose a point value (1.8, perhaps).

5. Watch the preview and adjust spacing if you like.

6. Click OK to make the changes or Cancel to abort them.

Creating Superscripts and Subscripts

Normally, any characters that you type are placed on an invisible line called the baseline. Superscripted characters are moved above the baseline; subscripted characters are placed below the baseline. While the obvious use for this is in equations and chemical formulas (H_2O, for instance), there are many other ways to use super- and subscripting.

For example, if you abbreviate ordinal numbers (e.g., 2nd for second), it looks really nice if the *nd* is superscripted and made a bit smaller. A nice new feature of Word is that it does just this formatting for you automatically. You don't even need to think about it. Just type along as you usually do, and whenever you type anything like **1st, 2nd,** etc., Word will make the change for you. You can turn off this feature if you like by visiting the Edit tab of the Options dialog box.

You can also use super- and subscripting to line up odd-sized bullets with adjacent text. As you'll soon see, it's possible to tweak the appearance of drop caps by super- or subscripting them (look ahead to the section called *Large Initial Caps, Drop Caps, and Dropped Words*).

There are two basic ways to super- and subscript. You can use Word's Super and Sub features or you can raise and lower the position of characters with Word's Position option in the Character Spacing tab of the Font dialog box. The first method changes the size of super- and subscripted characters in addition to their position. The dialog box method keeps the character size. (Typographical purists consider only the first to be "true" super- and subscripting.)

Using Superscript and Subscript

The Font dialog box lets you raise or lower characters. There are also keyboard shortcuts. Ctrl+= causes subscripting (lowering characters and reducing their size). The shortcut Ctrl+Shift+= superscripts (both raising and reducing the characters). Both of these shortcuts apply "automatic" spacing decisions made for you by Word.

To gain manual control over spacing:

1. Select the characters you wish to super- or subscript.

2. Choose Format ➤ Font.

3. Click, if necessary, to see the Character Spacing tab.

4. Choose Raised (or Lowered) from the Position list.

5. Specify the amount by which you want characters raised or lowered by using the By box or buttons.

6. Click OK to apply the changes or Cancel to lose changes.

Figure 9.9 shows an example of this. Characters are being raised (superscripted) 3 points.

TIP Sometimes line heights are not sufficient to display the tops and bottoms of super- or subscripted characters, making them appear cut off. Adjust the line spacing as described in Chapter 10 if this happens.

Character Color Choices

Even if you cannot display or print color, Word for Windows lets you specify twelve character colors plus black, white, or gray. You can then take copies of your disk files to color-capable hardware for display and printing. To specify a color follow these steps:

1. Start by selecting text or positioning the insertion point where you want to type colored text.

Figure 9.9 **These settings superscript 3 points without changing the size of the characters.**

2. Choose the desired color from the drop-down Color menu in the Font tab of the Font dialog box. If your monitor supports color, you will see color characters in the Preview area. If your monitor supports shades of gray, colors will be converted to grays.

3. Click OK to close the Font dialog box.

4. When you print, enable your printer's color or gray scale features if it has them.

   Remember, not all computers can display grays or colors, but you need not display color to print it. To see which color you've assigned to text when using a black-and-white monitor, select the text and visit the Font dialog box or use the Help button "cartoon" trick to read the name of the assigned color.

WARNING **Printed colors don't always match video display colors exactly. Before starting a big color print job, try a test printing to make sure of what you'll get.**

Part 2

Formatting Fundamentals

Using the Change Case Command

The Format ➤ Change Case command opens a dialog box that offers five choices:

Look closely at the dialog box. The capitalization style of each option illustrates the effect it produces. For instance, UPPERCASE changes all selected characters to uppercase letters, and the choice UPPERCASE itself appears all uppercase in the dialog box. Title Case changes the first letter of each selected word to uppercase, as illustrated in the dialog box.

WARNING Alas, the Title Case feature is not context-sensitive, so it capitalizes prepositions and articles, including *of, the,* and so on. If you need to observe this distinction and use Title Case frequently, consider creating a WordBasic macro (Chapter 34) to search for those words and lowercase them.

To change case with this feature, follow these steps:

1. Select the text you wish to change.

2. Choose Format ➤ Change Case.

3. Choose the desired case option.

4. Click OK.

When you change case using this dialog box, the characters themselves change to the specified case. It is just as if you had retyped them using the new capitalization scheme. Undo also works here.

NEW   If you make a mistake in typing and accidentally capitalize several letters at the beginning of a word (for example, typing TWain instead of Twain), you no longer need even worry about it, because Word will correct your mistake automatically. This doesn't eliminate the need for the Change Case command, but it will make your life easier.

Using the All Caps Option

The All Caps feature is found in the Font dialog box. It changes only the appearance of letters, without actually changing the letters themselves. For example, if you type the word *uppercase* and format it as All Caps, you'll see it as UPPERCASE; but a search for capital letters would not find it. Unlike the Format ➤ Change Case command, the All Caps option lets you type in lowercase and see uppercase letters as you work. Follow these steps:

1. Select the text you wish to change or position the insertion point for typing.

2. Choose Format ➤ Change Case.

3. Choose the desired case option.

4. Click OK.

5. Selected and/or subsequently typed text will appear in uppercase, but the underlying text will retain its actual capitalization.

Using the Small Caps Option

The Small Caps option in the Character Dialog Box can create some very interesting effects. Figure 9.10 shows some examples of Small Caps at work.

TIP   Remember that applying the Small Caps formatting option to text containing dingbats like those shown in Figure 9.10 will usually "capitalize" the dingbats, thereby changing the character that appears and prints. To fix this, select the dingbats and remove Small Caps formatting. Use Word's Replace command (described in Chapter 20) to do this if you have many changes to make.

ASK MR. FOSTER ▨ AMERICAN INDUSTRIAL REAL ESTATE
ASSN. ▨ FIRSTOURS CARLSON CORPORATION ▨ BEAR
STERNS ▨ BERGER & NORTON ▨ CABLE NEWS NETWORK
(CNN) ▨ CHILDRENS HOSPITAL LOS ANGELES ▨ SYBEX

SOUTHERN EXPOSURE

WRITTEN BY
GUY WIRE
DIRECTED BY
PHIL R. UPP
PRODUCED BY
MS. TAKE

⌀ CENTRAL VALLEY	10
⌀ SIERRA NEVADA	12
⌀ SACREMENTO AREA	14
⌀ MARIN COUNTY	22
⌀ CONTRA COSTA COUNTY	34

Figure 9.10 **These four samples of Small Caps character formatting show how easy it is to add punch and visual interest.**

Removing Character Formatting

Removing character formatting can be a simple or confusing task, depending on the situation. The six general ways to remove character formatting include:

▶ Toggling toolbar buttons, menu commands, and keyboard shortcuts

▶ Using the Remove Formats keyboard shortcut (Ctrl+spacebar)

▶ Changing to a different style

▶ Using the Font dialog box

▶ Using the Replace command to automate removal

▶ Choosing the Regular font style in the Font dialog box

Unfortunately, not all approaches work under all circumstances, and there are some land mines, particularly when styles are involved. Removing character formatting is easiest if you are not using Word for Windows styles other than Normal. See Chapter 14 to learn about Styles.

Toggling to Remove Character Formatting

You can use the Edit ➤ Undo command (Ctrl+Z) to undo formatting immediately after you've changed it. And you can remove most character formatting by applying it a second time. This process is called toggling (you've already encountered the toggling concept with toolbar buttons). For instance, if you select a bold word and click on the Bold toolbar button, the selected text will no longer be bold.

The Regular Font Style

The Regular font style in the Font tab of the Font dialog box will remove most character formatting. Simply select the text; then execute the choice.

Limitations of Toggling and Regular Font Style

The toggling and Regular font style techniques just described will remove formats and many combinations, such as bold or bold with underlines. In fact, toggling and the Regular font style should work with the following character-formatting features in any combination:

▶ Bold

▶ Italic

▶ Underline

▶ Double underline

▶ Word underline

- Dotted underline
- Strikethrough
- Outline effect
- Shadow
- Small caps
- All caps
- Hidden text
- Colors

However, the tricks will not tighten up characters that have been expanded, nor will they spread out characters that have been condensed. You cannot change fonts or their sizes this way, either. You'll need to visit the Font dialog box or use other specific controls.

Copying and Repeating Character Formats

The Format Painter button is a slick way to copy formatting and apply it to other characters. To apply character formatting, do this:

1. Select only the characters (but not the paragraph marker at the end of the paragraph) whose format you wish to copy.

2. Double-click on the Format Painter button in the Standard toolbar. The pointer will turn into a paintbrush and the status area will display instructions.

3. Drag across the text you want to format.

4. Release the mouse button and the text should reformat.

Typing Special Characters

Word for Windows makes it easy to type special characters and symbols not listed on your keycaps but available in most fonts. Let's look at the Symbol feature and then review the old reliable keyboard shortcuts.

The Symbol Command

The dialog box shown in Figure 9.11 appears whenever you choose
<u>I</u>nsert ➤ <u>S</u>ymbol. It has two tabs, Symbol and Special Characters.

Figure 9.11 **The two tabs in the Symbol dialog box (reached by choosing <u>I</u>nsert ➤ <u>S</u>ymbol).**

The dialog box shows you all available characters in the current font. Clicking on a symbol shows you a magnified, more readable version. Double-clicking inserts the character at the insertion point in your document. (Alternately, you can click on a character and then click on the Insert button, but that's more work.)

> **TIP** Once you've clicked to magnify a character in the Symbol dialog box, you can see magnified views of others by navigating with the arrow keys. This can eliminate the need for a lot of precision clicking. Also, once a character is highlighted, you can insert it by hitting ↵.

To see which symbols are available in different fonts, simply choose a font from the Font menu in the Formatting toolbar and use the Insert ➤ Symbol command to view the choices. Or, if the Symbol dialog box is already open, pick a font from the Font list in the dialog box.

The Special Characters tab provides a scrolling list of commonly used symbols and characters. Here too, double-clicking inserts the character at the insertion point.

> **TIP** The Special Characters tab in the Symbol window also lets you see (and change) keyboard shortcuts.

Typing Symbols from the Keyboard

If you know the key combinations, you can enter symbols right from the keyboard, bypassing the Symbol dialog box. For instance, to type the copyright symbol, hold down Alt and Ctrl and press the C key. There is also a new feature in Word that automatically converts what you type into symbols. For example, if you type (c), Word will change your typing to the copyright symbol: ©. These two might seem redundant; the first method is a bit quicker than the second because it takes a little time to make the conversion, but sometimes it's hard to remember those keyboard shortcuts for the faster way. Fiddle with them a bit to see which you prefer. Word now has a dozen or so symbols created by autoconversion. Here is a list of some of the more useful ones.

Type this...	...to insert this
:)	☺
:(	☹

Type this...	...to insert this
-->	→
<--	←
(c)	©
(r)	®
(tm)	™
--	—
. . .	...

Different fonts sometimes have different key combinations, so you will need to consult the documentation that comes with your fonts or use the Insert ➤ Symbol command to learn the combinations. Table 9.1 shows commonly used special characters and their keyboard shortcuts.

Name	Sample	Keys	Notes
Angstroms	Å	Ctrl+@+A	
Bullet	•	Alt+ 0149	
Copyright	©	Alt+Ctrl+C	
Dagger	†	Alt+0134	
Ellipsis	...	Alt+Ctrl+.	
em dash	—	Alt + Ctrl + NumLock + –	Longer than hyphen. Use numeric keypad minus key.
en dash	–	Ctrl + NumLock + –	Longer than hyphen, shorter than em dash. Use numeric keypad minus key.
Function, f-stop	*f*	Alt+0131	
Logical not	¬	Alt+0172	

Table 9.1 **Some of Word's commonly used special characters and their keyboard shortcuts.**

Name	Sample	Keys	Notes
Mu (lowercase)	μ	Alt+0181	A/k/a Micro
Much greater than	»	Ctrl+',>	Also European close quote
Much less than	«	Ctrl+',<	Also European open quote
Cent sign	¢	Ctrl+/,c	
Paragraph mark	¶	Alt+0182	
Plus or minus	±	Alt+0177	
Pound (currency)	£	Alt+0163	Top row, not keypad
Registered	®	Alt+Ctrl+R	
Section mark	§	Alt+0167	
Single closed quote	,	Ctrl+','	
Single open quote	'	Ctrl+','	
Trademark	™	Alt+Ctrl+T	
Yen (currency)	¥	Alt+0165	

*Table 9.1 **Some of Word's commonly used special characters and their keyboard shortcuts** (continued).*

For all special characters, first make sure a font containing the symbol is selected. For Alt+number combinations, turn on Num Lock and use the numeric keypad except where noted in the table.

International and Accented Characters

To type accented international characters (like the ñ in La Cañada) you use three keys. First you hold down the Ctrl key plus a key to tell your computer which accent to apply, then you press the character key for the character you wish to accent. For example, to umlaut an o, do the following:

1. Hold down the Ctrl key and press the colon (:) key (don't forget to hold down the Shift key).

2. Release all three keys.

3. Press the o (or Shift+O) key to get a small (or capitalized) umlauted o (ö).

   Incidentally, you can't accent just any old characters. Table 9.2 shows you the possibilities and their key combinations.

Name	Samples	Keys
Acute accent	áéíóú ÁÉÍÓÚ	Ctrl+' (apostrophe), letter
Circumflex	âêîôû ÂÊÎÔÛ	Ctrl+^, letter
Dieresis	äëïöü ÄËÏÖÜ	Ctrl+:, letter
Grave accent	àèìòù ÀÌÈÒÙ	Ctrl+ `, letter
Tilde	ãñõ ÃÑÕ	Ctrl+~, letter

Table 9.2 Word's accented characters and their keyboard shortcuts.

> **TIP** The keystroke combinations listed in Table 9.1 are shortcuts. If you forget them, you can always locate and insert accented characters with the Insert ➤ Symbol command.

Wingdings and Dingbats

Add some spice to your life. Use the little pictures found in the Wingdings font instead of plain old bullets. Wingdings are also great as list separators and as border decorations. You've already seen examples back in Figure 9.10, and you'll see others in later chapters. Consider purchasing and installing other "dingbat" fonts, which are often found in shareware packages at very low cost. Use the Insert ➤ Symbol command to see and insert them.

Bulleted List Command

There's a button on the Standard toolbar that looks like a bulleted list. It places plain old bullets in front of selected paragraphs and creates hanging indents (read about hanging indents in Chapter 10). The feature uses the current font.

 If you know you want a list before you start typing, there's a handy new automatic formatting feature of Word that you can take advantage of, automatically making what you type into a bulleted list. All you have to do is type an asterisk (*) and then a space or tab. When you hit the Enter key (↵), Word will turn the asterisk into a bullet (•) and set the spacing and all that stuff. Then, all you have to do is keep on adding things to your list. Word never tires of adding bullets, so don't be shy! Catalog your Xavier Cugat collection, like you've always wanted to.

Bulleting Existing Paragraphs

To bullet existing paragraphs, follow these steps:

1. Select the paragraph or paragraphs you wish to format.
2. Click the Bulleted List button. Word will create hanging indents and insert bullets in front of each selected paragraph.

Typing New Bulleted Lists

 The best way to make bulleted lists now is to let Word do the work for you, using the automatic bulleted lists feature. You can still use the Bulleted List button on the Formatting toolbar, but why do it yourself when Word is always ready to oblige? Follow these steps.

1. Begin by typing an asterisk (*) and then a space or tab.
2. Start typing. When you hit the Enter key (↵), word will turn the asterisk into a bullet (•) and set the correct spacing.

3. Repeat step 2 and continue until you've finished your list. That's all you have to do. Hit the backspace key when you're ready to return to ordinary paragraph text.

4. If, however, you've elected to use the Bulleted List button, you must now click it again to deactivate the feature.

Changing Bullet Styles

Word for Windows offers an astonishing array of bullet list options. You can even choose your own, nonstandard bullet characters. Here are the general steps. Experiment to find combinations you like. Use the Bullets and Numbering dialog box shown in Figure 9.12.

1. Select your list if you've already typed it.

2. Choose Format ➤ Bullets and Numbering.

3. Click to pick a style you like.

4. Click OK to change the style of the selected list.

5. Type additional list items or a new list, as necessary.

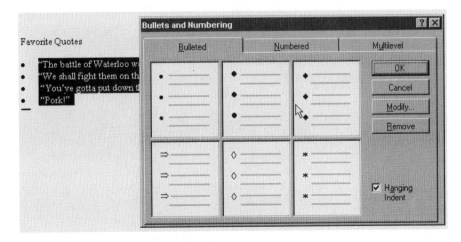

Figure 9.12 **Use this dialog box to modify the appearance of bulleted lists.**

Part 2

Formatting Fundamentals

Specifying Custom Bullets

Here's a nice way to spice up a dull list. Use Wingdings or other decorative characters instead of standard bullets:

1. Select your list if you've already typed it.

2. Choose Format ➤ Bullets and Numbering.

3. Click to pick a list style you like.

4. Click the Modify button to reveal the Modify Bulleted List dialog box, shown in Figure 9.13.

5. Change bullet positioning if you like by altering the dimensions in the Bullet Position area.

6. Pick a different type of bullet from the Bullet Character list.

7. To use bullets not shown in the Bullet Character box, click on the Bullet button.

8. When you see the Symbol dialog box, pick a Font that has interesting characters (Symbol or Wingdings for instance).

Figure 9.13 Use this dialog box to change spacing and pick new bullet shapes.

9. Double-click to select the desired character to use as a bullet. Here are some examples from the Wingdings font:

"Smart" or Typographer's Quotes

Word for Windows can automatically place curly quotes in documents when you type straight quotes. This gives your work a typeset look. Turn the option on before typing, as Word will not automatically change quote marks you've already typed.

1. Use the Tools ➤ Options command to display the Options dialog box.

2. Click on the AutoFormat tab to display the AutoFormat options.

3. Enable Smart Quotes by clicking to place a check in the option box.

4. Subsequently, when you type quotes, Word will convert them to curly opening and closing quotes (assuming that your chosen font has these characters).

TIP If you are creating a document that you plan to export (for use with different word-processing software, perhaps), turn off the Smart Quotes feature before creating documents containing quotes. Otherwise you'll risk confusing the other folks with strange codes instead of quotation marks.

Large Initial Caps, Drop Caps, and Dropped Words

Large initial caps are just what their name implies—big letters at the beginning of paragraphs. They are used as decorative flourishes. Drop caps are large initial caps that are dropped into a paragraph or into the margin next to a paragraph. They are often placed at the beginning of chapters and major topic transitions to catch your reader's eye. Dropped words are a variation on this technique. You create drop caps or dropped words by placing large initial caps or words in frames and positioning them to get the desired effect. Graphics can also be used as drop caps.

> **TIP** You can use Word's Drop Cap command to automate the process of creating drop caps and dropped words. Read about it in the following section.

Figure 9.14 shows a few examples. Read the text in each example to get an overview of how the effect was accomplished.

The process almost always looks easier than it is. It is very easy to fritter away the better part of a day lining up drop caps and the text they sit in. You'll often need to fiddle with paragraph formatting (line height and spacing settings), superscripts, subscripts, frame sizes, and font sizes. The Drop Cap feature does a pretty good job of minimizing this, but there will still be times when you will be tearing your hair out.

Using the Drop Cap Feature

You control drop caps from the dialog box shown in Figure 9.15. Reach it with the Format ➤ Drop Caps command.

The Drop Cap command is designed to work with single-spaced text only. It won't work in tables, headers, or footers. You won't be able to see the position of drop caps or create them in Outline view. You can't place drop caps in the margins of multicolumn documents, but you can place them within text in such documents. Narrow indents sometimes screw up the automatic drop cap feature. That said, here are the general steps:

1. Format the body text the way you like it. Be sure you are happy with things like margins, fonts, and so on, because if you change these, you will probably have to fiddle your drop cap's fine-tuning all over again. Single-space the text.

2. Select the character or characters you want to drop and choose the Format ➤ Drop Cap command. If you are not in Page Layout view, Word will prompt you to switch. You'll see the Drop Cap dialog box illustrated in Figure 9.15.

3. If you want to use a different font for the drop cap, choose it from the drop-down Font menu.

Word 's Drop Cap feature automatically creates frames, increases the size of the initial text and switches to Print Preview. It will place drop caps in the text or in the margin as shown here.

Drop caps can be created in a number of ways. This one was made by selecting just the letter D in 12 point New Century Schoolbook text and increasing it to 25 points. The D was framed with the Format menu's Frame... command. The Frame width was adjusted in the Frame dialog box. The D was then superscripted 6 points.

Large initial caps

Create these by choosing a larger type size for the first character. Minimize the resulting extra white space between the first and second lines by setting the lines' Space Before and Space After options to 0 points. You can use Frames to create similar effects.

Graphics can be used as drop caps too. This butterfly was pasted from the scrapbook, reduced in size, framed, then dragged into place from Print Preview. The From Text option was set to 0 in the Frame dialog box to tighten things.

Entire words can be dropped. This example was created with the Frame command on Word's Insert menu. First the word Entire was selected.

When you can't resist the urge to be decorative, consider using specialty fonts like Colonna MT shown here.

Figure 9.14 **Large initial caps and dropped words created using Frames, and character and paragraph formatting.**

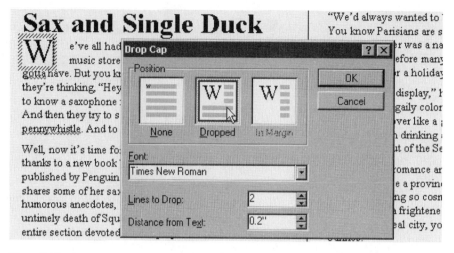

Figure 9.15   *Automatic drop cap options are specified in the Drop Cap dialog box.*

4. The Height box proposes the number of lines the cap will drop. For instance, 3 li means that the drop cap will be three lines tall and drop alongside the first three lines of text. Pick the desired number of lines from the drop-down line list, or alternately, type in an exact point size for the drop cap (36 pt, for instance).

5. Choose the Dropped Position option for traditional-looking drop caps or choose the In Margin choice to place drops in the margin.

6. When you click OK, Word places the specified text into a frame and positions the frame for you.

7. Use the character, frame, and paragraph tools, if you dare, to modify Word's settings.

TIP   You can use the Format ➤ Drop Cap command to drop graphics as well. Paste a graphic at the beginning of a line of text, drag, and if necessary, make it reasonably small. Then, with the graphic selected, use Format ➤ Drop Cap.

Tips for Creating Drop Caps

When creating drop caps, keep the following in mind:

▶ Do text formatting, make font decisions, and check spelling before you create drop caps.

▶ When using the Format ➤ Frame command, remember to specify a frame width so that text can flow around your drop cap.

▶ To remove the excess space that often appears beneath a drop cap frame, use negative line spacing (space less than the point size of the type being dropped) and subscripting, as you saw in the preceding example.

▶ To remove excess space to the right of frames, use the From Text option in the Frame dialog box.

Deleting Drop Caps

If you've just created a drop cap with the automatic Drop Cap command, Edit ➤ Undo will delete it. Otherwise you'll need to take the following general steps:

1. Highlight the drop cap and choose Format ➤ Drop Cap.

2. Click the None option and then click OK.

Typing Nonbreaking Spaces

In order to keep multiple words on the same line (someone's title and first and last name, for instance), you can use special spaces called nonbreaking spaces. To do this, simply hold down the Ctrl and Shift keys when you press the Spacebar.

Typing Hyphens and Dashes

To type hyphens, simply use the minus key (to the right of the zero key at the top of your keyboard). Hyphens typed this way will always print.

Typing Nonbreaking Hyphens

Nonbreaking hyphens keep hyphenated words together on the same line. Never press the minus key (–) to enter a nonbreaking hyphen! Instead, hold down the Ctrl and Shift keys and press the hyphen on the main keyboard.

Typing Em and En Dashes

Em dashes are used to indicate an abrupt change of thought—or did you know that already? En dashes are used to separate numbers. People often confuse hyphens and dashes. Type the longer em dashes by holding down Alt+Ctrl+– (the minus key on the numeric pad). In some fonts em dashes are very long and obvious. That's not always the case, though.

 Word has a new feature that automatically changes hyphens into dashes. When you type a hyphen, Word automatically changes it to an en dash (–). When you type two hyphens, Word changes it to an em dash (—). This is a handy way to make your documents look good without your having to do anything! Again, there are other ways to get en and em dashes; it's up to you what keyboard combos you want to try to remember.

Incidentally, em dashes get their name from their width. In most fonts an em dash is the length of a letter m. That's an easy way to remember what it's called. Shorter en dashes can be created with Ctrl+– (the minus key on the numeric pad).

TIP While dashes should always be longer than hyphens, in a few fonts they are not. You are not losing your mind after all. It's a "feature."

Typing Optional Hyphens

An optional hyphen will always be displayed whenever you have the Show Paragraph feature enabled, but it will print only if the word it is in sits on the right margin. Most people use Word's automatic hyphenation feature to enter optional hyphens, but you can enter them from the keyboard. Hold down the Ctrl key and press the minus key (–) on the main keyboard (not the one on the numeric pad).

TIP If you still have trouble remembering what's where, use the Special Characters tab in the Symbol dialog box, reached with the Insert ➤ Symbol command.

Automatic Optional Hyphenation

Word for Windows has an automatic feature that will work with you to place optional hyphens in words, based on certain built-in rules and a hyphenation dictionary. You can supervise the process or let Word take things into its own hands. If you use the automatic feature, there are some things you will want to do first.

WARNING Optional hyphenation is one of the last things you want to do when preparing a document. Finish everything else that affects line endings first. Otherwise, you will need to rehyphenate repeatedly.

Preparing to Hyphenate

Be sure that your document is complete and properly organized. Do the spelling check. Polish the appearance of your text (fonts, sizes, character expansion, etc.). Remove extra spaces. Apply justification, if that's part of your plan. Break the document into sections if you need them. Set up columns. Have someone else proofread your work one last time. You may, however, want to hold off on final page-break decisions until after hyphenation.

Entering Optional Hyphens

Word for Windows will hyphenate an entire document or just selected text. When you choose Tools ➤ Hyphenation, Word will open a small dialog box like the one in Figure 9.16. Choose automatic or manual hyphenation.

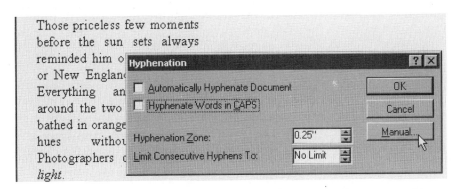

Figure 9.16 **The hyphenation dialog box.**

Part
2

Formatting
Fundamentals

Working from the insertion point, Word for Windows will move through your document (or selected text) looking for a possible word to hyphenate. In Figure 9.17 it has found the word *reminded*.

Those priceless few moments before the sun sets always re-minded him of fine brandy or New England in the fall. Everything and everyone around the two of them was bathed in orange and red and hues without names. Photographers call it *magic light*.

Manual Hyphenation: English (US)

Hyphenate At: re-minded

Yes   No   Cancel

Figure 9.17   **Word is suggesting that** reminded *be hyphenated between the* e *and the* m.

If you've chosen manual hyphenation, you will see a dialog box offering several alternatives. The Change button will place an optional hyphen between the *e* and *m*. The No Change button tells Word not to hyphenate this word and to continue. Cancel exits the hyphenation.

Optionally, you can move the hyphenation point yourself. Use your mouse to point to where you want to place the hyphen. Press the mouse button once. A nonblinking pointer will appear between the characters you've chosen. Click on the Change button to place the optional hyphen and continue the automatic search.

As you can see from Figure 9.18, Word has suggested several hyphenation points in our example. One of them is debatable. Some editors and style manuals will tell you not to hyphenate words in ways that leave only one syllable on a line, yet Word has done just that. There are few hard-and-fast hyphenation rules.

Those priceless few moments before the sun sets always reminded him of fine brandy or New England in the fall. Everything and everyone around the two of them was bathed in orange and red and hues without names. Photographers call it *magic light*.

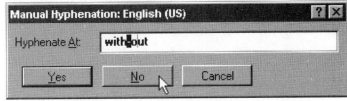

Figure 9.18   Word's automatic hyphenation feature may not solve all your problems.

Rejecting the suggested hyphen in *orange* creates a much nicer-looking paragraph, as you can see in Figure 9.19. The combination of manual and automatic hyphenation even found a home for the widow.

 TIP   If you like tight copy, you may want to run the auto-hyphenation feature and then fine-tune a bit by hand.

Figure 9.19   Sometimes replacing the suggested hyphenation can really improve the final appearance of the paragraph (especially in multicolumn formats).

Removing Automatic Hyphens

The Edit ➤ Undo Hyphenation (Ctrl+Z) command will be available to remove optional hyphens if you use it immediately after you run the auto-hyphenation feature. You can delete hyphens like any other character. Select them and cut or delete. Word's Find and Replace features will also help you delete hyphens of all sorts. See Chapter 20 for details.

TIP   If you don't want any hyphenation at all, choose Left alignment in the Format ➤ Paragraph dialog box. Many designers prefer the "ragged right" style for some kinds of text.

Chapter 10

Paragraphs, Line Spacing, Borders, and Shading

FAST TRACK

To delete a paragraph 242

double-click in the left margin to select the doomed paragraph and press the Backspace key. This will delete the paragraph and its ¶ mark. Alternately, you can select all text in the paragraph except the ¶ and delete it, which will leave the ¶ mark with its formatting information.

To modify the appearance of paragraphs 243

use the ruler, the Formatting toolbar, and the Paragraph dialog box.

To quickly modify the appearance of paragraphs 247

use one of Word's paragraph-formatting shortcut key combinations.

To set an automatic first-line indent 249

drag the top half of the triangular indent marker to the right to the desired position (Ctrl+M) or enter a setting in the First Line indent box in the Paragraph dialog box.

To increase or decrease the indents on selected paragraphs by one tab stop 250

use the Increase Indent and Decrease Indent buttons on the Formatting toolbar.

To create hanging indents 252

drag the top half of the triangular indent marker to the left to the desired position (Ctrl+Shift+M), or choose First Line in the Special box and enter a setting in the By box (in the Paragraph dialog box) that is farther left than the indent of the paragraph as a whole. Alternately, click the Numbered (list) button or the Bullets (list) button on the Formatting toolbar, which automatically creates a hanging indent.

To specify the alignment of selected paragraphs 253

use one of the four paragraph alignment buttons on the Formatting toolbar.

In this chapter we'll explore Word's paragraph-formatting tools, which you will use for adjustable line spacing, indentation, and text alignment. You'll see how to use Word's border features to create boxes and lines. Paragraph numbering, shading, and sorting are also discussed. You can save complex sets of formatting decisions as styles, as you'll see in Chapter 14.

Word's Paragraphs

Your English teachers taught you that a paragraph is a collection of sentences on a related topic. Word for Windows uses a somewhat more liberal definition. A Word paragraph can be a single text character, a graphic, or even a blank line consisting only of the paragraph mark (¶), which appears in your document when you press the ↵ key. (Click the Show ¶ toolbar button to display this and other nonprinting characters.) Paragraph-formatting features are an important part of Word's arsenal. Figure 10.1 contains five Word for Windows paragraphs, each ending with a paragraph mark. Can you find them all?

A·Word·paragraph·can·be·a·single·text·character,·a·graphic,·or·even·a·blank·line.¶

They·can·have·different·formats¶

¶

There·are·five·paragraphs·in·this·example·Can·you·find·them·all?¶

Figure 10.1 **Word paragraphs always end with a paragraph mark (¶).**

Each Word for Windows paragraph in your document can be uniquely formatted and need not contain text. For instance, the first paragraph in Figure 10.1 is single-spaced with the first line indented about $\frac{1}{2}''$. The next paragraph is right-justified. The third paragraph is a blank line created by pressing just the ↵ key. The fourth paragraph is centered. The final paragraph is a graphic (without text), followed by a paragraph mark. Notice that this last paragraph (the graphic) has been centered.

Creating Paragraphs

Each time you press the ↵ key you create a new paragraph. It's that simple. When you open a new document, Word for Windows applies the default paragraph settings stored as a style called Normal. It formats each new paragraph the same way until and unless you tell it to do otherwise.

Splitting Text into Multiple Paragraphs

If you want to split a lengthy section of text into two or more paragraphs, follow these steps:

1. Place the insertion point where you want the new paragraph to begin. (Be careful not to include unwanted spaces when splitting text.)

2. Press ↵. The text will split, and you'll see a paragraph mark if the Show ¶ feature is enabled. Note that the new paragraph will take on the characteristics of the one above. For instance, if the original big paragraph had a first-line indent, the two little ones also will.

Notice how, in Figure 10.2, the new paragraph takes on the same indentation characteristics as the preceding one.

Joining Paragraphs

It's easy to turn two paragraphs into one. Just delete the interceding paragraph mark and add any necessary space to separate the new neighbors. For instance, to rejoin the two short paragraphs in Figure 10.2, you'll need a space between the period after the word *topic* and the *W* in *Word*. The quick way to join these two paragraphs would be to select the unwanted paragraph mark and type a space to replace it. Follow these steps:

1. Turn on the Show ¶ feature to make things easier.

Position the insertion point; then press Enter

Figure 10.2   *To split one paragraph into two or more paragraphs, position the insertion point (watching for unwanted spaces) and press ↵.*

2. Delete the paragraph mark between the two paragraphs, adding space if necessary. Text above will take on the appearance of text below if the two paragraphs originally had different paragraph formatting.

Forcing New Lines without Using Paragraphs

Sometimes you'll want to force a new line without creating a new paragraph. The reasons will become more apparent as you start to use advanced Word for Windows features like paragraph numbering and styles with Next Style options, so tuck this trivia nugget away. To force new lines without creating new paragraphs, use the Shift+↵ key combination. Instead of a paragraph symbol, you'll see arrows like the ones in Figure 10.3.

Deleting Paragraphs

Think twice when deleting paragraphs. You can delete just the contents of a paragraph or delete the contents and the paragraph marker. If you

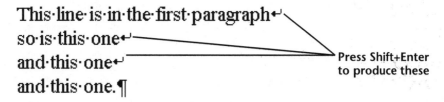

Figure 10.3 *Use the Shift+↵ feature to force new lines without starting a new paragraph.*

delete the marker, text above the old paragraph will take on the characteristics of the remaining paragraph below it. This is by design and is not a bug. If you accidentally delete a paragraph mark and create a problem, Undo (Ctrl+Z or the drop-down list) will usually return your heart rate to normal.

Adding Blank Lines between Paragraphs

You can create blank lines, typewriter style, by just mashing on the ↵ key all day. But hey, it's almost the year 2000. Instead, create white space between paragraphs, rather than adding blank lines. Use the Paragraph dialog box. As you'll soon see, this will give you better control over spacing between paragraphs and make it easier to keep paragraphs together. Read on.

Paragraph Formatting

You modify the appearance of paragraphs using the ruler, the Formatting toolbar, and the Paragraph dialog box. The ruler and Formatting toolbar are easy to use and readily available. When precise formatting is required, consider using the Paragraph dialog box rather than the ruler. Some formatting features have keyboard shortcuts.

TIP If you want to reformat only one paragraph, simply place the insertion point anywhere within the paragraph; then make formatting changes. There is no need to select the text in a single paragraph. To alter multiple paragraphs, select them first. Your changes will affect all selected paragraphs, including any partially selected paragraphs. Double-clicking at the left edge of a paragraph will select it.

As we did in the previous chapter, let's start with a quick tour of the paragraph-formatting tools; then we'll look at some everyday paragraph-formatting tasks.

Formatting with the Formatting Toolbar

The Formatting toolbar contains a number of handy paragraph-formatting tools. If it is not showing, bring it into view with the <u>V</u>iew ➤ <u>T</u>oolbars command. Figure 10.4 shows you the location and function of the ruler's paragraph-related features.

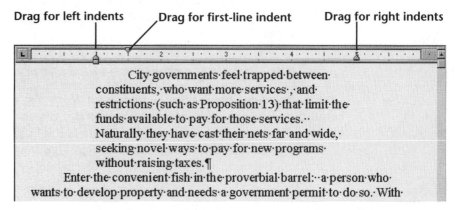

Drag for left indents   **Drag for first-line indent**   **Drag for right indents**

*Figure 10.4   **The Formatting toolbar places paragraph-formatting tools at your fingertips and also shows many paragraph settings options.***

You must tell Word for Windows which paragraph or paragraphs you wish to format before using the Formatting toolbar's tools. If you have only one paragraph selected, or if all of the selected paragraphs have identical paragraph-formatting options, activated paragraph options (like center) will be indicated with depressed buttons. But if you select dissimilar paragraphs, these indicators will not be accurate.

Moreover, if you select two dissimilar paragraphs (like those in Figure 10.4), you'll see subtle changes on the ruler. Indent handles will have dim outer edges, for instance. This is Word's way of saying it can't display two different settings at once.

Formatting with the Toolbar

Paragraph buttons on the Formatting toolbar include Align Left, Center, Align Right, Justify, Numbering (lists), Bullets (lists), Decrease Indent, Increase Indent, and Borders. Figure 10.5 shows the buttons. You've seen some examples of these buttons at work already.

Figure 10.5 *Paragraph-formatting buttons on the toolbar.*

Formatting with the Paragraph Dialog Box

The Paragraph dialog box shown in Figure 10.6 is reached by choosing Format ➤ Paragraph.

TIP Double-clicking on any indent marker will bring up the Paragraph dialog box!

The Paragraph dialog box lets you:

▶ Precisely specify line spacing (single, double, etc.)

▶ Precisely specify paragraph spacing (space before and after paragraphs)

▶ Dictate exact indentation measurements

▶ Turn off line numbering for specific paragraphs

▶ Specify text alignment (left, centered, right, or justified)

▶ Specify text-flow guidelines (widows, orphans, etc.)

▶ Suppress hyphenation

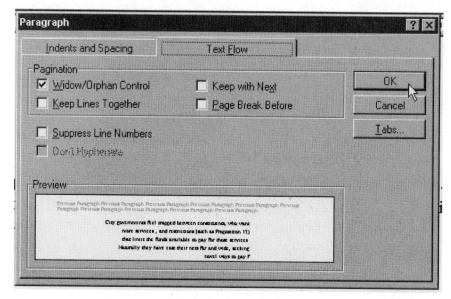

Figure 10.6   Reach the Paragraph dialog box from the Format menu or via hotspots. Both tabs are shown here.

When you enter measurements in the Paragraph dialog box, you can often use different units of measure for the same specification. For instance, you can specify line height in points (pt), lines (li), inches (in), picas (pi), or centimeters (cm). Each possible numeric entry in the Paragraph dialog box has a default unit of measure, which is shown in its entry box.

Part
2

Formatting
Fundamentals

NOTE Line Spacing shows a unit of measure when you select At Least or Exactly. When you select Multiple, you can enter a number and Word will assume you mean *li*.

WARNING It is possible to make entries in the Paragraph dialog box without specifying units of measure if you know the default unit of measure for each type of entry. For instance, the default for line spacing is points. Here's the rub. If you enter *2*, Word for Windows will assume you mean 2 points, not double spacing. To specify double spacing, you'd need to enter *2 li*. When you are uncertain about the default unit of measure for a paragraph specification, always enter the abbreviation for the unit of measure, to play it safe.

In United States Word versions, the default for horizontal measurements, such as indents, is inches. The default unit of measure for line and paragraph spacing is points. (There are 72 points per inch.)

Keyboard Formatting Shortcuts

There are numerous keyboard shortcuts for paragraph formatting. They are mentioned throughout this chapter and summarized in Appendix B.

A few keyboard shortcuts are additive. That is, instead of toggling when you press them more than once, they increase their effect. For example, pressing Ctrl+M indents a paragraph 0.5" from the left; pressing it twice indents the paragraph 1"; and so on.

Specifying Paragraph Formats

As promised, here are the steps for applying paragraph formats and everyday examples. Don't forget that it is possible to store and quickly recreate complex paragraph formats using Styles, as described in Chapter 14.

Indenting Paragraphs Automatically

There are a number of ways to indent paragraphs. Indents are *added* to margins, thereby increasing the white space and decreasing the text area for specific paragraphs. Thus, if you have a 1.0″ right margin and specify a right indent of 1.0″, your text will print 2.0″ from the right edge of the paper.

 WARNING   Don't confuse indenting with aligning. Aligning paragraphs is covered later in this chapter. Also, don't confuse indenting with margins.

The first line of each paragraph can be indented differently from other lines in the paragraph. First lines can be shorter than the others, creating regular indents, or longer than the others, creating *hanging* indents (sometimes called outdents). Once you change indents, each new paragraph you start by pressing ↵ will maintain the same indentation settings until you change them. Indented paragraphs can have other paragraph formatting as well. Figure 10.7 shows several indenting examples.

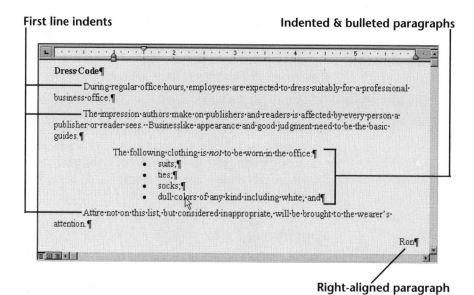

Figure 10.7   Several examples of paragraph indenting.

TIP Whenever you place the insertion point in a paragraph, the indent markers on the ruler move to show you the setting for the current paragraph.

Indenting with the Ruler

The quickest way to indent is to drag indent markers on the ruler. To adjust left and right paragraph indents from the ruler:

1. Place the insertion point in a paragraph or select multiple paragraphs.

2. Point to and then drag the appropriate triangular indent markers to the desired locations. (Drag on the bottom part of the left marker to set the overall left indentation.)

3. Watch the ruler's scale as you drag. It shows the position of the indent mark in relation to its respective margin. The bottom part of the left marker is divided by a black line. Click on the upper portion of the bottom part to move it independently of the other part.

4. You will see the text move when you release the mouse button.

5. Whenever you place the insertion point in a paragraph, the indent markers on the ruler move as necessary to show you the setting for the current paragraph.

Indenting with the Paragraph Dialog Box

The Paragraph dialog box lets you type in specifications for right, left, first line, and hanging indents. The default dimension in the United States is inches (in). By including the appropriate unit of measurement with your entry, you can specify points (pt), picas (pi), or centimeters (cm) instead. To adjust left and right paragraph indents from the dialog box:

1. Place the insertion point in a paragraph or select multiple paragraphs.

2. Open the Paragraph dialog box with the F<u>o</u>rmat ➤ <u>P</u>aragraph command or double-click on a hotspot.

3. Enter specifications for right, left, and/or first-line indents.

4. You will see the effects of your changes in the Preview box. Click OK when you are happy with the indentation.

5. Once you move indent markers, each new paragraph you start by pressing ↵ will maintain the same indentation settings until you change them.

Indenting with Keyboard Shortcuts

There are keyboard shortcuts that move the left indent marker. These are additive commands and can create nested paragraphs.

Command	Keystrokes
Center	Ctrl+E
Justify	Ctrl+J
Left align	Ctrl+L
Right align	Ctrl+R
Left indent	Ctrl+M
Remove left indent	Ctrl+Shift+M
Create hanging indent	Ctrl+T
Reduce hanging indent	Ctrl+Shift+T

Indenting with the Toolbar

  The Increase Indent toolbar button moves the left indent marker to the right the distance of one standard tab stop, and the Decrease Indent button moves it back the same distance. These are additive commands. Pressing Increase Indent twice indents farther than pressing it once. There are no toolbar buttons for the right indent marker.

Indents in Margins

It is possible to specify indentations that print in the right and/or left margins. Specify negative margin settings in the paragraph dialog box (**–0.5 in,** for instance) or drag indent markers into margins. Be patient. Horizontal scrolling is required when you drag indent markers into margins, and the process can sometimes be slow.

Indenting First Lines

You can indent the first line of a paragraph with the ruler, the Paragraph dialog box, or tabs. Tabs are generally the least efficient method.

First-Line Indenting with the Ruler

To set up automatic first-line indenting with the ruler, follow these steps:

1. Place the insertion point in a paragraph or select multiple paragraphs.

2. Drag the top half of the left indent marker. The text moves when you release the mouse button, and subsequently typed paragraphs will indent the same way.

First-Line Indenting with the Paragraph Dialog Box

To set up automatic first-line indenting with the Paragraph dialog box, follow these steps:

1. Place the insertion point in a paragraph or select multiple paragraphs.

2. Open the Paragraph dialog box (choose Format ➤ Paragraph or double-click on an indent marker in the ruler).

3. In the Special box, select First Line from the drop-down list and specify a first-line indent dimension in points (pt), inches (in), picas (pi), or centimeters (cm). Watch the preview to see the effect without closing the dialog box.

4. Click OK when you are happy with the indent.

First-Line Indenting with the Tab Key

You can create first-line indents with the Tab key. But it's extra work, because you'll need to remember to tab each time you start a new paragraph. Use the ruler or dialog box instead. And as discussed in Chapter 14, you can define a first-line indent as part of a paragraph style, available whenever you need it.

Hanging Indents

Sometimes you want to have the first line in each paragraph stick out. This is particularly useful for creating bulleted lists, numbered paragraphs, bibliographies, and so forth. The first line in a hanging indent is called (cleverly) a *hanging indent.* The subsequent lines beneath are called *turnover* lines. Figure 10.8 shows some examples.

NEW   Word has a new feature that automatically creates hanging indents for bulleted and numbered lists. All you have to do is type (at the beginning of a new line) an asterisk and a space or a number and a space, and Word automatically bullets or numbers all other entries in your list, complete with attractive hanging indents. The effect is similar to that shown in Figure 10.8.

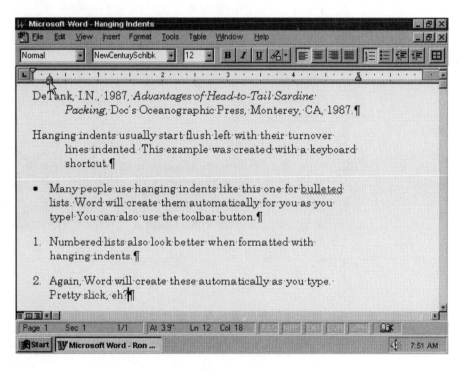

Figure 10.8   *Some examples of hanging indents.*

Hanging Indents with the Ruler

When creating hanging indents from the ruler, follow these steps:

1. Place the insertion point in the paragraph you need to format, select multiple paragraphs, or place the insertion point where you plan to begin typing hanging-indented paragraphs.

2. Set the position of the left (indented) edge of the turnover lines. To do this, with the ruler in view, drag the bottom half of the left indent marker to the right.

3. If you plan to indent the right edge of your paragraph(s), drag the right indent marker either now or later.

4. To create the hanging indent, drag the top half of the left indent marker to the left, past the turnover indent, and release the mouse button when you reach the desired point. The ruler will scroll to show you the hanging indent's position with relation to the rest of the paragraph.

Keyboard Shortcuts for Hanging Indents

There are keyboard shortcuts for moving the left indent. Use Ctrl+M to move the left tab marker to the right. Pressing Ctrl+Shift+M moves the marker to the left. Ctrl+Shift+N moves the indent back to the left margin. Movements are in the increments used for default tab settings (usually 0.5"). This is a great way to create nested indents! (Note that neither Ctrl+Shift+N nor Ctrl+Shift+M will go past the left margin.)

Aligning and Justifying Text

The four Formatting toolbar buttons that look like lines of text let you quickly justify, center, and right- and left-align. The lines in the buttons demonstrate the expected results. As always, you must first either select multiple paragraphs or place the insertion point in the paragraph you want to align.

Left Alignment

Left alignment is Word's default. Text sits right up against the paragraph's left indent position. If you have specified a first-line indent, the left alignment feature does not override it. Instead, it uses the specified first-line setting and then left-aligns the remaining text.

Centering

Clicking the Center button places the text or graphics smack dab between the indent markers for the paragraph being centered. If you want to center things between document margins, be sure the left and right indent markers are sitting on their respective document margins. Moving the first-line indent marker will affect centering.

 TIP Never use spaces to center. Always type words at the left margin and then click the Center button.

Right Alignment

 Clicking on the Align Right button places selected items flush against the right indent position for the paragraph. Use this feature for correspondence dates, inside addresses, and for added impact.

If you want to right-align something with the document's right margin, be sure the paragraph's right indent marker is sitting on the right document margin.

Justifying Text

 Clicking the Justify button causes Word for Windows to add space between words in the selected paragraphs. This results in what some people consider to be a typeset look.

Except for the last line in a paragraph, all of the justified lines will have exactly the same length and will all be flush left *and* right with the paragraph's left and right indent markers. Justified text can also have the first line indented.

If the uneven spacing and rivers of white space caused by justification annoy you, consider inserting hyphens to tighten up the text. See Chapter 9 for details.

Adjusting the Space between Lines

The Indents and Spacing tab of the Paragraph dialog box provides a drop-down list for simple but effective control of the space between lines under most circumstances. The preview area demonstrates the relative effect of single, one-and-a-half, and double line spacing. Single spacing causes 12-point line spacing, 1.5-line spacing is 18 points, and double-spaced lines will be 24 points apart. (There is little or no effect for text larger than 24 points.)

When you use these choices, Word for Windows will adjust the line spacing as needed to compensate for graphics, superscripts, and large or small type sizes. To force exact line spacing, use the At Least or Exactly choices described in a moment.

Single-Spacing Text

To single-space text, follow these steps:

1. Single spacing is Word's default. To reapply it to text spaced some other way, place the insertion point in a paragraph or select multiple paragraphs.

2. Press Ctrl+1 or choose Single in the Paragraph dialog box's Line Spacing menu. Selected text and subsequent typing will be single-spaced.

Double-Spacing Text

To double-space text, follow these steps:

1. To apply double spacing to text spaced some other way, place the insertion point in a paragraph or select multiple paragraphs.

2. Press Ctrl+2 or choose Double in the Paragraph dialog box's Line Spacing menu. Selected text and subsequent typing will be double-spaced.

Line-and-a-Half Spacing

To apply line-and-a-half spacing to text spaced some other way, follow these steps:

1. Place the insertion point in a paragraph or select multiple paragraphs.

2. Press Ctrl+5 or choose 1.5 lines in the Paragraph dialog box's Line Spacing menu. Selected text and subsequent typing will be one-and-a-half line spaced.

Specifying Exact Line Heights

Word for Windows automatically sets the appropriate amount of white space between lines for you unless you tell it to do otherwise. It even compensates for different-size characters on the same line by setting line spacing to the largest character.

But sometimes, you'll want to specify exact line spacing for one or more paragraphs. Increasing the spacing by a nonstandard amount can help you fill unused space when your copy runs a little short. Or, specifying slightly less than normal space between lines can help keep that last lonesome line from printing on its own page.

It's the Paragraph dialog box you need to visit. Here you tell Word for Windows that you want At Least or Exactly a specified amount of space.

1. Place the insertion point in a paragraph or select multiple paragraphs.

2. Open the Paragraph dialog box (choose Format ➤ Paragraph or double-click on any indent marker).

3. Choose Exactly or At Least from the drop-down list.

4. Enter a specification and a unit of measure (2.5 li, 26 pt, 1.5 in, 22 cm, etc.) in the At box. Watch the preview as you work.

5. Click OK to make the specified spacing change.

TIP If the tops or bottoms of characters are cut off, you may have set a line height that is too small. Revisit the Paragraph dialog box and increase the height.

Space before and after Paragraphs

Many people place white space between paragraphs by pressing the ↵ key several times—typewriter style. While this works just fine, there is a more efficient method.

The Paragraph dialog box (Format ➤ Paragraph) has an area in the Indents and Spacing tab called *Spacing*. It lets you define the amount of white space Word places before and after paragraphs. You can enter spacing settings in points (pt), inches (in), centimeters (cm), or lines (li). Thus, 12 points would be entered as *12pt*, 25 centimeters would be entered as *25cm*, and so on.

Each paragraph can have unique before and after spacing if you wish. One advantage to adding space this way is that the spacing before and after paragraphs does not change when you change the point size of your text. Another advantage is that you can use different spacing combinations for different purposes.

Headings often have different spacing requirements from body text, for instance. You may wish to create different Before and After paragraph spacing designs for figures and figure captions as well.

As you will learn in Chapter 14, you can save unique spacing specifications as part of a style, making it easy to keep the look of your documents consistent.

TIP When adding space, remember that if a paragraph has space added after it, and the paragraph beneath it has space added before, the white space between them will be the *combination* of the two settings. For example, if one paragraph has 12 points of spacing after it and its successor has 6 points of spacing before, the white space between will be 18 points. Therefore, it is wiser to use either one or the other, but not both.

Adding White Space before Paragraphs

To add a single line of white space before a paragraph, follow these steps:

1. Place the insertion point in a paragraph or select multiple paragraphs.

2. Press Ctrl+0 (zero).

To enter a specific amount of space before a paragraph:

1. Place the insertion point in a paragraph or select multiple paragraphs.

2. Double-click on any indent marker to open the Paragraph dialog box.

3. Enter new Before dimensions in the Spacing area in lines, inches, picas, etc. Selected paragraphs and subsequent ones will have additional amounts of white space before them.

To remove single lines of white space (originally created with Ctrl+0), press Ctrl+0 a second time.

Fine-Tuning Paragraph Spacing

While the ruler buttons are fine for most occasions, you may need to visit the Paragraph dialog box occasionally to get just the right look. Enter appropriate specifications in the Spacing Before and After boxes to fine-tune. You can observe the effect of your changes in the Preview box. Click OK when you are satisfied.

Space Before at Page Tops

When you print, Word for Windows ignores the Space Before setting in paragraphs that automatic pagination places at the top of a page. If you force a page or section break, however, Word retains this extra space. It will also retain the additional space if you check the Page Break Before option in the Pagination section of the Paragraph dialog box.

Borders and Shading

Word for Windows bristles with paragraph border and shading features. You can apply various border treatments and shading to single paragraphs or groups of paragraphs. For instance, all of the paragraphs in Figure 10.9 are surrounded by a common double-line border, while the last paragraph has a single line top border and shading.

You can have it fast.
You can have it cheap.
You can have it done right.

Pick any two of the above.

Figure 10.9   You can apply borders and shading to one paragraph or multiple paragraphs.

Creating Lines with the Border Command

Don't be fooled by the boxy-sounding name of this command. Format ➤ Borders and Shading can be used to create lines as well. Check out the samples in Figure 10.10.

There is even a new feature in Word that will automatically insert a border for you. While this can only be used for single or double lines, it is quite a handy shortcut for creating simple borders. All you have to do

Borders needn't be *boxes*. Use them to create *lines* like this one.

Lines *above* attract attention

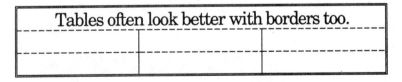

Lines below set things off

Consider leaving off left & right sides

Tables often look better with borders too.

Figure 10.10 **By leaving off parts of borders, you can create lines.**

is type three consecutive hyphens (---) or equal signs (===) on a new line and hit Enter (↵). Word will automatically make what you've typed into a single or double line, *and* set the leading to make it look nice! Pretty nifty, eh? Well, those smart young kids at Microsoft work day and night to keep you happy. This command can do some funky things if you use it several lines in a row. Experiment.

You adjust the horizontal *length* of borders or lines by adjusting a paragraph's width with indent markers or the Paragraph dialog box. It's also easy to control the distance between text and border lines. You can use borders to surround paragraphs, framed objects (like graphics), and tables.

The Borders Toolbar

 The Borders button on the Formatting toolbar brings up a handy Borders toolbar. (You can also display the Borders toolbar from the View menu by choosing <u>V</u>iew ➤ <u>T</u>oolbars.) You will see the changes in your document as you work. Here are general steps for using it:

1. Place the insertion point in the paragraph of interest or select elements to be formatted—multiple paragraphs, graphics, etc.

2. Adjust indents if necessary to define the desired width for the borders.

3. Reveal the Borders toolbar (use the Borders button or View menu), shown in Figure 10.11.

4. With the Borders toolbar open, choose the desired line thickness from its drop-down list.

5. Click on the button corresponding to the desired border (No Border, Outside, Inside, Right, Left, Bottom, or Top).

6. Pick shading, if you like, from the drop-down shading list.

7. Admire your work.

Figure 10.11 **The Borders toolbar.**

> **TIP**   You can mix line thicknesses and shading by reselecting different parts
> of the project and using different settings. Read on.

Custom Borders and Lines

Playing with borders and lines can be great rainy day entertainment. Just
don't get carried away on busy days or with a deadline looming. Before
you can effectively create custom borders, you must understand the
Border sample part of the Paragraph Borders and Shading dialog box,
highlighted in Figure 10.12.

The border sample changes to represent the border you are creating. For
instance, in Figure 10.12, the border specifications call for a thick black
line around the entire border and a 1.5-point magenta line separating
the two paragraphs. You specify lines (add and remove them) by clicking
on border guides. They look like dotted *T*'s and *L*'s. Two of them are
identified in Figure 10.12. Clicking on any of the three horizontal guides

**Part
2**

Formatting
Fundamentals

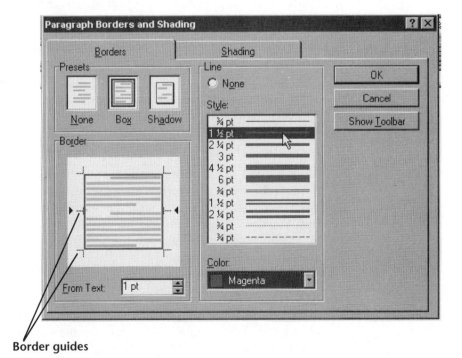

Border guides

Figure 10.12   *The Border sample portion of the Paragraph Borders and Shading dialog box.*

toggles horizontal lines. Clicking on vertical guides—well, you get the picture.

The little triangles that appear and disappear are called *selection markers*. They show you which border lines will be affected when you click a border guide. Don't worry, this will begin to make sense when you experiment on your own.

If you've selected multiple paragraphs (or tables) you'll be able to place lines between the different paragraphs (or table rows) thanks to those center border guides. And, as you've seen in the examples, it is possible to specify the line widths used for borders. It's even possible to combine different line styles in the same project. Here are the general steps for custom borders:

1. Place the insertion point in the paragraph of interest, or select elements to be formatted—multiple paragraphs, graphics, etc.

2. Open the Paragraph Borders and Shading dialog box (shown in Figure 10.12).

3. Click on the appropriate border guides in the sample to turn them on or off.

4. Click on the line type(s) you wish. Watch your document change as you work.

    TIP   Once you've created some favorite border combinations, consider saving them as glossary entries or styles. See Chapters 14 and 17 for details.

Increasing the Space between Borders and Text

To add extra space between the text contained within borders and the borders themselves, specify a measurement (in points) in the From Text portion of the Borders tab of the Paragraph Borders and Shading dialog box. You can do this when you are designing the border, or you can select an existing border and change the spacing later by visiting the Borders and Shading dialog box.

Controlling Border Width

A paragraph's indents (and the document's margins) control the width of a border. To change the border, select the paragraph(s) containing the border formatting and change the indents.

Shading

Shading can be added to paragraphs with or *without* borders. Use shading to create forms or just to add decoration. Be aware, however, that shading can look pretty raggedy on many printers. Test-print some samples before spending hours shading your favorite form or resume.

You can use either the Borders toolbar or the Paragraph Borders and Shading dialog box to add and change shading. To add paragraph shading, pick a shading percentage from the drop-down Shading menus or enter the first number of a percentage in the entry box.

For example, to choose a 40 percent shading, type **4** in the shading list box and press ↵. The smaller the percentage, the lighter the shading—100 percent is solid black.

TIP For settings that begin with the same number (e.g., 5 and 50), typing the number acts as a toggle. For example, typing *5* once selects 5; typing it a second time selects 50.

Removing Borders and Shading

While you can remove borders and shading either with the Borders toolbar or the Paragraph Borders and Shading dialog box, the toolbar's easier. Here are the general steps for using the dialog box:

1. Place the insertion point in the paragraph of interest or select elements to be shaded—multiple paragraphs, graphics, etc.

2. Open the Paragraph Borders and Shading dialog box with the Format ➤ Borders and Shading command.

3. Click on the Shading tab.

4. Scroll through the Shading list and select a percentage.

5. You will see the effects of your work in the Preview box.

6. Click OK.

7. Be sure to test-print new designs.

Here are the steps for removing borders or shading with the Borders toolbar:

1. Select the objects with the borders or shading you wish to remove.

2. Display the Borders toolbar (View ➤ Toolbars).

3. Click on the No Border button (it's the rightmost button).

4. If shading has been applied, choose Clear from the Shading list, or type **c** in place of the displayed percentage and press ↵.

NOTE Each paragraph can have its own tab settings. Read about tabs in the next chapter.

Tables and Paragraphs

As you'll see in the next chapter, tables can contain paragraphs. Generally, paragraphs in table cells behave like ordinary paragraphs.

Chapter 11

Tabs, Tables, Math, and Sorting

FAST TRACK

Word for Windows novices often either under- or overuse tabs. Primarily a quick way to position text or graphics, tabs have a lot of competition in Word for Windows. Some people use the spacebar instead of tabs. Lovers of Word's table features often abandon tabs altogether in favor of tables. This is probably a mistake too. Moreover, your typing teacher may have told you to use tabs to indent the first line of each paragraph. You may prefer Word's split left indent marker. Word's first-line indent feature is probably a better choice for that task. In this chapter you'll see some effective uses for tabs.

This chapter also shows you how to have Word for Windows do simple math calculations (a great way to compute and proof totals and subtotals in tabular typing). And you'll see how Word can sort things like phone lists. Finally, Word comes with a separate program called Equation Editor, manufactured by Design Sciences, Inc. It will be of particular interest to scientists and academicians. Microsoft ships a customized version of the program designed specifically for use with Word for Windows. This chapter introduces you to the Equation Editor and tells you how to obtain additional information or an even more robust version of the program.

Tabs

Tabs are great for creating quick, relatively simple lists, and they do some things in Word for Windows you can't do on a typewriter. For instance, they can help you exchange Word data with spreadsheets, databases, and other programs. Each paragraph in a Word document can have the same or different tab settings. So turn off that "Gilligan's Island" rerun, and let's explore the wonderful world of tabs and tab stops!

Word for Windows offers five specialized tab-stop types. They each work with tabs to help align text and are particularly useful for making simple columnar lists like the one in Figure 11.1.

Left Tab Stops

Left tab stops are like the plain vanilla ones you find on your old Smith Corona. Text typed at these tab stops bumps up against the left edge of the stop. A left tab was used to align the peoples' names (the third tab stop) in Figure 11.1.

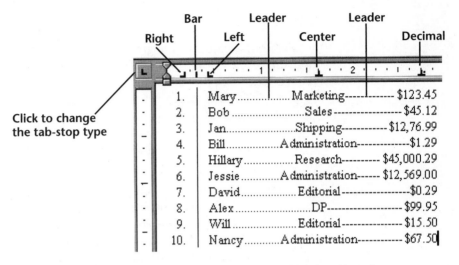

Figure 11.1   Word for Windows provides left, center, right, decimal, and bar tabs.

Center Tab Stops

A center tab stop centers your text around the tab stop. In Figure 11.1 the department names (at the fourth stop) are aligned with a center tab stop.

Right Tab Stops

Right tab stops position whatever you type to the left of the tab. As you can see in the first column of Figure 11.1, this is a great way to type long lists of numbers and have them line up.

Decimal Tab Stops

Decimal tab stops behave as you'd expect. They align columns of numbers on the decimal point and are perfect for simple financial reports.

Bar Tabs

The Bar button creates nice, thin vertical lines like the one you see separating the first and second columns in Figure 11.1. They aren't actual tab stops (that is, you cannot use them to align text), but they can be placed and moved like stops.

Tables vs. Tabs

Simple tabular columns are great if you have items that always fit on one line. But suppose that one of the departments in Figure 11.1 was the Department of Redundancy Department, for instance. If you use tabs, the title won't automatically wrap to fit the format. You would need to redesign the tab layout, shorten the department title, or cobble things up with a carriage return. Ugh. Long items like these give tab typists fits. As you will see later in this chapter, tables make it easy to deal with this and other problems.

Serious typists will probably choose table solutions over tabs most days. The price is speed and complexity. Word's table features can be slow at times, and you may scratch your head in the beginning. Tables require an understanding of tabs, too. So, for simple projects like the example here, you might want to stick with tabs alone, at least until you've mastered them.

Setting Custom Tab Stops

In the United States, at least, Word for Windows starts out each new document with tabs set at 0.5″ intervals. You can create custom tab locations to replace these.

Tab stops are always stored with the paragraph mark for each paragraph; thus, all of the rules about paragraph markers apply. If, for example, you set tab stops once and type ↵ at the end of each typing line, each new paragraph (line) will use the same tab stops as the preceding one until you tell Word otherwise.

Setting Tab Stops with the Ruler

You can set custom tabs as you type or use the standard tabs initially and then go back to fine-tune. Here are the general steps:

1. With the ruler in view, click the button at the left edge of the horizontal ruler repeatedly until it shows the icon for the desired tab-stop type (they are Left, Right, Decimal, and Center).

2. Click on the ruler where you want to place a tab stop. If you make a mistake, drag the stop off the ruler and try again.

3. When you type, press the Tab key to move the insertion point to the new tab positions. With Show ¶ turned on, you'll see fat arrows indicating each tab character you type.

```
→1. ┿ Mary.......→........Marketing------→----- $123.45¶
→2. ┿ Bob ..........→...........Sales --------→------- $45.12¶
```

Moving Tab Stops on the Ruler

To move tab stops before you've entered text, simply point to the stop of interest and drag away. If you have already entered text that uses the tab stops you want to move, first select all of the text before moving the tab stop.

For instance, if you had already typed the ten lines in Figure 11.1 and wanted to move the left tab stop for all of the lines, you would need to highlight *all ten* lines before moving the tab stop. Otherwise, some lines (paragraphs) would have different stops than others. Incidentally, you'd also want to highlight the paragraph mark *beneath* the last line if you plan to enter more items. Otherwise, the last paragraph marker wouldn't know about the change and subsequent entries would be off.

If you highlight paragraphs with different tab-stop settings, the tab stops will be dimmed. Only the stops for the top paragraph will be displayed.

Setting Tab Stops with the Tabs Dialog Box

While using the ruler is easy, you may want to use the Tabs dialog box for some projects. It provides ways to set tab stops precisely and offers some additional tab-related options. Figure 11.2 shows the Tabs dialog box at work.

You can reach the Tabs dialog box in any of these ways:

▶ Double-click any tab stop on the ruler.

▶ Choose Format ➤ Tabs.

▶ Click the Tabs button in the Paragraph dialog box.

Part
2

Formatting
Fundamentals

Changes default stops for current document

Clears a single tab   Clears all tabs in selected paragraphs

*Figure 11.2   **The Tabs dialog box gives you precise control and additional table-related features.***

▶ Double-click in the tab-stop area of the ruler to place a new left tab stop where you have clicked *and* bring up the Tabs dialog box. The position of the new tab stop will be shown in the Position area of the dialog box and will change as you move the tab stop.

WARNING   Remember to select all affected text and paragraph markers before moving tab stops. Undo (Ctrl+Z) will save you when you forget.

Units of Measure in the Tab Dialog Box

Measurements in the Tabs dialog box are assumed to be in inches unless you type another valid abbreviation (*cm* for centimeter, *pt* for point, or *pi* for pica). As an example, *5 cm* would position a tab stop five centimeters from the left margin.

There is also an alignment section in the Tabs dialog box, where you can change current tab-stop types. This is the only place where you can select a bar tab.

Leading Characters for Tabs

Word for Windows' *leader* characters are dots, dashes, and solid lines. These leaders precede tabbed entries, producing the effect demonstrated in Figure 11.3. You set them in the Tabs dialog box. They make it easy to read wide, sparsely populated lines without losing your place. Choose Leader 1 (the None option) if you want to remove leaders.

Part
2

Formatting
Fundamentals

Leader 1

.... Leader 2

------------Leader 3

_____ Leader 4

Figure 11.3 **Word provides tab leaders that make it easy to read lines without losing your place.**

To create leaders, follow these steps:

1. Select the paragraphs you want to pretty up.

2. Double-click on the tab where you want the leaders.

3. Choose the leader style you desire from the Tabs dialog box.

4. Click OK.

You can apply this effect when defining new tab stops or by double-clicking on existing stops to bring up the Tabs dialog box as an afterthought.

Default Tab-Stop Positions

The Word for Windows standard settings specify tabs every half-inch (0.5 in). You can change this for a single document by changing the setting in the Tabs dialog box. To change default tabs permanently, change and save stops in the Normal template, as described in Chapter 16.

Clearing Tab Stops

You can drag the occasional tab off the ruler if you don't need it. The Tabs dialog box provides facilities for clearing multiple tabs at once. If you do choose a specific tab, the Clear button in the Tabs dialog box will still remove it.

When Your Tabs Don't Line Up

Select all of the paragraphs that you want to conform and set identical tabs.

You might also consider using the Clear All button. It removes all custom tabs. Defaults remain. This can make an absolute mess of your pride and joy. Undo should work if you accidentally clear all custom tabs, but it is always a good idea to save your work before experimenting with major changes like these. Remember, these features work only on paragraphs you have selected.

Entering and Editing Tabular Data

Once you have set up tab stops, simply press the Tab key to reach the stop and begin typing. Word for Windows will position the text as you type. If you are typing at a center or right stop, text will flow appropriately as you type. When you type at decimal stops, the insertion point sits to the left of the decimal position until you hit the period key; then it hops to the right side. To leave an entry blank, simply tab past it by pressing the Tab key.

Tabs and Data Exchange

Tabs and carriage returns are often used by databases and spreadsheets, particularly when exchanging data with Macintosh computer users. Tabs usually separate fields in records and carriage returns usually separate the records themselves, as illustrated in this radio frequency database in Figure 11.4.

If you have a list of tab-separated names, addresses, and phone numbers, for instance, you might be able to export the list to your favorite database or time-management program by saving it as a text-only file. Check out the importing sections of your other program manuals.

```
"Air"→1  →  123.0250  →      →  "D"  →    →  "UNICOM·Helicopter··Air·to·Air··Busy·"¶
"Air"→2  →  128.7500  →      →      →    →  "Airport·Burbank·Approach·Control"¶
"Air"→3  →  128.1000  →      →      →    →  "Airport·Coast·Approach·Control"¶
"Air"→4  →  120.7000  →      →  "D"  →    →  "Airport·Edwards·Departures·&·Approach"¶
"Air"→5  →  121.8000  →      →  "D"  →    →  "Airport·Edwards·Departures·&·Approach"¶
"Air"→6  →  126.1000  →      →  "D"  →    →  "Airport·Edwards·Departures·&·Approach"¶
"Air"→7  →  132.5000  →      →  "D"  →    →  "Airport·Edwards·Departures·&·Approach"¶
"Air"→8  →  133.6500  →      →  "D"  →    →  "Airport·Edwards·Departures·&·Approach"¶
"Air"→9  →  134.0500  →      →  "D"  →    →  "Airport·Edwards·Departures·&·Approach"¶
"Air"→10 →  269.2000  →      →  "D"  →    →  "Airport·Edwards·Departures·&·Approach"¶
```

Figure 11.4 **Many applications can use tab-separated data created with Word. For database use, save files like these.**

Tables

Tables help you organize complex columnar information. Use them to create such diverse documents as forms, television scripts, financial reports, parts catalogs, and resumes. You can insert tables anywhere you need them in Word for Windows documents. Word's table feature, and the terminology used to describe it, will remind you of a spreadsheet.

Word tables consist of horizontal *rows* and vertical *columns*. You do the typing in areas called *cells*. Cells can contain text, numbers, or graphics. Text in cells can be edited and embellished as usual with Word's Formatting toolbar and ruler.

A number of table-specific features let you control the size, shape, and appearance of cells. Border and shading features are available. It is also easy to insert and delete rows and columns.

Tables can be created from existing text without needless retyping. Or you can use the table feature to organize information and then convert your table to text. You can even import and export spreadsheet data. A feature called the Table Wizard helps you automate table creation, but we'll wait to discuss it until after you understand the manual process. That's because you will often want to fine-tune the Wizard's results, so you'll need to become a wizard also. Figure 11.5 shows a typical Word for Windows table and its constituent parts.

Part 2

Formatting Fundamentals

Rows   Columns   End-of-row markers

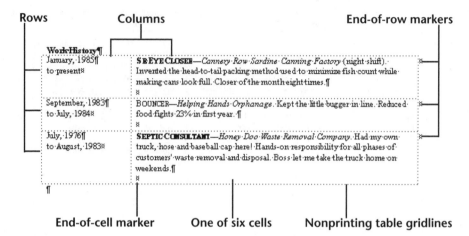

End-of-cell marker   One of six cells   Nonprinting table gridlines

Figure 11.5   **A typical table consisting of three rows, each containing two columns, for a total of six cells. The dotted cell gridlines will not print.**

 The dotted lines around each cell represent *nonprinting table gridlines*. You can add printing borders with the Format ➤ Borders and Shading command. The larger dots are end-of-cell and end-of-row marks. Click the Show ¶ button in the Standard toolbar to reveal them.

Creating a Simple Table

Word for Windows has several table features that you will love almost immediately. The first is the Table button, the second is an entire Table menu. Then, of course, there's the Table Wizard. Let's start with the button.

 TIP If you plan to add regular (non-table) text above a table in a new document, press ↵ once or twice *before* inserting a table. This will make it *much* easier to insert text above the table later. Then, if you haven't done so already, make any preliminary formatting decisions including the printer you plan to use, page orientation, margins, font, and so on. Word will consider these factors when inserting your new table. You can always change your mind later, but this step can greatly simplify things.

Using the Table Button

To create a table with the Table button, follow these steps:

1. Place the insertion point where you want to insert a table (ideally, *not* at the very beginning of a new, otherwise-empty document).

2. With the Standard toolbar in view, click the Table button, then drag while holding down the mouse button to highlight the desired number of rows and columns.

3. When the displayed grid represents the desired number of rows and columns, release the mouse button.

4. Word will insert an empty table.

> **TIP** Generally, it is best to guess at least how many columns there will be. Because Word determines the width of each column based on the number of columns and the space available, adding columns and getting them just the right width later on can be more difficult than simply adding rows.

Don't worry if you are uncertain about the exact number of columns or rows you'll need. You can always add or delete them later. Figure 11.6 shows the grid for eight two-column rows. Try to make your own 8 × 2 table with the button.

Using the Table Menu to Create a Table

You can use the Table ➤ Insert Table command to create tables. Here's how:

1. Position the insertion point where you want the table (ideally, not at the very beginning of a new, otherwise-empty document).

2. Choose Table ➤ Insert Table.

3. You'll see the dialog box shown in Figure 11.7.

4. Enter the desired number of columns and rows for your table.

5. Click OK.

Unless you specify a column width in the Column Width box, Word for Windows computes a column width automatically, taking into consideration the available text area in your document and the number of columns you've specified. Initially, all table columns are the same width, but you can change column widths using techniques described later in this chapter.

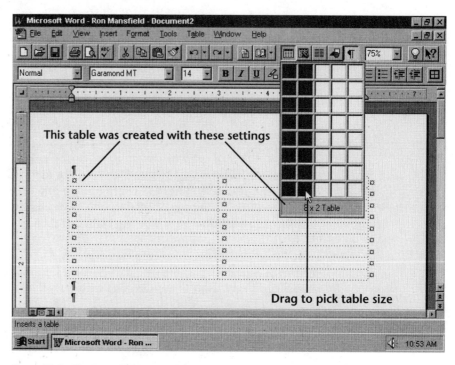

Figure 11.6   **The Insert Table menu box and the resulting table it creates.**

Figure 11.7   **You can use the Insert Table dialog box to define new tables or launch the Table Wizard (discussed later).**

Entering and Editing Text in a Table

With only the few exceptions noted in this chapter, you navigate, enter, and edit table text just as you do any other Word for Windows text. Use your mouse or arrow keys to position the insertion point, and then type normally. Think of the cell borders as margins. Word will automatically wrap text within the cell as you reach the right edge. Rows will automatically grow taller as necessary to accommodate your typing.

To move from cell to cell within a table, either use your mouse or use the Tab key to go forward and Shift+Tab to go backward. The insertion point will move left and down to the next row when you press Tab in the last column on the right side of a table, and it will move right and up one row when you Shift+Tab past the last column on the left. If you press Tab in the last cell of the last row, you will create a new row.

TIP   Because you use the Tab key to navigate in tables, you cannot simply press Tab to enter tab characters in cells. Instead, you need to hold down the Ctrl key while pressing Tab.

You can apply the usual character formatting to all or selected characters in a table. The familiar toolbar, ruler, and menu features all work here. Try recreating a personalized version of the to-do list shown in Figure 11.8. We'll use it for the rest of the exercises in this chapter.

Paragraphs in Cells

First-time table users are sometimes unaware of the important role that paragraphs play in tables. *A cell can contain more than one paragraph.* Create paragraphs in the usual way. While typing in a cell, press ⏎. If necessary, all of the cells in a row will increase in height to accommodate the extra paragraphs you create in a cell. If you haven't already done so, try adding the words *Home* and *Office* to all of the cells in the second column. Create two paragraphs in the process. Copy and paste if you like:

| Tuesday¤ | Home¶
Office ¤ |
| Wednesday¤ | Home¶
Office ¤ |

You can apply all of Word's paragraph formats to paragraphs in cells. Because cells can contain multiple paragraphs, they can also contain

Ron's To-Do List

Sunday	Home	
	Office	
Monday	Home	
	Office	
Tuesday	Home	
	Office	
Wednesday	Home	
	Office	
Thursday	Home	
	Office	
Friday	Home	
	Office	
Saturday	Home	
	Office	

Figure 11.8 **Try to add text to your first table.**

multiple paragraph formats. Thus, within a single cell you can have several different indent settings, tab settings, line-spacing specifications, styles, etc. For instance, the text in this cell was selected by double-clicking and dragging, made bold with the Formatting toolbar's Bold button, and centered using the Formatting toolbar's Center button. Try it.

¶

Ron's·To-Do·List

Selecting in Tables

As you've just seen, you can select characters, words, and other items in table cells using Word's usual mouse and keyboard features. In addition, Word also provides *table-specific* selection tools enabling you to choose whole cells, entire rows, columns, or areas.

Selecting Single Cells

The area between the first character in a cell and the left edge of the cell is called the *cell selection bar*. Clicking on it selects the contents of the entire cell. You can also select an entire cell by dragging with the mouse. Just be sure you include the end-of-cell mark in your selection:

Selecting Columns

To select a column, move the mouse pointer to the area at the top of a column called the *column selection bar*. You'll know you've arrived when the pointer changes into a large down-pointing arrow.

Click to select the entire column.

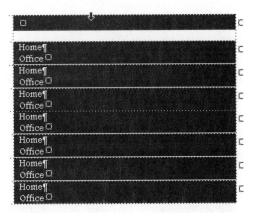

Holding down the Alt key while clicking anywhere in a column will also select the entire column. Selecting the bottom or top cell in a column and dragging up or down is somewhat tedious but will also work.

Selecting Rows

Double-clicking any cell-selection bar will select the entire row. Selecting the leftmost or rightmost cell in a row and dragging will also work.

Selecting Adjacent Groups of Cells

To select groups of adjacent cells, either drag through the cells or click in one cell and Shift+click in the others. For instance, to select all the "weekday" cells you could click in the Monday cell then Shift+click in the cell to the right of Friday. The 10 weekday cells would be selected:

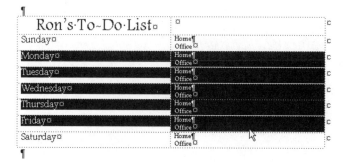

Selecting the Whole Table

To select an entire table, hold down the Alt key and double-click anywhere in the table. If your document contains multiple tables and they are not separated by paragraph marks, this technique will select all adjacent tables.

Do *not* use Word's Select All command to select a table, as this will also select paragraph marks and other things *outside* of the table.

TIP   **Word for Windows has a Select Table command on the Table menu. Its corresponding keyboard shortcut is Alt+5 on the numeric keypad (Num Lock has to be off for this to work).**

Modifying Table Designs

While Word's default table settings may be fine for simple typing tasks, you will eventually want to change column widths, overall table width, cell spacing, and so on. You'll want to insert, delete, and move rows and columns. As you can see from Figure 11.9, it is even possible to create professional-looking forms by modifying Word's standard tables.

Creating complex tables like this can be a little frustrating at first. It is a good idea to save your work before you experiment with new table formats. Beginners should consider working on copies of important documents. That said, let's look at a number of ways to modify standard table designs.

SALESPERSON	P.O. NUMBER	DATE SHIPPED	SHIPPED VIA	F.O.B. POINT	TERMS

QUANTITY	DESCRIPTION		UNIT PRICE	AMOUNT
				$ 0.00
				$ 0.00
				$ 0.00
				$ 0.00
				$ 0.00
				$ 0.00
				$ 0.00
			SUBTOTAL	$ 0.00
			SALES TAX	
			SHIPPING & HANDLING	
			TOTAL DUE	$ 0.00

Figure 11.9 **Create professional-looking forms by adding borders and adjusting row and column sizes.**

Table Borders that Print

An easy way to dress up a table is to add printed borders. The form in Figure 11.9 is an example of this. Select the cell or cells you wish to surround, then use the line-thickness portion of the Borders toolbar. Pick the desired combination of line thicknesses and apply the borders just as you would add them to Word for Windows paragraphs.

Adding Rows at the End of a Table

To add a new row at the end of an existing table, place the insertion point anywhere in the last cell (the one in the lower-right corner of your table) and press the Tab key. Word for Windows will insert a new row using the styles of the cells immediately above.

Adding Rows in the Middle of a Table

To insert a single row in the middle of a table:

1. Place the insertion point in the row *below* where you want the new row.

2. Click on the Table➤ Insert Rows command.

3. To add multiple rows, either repeat the Insert Rows command, press F4 (to repeat the previous insert action) as many times as you want rows, or try the alternate approach in the next step.

4. Select as many existing rows as the number of new ones you want to insert before making the insertion. In other words, if you want to add three rows, select the three existing rows beneath the desired insertion point, and then use the Table ➤ Insert Rows command. Word will insert three new rows.

Changing Row Heights

Normally, Word for Windows sets the height of each row automatically to accommodate the cell containing the tallest entry. For instance, if one cell in a row needs 2.0" to accommodate the text or graphic it contains, all of the cells in that row will be 2.0" high. All cells in a row must be the same height, but different rows can have different heights.

Dragging a Row to New Heights

To adjust the height of a row, follow these steps:

1. Click anywhere in the row you wish to resize.

2. In Page Layout view or Print Preview, move the pointer to the vertical ruler at the left edge of the screen, watching the pointer as you move it.

3. When it becomes an up-and-down arrow, use it to drag the row to the desired height.

4. Release the mouse button.

Resizing Rows with Cell Height and Width

You can also overrule Word's automatic row-height (and column-width) settings via the Table ➤ Cell Height and Width command. This is one way to create forms with fixed-sized entry areas.

There is no standard keyboard shortcut for this command, but experienced table typists often create their own. Figure 11.10 shows the Cell Height and Width dialog box.

To resize cells, follow these steps:

1. Place the insertion point anywhere in the row whose height you wish to specify. If you want multiple rows to share the same height, you can select all of them.

2. Choose the Table ➤ Cell Height and Width command.

3. Click on the Row tab, if necessary, to reveal its choices.

Figure 11.10   *Specify table row heights and column widths with the Table ➤ Cell Height and Width command.*

4. Use the drop-down list to choose Auto, At Least, or Exactly.

5. Enter the desired dimension in points, inches, centimeters, and so on. (The default is points.)

6. To change settings for previous or next rows, click the Previous Row or Next Row buttons.

7. Click OK to make the change and close the dialog box.

> **TIP**   If the exact height you specify is too small to accommodate the biggest entry in a row, the excessive text or a portion of the too-tall graphic will be cropped when printed. Simply increase the row height if this is undesirable.

Deleting Rows

To delete a row or rows of cells, select the row(s) to be deleted, then use the Table ➤ Delete Rows command. This will delete both the rows themselves (the cells) and their contents (text or graphics or whatever). To delete the *contents* of cells but leave the cells intact, use Word's usual text-deletion tricks (select text or graphics and press the Delete key, for instance).

Changing the Spacing between Rows

To change the amount of white space between the contents of rows, you must change the before and after spacing of the first or last paragraphs in the cells. (Don't confuse this with changing the *height* of rows, which is something else entirely.) Use the same techniques you use to add space between non-table paragraphs (see Chapter 10). Select the paragraph of interest, choose the Format ➤ Paragraph command, and specify Before and After spacing.

Inserting Columns in the Middle of a Table

To insert a single column within a table:

1. Select the column to the *right* of where you want the new column to appear.

2. Click the Table button in the Standard toolbar (notice how its name has changed to Insert Columns) or choose Table ➤ Insert Columns.

3. Word will add a new column but will not change the width of the earlier columns to accommodate it. In order to make the enlarged table fit on your page, you will probably need to adjust margins or column widths (described in a moment), or change page orientation. New columns usually retain the format of the old rightmost columns, but borders will not transfer.

> **TIP**   To insert multiple columns, select as many existing columns to the right of the desired location of the new columns as the number of new ones you want to insert. In other words, if you want to add three columns, select the three existing columns to the right of the desired insertion point, and then click on the Table button. Word for Windows will insert three columns.

Inserting Columns at the Right Edge of a Table

To insert a column at the right edge of a table:

1. Select an end-of-row marker.

2. Click on the Table button in the Standard toolbar (notice how its name has changed to Insert Columns), or choose Table ➤ Insert Columns.

3. A column is inserted at the right edge of the table.

Deleting Columns

To delete columns, follow these steps:

1. Select the column or columns to be removed. The choices on the Table menu change to include column-related commands.

2. Choose Table ➤ Delete Columns.

Changing Column Widths

You can change the widths of entire columns or selected cells within columns. Most changes can be made by dragging column markers on the table scale in the ruler. But you can make precise adjustments in the Table Cells dialog box.

Changing Column and Cell Widths with the Ruler

To change the width of an entire column, follow these steps:

1. Point to a column boundary.

2. The pointer will change shape.

3. Drag the column-width marker.

4. Watch the dotted line and ruler settings, then release the mouse button when it reaches the desired width.

If you hold down the Shift key while dragging, the column to the right changes size while the table's overall width remains unchanged. (Note that this affects two columns: the one being dragged and the one whose width is encroached upon.)

If you hold down Ctrl while dragging, all columns to the right change size, but the table's overall width does not.

TIP You can also drag the column markers on the ruler to change column widths. Just don't accidentally drag the cells' indent markers instead, as illustrated in Figure 11.11.

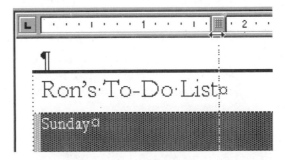

Figure 11.11   You can also change column widths by dragging these markers.

As you can see in Figure 11.12, it is possible to change the width of one or more cells by selecting them and visiting the Cell Height and Width dialog box. Specify a new width in the Columns tab.

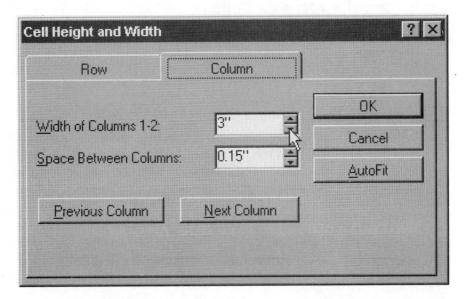

Figure 11.12   You can change individual cell widths or groups of cells with the Column tab in the Cell Height and Width dialog box.

TIP   When you are just learning, it's pretty easy to mess things up while dragging cell and column borders around this way, particularly if you change individual cell widths when you meant to change column widths. If multiple undos can't fix the problem, and you don't have a better, previously saved version, perhaps the AutoFit button can help. It's described next.

Changing Table Cell Widths with the AutoFit Button

The AutoFit button attempts to make cells snugly surround their contents. Therefore, it is best to use it after you've entered all of the information in your table or after you are done adding or deleting items. Follow these steps:

1. Select the cells you wish to resize or, more often, the entire table.

2. Choose Table ➤ Cell Height and Width.

3. Reveal the Column tab if it is not already in view.

4. Click on the AutoFit button.

5. Word will snug up the selected cells.

Merging Cells

Use the Merge Cells feature to combine the contents of multiple cells. This is a common way to make a heading in one cell span an entire table or selected group of columns. For example, you could merge the two cells in the top row of your To-Do list to form a heading like this that spans both columns:

As shown in Figure 11.13, you select the cells to merge, then choose Table ➤ Merge Cells, and the contents of the designated cells will merge. You may need to reformat text merged this way.

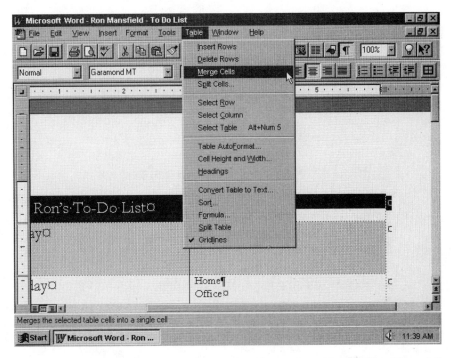

Figure 11.13 The contents of several cells can be merged together with the Table ➤ Merge Cells command.

Unmerging Cells

To split (unmerge) cells, follow these steps:

1. Place the insertion point in a merged cell.

2. Choose Table ➤ Split Cells. You'll be asked how many cells you want after the split.

Changing the Space between Columns

Word for Windows assigns cell widths based on the available text area and the number of columns you request. In the process, it sets aside a small amount of unprintable space between (actually within) each cell. This space takes away from the usable cell space. For instance, a $1\frac{1}{2}''$ column with $\frac{1}{4}''$ column spacing would have $1\frac{1}{4}''$ of usable space in the middle of each cell.

To change the space between columns, follow these steps:

1. Select the columns of interest.

2. Visit the Columns tab of the Cell Height and Width dialog box.

3. Type a new specification in the Space Between Columns box or use the arrows to flip through suggested choices.

4. Click OK.

AutoFormatting Tables

The Table ➤ Table AutoFormat command attempts to pick cell settings that make a presentable table. Whether it succeeds or not will vary with the project it's given and your definition of success. Personal taste plays a role too. For example, in a simple case like the one in Figure 11.14, AutoFormat successfully tightened up the table, added some nice-looking lines, and basically yupped it up.

But when the tables get big and slightly more complicated (containing merged cells for instance), things can get a little unpredictable.

WARNING   Before using the Table AutoFormat command, save your work to disk. That way if you get one of those "Insufficient memory to undo…" messages somewhere along the line, you'll at least have a disk copy of your "before" table.

Employee		Extension
Billie	Holiday	472
Dr. John		400
Robert	Benson	425
Robert	Johnson	450

Before Table
AutoFormat

Employee		Extension
Billie	Holiday	472
Dr. John		400
Robert	Benson	425
Robert	Johnson	450

After Table
AutoFormat

Figure 11.14   Before and after AutoFormatting a simple table.

Thus forewarned, here are the basic steps for using Table AutoFormat:

1. Enter, edit, spell check, reorganize, and otherwise finish with your table.

2. Save your document to disk.

3. Select the entire table (Alt+5 on the numeric keypad with Num Lock off).

4. Choose T<u>a</u>ble ➤ Table Auto<u>F</u>ormat.

5. Preview the format choices from the scrolling list, as shown in Figure 11.15, by highlighting their names one at a time. The ↑ and ↓ keys are handy here. Pay particular attention to how Word handles row and column headings in the preview examples.

6. Pick a style by highlighting it and click OK.

7. Behold—then undo and try again, if necessary.

Some (but not all) styles can add special effects to last columns or rows. This is a good way to highlight grand totals. Turn these effects on and off with their corresponding check boxes in the Apply Special Formats

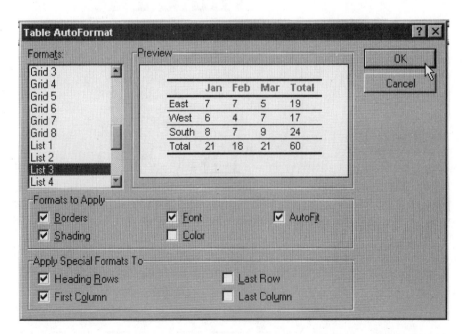

Figure 11.15 **Watch the previews of headings carefully when previewing automatic table style options.**

To area of the Table AutoFormat dialog box. You can also turn off many AutoFormat effects (borders, shading, etc.) the same way.

> **TIP**   Word's F*o*rmat ➤ *A*utoFormat command does not format tables. Use the T*a*ble ➤ Table Auto*F*ormat command instead.

Graphics in Tables

Tables aren't just for bean counters. Check out Figure 11.16.

Figure 11.16 is a two-column, one-row table with a graphic and a half-dozen different paragraph formats. Think of table cells as text and graphic containers; then set your imagination on turbo.

Make Big Money from

Tiny Sea Creatures !

Now you can turn a worldwide labor shortage into a real career opportunity. There are big bucks to be made in sardine eye closing.

Did you know that there are always openings in the canning industry? We need experienced eye closers now!

Day and night positions are available. **B**enefits include all the fresh sardines you can eat, and a free oil cloth apron...

Phone
1-800-EYE-SHUT

*Figure 11.16   **This is a two-column, one-row table!***

Importing Excel Worksheet Data as Tables

If you took offense at the bean-counter remark a moment ago, here's a tip designed to make your life easier and put me back in your good graces. You can import Excel worksheets as tables, and then edit and reformat them as necessary. The results can be pretty impressive, as you can see in Figure 11.17.

You can either copy and paste Excel worksheet cells (at which point they are converted to Word tables), or you can use more powerful tools like Link and Embed to give you live data that updates when you change your Excel spreadsheet. See Chapters 30 and 36 for details.

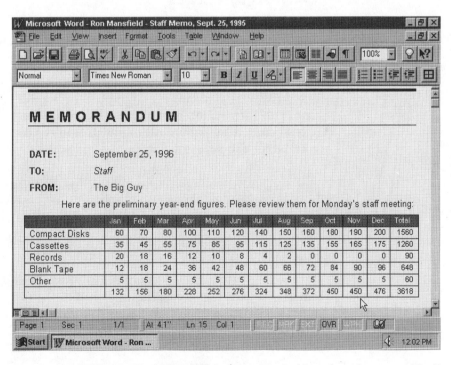

Figure 11.17   Either paste Excel cells, which become a Word table as shown here, or use Word's linking and embedding (described in Chapter 30).

Converting Tables to Text and Vice Versa

Sometimes you'll start a project using tabs and wish you'd created a table—or a coworker will give you some tabbed text. At other times, you will want to export things you've typed using Word's table feature for use with database and other programs that expect tab- or comma-separated (delimited) input. Word for Windows has solutions for all these contingencies.

Word makes it quite easy to convert back and forth from tables to text. You may need to do some cleanup before or after conversion, though. Always work on copies of your documents when you do this!

Converting Text to Tables

Highlight the text in your document that you want to turn into a table. Choose Table ➤ Convert Text to Table and click the appropriate option button in the resulting dialog box, shown in Figure 11.18.

Tab-Delimited Text

Click the Tabs button in the Convert Text to Table dialog box. Lines of text separated by paragraph marks or line breaks will become rows in your table. Tab-separated strings of text within those lines will become

Figure 11.18   *Word offers a number of conversion options. Pick the right one for your situation.*

cell entries in the row. Word for Windows will automatically create the necessary number of columns based on the maximum number of tabs in a line.

For instance,

```
Sony Corporation [Tab] 800-222-7669 [↵] SYBEX, Inc. [Tab]
415-523-8233 [Tab] Publisher [↵]
```

would create two rows with three columns, even though the last cell in the first row would be empty.

Comma-Delimited Text

Click the Commas button in the Convert Text to Table dialog box. Lines of text separated by paragraph marks or line breaks will become rows in your table. Comma-separated strings of text within those lines will become cell entries in the row. Word for Windows will automatically create the necessary number of columns based on the maximum number of commas in a line.

For instance,

```
Sony Corporation [Comma] 800-222-7669 [↵] SYBEX, Inc.
[Comma] 415-523-8233 [Comma] Publisher [↵]
```

would create two rows with four columns, even though the last two cells in the first row will be empty.

> **WARNING** Notice how the comma in *SYBEX, Inc.* created an unintentional column. While many database programs let you use quotation marks to solve this problem, Word does not.

Figure 11.19 shows part of the tab-separated text from Figure 11.18 after conversion to a table, editing, and formatting. Notice that the quotes surrounding the imported text have *not* been removed by Word's Text to Table feature. Use Replace to do this. See Chapter 20 for details.

Converting from Paragraphs

Click the Paragraphs button in the Convert Text to Table dialog box. If you ask Word for Windows to convert paragraphs to tables, it will propose a single column and create as many rows as you have paragraphs.

"Air"	1	123.0250	"D"	"UNICOM Helicopter Air to Air Busy "
"Air"	2	128.7500		"Airport Burbank Approach Control"
"Air"	3	128.1000		"Airport Coast Approach Control"
"Air"	4	120.7000	"D"	"Airport Edwards Departures & Approach"
"Air"	5	121.8000	"D"	"Airport Edwards Departures & Approach"
"Air"	6	126.1000	"D"	"Airport Edwards Departures & Approach"
"Air"	7	132.5000	"D"	"Airport Edwards Departures & Approach"
"Air"	8	133.6500	"D"	"Airport Edwards Departures & Approach"
"Air"	9	134.0500	"D"	"Airport Edwards Departures & Approach"
"Air"	10	269.2000	"D"	"Airport Edwards Departures & Approach"

Figure 11.19   Once you convert text to tables, you may need to clean it up.

Changing the number of columns will distribute paragraphs among the columns from left to right. In a two-column layout, the first paragraph would end up in the top-left cell of the new table, the second paragraph in the top-right cell, the third in the left cell of row two, and so on.

Converting Tables to Text

Select the table cells you wish to convert or use the Alt+double-click trick to select the whole table. Choose Table ➤ Convert Table to Text. Word will bring up a Table to Text dialog box, which asks if you want the table converted to paragraphs, tab-delimited text, or comma-delimited text. Pick one. If you pick the comma or tab options, Word will convert each row of your table into one line (a paragraph, actually). Cells in your old tables will become tab- or comma-separated items on the lines.

Remember that in-text commas will confuse Word for Windows. It would treat *SYBEX, Inc.* as two distinct entries. If you choose tab text, you will probably need to set new tabs after the conversion.

Choosing the paragraph option will convert each old table cell into at least one paragraph. If cells contain multiple paragraphs, the paragraph marks are retained during the conversion, so some cells will create more than one new paragraph.

The Table Wizard

The Table Wizard offers Word's simplest way of creating a table. It will ask you some questions and format your table. Let's suppose you want to make a ten-row table with a column for each month. Here are the basic steps:

1. Place the insertion point where you want the table. Tap ↵ once or twice if you've just opened a new document.

2. Choose Table ➤ Insert Table.

3. Click the Wizard button in the resulting dialog box.

4. You will be presented with a number of screens like this one, asking you questions:

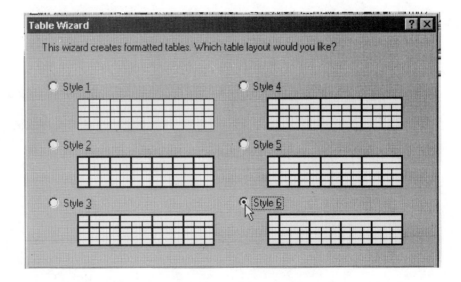

5. Look at each choice *carefully* and study the examples if they are given. Don't confuse *rows* and *columns* when the Wizard gives you choices. Try to imagine *your* data in the sample table formats.

6. Click on the Next button after each choice or Back to back up one screen.

7. When the Wiz runs out of questions, click Finish.

8. You'll be presented with the Table AutoFormat dialog box (which you read about earlier).

9. Cruise the format samples until you find just the right mood.

10. Click OK, wait a moment, and see what develops. Figure 11.20 shows the results of these requests:

   - Style 6

   - No heading, just 13 columns, Year 1996, quarters, then months

   - Repeat headings, center column headings in cells

   - No headings, just ten rows

   - Numbers: aligned on decimal

   - Portrait

   - Finish

   - Format: 3-D Effects 3

   - The names of the months changed to All Caps

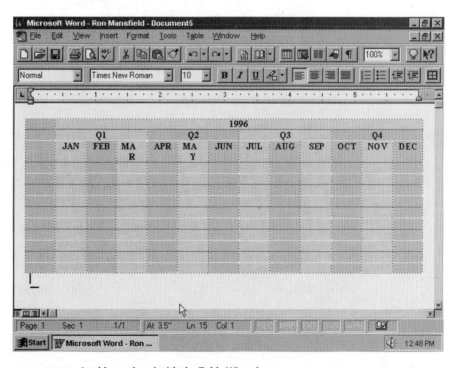

Figure 11.20   **A table produced with the Table Wizard.**

And that's why *manual* table skills were covered first in this book. At a minimum, you'll need to increase the width of the month columns and tidy up a few things before using the Wizard's creation. Fortunately, it's easy to do. Press on....

Table Tips

Here are some tips to help make you a more productive table editor. They cover a variety of subjects.

Print Format Samples

Today—before you have a rush job to do—create some sample tables using the automatic formats that appeal to you *and print them* on your printer(s). Some will look great. One or two may be unreadable. Find out before you are in a hurry.

Rearrange Rows in Outline View

With a table on-screen, switch to Outline view (View ➤ Outline). Move the pointer to the left edge of your table, as shown in Figure 11.21. The pointer shape will change.

You can drag rows to new positions using Word's Outline features. See Chapter 21 for more information about Outline view.

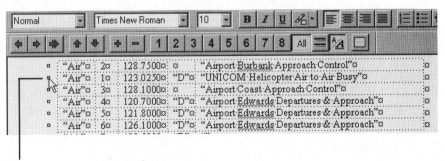

Drag rows to rearrange them

Figure 11.21   Drag rows in Outline view to rearrange tables.

Moving Cell Contents

To move the contents of cells, follow these steps:

1. Find or create empty destination cells in the appropriate quantity and configuration to hold the items you plan to move. For instance, if you plan to move a four-row-by-six-column collection of cells, you will need the same number of available cells in the same configuration (4×6) to receive the moved items.

2. Copy or cut the items of interest by highlighting them and using Edit ➤ Copy or Edit ➤ Cut or the keyboard shortcuts Ctrl+C and Ctrl+X.

3. Now you can either select the same cell configuration at the destination (four rows of six columns each in our example) or you can try a shortcut. Simply place the insertion point in the upper-left destination cell. (If you use this shortcut, do *not* select the cell.) Be sure to place the insertion point before the end-of-cell mark, then paste. All of the cells will flow into their new destinations, bringing their formatting information with them.

4. Delete unused columns using the Table ➤ Delete Columns command if necessary.

Styles and Tables

Word for Windows will use the current style (at the insertion point) when creating a new table. You can change the style of the whole table or apply different styles to different portions of the table.

Consider creating multiple styles if you plan to play with table formatting. For instance, you might have a style for table headings, another for standard text, another for decimal-aligned numbers, and so on. See Chapter 14 for more detail on styles.

Apply the new style to all appropriate paragraphs in your table by selecting the paragraphs and using the Formatting toolbar's Style menu. From then on, simply changing a style will change all table text formatted with the changed style.

Create AutoText Entries and Templates for Tables

If there are complex table setups that you reuse regularly, save them as Templates or AutoText entries. See Chapters 16 and 17 for details.

Repeating Headings on Multipage Tables

To repeat column headings on each page of a multipage table, tell the Wizard or follow these steps:

1. Select the row or rows you wish to use as headings (typically the top one or two).

2. Choose T<u>a</u>ble ➤ <u>H</u>eadings.

3. When a table spills over onto a new page, the headings will repeat.

 TIP If you insert manual page breaks, the heading will *not* repeat.

Use Tables to Create Forms

When you get good at manipulating tables, you can use them to create forms like the one shown in Figure 11.22. It's simply a combination of cells, borders, shading, and paragraph formats.

User Survey

Fill this out while at the user's desk			Network information (confidential)	
External Monitor?	Yes No	Screen size (diag):	User ID	Password
Color?	Yes No	Bits (8, 24, etc.): Grays:	Mail Name	Password
Printer	Laser Dot matrix		Groups	Sec Level
Please list software installed on this machine:			Interface type (Ethernet, etc.)	
			Zone & Port	
			Network User Training? Yes Date: No	

Figure 11.22 **Use tables to create forms like this one.**

Sorting in Word

Have you ever created something like an alphabetical list of employees and their phone extensions, and then needed a list of phone-extension assignments sorted by extension number? Most of us have small lists like these, and they always seem to be in the wrong order.

You could retype the old list or cut and paste, but the T<u>a</u>ble ➤ Sor<u>t</u> command or the Sort Text button on the Database toolbar might be a better solution.

Word for Windows can sort lines of tabular text, items you've entered in tables, or even paragraphs in a document. (If you're working in Microsoft Office, however, Excel and Access provide more powerful sorting tools.) The Sort command can be helpful when preparing data files for Word's Print Merge feature, discussed in Chapter 28.

> **WARNING**   As with some other Word features, Sort can make substantial changes to your document (read: ruin your hard work), so it is best to save before you sort. Consider practicing on copies of important files.

Sorting with the Database Toolbar

The Database toolbar contains some sorting buttons among other things. It looks like Figure 11.23.

To sort rows of text, select them and click on either the Sort Ascending or Sort Descending button. Word for Windows will sort based on the first letter(s) at the left of each line. Remarkably, if the first row (line) of text is bold or otherwise "looks" like labels, Word will not move it.

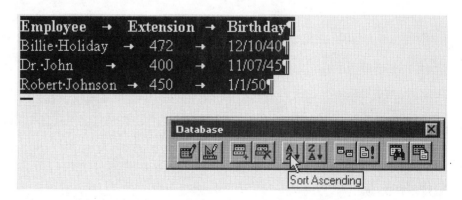

Figure 11.23   *The Database toolbar, while used mostly for Mail Merge products (see Chapter 28), can help with simple sorts too.*

To sort items in a table with the Database toolbar, follow these steps:

1. Save your work, just in case.

2. Place the insertion point in the column that you want to use as the "sort by" column.

3. Click the Ascending or Descending sort button.

4. Word will sort the entire table (all columns), leaving labels untouched.

   To learn more about the database capabilities and the rest of the buttons on the Database toolbar, read Chapter 33.

Sorting with the Sort Text Command

Word's Table ➤ Sort Text command will attempt to sort selected text alphabetically, numerically, or chronologically at your request. Sorts can be up to three levels "deep" (see Chapter 33). The Sort Text command can be used in free-form text but is much more powerful when used with a table. To sort a table with this command, follow these steps:

1. Save your work, just in case.

2. Place the insertion point in the table you wish to sort.

3. Pick Table ➤ Sort Text.

4. Word will highlight (select) the entire table.

5. You will see a dialog box like the one in Figure 11.24.

6. If you have labels at the top of your table, choose the My List Has Header Row option.

7. There will be up to three drop-down lists containing the column labels (if you have them) or column numbers (1, 2, and 3).

8. Specify the sort order by choosing the desired column for each sort level.

9. Choose a sort order for each column.

10. Tell Word whether the values in each column are text, numbers, or dates by choosing from the drop-down Type lists.

11. Click OK and Word will sort.

Figure 11.24   **Word lets you sort tables up to three levels deep.**

If you want the sort to be case-sensitive, or if you are sorting things not in a table, click the Options button in the Sort dialog box and make the appropriate choices in the Sort Options dialog box. It is shown in Figure 11.25.

Figure 11.25   **The Sort Options dialog box.**

Adding, Subtracting, Multiplying, and Dividing

Word's Table ➤ Formula command will add, subtract, multiply, and divide numbers you've typed in your documents. It is perfect for creating simple financial reports or for proofreading columns of numbers. The feature has some peculiarities, however; so if you plan to use it extensively, review the examples in this chapter and create some of your own before your next rush project.

Word's Built-In Math Capability

How often have you typed an important memo and made a math or typing error in a column of numbers? Word's Formula feature can minimize mistakes like these. In its simplest capacity, the command adds columns or rows of numbers in tables, but it can do much more. Read all about it in Chapters 32 and 33.

The Equation Editor

The Equation Editor is a more elegant way to create complex formulas. It helps you build formulas using palettes of math symbols and templates. The feature understands the rules and conventions for typesetting formulas, and it will do much of the formatting for you.

Starting the Equation Editor

The Equation Editor is a separate program that runs under Word's supervision. The program and related help file should be installed in your Commands folder. Choose Insert ➤ Object, go to the Create New tab, and double-click on Microsoft Equation to start it, as shown in Figure 11.26.

You assemble equations by typing text and picking templates and symbols from the palettes. The Equation Editor has a number of keyboard shortcuts, which are detailed in the program's context-sensitive help screens. Create equations by choosing elements from drop-down lists, as shown in Figure 11.27.

To receive online help about a particular palette or symbol, visit the Equation Editor's online Help menu.

Placing Equations in Word Documents

Closing the Equation Editor window pastes the equation you've created into your Word for Windows document at the insertion point.

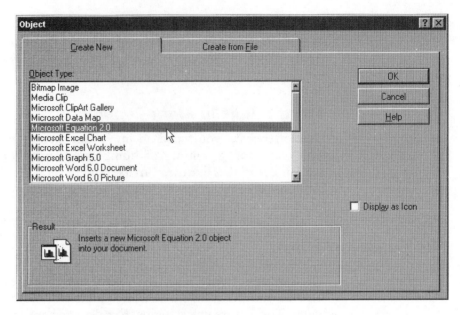

Figure 11.26   **Starting the Equation Editor.**

Figure 11.27   *Choose elements for your equations from the drop-down lists.*

Editing Equations in Word Documents

To edit equations, follow these steps:

1. Double-click on the equation in your document to open the Equation Editor window.

2. Make the changes.

3. Close the Equation Editor window to replace the old equation with the new.

Upgrading the Equation Editor

If you work a lot with equations, there is an even more powerful version of this program available from Design Sciences, Inc. Their address is 4028 Broadway, Long Beach, CA, 90803. Or you can phone them at (800) 827-0685.

Chapter 12

Headers, Footers, Page Numbers, and Footnotes

FAST TRACK

Word's *headers* and *footers* are places to put repetitive information in a document's top and bottom margins. Logically enough, headers print at the top, footers at the bottom. (Don't confuse footers with *footnotes*, which are different.)

You can use headers and footers to print something simple on each page, such as your name, or something complex, such as a graphic. Style elements such as formatted text, dates, and automatic page numbering can all be included in headers or footers.

Headers and footers can be identical on all pages in your document, or you can specify different contents for each section of the document. Odd and even pages can have different designs if you wish. The first page of each document or each section can be unique.

It is possible to apply virtually any paragraph or character style using the Formatting toolbar and rulers in headers and footers. You can also place framed items and frame anchors in headers or footers. They will repeat on all pages thereafter.

In this chapter you'll also learn about Word's footnote features, which are equally powerful and easy to use. You can enter, edit, and view footnote numbers in a variety of formats. Word for Windows simplifies inserting, deleting, and moving footnotes by automatically numbering and renumbering them as necessary.

Entering Basic Headers and Footers

In Word for Windows, header and footer editing always takes place in Page Layout view. You work right in the header and footer area of your document after double-clicking to undim it, or switching from Normal view with the Header and Footer option on the View menu.

Headers and footers are also displayed in Print Preview, but when you attempt to open a header or footer in Normal view or Print Preview, Word for Windows switches you to Page Layout view and displays the Header and Footer toolbar.

To enter a header that repeats on all pages in your document:

1. Choose View ➤ Header and Footer or double-click in the header area of the first page to be modified in Page Layout or Print Preview.

2. Word will switch to Page Layout view if it is not already there and display the Header and Footer toolbar.

3. Create and edit header text as you would any other. You can paste graphics, apply styles, and otherwise format your work normally. Figure 12.1 shows an example.

4. Use the automatic page number, time, and date features described later in this chapter.

5. Double-click in the main document to return to work there.

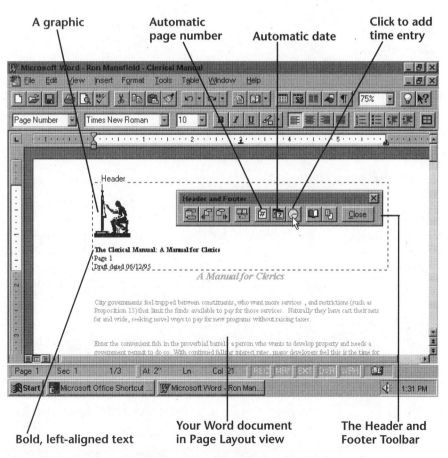

Figure 12.1   A header window can contain stylized text, borders, shading, and graphics.

Part
2

Formatting
Fundamentals

> **TIP**   Unless you already have a header, double-clicking can be cumbersome. So, until you have a header, it's probably best to use the menu command.

Footers are entered the same way as headers, except that you work in a Footer window:

1. Choose <u>V</u>iew ➤ <u>H</u>eader and Footer or double-click in the footer area of the first page to be modified in Page Layout or Print Preview.

2. Word will switch to Page Layout view if it is not already there and display the Header and Footer toolbar.

3. Click the leftmost button on the Header and Footer toolbar to switch to the Footer pane.

4. Create and edit footer text as you would any other. You can paste graphics, apply styles, and otherwise format your work normally.

5. Use the automatic page number, time, and date features described later in this chapter.

6. Double-click in the main document to continue working there.

Adding Dates, Times, and Simple Page Numbers

In Figure 12.2 I've inserted a page number in a footer by clicking on the page-numbering icon. It was centered with the Formatting toolbar's Center button. You could use other formatting tricks as well—adding some space before the page number with the Paragraph tab's Space Before option, for instance.

> **TIP**   You can place *fields* in headers or footers so that things like authors' names, file names, date last saved, and other information can appear automatically. See Chapter 32 for details.

Rulers and Toolbars in Headers and Footers

Use your regular document ruler or Formatting toolbar when working in header and footer windows. Margins, indents, tabs, and all the other tools work as you'd expect. The Header and Footer toolbar's functions are shown in Figure 12.3.

Figure 12.2   Use toolbars to enter and position things like page numbers.

Figure 12.3   The Header and Footer toolbar functions.

Headers and Footers in Print Preview

It is a good idea to switch to Print Preview occasionally when designing headers and footers. You can get a good approximation of how headers and footers will print and spot potential problems (like the footer that appears only on odd pages in Figure 12.4).

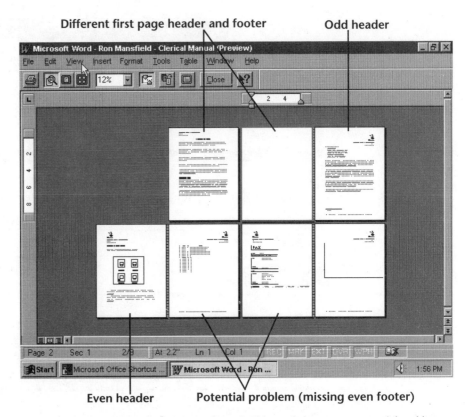

Figure 12.4   *Use Print Preview to view your work. This can help you spot potential problems so you can fix them before printing.*

TIP   Remember that many printers cannot print at the very edges of the paper and that it is possible to position a header or footer in nonprinting areas. If you have selected the correct printer at the start of the project, Word does a pretty good job of showing you when a header or footer will be cut off by your printer.

Take another look at Figure 12.4. Because this document will be printed two-sided and then bound, mirrored margins and odd/even headers and footers have been specified. Notice also that the table of contents page does not have a header or footer and the back side of that page (the even page) is blank. Read on to learn how to accomplish these effects.

Even and Odd Headers and Footers

To create different even and odd headers or footers:

1. Place the insertion point in the section where you want the odd/even effect to begin (read more about sections in Chapter 13).

2. Open the Page Setup dialog box (double-click in a blank part of a ruler or choose File ➤ Page Setup).

3. Visit the Layout tab.

4. Check the Different Odd and Even choice in the Headers and Footers area.

Headers and Footers
☑ Different Odd and Even
☐ Different First Page

Odd Page Header

Odd Page Footer

Even Page Header

Even Page Footer

You now have four header and footer areas in Page Layout view. Their names will change from page to page.

Different First Page Headers and Footers

The Layout tab in the Page Setup dialog box contains a choice called Different First Page. (Chapter 13 goes into more detail about sections.) To create unique headers and footers for the first page of your document:

1. Place the insertion point in the section where you want the different first page effect to begin (read more about sections in Chapter 13).

2. Open the Page Setup dialog box (double-click in a blank part of a ruler or choose File ➤ Page Setup).

3. Choose the Layout tab.

4. Check the Different First Page choice in the Headers and Footers area. You'll have different header and footer areas on the first page. Their names will be visible in Page Layout view:

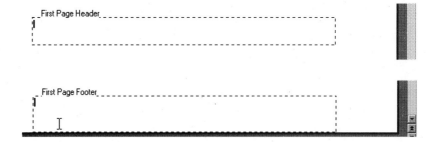

5. Create different headers and footers for the first page in Page Layout view.

Page Numbering

Word for Windows offers a variety of tools to help you automatically number pages. You are given many page-numbering format and style choices. It's possible to position page numbers nearly anywhere that pleases you. Let's explore these features and discuss the effects of document sections and pagination on page numbering.

TIP Word for Windows provides two page-numbering techniques. Both have advantages and disadvantages. Normally, you will use only one for a particular document. Otherwise, you might end up with two or more sets of page numbers!

The Header and Footer Toolbar Method

As you've seen already, Word for Windows makes it easy to place page numbers in headers and footers. To add page numbers using the header/footer method:

1. Open a header or footer by double-clicking on it in Page Layout view.

2. Click on the page-numbering button in the Header and Footer toolbar.

3. A number will be inserted for you in your header or footer at the insertion point.

4. Like anything else placed in headers and footers, page numbers can be formatted, repositioned, surrounded with borders, accompanied by text, and otherwise embellished.

Word for Windows uses the standard header or footer style to format page numbers placed therein. You can override this by applying additional character and paragraph formats or by changing the standard header or footer style (see Chapter 14).

Headers and footers have tab stops, which you may find useful for page-number positioning.

The Page Numbers Command

The Insert ➤ Page Numbers command provides a wider variety of numbering options. It reveals the Page Numbers dialog box and lets you quickly reach the Page Number Format dialog box, shown in Figure 12.5.

1. Start by placing the insertion point in the section you want to number.

2. Display the Page Numbering dialog box by choosing Insert ➤ Page Numbers.

3. Word suggests page numbers in the bottom-right corner of your document ($\frac{1}{2}''$ from the bottom and right edges of the paper), but you can specify different positions with the Position and Alignment drop-down menus. Watch the Preview area as you work.

4. Choose whether to place a page number on the first page by clicking to add or remove the corresponding check mark.

5. Either click OK or click on the Format button to review other page-numbering options.

Page-Numbering Formats and Styles

Word for Windows supports five page-number formats. Standard Arabic numbers (1, 2, 3, …) are the default. It is also possible to number with capital Roman numerals (I, II, III, …) or with capital letters (A, B, C, …). Lowercase formats are also provided (i, ii, iii, … and a, b, c, …).

Specify number formats in the Page Number Format dialog box reached by clicking the Format button in the Page Numbers dialog box (Insert ▶ Page Numbers), as shown in Figure 12.5. All of the formats are available, regardless of which page-numbering technique you choose.

You can use Word's many character- and paragraph-embellishment features to spruce up page numbers. Pick the font of your choice, make numbers bold, align them, put boxes around them. Text can appear next to the numbers (*Page 1*, for instance).

After inserting page numbers, switch to Page Layout view and change their appearance.

Figure 12.5 *The Page Number Format dialog box.*

TIP Documents containing multiple sections can have different formats in each section. If you want all sections to have the same format, most kinds of formatting (typefaces, font sizes, styles) will be applied to the whole document as usual, but when designating formats in the Layout tab of the Page Setup dialog box, be sure to change This Section to Whole Document in the Apply To area, as always when handling any aspect of multiple-section documents in this dialog box.

Chapter Numbers in Page Numbers

If you use Word's standard heading styles, and if you use one of the headings for chapter titles, you can have Word for Windows include chapter numbers with your page number (*2-36*, for instance). You can specify one of five separators—hyphens, periods, colons, en dashes, or em dashes.

 TIP Don't confuse hyphens with en dashes and em dashes. Both are longer than hyphens. En dashes (–) are typically used to indicate ranges of numbers, and em dashes (—) are used to show breaks in thought.

You set up chapter page numbering in the Page Number Format box, in the section called Use Separator:

Managing Starting Page Numbers

Usually you will want Word for Windows to place the number 1 on your first printed page, but not always. For example, many people prefer their multipage letters to be printed without a 1 on the first page. They still want the second page to be numbered 2, the third 3, and so on. Let's call this *first page number suppressed*.

Or you may wish to start each new section in a multisection document with 1. Let's call this *restart sections with 1*.

Sometimes you may want your first page to be printed without a number (a cover page, for instance) and then the next page to contain the number 1. Let's call this *begin second page from 1*.

Finally, you might want to use some other number for the first page, like 25 or 100. This is helpful when you are combining your work with other documents. Let's call that *starting page other than 1*.

Note that in all the following examples, we assume that your document does not already have page numbers.

First Page Number Suppressed

This one's easy.

1. Place the insertion point in the desired section.

2. Open the Page Numbers dialog box with the Insert ➤ Page Numbers command.

3. Remove the check mark from the Show Number on First Page box:

4. Click OK.

Restart Sections with 1

To restart each section at page 1, follow these steps:

1. Select all sections that you want to start with page 1. Open the Page Number dialog box, reached with the Insert ➤ Page Numbers command.

2. Click on the Format button to reach the Page Number Format dialog box.

3. Check the Start At box.

4. Specify the number each section will start with (1 in this example).

Removing Page Numbers

Simply open the header or footer containing unwanted page numbers and delete one. The rest of the page numbers in the section will disappear. To delete all of the page numbers in a multisection document, follow these steps:

1. Open a header or footer containing page numbers.

2. Choose Edit ➤ Select All or use the Ctrl+A shortcut.

3. Delete a page number. The rest will disappear.

Footnotes and Endnotes

Word for Windows lets you create simple *footnotes* or *endnotes* and personalize their appearance. Although the following sections refer only to the more common footnotes, the various techniques for working with both types of notes are the same.

Easy Automatic Footnotes

Figure 12.6 shows an automatic (default) Word for Windows footnote. It should take you less than ten seconds to add your first footnote to existing text.

Follow these steps:

1. Start by placing the insertion point where the footnote marker is needed (after the words *data lines* in our example).

2. Choose Insert ➤ Footnote.

3. You can dismiss the Footnote and Endnote dialog box by clicking OK, because Word's defaults are fine for this project.

4. If you are in Normal view, a second window pane opens where you do the footnote typing:

Typically, foupplex jacks are used. The top two j
and/or modems (voice lines) and the bottom two jacks a
(data lines).[1]

The data jacks[2] are color coded. Red normally de
denotes Ethernet. The actual *wiring* of the red and blue c

All Footnotes   Close

Notes

[1] A few locations (such as the library) have two sets of duplex jacks
lines.
[2]

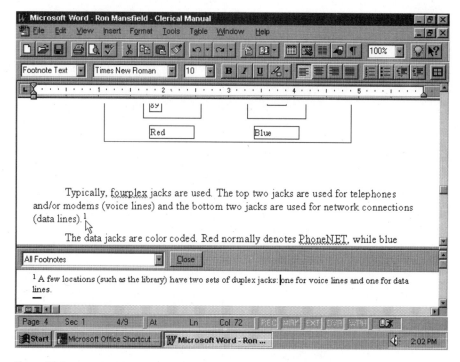

Figure 12.6   Standard footnotes like these require very little effort.

In Page Layout view you type right where the footnote will print—usually between the text and footer:

> • Fat, silver RJ-45 to I
>   patching.

5. In either case, the insertion point automatically moves to the proper place for you to type the footnote. Type it.

6. To return to the main document, click the Footnote window's Close button, move the insertion point with the mouse, or press Ctrl+Alt+Z.

Viewing Footnotes

Footnotes are always displayed in Page Layout view and Print Preview. If they are not visible in Normal or Outline view, choose View ➤ Footnotes. Word for Windows will open the footnote pane.

If you are constantly entering or referring to footnotes in Normal view, you can leave the footnote window visible while you work. Scrolling in your document will cause corresponding scrolling in the footnote window. Use the footnote scroll bars if necessary to view notes. Feel free to resize the footnote window to suit your taste and screen size. Drag the bar separating the two windows the same way you resize other Word for Windows split screens (point to the Split box and drag).

To hide the footnote window, choose View ➤ Footnotes and remove the check mark next to the command, or click the Close button.

TIP Double-clicking on a footnote marker in your document will display the footnote pane and place the insertion point at the beginning of the footnote. If necessary, Word for Windows will open the footnote pane and scroll to the appropriate note. Also, clicking on a reference marker in the footnote pane will cause the main document to scroll to the reference.

Inserting Footnotes ahead of Existing Ones

Whenever you insert (or delete) footnotes, Word for Windows renumbers the existing ones properly. Just position the insertion point and choose Insert ➤ Footnote or press Alt+Ctrl+F. (This quick key combo is especially useful because it bypasses the dialog box.) Word for Windows will take it from there. To delete a footnote, just delete its number in the text. Again, Word will do the dirty work.

Editing and Personalizing Footnotes

You can copy, move, or delete entire footnotes as easily as you would a single character.

1. Select the footnote marker of interest in the document text. (This might take a steady hand, particularly if you have drag-and-drop enabled.)

2. Cut, copy, paste, or drag-and-drop the footnote mark.

3. Word does the rest. If you have used AutoNumbering, Word will update the numbers in your text and in the corresponding footnotes. If you copy and paste a mark, a corresponding new footnote will magically appear in the right spot in your footnotes. Deletion works as you would expect.

Editing Footnote Text

Visit the footnote pane in Normal view or the footnote itself in Page Layout view. Cut, paste, and drag-and-drop away to your heart's content. (Note that you cannot delete a footnote in this pane; you must cut the footnote mark in the document text if you wish to delete or move it.)

Footnote Text Style

You can embellish selected footnote text as you would expect. Highlight the text of interest, then use the ruler, Formatting toolbar, or format-related menu choices (bold, italic, and so on).

To change the size or font or other footnote style elements for all footnotes, you must modify the Microsoft standard footnote text style, since manually formatting existing footnotes will not affect new footnotes. (Footnote text is based on the Normal style.) To change the footnote-reference marks, modify the footnote-reference style.

Personalizing Footnotes

Word for Windows lets you modify many footnote parameters via the Insert ➤ Footnote command and the Note Options dialog box. Here's the general procedure:

1. Choose Insert ➤ Footnote.

2. If you want to mark each footnote with a symbol instead of numbering them, use the Symbol button to select a footnote symbol character. Click OK in the Symbol dialog box when you've made your selection.

3. Click Options to bring up the Note Options dialog box, shown in Figure 12.7.

4. Click to switch to the All Footnotes tab, if necessary.

5. Specify note placement, number formats, starting numbers, and starting points.

6. Click OK.

Figure 12.7 *Personalize footnote appearance using the Footnote choices in the All Footnotes tab of the Note Options dialog box.*

Controlling Footnote Numbering

Footnote numbering can restart on each page if you check the Restart Each Page button in the Footnotes area of the All Footnotes tab of the Notes Options dialog box.

Footnote Position

You can also use the Note Options dialog box to specify where footnotes and endnotes should be placed. It has two tabs: All Footnotes and All

Endnotes, each with a Place At drop-down list. Positions available for Footnote are:

- At the bottom of each page (the default)
- Directly beneath the last text on a page

Positions available for Endnote are:

- At the end of a section in multisection documents
- At the end of your document

Incidentally, in multicolumn sections, footnotes print below each column.

Footnote Separators

The little black lines that separate document text from the footnotes themselves are cleverly called *footnote separators*. Edit them as follows:

1. Switch to Normal view.

2. Choose View ➤ Footnotes to display the Footnote pane.

3. Choose Footnote Separator from the drop-down list.

4. This is just like any other Word window. You can edit the length of the line (it's a paragraph). Insert a graphic, if you like. You can even use Word's drawing tools here. Double lines look nice. Use Word's Paragraph Border feature to create them. It is possible to use a ruler and the Formatting toolbar in the separator window.

5. Click Close (or Reset to restore the standard separator).

When you are happy with your creation, close the separator window and view the results in Print Preview or Page Layout view.

Footnote-Reference Marks

Footnote-reference marks appear wherever you place them in your document's text area and at the beginning of each footnote in the footnote area itself.

By default, Word for Windows uses numbers for reference marks. This is the AutoNumber button in the Numbering section of the Footnotes and Endnotes dialog box. You can customize the numbering, though, by clicking the Custom Marks button and typing in your own characters or selecting them from the Symbol dialog box (display it by clicking the Symbols button). Up to ten characters can be used as footnote reference marks. To use one of Word's default numbering styles, click the Options button to bring up the Note Options dialog box. Then choose the style you wish from the Number Format dialog box. When you click OK, your selection will become the default.

Footnote Continuation

Continuation separators appear whenever footnotes carry over onto the next page. These notices can be modified the same way you change regular separators as described in the previous section.

Endnotes

Endnotes are much like footnotes, except that they appear at the end of a document. Use the same basic procedures as you do for entering, editing, and moving footnotes. When working in the Note Options dialog box, choose the All Endnotes tab.

Footnote Tips and Cautions

Here are some tips and caveats on using footnotes:

▶ Whether or not Automatic Spell Checking is turned on, spelling errors have a hard time hiding from Word. It checks your spelling even in footnotes. No need to do anything special. Just click the Spelling button and Word will display any unrecognized words it finds in the footnote pane.

▶ Do not place index or table-of-contents entries in footnotes. They will be ignored.

▶ Word's new Find and Replace features can help you search for and reformat footnotes. See Chapter 20.

▶ Save frequently used footnote entries and use AutoText to eliminate tedious retyping. See Chapter 17.

Chapter 13

Formatting Your Work with Section Breaks

FAST TRACK

In earlier chapters you've seen many examples of Word's powerful formatting capabilities. In some types of documents you'll want the same formatting decisions to apply from beginning to end; in other types, such as newsletters and the like, you may want to change page orientation or margins for some parts. Word for Windows offers the *section* feature to let you change major formatting features at places you decide in your document.

You must start a new section whenever you need to:

▶ Change page orientation within a document

▶ Change margins in part of a document

▶ Turn line numbering on or off

▶ Change footnote appearance or numbering, or suppress notes

▶ Change the appearance of headers and footers

▶ Change the format, position, or progression of page numbers

While the exact sequence of events will vary with your project and needs, in general you will:

1. Place the insertion point where you want a new section to begin.

2. Use the Insert ➤ Break command to create the new section.

3. Make the desired formatting and other changes for that section.

4. Perhaps create other sections farther down in the document.

You'll see practical applications of sections in a moment. There are no hard and fast rules about *when* to create new sections. Experienced Word for Windows users often create ten or twenty sections in a one-page document. Others use a single section for an entire 100-page report.

Occasionally, Word for Windows will insert section breaks for you—when creating an automatic table of contents, for instance. Mostly, you'll insert them yourself.

Inserting Section Breaks

To insert a section break, follow these steps:

1. Prepare to create a new section by placing the insertion point where you want the break to occur. It's a good idea to press Enter before inserting

a section break so the break doesn't come between a paragraph's text and its paragraph mark.

2. Next, choose <u>I</u>nsert ➤ <u>B</u>reak. In the Section Breaks area, double-click on the particular text flow option you want to use to insert the break. For instance, if you want to insert a section break and have succeeding text start a new page, double-click Next Page. To have text resume without a page break, double-click Continuous.

3. You'll see a double-dotted, nonprinting line containing the words *End of Section* at the insertion point on your screen (see Figure 13.1). The status area reflects section numbers as you move the insertion point or scroll to pages in the new section.

Part 2

Formatting Fundamentals

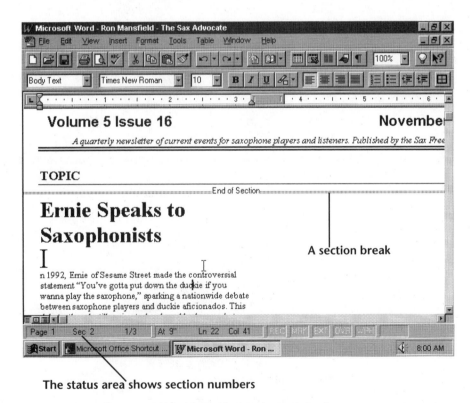

The status area shows section numbers

Figure 13.1 **Sections are marked with double-dotted nonprinting lines.**

Sections as Chapter Elements

For the largest Word projects, such as book-length manuscripts, it's usually best to make each chapter a separate document file. In medium-size documents such as reports, however, it is very common to create a new section for each chapter. This makes it possible to change header and footer information like chapter names. If you were creating an employee handbook, Chapter 1's header might contain the words *Welcome new employees,* while the headers in Chapter 2 might say *Your health plan explained,* and so forth.

Sections also make it possible to customize page numbers within chapters. Your document's front matter might be numbered in lowercase Roman numerals (i, ii, iii, and so on). Pages within chapters might contain chapter-related numbers that restart at the beginning of each chapter (1-1, 2-1, and so on). As you'll recall, you can use different page-numbering styles in each section of your document, and you can restart page numbering at the beginning of any new section.

The Layout Tab in Page Setup

You reach the Layout tab in the Page Setup dialog box by double-clicking on the section break at the end of the section you wish to change. You can also place the insertion point in the section being designed and choose File ➤ Page Setup; then click on the Layout tab.

Many of the choices in the Layout tab are covered elsewhere in this book, but the Section Start drop-down menu contains a number of section-specific items worth exploring. It is shown here:

NOTE   The options listed in the Section Start drop-down menu are the same as those in the Break dialog box (reached by choosing Insert ➤ Break).

This is how you tell Word for Windows where you want it to start printing the various sections of your document. You can make a different choice for each section. Here are explanations of your options.

Continuous

Continuous is Word's default section printing strategy. Text from preceding sections will occupy the same page as the designated section, if there is enough room for the text from both sections.

Next Page

Word for Windows will always start new sections on new pages with this choice.

Even Page

Word for Windows starts printing the new section on an even-numbered page, even if it means leaving an odd-numbered page blank.

Odd Page

Word for Windows will start the new section on an odd-numbered page. This is a great way to ensure that new sections start on right-hand pages when designing documents for two-sided printing.

Apply To

Another area worth scrutinizing is the Apply To portion of the Layout tab. It lets you tell Word how far to go with your requested changes.

This Section

If you check This Section, the changes will affect only the section containing the insertion point.

This Point Forward

This Point Forward makes the changes effective from the insertion point to the end of the document (or until you make other Layout tab changes at some further point).

Whole Document

This choice makes the changes document-wide.

Copying Section Breaks

Section-formatting information is stored with section breaks in much the same way as paragraph formatting is stored with paragraph marks (¶). And you can copy section information by copying and pasting section breaks. It is even possible to place section breaks as AutoText items. See Chapter 17 for details.

Section breaks differ from paragraph marks in that a section break controls the information below it, while a paragraph mark controls the information that precedes it.

Click on a break to select it. A thick insertion point will straddle the break line. You may find it easiest to do this in Normal view. Once a break is selected, you can then copy, cut, etc.

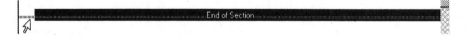

Deleting Section Breaks

Select a section break as just described. Then press the backspace or Delete key. Text before the removed section break will take on the characteristics of the following material. It may take a moment for Word for Windows to reformat and repaginate the document. Watch the status line and be patient.

Changing Page Orientation with Breaks

Section breaks make it possible for you to mix portrait and landscape page orientations in the same document. For instance, you could have a three-page memo with pages one and three in portrait mode (the text, perhaps) and the middle page in landscape mode (a wide spreadsheet, perhaps). Figure 13.2 illustrates the general concept with an article example.

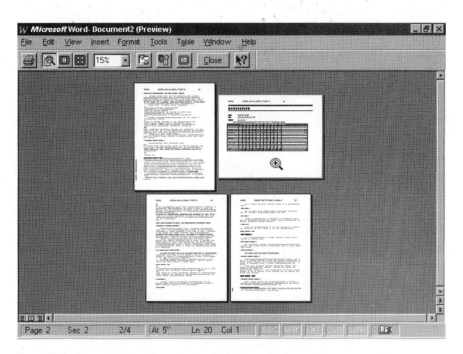

Figure 13.2   Use sections to change page orientation mid-document.

 NOTE   Word for Windows flips headers, footers, page numbers, and other marginalia for you unless you override this. Therefore, if you've placed page numbers at the bottom of your pages, the landscape page(s) will have numbers at the right edge of the paper so that they read like the rest of the (flipped) text on the page(s).

Part
2

Formatting
Fundamentals

Here are the general steps for changing orientation:

1. Position the insertion point where you want the break to occur.

2. Choose Insert ➤ Break.

3. Choose the Next Page option.

4. Click OK.

5. Move the insertion point to where you want the orientation to change again (if you do)—the beginning of page 3 in our example.

6. Insert another Next Page section break there.

7. Position the insertion point in the section you want to change to landscape orientation.

8. Visit the Paper Size tab in Page Setup (double-click in an unmarked part of the ruler or choose File ➤ Page Setup), and mark the Landscape button in the Orientation area, first making sure the Apply To drop-down menu says This Section.

9. Make other page layout choices in the other Page Setup tabs.

10. Preview, then print your work.

TIP You can center a spreadsheet (or any landscape-oriented item) between the top and bottom margins of its page with the Vertical Alignment setting in the Layout tab of the Page Setup dialog box. Choose Center to create this effect.

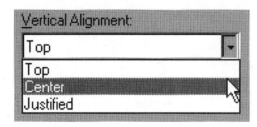

Time-Saving Section Tips

Here are some time-saving tips on using section breaks:

▶ Documents start out as one big section, and it is often best to wait until you are nearly finished with a document before breaking it into smaller sections. Do, however, think about the divisions in your document early on.

▶ Section formatting you apply when there is only one section affects the *entire* document. For instance, header and footer choices will be applied throughout.

▶ Set up templates and AutoText entries for complex section designs. See Chapter 17.

▶ One really great use of section breaks is to vary the number or formatting of columns with a document such as a newsletter, using the techniques discussed in this chapter.

Part
2

Formatting
Fundamentals

Chapter 14

Using Paragraph Styles and AutoFormat

FAST TRACK

Word's *style* features are responsible for much of its power and popularity. They also confuse and initially frustrate most new users. It is possible to plug along in Word for Windows for the rest of your life without knowing a whit about styles. That would be a shame, though. Learning about Word's standard styles, custom styles, and concepts like Normal style and base styles can save you hundreds or even thousands of hours.

NOTE In case you want to review character styles, please see Chapter 9. This chapter covers paragraph styles, which can include aspects of character styles, but apply to entire paragraphs, and, as such, include issues such as space before and after, margins, and leading.

But things aren't as complicated as they seem. The two kinds of styles in Word for Windows—paragraph styles and character styles—are the equivalent of its two kinds of formatting, paragraph and font. If you understand these, you are on your way towards mastering styles. If you are not yet comfortable with font and paragraph formatting, you should have a look at Chapters 9 and 10 before tackling styles.

When you couple your knowledge of styles with Word's AutoText, AutoCorrect, AutoFormat, and template features (covered elsewhere in this book), Word for Windows can make you a dramatically more efficient author, typist, and desktop publisher. If you work with other people on large, complex projects, or if your organization wants a uniform look for all of its printed documents, styles are essential.

Some styles do more than just change the appearance of text. For example, Heading styles make it easier to create a table of contents.

It's important to understand what styles are and how to modify them before you turn Word's AutoFormat feature loose on your documents. That way you can fine-tune things. Consume this chapter a little at a time. Try a few style experiments when you are not working on a rush project. Play with noncritical documents or use copies of important documents. If your eyes begin to glaze over or you find yourself pounding the desk with your fist, take a break. It will all make sense sooner than you think, and then all kinds of things will be easier than they ever were before. The surprising secret about styles is that once you learn to use them, they are *fun*.

What Are Styles?

Styles are collections of paragraph- and character-formatting decisions that you or others make and save using meaningful names. Styles make it easy for you to reuse complex formats without laboriously recreating them each time. There are "built-in" styles available in all Word documents. And each document can have its own collection of custom styles. The letter shown in Figure 14.1 illustrates nine different styles.

All of the styles in Figure 14.1 are from Word's standard "gallery" of styles. In fact, the letter was created using one of the letter templates provided by Word. (*Templates* are simply collections of styles, sometimes with boilerplate text, designed to get you quickly working on everyday tasks.)

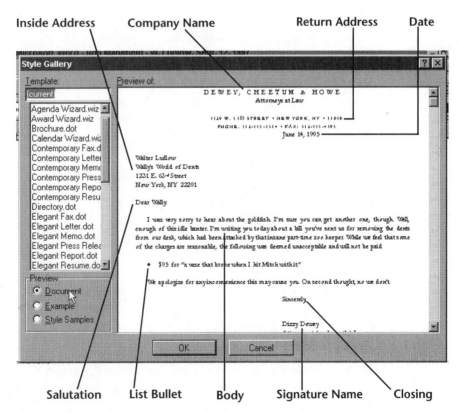

Figure 14.1   This document uses many different styles.

Some styles in the example are very simple. For instance, the style used for the body of the letter is called Body. It's just like the default text you use for typing except that Word for Windows adds a first-line indent and twelve points of white space at the end of each paragraph. This "space after" separates paragraphs from each other without your needing to type extra carriage returns. So you see, many of the formatting choices are ones you're already familiar with.

The Company Name style is more complex. It is body text plus 10.5 pt Garamond, all caps, expanded 3.75 pt, centered, 2 pts after, with Keep Lines Together enabled, center horizontal... You get the idea. It's got more goodies.

As you will see later in this chapter, creating and naming your own styles like these is very easy. Developing clever style *strategies* takes much more forethought. Here's how it all works.

Applying Styles from the Formatting Toolbar

Because Word for Windows comes with built-in styles, you can easily apply them to one or more paragraphs. Here are the general steps.

1. Either place the insertion point in a paragraph or select several paragraphs.

2. Scroll through the drop-down style list on the Formatting toolbar to pick the desired style.

The available items in the list will vary from document to document for reasons you'll soon understand.

3. Click on a style name to apply it to the selected text. Your text will be reformatted using the selected style.

4. Use <u>E</u>dit ➤ <u>U</u>ndo if you don't like the results.

TIP   When the drop-down list is long, type the first letter of the style's name. The list will scroll to the proximity of your desired style.

Applying Styles from the Keyboard

A few of the commonly used styles have their own keyboard shortcuts. To use them, select text or place the insertion point in the paragraph to be styled and use one of the following key combinations:

Style	Keystrokes
Normal	Ctrl+Shift+N
Heading 1	Alt+Ctrl+1
Heading 2	Alt+Ctrl+2
Heading 3	Alt+Ctrl+3
List Bullet	Ctrl+Shift+L
Style shown in toolbar	Ctlr+Shift+S

TIP   The <u>E</u>dit ➤ <u>R</u>epeat keyboard shortcut (Ctrl+Y) works when applying styles. After you apply a style once, you can move the insertion point to other paragraphs and press Ctrl+Y to apply the new style where needed.

Defining Your Own Styles from the Formatting Toolbar

You can define your own styles, and many experienced users do that. But before spending hours reinventing the wheel, check out the styles already provided by Word. In fact, new styles you define are always based upon existing styles. When you have satisfied yourself that what you need doesn't exist, try the following steps:

1. Display the Formatting toolbar if it is not already in view.

2. Format at least one paragraph with all of the characteristics you want to record in the new style.

3. Place the insertion point in the formatted paragraph whose style you'd like to capture. Make any last-minute changes if necessary.

4. As shown here, click *once* on the style box (the name portion of the drop-down style-name list). The style box will be highlighted, indicating that you can type a new style name.

5. Type a meaningful, unique style name and press ↵. Word will save the style information and add the new name to the drop-down style list for the current document.

 TIP   You can no longer type the first few characters of a style name to apply it as you could in earlier Word versions.

Style Name Considerations

Style names can be up to 253 characters long, but shorter is often better. Names can contain any legal characters except backslashes (\), braces ({}), or semicolons (;).

 WARNING   Word cares about capitalization in style names. For example, *Figure* and *figure* are two different names. Try to be consistent when naming similar styles in different documents. You'll learn why later in this chapter.

The Style Dialog Box

For styles, as is often the case with Word for Windows features, there is a dialog box that contains powerful options not found on the Formatting toolbar. Reach the Style dialog box by picking Format ➤ Style. You will see something like Figure 14.2.

Figure 14.2 **The Style dialog box.**

This dialog box lets you define new styles and rename, explore, list, or delete existing ones. It serves other purposes, as you will soon see.

Defining Styles in the Style Dialog Box

To define a style via the Style dialog box, follow these steps:

1. Format at least one paragraph with all of the characteristics you want to record in the new style.

2. Select (or place the insertion point in) a paragraph containing the desired format.

3. Open the Style dialog box.

4. Click on the New button.

5. Type a legal style name in the box provided.

6. Make sure the Based On box shows the appropriate base style, as discussed under "Basing One Style upon Another" later in this chapter.

7. Click on OK to save the style.

Defining Keyboard Shortcuts for Styles

Word for Windows lets you assign keyboard shortcuts from the Modify Style Dialog box (reached with the Modify button in the Style dialog box) You can also use the Keyboard tab of the Customize dialog box (reached with <u>T</u>ools ➤ <u>C</u>ustomize). See Chapter 36.

Basing One Style upon Another

This time-saver is often a source of bewilderment for newcomers. It occasionally catches old pros off guard too. Word for Windows lets you build upon styles or base one upon another. You've seen examples of this in the sample customer letter at the beginning of the chapter. The letter's style called Body is built by starting with the Normal style and adding instructions to indent the first line of each paragraph. In other words, the style Body is based on the style Normal.

If you change the Normal style so that it uses Times New Roman instead of Arial, any paragraphs formatted with the Body style will change to Times New Roman too. That's both good news and bad news.

Word for Windows watches as you develop new styles and bases new styles on the styles you modify. For instance, if you type the last paragraph of a letter in a style that produces indented paragraphs and decide when you get to the end of the last paragraph in your letter that you want to create a new closure style, you might be tempted to press ⏎ to start a new paragraph, then drag the left indent marker to the left before typing *Sincerely*. If you then create a style named Closure based on the *Sincerely* line, Word will base that new style on the indented Body style, because that's the style you modified to create Closure. No problem at the moment, but wait.

If you ever change the distance that the Body style indents first lines, the Closure paragraph will move too.

Unless you are careful, you can create quite a chain reaction this way. Experienced users try to create one or two fairly simple base styles and tie most of the rest of their styles to those base styles, rather than basing each new style on the previous style. In our example, we could avoid the chain reaction effect by choosing Normal as the Based On style when defining the Closure style.

The Modify Style dialog box, shown in Figure 14.3, lets you force specific styles to be based upon other styles of your choosing. It is important to use this box, because if you don't, your new style will by default be based upon the style of the paragraph the cursor is in, which may not be the right one.

Salutations will follow Inside Address

Tells which style to use as a basis for the new one

Figure 14.3 **Word lets you specify which style each style is based upon.**

To change an existing style's base, follow these steps:

1. Choose Format ➤ Style.

2. Select the style whose base you want to change.

3. Click the Modify button.

4. When you see the Modify Style dialog box, choose a base style from the Based On list.

5. Make any other necessary changes in the Modify Style dialog box.

6. Click OK when you're done.

TIP   To add a style you've *created* to the template upon which the document you are working on is based, enable the Add to Template option in the Modify Style dialog box. Many people find this unassuming little box easy to forget—but it is essential if you want your new or modified style to be available to future documents.

What's the appropriate base style? That will vary with your project. At first, you may find it less confusing to base all of your styles upon Normal. Then experiment and observe carefully. You will soon learn from experience which combinations work best for you. Newcomers, beware. Play with *copies* of important documents, especially if it is ten minutes before the Federal Express person is due to pick up your document.

Next Style

Frequently, you can predict the order in which styles will be used. When you type letters, for instance, you know that the To style will always be used after the From style. In reports and manuals, headings are usually followed immediately by body text, and so on.

The Modify Style dialog box lets you specify which style Word will flip to when you finish typing a paragraph and press ↵. Often, you want a paragraph to be in the same style as its predecessor. This is the default condition when creating styles.

But it is possible to specify different next styles. Follow these steps:

1.   Choose Format ➤ Style.

2.   Select the style you plan to modify.

3.   Click the Modify button.

4.   When you see the Modify Style dialog box, choose a "next" style from the Style for Following Paragraph list, shown in Figure 14.3.

5.   Make any other necessary changes in the Modify Style dialog box.

6.   Click OK when done.

Finding Out Which Styles Have Been Used

The obvious way to sniff out styles is to place the insertion point in the text of interest and look at the Formatting toolbar indicators (the style list, which buttons are depressed, and so on). But there are several ways besides the obvious to see which styles and character formatting have been applied. The first is to print out a style list.

Printing Out a Style List

It is often useful to have a printed list of styles and their descriptions. This can help you keep things consistent in a large organization, and it can help you troubleshoot formatting problems in complex documents. To print style information:

1. Open the document of interest.

2. Choose <u>F</u>ile ➤ <u>P</u>rint or use the Ctrl+P keyboard shortcut.

3. Choose Styles from the drop-down Print What list.

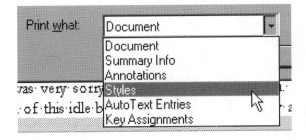

4. Click OK.

Open a document and print out a style list of your own. Take a moment to examine it. Pretty slick, eh?

The Style Gallery

This feature is a little like the Smithsonian Institute. You can spend days exploring it and learn something new each visit. It's an excellent place to see the seemingly endless collection of styles provided with Word's templates. The first figure in this chapter showed one use of the Style

Gallery (previewing the effect of a template style on your document). Figure 14.4 shows another way to use the Gallery.

By clicking the Style Samples button in the Style Gallery, shown in Figure 14.4, you can see examples of all of the styles for a document or template. If you are currently working on a project, you can also see how the project would look if you applied styles from various templates. If you like what you see, you can even have Word for Windows automatically apply the styles to your current project. You do not need to have a project in the works to visit the Gallery, but if you think you might want to reformat something, open that document first and make it the active Word project before you begin. Here are the general steps.

Pick templates to see their style collections

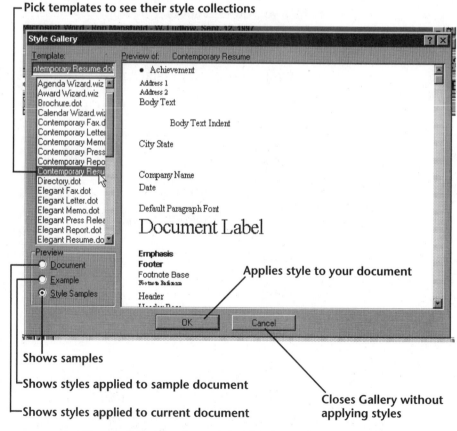

Applies style to your document

Shows samples

Shows styles applied to sample document

Shows styles applied to current document

Closes Gallery without applying styles

Figure 14.4 *The Style Gallery showing you examples of a template's predefined styles.*

1. Open a Word project if you think you might want to reformat it.

2. Open the Gallery with the Format ➤ Style Gallery command.

3. Click the Style Samples button.

4. Pick a style from the Template list.

5. Wait a moment while Word displays the samples.

6. Choose different template names if you wish to see samples of other style collections.

7. Click the Document button if you want to see the styles automatically applied to the current document you have open.

8. Click OK to close the gallery *and apply the new styles* or Cancel to close the gallery without changing your document.

Reveal Formats—the Cartoon Balloon

Another way to see style settings is to use Word's Reveal Formats command, or what I call the style "cartoon balloon." Here's how it works.

1. Click once on the Standard toolbar's Help button.

2. The mouse pointer gets a big question mark.

3. Point to a paragraph of interest and click to read about formatting, as illustrated in Figure 14.5.

4. Click the Help button again to turn off the Reveal Formats display.

Displaying Format Names On-Screen

Here's another interesting trick. You can display style information at the left edge of the screen in something called the *style area*, illustrated in Figure 14.6.

Here is how it works:

1. Switch to Normal or Outline view.

2. Choose Tools ➤ Options.

3. Visit the View tab.

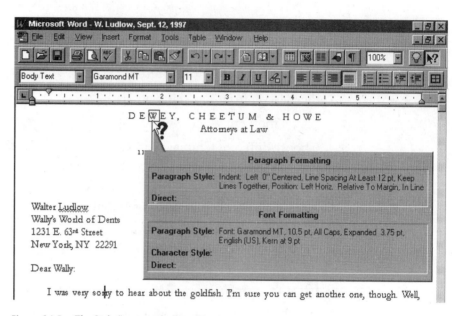

Figure 14.5   **The Style "cartoon balloon" in use.**

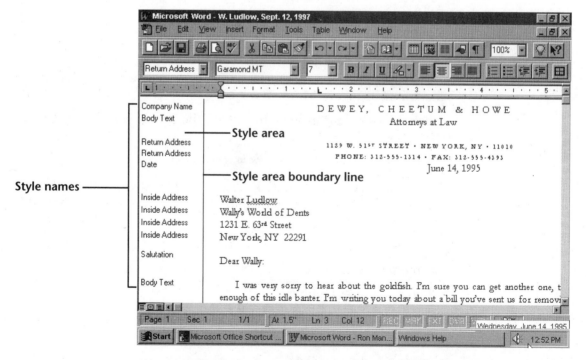

Figure 14.6   **You can see format names in the style area if you enable it.**

4. Pick a style-area width (1″, perhaps) from the Style Area Width section of the View tab. Figure 14.7 shows where to do this.

5. Click OK.

6. Style names will appear at the left of the screen in Normal and Outline views.

7. To remove them, repeat steps 1 through 5, choosing 0 (zero) for the Style Area Width.

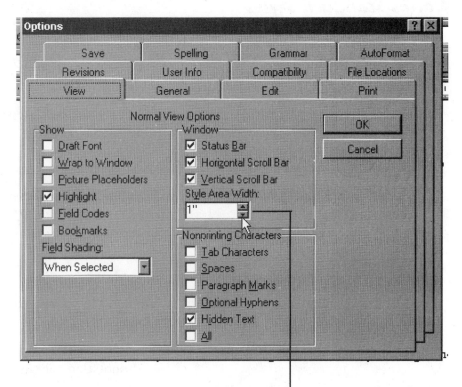

Specify style-area width here (0 means no style area)

Figure 14.7 Specify the width of the style area in the View tab of the Options dialog box (Tools ➤ Options).

When and Where Styles Are Saved

Styles are saved with your document and they are saved only when you save the document. This is yet another good reason to get in the habit of saving early and often. If your computer crashes after you've spent several hours setting up a complex collection of new styles, or if you accidentally click No to the Save Changes? prompt when you close a document, you will not be happy.

Word's Standard Styles

Word's designers have created hundreds of standard styles that are used by its footnote, outline, index, table-of-contents, page-numbering, header, and footer features.

Many of the templates for letters, brochures, newsletters, and other documents have their own predefined styles. Take some time now to open a few documents based on these templates and explore their styles. As a starter, try this:

1. Choose File ➤ New.

2. Click on the Reports tab and double-click on Contemporary Report.

3. Take a few moments to look it over. Could you use this template as is? How might you modify it to make it more useful?

Styles that Word Applies Automatically

Word applies certain styles automatically, as listed here:

Style	When Word Applies
Annotation Text	Comments inserted by the Annotation command
Annotation Reference	Initials of person who inserted the comment
Caption	Captions and table and figure titles
Footer	Footer info
All Footnotes	Text in a footnote

Style	When Word Applies
All Endnotes	Text in an endnote
Footnote Reference	Numbers and characters used as reference marks
Endnote Reference	Reference marks
Header	Header info
Index l–Index 9	Index entries created with the Index And Tables
Line Number	Automatic line numbers
Macro Text	Text of a WordBasic macro
Page Number	Automatic page numbers
TOC 1–TOC 9, Table of Contents	TOC entries
Table of Figures	Automatic figure numbering

Additional Formatting and Styles

It is possible to override or embellish styles with additional character formatting. But there are some caveats.

You already know how to make character-based changes from the Formatting toolbar, and the changes will work in styled paragraphs. But they interact with formatting elements in your styles. Read on.

Reapply/Redefine Styles

If you ask Word for Windows to apply a style to a paragraph that already uses that style (applying Normal to an already Normal paragraph, for instance); you will be visited by this strange and powerful dialog box:

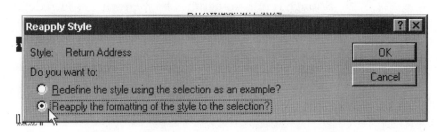

To Restore Styles

This box serves two purposes. First it lets you reapply a style to a paragraph that you have inadvertently messed up. Suppose you accidentally dragged the first-line indent marker in a Body paragraph and the paragraph no longer looks like the others. By choosing the Body style again from the Formatting toolbar you will get a chance to reapply your Body style and repair the errant paragraph. Follow these steps to restore a style:

1. Select the paragraph, paragraphs, or characters you wish to restore.
2. Choose the desired style from the Formatting toolbar's list.
3. If asked to reapply or redefine, pick Reapply.
4. Click OK.

To Redefine a Style

The second use of this dialog box is to let you quickly redefine a style. Suppose you hate the first-line indent you've used for body text. Change the indent in any one Body style paragraph; then pick Body from the Style list. Click on the Redefine button and click OK. Word for Windows will redefine the Body style using the new indent from your sample paragraph. All of your Body paragraphs will be changed. To redefine a style, follow these steps:

1. Select any paragraph or character formatted with the style to be changed.
2. Make the desired appearance changes (indents, underlining, etc.).
3. From the Formatting toolbar's list, choose the style *originally* used for the formatting.
4. When you see the Redefine/Reapply choice, choose Redefine.
5. Click OK.

Strange things sometimes happen when you redefine or reapply styles to manually embellished paragraphs, however. While the interaction of manually applied formatting and styles may seem almost random sometimes, it is not. Read about it at the very end of this chapter.

Deleting Styles

You cannot delete Word's built-in styles (headings and Normal, for instance), but you can remove custom ones you've created and many of the fonts provided with Word's templates. Unwanted styles can be deleted by selecting them in the Style dialog box and clicking the Delete button, as shown in Figure 14.8.

Select a style...   **... Then click to delete.**

Figure 14.8 **Deleting unwanted styles.**

You will be asked to confirm; press OK. All paragraphs formatted with a deleted style will revert to the document's Normal style. Follow these steps:

1. Open the Style dialog box with Format ➤ Style.
2. Click on the style you want to delete in the Styles list (scroll, if necessary).
3. Click Delete.
4. Click Yes to confirm the deletion.
5. The style will be deleted from the current document.

TIP   You can use the Undo list pulled from the Standard toolbar to replace accidentally deleted styles.

Renaming Styles

Styles can be renamed in the Style dialog box. Follow these steps:

1. Open the Style dialog box with the Format ➤ Style command.
2. Click on the style you want to rename in the Styles list (scroll, if necessary).
3. Click the Modify button.
4. You will see the Modify Style dialog box (shown earlier, in Figure 14.3).
5. Edit the name in the Name box.
6. Make any other desired changes while in the Modify Style dialog box.
7. Click OK.

Word will not let you change a style's name to one that already exists in the document. If you try to do so, a message will appear, informing you the name already belongs to another style. Click OK and type in another name.

Remember—Word for Windows cares about capitalization when you name styles. The names *Salutation* and *salutation* are not the same.

Finding and Replacing Styles

Style-change junkies rejoice. Word for Windows lets you search for and replace styles. While Word's powerful Replace feature is fully described in Chapter 20, here's a quick style replacement how-to:

1. Open the Replace dialog box with the Edit ➤ Replace command or use the Ctrl+H keyboard shortcut.
2. Place the insertion point in the Find What box.
3. Choose Style from the drop-down Format menu (see Figure 14.9).

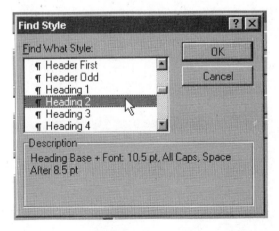

Figure 14.9   The Replace feature lets you locate or swap styles.

You will be presented with a list of possible styles in the Find Style dialog box:

4. Pick the style you wish to replace (Heading 2, for instance) and click OK. The name of the style will appear in the Format portion of the Find What area.

5. Move the insertion point to the Replace With portion of the dialog box.

6. Choose Style from the drop-down Format menu again.

7. Choose the new style from the resulting Replace Style dialog box list (Heading 1, for example):

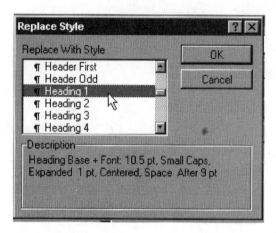

8. Click OK.

9. Tell Word whether you want to search the whole document (All), up from the insertion point, or down from the insertion point.

10. When you are ready, click Find Next and Replace, or Replace All, as appropriate. For instance, to replace all Heading 2 style occurrences with Heading 1 styles, you'd pick Search: All and Replace All:

NOTE Chapter 20 covers finding and replacing in detail. If you can't wait, experiment on copies of important documents rather than the real things. And be sure you turn off format searching when you are finished. Word will continue to search only for text in the style you've specified until you click No Formatting.

Transferring Styles to Other Documents

After you've spent time setting up complex styles, it would be nice to re-use them in new projects. Word for Windows provides several ways to do this. For repetitive tasks, consider setting up Template documents containing styles, as described in Chapter 16, and AutoText entries, described in Chapter 17.

If you have just a style or two you want to copy from one document (the source) to another (the destination), follow these steps:

1. Copy some text from the source document containing the style of interest and paste it into the destination document needing the style. If it is a paragraph style, be sure to include the paragraph mark in your selection.

2. Word will bring over the style with the text.

WARNING Remember that if the destination document has a style name identical to the style being copied from the source, the destination document will reformat the incoming text rather than take on the new style. Moreover, if you copy more than fifty styles at once, the source document's entire style sheet will be automatically copied to the destination document.

It is also possible to merge different style sheets, which copies unique styles from one document to another and modifies styles with identical names.

Think of the document containing styles you want to copy as the *source* document and the document receiving the new styles as the *destination* document. Here's how to merge style sheets:

1. With styles properly named and saved, work in the source document.

2. Open the Style dialog box with the F_ormat ➤ _Style command.

3. Click on the Organizer button to open the Organizer dialog box, shown in Figure 14.10.

4. Pick the Styles tab if it is not already foremost.

5. Note the two Styles Available In text boxes at the bottom of the Organizer dialog box. If the name of the destination file is not available in the Styles Available In box on the left, click the Close File button beneath. It will change into an Open File button. Choose the desired source file using standard Windows file-opening techniques.

6. The file Normal will probably be specified as the destination or To file on the right-hand side of the dialog box. This is telling you that Word wants to copy new styles to the Normal template to make them available to all new documents. If you want to make the style or styles you are copying globally available, leave the To setting as Normal. If you want to add the style(s) to just a selected document or template, click the *right* Close File button (note that there are two). It will change to an Open

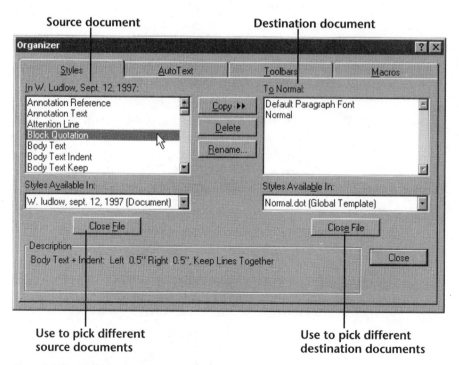

Figure 14.10   The Organizer dialog box.

File button. Choose the desired destination file using standard Windows file-opening techniques.

7. When the source and destination files have been properly identified, pick the styles you wish to copy in the left-hand scrolling list. Click to choose a single style, Shift+click to select ranges, or hold down the Ctrl key while you selectively click on noncontiguous styles.

8. With the desired styles selected, click Copy.

9. Use the Delete or Rename keys as necessary.

10. Open other source or destination files as necessary, then click Close when you're done.

Tips for Transferring Styles

Here are a few tips worth noting. First, you should save any changes to the source document before attempting to copy styles. This records the current styles for the source document. Next, inspect the source and destination documents for possible style-name problems. Remember that Word for Windows styles are case sensitive—*body* and *Body* are different style names. As you may have guessed, this can work for or against you. Consider printing out style sheets for both the source and destination documents and comparing them *before* you copy styles.

If the destination document has a style name identical to the style being copied from the source, the destination document will reformat the incoming text rather than take on the new style. Moreover, if you copy more than fifty styles at once, the source document's entire style sheet will be automatically copied to the destination document.

TIP   Other Word commands that exchange style information will bring over styles as necessary. For instance, Subscribe, Link, AutoText, and Paste Special all attempt to bring styles with them.

A Few More Style Tips

Here are a few tips on using styles:

▶ Get to know the styles provided in Word's templates before creating your own.

▶ Establish organization-wide style sheets and style-naming conventions. This will make it easy for groups of people to work on projects together.

▶ When experimenting with styles, work on document copies. This is particularly important for new users working on complex documents containing interrelated styles.

▶ Establish one or two base styles for complex documents. They need not be based on Word's Normal style, particularly if the look of the document is radically different from your normal work.

▶ Because Word's AutoFormat feature (described shortly) works only on text that has been formatted with styles, you'll want to get in the habit of using at least the Normal style when you type. Fortunately, this happens automatically unless you tell Word for Windows to do otherwise, as Word always formats typing in your new documents as Normal. If you import documents from other programs or import plain ASCII text, however, you'll probably need to select it and apply at least Normal style.

AutoFormat

AutoFormat inspects your document and suggests formatting changes that you can accept or reject. Consider this "before" glimpse at a report that was formatted entirely in Normal:

··What's·Wrong·Here?¶
¶
Introduction¶
City·governments·feel·trapped·between·constituents,·who·want·more·services·,·and·restrictions·(such·as·
Proposition·13)·that·limit·the·funds·available·to·pay·for·those·services.··Naturally·they·have·cast·their·nets·
far·and·wide,·seeking·novel·ways·to·pay·for·new·programs·without·raising·taxes.¶
With·increasing·frequency,·government·agencies·have·refused·to·issue·permits·to·local·politicians·bent·on·
some·pet·municipal·project·by·paying:¶
    →   linkage¶
    →   impact¶
    →   other·payments¶
The·fee·is·supposed·to·be·used·to·replenish·the·community·assets·to·repair·highways·and·provide·for·other·
related·infrastructure·maintenance,·but·the·truth·is·that·the·only·connection·some·of·these·fees·have·to·with·a·
given·project·is·that·the·city·government·knows·who·has·the·deep·pockets.¶
¶
The·State·View¶
Enter·the·convenient·fish·in·the·proverbial·barrel:··a·person·who·wants·to·develop·property·and·needs·a·

Word for Windows can locate and reformat headings, change straight quotes to curly quotes, and more. Here are the general steps and an example of AutoFormat at work:

1. Open the document you wish to reformat.

2. Choose F<u>o</u>rmat ➤ <u>A</u>utoFormat. You will see this dialog box:

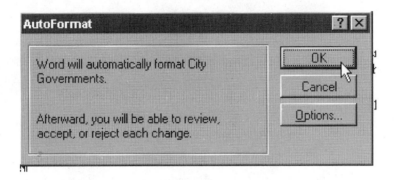

3. If you wish to change the way AutoFormat works, click the Options button. Click to tell which formatting tasks you don't want it to perform. For instance, if you don't want Word to preserve any Styles you've already applied, click to remove the check from the Styles box.

4. When you have specified any necessary changes to Word's usual Auto-Formatting habits, click OK to be taken back to the AutoFormat dialog box.

5. Click OK in the AutoFormat dialog box.

6. Word will go to work. In a few moments, you'll see this dialog box:

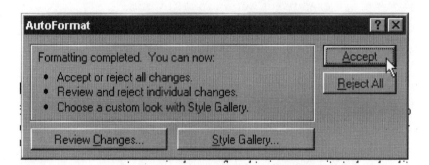

7. To see and review each proposed change, choose Review Changes. To apply further formatting via the Style Gallery click the Style Gallery button; otherwise, simply accept or reject all changes.

8. Inspect your finished product carefully to be sure that you got what you wanted.

   Typically, you'll want to polish Word's work. For instance, take a look at two of the pages in our sample document (see Figure 14.11).

   AutoFormat removed all those spaces in the first line and centered it, figuring out that it was a document title. AutoFormat spotted likely paragraph headings, increased their point sizes, changed their fonts, and added paragraph spacing nicely. It did not recognize the tabbed list as a candidate for bulleting, though, and therefore did not add bullets.

   So, while AutoFormat does a nice job considering that this whole document was formatted as Normal text, you can still add some polish to all but the simplest projects.

Manual Formatting and Styles

As promised, here's an explanation of how styles and manual formats interact (although, perhaps *collide* is a better word). Don't feel bad if this seems confusing. It is. First, there are some important concepts to review:

▶ By now, you should know the difference between font and paragraph formatting. Paragraph formatting describes things that happen to all of

Part 2

Did not bullet list

Spaces removed and formatted as a title

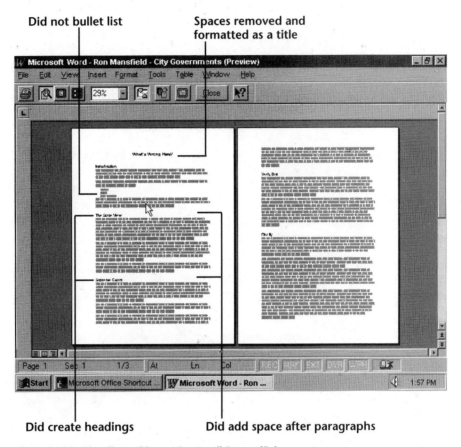

Did create headings

Did add space after paragraphs

Figure 14.11 **The effects of formatting an all-"normal" document.**

the characters in a paragraph—like indenting and line spacing. Font formatting can be applied selectively to all, or to just a few, characters in a paragraph. For this reason, some former versions of Word called font formatting "Character formatting," and this might still be the better name for it.

▶ You'll probably remember that some character-formatting choices toggle. Specifying bold twice, for instance, turns bold character formatting on and then off. Other character-formatting features don't toggle. Choose Helvetica twice, for example, and nothing interesting happens.

Now for the interesting stuff. When you use menu choices, the Formatting toolbar buttons, or keyboard shortcuts to specify formatting, you are doing something called *manual* formatting. When you use a style to format text, that's called (yep) *style* formatting. There's a difference, as you will soon see.

When you initially define a new style, Word for Windows looks at any paragraph and character formatting you've done and memorizes a collection of your manual-formatting decisions. If all of the text in the sample paragraph(s) is identical, that's a no-brainer.

But what if you ask Word to a create a style from a sample paragraph or paragraphs containing inconsistent formatting? What should it do, for instance, about bold if some of the text in the sample paragraph is bold and some isn't—ignore bold formatting, make everything bold, lock up your computer? And what if some of the lines you've selected for the sample are single-spaced and others double-spaced? Or how about inconsistent spacing before and after selected paragraphs, or wacky indents? (Variety has its price.)

Word for Windows needs to come to some conclusions about these inconsistencies because when you apply styles, they must format all of the specified text consistently.

Sooooo, Word looks at the first 255 characters in your sample text and decides whether or not to include their manually applied formatting as part of the style. If a particular manual format (bold, for instance) appears in at least half of the first 255 characters of your sample, it becomes part of the style. Suppose, for example, you have a 600-character paragraph and at least 128 of the first 255 characters are bold. The style will include bold as one of its formatting features.

Any text you subsequently apply this style to will receive bold formatting. However, if at least 128 of the first 255 characters are not bold, the style will not contain bold formatting, even if the last 300 characters in the text sample are bold. So far so good? Read on.

Once you've defined a style (1″ left and right indents, plus all bold text, for instance), selecting unformatted, plain vanilla text, and applying the new style will make the text conform to the style's formatting definitions (indented, bold text, in our example).

But what if the text you apply this style to already has other manual formatting like bold or italic—or what if you later try to apply manual formats to text you've formatted with your indented bold style? "Well," as President Clinton says, "that depends."

Let's take it one situation at a time—but first, a word or two about formatting *layers*, as Microsoft likes to call them.

Formatting Layers

Suppose you use a style to format otherwise plain-vanilla text. You would be applying something Microsoft refers to as the *style-formatting layer*. The once-plain text would take on the formatting characteristics defined by the style (indented, bold Times, let's say).

Then, suppose you manually format some of those same characters—italicize a word or two, increase the point size of the first character, and so on. You've added something called the *manual-formatting layer*.

Format Layers and the Replace Command

What's that? You wonder about Word's Replace command and format layers? Your concern is justified. When you run around globally replacing styles or manually applied formatting with the Replace command (described in Chapter 20), you'll need to keep in mind Word's behavior when it encounters combinations of manual formatting and styles. The Replace command causes the same toggling and other behavior problems as human intervention.

Removing Styles and Retaining Formats

Occasionally you might want to remove all of the styles in a document without affecting the appearance of the document. You'll want to remove the Bold Indent style you've created, for instance, but you want the text to remain bold and indented. Some people do this before sharing Word for Windows documents with WordPerfect DOS users, for example. Here are the steps:

1. Save your document with the Rich Text Format choice in the Save As dialog box. (It's in the Save File as Type scrolling list.)

2. Word will save the document. The resulting document can be used by Word for DOS, WordPerfect for DOS, and many other DOS word-processing programs.

Part
2

Formatting
Fundamentals

Time
Savers

Chapter 15

Envelopes, Labels, and Simple Mailing Lists

FAST TRACK

To suppress the printing of return addresses (for preprinted envelopes) *381*

either leave the Return Address area blank, or, if you have a return address typed there, click to place an X in the Omit box.

To print an envelope *381*

open the Envelopes and Labels dialog box by choosing the Tools ➤ Envelopes and Labels command. Then insert an envelope in your printer and click on the Print button.

To add an envelope page to the beginning of your document *382*

click on the Add to Document button in the Envelopes and Labels dialog box. Word takes care of all the details.

To change an inside address *383*

open the document and make the address change in the inside address. Or open the Envelopes and Labels dialog box (Tools ➤ Envelopes and Labels) and click the Change Document button. The envelope will be changed.

To specify envelope sizes (both standard and custom), fonts used for delivery, return addresses, and more *383*

use the Envelope Options tab or the Envelopes and Labels dialog box.

To print simple labels *385*

open the Envelopes and Labels dialog box with the Tools ➤ Envelopes and Labels command. Click on the Labels tab if it is not already foremost. Type an address in the big box and choose the desired options in the main Labels tab. To select different label sizes, click either on the picture of a label or the Options button. Insert a label or sheet of labels in your printer. (Make sure the label isn't too small for your printer.) Click on the Print button.

t's ironic that expensive computers make the simple task of envelope and label printing more difficult. Many offices keep typewriters around just for this reason. Sound familiar? Computerized envelope printing is not so bad once you get the hang of it, and you can set up documents that remember the recipe for you. In Word, there are envelope, label, mail, and list-management features that you'll find quite useful. Before we get into the details, here are some general tips:

- Use window envelopes whenever possible to avoid envelope printing altogether. Set up letterheads, invoices, and similar documents with the inside address properly positioned for standard window envelopes.

- Ask your letterhead designer to take your computer printer into consideration when picking paper stocks and envelope designs.

- Pick envelopes designed for your printer. These supplies are easier to find now, and many office-supply stores and mail-order paper sellers stock them. (Try Paper Direct, for instance—800-272-7377.) Laser-friendly envelopes have special flaps and flap glue that minimize jamming. Ink-jet–savvy envelopes are made of paper stock that won't fuzz up your characters.

- Purchase an envelope tray or feeder for your envelopes if you print a lot of them.

Printing Envelopes

Word can print addresses on envelopes by looking for the addresses in your documents (the inside address of a letter for instance), or you can type an address in the Envelopes and Labels dialog box, as illustrated in Figure 15.1.

  A nifty new feature of Word is the Insert Address button, found on your Standard toolbar and in the Envelopes and Labels dialog box. Click on this to access your Personal Address Book (if you have created one), where you can choose addresses to paste into documents or into the Delivery and Return Address boxes of the Envelopes and Labels dialog box.

Click to insert an address from your Personal Address Book

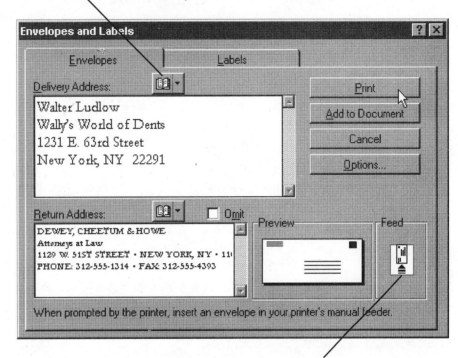

Click to choose a different orientation or position

Figure 15.1   Word can find addresses in your document; or you can use the Insert Address button or type them in.

You reach the Envelopes and Labels dialog box with the Tools ➤ Envelopes and Labels command. The dialog box lets you:

▶ Print envelopes containing one time addresses that you type into the dialog box itself.

▶ Copy an address from your document for envelope printing.

▶ Insert addresses from your Personal Address Book with the Insert Address button.

▶ Type envelope addresses and then insert them into your letters or other Word documents.

Setting Up a Return Address

If your envelopes have preprinted return addresses, you can skip this task. But if you want to use plain envelopes and have Word print your return address in the upper-left corner of envelopes, do this:

1. Choose the printer you plan to use if you have more than one.

2. Open the Envelopes and Labels dialog box by choosing Tools ➤ Envelopes and Labels.

3. Click on the Envelopes tab if it is not foremost. You'll see the dialog box shown in Figure 15.1.

4. If Word finds an address in the current open Word document, you will see it in the Delivery Address portion of the dialog box

5. Use the Insert Address button or type your return address in the large box labeled Return Address. (Part of the address may be already filled out automatically, based on your Word User Info.)

6. When you are happy with the spelling and appearance of your return address, try test printing on a plain #10 ($4.125'' \times 8^{1}/_{2}''$) envelope. Word assumes that you can center-feed envelopes in your printer. If that's not possible, click on the envelope in the Feed section of the dialog box to bring up the Envelope Options dialog box, shown in Figure 15.2.

7. Select a combination that will work with your printer; then click OK. Word is pretty smart about knowing the options for your specific printer, though, so they should be okay.

8. Place an envelope in your printer.

9. Back in the Envelopes tab of the Envelopes and Labels dialog box, click Print.

TIP Word will make a guess as to what the delivery address is, and usually it hits it. If, however, you have several addresses in your document, Word might get confused. One way around this is to select the correct delivery address before you choose the Tools ➤ Envelopes and Labels command.

Figure 15.2 **You can change the envelope printing options in the Envelope Options dialog box.**

Suppressing Return Addresses

If you always plan to use envelopes that contain preprinted return addresses, you can make sure that nothing prints by making the Return Address area blank. Or you can have a return address typed there and suppress its printing by clicking to place a check in the Omit box.

Printing Envelopes with New Addresses

You can either choose an address with the Insert Address button, type an envelope address directly into the Envelopes and Labels dialog box, or select an address in your letter or other Word document and then open the Envelopes and Labels dialog box. Here are the general steps for envelope printing:

1. Select the address in your document if there is one.

2. Open the Envelopes and Labels dialog box by choosing the Tools ➤ Envelopes and Labels command.

Part
3

Time Savers

3. If you selected an address in step 1, you'll see it in the dialog box; if not, use the Insert Address button or type an address in the Delivery Address box.

4. Insert an envelope in your printer.

5. Click on the Print button.

Adding an Envelope Page to Documents

Clicking on the Add to Document button in the Envelopes and Labels dialog box adds an envelope page to the beginning of your document. Word takes care of all the details. You can see what it does by switching to Print Preview with two pages showing, as illustrated here in Figure 15.3.

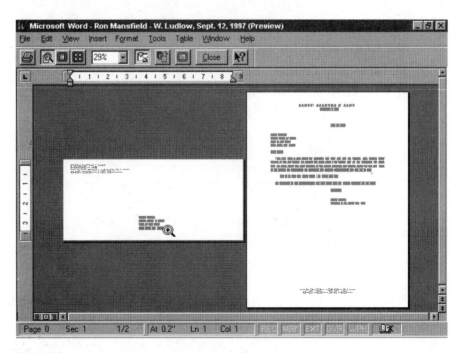

Figure 15.3   **Word will add an envelope to your document file if you so desire.**

Changing Addresses

Once you've inserted an envelope page in your document, you can change the envelope and inside address at any time. Here's how:

1. Open the document.

2. Make the address change in the inside address. You can use the Insert Address button for this.

   or

3. Open the Envelopes and Labels dialog box (Tools ➤ Envelopes and Labels). Make the address change in the inside address. You can use the Insert Address button for this.

4. Click the Change Document button. The envelope will be changed.

> **WARNING**   If you change the Delivery Address in the Envelopes and Labels window and then click the Change Document button, Word will update the envelope but not the inside address, so be careful. It's better to make the change in the document, not the Envelopes and Labels window.

Envelope Sizes, Fonts, and Other Options

Word lets you specify envelope sizes (both standard and custom), fonts used for delivery and return addresses, and more. The options are selected in two tabs located in the Envelope Options dialog box. Let's look at the Envelope Options tab first. It is illustrated in Figure 15.4.

Envelope Size

Choose from any of the standard sizes listed in the drop-down list or specify a custom size by typing dimensions or selecting Custom Size in the drop-down list in the Envelope Size dialog box:

Obviously you'll need to specify dimensions that your printer can handle.

Part
3

Time Savers

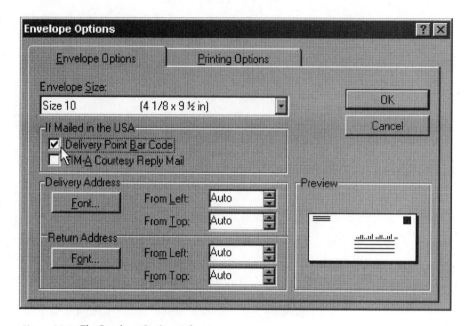

Figure 15.4 **The Envelope Options tab.**

Bar Codes to Speed Postal Delivery

If you are planning to send mail within the United States, you can ask Word to print bar codes on your envelopes. These will speed automated mail sorting. Two coding techniques are provided—POSTNET for regular mail and FIM-A for "courtesy reply" mail. Both types of codes are illustrated in Figure 15.5.

Place a check in the box or boxes you desire. Word will do the rest, calculating the bar code from the mailing address.

Fonts and Address Positioning

Use the Font buttons to choose the desired fonts for the delivery and return addresses. They bring up the Envelope Address Font tab, which lets you specify fonts, font sizes, colors, character formatting, etc.

The dimension boxes in the Delivery Address and Return Address sections of the Envelope Options tab let you specify address spacing. Auto makes Word do all of the work. You can type new dimensions or use the triangles to change dimensions. Watch the preview as you work.

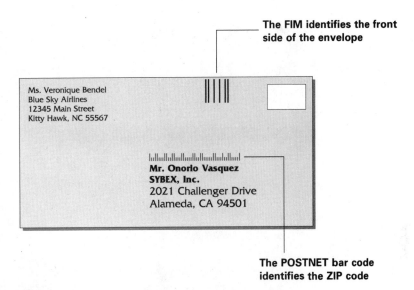

The FIM identifies the front side of the envelope

Ms. Veronique Bendel
Blue Sky Airlines
12345 Main Street
Kitty Hawk, NC 55567

**Mr. Onorio Vasquez
SYBEX, Inc.**
2021 Challenger Drive
Alameda, CA 94501

The POSTNET bar code identifies the ZIP code

Figure 15.5   Here are the two types of bar codes.

The Care and Feeding of Envelopes

You've already seen the Printing Options tab in the Envelope Options dialog box, but it deserves a second look. As you can see in Figure 15.6, this is where you tell Word how you plan to feed envelopes.

The choices vary with the chosen printer. If you have multiple trays, you specify the tray containing envelopes (upper, lower, etc.). Click Reset to return to the default settings for the chosen printer.

Labels

Label printing is a lot like envelope printing except that you have even more options. For instance, you can print single labels or sheets of labels. Word "knows" the dimensions for many different industry-standard stocks from Avery and others. For instance, you'll find Word knows how to print:

▶ Audio tape labels

▶ Business card perf stock

▶ Diskette labels

Part
3

Time Savers

*Figure 15.6 **Pick envelope-feed options here in the Printing Options tab of the Envelope Options dialog box.***

▶ File folder labels

▶ Mailing (address) labels

▶ Name tags

▶ Postcards

▶ Ready indexes

▶ Rotary (Rolodex) cards

▶ Shipping labels

▶ Videotape labels

▶ WorkSaver tabs

Printing Labels

Simple label printing is a lot like envelope printing. Here are the general steps:

1. Select the address in your document if it has one.

2.   Open the Envelopes and Labels dialog box with the <u>T</u>ools ➤ <u>E</u>nvelopes and Labels command.

3.   Click on the Labels tab if it is not already foremost. You'll see the options illustrated in Figure 15.7.

4.   If you selected an address in step 1, or if Word finds one on its own, you'll see it in the dialog box; if not, type an address in the big box or use the Insert Address button.

5.   Choose the desired options in the main Labels tab. To print a single label on a multilabel sheet, click on Single Label and specify the row and column location of the label. Choose to print or not print the bar code and return address.

6.   To select different label sizes, click either on the picture of a label or the Options button. You'll see the choices illustrated in Figure 15.8.

The Insert Address button

Prints labels

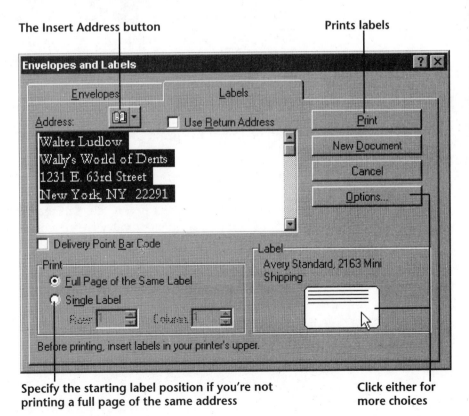

Specify the starting label position if you're not printing a full page of the same address

Click either for more choices

Figure 15.7   *The Labels tab.*

Pick a printer here　　　**Pick a tray**　　　　　**Takes you back to the Label tab**

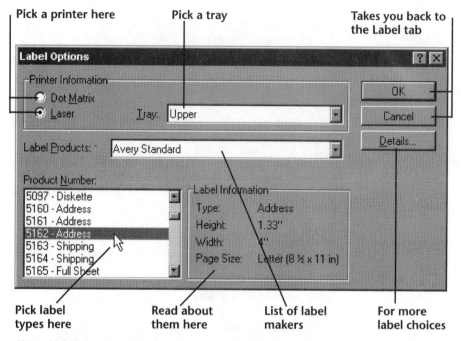

Pick label types here　　　**Read about them here**　　　**List of label makers**　　　**For more label choices**

Figure 15.8　*The Label Options dialog box.*

7. Pick the label maker, label product number, and printer type. For more detailed options, press the Details button to see the choices in Figure 15.9.

8. Fine-tune Top and Side margins here if your printer prints *all* of the labels of the current type too high or too far left or right. The other settings are probably correct if you selected the correct label type back in step 6. When you have made all of your choices, click OK once or twice as necessary to return to the Label tab of the Envelopes and Labels dialog box.

9. Insert a label or sheet of labels in your printer. (Make sure the label isn't too small for your printer.)

10. Click on the Print button.

Takes you back to the Label Options dialog box ⎯⎤

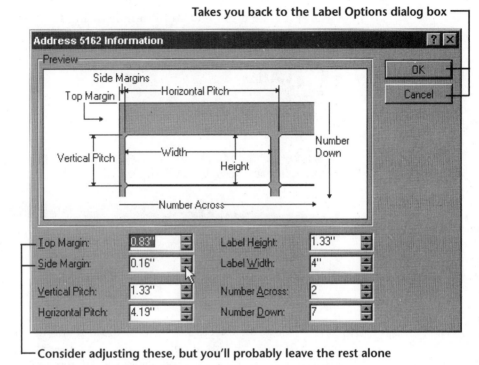

Consider adjusting these, but you'll probably leave the rest alone

Figure 15.9 **Additional label details.**

> **TIP** Normally, you can put partially used sheets of laser labels through your printer once or twice more, but you run the risk of jamming and possibly damaging your printer. It's often better to print full sheets and file the unused labels for the next time you mail something to the same recipient.

Including Graphics on Envelopes

You can print graphics on envelopes. It's a great way to add logos, special messages, business reply art, and so on. Here are the general steps:

1. Select the Envelope tab in the Envelopes and Labels dialog box reached with Tools ➤ Envelopes and Labels.

2. Click on either the Add To Document or the Change Document button.

3. Switch to Page Layout if not already there.

4. Paste or create a graphic and frame it (using the <u>I</u>nsert ➤ <u>F</u>rame command); then move it into position as you would any other framed item:

5. Make any other changes that you like (rearrange or reformat lines of text in the inside address, for instance).

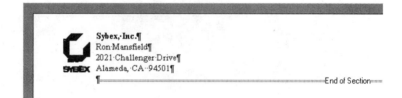

At this point, the envelope is one-of-a-kind, and in a separate section at the top of your current document. You can either save the document and print the envelope along with the rest of the document, or save the document as a template for repeated use (see Chapter 16). But there's one other possibility. If you want the artwork to appear on *all* of your envelopes, you can select the art and create a special AutoText entry called EnvelopeExtra 1 or EnvelopeExtra 2. Use the techniques described in Chapter 17 to create AutoText entries.

Envelopes, Labels, and Long Mailing Lists

When mailing to many different addresses, consider using Word's Mail Merge feature. It is described in Chapter 28.

To preview envelopes, follow these steps:

1. In a document, type the name, address, etc., that you want on the label.

2. Format the information, adding graphics if you wish.

3. Select the label, including the graphic.

4. Open the Envelopes and Labels dialog box.

5. Select the right label size and make any other appropriate changes.

6. Click on New Document on the Labels tag, and your labels will appear in a document, which you can preview.

   It is a good idea to practice on plain white paper and hold test pages up to the light in front of a sheet of labels or an envelope to see how things will line up.

Wish List

There is no easy way to insert art or change the font, size, or other elements of character appearance in the Labels tab (although you can do these things with envelopes). This means that name tags, video-spine labels, and similar specialty labels are going to look pretty boring.

There is a workaround to this problem (use the Add to Document button, then edit the individual labels in the document), but it probably isn't appropriate if you're running big jobs.

TIP   Formatting all labels in a given document is a breeze. Select them all, make them look terrific, and then print. They won't look different from each other, but the labels for a given mailing, name badges for a conference, etc., can have a great look unique to that mailing or conference.

Chapter 16

Templates, Wizards, and Sample Documents

FAST TRACK

Word's *templates* are read-only documents containing styles and other design elements that you can use to create or restyle your own documents. *Wizards* are computerized assistants. Like you, Wizards also use templates to create documents, after asking some questions and making a few design decisions on their own. The following Wizards are supplied with Word:

Agenda

Award

Calendar

Fax

Letter

Memo

Newsletter

Pleading

Resume

Table

In addition, some Word templates have pointers embedded right in their example text that explain how to personalize them to suit your own needs. These are called *sample documents*, and they are great learning tools. If you did a complete installation of Word, these files are all located in their own subfolders within the folder called Templates.

Look for the Templates subfolder in your MSOffice folder. Let's begin our tour with templates.

Templates

There are at least four different ways to use templates:

▶ Start a new project based on a template shipped with Word

▶ Modify an existing project by choosing a template and completely reformatting your work in the template's styles

▶ Copy selected styles from templates for use in a project

▶ Create and save new templates of your own

> **NOTE** All new documents are based on Word's Normal template, unless you specify otherwise. As discussed in Chapter 14, Normal includes hundreds of predefined styles, and it may suit your needs just fine. To make your documents look really snazzy, though, consider using Word's other templates.

If you want to make a template for your own work, here's how:

1. Click the Open button on the Standard toolbar and locate the template upon which you want to base your own template.

2. Be sure the Document radio button is selected and click OK.

3. Make any formatting, design, or other decisions you want stored in the template.

4. When you go to save the document, select the Word Template file type in the Save as Type list, then click OK. Whenever you open the document from now on, it will have the styles and design elements you've specified.

Template Types

Word's standard templates come in up to three different "flavors." Microsoft refers to these as *Template types*:

▶ Contemporary

▶ Elegant

▶ Professional

Part 3

Time Savers

Each type uses fonts and effects chosen to give a document a different "mood." For instance, the Contemporary Letter template uses Times New Roman, while Professional uses Arial. The Company Name style in the Contemporary Letter template includes shading, while the Elegant type does not, and so on.

By always using templates of the same type, you can give your work a consistent look. And when creating other documents based on templates, you can copy the existing styles using the tricks you learned in Chapter 14.

> **TIP** No matter what kind of document you want to create (newsletter, manual, invoice, time sheet, press release, brochure, etc.), chances are Word has a template for it. Since these templates were intended to be used together, some even sharing a common design, one way to ensure some consistency within your company is to standardize the use of Word's templates.

Many templates come in the three types discussed above, but not all templates come in all types. For instance, there is only one invoice type, simply called Invoice. Here is a list of Word's templates, divided into those available in Contemporary, Elegant, and Professional and those with only one type:

Available in All Three Types	Just One Type
Fax	Brochure
Letter	Directory
Memo	Invoice
Press Release	Manual
Report	Newsletter
Resume	Purchase Order
	Thesis
	Weekly Time Sheet

Using Templates

Once you know what each template looks like, you can quickly start new projects by picking the appropriate template whenever you start. Choose

<u>F</u>ile ➤ <u>N</u>ew and click the tab you wish in the New dialog box. Then just pick the template you wish by name:

Notice that you can preview templates here. You can also start Wizards from the New dialog box. Double-click on your choice; then simply add your own text by clicking on the appropriate areas of the template and replacing the labels with your own words.

Memorandum

To: John, Paul, George and Ringo

CC: [Click here and type name]

From: [Click here and type name]

Date: June 15, 1995

But first, it's helpful to know what the various templates look like. You could load each one and take a look, but there's an easier way.

Exploring Templates

Use the Style Gallery, reached with the Format ➤ Style Gallery command, to preview templates. Here are the general steps.

1. Open a new document with the File ➤ New command.

2. Choose Normal (the Default template).

3. Choose Format ➤ Style Gallery. You will see a window like the one in Figure 16.1.

4. Pick the template that you want to see from the scrolling list.

5. Click the Example button in the Preview area to see a preview of the template's appearance.

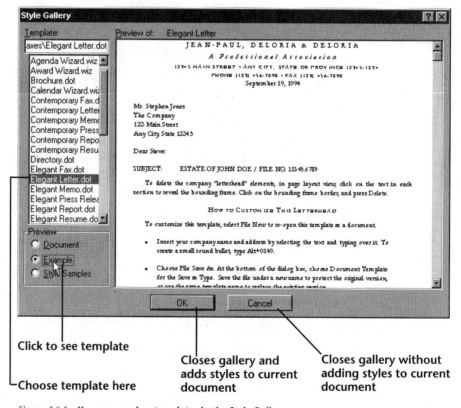

Figure 16.1   *You can preview templates in the Style Gallery.*

6. Scroll to make sure you see the entire template. They are often several pages long.

7. Click Style Samples to see the names of styles displayed in the styles themselves. Unfortunately, these are often too small to read.

8. When you are done previewing, click Cancel. (Clicking OK copies the styles to your current document but does not load the other template elements—the boilerplate text, etc.)

Modifying Templates

You can change templates just as you would any other Word documents. The only difference is one additional step you must take when saving your work. Suppose you want to update the Professional letter template to include your company logo. Follow these steps to see how:

1. Use the File ➤ New command to open a new document based on the Professional Letter template:

2. Make the changes, such as adding your logo and other embellishments.

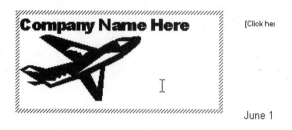

[Click here and type recipient's address]

3. Print out a sample and check your work.

4. When you are satisfied, choose <u>F</u>ile ➤ Save <u>A</u>s.

5. Type the same file name as the old template if you want to replace that template, or type a new file name to keep *both* the old and new. Make sure you choose Document Template in the Save As Type box:

    TIP If you always save modified templates under new names, you'll have the original templates available for modifying in different ways should the need arise.

Prewritten Business Letters

Word comes with a number of prewritten letters for various occasions. They are generally accessed via Letter Wizard, which is described in detail in Chapter 27. When you elect to use a prewritten letter, you will be prompted for details specific to you and your purposes. Whether the letters will work for you is a matter of taste and circumstance.

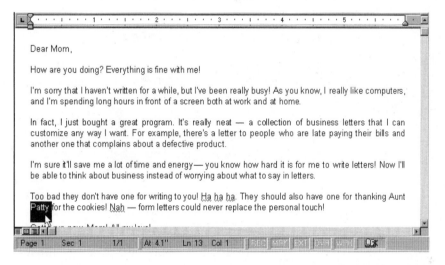

Over a dozen "canned" letters are provided with Word. These include:

Apology for delay

Announcement of price increase

Collection letter

Complaint under investigation

Credit report request

Direct mail

Lease expiring

Letter to Mom

Order cancellation

Press release

Resume cover letter

Returned check (firm request for payment!)

Thanks for inquiry

Thanks for job application

Thanks for the suggestion

Tips for Using Templates

▶ Word often gets information from the User Info tab in the Options dialog box (reached with the Tools ➤ Options command). Make sure your info is up-to-date by visiting that tab.

▶ In templates with inside addresses, signature blocks, and other multiline items, consider the Shift+↵ trick to keep lines all in the same paragraph. This eliminates unwanted "space before" in each address line, for example.

▶ Switching types (from Elegant to Professional, for instance) can give your documents a whole new look. And you can mix and match styles by copying selected styles from other documents.

▶ Some of the more complex templates (like Manual) use a wealth of Word features, including table of contents, index entries, etc.

▶ Don't forget other time savers such as the Tools ➤ Envelopes and Labels command. They work with templates, too.

▶ Use Find and Replace to speed the task of changing things like product names that repeat many times in the same document.

Wizards—The Computer Wants Your Job

You've seen Wizards at work elsewhere in this book, but because they often use templates, they are worth mentioning here, as well. Wizards ask you questions and then use your responses to design documents for you. Take the Calendar Wizard, for instance. You start Wizards with the

File ➤ New command. Pick the Calendar Wizard from the scrolling list, and it will appear:

 TIP Turn off the Show ¶ feature for better-looking previews.

You'll be asked questions about your hopes and dreams for the new document. Do you want portrait or landscape orientation? Would you like to leave room for a picture or other graphic? Do you want fries with that? You get the idea.

All the while, Word shows you a preview, making changes as you answer questions. The preview is very useful because you can try several different settings in each window to see which you prefer. When you click the Finish button, the Calendar Wizard works its magic (see Figure 16.2).

For more on Wizards, see Chapter 27.

Figure 16.2   **The Wizard's work.**

Chapter 17

End Monotony with AutoText, AutoCorrect, and Insert

FAST TRACK

then click the AutoText toolbar button, press the F3 function key, or type **Alt+Ctrl+V***; or, choose* Edit ➤ AutoText *(you'll see a preview) and then pick an entry from the scrolling name list by either double-clicking or clicking once and then clicking the Insert button or pressing ↵.*

To edit an AutoText entry 411

*insert the entry in a document. Edit and reformat it as necessary. Select the corrected entry and any necessary punctuation, paragraph marks, spaces following, etc. Visit the AutoText dialog box (*Edit ➤ AutoText*). Rename the entry, if necessary, and click the Add button. Answer Yes to the "Do you want to redefine" question.*

To delete an AutoText entry 411

*open the AutoText dialog box (*Edit ➤ AutoText*). Select the doomed item from the scrolling list. Look in the Preview box or insert the entry and check to be certain that this is the entry you wish to delete. Click Delete.*

To create your own AutoCorrect entries 416

open the AutoCorrect dialog box with the Tools ➤ AutoCorrect *command. Type the "name" (the text string you wish to replace) in the Replace box. Type the replacement in the With box (or see the tip that follows).*

To delete an AutoCorrect entry 418

*open the AutoCorrect dialog box (*Tools ➤ AutoCorrect*). Select the victim. Click the Delete button. The entry will be deleted.*

To cut a selection to the Spike 421

press Shift+F3.

To insert and clear the Spike 422

press Ctrl+Shift+F3.

To insert without clearing the Spike 422

type **spike** *and then press F3.*

Word for Windows offers three convenient ways to store, retrieve, and insert frequently used text, graphics, and other document elements. The techniques employ Word's AutoText, AutoCorrect, and Insert commands. Each has strengths and weaknesses. Read about all three approaches before you develop a strategy and spend hours personalizing your computer.

AutoText

The *AutoText* feature provides an easy way to store and retrieve "boilerplate" text, graphics, addresses, letter closings, memo distribution lists, tables, logos, and just about anything else that you can create with Word for Windows.

You can store AutoText entries with the Normal template so that they are always available, or with other templates for specialty projects.

Users of older Word for Windows versions (2.0 and earlier) will notice that there are no Microsoft "standard" AutoText entries analogous to those in the old Glossaries. These functions (inserting dates and times, for instance) are handled in other ways, described elsewhere in this and other chapters.

Creating AutoText Entries

To create an AutoText entry, simply select whatever you wish to memorialize, then choose Edit ➤ AutoText. You'll see a dialog box like the one in Figure 17.1.

If you want to store the paragraph formatting with the entry, be sure to include paragraph marks in your selection. (Even if you store an entry *with* paragraph formatting, you can later insert the entry *without* formatting if you wish.) Click on Add.

TIP If you find that you make AutoText entries frequently, consider adding the AutoText button to one of your toolbars. It looks like a keyboard with a finger pointing at it. See Chapter 36.

Select ¶ marks if you want
to save formatting

Word proposes a name,
which you can change

You'll see part of the entry here

Choose All Documents or attach the
entry to a particular document

Figure 17.1   Name and store AutoText entries with the Edit ➤ AutoText command.

Saving AutoText Entries

To save an AutoText entry, follow these steps:

1. Before saving an entry, you are given a chance to review and change the
    automatic entry name that Word for Windows assigns. To change the
    name, just type a new one in the name box. Names can be up to 32
    characters long, and spaces are permitted.

2. If you want an entry to be available whenever you use Word, leave the
    default choice All Documents (Normal.dot) in the drop-down "avail-
    ability" list. To attach an entry to a different template, pick one from the
    drop-down list.

3. Click the Add button.

> **TIP** It is often good to select the space *after* text being memorialized when creating an AutoText entry (that is, the single space created by the spacebar, not the blank line created by the paragraph return). This will save you from typing a space each time you insert the entry later.

Using AutoText Entries

Once you've saved some AutoText entries, you can insert them using several different techniques. Always begin by placing the insertion point where you want the entry to be placed. If you need spaces or tabs before the entry, it is easiest to type them first. When the insertion point is properly positioned, do one of the following:

▶ Type all or part of an AutoText entry's name; then press F3.

▶ Type all or part of an AutoText entry's name; then type Alt+Ctrl+V.

▶ Choose Edit ➤ AutoText (you'll see a preview); then pick an entry from the scrolling name list by either double-clicking or clicking once and then clicking the Insert button or pressing ↵.

In any event, Word for Windows will insert the entry. Edit it as you would any other text or graphic or other document element.

Forcing Plain Text

You can have an AutoText entry take on the appearance of the text at the insertion point in the current document, even if you saved it with its own formatting. To do so, choose Plain Text in the Insert As box of the AutoText dialog box:

Editing AutoText Entries

To edit an entry, follow these general steps:

1. Insert the entry in a document.

2. Edit and reformat it as necessary.

3. Select the corrected entry and any necessary punctuation, paragraph marks, spaces following, etc.

4. Visit the AutoText dialog box (Edit ➤ AutoText).

5. Restore the entry's name in the Name box, if necessary.

6. Click the Add button.

7. Answer Yes to the "Do you want to redefine" question.

Deleting AutoText Entries

Deleting AutoText entries is as simple as you'd expect (and hope). Follow these general steps:

1. Open the AutoText dialog box (Edit ➤ AutoText).

2. Select the doomed item from the scrolling list.

3. Look in the Preview box or insert the entry and check to be *certain* that this is the entry you wish to delete.

4. Click Delete.

WARNING Word does not ask if you *really, really* want to delete AutoText entries, and Undo *will not work* here, so stay awake, particularly if you have a lot of similar-looking entries or entries with similar names.

Shortcuts for Frequently Used Entries

You need not type an entire entry name when specifying it. You need only type enough characters to uniquely identify the entry. For instance, if you have an entry called *Mansfield* and another called *Manhole*, typing **Mans+F3** would insert the *Mansfield* entry while **Manh+F3** would get you *Manhole*.

TIP If you like the previously described AutoText entry shortcut, keep it in mind when *naming* entries. Make the first few characters in an entry name as unique as possible.

It is also possible to assign keyboard shortcuts (hot keys) and to create Toolbar buttons for your favorite AutoText entries. See Chapter 36 for details.

Converting Old Glossaries to AutoText

If you've upgraded from a previous Word for Windows version, your Normal template has inherited any glossary entries that were in your earlier Normal template, and they are readily available as AutoText. If you made glossary entries in other templates, they will also work with newer versions of Word for Windows. Simply open a document using the old templates.

EnvelopeExtra Entries

Word for Windows normally lets you use any names you like for Auto-Text entries. There are two exceptions. Word reserves the names Envelope-Extra1 and EnvelopeExtra2 for a special purpose (see Chapter 15). If you give items these names, they will appear on envelopes each time you print them. For example, you might select a logo, and perhaps return address text, then name it EnvelopeExtra1, as shown Figure 17.2.

Thereafter, whenever you use Word's Envelope and Labels command, it will insert the contents of EnvelopeExtra1 and EnvelopeExtra2, if they exist. Figure 17.3 shows the results of including the EnvelopeExtra1 entry shown in Figure 17.2.

To delete these entries forever, delete them as you would any other entry. To temporarily disable them, rename them. Remember, you can create different entries for different templates, so you can have multiple EnvelopeExtra1 and EnvelopeExtra2 entries for different projects. For instance, you could have one template with an entry like *Your newsletter is enclosed* and another that says *Here is the literature you've requested* and so on.

Figure 17.2 **Word reserves the AutoText entry names EnvelopeExtra1 and EnvelopeExtra2 for envelope printing.**

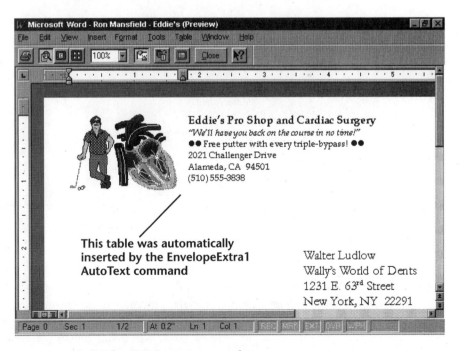

Figure 17.3 **An EnvelopeExtra1 entry on an envelope.**

Part
3

Time Savers

Printing Lists of AutoText Entries

To see printed examples of all AutoText entries and their full names, follow this procedure:

1. Open a new document using the template of interest (Normal, for instance).

2. Open the Print dialog box (Ctrl+P or File ➤ Print).

3. Choose AutoText Entries from the Print What list, as shown in Figure 17.4.

4. Having made sure your printer is ready, click OK or press ⏎.

5. The list will present itself.

Figure 17.4   Choose AutoText entries to print out a list.

AutoCorrect

I suspect that *AutoCorrect* started out with one purpose in life, and then someone discovered a second use for it. (I call these discoveries "hey lookits," as in "Hey look at what this can do!")

The primary reason for AutoCorrect is to fix typos like *teh* when you meant to type *the*. Word for Windows will watch you type and change things for you.

You can create your own entries, and there are some predefined entries. For instance, if you type **(r)** or **(R)**, Word will replace those characters with the registered symbol (®).

new

Word's AutoCorrect feature is now even more robust than before. Now Word will correct what it believes to be Caps Lock key errors, as well as insert correct plural and possessive forms of AutoCorrect entries you have assigned. More symbols have been added that are changed automatically (such as arrows and smiley faces), and Word will now format ordinal numbers (such as *2nd*) and fractions (such as $\frac{1}{2}$) in fancy typesetter's style. Keep in mind that AutoCorrect is different from the Automatic Spellchecking option, which doesn't correct misspelled words, but flags unfamiliar words (with red underline) as you type. If you want Word to actually correct your own personal pet-peeve typos or misspellings, AutoCorrect is the tool for the job.

To use the built-in entries, you just type along as usual. Word for Windows will make changes when it thinks they are needed. You can see a list of the current autocorrections by scrolling in the AutoCorrect dialog box (reached with the Tools ➤ AutoCorrect command), shown in Figure 17.5.

Other Uses of AutoCorrect

Here's the hey lookit. In addition to correcting typos, you can use Auto-Correct to convert "shorthand" into longer text strings. For instance, you could tell Word for Windows that you want it to replace *aka* with *also known as*, or replace *mwg* with *Mr. William Gates*, and so on. You can even insert text and graphics this way. Type *sylogo*, for instance, and insert the Sybex logo (see Creating Your Own AutoCorrect Entries, next).

The primary difference here is that *AutoCorrect* will *always* make the replacement when you type a defined string of characters followed by a space. *AutoText* waits for you to press the F3 key before it takes over.

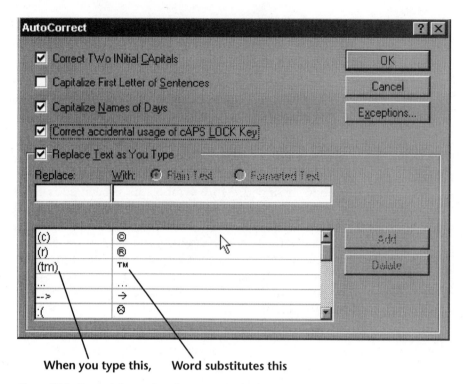

When you type this,   Word substitutes this

Figure 17.5   *See and change AutoCorrect entries in the AutoCorrect dialog box.*

Creating Your Own AutoCorrect Entries

When creating your own AutoCorrect entries, there is one potential land mine, which is that AutoCorrect will always blindly replace certain text strings with other text strings. For example, if you want to change each occurrence of *add* with your inside address, and you assign *add* as the name for this autocorrection, things will work fine until the first time you type a sentence like *Please add my name to the carpool list.* Then you'll get your address smack in the middle of an otherwise perfectly good sentence. Because of this potential problem, it's probably safest to use AutoText for inserting boilerplate and save AutoCorrect for true corrections. If you do use AutoCorrect for insertions, use care when defining the text that AutoCorrect will react to (the name for each entry) and give some thought to whether the text string you're replacing is likely to occur in cases other than those where you'd want it replaced.

Try to use names that are uncommon, yet easy to remember. If you get hooked on AutoCorrect, consider preceding all of your entry names with some unusual character that will never appear in normal text, like a backslash (*add* for instance). Names can be up to 31 characters long. That said, here are the steps:

1. Open the AutoCorrect dialog box with the <u>T</u>ools ➤ <u>A</u>utoCorrect command.

2. Type the "name" (the text string you wish to replace) in the Replace box.

3. Type the replacement in the With box (or see the tip that follows).

4. Click Add.

5. Make any other entries or changes.

6. Click OK when done.

TIP If you select the text (or graphics and other things) you want to use as the replacement item before you open the AutoCorrect dialog box, it will appear in the With portion of the box when it opens. If the items are formatted, you'll be given the choice of pasting the items as formatted or not.

Editing AutoCorrect Entries

To modify an AutoCorrect entry, follow these steps:

1. Correct the entry in a document and select it.

2. Open the AutoCorrect dialog box (<u>T</u>ools ➤ <u>A</u>utoCorrect).

3. Type the old Replace name.

4. When the Replace button undims, click it.

5. Answer Yes to the "Do you want to redefine" question.

6. The entry will be updated.

Deleting AutoCorrect Entries

To delete an AutoCorrect entry, follow these steps:

1. Open the AutoCorrect dialog box (Tools ➤ AutoCorrect).

2. Select the victim.

3. Click the Delete button.

4. The entry will be deleted.

Automatic Correction

In addition to fixing things as you type them, you can run the AutoCorrect feature at any time to inspect and clean up documents. Use the AutoCorrect dialog box to choose the options you wish Word to use, as shown here:

Insert Commands

Word's Insert menu has a number of useful choices that can do things similar to AutoText, AutoCorrect, and the now-defunct Word Glossary command. While you'll find more about this topic in Chapter 32, let's take a quick look at a few of the commands here.

Insert ➤ Date and Time

The Insert ➤ Date and Time command gives you a wide choice of date and time formats, as shown here.

If you check the Insert As Field box, Word for Windows will place a date or time field in your document. Then Word for Windows will update the date and time whenever you *print* your document. See Chapter 32 for details.

Insert ➤ File

The Insert ➤ File command lets you place the entire contents of any file into the open document. It places the file at the insertion point. Word for Windows can insert other Word documents, documents created by many other word processors, graphic files, plain text files, and more. When in doubt, give it a try.

The Insert ➤ File command brings up the File dialog box. Just pick the file of interest and click OK. Word will insert it. You may need to reformat it after insertion.

 TIP Save your work before inserting files, just in case.

Insert ➤ Picture

The Insert ➤ Picture command brings up the Insert Picture dialog box, shown in Figure 17.6.

Part
3

Time Savers

Choose drives and folders from here

This will place the selected graphic at the insertion point

Figure 17.6   Preview and choose the picture you wish to insert.

Use the Insert Picture dialog box to preview pictures. When you click OK, a full-sized version of the selected graphic will be pasted at the insertion point in your current Word document.

Crop, resize, and move the graphic if necessary using the techniques you learned in Chapter 5.

Insert ➤ Field

The Insert ➤ Field command lets you insert fields that can automate many aspects of document preparation. For instance, the FileName field will insert the file's name in your document. A *field* is an object in your document that inserts information. With fields turned off, you will simply see their results; however, if you turn fields on in the View tab of the Options dialog box, you will see the field instructions themselves.

You'll learn a lot more about fields in Chapter 32.

The Spike

There are several other ways you can move things around in Word. Document scraps (discussed next) are ubiquitous to Windows 95 applications. Word itself, though, has a built-in tool for cutting and pasting, called the Spike. The Spike is a special, preset AutoText entry. You use it to collect a series of selections into a list and then insert them all in one place, in the order that you "spiked" them.

To cut something (text or graphics) to the Spike, first select it in any of the normal ways. Then press Ctrl+F3. The selection will disappear. Repeat this process as often as you like to stack up a series of selections in the Spike.

There are two ways to insert the Spike's contents into a document. You can insert the contents and clear the Spike at the same time, or you can insert the contents without clearing the Spike. Use the latter method when you want to insert the Spike contents elsewhere or continue adding items to the Spike.

Insert and Clear the Spike

To insert the contents of the Spike and clear it out at the same time, first place the insertion point where you want the contents to appear. Then press Ctrl+Shift+F3. The contents will appear in the order that you spiked them, each as a separate paragraph (separated by paragraph marks).

Insert without Clearing the Spike

To insert the contents of the Spike without clearing it, place the insertion point at the beginning of a line or between two spaces. Then type **spike** and press F3 or Alt+Ctrl+V. The contents will appear in the order you spiked them, each as a separate paragraph.

Spike Summary

So, just to review:

To Do This...	...Type This
Add a selection to the Spike	Ctrl+F3
Insert and clear the Spike	Ctrl+Shift+F3
Insert but don't clear the Spike	**spike** *and then* F3

Document Scraps

Windows now lets you place scraps of documents on the Windows desktop. Scraps are bits of text or graphics that you have copied and placed in files on the desktop. The nice part is, this feature is a no-brainer. Scraps can be pasted into other documents or programs. You can think of scrap documents as automatically saved Clipboard files. But you don't lose one scrap when you save another, unlike Clipboard entries; also, since scraps are saved to files, you can move them around and put them in folders on disk for later use.

NOTE   Only programs that support OLE can make and use document scraps.

Creating Document Scraps

Creating a document scrap couldn't be easier. All you do is select the text, graphics, or other data you want to save. Then just drag it out to the desktop. Windows will then make a new file right on the desktop. You can rename, delete, or move the scrap as you see fit.

TIP You can view a document scrap simply by double-clicking on it. Once it is open, you can select text and edit it just like any other document.

Inserting Document Scraps

Once you have a scrap or two on the desktop, inserting the contents of a scrap is quite straightforward. Just click on the scrap and drag to where you want it inserted. A copy of the scrap's contents will be inserted in your destination document, leaving the original scrap untouched. This is handy, because you can reuse a scrap over and over.

Scraps vs. the Spike

No doubt the advent of Windows 95 will spark a heated debate about which is better, scraps or the Spike. Probably the Spike is best for cases where you want to keep adding little bits of information, while scraps are better for information that you wouldn't want to lose. Experiment. Be brave!

Tips and Strategies

Here are some tips for using the time-saving features discussed in this chapter:

▶ In my humble opinion, you should use AutoText, the Insert commands, and Templates for inserting things; use AutoCorrect only for its named function—correcting typos. If you *do* use AutoCorrect for heavy-duty boilerplate insertions, be certain that the names are uncommon and distinct.

▶ Set up keyboard shortcuts for regularly used AutoText entries.

Part 3

Time Savers

▶ Consider adding buttons to a toolbar for the AutoText command itself and for the really frequent entries. Visit the Toolbars tab in the Customize dialog box (Tools ➤ Customize), and scroll to the AutoText category. (See Chapter 36 for details.)

Next stop, Word's Thesaurus, where you'll learn how to find just the *right* word.

Chapter 18

Using the Thesaurus to Find the Right Words

FAST TRACK

highlight the word or phrase you wish to replace, or position the insertion point in a word, and then choose <u>T</u>ools ➤ <u>T</u>hesaurus. If you haven't chosen a word, Word for Windows will choose the closest one. Clicking on a meaning in the Meanings list displays related synonyms in the Synonyms scrollable list. Clicking on a particular synonym places it in the editable Replace with Synonyms area of the Thesaurus dialog box. If you don't like any of the choices, clicking Cancel will close the thesaurus window and take you back to your unchanged document.

English is a rich language. There are many ways to say the same thing, yet we all tend to use a few words and phrases repeatedly. Word's *thesaurus* can help you add interest and texture to your prose. It gives you lists of synonyms (words that mean the same thing), and then lets you quickly replace your original word with the alternative of your choice. Sometimes Word for Windows can offer antonyms (words with opposite meanings). Word's thesaurus also contains common phrases like *in consideration of* and *at rest*.

The Thesaurus command lives on the Tools menu and its keyboard shortcut is Shift+F7.

 TIP If you frequently use the thesaurus, consider adding a Thesaurus *button* to your toolbar. It's easy. Chapter 36 shows you how to assign any item to a toolbar button.

Looking Up Words and Phrases

To use the thesaurus, highlight the word or phrase you wish to replace, or position the insertion point in a word, and then choose Tools ➤ Thesaurus. A dialog box will appear, similar to the one shown in Figure 18.1.

 TIP If you don't select a word and the insertion point is not in a word, the thesaurus feature will pick the word closest to the insertion point.

If you haven't done so already, Word for Windows will highlight the word in your document and place it in the Thesaurus dialog box next to Looked Up. This word (or phrase) is referred to as the *original* word.

If your original word has more than one meaning, the various meanings and their parts of speech will appear in the Meanings scrollable list. Clicking on a meaning in the Meanings list displays related synonyms in the Synonyms scrollable list. In Figure 18.1 the thesaurus offers five meanings for *paper*. Clicking on *newspaper* displays its synonyms.

Clicking on a particular synonym for *newspaper* (*tabloid*, for instance) places the synonym in the editable Replace With Synonym area of the Thesaurus dialog box. If you don't like any of the choices, clicking Cancel or pressing Esc will close the thesaurus window and take you back to your unchanged document.

Figure 18.1 *Word's thesaurus suggests synonyms and antonyms for highlighted words or phrases.*

Replacing Words and Phrases

After exploring the various potential replacement words or phrases suggested by Word for Windows, you can replace your original word by following these steps:

1. Highlight the suggested replacement you like best. It will appear in the Replace With Synonym box.

2. Click the Replace button in the thesaurus window. Word will replace the highlighted text in your document with the contents of the Replace with box; then the thesaurus window will disappear.

3. If you don't like the results, the Edit ➤ Undo Thesaurus command is available, provided you act immediately.

Sometimes if you highlight a phrase, Word for Windows can suggest synonyms. Try it by highlighting the words *at rest*, for example. Watch carefully whenever you use the thesaurus to replace highlighted phrases, because it doesn't always do what you expect:

Related Words and Phrases

Frequently, Word's thesaurus will not contain an exact match for your original word. This can happen if you've misspelled a word. In that case, you will probably see an alphabetical list of words in place of the Meanings list. Pick the correct word from the list or return to your document and correct the spelling error and then try the Tools ➤ Thesaurus command again.

You will also have trouble matching certain tenses of words. For instance, if you attempt to replace *ambled,* Word for Windows will tell you to seek related words, as shown in Figure 18.2, because it contains the word *amble* but not *ambled.*

Clicking on a related word in the scrollable Related Word list will place it in the Replace With box. For instance, double-clicking on the Related Words choice in the list on the left will reveal a list of related words on the right, as shown in Figure 18.3. Once you have the related word in the Replace With box, click on the Look Up button to find synonyms and antonyms.

When you find a related word (*meander,* for instance), click on it to move it to the Replace With box; then edit the word to suit your needs before clicking Replace. For instance, you'd probably want to add *ed* to *meander* in our example.

Figure 18.2 **You may need to use a related word in the thesaurus and then edit it.**

Figure 18.3 **With the related word moved to the Replace With box, click Look Up to peruse a list of synonyms.**

Restoring the Original Word

Clicking on the Looked Up list in the Thesaurus dialog box will let you go back to earlier choices. The top of the list contains the original word. Click to restore it. You can also use Undo to restore your original word.

Finding Antonyms

Frequently, Word for Windows can help you find antonyms. When they are available, the word *Antonyms* appears at the bottom of the scrollable Meanings list. Click on Antonyms to display a list of them on the right side of the thesaurus window. As you can see in Figure 18.4, the name of that list changes from Synonym to Antonym, and the list contains potential antonyms for the word in the Replace With box.

Figure 18.4   The thesaurus can suggest antonyms, too.

Spelling Help from the Thesaurus

While Word's thesaurus doesn't actually contain definitions, you can sometimes use it to help pick the appropriate spelling of confusing words like *which* and *witch* or *weather* and *whether*. Look up the words in question and compare synonyms to help you pick the right spelling. Figure 18.5 illustrates this.

Figure 18.5   Use the thesaurus to eliminate confusion over words like weather and whether.

Exploring the Thesaurus

Here are some guidelines for exploring the thesaurus:

▶ It is possible to really meander around in the thesaurus! A single click on any word (either in the left or right lists) places a new word in the Replace with box. Then you can click on Look Up and go from there.

▶ Double-clicking on a synonym in the Meanings area places that word in both the Replace With and Meanings spaces.

▶ Double-clicking on a Meanings word places just that word in the Replace With space.

Part
3

Time Savers

Chapter 19

Checking Spelling, Word Counts, and Grammar

FAST TRACK

start the Spelling tool with the F7 shortcut or by picking Tools ➤ Spelling. Unless you've selected only a portion of your document to check, Word for Windows scans down, beginning at the insertion point, and will ask if you want to go back to the top of the document to continue checking, if necessary. The Spelling tool looks for words that it cannot find in its open dictionaries. When it spots a word that it can't match, Word highlights the questionable characters, scrolls the document so that you can see the problem word in context, and offers you a number of choices.

type a replacement in the highlighted Change To box and press ↵ or click the Change button. Word will replace the problem text with the new text you have typed in the Change To box and then continue spell checking. To change the word throughout the document that you are checking, click Change All instead of pressing ↵ or clicking Change.

To create a new custom dictionary 443

visit the Spelling tab in the Options dialog box either by choosing
Tools ➤ _Options_ or by clicking the Options button in the Spelling
dialog box. Click New to create a new dictionary. You will be
prompted for a dictionary name. Type a new name containing up
to 32 characters. Open the folder where you want to store the
dictionary (it is best to keep custom dictionaries with the main
dictionary). Click Save.

To count the number of words in your document 446

choose the _Tools_ ➤ _Word_ Count command. Word will scan an
entire document or just text you've selected, counting pages,
words, characters, paragraphs, and lines. If you place an X in the
appropriate box, it will include footnote and endnote text when
counting.

To check grammar and style 446

choose _Tools_ ➤ _Grammar_. Unless you select a portion of your
document, Word will attempt to check the whole thing. Working
from the insertion point, Word will highlight a portion of your prose
(usually a sentence) and evaluate it. There may be a slight delay.
If Word spots questionable spellings, you will be given the opportunity to correct them or tell Word to ignore them. Once spelling
issues have been dealt with, Word will use its Grammar dialog box
to point out questionable style and grammar issues. The text being
considered is listed in the scrolling Sentence box.

To accept Word's suggested changes 448

double-click on its suggestion or click the Change button to apply
the change. When Word is unable to make changes by itself, the
Change button will be dim. When the Grammar tool finishes
checking, it will tell you so. Use the Cancel button to exit sooner.
If you have the Statistics option turned on, you'll see a readability
report.

new **W**ord provides a powerful Spelling tool that lets you check the spelling of an entire document, including headers, footers, and hidden text. A great new feature of Word is that you can choose to have the spellchecker run automatically. If you elect to do this, Word will spellcheck your documents as you type them, flagging unfamiliar words with red, squiggly underline. You can run a regular spelling check later to correct or ignore these words, or you can actually fix them "on the fly." Simply right-click on the word in question to see a list of possible replacements:

was bubbling over like a glass of the fizzy stuff. They must have been drinking a lot of it, too, 'c fishing them out of the Seine every ten mi

> fizz
> **fuzzy**
> **frizzy**
> **dizzy**
> **tizzy**

With all of its romance and intrigue, Rosc finds Paris to be a provincial city at heart. about Paris being so cosmopolitan and int it's really just a frightened young city tryi If you want a real city, you have to go to Cannes."

> Ignore All
> Add

> Spelling...

If one of the replacement words is correct, just click on it. Otherwise, you can tell Word to ignore all future occurrences of the word or to add it to the dictionary. If you're feeling spry, you can even bring up the full-featured Spelling dialog box.

TIP If you *absolutely* hate the automatic spellchecker, you can easily disengage it. Go to the Options dialog box (Tools ➤ Options) and click to bring the Spelling tab forward. Then remove the check from Automatic Spell Checking.

Using the automatic spellchecker is probably the safest and quickest way to ensure that your spelling is perfect, but if you prefer to do a single spelling check of your whole document at the end, you can do that instead. The rest of the spell-check information of this chapter is devoted to using the full-featured Spelling dialog box to check your documents. Note that the automatic spellchecker and the Spelling dialog box both use the same dictionary.

Unlike the printed dictionary on your desk, Word's checker does not contain definitions. It does not consider words in context. While it knows that *two*, *too*, and *to* are all proper spellings, it cannot warn you of their improper use. For instance, Word's Spelling tool would not object to the sentence *She went two the bank too get a to dollar bill*.

What it *can* do is offer suggested spellings with uncanny accuracy. Misspellings are usually replaced with just a mouse click or two. You can add and edit your own custom dictionaries, which might contain proper nouns, technical terms, and other specialized words or numbers. You'll learn how to use all of these features in this chapter.

We'll also explore the Tools ➤ Word Count command. It's a way for authors to quickly determine the number of characters, words, lines, and paragraphs in documents and footnotes.

Finally, we'll look at the Grammar tool. It can help you spot many common writing errors and evaluate your document's readability.

Setting Up the Spelling Checker

The first time you use the Spelling tool it's a good idea to ensure that it is set to use the proper dictionary—English (US) in the United States. Here are the steps:

1. Choose Tools ➤ Language.

2. Scroll to the desired language—probably English (US)—and select it by double-clicking or clicking once on the name and once on OK.

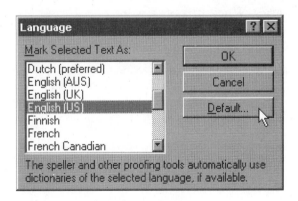

Part
3

Time Savers

3. Click the Default button.

4. Answer Yes to the confirmation.

5. Click on OK.

> **WARNING**   You can format certain text (foreign language or technical, for example) as "no proof" text, which means Word will skip it during spelling checks. If you don't instruct Word to use a dictionary, though, you might think Word has spellchecked your document and found nothing wrong; unlike earlier versions, Word for Windows 95 does not inform you of this.

> **TIP**   You can assign different languages to different templates if you frequently use more than one language.

Checking Spelling

Start the spelling checker with the F7 shortcut, the toolbar button, or by picking Tools ➤ Spelling. The Spelling dialog box appears, as shown in Figure 19.1.

Unless you've selected only a portion of your document to check, Word scans the whole thing, beginning at the insertion point, and will ask if you want to go back to the top of the document to continue checking, if necessary.

The Spelling tool looks for words that it cannot find in its open dictionaries. When it spots a word that it can't match, Word highlights the questionable characters, scrolls the document so that you can see the problem word in context, and offers you a number of choices.

> **TIP**   The checker will confine itself to single words or phrases if you select items of interest before issuing the Spelling command. Of course, if you have automatic spelling enabled, right-clicking on a flagged word will offer you some choices.

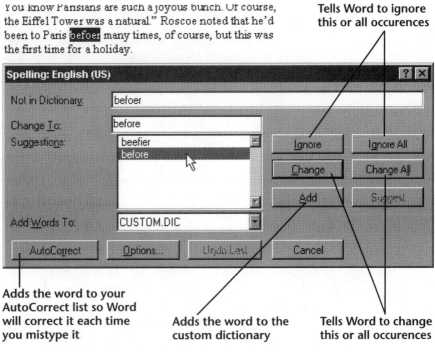

You know Parisians are such a joyous bunch. Of course, the Eiffel Tower was a natural." Roscoe noted that he'd been to Paris befoer many times, of course, but this was the first time for a holiday.

Tells Word to ignore this or all occurences

Adds the word to your AutoCorrect list so Word will correct it each time you mistype it

Adds the word to the custom dictionary

Tells Word to change this or all occurences

Figure 19.1 The spelling checker lets you pick suggested replacement words, type your own corrections, ignore unrecognized words, or add words to your custom dictionaries.

Typing Your Own Changes

If you want to change a misspelled word only once:

1. Type a replacement in the highlighted Change To box.

2. Press ↵ or click the Change button. Word will replace the problem text with the new text you have typed in the Change To box and then continue spellchecking.

To change the word throughout the document that you are checking, click Change All instead of pressing ↵ or clicking Change. If the new word you've typed is something you want Word to recognize in all of your documents, see the section "Custom or User Dictionaries," later in this chapter.

Part 3

Time Savers

Word's Suggested Changes

If you have suggestions enabled (check the Always Suggest option in the Spelling tab of the Options dialog box), Word will usually list one or more possible spellings, placing what it thinks is the best guess in the Change To box. If the default is not enabled, you can always ask for suggestions by clicking Suggest. Other suggestions, if any, will be listed in the scrollable Suggestions box. This may take a moment. You'll know Word has finished looking for alternative suggestions when you see either (End of Suggestions) or (No Suggestions) in the Suggestions list.

If you agree with Word's best guess, simply click the Change button to change this occurrence or click Change All to change this and all succeeding occurrences of the word. The Spelling tool will replace the word and continue examining your document.

Word's best guess is usually, but not always, right, as you saw in Figure 19.1. If one of the alternative suggestions is correct (the word *before* in Figure 19.1), simply double-click on the desired word to replace the misspelled word or click on it once to move it to the Change To box, then click the Change or Change All button as necessary. Sometimes, however, Word's guesses will be bizarre or comical (e.g., *broccoli* for *Berkeley*), so be sure you read the replacement text carefully.

Overruling Suggestions

Sometimes Word won't make correct suggestions, or you might want to correct the problem yourself without retyping the entire word or phrase. For instance, Word may spot two run-together words like the ones shown in Figure 19.2.

When it has no suggestions, Word moves the problem text to the Change To box where you can edit it yourself (place a space between the two words, for instance).

Ignoring Flagged Words

Sometimes Word will spot a word that is properly spelled, but that isn't in its open dictionaries. Proper nouns, technical jargon, and typesetting codes are examples.

Figure 19.2   Problem text can be edited right in the Change to box.

If you want Word to ignore the text only once, click the Ignore button. Word will leave the word or other text string as you typed it and continue spellchecking. To ignore the word throughout the document you are checking, click Ignore All. (If the word is something you want to ignore in all of your documents, you may want to add it to a custom dictionary.)

NOTE   The Spelling tool's Ignore All button ignores words for your *entire* Word session. That is to say, if you tell Word to ignore a word in the morning, it will ignore the word all day in each document you check, unless you exit Word or use the Reset Ignore All button in the Spelling tab (of the Options dialog box), as shown in Figure 19.3.

Custom or User Dictionaries

Most of the words used by the Spelling tool are located in a dictionary that comes with your Word program. In the United States, Word is shipped with a dictionary called the US English Dictionary. It is kept in the Commands folder. You cannot make changes to this dictionary.

You can, however, maintain one or more of your own *custom* dictionaries. Word checks only open dictionaries. The more dictionaries you have open, the slower spellchecking will be.

Figure 19.3   Reach the Spelling tab either by choosing Tools ➤ Options or by clicking the Options button in the Spelling dialog box.

The Standard Custom Dictionary

When you install Word, the installation program places an empty Custom Dictionary in your Commands folder. The default name for the dictionary is Custom.dic. It is opened and used whenever you spellcheck unless you instruct Word otherwise. This is where you will want to keep most proper nouns, trademark names, etc.

Word will place words in the Custom Dictionary whenever you click the Add button while spellchecking. (The first time you add a word, you may be asked to create a custom dictionary.) Normally, Word places a dictionary called Custom.dic in the Proof subfolder. You can overrule this default use of the Custom Dictionary by using the drop-down Add Words To list to specify a different dictionary.

Custom dictionaries handle capitalization as follows. If you add a word to a dictionary as all lowercase, it will be recognized later, regardless of whether it is typed as all lowercase, all uppercase, or with an initial capital letter. If you enter a word with only the first letter capitalized, Word will recognize the word when it later appears in all caps or with a leading cap, but will question the word if it is all lowercase. Unusual capitalizations, like *AutoCAD*, will be questioned unless they are stored in the dictionary exactly as they should be.

Creating Additional Custom Dictionaries

If you work on unusual projects that involve technical jargon, typesetting codes, etc., you might want to create one or more additional specially named custom dictionaries, which you can turn on or off in the Custom Dictionaries dialog box, reached from the Spelling tab of the Options dialog box. To create a new custom dictionary, follow these steps:

1. Visit the Spelling tab in the Options dialog box either by choosing Tools ➤ Options or by clicking the Options button in the Spelling dialog box.

2. Click the Custom Dictionaries button to bring up the Custom Dictionaries dialog box, as shown in Figure 19.4.

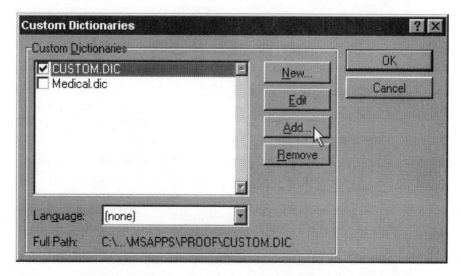

Figure 19.4   You can add and edit custom dictionaries in the Custom Dictionaries dialog box.

Part
3

Time Savers

3. Click New to create a new dictionary. You will be prompted for a dictionary name.

4. Type a new name containing up to 32 characters.

5. Open the folder where you want to store the dictionary (it is best to keep custom dictionaries with the main dictionary).

6. Click Save.

Opening and Closing Custom Dictionaries

To be available to the Spelling tool, a dictionary must be open. Place check marks next to both custom dictionaries in the dialog box to make both open and available for the Spelling tool to use. Click in the box next to the desired dictionary to open or close it. A check mark means it's open.

To open dictionaries that are not in the folder containing the main dictionary, click the Add button. Show Word where the desired dictionary is, using standard Windows folder-navigation techniques.

Editing Custom Dictionaries

To add items to a custom dictionary, click Add when the Spelling tool encounters a word of interest or create a separate Word document containing all of the words you want to add. Spellcheck this document, adding each unrecognized word.

If you accidentally add a word to a custom dictionary, it is a good idea to delete it, as extra words mean more searching time during your spelling checks. And if you add misspelled words, they will no longer be challenged by the checker. Removing words from a custom dictionary is slightly more involved than adding them.

1. Choose the dictionary you wish to edit in the Custom Dictionaries dialog box, reached from the Spelling tab in the Options dialog box (Tools ➤ Options).

2. Click the Edit button.

3. If automatic spellchecking is on, a dialog box will appear, as shown in Figure 19.5, offering to let you edit the dictionary as a regular Word document but warning you that automatic spellchecking will be turned off. Click OK.

Figure 19.5 Word lets you edit custom dictionaries as Word documents. Click Edit in the Custom Dictionaries dialog box (reached from the Spelling tab of the Options dialog box).

Word will close all open dialog boxes and bring up the dictionary as a regular Word document.

4. Edit the dictionary.

5. Save it with the Save command (Ctrl+S).

TIP The Spelling tab provides other spelling options, which should be self-explanatory. Choose Help to learn more from Word's online help feature.

Speeding Up the Spelling Checker

Here are some tips for speeding up your spellchecking:

▶ Use that automatic checker, by golly!

▶ To do regular spellchecks, place the insertion point at the beginning of your document (Ctrl+Home) and check in Normal view.

▶ If you are a good speller with a slow computer and are mostly looking for typos, either use the automatic checker or consider turning off suggestions to speed checking in the regular Spelling dialog box. (Visit the Spelling tab in the Options dialog box reached with Tools ▶ Options.)

▶ Keep custom dictionaries fairly small (one to two hundred words, perhaps).

▶ Split larger custom dictionaries into smaller ones by categories that match different kinds of work you do (legal, technical, etc.). Open just the one(s) you need.

Part
3

Time Savers

The Word Count Command

The Word Count command is found in the Tools menu. Simply choose the command to start the process. Figure 19.6 shows typical results.

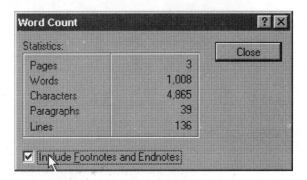

Figure 19.6   *The Word Count feature also counts characters, lines, paragraphs, and pages, both in the main text and in footnotes, if you so desire.*

TIP   There are more occasions for counting words than you might realize. If you are copyfitting and have to write a specified number of words, for example, this can be very important. And how many times on application forms have you seen the words "Write a 300–500 word essay on..."?

Tools ➤ Word Count will scan an entire document or just text you've selected. It counts pages, words, characters, paragraphs, and lines. If you place a check in the appropriate box, it will include footnote and endnote text when counting. It does *not* count words in headers and footers. Also, you must display invisible text to include it in the count.

Checking Grammar and Style

Word's Grammar tool evaluates style and points out many, but not all, grammatical errors. It can often suggest changes and even make some of them for you. Word uses collections of rules when analyzing your documents. You can turn off specific rules that annoy you or cramp your style. Word will explain and demonstrate the rules for you.

Statistics and readability indexes are created at the end of a grammar-checking session. These help you determine whether the writing style is appropriate for your audience.

Because the Grammar tool needs to work with properly spelled documents, it sometimes activates Word's Spelling tool when it encounters unfamiliar words.

Word is not a complete replacement for a human editor. For instance, it will not catch things like missing periods at the end of sentences or double spaces between words.

The fact that Word considers parts of speech when checking grammar might make you believe that it understands what you've written. This is not the case. For instance, the nonsense phrase *Eye sea sum tins knot write hear* passes the grammar check successfully.

None the less (oops, Word prefers *Nonetheless*), the checker will help you spot many common problems and can help you polish your style.

TIP If you never use the Grammar tool, save some disk space and RAM by reinstalling Word without it. See Appendix A.

You may want to save your document just before grammar checking or run the check on a copy of your masterpiece. While grammar and style changes are often reversible with Undo, this is not always the case. Also be sure that you've specified a language for proofing as described at the beginning of this chapter.

To check grammar and style:

1. Save your work and move the insertion point to the beginning of your document.

2. Choose <u>T</u>ools ➤ <u>G</u>rammar. Unless you select a portion of your document, Word will attempt to check the whole thing.

3. Working from the insertion point, Word will highlight a portion of your prose (usually a sentence) and evaluate it. There may be a slight delay. If Word spots questionable spellings, you will be given the opportunity to correct them or tell Word to ignore them.

4. Once spelling issues have been dealt with, Word will use its Grammar dialog box to point out questionable style and grammar issues. The text being considered is listed in the scrolling Sentence box. Suggestions and

observations are made in the scrolling Suggestions box. For example, in Figure 19.7, the Grammar tool doesn't like *he'd*.

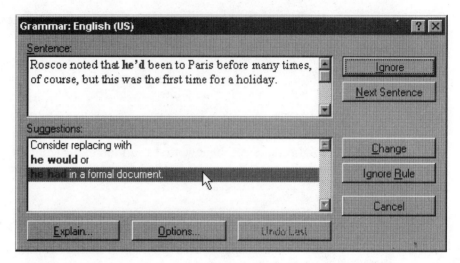

Figure 19.7 **Word finds this document not wordy enough for purposes of formality.**

Accepting Word's Suggestions

In Figure 19.7, Word is suggesting *he would* as a replacement for *he'd*. When Word makes specific suggestions like this, you can double-click on its suggestion or click the Change button to apply the change. This example shows that when your meaning is ambiguous (to Word anyway), it might make suggestions that are wrong. If the first suggestion were taken here, the sentence would read *Roscoe noted that he would been to Paris...* which is nonsense to everyone but Word. When Word is unable to make changes by itself, the Change button will be dim.

When the Grammar tool finishes checking, it will tell you so. Use the Cancel button to exit sooner. If you have the statistics option turned on, you'll see a readability report.

Making Manual Changes

Many of the problems the checker spots need your intervention. To make manual changes, type right in the Grammar window's Sentence box.

Click the Change button when done. The Grammar tool will make the change and continue checking.

Ignoring Suggestions

The Ignore button in the Grammar dialog box instructs Word to ignore the current occurrence of a problem but will not prevent the Grammar tool from pointing out similar problems in the future.

You can skip to the next sentence without making changes to the current one by clicking on the Next Sentence button. Clicking Ignore Rule in the Grammar dialog box tells Word to stop using the current rule with the current document. For example, to stop reminders about passive voice, click the Ignore Rule button the first time Word points out a passive construction.

To turn off passive-voice checking for all your projects, turn off the rule (called Passive Verbs Usage) in the Grammar tab of the Options dialog box, as described next.

Changing Preferences

You can turn rules on and off by clicking on the Customize Settings button in the Customize Grammar Settings dialog box, reached from the Grammar tab in the Options dialog box, as shown in Figure 19.8.

Here you can fine-tune Word's grammar pickiness. Rules are listed in two categories—Style and Grammar. Pick a list to scroll by clicking on the appropriate button. Check marks next to a rule mean the rule will be enforced. Clicking near a check mark toggles it on and off. For more information about a rule, highlight it and click on the Explain button:

> **Grammar Explanation** ✕
>
> **Rule: Gender-Specific Expressions**
> These rules flag gender-specific expressions, many of which describe occupations or professions. For example, one rule will flag a sentence like 'We are planning to hire two anchormen for the 11 o'clock news,' because 'anchormen' is a gender-specific expression; it suggests the terms 'anchor', 'newscaster', and 'commentator' as alternatives.
> Unlike the terms in the Sexist rule set, gender-specific expressions do not necessarily have negative connotations like condescension or hostility. However, some people consider the use of gender-specific terms to be sexist, and this rule set exists to make it possible for you to replace them with gender-neutral alternatives if you choose.

*Figure 19.8 **Reach the Customize Grammar Settings dialog box from the Grammar tab of the Options dialog box (choose Tools ➤ Options or click Options in the Grammar window).***

Document Statistics

There are liars, damned liars, and statistics. Word can provide the latter, as illustrated in Figure 19.9. Document statistics appear after the Grammar tool has finished scanning your document.

The Readability feature will count words, paragraphs, and sentences, then calculate the average number of characters per word and similar trivia. Several readability statistics are computed, including a count of passive sentences, Flesch Reading Ease, the Flesch-Kincaid Grade Level, the Coleman-Liau Grade Level, and the Bormuth Grade Level. Click the Help button in the Readability Statistics window for a brief explanation of these statistics.

Readability Statistics ☒

Counts:

Words	1,005
Characters	4,873
Paragraphs	37
Sentences	62

Averages:

Sentences per Paragraph	1.7
Words per Sentence	16.2
Characters per Word	4.6

Readability:

Passive Sentences	4%
Flesch Reading Ease	59.4
Flesch-Kincaid Grade Level	8.5
Coleman-Liau Grade Level	12.0
Bormuth Grade Level	9.8

[OK]   [Help]

Figure 19.9   **Word can try to quantify your writing style.**

The Grade Level measurements assign a (US public school) grade level. The higher the index, the tougher the reading. Imagine how much better Shakespeare might have been, given tools like these. To write passively, or not. That is the question.

Part
3

Time Savers

Chapter 20

Finding
and Replacing

FAST TRACK

Every contemporary word-processing product has a way to quickly locate and replace specific text strings (collections of words, numbers, and other characters). Lawyers use these features (sometimes called *global replace features*) to do things like finding each occurrence of *Marion Morrison* in a contract and replacing it with *John Wayne*.

Some typists enter shorthand or acronyms for lengthy items when they draft. Then, while polishing the document, they replace the shorthand with the actual text. For instance, you might initially type *DRD* in the draft of a government document, then have Word find and replace each occurrence of *DRD* with *Department of Redundancy Department*.

TIP If you do a lot of this, consider using Word's AutoCorrect feature instead. It will replace acronyms as you type them.

Word provides two separate commands, called <u>E</u>dit ➤ <u>F</u>ind (Ctrl+F) and <u>E</u>dit ➤ R<u>e</u>place (Ctrl+H). Find is really just an evolutionary predecessor to Replace.

A slick new feature of Word is that Find and Replace can both search for *word forms*. What this means is that you can, for instance, search for all tense and person forms of verbs. So instead of having to make separate searches for *fly*, *flew*, and *flies*, you just search for *fly* and check the Find All Word Forms box. Replace takes this one step farther. You can now replace words *with their proper forms!* This is so cool it's positively scary. If you want to replace all occurrences of any form of the verb *to fly* with the verb *to walk*, you just type **fly** in the Find what box, **walk** in the Replace with box, and check Find All Word Forms. Word will replace *fly* with *walk*, *flew* with *walked*, *flies* with *walks*, etc. Now who could ask for more than that?!

With Word you can search for, and then replace or remove, special characters like paragraph marks, optional hyphens, or footnote-reference marks.

A form of wild-card searching is permitted, letting you insert question marks in search requests to work-around minor spelling variations. Asking Word to find **Sm?th**, for instance, would find both *Smith* and *Smyth*. You can search for ranges of numbers using a similar technique. Word's designers refer to this process as searching for *unspecified letters* and *unspecified digits*.

Occasionally, Word's find and replace features can be used to reformat documents. You might, for instance, search for all occurrences of two consecutive spaces and replace them with a single space. But Word can do much more than that. The Find and Replace commands can do the following:

▶ Help you find all or selected paragraphs formatted with a particular style and apply a different style.

▶ Remove things simply by telling Word to search for the item you wish to delete and replace it with nothing.

▶ Search your entire document or selected portions. You specify the direction of the search (up or down).

The Art of Finding

The Find feature helps you quickly locate text, formats, special characters, and combinations thereof. It lets you search selected parts of your document or the whole enchilada. Simple find requests can locate text regardless of format. It's also easy to ask Word to search for very specific things, like occurrences of the word *Liberace* formatted in bold, blue, 24-point Playbill.

You need not limit your searches to text. You can look for section marks, graphics, paragraph marks, and more. When using the Find command (as opposed to Replace), Word finds what you've requested, then scrolls to the found item and its surrounding text without modifying anything.

You must click in the document window to work with the found item. You can leave the Find dialog box out on your screen as you work, flipping between it and your document window. Figure 20.1 shows the Find dialog box.

Here's a general overview of the Find dialog box. (Details will follow.) To do a search:

1. Choose Edit ➤ Find.

2. Specify text and special characters (if any) to find.

Find What: B B King

Part 3

Time Savers

Figure 20.1   The Find dialog box (Edit ➤ Find) lets you specify search criteria.

3. Specify formatting characteristics (if any) to find.

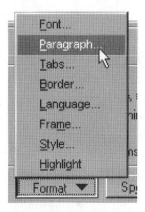

4. Tell Word where to search and in which direction.

5. Use the Special menu to search for things like section breaks, paragraph marks, etc.

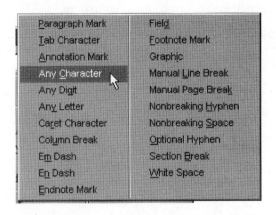

6. Check off any special search requests like Match Case or Find All Word Forms.

7. Click Find Next to start the search.

8. When Word finds what you want, return to the document.

9. To find again, press Enter on the numeric pad (if you're still in the document) or click on the Find Next button in the dialog box.

Like any good computer program, Word takes your requests quite literally, so you will need to understand each Find option fully to locate exactly what you want.

For example, if Word searches using the criteria specified in Figure 20.1, it will find *B B King* and *b b king*, but not *B.B. King*, *BB King*, or *Burger King*.

There are ways to get Word to find each of these text strings, of course. Just realize that you may need to carefully formulate and test your search strategy. In some cases, you will need to perform multiple searches to find similar but subtly different text strings.

Word will automatically search in headers and footers. For multisection documents, you may need to open and search headers and footers in each section. If your search plans include things like paragraph marks or hidden text, the hidden text must be visible on the screen.

 TIP   Consider proofing your document or at least running the spelling checker before important, major searches. If you spell *banana* correctly six times and incorrectly once, Word will find only six of your seven bananas.

Finding Text

Choose Edit ➤ Find or use the Ctrl+F shortcut. Move to the text area of the Find What box and type enough text (a maximum of 255 characters) for an accurate, unambiguous search. For instance, suppose you wanted to find the word *man*. Entering **man** in Find What would cause Word to find the words *man, Man, Mansfield, reprimand, manhole,* and *man* at the end of a sentence (followed by a period, question mark, etc.).

Placing a space after **man** in your Find request would eliminate the unwanted *Mansfield, reprimand,* and *manhole,* but would also prevent you from finding *man* at the ends of sentences because periods, question marks, and such are not spaces.

That's the reason for the Match Whole Word Only check box in the Find dialog box. If you type **man** (no space) in the Find What area and check Find Whole Words Only, Word will locate only *man, Man,* and *man* at the end of sentences.

The Match Case check box instructs Word to look for exact capitalization matches. If you type **postscript** in the Find What area and check Match Case, Word will not find *POSTSCRIPT, PostScript,* or even *Postscript* at the beginning of sentences.

Extra spaces, nonbreaking spaces, and forced page breaks can also get in the way of searches. See the section "White Space" later in this chapter to see how to work around this.

Finding Special Characters

The Special drop-down list is a convenient way to enter certain special characters like tab marks, nonbreaking spaces, etc., when constructing a search request. Place the insertion point in the Find What box where you want the special character to go, and choose the desired character from the drop-down list.

Find requests can combine regular text and special characters. For instance, you could ask Word to search for occurrences of *Bob* followed by two tab marks. Many of the special characters in the drop-down list are self-explanatory. Let's look more closely at the ones that are not. Some are extremely useful.

White Space

Here's one to keep you awake nights. Suppose you are searching for two words together, like *Microsoft Corporation*. Suppose further that sometimes you used nonbreaking spaces to separate the two words. Other times you've just typed regular spaces. Occasionally, you typed two spaces between the words by mistake. Unless you use Word's White Space feature, you will not find the occurrences of *Microsoft Corporation* containing nonbreaking spaces or two spaces!

So, to do it right, insert Word's White Space special character in your search string. In our example, you'd start by typing **Microsoft** in the Find What box. Then, without touching the spacebar, choose White Space from the Special menu. The White Space code (^w) will appear next to *Microsoft*. Type **Corporation**. Your finished search string would be *Microsoft^wCorporation*. That should do it.

Any Letter

The Any Letter character lets you overcome some nasty problems too. Suppose you've used accented characters sometimes but not always. *La Cañada* and *La Canada* are not the same thing to Word when it searches. A search for *La Ca^*ada* will find both. Enter the Any Letter character from the Special drop-down menu the same way you entered the White Space character. You can type in these characters as well as choose them from the menu.

Any Digit

This special character will sometimes help you find numbers within ranges. It might be helpful for finding specific groups of part numbers or zip codes.

> **NOTE**   When using Any Digit once with the Replace feature, Word will find all occasions but only highlight the first two digits. So, when you use Replace, you must handle this differently. With the Find feature, it doesn't matter.

For instance, the search string **99^#** would find any number between 990 and 999. The specification **1^#** would find the combinations *101* and *11* in *111*. It would also find *1000*, but not *1,000*, because Word treats numbers as text, not numeric values, in searches like these. Commas confuse things. Ah, computers.

Finding Sound-Alikes

Word can attempt to locate words that sound alike but are spelled differently (*smith, smyth, but,* and *butt,* for instance). This is an imprecise art at best, because even things that are *spelled* the same *sound* different in various parts of any country. (If you doubt this, ask a Bostonian, New Yorker, and Chicagoan to pronounce the word *car.*)

At any rate, the Sounds Like option can sometimes round up useful word variations and misspellings.

It is difficult to predict whether a sound-alike will match the word you're looking for, as Word is less than forthcoming about how it applies criteria. Presumably, it distinguishes consonants from vowels and then compares parts of the word in question to a table of equivalent sounds. Search for *kerection* and you'll find *correction,* but search for *cerection* and you won't. Go figure.

The real purpose of this option is to cut you some slack if you're not absolutely sure about how to spell a word. If you're searching and finding nothing, but you're sure the word is in there somewhere, check Sounds Like and try again. (Then note how to spell the word for future reference.)

Pattern Matching

To perform advanced searches for combinations of things (such as both *bet* and *bat*), you use characters called *operators*. They will remind you of wild cards. For instance, to find either *bet* or *bat*, you would place **b?t** in your Find What box and check Use Pattern Matching. If you forget to check Use Pattern Matching, the results will not be what you expect. Here's the list of operators you can use with Word and what they help you do:

Operator	Lets You Find
?	A single character: **b?t** finds *bet* and *bat*.
*	Any string of characters: **b*d** finds *bed*, *befuddled*, and *blood*.
[characters]	Any of the characters in brackets: **b[eo]d** finds *bed* and *bod* but not *bid*.
[character–character]	Any character in the range: **b[a–i]d** finds *bed* and *bid* but not *bod*.
[!character]	Any single character except the one in brackets: **b[!i]d** finds *bed* and *bod* but not *bid*.
[!characters]	Any single character except the ones in brackets: **b[!ie]d** finds *bad* and *bud* but not *bid* or *bed*.
[!character–character]	Any single character *except* those in the specified range: **b[!a-i]d** finds *bud* and *bod* but not *bad* or *bid*.

Part
3

Time Savers

Operator	Lets You Find
character{*n*}	Any *n* occurrences of the preceding character: **ble{2}d** finds *bleed* but not *bled* (or for that matter, *bleeeeed*). What's the purpose of this? Well it only makes sense if you're looking for a long string of a repeated character. In that case it would save you some typing. Otherwise, it seems silly: *ble{2}d* requires more typing (not to mention unusual characters) than *bleed* does!
character{*n*,}	At least *n* occurrences of the preceding character: **ble{1,}d** finds *bled* and *bleed*.
character{*n*,*m*}	At least *n* occurrences of the preceding character and no more than *m*: **1{1,2}5** finds both *15* and *115* but not *1115*.
character@	One or more occurrences of the preceding character (thus, @ is equivalent to {1,}): **ble@d** finds *bled* and *bleed*.
<text	The beginning of a word: **<man** finds *manhole* and *manage* but not *human*. (This works better than putting a space in front of the text, as it deals with exceptions such as the beginning of a paragraph.)
text>	The end of a word: **in>** finds *in* and *herein* but not *interfere*. (Likewise, this works much better than putting a space after the text, as it covers words that end at a period or other punctuation.)

To search for characters that are also used as operators ({, !, *, etc.), separate them with a backslash. For instance, to find the asterisk, search for *.

Notice that the ? symbol with Pattern Matching is equivalent to the ^? special character without it, just as the * symbol with Pattern Matching has the same effect as the ^* symbol without it.

All of the above operators can be combined, so, for example, **<ble@d** finds *bleeding-heart*, but not *nosebleed* or *doubled*. If you combine several of these operators, you can use brackets to clarify which operations Word must evaluate first. Brackets can also go inside other brackets, though I hope for your sake that it is never necessary!

Find All Word Forms

A great new feature of Word is that Find can search for *word forms.* What this means is that you can, for instance, search for all tenses and person forms of verbs. So instead of having to make separate searches for *drink*, *drank*, and *drunk*, you just search for *drink* and check the Find All Word Forms box. This is really uncanny the first time you see it!

It's incredibly slick, too. Word seems to know most forms of most of the common verbs, as well as many irregular ones. For instance, if you enter **be** as the Find What text, Word will find all forms and tenses of the verb *to be!* That is, it will find *are, is, were, was, am,* and so on.

Find All Word Forms works with nouns, too, and is especially useful for nouns with irregular plurals, such as *goose* and *geese*. The only challenge where Word seemed overmatched was with adjectives from proper nouns. When I tried *Shaw* and *Shavian*, Word found *Shaw* but flagged *Shavian* as a misspelling. Same with *Liverpool* and *Liverpudlian*.

The Art of Replacing

To replace, follow these general steps:

1. Save your work.

2. Choose <u>E</u>dit ➤ <u>R</u>eplace or press Ctrl+H.

3. Create search criteria using the techniques discussed in the previous section.

4. Specify the desired replacement text, formats, etc.

5. Tell Word where to search and in which direction.

6. Click Find Next or Replace All to start the replacement.

7. Confirm the replacements.

> **WARNING** It is a good idea to save your work before using the Replace feature. If you are working on a complex, important project, you might want to use a copy rather than the original document as it is much easier to screw up a document with Replace than it is to repair it.

As you can see from Figure 20.2, the Replace dialog box looks like the Find dialog box, with additional features. Word lets you confirm each replacement before it happens, or it will find and replace without your intervention.

Just as you can search for text, formats, styles, and special characters, you can also replace them. For instance, you could replace *Marion Morrison* with *John Wayne*.

Figure 20.2 *The Replace dialog box resembles the Find box, with added features.*

Or you could change each occurrence of two consecutive paragraph marks to a single end-of-line marker, or change the style of certain paragraphs from chapter-heading style to appendix style. It is even possible to replace text with graphics. Here are examples of each technique.

Replacing Text with Text

To simply replace text (like changing *Marion Morrison* to *John Wayne*) without altering formats or styles, start by entering the text to find and the desired replacement text. For instance, you might enter *Marion Morrison* in the Find What box and *John Wayne* in the Replace With box. Follow these steps:

1. Save your work.

2. Choose Edit ➤ Replace (Ctrl+H).

3. Visit the Search drop-down menu to tell Word if you want it to search from the insertion point forward or backward, or the entire document.

4. Use the Find What box to specify the search item and the Replace With box to specify its replacement. When your instructions are complete, click Find Next. Word will search the document (or the selected portion) for things matching your Find criteria and propose the next replacement. The Replace button will undim, and your document screen will scroll to reveal the first potential replacement point.

> **WARNING** If there are any formats or styles listed under the Find What or Replace With boxes, click No Formatting with the insertion point in the appropriate place (Find What, Replace With, or both). This way, Word will not alter the style or format of the document. If you *do* want to replace one style or format with another, make sure that both Find What and Replace With accurately reflect your choices.

5. If you want Word to make the change it is proposing, click Replace. To skip the change, click Find Next. To make the change and let Word continue uninterrupted, click Replace All. Word will make the rest of the replacements nonstop, probably too quickly for you to even see them. A message will display the number of replacements made.

6. Check your work. Undo will work here for all the replacements if you used Replace All, but only for the last replacement if you were monitoring the replacements. This is a big reason for saving your document just before running Replace.

Replacing Formatting

Suppose you have italicized words scattered throughout your text and decide to change all of them to underlined words. Start by removing any text from the Find What and Replace With boxes. (This is because you want Word to find all italicized text, not just words in the Find What box that are italicized.) Then follow these steps:

1. Specify the character attributes you want Word to find (italics for example). You can do this in one of several ways. Always start by placing the insertion point in the Find What entry box. Then specify the Italic format from the Standard toolbar, by entering the Ctrl+I keyboard shortcut, or by pulling down the Format list in the Replace dialog box. From there, choose Font, then click in the Italic option of the Font dialog box.

TIP   Using keyboard shortcuts or toolbar buttons is often the quickest way to specify formatting.

The word *Italic* (or whatever) will appear beneath the Find What box.

2. Next go to the Replace With box and choose a new format (Underline in this example). To prevent Word from changing italic to italic underline, double-click the Italic button on the Formatting toolbar so that the Format information under the Replace With box reads **Not Italic, Underline.** Figure 20.3 shows how your dialog box should look after this maneuver. Note that toolbar buttons and keyboard shortcuts "cycle" through three phases; for example: italic, not italic, no formatting.

3. Let 'er rip! Either tell Word to Replace All or supervise each replacement as before.

You can also change the formatting of specific text only for that text or combine the replacement of text and formatting. To change the formatting of specific text, type the text you want to change in both the Find What and Replace With boxes. Click on the Find What format box and select the type of formatting the text has now. Then click on the Replace

Figure 20.3 **This combination will change all italicized text to underlined text.**

With format box and select the type of formatting you want to give to the text.

Changing both text and formatting at the same time is just as easy. Suppose you want to replace every instance of the italicized word *ennui* with the unitalicized word *boredom*. That would be simple. Just type **ennui** in the Find What box and select Italic formatting. Then type **boredom** in the Replace With box and click the Italic button on the Formatting toolbar twice to select Not Italic. Then proceed with Replace as normal.

Replacing Styles

If you want to change the style of certain paragraphs, the Replace command can help:

1. Click on the Format button.

2. Choose Styles.

3. You will see a list of your document's styles and descriptions, as shown in Figure 20.4.

4. Pick styles for both the find and replace criteria, then proceed as usual.

Part 3

Time Savers

Figure 20.4 **Specify styles to find and replace with the Replace Style dialog box.**

In this example, paragraphs formatted with the Heading 3 style will be reformatted using the Heading 2 style. Because any custom styles you've defined (see Chapter 14) will appear in the Styles list, you can use this technique to apply these styles quickly and accurately.

Combining Replacement Tasks

Within reason, it is possible to combine search and replace instructions to restrict actions. For instance, assuming you had a document with appropriate styles, you could italicize all occurrences of *Gone with the Wind* in the body text of your report, while leaving the same words alone when they appear in headings, the table of contents, and the index.

You would do this by typing **Gone with the Wind** in the Find What box and specifying body text as its style. Then specify Italic as the format in the Replace With box. (You could type **Gone with the Wind** and specify body text style again in the Replace With box, but you don't need to.)

Again, computers are very obedient but not very clever. Undo should help you recover from most disasters, but it's a good idea to work on copies of important documents just in case.

With all the different possibilities of finding text or formatting or both and replacing it with other text or formatting or both, you might sometimes find it hard to think through what exactly will change. Table 20.1 outlines how the different choices interact with each other.

If You Find	And Replace It with	You Get
text	text	all Find text replaced with Replace text
text	format	all Find text formatted
text	text and format	all Find text replaced with formatted Replace text
format	text	all formatted text replaced with Replace text in same format
format	format	all formatted text given new format
format	text and format	all formatted text replaced with Replace text in new format
text and format	text	all formatted Find text replaced with Replace text in same format
text and format	format	all formatted Find text given new format
text and format	text and format	all formatted Find text replaced with Replace text in new format

Table 20.1   Combining Text and Format Options in Replace

Part
3

Time Savers

So, for example, if you type **ennui** in the Find What box, choose Underline formatting, then put nothing in the Replace With box and choose both Italic and No Underline (click the Underline button on the Formatting toolbar twice), then every underlined instance of *ennui* in your document will become italicized, but the word won't change.

Search

You have several choices for how Word will search your document for words you wish to either find or replace. These options are found under the Search drop-down menu in the Find and Replace dialog boxes. Up searches back toward the beginning of the document, while Down searches toward the end. All searches the entire document, as you would expect.

If you choose Up or Down, Word will search until it gets to the beginning (or end) of the document, and then tell you it has reached the end of the document and ask if you want it to continue the search. If you choose Yes, it will continue in the same direction from the other end of the document until it reaches the place you started from. If you choose No, it will end the search. Why would you want to end the search? Well, you may know that the word you're searching for occurs several times in the beginning of your document, and you may not want to change any of those earlier instances.

Another way to limit the range of the search is to select a portion of the document before selecting Replace. Word will search just the selection first. Then it will ask if you want it to continue the search in the rest of the document. Choose No to end the search then.

If you stop in the middle of a Replace to, say, correct something else you've noticed, be sure to deselect the last found word before resuming the Replace. Otherwise, Word will begin the Replace again by searching just the selection (the last word found). This does no harm, but always having to click on Yes to continue the search gets boring.

Resume the Replace by clicking on the Find Next button.

Using the Clipboard with Find and Replace

The Clipboard can be used for several interesting Find and Replace tasks. For instance, you can copy text from your document to the Clipboard, then paste it into the Find What or Replace With boxes. This is a great way to find or replace long passages or obscure characters like umlauted letters or math symbols. It is even possible to overcome the 255-character limitation this way.

Word also lets you replace text with graphics that you've placed on the Clipboard. Figure 20.5 illustrates how that is done.

1. Copy a graphic to the Clipboard.
2. Visit the Replace dialog box.
3. Enter Find What criteria.
4. Click on the Replace With portion of the dialog box.
5. Choose Clipboard Contents from the Special list.
6. Replace as usual.

Figure 20.5 **It is possible to replace text with graphics on the Clipboard.**

Part
3

Time Savers

Tips for Replacing

Here are some tips for replacing efficiently:

▶ The Replace command uses considerable memory if you make a lot of changes. It is a good idea to perform a normal save after making sure that your replacements are satisfactory.

▶ Undo will undo all changes if you use Replace All, but only your last change if you have been supervising with the Find Next button.

▶ If you've used styles in your document, you may find it easier to make wholesale style changes by redefining or reapplying styles rather than using Replace.

▶ The Find All Word Forms feature works as you might hope when replacing. You can search for forms of one word, and Word will replace them with all the correct forms of another word! For example, you can instruct Word to replace all forms of (the verbs) *drink* with *fish* and it would replace *drink* with *fish*, *drank* with *fished*, *drunk* with *fished*, and so forth.

▶ You can specify any character in Find or Replace strings by typing **^n**, where *n is the ASCII (decimal) code for the character of interest.*

▶ Remember to click No Formatting when specifying new search criteria in the Find What and Replace With boxes.

▶ All of the special characters (paragraph markers, tabs, etc.) can be represented by caret codes that you can enter directly from the keyboard into the Find What box, the Replace With box, or both. This is often the quick way to go. Table 20.2 shows a handy reference list of special-character codes. Notice that they all require lowercase characters.

TIP There are drop-down lists in the Find What and Replace With fields that show your last four entries. You can save some typing and time by choosing from these lists.

Character	Code	OK in Find What Box?	OK in Replace With Box?
Annotation mark	^a	Yes	No
Any single character	^?	Yes	No
Any single digit	^#	Yes	No
Any single letter	^$	Yes	No
ASCII character number *nnn*	^O*nnn*	Yes	Yes
Caret character	^	Yes	Yes
Clipboard contents	^c	No(text only)	Yes (text or graphics)
Column break	^n	Yes	Yes
Contents of the Find What box	^&	No	Yes
Em dash (—)	^+	Yes	Yes
En dash (–)	^=	Yes	Yes
Endnote mark	^e	Yes	No
Field code	^d	Yes	No
Footnote mark	^f	Yes	No
Graphic	^g	Yes	No
Manual line break	^l	Yes	Yes
Manual page break	^m	Yes	Yes
Nonbreaking hyphen	^~	Yes	Yes
Nonbreaking space	^s	Yes	Yes
Optional hyphen (activated)	^-	Yes	Yes

Table 20.2 Special Characters and Their Find and Replace Codes

Part
3

Time Savers

Character	Code	OK in Find What Box?	OK in Replace With Box?
Paragraph mark	^p	Yes	Yes
Section break	^b	Yes	No
Tab	^t	Yes	Yes
White space	^w	Yes	No

Table 20.2   *Special Characters and Their Find and Replace Codes (continued)*

How Replace Interacts with Styles

Be aware that just as manually applied formatting and styles interact when you change styles or formatting yourself, they interact when the Replace command makes changes.

As explained at the end of Chapter 14, Word makes a distinction between manual formatting (formatting you apply directly from the toolbar or Font menu) and style formatting (formatting that is applied to text as part of a style definition). When you define a style based on a manually formatted selection, Word tries to include in the style any kind of formatting that is applied to the majority of the selection (actually the first 255 characters of it, to be pedantic). Any manual formatting applied intermittently is interpreted as just that, manual formatting layered on top of the style formatting.

Replace operations can include combinations of style formatting and manual formatting. Searches for boldface text, for example, will find text you've made bold manually as well as text that has been formatted with a style that includes bold. You can search for any combination of style formatting and manual formatting and replace with any other combination.

If you combine both types of formatting under the Find What box, Word will find any examples that have the style formatting and match the manual formatting. If you combine both types of formatting under the Replace With box, Word will apply the style formatting first, then layer the manual formatting on top of it. Of course, you can also use different combinations of either or both in the two boxes. Table 20.3 shows how the two types of formatting interact during the Replace operation.

To make matters worse, you additionally have the option of including text or not in either of the boxes, along with any combination of formatting. Realistically, you shouldn't need to get involved in such complicated, twisted operations.

If You Find	And Replace It with	You Get
manual formatting	manual formatting	all formatted text given new formatting
manual formatting	style formatting	all formatted text given style formatting in addition to manual formatting
manual formatting	manual and style formatting	all formatted text given style formatting and new manual formatting layered on top
style formatting	manual formatting	all text in that style given manual formatting in addition to the style formatting
style formatting	style formatting	all text in the old style given the new style
style formatting	manual and style formatting	all text in the old style given the new style and the manual formatting layered on top

Table 20.3   Combining Manual and Style Formatting in Replace

Part
3

Time Savers

Chapter 21

Get Organized
with Outline View

FAST TRACK

Word's *Outline* view, available from the View menu (Ctrl+Alt+O), is really more than a view. It's a collection of tools designed to help you plan, create, and reorganize long documents. It does this by letting you expand or contract the amount of detail you see on your screen. Figure 21.1 illustrates Outline view.

The top window in Figure 21.1 shows part of a document in Normal view. The bottom window shows the same document in Outline view with all of the body text collapsed (not revealed). Because only paragraph headings are visible in the bottom window, it's easy to see the overall organization (the outline) of the document. As you will soon see, Outline view lets you control how much detail you see. For instance, you can view the first line of text following each heading if you wish.

Notice also that headings in Outline view are indented, giving you a better idea of the document's organization. Each new level is indented $^1/_4$" from the preceding one.

It's a snap to reorganize documents in Outline view. If you want to move all of the paragraphs having to do with Landing Gear so they appear before Tail, simply drag the Landing Gear heading marker using the Outline view's special pointer. This will move all corresponding paragraphs, called the heading's *subtext*.

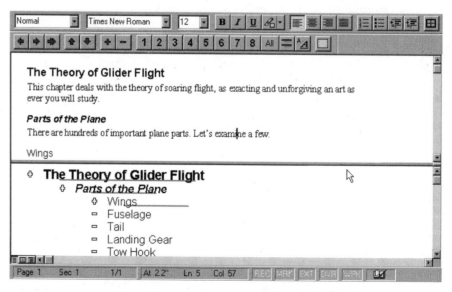

Figure 21.1   Outline view (bottom) lets you get a bird's eye view of large documents (top).

Finally, you can quickly *promote* or *demote* portions of your document (that is, change a level 2 head to level 3, or vice-versa) using the Outline view tools, found on the Outline toolbar.

Styles and Outlines

In order to use Outline view, you first need to format your headings using Word's standard-heading styles (Heading 1 through Heading 9). Even if you didn't use these styles when you created a document, it is easy to reformat with them. And, as you probably know, you can change the appearance of standard headings if you don't like Word's standard styles. (See Chapter 14 for more about styles.)

What You See in Outline View

Outline view presents a number of unique elements, not seen in other views. First there is the Outline toolbar, at the top of the screen. Also, the mouse pointer changes to a compass shape when it is poised to move a heading and its text.

Another difference is that on-screen text is often underlined with an unusual line style. This does not indicate text that will be underlined when printed. Rather, it indicates that there is collapsed subtext beneath it.

Large plus signs, boxes, and dashes appear next to many headings in Outline view. Boxes tell you that you are looking at body text; pluses indicate headings containing subtext; and minuses denote headings without subtext.

The Outline Toolbar's Tools

Figure 21.2 summarizes the Outline toolbar's unique tools. They promote and demote heading levels, hide or reveal body text, and turn formatting on and off.

The best way to understand the effect of these tools is to open a document containing standard Word headings in Outline view and experiment. If you don't have a document of your own, create one or use the Business Report from the Sample Documents folder. The rest of this chapter describes the various Outline view tools, offering tips on how to use them.

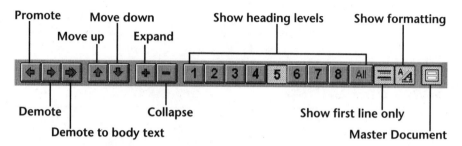

Figure 21.2   Buttons on the Outline toolbar promote and demote headings and reveal or hide text and formatting.

Creating and Editing Outlines

When you start typing a new document in Outline view, Word assumes the first thing you want to type is a level 1 heading. Each new paragraph you type will take on the heading level of the previous paragraph.

One strategy is to type all of your top-level headings first, and then go back and insert headings in progressively lower heading levels. Another approach is to type all your document's headings in sequence, promoting and demoting as you go. It is even possible to type the entire document (all headings and text) in Outline view without doing a traditional outline first. (Of course, if you do this, you lose much of the benefit of outlining, particularly the opportunity to see all your headings in sequence and verify that they make sense.)

TIP   The outlining approach you choose is largely a matter of personal preference. In any scenario, you will need to know how to promote and demote headings and text.

Promoting and Demoting

  The two arrows at the left end of the Outline toolbar are used to promote and demote headings. Place the insertion point in the heading you wish to promote or demote. Click the right arrow to demote, or the left arrow to promote. Figure 21.3 shows this at work on a new outline originally typed with everything at level 1.

All headings at top level ————

Click once to demote
current heading

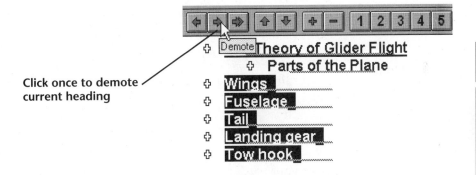

Click twice to demote
two levels

The results

Figure 21.3 **The right arrow demotes selected headings while the left arrow promotes them.**

Here we placed the insertion point in the *Parts of the Plane* heading and clicked the right arrow once. Then we highlighted the headings *Wings* through *Tow hook* and clicked the right arrow twice, which demoted them two levels. The results are shown at the bottom of Figure 21.3. We have left the *Theory of Glider Flight* heading at the top level; *Parts of the Plane* is now the next level down, and *Wings* through *Tow hook* are at heading level 3. (You could confirm this by switching to Normal or Page Layout view.)

Promoting works as you'd expect. With the insertion point in a heading, click the left arrow to turn a level 3 heading into a level 2 heading, and so on.

Outlining Existing Documents

To outline existing documents, follow these steps:

1. Open your document in Outline view.

2. Place the insertion point in each heading and promote or demote them as desired.

3. Save your work.

4. Use the viewing techniques described next to view and rearrange the organization of your document.

Expanding and Collapsing Outlines

One of the main reasons to use Outline view is to get a collapsed overview of a document's contents. Do this by turning on Show First Line Only, and then expanding and collapsing views with the numbers and buttons on the Outline toolbars.

For instance, Figure 21.4 shows our Glider book in a bit more detail than the view in previous figures. The first line of text beneath each heading has been revealed.

  This was accomplished by clicking on the Show First Line Only button (just to the left of the Show Formatting button) on the Outline toolbar. Clicking the All icon—just to the right of the number 8—reveals all headings and text.

 The document's true heading styles are apparent in Figure 21.4. The Show Formatting button at the end of the Outline toolbar turns character formatting on and off.

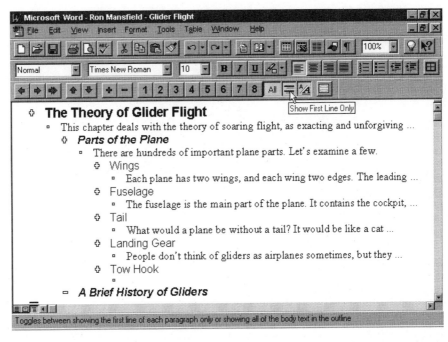

Figure 21.4   Click the All Text or First line icon on the Outline toolbar to show the first line of text beneath each heading.

Clicking on the numbers 1 through 8 in Outline view hides or reveals the levels of your document. For instance, in our sample document, clicking on 1 will reveal only level 1 headings (the *Theory of Glider Flight*). Clicking on the 2 would reveal both level 1 and level 2 headings (*Parts of the Plane* and *A Brief History of Gliders*).

Split Views

Figure 21.5 illustrates a strategy for working on large documents. You can split the screen and show your document in Page Layout view in one half of the window and Outline view in the other.

To split a window this way, double-click on the Split bar. Then drag it up or down to change the size of the two areas. Each part of the screen has its own scroll bars. Double-clicking on the Split bar (in the scroll area) or dragging the bar in the pane of a split window returns you to a single window.

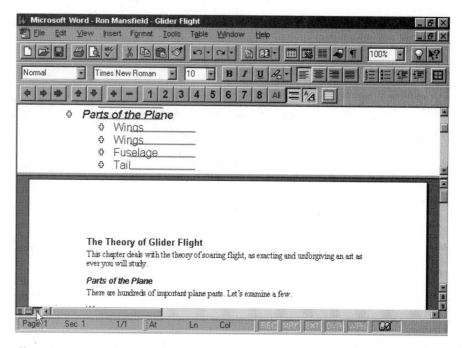

Figure 21.5 Splitting the screen lets you work in Outline and Page Layout views at the same time.

TIP When you double-click the Split bar to unsplit a document divided into two panes, the pane where you had the insertion point will become the full page. So be careful! If you are taken away from where you want to work, pressing Shift + F5 (Go Back) might help.

Moving Paragraphs

With the outline collapsed, you can move collections of paragraphs (*subtext*) by moving their associated headings. When you move a heading, *all* the lower-level heads and text below it will be moved along with it. This makes it easy to move entire chapters or sections without needing to select the text. Think of this feature as drag-and-drop on steroids. Figure 21.6 shows how it works.

Placing the pointer over the left edge of a heading changes the pointer's shape. It will look like a compass. Click and drag, and a large right arrow will appear along with a dotted line, like the ones shown in Figure 21.6.

Figure 21.6   Drag outline headings to move them and all their related subtext.

Drag the line and the pointer to where you want to move the text. Release the mouse button and the document will be reorganized.

The up- and down-pointing arrows on the Outline toolbar will also move items up and down. Highlight the headings; then click on the appropriate arrow.

> **TIP**   You can use Outline view to maintain alphabetical order in documents such as glossaries, membership directories, and the like. Make sure the headings to be alphabetized are all at the same level (preferably Heading 1). Collapse the outline to that level and select the headings. Then select Table ➤ Sort Text and click OK with the default sorting options. You can repeat the sort after adding new entries.

Dragging to Change Levels

You can also drag to change the indent level in Outline view. When you do, the pointer arrow changes, and you'll see a guideline that indicates the pending indent level as shown in Figure 21.7.

Figure 21.7   You can drag to change indent levels in Outline view.

Rearrange Tables by Dragging Rows

When you view a table in Outline view, it is possible to move rows by dragging them. This is illustrated in Figure 21.8.

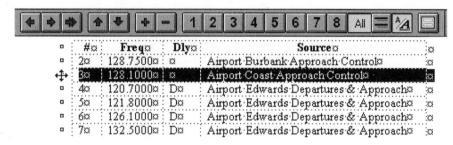

Figure 21.8   *Outline view is a handy place to rearrange Word tables by dragging rows.*

Numbering Headings in Outline View

You can number headings in any view, but Outline view makes it easiest to see their sequence. Figure 21.9 illustrates this.

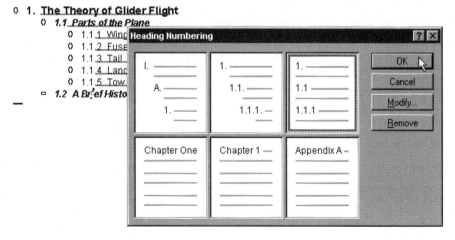

Figure 21.9   *You can use the Format ➤ Heading Numbering command in Outline view.*

The basic steps are:

1. Choose Format ➤ Heading Numbering.

2. Click on a sample to select the numbering format you desire, or choose Modify for custom-numbering choices.

3. Click OK.

4. Word will renumber immediately whenever you rearrange your outline. Whenever you add a heading it will automatically be numbered, as shown in Figure 21.10.

⊹ 1.1.4 Landing·gear¶
⊹ 1.1.5 Tow·hook¶
▭ 1.2 Thermals—Rising·Hot·Air¶

Figure 21.10 **When you add headings, they will be numbered as you have specified.**

Outlines and Tables of Content

Because Outlines use (assign to headings) standard Word Heading styles, you can quickly create a table of contents based on your outline. The table will include each heading. See Chapter 23 for more information about tables of contents.

Printing Outlines

Printing in Outline view creates a document containing only the levels you see on the screen. Collapse the document to the desired level, then use the File ➤ Print command or Ctrl+P shortcut. Even if just the first line of text appears, Word will print the whole paragraph.

Desktop Publishing

4

Chapter 22
Multiple Columns

FAST TRACK

To create different numbered columns (even on the same page)   495

select the text to be "columnized" and specify column settings with the Columns toolbar button or dialog box. Word will apply the settings only to the selected text and insert necessary breaks automatically.

To drag columns to different widths using margin markers   496

place the insertion point in the desired column and, in Page Layout view, display the rulers if they aren't already on-screen. Drag any margin boundary marker, and the columns will adjust to their new width.

To add decorative lines between columns   497

place the insertion point in a column that you wish to decorate. Then choose Format ➤ Columns and choose Line Between.

To force column breaks   497

place the insertion point where you want the column break, then choose Insert ➤ Break, specify Column, and click OK. You remove breaks by highlighting them and pressing Delete.

To "even out" uneven columns   497

place the insertion point after the last character in the text and choose Insert ➤ Break. Choose Continuous in the Sections area. Then click OK, and the column bottoms will align.

To remove columns from an entire document   499

select all of the text and use the toolbar's Columns button to specify a single column.

To remove one of several column specifications in a multiple-section document   499

place the insertion point in the unwanted column and then use the Columns button.

Most people find short lines of text easier to read than long ones. That's one reason newspapers and book designers frequently use side-by-side snaking *columns*. Text flows from the bottom of one column to the top of the next until a page is filled; then it flows onto the next page.

Creating Multicolumn Documents

Word makes it easy to arrange your text in columns like these. The Standard toolbar's Columns button lets you choose from one to six columns (single is the default). If that's not enough, the Columns dialog box lets you specify up to forty-five columns (for *really* wide sheets of paper). It also provides a way to adjust the amount of white space between columns.

TIP When you start with a new document, the toolbar button lets you choose up to six columns for a portrait page, or eight for landscape orientation. If you use the Columns dialog box to increase the number of columns, the toolbar button will show up to the highest number you've assigned.

In a single-section document, all pages must have the same number of columns. But, by breaking a document into multiple sections, you can have as many different column designs as you have sections. Note that Word inserts section breaks automatically.

Word automatically adjusts column widths to accommodate your chosen page size, orientation, and document margins. You can overrule these decisions.

It is possible to use indents within columns. You can edit columnar text just as you do any other. When you work in Page Layout view, you will see side-by-side columns as they will print. When working in Normal view, you will see text in the appropriate column width, but you will not see the columns in position next to each other. Scrolling is faster in Normal mode, so it's ideal for editing, while Page Layout view is better for formatting.

Word's column feature allows for columns in a section to be of varying widths. You can drag columns or specify their widths precisely from your keyboard.

Simple Column Creation

Here's an easy way to create up to six columns (or eight for landscape orientation) if your document has only one section and if you want the same number of columns throughout the document:

1. Make any page setup, margin, and other design decisions that will affect the amount of text area on your page.

2. Click on the Columns button near the right edge of the Standard toolbar. As you can see in Figure 22.1, you *drag* across it to select the desired number of columns.

3. When you release the mouse button, Word automatically determines the appropriate width of columns and the amount of white space between them based on the page and document settings. You can see the columns as they will print in Page Layout view and Print Preview. You will see a single column only in Normal view.

Drag to specify from 1 to 7 columns

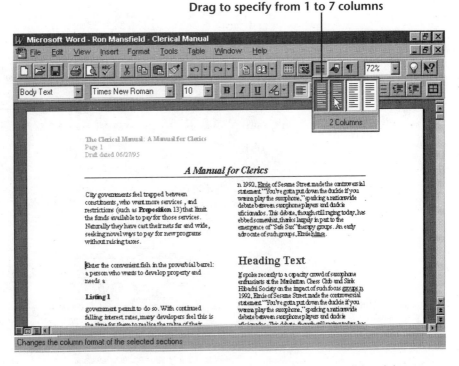

Figure 22.1 **The Columns toolbar button puts up to seven-column text a click-and-drag away.**

Changing margins, page size, orientation, indents, and related settings will cause corresponding changes in column widths and spacing. The zero point on the ruler is always at the left edge of the column containing the insertion point. Clicking in the left column would move the zero point of the ruler to the left edge of the left column. Indents work as you'd expect within columns.

Using the Columns Dialog Box

You can create more than eight columns (up to forty-five in either orientation) and specify the desired amount of white space between columns by using the Columns portion of the Columns dialog box. You can also specify decorative lines between columns here. And you can create adjacent columns of differing widths.

Reach the Columns dialog box by choosing Format ➤ Columns. Figure 22.2 shows the specifications for two columns with different widths. Notice that you can preview the results of choices made in this dialog box.

Figure 22.2 *You can precisely specify the number of columns and the spacing in the columns box.*

Different Column Designs in the Same Document

You can have different column designs in different parts of a document. For instance, part of a page could be a single column with the rest two or three columns.

Word makes it easy to specify where new column settings should begin and end. Essentially, all you need to do is select text and specify a column design for the selected text. Word will format the columns, insert section breaks, etc.

For example, to create the effect shown in Figure 22.3, you need to take the following steps:

1. Select the text to be "columnized."

Part 4

Desktop Publishing

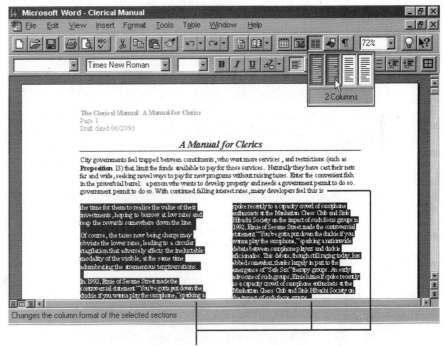

If you select text first, Word inserts the necessary breaks automatically.

Figure 22.3   Select text and then specify desired column settings.

2. Specify column settings with the toolbar button or the Columns dialog box (described next). Word will apply the settings only to the selected text and insert necessary breaks.

Controlling Column Width

Word initially sets the widths and spacing for you. It's possible, however, to drag columns to different widths using *margin markers*. Here's how. Follow along in Figure 22.4.

Figure 22.4   **Drag margin markers to change column widths in Page Layout view.**

TIP   Some people find the Columns dialog box (choose Format ➤ Columns) more straightforward for adjusting column widths. The ruler method is quicker, but if you prefer, you can use the Columns dialog box to type in actual column widths.

1. Place the insertion point in the desired column.

2. From Page Layout view, display the rulers if they aren't already on-screen.

3. Drag any margin boundary on the ruler, and the columns will adjust to their new width.

TIP   When creating columns of justified type, spacing within the text can get a little raggedy. Consider using unjustified text or optional hyphens to tighten up columns.

Adding Decorative Lines between Columns

Use the Columns dialog box if you want to add decorative lines between columns. There is only one line style.

1. Place the insertion point in a column that you wish to decorate.

2. Choose Format ➤ Columns.

3. Choose Line Between.

Controlling Column Breaks

Use Word's Keep Lines Together and Keep with Next Paragraph features to prevent unwanted breaks. Sometimes, you will want to force breaks. For example, the last page of a two-column document may end with uneven columns because Word will completely fill the left column before putting text in the right column.

Use Word's Insert ➤ Break command to force column breaks. Place the insertion point where you want the column break, then choose Insert ➤ Break, specify Column, and click OK. You remove breaks by highlighting them and pressing Delete.

Balancing Column Endings

Sometimes you'll have uneven column endings on the last page of a document or section. Figure 22.5 illustrates this problem (and no, you are not going blind—the text is *greeked*).

If you wish to "even out" the columns, do the following in Page Layout view:

1. Place the insertion point after the last character in the text.

2. Choose Insert ➤ Break.

3. Choose Continuous in the Sections area.

4. Click OK. The column bottoms will align as shown in Figure 22.6.

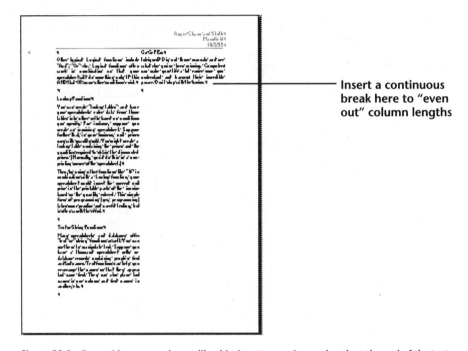

Insert a continuous break here to "even out" column lengths

Figure 22.5   **To avoid uneven columns like this, insert a continuous break at the end of the text.**

Figure 22.6   **Flush column bottoms.**

Don't Forget Tables as an Alternative

While Word has made it easy to create and edit multiple columns, there are times when it will be easier for you to use tables instead of columns. This is particularly true for things like resumes and "television-style" scripts where side-by-side items should always maintain the same horizontal relationship.

Removing Columns

To remove columns from an entire document, select all of the text and use the toolbar's Columns button to specify a single column. To remove one of several column specifications in a multiple-section document, place the insertion point in the relevant section and then use the toolbar button.

TIP If you have inserted section breaks for the sole purpose of dividing areas of text with different column layouts (or if Word inserted them automatically), it is a good idea to clean up your document by deleting the breaks.

Part 4

Desktop Publishing

Chapter 23

Creating Tables of Contents and Indexes

FAST TRACK

begin by formatting your document's headings with Word's standard heading styles. When you have typed and proofed your document and are happy with margins, headers, footers, and other design elements (especially those that affect page breaks), place the cursor where you want the Table of Contents and pick Insert ➤ Index and Tables. You will see the Index and Tables dialog box. Choose the Table of Contents tab if it is not already foremost. Preview the available formats by clicking in the Formats list and watching the Preview area. Pick one. Choose the number of levels you wish to include. If you wish to include a tab leader (dashes or dots, for instance), choose the style from the drop-down list. Click OK or press ↵. Word will compile the new TOC.

To turn index entry levels on and off with the Table of Contents Options dialog box 507

open the Index and Tables dialog box (reached with Insert ➤ Index and Tables) and go to the Table of Contents tab. Click the Options button. Turn off headings by removing numbers from the Show Levels box. Change levels by typing in the Show Levels box.

To update a TOC after you've made changes to your document 507

click in the TOC to highlight the entire TOC (it will turn gray). You'll see a dialog box, where you'll have a choice of whether to Update Page Numbers only or the Entire Table. Decide which you prefer and click OK.

To update (recompile) an index 510

click anywhere in the index to select it. Press the right button to see Word's mini-menu. Choose Update Field. Word will repaginate the document, then recompile and update the index.

To change the appearance of index entries 511

click anywhere in the index to select it, then visit the Index and Tables dialog box (Insert ➤ Index and Tables) and choose the Index tab. Click on format names and watch the preview box. (Use ↑ and ↓ to speed selection of different format names if you like.) When you find one you like, click OK to apply the new format to the index.

To have Word for Windows automatically index a document 512

create a new document, called a concordance file, with the New command. Insert a two-column table. Type all index entries in the first column. They must be identical to text Word will find in the document you intend to index. In the second column, type all index entries as you wish them to appear in the index. Open the document to be indexed. Choose Insert ➤ Index and Tables. Visit the Index tab of the Index and Tables dialog box. Click the AutoMark button. Choose the concordance file from the resulting "Open" dialog box. Click OK.

Word's slick automated features make creating a *table of contents* (TOC) for your documents a snap. If you format your headings using Word's standard heading styles or Outline feature, the Insert ➤ Index and Tables command will quickly compile (create) a simple but very usable table of contents and place it in a new section at the beginning of your document.

It is also possible to manually select items to appear in your table of contents. You do this by identifying words and phrases in your document using hidden text codes called *TOC Entry* codes. You can control the appearance of the table of contents as well. Your TOC can have one or multiple levels.

The Insert ➤ Index and Tables command and the hidden *Index Entry* codes work together to produce equally simple or distinctive *indexes* at the end of your document.

 TIP If you plan to create an index for your document, you may want to create it before you create the table of contents so that it will show up as an entry in your TOC.

In this chapter you'll also learn how to create tables of authorities for legal documents, and tables of figures for illustrated documents.

Creating a Table of Contents

Figure 23.1 shows a simple table of contents containing only paragraph headings, created using Word's standard Heading 1 through Heading 3 styles.

Notice that Word has placed the TOC in its own new section at the beginning of the document. It has automatically inserted tabs, leading dots, and page numbers. To format and indent the new table of contents, it has used TOC styles corresponding to the standard heading styles. Thus, headings in the document formatted with standard Heading 3 will appear in the TOC formatted with a standard style called TOC 3.

To create a table of contents, follow these general steps:

1. Begin by formatting your document's headings with Word's standard heading styles.

==End of Section==

Figure 23.1 **You can produce simple multilevel TOCs using Word's standard heading styles.**

Part
4

Desktop Publishing

TIP These styles can be added to your Formatting toolbar's drop-down style list by visiting the Style dialog box. See Chapter 14 for more about styles.

2. When you have typed and proofed your document and are happy with margins, headers, footers, and other design elements (especially those that affect page breaks), place the cursor where you want the Table of Contents and pick Insert ➤ Index and Tables. You will see the Index and Tables dialog box, as shown in Figure 23.2.

3. Choose the Table of Contents tab if it is not already foremost.

4. Preview the available formats by clicking in the Formats list and watching the Preview area. Pick one.

5. Choose the number of levels you wish to include in the TOC.

6. If you wish to include a tab leader (dashes or dots, for instance), choose the style from the drop-down list.

Figure 23.2   The Index and Tables dialog box with the Table of Contents tab foremost.

7. Click OK or press ↵. Word will compile the new TOC. It starts by repaginating your document. Then it will insert the TOC at the insertion point.

> **NOTE**   If you've already created a TOC for the document, Word will ask if you want to replace it. If you choose "No," you will end up with *two* TOCs at the beginning of your document. (This is a way to create two levels of content detail like the Contents at a Glance and regular TOC at the beginning of this book.)

Including Non-Heading Styles in Your TOC

Word lets you easily specify non-heading heading styles for inclusion in your TOC. For example, suppose you create and define a style called Chapters, and you want it to be "above" Heading 1 in your TOC. You can use the TOC options to accomplish this.

1. Create and define styles for items you wish to include in the TOC.

2. Format the material using these styles.

3. Open the Table of Contents tab in the Index and Tables dialog box (reached with Insert ➤ Index and Tables).

4. Click on the Options button.

5. You will see a scrolling list of all of the styles in the current document, as illustrated in Figure 23.3.

6. Assign "levels" to the styles you wish to include in the TOC, as illustrated in Figure 23.3, where Chapters will be the first level, Heading 1 the second, and so on.

7. Make any other formatting choices and create the TOC as usual.

Figure 23.3 **A list of styles.**

Changing a TOC's Appearance

Notice how some of the styles apply things like all caps and small caps formatting for different levels. Some styles include underlines. If it bothers you that, for example, some headings have both underlines and leader characters (like the top-level headings in Figure 23.2), remove one or the other format and redefine the style using standard Word techniques.

You can edit the resulting TOC as you would any other text in your document. Feel free to make characters boldface, change line spacing, etc. As you'd expect, changing the style definitions for styles 1 through 9 will change the appearance of your TOC. There's an easy way to do this in Word:

1. Visit the Table of Contents tab in the Index and Tables dialog box (reached with Insert ➤ Index and Tables).

2. Pick the From Template option from the Formats list.

3. Click the Modify button.

4. You will see the Style dialog box, illustrated in Figure 23.4.

5. Pick the style you wish to modify by clicking on it in the scrolling list.

6. Click the Modify button.

7. You'll see the Modify Style box.

8. Make the desired changes to the style using the drop-down lists and the Format button (which takes you to familiar formatting dialog boxes).

9. Work your way back to the Index and Tables dialog box and click OK.

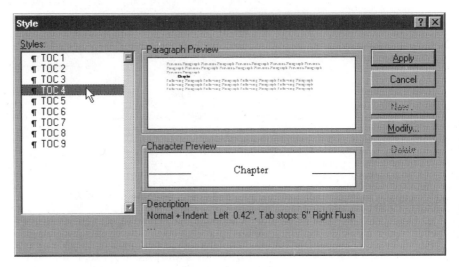

Figure 23.4 **The Style dialog box.**

Restricting Levels

In a document with numerous heading levels, you probably don't want to include all the levels in your TOC. To suppress the printing of all of the levels past a certain point (everything after 5, for instance), specify the levels you wish to print in the Show Levels portion of the Table of Contents tab:

You can also turn levels on and off with the Table of Contents Options dialog box.

1. Open the Index and Tables dialog box (reached with Insert ➤ Index and Tables) and go to the Table of Contents tab.

2. Click the Options button (for From Template only).

3. Turn off headings by removing numbers from the Level box.

4. Change levels by typing in the Level boxes. For instance, in this example Heading Level 3 will not print, and headings 4 and 5 will print as levels 3 and 4.

Available Styles:	TOC Level:
Header	
✓ Heading 1	1
✓ Heading 2	2
Heading 3	
✓ Heading 4	3
✓ Heading 5	4

Updating a Table of Contents

You can update a TOC after you've made changes to your document. You'll be given the choice of just changing page numbers or updating the entire TOC. Here are the general steps:

1. Click in the TOC to highlight the entire TOC (it will turn gray).

Part 4

Desktop Publishing

2. Press F9. You'll see a dialog box like this one:

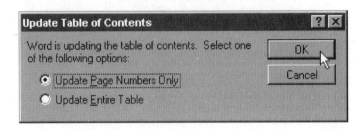

3. Choose Update Page Numbers Only or Update Entire Table.

4. Click OK.

   TIP   You can also update your TOC by clicking the right mouse button and selecting Update Field from the drop-down menu.

Creating an Index

Word compiles indexes on demand and places them at the end of your document in new sections that it creates for this purpose. You tell Word which words or phrases to include either by marking them in the document or by creating a separate list and then Automarking them. Whichever method you use, marking an index entry creates a code called an XE or Index Entry field.

Marking Index Entries

Word makes it easy to create an index. Simple indexes can be created by selecting text, issuing the Alt+Shift+X keyboard shortcut, and choosing a few options. Word then compiles and styles an index and places it at the document's end. Here are the basic steps:

1. Start by making sure that you are done proofing, fiddling with margins, page endings, and the like.

2. Select (highlight) a word or phrase you want to use as an index entry.

3. Press Alt+Shift+X.

4. You'll see the Mark Index Entry dialog box, as illustrated in Figure 23.5.

Figure 23.5   The Mark Index Entry dialog box can be reached with Alt+Shift+X.

5. Click Mark to mark just this entry, or Mark All to mark all occurrences. (Word will scan the document, marking all occurrences, and the status area will tell you how many were found.) Edit the entry and add a subentry. You can also include a cross-reference at this time ("See...").

> **WARNING**   The Mark All choice, while tempting, carries risks. It may include trivial as well as significant occurrences or words, which is considered bad indexing practice.

6. The Mark Index dialog box remains visible so that you can scroll to other text and mark it or simply type words to be indexed into the Main Entry section of the dialog box. For example, you might flag an occurrence of *garden slender salamander* and add *Amphibians* as the main entry.

7. Repeat steps 2 through 6 until you have specified all desired entries.

8. Click on Close to close the dialog box.

9. Place the insertion point where you want the index (typically at the end of your document).

10. Choose Insert ➤ Index and Tables.

11. Visit the Index tab of the Index and Tables dialog box, as shown in Figure 23.6.

12. Pick an index style using the scrolling Preview area as your guide.

13. Double-click on the name of the desired style or click once on a style name and once on OK.

14. Word will repaginate the document and then create an index that will be placed at the insertion point.

Choose a style here   Preview index formats here

Figure 23.6   The Index tab of the Index and Tables dialog box.

Updating Indexes

Each time you visit and close the Index tab in the Index and Tables dialog box, Word will ask if you want to replace (recompile) the selected index. Click Yes if you do (and you probably will want to). But there's also a shortcut worth knowing:

1. Click anywhere in the index to select it.

2. Press the right button to see the mini-menu:

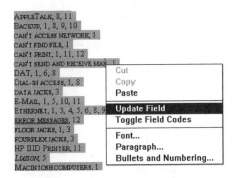

3. Choose Update Field. Word will repaginate, then recompile and update the index.

 WARNING Again, the index should be generated as the last thing done with your document. Updating it can be useful, because you can update an index to reflect other changes in your document, but the procedure should be done with care.

Formatting Indexes

The easy way to change the appearance of index entries is to pick a different index format choice from the scrolling Formats list in the Index tab of the Index and Tables dialog box. Watch the Preview area of the dialog box as you shop.

1. Click anywhere in the index to select it.

2. Visit the Index and Tables dialog box (Insert ➤ Index and Tables) and choose the Index tab.

3. Click on format names and watch the preview box. (Use ↑ and ↓ to speed selection of different format names if you like.)

4. When you find one you like, click OK to apply the new format to the index.

It is also possible to change the standard index styles (Index 1–Index 9). Here are the general steps for customizing index styles:

1. While in the Index tab of the Index and Tables dialog box, select From Template and click the Modify button, which reveals the Style dialog box.

2. Pick an index style you wish to modify from the Style list (Index 1, for instance).

3. Click the Modify button in the Style dialog box.

4. Use the resulting Modify Style dialog box to change the appearance of the style. (For instance, to apply Small Caps formatting, pick Font from the list revealed by the Format button.)

5. Work your way back to the Index tab by clicking OK as necessary (or press Esc).

6. Answer Yes to the "replace selected index" question. The index will be restyled. (Undo will work if you don't like the results.)

Creating Automatic Indexes

It is possible to have Word automatically index a document without your needing to visit the text manually. You do this by creating a list of terms you wish to index (called a *concordance* list). Concordances are often best used as supplements to automatic indexes, to take care of entries that might otherwise be missed. Here are the general steps:

1. Create a new document with the New command.

2. Insert a two-column table (with the Table button, perhaps).

3. Type all index entries in the first column. They must be identical to text Word will find in the document you intend to index. (For this reason, it's often easier to just go into the document and look up the terms.) Capitalization counts. (*Network Troubleshooting* might be a typical entry.)

4. In the second column, type all index entries as you wish them to appear in the index (*Troubleshooting: network*, for instance).

5. Save the document.

6. Open the document to be indexed.

7. Choose Insert ➤ Index and Tables.

8. Visit the Index tab of the Index and Tables dialog box.

9. Click the AutoMark button.

10. Choose the concordance file from the resulting "Open" dialog box.

11. Click OK.

12. Word will mark the entries for you.

Tables of Authorities

For legal documents, Word can help you automatically create Tables of Authorities. It provides commonly used categories, including:

▶ Cases

▶ Statutes

▶ Other Authorities

▶ Rules

▶ Treatises

▶ Regulations

▶ Constitutional Provisions

You can control the appearance of the entries and the table itself. Word will even help you seek out items to be included in your table.

Creating Entries

Always type a long citation as your first entry in a legal document—*Mansfield v. Newman, 45 Wn 2d 412 (1994)*, for instance. Subsequent entries can be short versions like *Mansfield v. Newman*. Once you've typed all of the entries:

1. Scroll to the first long entry.

2. Select it.

3. Press Alt+Shift+I to bring up the Mark Citation dialog box, like the one in Figure 23.7.

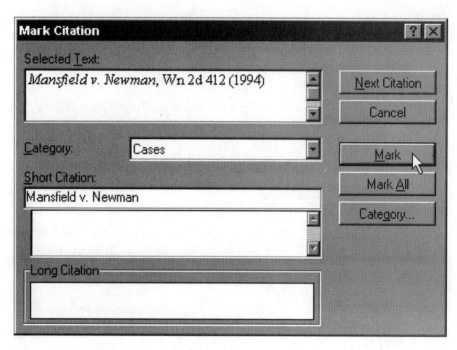

Figure 23.7   **The Mark Citation dialog box.**

4. Type your selected text in both the Selected Text and Short Citation boxes, if necessary.

5. Edit the Long Citation and format it if you like; you may use only the keyboard shortcuts here (Ctrl+B, Ctrl+I, etc.), as using the buttons formats the text *in the document*.

6. Pick a category (Cases, for example).

7. Edit the Short Citation so that it matches those in your document, *Mansfield v. Newman*, for instance.

8. Click the Mark button to visit each potential citation or Mark All to mark them automatically.

9. To find the next citation to mark, click Next Citation. Word will search for legalese (*v.*, *in re*, etc.) and display possible citations. When you find one, repeat steps 2 through 8.

10. When you've marked all the citations, click Close.

Generating the Table of Authorities

To format and compile the actual table, visit the Table of Authorities tab in the Index and Tables dialog box. Follow these steps:

1. Choose <u>I</u>nsert ➤ Inde<u>x</u> and Tables.

2. You'll see a dialog box like the one in Figure 23.8.

3. Pick a format from the Format list.

4. If you want Word to replace five or more page references with *passim,* choose that option.

5. Click OK. Word will compile the table.

Figure 23.8   The Table of Authorities tab.

Updating a Table of Authorities

Place the insertion point anywhere in the table of authorities, then press F9. Word will update the table to include any recent insertions, deletions, etc.

Custom Styles and Categories

Word lets you change the appearance of the styles used for TOAs. It also lets you create and edit category names. Consult the online help for details.

Tables of Figures

Word will help you create tables of figures and other elements based on captions and bookmarks. Assuming you've captioned the figures in your document with the Insert ➤ Caption command, the process is quite simple:

1. Place the insertion point where you want the table to appear.

2. Choose Insert ➤ Index and Tables.

3. Display the Table of Figures tab if it is not in view. It will look like Figure 23.9.

4. Select the desired caption label from the scrolling list.

5. Select a format for the table.

6. Visit the Table of Figures Options dialog box if necessary to pick the style you want Word to use as the basis of the table.

Figure 23.9   **The Table of Figures tab.**

7. Back in the Table of Figures tab, make other option choices (Show Page Numbers, etc.).

8. Click OK.

9. Word will compile a table and place it at the insertion point.

Updating a Table of Figures

Place the insertion point anywhere in the table of figures; then press F9. Word will update the table to include any recent insertions, deletions, etc.

Chapter 24

Working with Large Documents and Team Projects

FAST TRACK

To define text as hideable ("hidden") 529

select the desired text. Visit the Font dialog box (choose Format ➤ Font). Check Hidden in the Effects area. Click OK to set. Before printing, check the Hidden Text choice in the Print tab of the Options dialog box (Tools ➤ Options) if you want the hideable text to print.

To create annotations 531

place the insertion point in your document or select the item you wish to discuss. Pick Insert ➤ Annotation (not View ➤ Annotations). You'll see the annotation pane. Word will insert your initials as hidden text. Type the note. Either choose Close or leave the pane visible as you work.

To view annotations 532

double-click on the annotation mark of interest in your document or use the View ➤ Annotations command. (If you don't see marks, reveal them with the Standard toolbar's ¶ button.) To view the next or previous annotation, scroll in the annotation pane. To filter annotations so that you see only those from a particular author, pick the initials of interest from the annotation pane's drop-down list. Close the annotation pane with the Close button.

To password-protect a document 532

choose Tools ➤ Protect Document. The Protect Document dialog box will appear. Choose the protection you desire (for example, Annotations). Enter a clever password. Repeat it when Word asks. Click OK or press ↵. Remember it.

To have Word mark your revisions 535

start with a draft document and turn on revision marking by checking the Mark Revisions While Editing option box in the upper-left corner of the Revision Marks dialog box. As you work, Word marks your revisions using embellishments you specify by selecting Options in the Revision dialog box. Print and distribute (or e-mail) your marked-up draft with the revisions.

One person's large document is another's small one. Word has the ability to create documents of virtually any length. At some point, however, you will find that Word's performance degrades as your document size increases. This is particularly true of older, slower computers with limited RAM and slow hard disks.

Many people routinely work with documents containing hundreds of pages. But if you are disappointed by your computer's performance (scrolling speed, spell checking, autosave, etc.), you might want to split a single document into multiple documents. Another reason to split documents is to have different people work on different parts of the project. After everyone is done, you'll probably want to print the whole body of work as if it were one document.

Sometimes people create parts of a long document at various sites and then combine them. Whether you start out with a bunch of small documents and combine them, or split a big document for whatever reason, chances are you'll want to print the completed work as a whole. You *can* combine all the parts and treat the resulting large document as a single entity. Or, you can keep the document broken into multiple sections and use Word's *Master Document* feature.

Group work sometimes causes confusion, so Word offers a number of ways to annotate text and share your thoughts with other authors working on the project. You can even exchange voice notes with each other if you have the right gear.

There are two important things to watch whenever there's more than one "cook in the kitchen"—consistency of appearance and correct page numbering across document parts. This chapter discusses both of these potential problem areas.

Planning for Large Documents

If you know you are going to create a large document, then use templates, AutoText entries, and possibly a set of author's instructions, to create the multiple parts.

TIP   Another good idea would be a hard-copy style sheet for the project and a file-routing strategy and directory structure. That way, everyone will be able to see which versions of a file are old (*foul copies*, as copyeditors used to say), which are being revised, and which are final.

If other people will be working on parts of the document, provide them with copies of your templates, and possibly copies of your custom spelling dictionaries and special fonts. The more alike your computers are, the fewer problems you will have during the crunch.

Develop a strategy. Decide how you plan to number figures, tables, and other design elements. Test these strategies on "mini" versions of your document containing a few samples of each element you plan to use (headers, footers, page numbers, tables, figures, figure captions, paragraph headings, etc.). Work out the bugs with twenty or thirty pages before typing and formatting hundreds.

Consider making logical breaks at the beginning of chapters or sections. Use Word's standard styles and templates and the Style Gallery whenever possible. Put one person in charge of rounding everything up.

Combining Documents with Insert ➤ File

The obvious way to round up multiple files to create a long document is to use the Insert ➤ File command. It places specified files at the insertion point in your document. You are presented with the familiar file selection dialog box where you pick the next file to be inserted. If necessary, Word will attempt to convert files coming from non-Word authors.

You might be wondering why you wouldn't always use Insert ➤ File, as opposed to using the master document feature. The advantages of master documents are two:

▶ Since the master document doesn't actually contain the documents (only "references" to them, sort of like Windows shortcuts), you don't end up with enormous documents.

▶ It's much easier to move things around in a master document, since the feature is specifically designed to be a tool for organizing large documents. For example, moving an entire chapter often requires only a simple click and drag.

When you use Insert ➤ File, how Word handles things like headers, footers, styles, and other formatting issues will depend upon the source files. Here again, it's best to test before the crunch.

WARNING   Word is likely to imitate the look of the original format, but not with styles. It is therefore advisable to attach standardized styles initially, even though it's a bit of a bother.

Master Document Features Facilitate Teamwork

You can use a *master document* and *Master Document* view to divide a long document into shorter subdocuments. This facilitates workgroup editing, and it makes it easier to format, organize, and number pages. Master documents facilitate other tasks like cross-referencing and creating an index or table of contents. Master documents handle many details for you, including the automatic naming of subdocument files. Master documents are perfect for workgroups sharing a file server. Placing the master document on the server lets everyone work on the entire document or its parts without worrying about the location or names of the subfiles.

Creating a Master Document

You can either create a master document at the time you start a new project or turn an existing document into a master document. It's also possible to combine multiple documents to create a master.

Creating a Master Document for a New Project

Here's an easy way (but not the only way) to create a new master document at the time you begin a project:

1. Open a new document using the template you want as the starting point for your project.

2. Choose <u>V</u>iew ➤ <u>M</u>aster Document. Your screen will look like Figure 24.1.

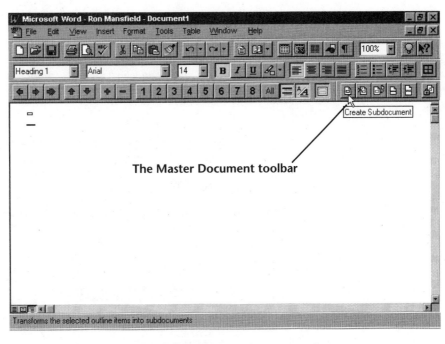

Figure 24.1   Master Document view and the Master Document toolbar.

3.   Word displays the Outline tools described in Chapter 21 and the Master Document toolbar, nestled at the right end of the Outline toolbar. Figure 24.2 details the button names.

4.   Create an outline for your master document using the techniques described in Chapter 21.

Figure 24.2   The Master Document toolbar.

Part 4

Desktop Publishing

TIP Assign Word's Heading 1 style *only* to the entry that you wish to use as the start of each subdocument. For example, if you wanted each chapter to be a subdocument, apply the Word style Heading 1 to chapter heads (and to chapter heads only) as shown in Figure 24.3.

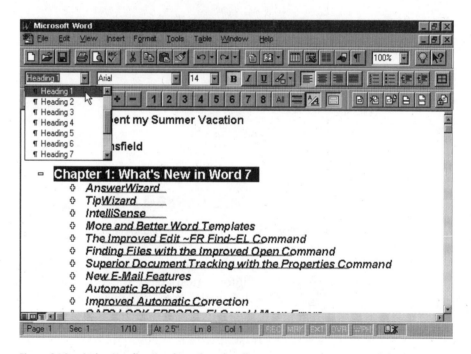

Figure 24.3   Assign Heading 1 only to those headings you want to start new subdocuments.

5. Select *all* of the headings you wish to subdivide, being sure to include the heading you wish to use at the start of each subdocument (the first Heading 1 entry, for example). This heading should be the first item selected. Do not select anything you don't want to be part of the subdocument. Because this is a new outline, we don't have any text yet. Text you subsequently create will be part of the subdocument.

TIP   Collapsing the outline to the top level makes it easier to select the headings and their related text. Figure 24.4 illustrates this concept.

□
□ How I spent my Summer Vacation
□ by
□ Ron Mansfield
✥ **Chapter 1: What's New in Word?**
✥ **Chapter 2: Creating Your First Document**
✥ **Chapter 3 Viewing and Navigating**

Figure 24.4   Select only headings you wish to divide. Make sure the first thing selected is a heading at the "top level"—that is, the level you wish to use as the starting point for each new subdocument.

6. Click the Create Subdocument button on the Master Document toolbar.

7. Word will insert break lines and split the entire project up into subdocuments. You'll see little subdocument icons next to each subdocument break point as shown in Figure 24.5.

> **NOTE**   It's easy to make an existing document into a master document. You just open it in Master Document view, use the outlining tools to display it as an outline, and then follow steps 5–7 above.

Turning an Existing File into a Subdocument

Once you've created a master document it is easy to insert old Word (and many other) documents. Here are the general steps:

1. While in Master Document view, position the insertion point where you want the subdocument document to be placed.

2. Click the Insert Subdocument button on the Master View toolbar. It's the third button from the left.

3. Use the resulting Insert Subdocument dialog box just as you'd use Word's Open dialog box—find the document of interest and click OK.

4. Word will add the document, converting it from another format (like WordPerfect) if necessary.

5. If the incoming document and master document were based on different templates, the incoming work will take on the characteristics of the master document.

Subdocument icons

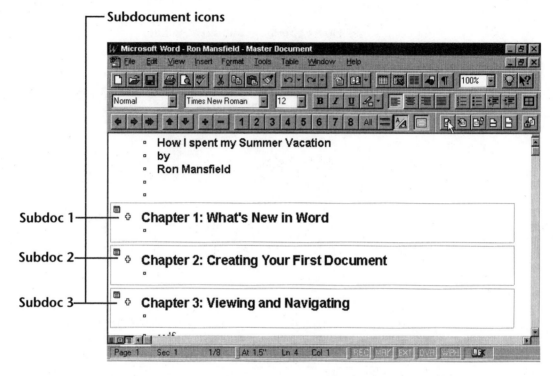

Subdoc 1

Subdoc 2

Subdoc 3

Figure 24.5   The master document now contains three subdocuments—one for each chapter. The book title and author name are saved in the master document.

NOTE   If you later open an external document without using Master Document view, the document will retain its old formatting (based on its original template instead of the master document's template).

Saving Masters and Subs

When you save your master document for the first time, Word assigns file names and locations to the subfiles as well. It does this by using characters from the first heading in each subdocument. When headings are similar, Word assigns numbers as part of the file name to differentiate the different subdocuments.

For instance, in our book example, all the first headings begin with *Chapter(space)*, so Word will assign numbers at the end of each file name. In a perfect world, that would mean that the subfile for Chapter 1 would be automatically named Chapter 1, subfile 2 would be Chapter 2, and so on. But that ain't necessarily so. Read on...

A File-Naming Gotcha

If the subfolder to which you are saving already *has* files named Chapter 1, Chapter 2, and so on, Word will use different numbers for the subchapters. This means that it's possible to end up with a subdocument containing Chapter 1 but named Chapter 4, and a Chapter 2 subdocument called Chapter 5, ad nauseam. Never (ever, ever) trust a computer to name your files for you without checking up on it.

To rename a subfile, follow these steps:

1. Double-click on the subfile icon of interest to open it.

2. Choose <u>F</u>ile ➤ Save <u>A</u>s.

3. Pick a more fitting name.

4. Click OK.

5. Rename all the subdocuments this way before closing the main document.

 WARNING   Never change subdocument file names in Windows Explorer or any other way except via the Save As command as just described. You'll confuse Word and raise your blood pressure.

Working with a Master Document

So, now what? All that work and what does it buy? Here's the deal. You can switch to Master Document view to get the big picture. Rearrange things just as you do in Outline view. Create cross-references for multiple subdocuments. You work on Chapter 1 while somebody at the other end of the network fiddles with Chapter 2. Spell-check and reformat the whole mess at once. Make sweeping style changes. Save a tree; print preview all 200 pages.

You can make sweeping changes by working in Master Document view or change just a subdocument or two in Normal view. Remember to switch to Master Document view before attempting project-wide changes.

Don't forget that the section breaks Word inserts for each subdocument will play a part in things like header and footer designs. Give some thought to whether you want to design headers and footers before or after breaking a large document into subdocuments.

Incidentally, there are some things to remember when working with other people on the same project across a network. You may not be able to change subdocuments that you or others have currently opened elsewhere. Word lets you know when this will be a problem in two ways. First, you'll see a little padlock beneath certain subdocument icons as shown here:

Chapter 1

The other sure-fire sign of trouble is an alert like this one:

This command is not available because the document is locked for edit.

There are two possible reasons for this. Either you are not the original author of the subdocument, in which case it will need to be unlocked (with the appropriate password), or the subdocument is already in use by you or someone else.

If you are the culprit, close the window containing the subdocument or start the search for your partner in crime elsewhere on the network. Make sure that your network's and Word's file protection are set to give access to those with a need to know, read, and write. Learn any necessary passwords. Contact your network manager and the subdocument author(s) for assistance.

Printing Masters and Subs

To print an entire document:

1. Open the master document.

2. Switch to Normal view.

3. Print Preview if you like.

4. Print.

To print the whole project's outline, switch to Master Document view, reveal the desired levels of detail as you would in Outline view (see Chapter 21 for details), and then print.

 TIP   You can open a subdocument by double-clicking on its icon.

To print just a subdocument, open it as you would any other document and print. Be advised however, that if you use any of Word's handy cross-referencing features (described in Chapter 25), the references will probably not be properly updated, and you may see error messages unless you print from the master document.

Annotations

Are you one of those people like me with Post-it notes stuck all over your documents? Word offers several alternatives. Hidden text is one option; another is *voice annotations*, a way to record and play back sounds attached to specific locations in Word documents if your computer is sound-capable. Footnotes can also be used for this purpose if they are not being used for anything else—provided someone deletes them before the document gets printed!

Finally, Word's text annotation and Revisions features let you document changes as you work.

Using Hidden Text for Notes

Hidden text might be better named *hideable* text, as it is not always hidden. In fact, many people leave hidden text in view most of the time. So, with apologies to Microsoft, let's call it hideable text here.

Authors often use hideable text to make notes to themselves or to colleagues. They leave the notes in view while working, then hide them when they print their work. Figure 24.6 shows an example of a hideable note.

In the example, *Too much description here. Trim it* is hideable text. As you can see, it is possible to embellish hideable text just as you can embellish regular text.

To define text as hideable:

1. Select the desired text.

crashed headlong through the window of the tiny Himalayan hut wher
we'd been bivouacked for more than three months.

Too much description here. Trim it.

Sinewy vines crept their way stealthily over the verandah toward the f
gentleman (not the one from Kuala Lumpur, the other one) who was

Figure 24.6　Hideable text has dotted lines under it unless you check the Hidden Text box in the View tab of the Options dialog box.

2. Visit the Font dialog box (choose Format ➤ Font).

3. Check Hidden in the Effects area:

4. Click OK to set.

5. When printing, click on Options in the Print dialog box (File ➤ Print) and check the Hidden Text option in the Include with Document section of the Options dialog box.

> **TIP** The keyboard shortcut to define selected text as hideable is Ctrl+Shift+H. This command is a toggle; if you use it with text already marked as hideable, the text will revert to non-hideable.

Showing and Hiding Text

To show or hide text, follow these steps:

1. Use the View tab in the Options dialog box (reached with Tools ➤ Options).

2. Enable or disable the Hidden Text feature by clicking to add or remove a check.

3. Click OK.

 TIP If you find yourself toggling hidden text frequently, add the Show Hidden Text command to a menu or the toolbar. You may wish to define a keyboard shortcut as well. See Chapter 36 to learn how.

Text Annotations

This feature lets you add reminders to yourself and notes to others collaborating on your document. The notes can be completely hidden, flagged, or displayed and printed. When you are done with them, they can be deleted or incorporated into your final document.

Inserting Annotations

Creating annotations with Word couldn't be easier. Follow these steps:

1. Place the insertion point at the place in your document where you want to insert the annotation or select the item you wish to discuss.

2. Pick Insert ➤ Annotation (*not* View ➤ Annotations).

3. You'll see the annotation pane.

4. Word will insert initials (yours, assuming your initials are in the User Info tab of the Options dialog box) as hidden text.

5. Type the note.

6. Either choose Close or leave the pane visible as you work.

Part 4

Desktop Publishing

TIP If you don't see your initials in the document or in the drop-down From list, visit the User Info tab in the Options dialog box and type your initials in the initials area. Click OK.

Viewing Annotations

You view annotations with the <u>V</u>iew ➤ <u>A</u>nnotations command. (Notice that *this* command is plural while the one on the Insert menu is singular, because you insert annotations one at a time but can view several at once.)

1. Double-click on the annotation mark of interest in your document or use the <u>V</u>iew ➤ <u>A</u>nnotations command. (If you don't see marks, reveal them with the Standard toolbar's ¶ button.)

2. To view the next or previous annotations, scroll in the annotation pane.

3. To filter annotations so that you see only those from a particular author, pick the initials of interest from the annotation pane's drop-down list.

4. When you are done, close the annotation pane with the Close button or leave it open while you work.

NOTE If the author of an annotation highlights text or other document elements when creating the note, those items will be highlighted again when you read the annotation. This is not the same thing as selecting before editing. If you wish to edit a highlighted item, you'll still need to select it.

Editing and Protecting Annotations

You can change any existing annotation, even if you are not the author of the annotation. Hmmm... Startled?

NOTE This procedure for adding password protection is appropriate for any document you are working on in Word.

Actually, it is possible for authors to password-protect annotations (and revision marks) with the <u>T</u>ools ➤ <u>P</u>rotect Document command. If you work with the "ethically challenged," protect your annotations and revisions thus:

1. Choose <u>T</u>ools ➤ <u>P</u>rotect Document. The Protect Document dialog box will appear:

2. Choose the protection you desire (in this case, Annotations).

3. Enter a clever password.

> **WARNING** Punctuation counts when entering passwords; so does capitalization. *watergate, Watergate,* and *WATERGATE* are all different (and dumb) passwords. A good password is something like your dog's name and age or something equally obscure that no one is likely to know, such as the name of the Speaker of the House. Also, beware of the Caps Lock key. Because Word does not indicate in the status area whether Caps Lock is on or off, you have to be especially careful when creating passwords.

4. Repeat it when Word asks.

5. Click OK or press ↵.

> **TIP** If one person is responsible for collating all changes to your document, that person should have all the passwords.

6. Remember it....

Incorporating Annotations

You can copy and paste text from the annotation pane into the document. Drag-and-drop works here too!

Printing Annotations

To print just the annotations, visit the Print dialog box (Ctrl+P) and choose Annotations from the Print What list:

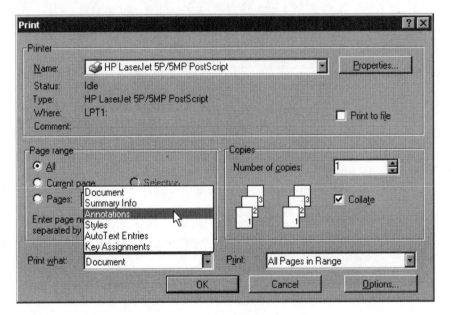

To print a document and its annotations, choose Document in the Print dialog box's Print What list, then click the Options button to reveal the Print tab. Choose Annotations from the Options list:

NOTE   This choice will be unavailable if you have selected Annotations in the Print What box back in the Print dialog box.

Moving and Removing Annotations

Feel free to move and delete annotations by treating their annotation marks as you would any other character in a document. Select them, drag and drop, delete, copy, etc. (Of course, you can do this only if the document is not password-protected or if you know the password.)

Revision Marks

Revision marks show who did what, when, and where—an audit trail of changes, if you will. Revision marks can include strike-throughs, underlining, double underlines, bold characters, and so on. You get to decide how revisions will be marked.

When several people edit a document, Word assigns their reviewer's marks and labels different colors to help keep things straight. Revisions can be displayed and printed, protected, hidden, incorporated in the text, or deleted altogether. You can merge revisions from several copies of a document into one "consolidated" document file. Let's have a look.

TIP   Word uses only eight colors for marking revisions, so if you have more than eight contributors, things can get a little confusing. Consider using one color for each workgroup (marketing, accounting, etc.) and specify colors on each group's machines by using the Revisions tab of the Options dialog box, described later in this chapter and in Chapter 36.

Using the Tools ➤ Revisions Command

The Tools ➤ Revisions command reveals the dialog box shown in Figure 24.7.

1. Start with a draft document and turn on revision marking by checking the Mark Revisions While Editing option box in the upper-left corner of the Revision Marks dialog box.

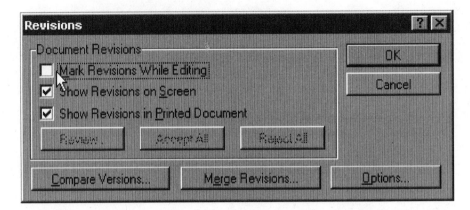

Figure 24.7   **Turn on revision marks in this dialog box.**

2.   As you work, Word marks your revisions using embellishments you specify by selecting Options in the Revision dialog box. At this point you will see old and new text whether you have deleted it or not. In Figure 24.8, newly inserted text is underlined and deleted text is marked with strike-through lines.

```
    To the best of my recollection, I never inhaled used
illegal substances while in this country.
```

Figure 24.8   **Revisions are marked for review.**

3.   Print and distribute (or e-mail) your marked-up draft with the revisions.

> **TIP**   To force automatic revision tracking, open the Normal template, enable revision tracking, and save the changes as Normal (thus replacing the old Normal template). If you work in a group, make sure everyone's Normal template is modified.

Reviewing Revisions

Here's how to review revisions whether you or someone else created them:

1. Open the document.

2. Unmodified text, modified text, and revision marks will show. If you have a color display, revisions will be in one or more colors.

3. Choose Tools ➤ Revisions. You'll see the dialog box shown back in Figure 24.7.

4. At this point you can click the Accept All button to accept all revisions, Reject All to reject all revisions, or Review to consider revisions one at a time.

5. If you choose Review, you'll see the dialog box illustrated in Figure 24.9.

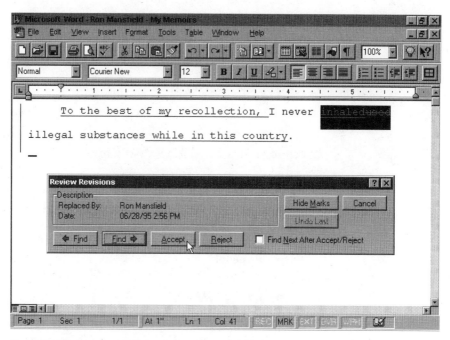

Figure 24.9   *Review, accept, or reject individual changes from here.*

6. You'll see who made the change and when. You can accept or reject the change, or procrastinate by moving on or closing the dialog box without making a decision. When you accept, the related revision marks and deleted text will disappear. Inserted text will take its rightful place.

7. Move from revision to revision with the two Find buttons. A check in the Find Next box moves you to the next revision after accepting or rejecting a change. Undo—well, it undoes.

8. Cancel will close the dialog box for you.

Comparing Documents

If revision marks were not turned on when a document was edited, you can review the changes by comparing the edited version with the original file. The files must either have different file names or reside in different directories. Here are the general steps:

1. Open the *edited* document.

2. Choose Tools ➤ Revisions.

3. Click Compare Versions.

4. Type or select the name and location of the *original* file.

5. In the edited version, all the revisions will now be marked, and you can accept or reject them individually or all at once.

 NOTE   If the original has been edited since the copy was made, both sets of revisions are marked, but are not distinguished from one another unless the revisions are made in different colors. Since it's common for several people to be editing the same file, it's a good idea to assign specific colors to specific people.

Customizing Revision Marks

Word lets you specify colors, revision-mark types, and more from the colorful Revisions tab of the Options dialog box. Reach it with the Tools ➤ Options command or with the Options button in the Revisions dialog box.

Notice that there is now a Highlight Color option. This uses the Highlighting tool from the Formatting toolbar to highlight text that you want other to pay particular attention to.

Voice Annotations—Maybe...

Some computers contain audio boards that let you record sounds to disk and then play them back. Word provides a built-in software feature that lets you record voice annotations. It saves these annotations with your Word documents. But before you toss out your pocket dictating machine, there are some things you should know. Sound files are pretty big. There are RAM considerations as well. Not all sound boards are Word-compatible. Once the appropriate sound-recording hardware is installed and configured (check your manuals for these things), if you give a file to others, they must also have properly installed, compatible sound boards to listen to your voice notes.

Part
4

Desktop Publishing

Recording Voice Annotations

Word makes it easy to record voice annotations. Here are the steps for recording voice annotations on an audio-capable computer:

1. Place the insertion point where you want to attach a voice annotation (after a text annotation, perhaps) or select an item you wish to discuss.

2. Choose <u>I</u>nsert ➤ <u>A</u>nnotation.

3. The annotation pane will appear, complete with a button that looks like a cassette recorder. It's called the Insert Sound Object Button.

4. Click on the button to begin recording.

5. Follow the recording instructions that came with your sound board.

6. If Word asks you whether to update the sound object, answer Yes.

7. Either close the annotation pane or leave it open if you wish to add other annotations.

Playing Voice Annotations

You must have a properly installed audio board to play sounds. Begin by choosing <u>V</u>iew ➤ <u>A</u>nnotations. Double-click on the icon for the sound you wish to hear.

Pen Annotations

You can write directly in the annotation pane if you have a pen-equipped computer. Word treats the writings as graphic objects. Install the Pen Annotation button in one of your toolbars so that you can click it before writing. See Chapter 36 to learn more about adding toolbar buttons and consult your hardware manuals regarding pen features.

Merging Revisions and Annotations

Sometimes you will want to combine revisions or annotations from multiple authors playing pass-the-floppy or the network equivalent. Here are the general steps.

1. Open the document containing the revisions or annotations (from a coworker, perhaps).

2. Choose <u>T</u>ools ➤ R<u>e</u>visions.

3. Click Merge Revisions.

4. Specify the original document (the one that will be receiving the additions) in the Original File Name box.

5. Word will incorporate the changes. If your coworker used revision marks when making the changes, those marks will appear in the merged document.

WARNING Word can sometimes make changes you won't like when you merge. It's a good idea to work with a copy of your "original" document when merging, particularly if you work with the Automatic Save feature enabled. Automatic Save can be overridden by closing without saving, but why take a chance?

Routing Documents

While we are on the subject of teamwork, it is worth noting that if y'all are connected to a network, Word can help you play "pass the document." Check out the great new Routing feature discussed in Chapter 31.

Part 4

Desktop Publishing

Chapter 25

Bookmarks, Captions, and Cross-Referencing

FAST TRACK

either move the insertion point to the item of interest or select the item. Choose Edit ➤ Bookmark (Ctrl+Shift+F5). You'll see the Bookmark dialog box. Give the bookmark a unique name consisting of up to 40 characters. Spaces are not allowed, so use an underscore instead. Click Add. (If the button is dimmed, check to see that the name is less than 40 characters long and contains no spaces.) Create more bookmarks or close the box. Clicking the Add button will also close the dialog box.

visit the Bookmark dialog box. Choose the desired bookmark name. Click the Delete key; then click Close. The bookmark disappears and the previously marked items remain.

turn on Bookmark markers in the View tab. Select the item and both bookmark markers. Delete as usual (Cut, press Delete, etc.). The mark and the items(s) will disappear.

To add a caption manually 548

select the item to be captioned. Choose Insert ➤ Caption. You'll see the Caption dialog box. Word proposes a caption label that you can accept as is or edit. For example, you can type descriptive text. Change the default appearance options, if you wish, by visiting the Position List and Numbering dialog box. Click OK to insert the label. Be patient, it takes a moment.

To add a series of captions automatically 550

choose Insert ➤ Caption and click AutoCaption. Pick one or more types of items to automatically caption. Pick a label type from the Use Label list or create your own with the New Label button. Pick a position for the label (above or below the item). Change the numbering scheme if you like. Repeat these steps for each different type of caption you want. Click OK.

To create new label types 551

use the New Label button in the Caption and AutoCaption dialog boxes.

To include chapter and similar numbers in automatic captions 551

format all of the Main headings (Chapters, for example) as Heading Style 1. Choose Format ➤ Heading Numbering. Make sure a numerical numbering style is in use (not Chapter One, for instance). Visit either the Caption or AutoCaption dialog box. Choose the Numbering button. When you see the Caption Numbering dialog box, choose Include Chapter Numbers. Return to your document by clicking OK as needed.

To update cross-references immediately 553

press F9. They will also be updated when you switch to Print Preview or print.

Word's bookmarks let you name specific points or areas of your document. Use bookmarks to identify the beginning of chapters, tables, spots that need work, the place where you left off, and so on. You can mark a place, a character, ranges of characters, graphics, or just about any other Word document element. You can then tell Word to go to those specific points without a lot of scrolling and searching. You can also use bookmarks to indicate ranges of pages in indexes.

Captions are the words that appear next to a figure in your text, identifying the figure and perhaps explaining what it is supposed to be illustrating. (The descriptive part of the caption is optional, but it's a good idea.)

Cross-references let you refer to different places in your document and have Word keep track of those references when things change. For example, if you say *see Figure 3*, and then add a new figure between the old figures 2 and 3, Word will automatically renumber the figures and the in-text references to them.

Bookmarks

To use bookmarks, you simply locate things of interest, define them as bookmarks, and visit them as necessary. Here are the general steps.

Defining Bookmarks

To define a bookmark, follow these steps:

1. Either move the insertion point to the item of interest or select the item.

2. Choose Edit ➤ Bookmark (Ctrl+Shift+F5). You'll see the Bookmark dialog box, shown in Figure 25.1.

3. Give the bookmark a unique name consisting of up to 40 characters. Numbers are allowed, but not as the first character of the name. Spaces are *not* allowed, so use an underscore instead, as illustrated in Figure 25.1.

4. Click Add. (If the button is dimmed, check to see that the name is less than 40 characters long, does not begin with a number, and contains no spaces.)

5. Create more bookmarks or close the box. Clicking on Add also closes the dialog box.

Figure 25.1   **Creating a bookmark.**

Going to a Bookmark

Once you've defined a bookmark, you can go to it in one of two ways. If you select Edit ➤ Go To and choose Bookmark from the Go to What list, you'll see a scrolling list of bookmarks (as illustrated in Figure 25.2).

Figure 25.2   **Double-click on a bookmark's name either in the Go To or Bookmark dialog box to go to it.**

Click on a bookmark's name and click the Go To button to go there. If you click the Go To button in the Bookmark dialog box (Edit ➤ Bookmark), however, Word will go to the selected bookmark without displaying the Go To dialog box.

In the Bookmark dialog box, you can sort the list either by name or by the relative location of the bookmark in the document:

TIP If you have only one bookmark in a document, double-clicking on Bookmark in the Go To What list will take you directly to that bookmark. A single bookmark may be all you need if you simply want to mark your place as you work; just remember to update its location before you move around or close the document. To move a bookmark, choose Edit ➤ Goto, make sure the bookmark's name is selected (it will be if there is only one), and click Add. The bookmark will move to the current insertion point, and you can quickly jump to that location to resume work next time you open the document.

Viewing the Marks Themselves

Word also lets you display in-document markers that tip off the location of bookmarks. Choose Tools ➤ Options, visit the View tab, and check the Bookmarks option in the Show area.

Large square brackets will then indicate the beginning and ending of a bookmarked area. For instance, the entire heading *Patch Panel* is a bookmark:

¶
[Patch·panel]¶

Data·jacks·are·

> **NOTE** If you select text before setting a bookmark, you'll get something that looks like [ ]. If you don't select text, though, you'll get something that looks like a big *I*.

As you can see, these markers can get in the way of the text, so you may want to turn them off and use Edit ➤ Go To when you just want to resume work at a bookmarked location, for example.

Working with Bookmarked Items

It's often easiest to work with bookmarked items and see the effect of your work if you have the bookmark markers displayed.

If you move a bookmarked item, the mark moves with it, even to another document (as long as this won't create a duplicate bookmark name in the destination document).

Deleting the entire text or other items between two bookmark markers deletes the bookmark as well. (Say that five times fast.)

To add things and have them included with the bookmark, insert them within the bookmark marks. To insert things and not have them included, place the insertion point to the right of the bookmark marker.

You can use bookmark names in some field operations (described in Chapter 32), so it is even possible to perform computations and do other tricks with marked items.

Deleting Bookmarks

To delete a mark *but not* the marked item(s), follow these steps:

1. Visit the Bookmark dialog box.

2. Choose the desired bookmark name.

3. Click the Delete key.

4. Click Close. The bookmark disappears and the previously marked items remain.

To delete a bookmark *and* the items it marks:

1. Turn on Show Bookmarks in the View tab.

2. Select the item and both bookmark markers.

3. Delete as usual (Cut, press Delete, etc.). The mark and the items(s) will disappear.

Captions

If you write long documents with numbered figures, tables, and other elements, are you gonna love this feature! It automatically numbers things, lets you label them, and renumbers them if you move them or otherwise change their sequence in a document. There are a variety of appearance options as well.

Adding Captions

You can either manually caption the occasional item or turn on automatic captioning. To add a caption manually:

1. Select the item to be captioned.

2. Choose Insert ➤ Caption.

3. You'll see the Caption dialog box, illustrated in Figure 25.3.

4. Word proposes a caption label that you can accept as is or edit. For example, you can type descriptive text, as shown in Figure 25.3.

Figure 25.3 **Manually inserting a caption.**

5. Change the default appearance options, if you wish, by visiting the Position List and Numbering dialog box.

6. Click OK to insert the label. Be patient; it takes a moment.

To add captions automatically to items of a particular type (all Excel Charts, for instance), use the AutoCaption dialog box, reached with the AutoCaption button in the Caption dialog box. The AutoCaption dialog box is illustrated in Figure 25.4.

Word can recognize and automatically caption the following types of files:

▶ Most graphic files

▶ Microsoft drawings

▶ Microsoft equations

▶ Microsoft Graphs

▶ Microsoft WordArt

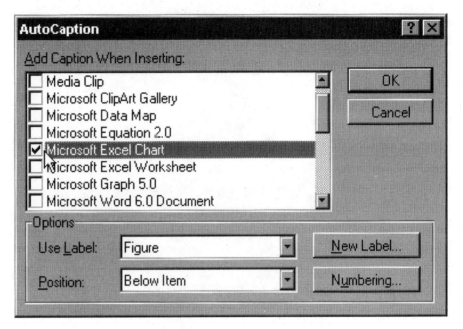

Figure 25.4   **The AutoCaption dialog box.**

▶ Inserted Word documents

▶ Microsoft PowerPoint presentations and slides

▶ Paintbrush pictures

▶ Sounds

▶ Excel charts and worksheets

▶ Video clips

▶ MIDI sequences

▶ And much more

   To automatically caption things, follow these steps:

1. Choose Insert ➤ Caption.

2. Click AutoCaption.

3. Pick a type of item to be captioned. You can pick more than one type for the same caption label (for instance, you can pick Excel charts and

PowerPoint slides to be captioned as Figures). Inserting either will have the same effect.

4. Pick a label type from the Use Label list or create your own with the New Label button.

5. Pick a position for the label (above or below the item).

6. Change the numbering scheme if you like.

7. Repeat steps 3 through 6 for each different type of caption you want.

8. Click OK.

After you've turned on AutoCaption and defined the appearance options, Word will automatically label any insertion that meets the Auto-Caption criteria. You can then add descriptive text to the captions.

If you move a figure and its label, Word will not immediately update the figure labels. But it *will* update figure numbers whenever you ask to print or switch to Print Preview. To force an immediate update, select all of your text (Ctrl+A) and press F9.

To revise a caption, just edit it like any other text. To change all of the captions of a given type (*Figure* to *FIG*, for instance), select a caption in text, visit the Caption or AutoCaption dialog box, and pick a different label from the Use Label List.

To create new label types (*FIG*, for example), use the New Label button in the Caption and AutoCaption dialog boxes.

Including Chapter and Other Numbers in Captions

You can include chapter and similar numbers in automatic captions if you like. Here are the general steps:

1. Format all of the Main headings (Chapters, for example) as the Heading 1 style.

2. Choose Format ➤ Heading Numbering. Make sure a numerical numbering style is in use (*Chapter 1*, for instance, not *Chapter One*).

3. Visit either the Caption or AutoCaption dialog box.

4. Choose the Numbering button.

5. When you see the Caption Numbering dialog box, choose Include Chapter numbers.

6. Click OK as needed to exit the dialog boxes.

Cross-References

Cross-referencing lets you say things like *see Chapter 9 for details*, and then have Word automatically update the reference if you change the chapter number. Cross-references are not limited to chapter numbers; they can refer to just about anything, including headings, footnotes, endnotes, captions, etc. You can cross-reference items in different documents, as long as they are in the same master document (see Chapter 24).

Creating Cross-References

Here are the general steps for creating cross-references:

1. Begin by typing the in-text reference followed by a quotation mark (**See** ", for example).

2. Choose <u>I</u>nsert ➤ Cross-<u>r</u>eference. You'll see the Cross-reference dialog box, illustrated in Figure 25.5.

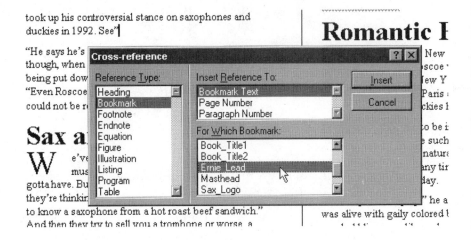

Figure 25.5 **The Cross-reference dialog box.**

3. Pick the Reference Type that will tie the in-text reference to the item you wish to reference (Bookmark, for instance).

4. Choose the type of item to be referenced (Bookmark Text, for example) from the Insert Reference To list.

5. Choose the item you wish to reference from the scrolling For Which list.

6. Click Insert. You'll see some new information at the insertion point. This is actually a field. (See Chapter 32 to learn more about fields.)

7. Click Close or add other cross-references first, then close.

Once you've created cross-references, they will be updated when you switch to Print Preview or print. To update immediately at any time, select the entire document and press F9.

If you delete an item that is referenced, Word will alert you.

Chapter 26

Using Specialty Paper Stock

FAST TRACK

To apply a paper size, orientation, or source to a section 561

first create the section. Put the insertion point within the section. Select File ➤ Page Setup and choose the settings you want. Make sure This Section is selected in the Apply To drop-down list box and click OK.

To create a section break as you apply your new settings 562

place the insertion point where you want the break to appear and then select File ➤ Page Setup and choose the settings you want. Select This Point Forward in the Apply To drop-down list box and click OK.

To create two section breaks before and after your new settings 563

first select the text you want to get the new settings. Then select File ➤ Page Setup and choose the settings you want. Make sure Selected Text is showing in the drop-down list box and click OK.

To change the normal paper size, orientation, or source 564

select File ➤ Page Setup and choose the settings you want. Then click the Default button. Click Yes on the dialog box that appears. Then click OK.

To maintain several custom sizes 564

create each size in a different new document and save each document as a template.

Special documents often require special printing stock and unusual kinds or sizes of paper. If you lay out a three-fold brochure, for example, you may decide that you'd rather print on thicker card stock instead of the usual paper. With the right kind of paper stock, you can print your own Rolodex-style cards or produce odd-sized mailings.

Word doesn't offer too many built-in paper choices. They're all variations on standard letter, legal, or European page sizes, or typical envelopes; and they work for most users most of the time. But when you do have a special need, Word allows you to customize the paper-size settings, so you can just measure your paper stock and enter the correct dimensions manually.

Before we get into designing your paper size, let's first run through the basic procedures for choosing a paper size (or orientation).

Selecting a Paper Size and Orientation

You choose your paper size and orientation setting from the Page Setup dialog box. To get there, select File➤ Page Setup.

> **TIP** It's best to make your paper size and orientation selections, along with your other page-setup choices, before you start typing up your document. It's easy to change these settings at any point, but by starting with the correct dimensions, you'll be able to see right away what your layout will look like and avoid unpleasant surprises.

This brings up the Page Setup dialog box. Select the Paper Size tab (see Figure 26.1).

The Paper Size box and the Width and Height boxes are interconnected. The Orientation setting also affects the Height and Width boxes. If you choose Letter ($8^1/_2 \times 11$ in), the default choice, the Width will automatically set itself to 8.5″ and the Height to 11″ (as long as the Orientation is Portrait).

Choosing a Different Orientation

Orientation indicates the way the paper is turned relative to the text on it. (Of course, the paper doesn't actually turn in a different direction in your printer—the printer turns the text instead.) Portrait is the usual

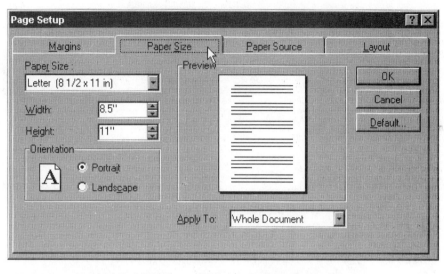

Figure 26.1   The Page Setup dialog box with the Paper Size tab foremost.

vertical orientation of a letter page. Landscape is the alternative, wider than it is high.

If you click the Landscape button in the Orientation area, the Width and Height figures will do a switcheroo. The numbers stay the same, because the paper size has not changed, but they switch places.

Look also at the Preview area. It's more than a simple, static picture of a dummy page. It responds and changes to reflect the choices you make in the other boxes. When you click Landscape, the picture changes and the dummy text spreads out to fill the new shape.

Choosing a Different Paper Size

Choosing a built-in paper size is as simple as clicking the Paper Size drop-down list and choosing one of the options listed there. Try selecting Legal ($8^1/_2 \times 14$ in) in and notice how the Preview changes. Then try selecting Envelope #10 ($4^1/_8 \times 9^1/_2$ in) and look at the Preview.

Part
4

Desktop Publishing

NOTE   Many settings depend upon your printer, so what you see here might not be exactly what you see on your screen. Don't worry about these minor differences.

Now try selecting Custom Size in the Paper Size list box (it's the last choice). Nothing happens—whatever Height and Width went along with your last Paper Size choice are still there. Custom Size doesn't mean any specific Height and Width. It means you can specify the size you want. We'll look at creating your own custom paper size next.

Creating Custom Paper Sizes

If none of the built-in paper sizes is appropriate for your desktop publishing project, then you'll just have to roll up your sleeves and create a custom size. It's actually remarkably easy.

First, measure the paper stock you'll be using. (Perhaps the measurement is given on the packaging, but it never hurts to measure it for yourself.) Jot down the height (the long dimension) and the width.

Then select File ➤ Setup and click the Paper Size tab. Select Custom Size in the Paper Size box or just change the Height and Width settings.

If you change one of these by .2″ or more from a standard size, Custom Size will be selected automatically:

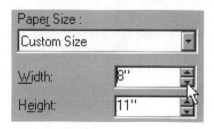

You can enter your measurements directly or click the spin arrow buttons to inch (actually tenth of an inch) your way to the correct dimensions.

It's often easier just to type them in. The Preview will adjust as you change the measurements, and it's a good idea to eyeball it and make sure that it looks proportional to the paper you're using (just to avoid gross errors).

When you've chosen the Paper Size and Orientation that you want, click OK. Depending on the size or orientation you've chosen, the zoom percentage might change. (You can change it back if you prefer with the Zoom Control tool or Zoom on the View menu.)

See the following sections for how to choose a different paper source, apply your custom size to just part of a document, or make your new size the default.

Part
4

Desktop Publishing

TIP   For rotary card (Rolodex-style) stock or other specialty paper sizes with more than one unit to the page, you'll find it easier to pretend you're making custom mailing labels. You still have to measure your basic unit size. Mailing labels are explained in Chapter 15 (and mail merges with label documents are covered in Chapter 28), but here's the quick-and-dirty run-through: Select Tools ➤ Envelopes and Labels, click the Labels tab, and click the Options button. Select Custom Laser in the Product Number box and then click the Details button. Enter the measurements for your paper stock and then click OK twice and click Print.

Specifying the Paper Source

If you're planning to print on a nonstandard paper stock, you might want to select a different option for the paper source. By default, all the pages of your document will be printed from the default tray (usually the upper tray, if there's more than one) of your printer. To choose a different source, select File ➤ Page Setup and select the Paper Source tab (or just click the Paper Source tab if the Page Setup dialog box is already on the screen), as shown in Figure 26.2.

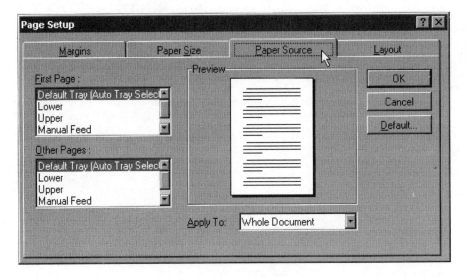

Figure 26.2   The Paper Source tab of the Page Setup dialog box. Specify a source for the first page and the rest of the document here.

If the first page is going to be treated as different from the rest (printed on different paper, for example), then you can select a different option in the First Page list box. Otherwise, select the same options in both the First Page and the Other Pages list boxes.

The available options will vary depending on your printer. For a standard, HP LaserJet 5P/5MP PostScript printer, the options are:

▶ Default Tray (Auto Tray Select)

▶ Lower

▶ Upper

▶ Manual Feed

▶ Auto Tray Select

Select Upper only if you have both a lower and upper tray (the lower tray is the default) and you want to use the upper tray. The manual feed option is there so that you can feed in a different kind of stock (envelope or other) while keeping your normal paper in the default tray. You might have another option, such as Envelope, if you have a special envelope feeder.

Applying a Different Paper Size to Part of a Document

If you need part of a document to be printed on a different type of paper, in a different orientation, or on paper fed from a different source, you can break your document into sections and then choose different Page Setup options for each section.

NOTE   Document sections are covered in Chapter 13.

There are two ways to do this. You can create your section breaks first, or you can apply your new Page Setup settings to just part of your document and force Word to create section breaks for you.

Making a Section Break Ahead of Time

To insert a section break ahead of time, first place the insertion point where you want the new section to start. You can make a selection, but the section break will be inserted at the beginning of the selection just as if the insertion point was there.

Then select Insert ➤ Break. This brings up the Break dialog box:

Select Next Page in the Section Breaks area and then click OK. If you're going to want another section break, either to go back to the original settings or to apply a third set of Page Setup options, move the insertion point to the next breaking place and repeat this process.

> **TIP**   If you want one section in the middle of a document to get a different page setup and the rest to stay the same, use the method described in *Applying New Page Setup Settings to a Selection*, coming up.

Now put the insertion point in the section you want to change (if you've just added a single section break, then it should already be in the right place) and follow the instructions in *Selecting a Paper Size and Orientation* earlier in this chapter.

Applying New Page Setup Settings from "This Point Forward"

If you know that you'll want different Page Setup settings to apply from a certain point through the end of a document (or up to the point where you next make some changes), then you don't need to make your section break first.

Instead, just put the insertion point where you want your new settings to take hold. Then select File ➤ Page Setup. In the Page Setup dialog box, choose your settings and then select This Point Forward in the Apply To drop-down list box. Then click OK. Word inserts a section break where the insertion point was and applies your settings in the new section.

NOTE   If you select This Point Forward in any tab of the Page Setup dialog box, your selections in all the other tabs will also be applied from the insertion point forward when you click OK. However, if you want to apply one setting to the entire document and settings from another tab just from this point on, select File ➤ Page Setup and choose your universal settings, making sure to apply them to the Whole Document, and click OK. Then select File ➤ Page Setup again and choose your local settings, making sure to apply them from This Point Forward.

Applying New Page Setup Settings to a Selection

If you know for sure that your special Page Setup settings should apply to a limited portion of your document, such as a Landscape-oriented spreadsheet or chart in a report, then you don't need to make the section break first. Instead, just select the text that will constitute your new section and then select File ➤ Page Setup. In the Page Setup dialog box, choose the settings that you want in whatever tabs you want and make sure Selected Text is showing in the Apply To drop-down list box. Then click OK. Word inserts a section break before and after your selection, applying your settings to the section in between while keeping the old settings in sections before and after the new breaks.

NOTE   If you select Selected Text in any tab of the Page Setup dialog box, your selections in all the other tabs will also be applied to the selection when you click OK. However, if you want to apply one setting to the entire document and settings from another tab just to selected text, select File ➤ Page Setup and choose your universal settings, making sure to apply them to the Whole Document, and click OK. Then select File ➤ Page Setup again and choose your local settings, making sure to apply them to Selected Text.

What Happens When You Delete Section Breaks?

If you delete a section break, the settings for the following section get applied to the preceding section. This is because the Page Setup settings are stored in the section break character. If you delete that character, the

Part
4

Desktop Publishing

sections before and after the break are joined into one, and the settings for the latter apply.

Changing the Default Paper Size or Orientation

If, for whatever reason, you plan to use a different paper size or orientation most of the time, you can make those settings the default, either for the Normal template or for a custom template you create for this purpose. This way, all new documents (at least all new ones based on the present template) will have that paper size and orientation.

To do this, select File ➤ Page Setup and choose the settings that you want to be the default (in whichever tabs you want). Then click the Default button, on the right.

This will bring up a dialog box like the following:

Click Yes if you're sure or No to change your mind.

> NOTE   All you really do if you click the Default button is save your Page Setup settings in the template on which the current document is based (in the illustration, Normal). You could achieve the same effect by opening the template, selecting File ➤ Page Setup there, choosing your settings, clicking OK, and then saving the changes. The Default button is just a shortcut.

Maintaining Several Different Custom Paper Sizes

The Page Setup dialog box will allow you to establish only one kind of Custom Size (per section), so if you want to have more than one preset Custom Size available, you'll have to create a different template for each one. Just start a new document, select File ➤ Page Setup, and choose the settings you want. Then select File ➤ Save to save the document. In the Save As dialog box, choose Document Template in the Save File as Type drop-down list box. Give the template a name and click OK.

Then, when you want to use that kind of paper stock, just create a new document based on the template you saved. You can create as many templates as you need.

Part
4

Desktop Publishing

Chapter 27

The Document Shop

FAST TRACK

This chapter shows you how to construct useful documents in minutes, using Word's Wizards, templates, "canned" documents, and other tools. The common theme here is that Word does most of the busy work (tabs, fonts, leading, borders, and other formatting issues), leaving you to create, customize, and add your own personal touch. These features are sometimes confusing, even to Word experts, but there are really only three things you need to understand:

➤ Wizards are automatic programs that run within Word to help you set up specific types of documents. These include letters, memos, awards, calendars, agendas, and so forth. You use Wizards to create documents "on the fly," telling Word how you want things to look each step of the way.

➤ Templates are documents with special formatting and often a distinctive design. You can base all your documents upon templates to ensure a consistent look. Usually you fill in all the text in these, but some text may be filled in for you (such as the word *Fax* at the top of the Fax template). The three-fold brochure is an example of a template.

➤ There are more than a dozen templates with "canned" text, such as price increase announcements, thank-you letters, credit report requests, and many others. You fill in the specifics, but Word takes care of all the formatting and most of the wording. These are accessed through Letter Wizard.

And for those few projects, such as organizational charts and phone lists, where Word doesn't have a Wizard or template, you can take advantage of Word's vast array of tools to do the job quickly and easily. We'll look at these projects specifically at the end of the chapter.

 NOTE Throughout the chapter you'll be told to use the File ➤ New command to reach the New dialog box. The Ctrl+N shortcut and New toolbar button both bypass the New dialog box when opening a new document, and therefore cannot be used to access templates and Wizards.

Wizards

Wizards are very complicated macros that run within Word to help you set up specific types of documents. All Wizards work the same way: they ask you questions about the document you want to make and then follow your every command. What's really nice is that Wizards show you how the document is going to look as you go along, so you can play "what if" games to see which designs you like the best. You can even back up as you are creating your document, changing previous format or design decisions.

Word comes with the following Wizards:

Agenda

Award

Calendar

Fax

Letter

Memo

Newsletter

Pleading

Resume

Table

We'll work through an entire Wizard project here, just to help you get the hang of it. Since all Wizards work alike, you can then use any of the others to create documents as the need arises. Our sample project will use the Award Wizard. Here's how to create an award with it:

1. Select File ➤ New (again, the New Document button won't work here). This will bring up the New dialog box. Click the Other Documents tab to bring it forward (see Figure 27.1).

2. Select Award Wizard.

3. Click OK. This opens a new document based on the Award Wizard template. The Wizard displays a dialog box (see Figure 27.2).

4. Select one of the four styles for your award. To preview the different styles, click on them one after another and wait for the sample to update itself.

5. When you've chosen the style you want, Click the Next>> button. The dialog box changes to ask you some more questions (see Figure 27.3).

6. Select Portrait if you want that orientation or leave the first question's answer as Landscape if you prefer.

Figure 27.1   **The New dialog box with the Other Documents tab foremost.**

Figure 27.2   **The first Award Wizard dialog box. Select the type of award you wish to make.**

Figure 27.3 *Decide whether you want the award to have Portrait or Landscape orientation.*

7.   Click Yes to the second question if you have special bordered paper to print your award on. (If you do, you'll still want to do a test print on normal paper to see if the layout fits. More on this shortly.)

8.   Click the Next>> button. The dialog box changes again (see Figure 27.4).

9.   Type the name of the recipient in the first text box and the title of the award in the second.

10. Click the Next>> button to see the screen shown in Figure 27.5.

11. If you want your name to be first among the presenters of the award, click the Add button. Otherwise, type a different name and then click the Add button. Repeat as often as necessary. If you add a name by mistake, highlight the wrong name and click the Remove button.

12. Click the Next>> button.

13. If you want to enter a name for the presenting organization, click Presented By and then type an organization name in the text box.

14. Click the Next>> button.

Figure 27.4   *Enter a name and title.*

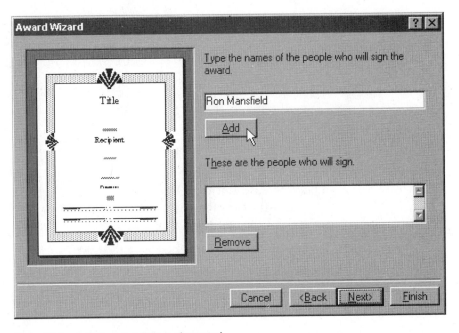

Figure 27.5   *Add signature lines to the award.*

15. Type the date of the award in the first text box (or accept the default current date, if that's appropriate).

16. If you want additional text on the award, type it in the second box. If you want none, delete the dummy text suggested by the Wizard. (If, by some amazing coincidence, "For extraordinary work" is exactly what you would have added yourself, then just leave it.)

17. Click the Next>> button. Your hard work is done! The Wizard lets you know you're finished (see Figure 27.6).

18. If you plan to fine-tune your award immediately after creating it and want the Wizard to display a list of Word's related Help topics, click *Yes, display Help as I work*.

19. Click Finish. The Wizard creates your award (see Figure 27.7).

20. Click the Print button to print the award.

> **TIP** If you *do* have bordered paper of your own, print the award on plain paper first and then hold the sample up to the light with the bordered paper as an overlay. If the text does not fit the border properly, play around with the margins of the award document and print it out again. Repeat until it fits and *then* print the award on your special paper.

Figure 27.6 *The Wizard lets you know you're done and offers continued help.*

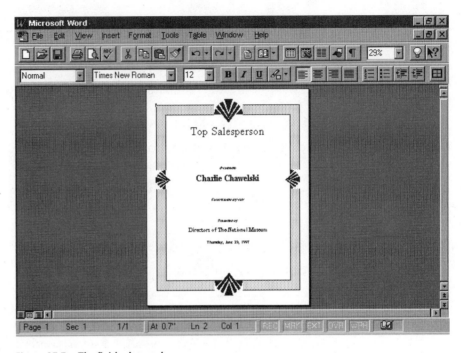

Figure 27.7   **The finished award.**

Templates

Word provides many excellent templates to help ensure a consistent and professional look in your documents. Templates generally have special formatting and a unique design. Many templates have dummy text to guide you in using them. For example, you'll see a field marked *Click Here to Insert Your Name* and you just follow directions. Some templates will even have extended passages explaining how you can format and customize them.

Word's most common templates (letter, memo, etc.) come in three different types: Contemporary, Elegant, and Professional. Others come in only one type. Here is a catalog of templates that come with Word.

Available in All Three Types	Available in Only One Type
Fax	Brochure
Letter	Directory

Available in All Three Types	Available in Only One Type
Memo	Invoice
Press Release	Manual
Report	Newsletter
Resume	Purchase Order
	Thesis
	Weekly Time Sheet

NOTE   There will often be more than one way you can do a project in Word. For example, you can create a letter either by opening a template or by using a Wizard. Which technique you use depends largely upon your own preferences.

We'll work through a simple template project here to give you a feel for how to use them. Since most templates work the same way, you can use any of the others as needed. Let's look at the Invoice template, which has form fields that make filling it out quick and easy. You have to customize the template the first time you use it (unless your company happens to be called Your Company Name Here), but even that's not too rough.

1. Select File ➤ New (again, the New Document button won't work here). This brings up the New dialog box. Click the Other Documents tab to bring it forward (see Figure 27.8).

2. Select the Invoice template as shown in Figure 27.8 and click OK. This starts a new document based on the Invoice template.

3. The document is a protected form, so to change it, you need to unprotect it. Select Tools ➤ Unprotect Document.

4. Replace the dummy text (Your Company Name Here, etc.) with your own information (see Figure 27.9).

5. Also personalize the information at the bottom of the invoice (see Figure 27.10).

*Figure 27.8   **The Other Documents tab of the New dialog box.***

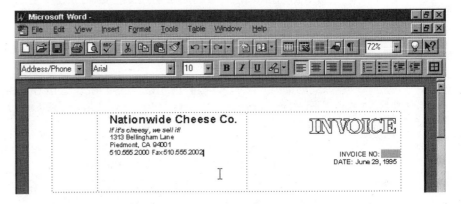

*Figure 27.9   **Replace the dummy text with your own information in the company name, slogan, address, and phone number areas.***

TIP   Currently, the sales tax field near the bottom of the invoice is a straight text field, for which you must calculate the sales tax separately and type it in. You can make Word calculate the tax automatically if you want. Click the right mouse button over the field and select Form Field Options. Then select Calculation in the Type drop-down list box and enter subtotal*(t) after the = sign in the Expression box, substituting your local sales tax rate for *t*. Then click OK.

Figure 27.10 **Enter your company name and the name of a contact at the bottom of the invoice.**

6. Restore protection to the document (because you want it to be a new template) by selecting Tools ➤ Protect Document. This brings up the Protect Document dialog box:

7. Make sure Forms is selected and click OK.

8. Select File ➤ Save As. When the Save As dialog box appears (see Figure 27.11), type a new file name and select Document Template in the Save File as Type drop-down list box.

Now, whenever you want to fill out an invoice, select File ➤ New and choose your customized invoice template. Then enter the particular information required, such as the invoice number; charge-to and ship-to names; information about the sale; number of units, description, and price per unit; sales tax; and shipping costs. When your invoice is complete, save and print it.

Three-Fold Brochure

One of the most useful templates in the Word stable is Brochure. This template is formatted in such a way that, when you print it out, you can

Part 4

Desktop Publishing

Figure 27.11   **Save your modified template as a Document template.**

fold it over (like a letter) to create slick and professional-looking brochures. Let's check it out now.

Before starting to make your three-fold brochure in Word, you should first plan it out on scratch paper. There are six panels to a three-fold brochure, three per side of the paper stock. On the outside, there's the inner flap, the back, and the outer flap. There are also three panels on the inside (see Figure 27.12).

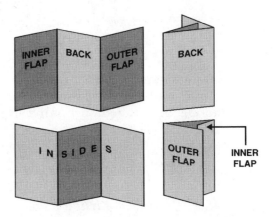

Figure 27.12   **Before trying to create your brochure, plan it out on paper, thinking about what will be on each side.**

To use Word's Brochure template to create the three-fold brochure:

1. Select File ➤ New (the New Document button won't work here). This will bring up the New dialog box. Click the Publications tab to bring it to the front.

2. Select Brochure.

3. Click OK. This opens a new document based on the Brochure template.

This template provides a set of preset styles and some style gallery settings. The document opens in Page Layout View, so you'll instantly see that the page has a landscape orientation.

new In previous versions of Word, you had to specify columns with the brochure template. Now, however, the columns are preset, and there is even dummy text on which you can base your own brochure (see Figure 27.13). Enter the text for the inner flap, using the dummy text as a guide. Try out the different preset styles that Word provides to see if any suit your needs.

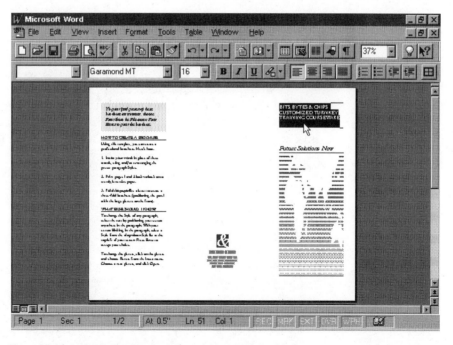

Figure 27.13 **Word's Brochure template comes complete with dummy text you can use as a guide in creating your own brochures.**

TIP   If what you type for the inner flap spills past the first column and runs into the second, play around with the font size and line spacing (or edit the text) to make it fit.

All you have to do is highlight dummy text and type your own text in. Feel free to add graphics and your logo. There are even instructions on how to customize the brochure printed right on it.

From time to time, switch to Page Layout view to see how your contents are fitting on the page as a whole. If your text ends too high on the panel, go back to the top and press Enter a few times to move it down. Be sure to save often, giving your document a meaningful name the first time you save it.

When you are done, print the two pages and then take them to a copy shop or service bureau to produce the actual brochures on card paper, fold them, and have them stapled if necessary.

Canned Letters

Most templates are set up for you to enter information and other text. Word also comes with about fifteen templates with "canned" text. That is, they are standard business letters already written for you! This way, if you don't like to write or are to busy to do so, you can let Word do it for you. For example, there is one canned template for a complaint under investigation. There is another that is a resume cover letter. And for those of you who just *can't* find the time to write, there's even a letter to Mom! Here is a list of the canned letters included with Word.

Apology for delay

Announcement of price increase

Collection letter

Complaint under investigation

Credit report request

Direct mail

Lease expiring

Letter to Mom

Order cancellation

Press release

Resume cover letter

Returned check (firm request for payment)

Thanks for inquiry

Thanks for job application

Thanks for the suggestion

These templates are accessed via the Letter Wizard, which works as described above in the section on Wizards. Follow these steps:

1. Select File ➤ New (the New Document button won't work here). This will bring up the New dialog box. Click the Letters & Faxes tab to bring it to the front.

2. Choose Letter Wizard and click OK. This will start Letter Wizard.

3. In the first Letter Wizard dialog box, click the Select a Prewritten Business Letter button and click Next>>.

4. Word will then ask you to select the letter you want to use as well as the usual Letter Wizard questions, as shown in Figure 27.14. Choose one of the options and click Next>>.

5. Then just fill in the specifics and Word does the rest.

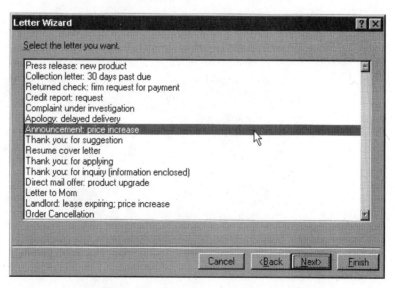

Figure 27.14 Choose the prewritten business letter that you want to use.

Organizational Chart

Word doesn't provide a Wizard or template for making an organizational chart, but if you have the MS Office suite, your best bet is to choose Insert Object and select MS Organizational chart 2.0, a handy little applet that specializes in this area. But even if you don't have this applet, an organizational chart is pretty easy to do by hand. And with Word's color capabilities, you can make really snazzy looking organizational charts. Here's how:

1. First sketch out a rough approximation of the organizational chart, so you can get an idea of the number of boxes you'll need in the bottom row and the number of levels in the chart.

> **TIP** If the chart is going to be wide, choose Landscape in the Page Setup dialog box.

2. Multiply the number of boxes in the bottom row by three and subtract one (so if there will be four boxes, $4 \times 3 = 12 - 1 = 11$). This is the number of columns you'll need to start with.

3. Multiply the number of rows by three and subtract two (so if there are three rows, $3 \times 3 = 9 - 2 = 7$). This is the number of rows you'll need to start with.

4. Start a new document (click the New Document button).

5. Select Table ▶ Insert Table. This will bring up the Insert Table dialog box:

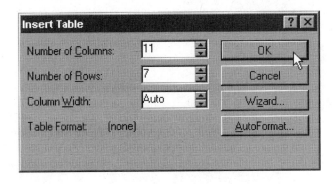

6.   Type **11** for the number of columns and 7 as the number of rows. Then click OK. Word inserts the table you specified (see Figure 27.15).

Figure 27.15   **The empty table.**

7.   Select the entire table (or even the whole document), and choose a nice large font size (at least 12 points) and center alignment (click the Center button on the Formatting toolbar).

8.   Join the first two cells in the bottom row of the table by selecting them both and then selecting Table ➤ Merge Cells.

9.   Skip a cell and then do the same thing for the two after the one you skipped. Repeat this process until the bottom row consists entirely of double-width cells separated by single cells.

10.   Enter the titles of the people represented by the boxes in the bottom row (see Figure 27.16).

11.   Leaving *two* blank rows above the boxes you've already entered, merge together cells in the next row up. You'll need to center these boxes over the boxes below that relate to them and include at least two cells in each box.

12.   Enter titles in this next row up (see Figure 27.17).

13.   Repeat this process as many times as necessary until you have created the single box at the top of the chart.

14.   Now select a box containing a title (select the entire cell, not just the paragraph of text inside it).

Part
4

Desktop Publishing

Figure 27.16   **The bottom row of the organizational chart.**

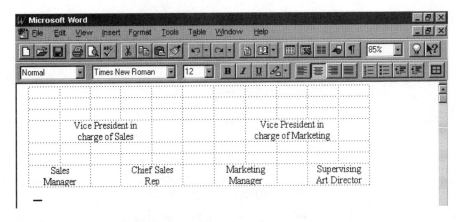

Figure 27.17   **The next row up of the organizational chart.**

15. Select Format ➤ Borders and Shading. This brings up the Cell Borders and Shading dialog box (see Figure 27.18).

16. Choose a border style for the box and then click OK.

17. Repeat this process for all the other boxes (or take a shortcut by selecting each box and pressing R4, Repeat Action—if adding the border is the last thing you did). When you are finished, your chart should look like Figure 27.19.

Figure 27.18   *Choose a border style for your box in the Cell Borders and Shading dialog box.*

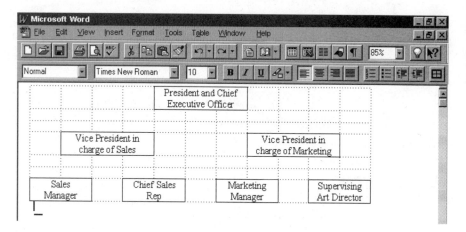

Figure 27.19   *Put borders around all your boxes.*

This next part is tricky:

18. For each box without an empty table cell edge directly below its middle (that is the President and two Vice President boxes in the illustration), select the empty cell directly below the middle of the box and one of the empty cells next to it.

19. Then drag the divider between those two empty cells to a point directly below the middle of the box, as shown:

20. Repeat as often as necessary.

21. Do the same to center cell dividers above boxes.

 22. Now click the Borders button at the right edge of the Formatting toolbar. This brings up the Borders toolbar.

23. Now select cells and add borders to them using the partial-border buttons in the Borders toolbar to add the lines between the boxes, as shown in Figure 27.20.

 TIP   Place the horizontal lines first, selecting rows of cells and adding partial borders above or below them as appropriate. Then select single cells to add the vertical lines.

24. Click the Borders button again to remove the Borders toolbar. Your organizational chart is complete (whew!). Figure 27.21 shows a completed organizational chart with table gridlines not showing.

Phone List

One nice thing about making a list of phone numbers on your computer is that you can easily update it in the future, changing numbers, adding new people, and so on. Word has no template or Wizard for making a simple phone list, but it's pretty easy.

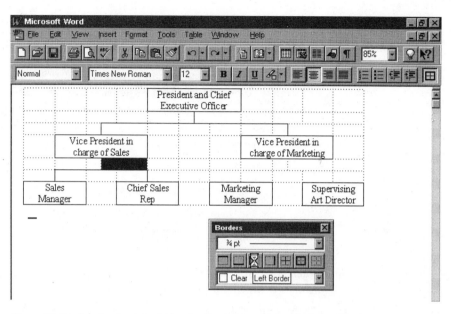

Figure 27.20 Select cells and add borders to them to create the lines of authority between the boxes.

Figure 27.21 The completed organizational chart.

TIP   Though Word does not have a template for a simple phone list, it *does* have a template for a fancy directory. If you want a really jazzy phone list that you intend to publish and distribute outside your company or organization, you might want to use the Directory template, which you access as described in the section on templates earlier in this chapter.

1.   Start a new document (click the New Document button).

2.   Type **Phone List** and format it in some nice large size and clear font.

3.   Press Enter and then select the blank line below the words *Phone List*.

4.   Click the Columns button on the Standard toolbar and create two columns with it. This creates a section break and then a two-column layout thereafter.

5.   Click the square at the left end of the Ruler twice to change the symbol in it to the right-aligned tab symbol.

6.   Click in the Ruler above the first column and drag the tab symbol to the right edge of the first column:

7.   Select Format ➤ Tabs. This brings up the Tabs dialog box (see Figure 27.22).

8.   Click the number 2 option in the Leaders area of the Tabs dialog box to make the tab a dot-leader tab; then click OK.

9.   Type the first name you want in your phone list.

10. Press Tab.

11. Type the person's phone number.

12. Press Enter. Your first entry will look like Figure 27.23.

13. Repeat Steps 9 through 12 as often as you like (you might want to collect all your scraps of paper first) to complete your phone list for now. Figure 27.24 shows a filled phone list.

Just amend your phone list as people's numbers change or as you want to add or delete individuals from the list. Now isn't that a lot handier than the old daytimer?!

Figure 27.22   Make the tab you just created a "dot leader" tab in the Tabs dialog box.

Figure 27.23   The first entry in my phone list.

Figure 27.24   *My filled-in phone list.*

Power
Tools

Chapter 28

Mail Merge—
Creating Custom
Documents

FAST TRACK

Word's Mail Merge feature lets you quickly create personalized correspondence and other documents by combining (*merging*) information from two different files. For instance, you could merge a list of names and addresses from one file (your *data document*) with a form letter in another file (your *main document*) to produce a number of personalized form letters.

Never going to do a mail merge? What about producing a catalog, a form, or an invoice—or even a whole bunch of labels or name tags? Mail Merge can help with all these tasks. You could even personalize a Christmas letter to all your relatives, tailoring the news to what each one would be interested in. That beats a business letter for entertainment any day, so we'll use it as an example in this chapter.

You insert data instructions (*fields*) in the main document wherever you want information from the data source to appear in your merged documents. For instance, for this Christmas letter to your friends and relatives, you could use fields to create suitable salutations for each one. Instead of writing plain old boring "Dear" to each victim, you could have a salutation field containing any number of greetings. Then you could have a name field for the hapless recipient of the letter. And then, if you wanted, you could have a third field (to appear on the same line) of further greeting. This way, you could produce such salutations as "Hi, Joe Bob, how's it going?" and "My darling little Rosemary, how much you've grown this year!" as well as the staid "Dear Aunt Edna." How's that for variety?

Once the main document and the data source are prepared, you're ready to merge them. The Mail Merge Helper lets you send merged documents directly to your printer or save them to a file for editing and later printing.

In either case, Word will automatically take care of things like word wrap and pagination for each new document. Figure 28.1 shows an overview of the elements in a mail-merge project.

Thanks to Word's Mail Merge Helper, merging is relatively painless, though you still need to pay plenty of attention to what you're doing. Some planning beforehand doesn't hurt either, but it's not absolutely essential. That said, let's get into it.

The header source (containing field names)

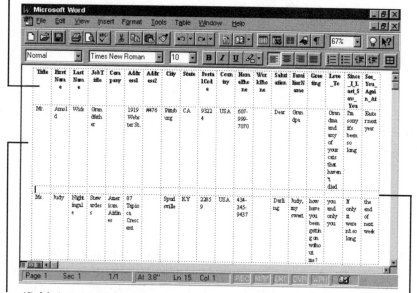

Data (fields in records) **An empty record**

Mail Merge Helper toolbar

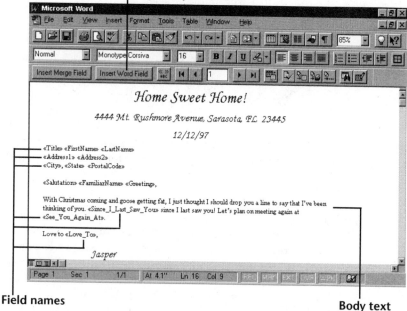

Field names **Body text**

Figure 28.1 Mail-merge projects require a data source (top) and a main document (bottom) to produce new documents that contain information from both.

NOTE   Unfortunately, a book this size cannot cover all the variables involved in mail merges. Sometimes you'll find it easier to copy a form letter a few times and paste in the names and addresses of the recipients rather than perform an entire mail merge. Take a quick reality check before turning blindly to the Mail Merge Helper.

About Data Sources and Main Documents

Data sources are organized collections of information—databases—stored as Word tables. As you'll see in this chapter, the Mail Merge Helper leads you step by step through the creation of a new data source if you don't already have one.

Word can also use data from other applications, such as Microsoft Excel or Microsoft Access. All data sources, no matter where they come from, contain *records* and *fields*. For instance, an employee data source would usually contain one record for each employee. Each record would contain multiple fields—one field for the employee's first name, one for the middle initial, one for the last name, one for each part of the address, and so on.

Main documents, as mentioned above, contain the text of your project (the body of a letter, for instance), fields, and merge instructions.

Using Main Documents from Earlier Versions of Word

You can use main documents from earlier versions of Word—for example, version 6.0x—with no problem. Simply open the document in Word 95 and proceed as normal.

NOTE   When you open a main document in Word, it will bring with it the association (to its data source) with which it was last saved. If you use a previously created main document, remember to attach to it any new data source that you want to use. You'll see how to do that later in this chapter.

Using Main Documents from Other Applications

You can use a main document from another application by opening that document in Word and converting its contents to Word. However, field names and formatting from some applications may not translate well into Word format. Check the fields in your main document and adjust them if necessary before completing the merge.

If you experience problems, try pasting the main document into Word as plain text and then applying the formatting and entering the field names.

Using Data Sources from Other Applications

You can use data sources from other applications in your Word merges. For example, if you have data in a Microsoft Excel spreadsheet, you can insert either the whole worksheet or just a range of cells. If you have Microsoft Access, you can open a database and insert records from a table or a selection of records defined by a query.

After opening a data source in another application, make sure that the merge fields in your main document match the field names in the data source.

Creating Your First Mail-Merge Project

The best way to learn how to create a merge document is to try one. Consider working along as you read the rest of this chapter.

Project Overview

For each new mail-merge project, you'll need to:

▶ Create or have available a data source

▶ Enter information into the data source

▶ Create and proof the text of your main document

▶ Insert fields into your main document

▶ Check for design and data-entry errors

▶ Merge the data source and main document and print the merge documents

For your first mail-merge project, Word's Mail Merge Helper runs you through the process of creating your data source and main document in a given order. If this feels like wearing a straitjacket, don't worry—on subsequent projects you can vary the order in which you complete the steps. For instance, you can create the main document first and then create a data source, or vice versa.

Because data sources in Word are simply documents containing tables, you can add information and edit them at any time before doing the actual merge. Once you get comfortable with merging and its possibilities, feel free to do things in any workable order that pleases you.

While you don't need to type your main document first, it's often helpful to make a draft to get a sense of which information you will need from your data sources and where to insert it.

NOTE If you already have a data source, simply open it or adapt it for the new project. (Adapting here usually means querying to select relevant fields and records.)

Planning Your Data Document

Designing a useful and easy-to-maintain data source is one of the most important parts of a new mail-merge project. With a little ingenuity, you can use the same data sources for a number of projects.

For instance, if you plan to use an employee data source to send letters or memos, you might want one field for the employee's full legal name and another for an informal salutation. That way, you could address mailing envelopes to Dr. Tyler Z. Gradgrinder and have the salutation of the letters or memos read *Dear Ty* or *Dear Doc*.

At first glance, it might seem a good idea to create a single field for all the address information needed for letters and labels. Then you could type everything—the recipient's name, company name, street address, city, state, and zip code—in that single field, insert that field in your main documents for form letters and envelopes, and merge merrily away. The problem with this approach comes when you need to break up the information you put in that field—for example, to produce a quick list of employees (without their full addresses) who live in a particular city who might appreciate ride-sharing.

It's far better to break your data up into multiple fields. Create separate fields for recipients' first and last names. Then you can use Word's Sort feature to produce alphabetized lists or labels sorted by last name. Break addresses down into five or six fields, as Word's Mail Merge Helper encourages you to do: street address, apartment number (if any), city, state, country (if you're international), and zip code. Putting city, state, country, and zip code in their own fields gives you enormous flexibility—you can easily find out who all your customers are in, say, Anaheim, Colorado, or Mexico.

> **TIP**   Test your new design with small data documents containing a dozen or so representative records. Try your sample data source with a number of different main documents, or have an experienced print-merge user look over your new design before you spend hours entering data into your first data source. Consider keeping sample main documents and data sources at hand in a test folder so you can perform quick tests on new merge projects you put together.

Using the Mail Merge Helper

Word's Mail Merge Helper guides you through the steps of merging documents. The process seems a little convoluted the first time, but it works well. Once you've tried it once or twice, you'll be merging merrily with the best of them.

> **NOTE**   In the following sections, we'll discuss how to perform the different stages of a mail merge by using the Mail Merge Helper, because this is the easiest way to merge. We'll indicate parenthetically how you can proceed without using the Mail Merge Helper.

To start the Mail Merge Helper, select Tools ➤ Mail Merge. The Mail Merge Helper dialog box appears, as shown in Figure 28.2. Note the instructions in the box at the top telling you to click the Create button to set up the mail merge. Watch these instructions as you proceed with subsequent stages of the mail merge. If you're ever confused about what to do next, consult this box.

Part
5

Power Tools

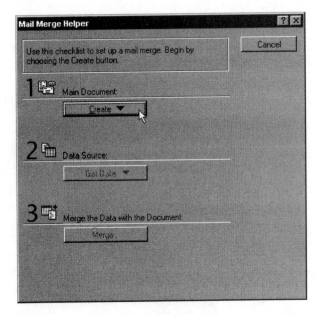

Figure 28.2   **The Mail Merge Helper dialog box. Instructions are in the top-left corner.**

The first step in the mail merge is to create your main document, as the type of main document governs the subsequent choices you can make in the Mail Merge Helper. Form Letters, Mailing Labels, Envelopes, and Catalogs have different components, so the Mail Merge Helper offers you different choices of data source.

Starting Your Main Document

To start your main document, follow these steps:

1. Select the Create button to start creating your main document. A list will drop down offering you four choices—Form Letters, Mailing Labels, Envelopes, and Catalog:

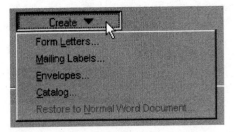

2. Select the type of main document you want. (In the example, I've chosen Form Letters.) A dialog box will appear offering you the choice of the active window or a new main document:

3. Select the window you want to use. If you're starting from a new document, as in the example, or if the active window contains information for your main document, choose the Active Window button. If your active window contains valuable information that has nothing to do with the mail merge, choose the New Main Document button.

    *   If you choose the New Main Document button, Word will open a new document. The previously active document stays open—Word does not save or close it.

    Regardless of which button you chose, Word will return you to the Mail Merge Helper dialog box for the next stage of the mail merge, arranging the data source. You'll see that the space below the Create button now lists the information you've entered so far—the type of merge and the main document to use:

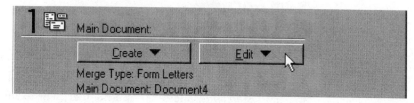

    The information box at the top of the Mail Merge Helper dialog box tells you that the next step is to specify the data source. Let's do it.

Specifying the Data Source

Next, you need to specify the data source and arrange in it the fields that will be available to your main document for the merge.

1.   Click the Get Data button to display a list of options for your data source:

2.   If you already have a data source that you want to use, select Open Data Source. If you want to create the data source, select Create Data Source. If you want to use your Address Book, then choose the Use Address Book option.

If you chose Open Data Source or Use Address Book, skip ahead a section. If you chose Create Data Source, read the next section.

Creating a Data Source

The dialog box that appears when you choose Create Data Source contains a list of commonly used field names for the type of mail merge you're performing. Figure 28.3 shows the Create Data Source dialog box for form letters.

Adding a Field Name

Here's how to add field names to the list in the Field Names in Header Row box:

1.   Type the name in the Field Name box.

> **NOTE**   Field names can be up to 40 characters long and can contain letters, numbers, and underscores (_). Field names *cannot* contain spaces or hyphens and must start with a letter (not a number). For example, What_We_Discussed_At_Yesterday's_Meeting is an acceptable field name (and might remind you better of the field's purpose than MeetingTopic), but 1994_May_15_Meeting is not. Bear in mind that the ends of very long field names may not show in the Field Names in Header Row box, so it can be confusing to have long field names that differ only at their ends.

Figure 28.3 **The Create Data Source dialog box offers a list of commonly used field names. Chop and change these at will.**

2. Click the <u>A</u>dd Field Name button. The new field name is added at the bottom of the list.

3. To move the new field name to a different position in the list, make sure it's highlighted and click the Move arrow buttons.

   You can see the field names that I've entered for my Christmas mail merge at the bottom of the list in Figure 28.4.

Removing or Modifying a Field Name

When a main document is changed, you may need to remove some field names from the data source (just to reduce clutter and avoid confusion) or modify others:

1. In the Field <u>N</u>ames in Header Row box, highlight the field name you want to remove by clicking it with the mouse or by scrolling to it with the scroll bars or the down arrow. Then click the Remove Field Name button. The field name will be removed from the Field Names in Header Row list and will appear in the Field Name box.

Figure 28.4 New field names for my sample mail merge.

2. To modify the field name, make your changes in the <u>F</u>ield Name box and then click the Add Field Name button.

Rearranging Field Names

To rearrange the field names in the Field Names in Header Row box, highlight the field you want to move and click the Move up and down arrows beside the Field Names in Header Row box to move the highlight field up or down.

Saving Your Data Source

When you've finished adding, removing, and arranging fields, click OK to save your data-source. In the Save Data Source dialog box that appears, enter a name for your data-source file and select OK to save the file. Word will save the data-source file under the name you give.

Editing the Data Source

Word now checks your data source to see if it contains records. If it doesn't, Word will display a dialog box informing you of this and inviting you to edit the data source or the main document, as shown below. Choose the Edit Data Source button to edit your data source.

Opening a Data Source

To open an existing data source, select Open Data Source from the Get Data drop-down list. The Open Data Source dialog box works just like the File Open dialog box: Select the document you want to use and click OK. Word will open the document and return you to the Mail Merge Helper dialog box.

NOTE   If you want to use a data source from another application, such as Microsoft Excel or Microsoft Access, simply choose it at this point and use the application's techniques to select the data records you want to use.

Entering Your Records

In the Data Form dialog box that Word displays (see Figure 28.5), enter the details for each of your records by typing text into the boxes. Press Tab or ⏎ to move from field to field. To move backwards, press Shift+Tab.

TIP   It is a good idea to enter a few records at this point, if you don't have any. The following steps will be much clearer if you can try out the buttons yourself.

Here's how to alter the records in the Data Form dialog box:

▶ To add a new record, choose the Add New button.

▶ To delete a record, choose the Delete button.

▶ If you realize you've trashed a record (by entering data in the wrong place or whatever), click the Restore button to return its entries to their previous state.

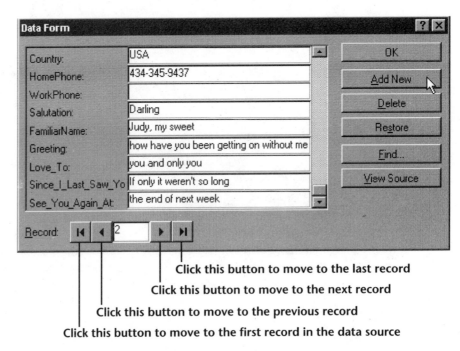

Figure 28.5 *Entering data in the Data Form dialog box.*

► You can also use the arrows at the bottom, marked in Figure 28.5, to move around the records.

To Find a Record

Word's database functions offer great flexibility in searching. You can search for any word or part of a word in any of the fields.

To find a record, follow these steps:

1. Click the Find button. The Find in Field dialog box will appear:

2. Type the word or words you want to find in the Find What box.

3. Click the arrow at the right end of the In Field box to drop down the list of field names and select the name of the field you want to search.

4. Click the Find First button. Word will search for and display the first record it finds containing the word or words in the selected field.

5. If this is the record you were looking for, click Close to close the Find in Field dialog box. If not, click the Find Next button to find the next occurrence of the text.

6. When you've finished entering or updating your records, click OK to close the data source and save the changes. Now you're ready to edit your main document.

> **TIP** If the Find in Field dialog box is hovering annoyingly over the field you're trying to read, grab it by clicking anywhere in its title bar, then drag it to a more convenient location on the screen.

You can also edit your data file directly (if the Data Form dialog box is on the screen, click OK to close it). You can simply type in the cells of the table as you would normally. (Don't worry about word wrap—or anything cosmetic for that matter.)

You'll also notice that Word automatically includes the Database toolbar in any data-source document:

Here's what the buttons on the Database toolbar do:

Icon	Name	Function
	Data Form	Brings up the Data Form dialog box (the one that appeared when you first created the data source)
	Manage Fields	Lets you add, remove, or rename fields

Icon	Name	Function
	Add New Record	Inserts a new record (row) in the data-source table
	Delete Record	Removes the current record (row) from the data-source table
	Sort Ascending	Sorts all the records (rows) in the data source in ascending order, based on the current field (column)
	Sort Descending	Sorts all the records (rows) in the data source in descending order, based on the current field (column)
	Insert Database	Inserts records from a data source
	Update Fields	Updates the contents of selected *field codes* (such as links to database documents)
	Find Record	Searches for a record with specified text in a specified field
	Mail Merge Main Document	Switches you to the main document

Sorting the Data Source

If your data source grows large, you might find it useful to sort the records. This has several advantages: it makes searching through the data source manually easier, it gives you a way to keep tabs on the progress of a large print job, and it lets you take advantage of US Post Office bulk mail rates that require sorting by ZIP code.

Sorting a data source is easy.

1. Put the insertion point in the field (column) you want to sort on. It doesn't matter which record (row) you put it in.

2. Click either the Ascending Sort or Descending Sort button on the Database toolbar. (For normal alphabetical order, click Ascending Sort.)

Finding a Record in the Data Source

If your data source is very large and you don't feel like sifting through it manually to find a particular record, click the Find Record button on the Database toolbar. This will bring up the Find in Field dialog box, which you can use as discussed under *To Find a Record* earlier in this chapter.

Inserting or Removing Fields or Records in a Data Source

If you maintain a data source long enough, you're going to have to make changes to it from time to time. The Database toolbar gives you easy shortcuts for managing your fields and records.

Inserting, Removing, or Renaming Fields

Before fooling around with your fields, save a backup copy of your data source in case things go seriously awry. Then, to make changes to the fields in your data source, click the Manage Fields button on the Database toolbar. This brings up the Manage Fields dialog box:

Manage Fields	? X
Field Name:	**Field Names in Header Row:**
	Title
	FirstName
Add >>	LastName
	JobTitle
Remove	Company
	Address1
Rename...	Address2
	City
	OK
	Cancel

You can make all your field changes from this one dialog box.

▶ To insert a new field, type the field name in the Field Name box and then click the Add >> button. (The field will be added at the end of the list—at the right side of the data table. There's no shortcut for moving a field after you've created the data source, though you can move it by selecting the entire column and dragging it to a new location in the table.)

▶ To remove a field and all the data in it, highlight the name in the Field Names in Header Row list box and then click the Remove button. Then click Yes to confirm that you *really* do want to do this.

▶ To rename a field, highlight the old name in the Field Names in Header Row list box and then click the Rename button. This brings up the Rename Field dialog box:

Type a new field name and then click OK.

When you are done, click OK in the Manage Fields dialog box. If you'd like to undo your changes, click Cancel (or press Esc) instead.

NOTE   You can also make any of these changes directly, simply by editing the table in the data source. Somehow, though, it seems easier and less risky to use the Manage Fields dialog box to make these changes.

Inserting or Removing Records

Data sources inevitably grow (though you occasionally need to prune them back as well) as new names are added to your mailing list or new records in general. The Database toolbar makes it easy to add or remove records when the time comes to make these changes.

TIP   You can always add a new record to the end of a data-source table simply by pressing Tab in the last field of the last record. Also, the Data Form dialog box (Figure 28.5) has an Add New button. Click it to add a record to the end of the data-source table.

▶ To add a record to the end of the data-source table, click the Add New Record button on the Database toolbar.

▶ To delete a record, first select it. Then click the Delete Record button on the Database toolbar. To delete several records at once, select them all and then click the Delete Record button.

Inserting Data from Another File

If you've already got the data you need for your merge in an existing file—a word-processing, database, or even a spreadsheet document— then you can insert this data into your data source. There are two ways you can do this. You can simply insert the data directly into your data source, or you can insert field codes that link your data source to the database file. (Chapter 30 explains links and Chapter 32 fields.)

The benefit of inserting field codes is that you can update the information automatically when it changes in the original database file. If you know you'll never need to update it, you can simply insert the data directly. Either way, do this:

1. Click the Insert Database button on the Database toolbar. This brings up the Database dialog box:

Database   ? ✕

Data Source:

    [Get Data...]   [Cancel]

Data Options:

    [Query Options...]   [Table AutoFormat...]

Insert the Data into the Document:

    [Insert Data...]

---

2. Click the Get Data button. This brings up the Open Data Source dialog box, which works just like the Open File dialog box. Select the document you want to use and click OK.

For some types of files, such as spreadsheets and databases, Word will display a dialog box that allows you to select just part of the data from the other file for insertion.

3. If you want to limit the data from the other file in some way, click the Query Options button on the Database dialog box. This brings up the Query Options dialog box:

From this dialog box, you can filter the records, sort the records, and select which fields to import.

To limit the records imported into your data source, choose a field from the Field drop-down list box (or just type the first letter of the field you want, repeatedly if necessary). Then press Tab and choose a comparison in the Comparison box (such as Equal to, Greater than—b is greater than a—and so on). Then press Tab again and enter a value to compare the field with.

If you want to add more conditions to your query, accept And as the relationship or select Or in the little unnamed box to the left of the second row. Then repeat the process for the Field, Comparison, and Compare To boxes.

To sort the records in the other data file before importing them, click the Sort Records tab in the Query Options dialog box. Choose a field to sort on in the Sort by drop-down list box and then accept Ascending order or select Descending. If you want to add secondary and tertiary sort criteria, select fields and sort order in the next two boxes.

> **NOTE** For those of you who aren't familiar with database sorting, it simply means switching the records around into an order that you find useful, based on information in one or several of the fields. For instance, you might sort all the records by zip code if you wanted to do a mailing to only one zip code. Usually records are sorted alphabetically by last name.

To select fields to import, click the Select Fields tab in the Query Options dialog box. Word starts you off with all the fields selected. To remove one, highlight it and click the Remove button. To remove them all and start over, click the Remove All button. That will change the buttons to Select and Select All. Then highlight and select the fields you want. If you don't want a header row of field names in the imported data, uncheck Include Field Names.

When you are done with the Query Options dialog box, click OK.

4. When you are ready, click the Insert Data button at the bottom of the Database dialog box. This brings up the Insert Data dialog box, giving you one more control over the import procedure:

5. If you want to import only certain records from the data file (and you know which ones they are by number), enter the numbers of the first and last records you want in the From and To boxes of the Insert Data dialog box. (You can always remove records after importing, as explained above in Inserting and Removing Records.)

6. If you want to insert linked data into your data source instead of straight text, check Insert Data as Field.

7. When you are ready, click OK.

8. If you already had data in your data source and the insertion point was in the table, then Word will warn you that the data table will be replaced with the imported data. If you want this, click Yes. If not, click No and then move the insertion point past the original table (or start over with a new data document).

If you chose to insert linked data, then you can update any entry by selecting it and clicking F9. To unlink the data and turn it into regular text, select the entire table and press Ctrl+Shift+F9.

Editing the Main Document

Once you've used the Helper to create the data document, you'll want to turn your attention to the Main document. Main documents contain the following:

▶ Text and punctuation

▶ Merge instructions and field names that Word uses to merge data

Figure 28.6 shows a main document for our sample mail merge. We'll discuss the various elements in detail.

Text in Main Documents

Use Word's word-processing and graphics features to create the text and design elements for your main document. In the sample, a suitably sickly letterhead was created by typing the return address in Monotype Corsiva and centering it. (The first line was increased to 24 points, and the second to 16 points.)

The body of the letter was typed (in 10-point Times New Roman) using regular Word techniques, with data instructions containing field names and other merge devices inserted as needed, as explained below.

Inserting Data Instructions

The Mail Merge Helper makes it easy to insert field names and other data instructions in your main documents. Just place the insertion point where you want to insert a data instruction, then pull down the appropriate list from the Mail Merge toolbar and pick the item to insert.

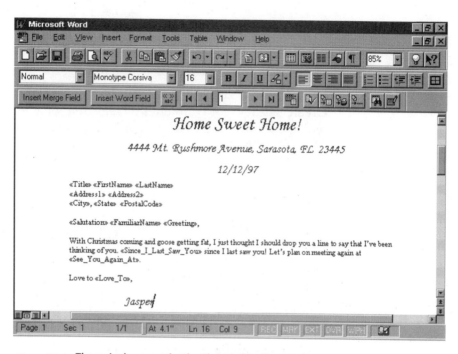

Figure 28.6 **The main document for the Christmas mail-merge letter.**

For example, to insert the Title field name shown in Figure 28.6, you would place the insertion point on a new line at the beginning of the document (below the header). Then click the Insert Merge Field button on the Mail Merge toolbar to display the list of field names available in the associated data source. Next select the appropriate field name, and Word will insert it into the document. (The guillemets « and » come free with the field name.)

When preparing the text of a main document, remember to include things like spaces between field names and any required punctuation following them. Running people's first and last names together will spoil the effect of your carefully personalized letters. You know the feeling if you've ever been insulted by Publishers' Clearing House.

As you'll see in a moment, you can use combinations of merge fields from the Insert Merge Field button and Word fields from the Insert Word Field button (both on the Mail Merge toolbar) with text typed from the keyboard to put together powerful merge instructions.

Try It

Take a moment to create a main document for a merge yourself. The steps below refer to the sample letter in Figure 28.6. Use these instructions for general guidance.

1. Create a header for your letter by selecting <u>V</u>iew ➤ <u>H</u>eader and Footer, typing the return address, and applying such formatting as you see fit. If you want to include the date, click the Date button on the Header and Footer toolbar.

2. Close the header by clicking the Close button on the Header and Footer toolbar.

3. With the insertion point at the beginning of the document, insert the Title field by clicking on the Insert Merge Field button and selecting Title from the drop-down list. Don't press ↵ yet—the Title, FirstName, and LastName fields all belong on the same line.

4. Type a space to separate the Title and FirstName fields.

5. Use the Insert Merge Field drop-down list to insert the FirstName field.

6. Add a space and insert the LastName field.

7. Now press ↵ to start a new line.

8. Add the Address1, Address2, City, State, and PostalCode fields, together with whatever punctuation and spacing they need.

9. On a new line, insert the Salutation field, a space, the FamiliarName field, another space, and the Greeting field.

10. Type the body of your letter, including any merge fields that you need.

11. Save your main document.

12. If you didn't enter any data in your data source earlier, switch to it. If necessary, crank up the Mail Merge Helper by choosing <u>T</u>ools ➤ Mail Me<u>r</u>ge; then choose Edit in the Data Source step:

13. Add a few names and addresses. Try leaving the Address2 field blank in at least one record so you can see how it handles blank lines.

Testing and Proofing

Before firing up the Mail Merge Helper and churning out a whole batch of letters, proofread your work. Use Word's spell checker and grammar tools (see Chapter 19 for more information on these). Make any necessary corrections. Remember that Word will faithfully copy every error in your main document into every single copy it merges.

 Next run the Mail Merge Helper's error-checking program. Choose the Check Errors button from the Mail Merge toolbar. The Checking and Reporting Errors dialog box will appear:

For now, choose the first option, *Simulate the merge and report errors in a new document.* Word will check your data source and main document for errors (such as missing data fields in the data source and misspelled field names in your main document). If Word finds no errors, you will see a happy dialog box telling you that no mail merge errors have been found. If errors are found, correct them.

As a final check, consider merging some or all of your documents to a file and inspecting them, rather than printing them all at once. We'll look at how to do this in just a moment. First, let's look at Word's sorting and filtering features.

Sorting Merged Documents

Usually, records are merged in the order they occur in your data source, but Word's Mail Merge Helper lets you sort the records during the merge. In addition, Word lets you use filters to restrict merging to records containing certain data. (Filtering is discussed in the next section.)

To sort records before you perform a merge, follow these steps:

1. Open the Mail Merge Helper dialog box and choose the Query Options button. The Query Options dialog box will appear (see Figure 28.7).

2. Click the Sort Records tab to enter your sorting preferences.

3. In the Sort By area, click the down arrow, then select a field to sort by from the list that appears.

4. Select a field for one or both Then By fields if you want to refine your sort further.

5. When you've defined the sort to your satisfaction, click OK. If you mess things up, click the Clear All button to clear the fields and start again or click Cancel to escape from the dialog box.

Figure 28.7 *The Query Options box is where you choose sorting and filters for the merge you're about to perform. I'm going to sort my relatives by FamiliarName and then LastName.*

Filtering Merged Documents

If you're not content with sorting your records, you can *filter* them as well—that is, you can specify criteria for including or excluding certain records from the merge. Filtering gives you a lot of flexibility in removing entries from the merge that for any reason you don't want to use. For instance, if I thought that my sister would never speak to me again if I sent her a form letter for Christmas, I could exclude her record from the merge to safeguard myself.

Here's how to set up filtering:

1. Pull up the Mail Merge Helper dialog box and choose the Query Options button. The Query Options dialog box will appear.

2. Select the Filter Records tab.

3. In the Field column of the first row, choose the field you want to use as a filter.

4. In the Comparison column of the first row, drop down the list of filtering comparisons to choose one. This is what they do:

Comparison	Effect
Equal to	The contents of the data field you chose must match those of the Compare To box.
Not Equal to	The contents of the data field you chose must not match those of the Compare To box.
Less Than	The contents of the data field you chose must be less than those of the Compare To box.
Greater than	The contents of the data field you chose must be greater than those of the Compare To box.
Less than or Equal	The contents of the data field you chose must be less than or equal to those of the Compare To box.
Greater than or Equal	The contents of the data field you chose must be greater than or equal to those of the Compare To box.
Is Blank	The merge field must be empty.
Is Not Blank	The merge field must not be empty.

Part
5

Power Tools

5. In the second row, choose And or Or in the first column to include additional or complementary criteria for filtering.

6. Repeat steps 3, 4, and 5 for more rows as necessary to refine your criteria further.

7. When you've defined the filtering criteria to your satisfaction, select OK. If you mess things up, select Clear All to start again or Cancel to escape from the Query Options dialog box.

> **NOTE** When you filter a data field that contains text, Word compares the sequence of characters based on the ANSI sort order. Because *antelope* precedes *zebra* alphabetically, Word considers it "less than" zebra. So if you wanted to retrieve data records for only the second half of the alphabet, you could specify LastName Is Greater Than M. If you mix numbers with letters, Word compares the numbers as though they were a sequence of text characters.

Printing Merged Documents

When you've specified any filtering and sort-ordering that you want, you're ready to run the mail merge.

1. Start the merge process by making your main document the active document (click in it if necessary).

2. Click the Merge button in the Mail Merge Helper dialog box to bring up the Merge dialog box (see Figure 28.8).

Figure 28.8   *The Merge dialog box—the culmination of your quest... Choose your final options here.*

3. You can either merge directly to your printer by selecting Printer in the Merge To box, or you can have Word merge to a new, untitled document that will contain all of the merge documents by selecting New Document.

4. Select the Records to Be Merged by choosing either All or From and To. If you choose From and To, specify the record numbers for the merge to start and stop at.

5. The default is not to print blank lines when data fields are empty. If you *do* want to do this—perhaps you have a reason, like to show gaps in your data source—choose the *Print blank lines when data fields are empty* option.

6. When all is set to your liking, click Merge. The mail merge will finally take place.

When the mail merge is finished, close the Mail Merge Helper dialog box. If you merged to a new document, it should be on-screen now. If you merged to a printer, the printer will be churning out your merged documents. Either way, check your output carefully before inflicting it on your victims. The law of mass mailing clearly states that you'll only notice an egregious error *after* you've mailed the whole batch.

If you have unsaved changes in your main document, Word will invite you to save them.

Specifying Header Options

The header row is the row of fields at the top of a data source that identifies each kind of information in the data source—the Title, FirstName, and LastName fields and so on.

Why would you want to reuse a header? Well, you could then use the same header source with more than one data source. If you can't change the merge fields in a data source to match the names of the merge fields in a main document (the file might be read-only), you can use a header source that contains matching merge fields.

To specify a header source:

1. Choose the <u>G</u>et Data button in the Mail Merge Helper dialog box and select Header Options. The Header Options dialog box will appear (see Figure 28.9).

Part
5

Power Tools

Figure 28.9 *In the Header Options dialog box you can open an existing header source or create a new one.*

2. In the Header Options dialog box, choose Create to create a new header source. Or choose Open to open an existing header source; then skip ahead to step 5.

3. If you chose Create, the Create Header Source dialog box will appear. This works just like the Create Data Source dialog box we discussed under *Creating a Data Source* earlier in the chapter. Add, remove, and rearrange the fields to your satisfaction; then click OK.

4. In the Save Data Source dialog box that appears, give your header source a name and click OK. You'll be returned to the Mail Merge Helper dialog box, and the header source you created will now appear under the Get Data button.

5. If you chose Open, the Open Header Source dialog box will appear. Select the header source you want to use and click OK. You'll be returned to the Mail Merge Helper dialog box, and the header source you created will now appear under the Get Data button.

6. Word will check the header source against the data source and warn you if the data source contains too many data fields, as shown below. The Merge button on the Mail Merge Helper dialog box will be dimmed, indicating that you cannot yet run the merge.

7. If the data source contains too many fields, edit the data source or header source so that they match.

Checking for Errors in Your Data Source

 To check your data source for errors (such as inconsistencies between the fields in the source and fields in the main document), click the Check Errors button on the Mail Merge toolbar (the one with the check mark on it). If you can't find it, maybe you're looking in the wrong document. Open the main document. Then click the Check for Errors button on the Mail Merge toolbar. This brings up the Checking and Reporting Errors dialog box:

There are three options. Choose the first if you don't want to actually do the merge yet, just see what might go wrong if you did. Word will list any errors in a new document. The second option, the default, merges the data and main documents and reports errors to you in a dialog box as they occur. The third option proceeds with the merge and lists the errors in a new document.

If Word encounters no errors, it will report that fact to you when it's done. Correct any detected errors when the check is completed. The most common problems involve different numbers of fields in different records. All records must have the same numbers of fields, and that number must match the number of field names.

Merging onto Letterhead

If you want to print your form letters on letterhead (either preprinted or created by including a header in your main document), you have to make sure that the text begins low enough on the first page to leave room for the letterhead itself. It's easy, though:

1. Go to the top of your main document.

2. Select File ➤ Page Setup.

3. Click the Margins tab.

4. Type a new top margin, large enough to clear the letterhead contents.

5. Click OK.

6. Go to the bottom of the first page.

7. Select Insert ➤ Break.

8. On the Break dialog box, click Next Page.

9. Click OK.

10. Select File ➤ Page Setup.

11. Reenter the original top margin.

12. Click OK.

If you don't have letterhead stock, you could skip steps 5 and 6 and then select View ➤ Header and Footer and create a letterhead (by typing and formatting text and inserting graphics such as a logo, if necessary) in the header area. When you're done, click Close.

Using Different Data Sources with a Single Main Document

You can create a master main document and merge different data sources into it. The procedure for attaching a new data source to a main document is essentially the same as the original procedure. Click the Mail Merge Helper button on the Mail Merge toolbar. This brings up the Mail Merge Helper dialog box (shown earlier in Figure 28.2). Click the Get Data button and select Open Data Source (or Create Data Source if you want to create the new data document on the fly).

That's it. The new data source is attached to the main document. Check the new data source for errors right away, in case the fields don't match up perfectly. Repeat the procedure to reattach the original data source at any time.

If you need to use different database documents as data sources, then you might want to attach a header file to your main document. A header file only needs to contain the field names (though it can be a complete data source in its own right and still function as a header file for another source). The new data source must have the same number of fields as the header file, *but* it does not need to have a header row of its own to identify the fields.

To attach a header file, click the Get Data button in the Mail Merge Helper dialog box and choose Header Options. This brings up the Header Options dialog box:

Click the Open button to open an existing data source as a header file or click the Create button to create a new one.

If you click Open, this will bring up the Open Header Source dialog box (which looks uncannily like the Open Data Source dialog box). Select the file you want to use and click OK.

If you click Create, you'll see the Create Header Source dialog box:

This looks about the same as Create Data Source, and it works the same way, too. Type field names and click Add Field Name to add them to the field-name list. Highlight existing field names and click Remove Field Name to delete them.

When you are done, click OK. The Save Header Source dialog box (much like the Save Data Source dialog box, of course) will appear. Type a file name and click OK.

After you attach a header source, you must still attach a data source (and it should not have a header row of its own, as it will be misinterpreted as a record).

Using Word's Merge Instructions

Word provides a number of ways to change its mail-merging behavior based on the contents of individual records in your data source. As you've just seen, it can eliminate unwanted blank lines in merged documents. It can insert special text if certain conditions are met, or stop during each merge to let you enter unique text from the keyboard. If you decide to use these features, be prepared to spend some time experimenting and troubleshooting.

Ask

The Ask feature causes Word to stop during the merge each time a new record is merged to prompt you for keyboard input to be printed.

Ask is normally used to include in merged documents data that has not been stored in the data document. Suppose, for example, that you were creating ten welcome letters to bungee jumpers, like the one in Figure 28.10, and that you wanted to enter a date and time for each jumper's first lesson. Suppose further that your data document does not contain a field for first lesson dates and times.

Setting Up an Ask Entry

When designing your main document, move the insertion point to where you want the information entered for the Ask field to appear. Then pick Ask from the Insert Word Field drop-down list on the Mail Merge toolbar. Word displays the Insert Word Field: Ask dialog box (see Figure 28.11).

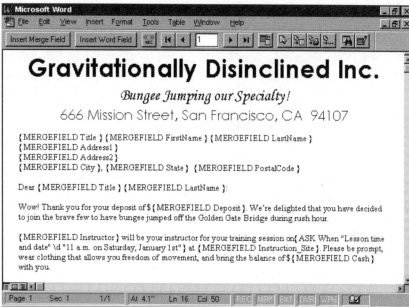

Figure 28.10 *This form letter (top) uses merge instructions to ask the operator for information from the keyboard, as you can see when Field Codes are revealed (bottom).*

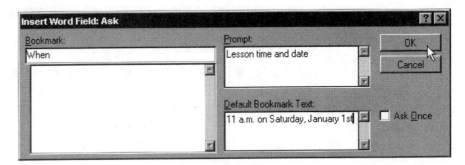

Figure 28.11   The Insert Word Field: Ask dialog box creates prompts for keyboard entries when you merge.

Use this dialog box to create a new field unique to the main document (not the data source). In the Bookmark field, type a name for the bookmark. This gives you quick access to the field. In the Prompt box, enter the text that you want to appear on-screen during the merge to prompt the operator to enter appropriate information. In the Default Bookmark Text box, you can enter default text that will appear to guide the operator. When you're done, click OK.

Word gives you a preview of the dialog box that will appear:

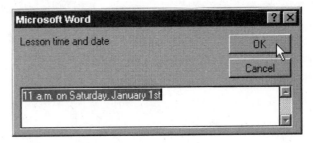

Choose OK if it's all right; otherwise, choose Cancel. Be aware, though, that Cancel doesn't return you to the dialog box. It cancels Ask and you have to start over from scratch. It is a good idea to proof your work carefully while in the dialog box.

Word inserts the Ask instruction at the insertion point. To view the Ask field, display field codes (select Tools ➤ Options, choose the View tab, check the Field Codes box, and click OK).

Using Ask

When you actually merge your ten letters (to continue the bungee jumping example), you'll see a dialog box like the one shown above for each letter. In it you enter the date and time for each bungee jumper; then click OK or press ↵.

Set Bookmark

Set Bookmark, like Ask, inserts a field unique to the main document (i.e., not in the data source). But the value you define for it is used for all documents being merged—you don't get to enter a different value for each one. For instance, you could use it to insert Winter in everyone's Semester field in winter, Summer in summer, and so on.

Inserting a Set Field Name

When designing your main document, move the insertion point to where you want the Set information to appear. Pull down the Insert Word Field list on the Mail Merge toolbar and choose the Set Bookmark command. Word displays the Insert Word Field: Set dialog box, as shown in Figure 28.12.

In the Bookmark box, type the name of the bookmark you want to create. If you want to specify a default value for any mail merge main document you create, enter that in the Value box. Click OK to accept the bookmark name and value. Word inserts the Set information in your document at the insertion point.

Figure 28.12   *The Insert Word Field: Set dialog box.*

Using Set

When you actually merge your documents (ten letters, for instance), Word automatically prints the defined Set value in each letter at the points where you've inserted the field names.

If...Then...Else...

You can use If...Then...Else... to make Word do different things based on conditions it finds in fields in your data sources. For example, you could enter a field in the bungee-jumping letter to check whether the would-be jumper had paid a deposit. If the condition was met, your Then instructions could make Word thank the jumper for the deposit and request the balance of the fee; otherwise, your Else instructions would cause Word to request the full fee.

To insert an If...Then...Else... field, click on the Insert Word Field drop-down list on the Mail Merge toolbar.

This brings up the Insert Word Field: IF dialog box:

So, say you're sending out collection letters and you want to vary some of the language you use, depending on how overdue your invoices or bills are. You'd need to maintain an age field for overdue bills and then include an If...Then...Else expression that If the overdue bill's age was greater than 90 days, Then a sentence containing strong language would be included, Else a more conciliatory sentence would be included instead.

This means that in the Insert Word Field: IF dialog box, you'd select the Age field in the Field Name box, select Greater Than in the Comparison box, and enter **90** in the Compare To box. Then you'd type something like "Please remit immediately to protect your credit rating!" in the Insert this Text box and something like "Did you forget?" in the Other-wise Insert this Text box. Then click OK.

Fill-In...

Fill-in... prompts for text to be inserted at the location of the field in one document. For more than one document, use Ask instead. To insert a Fill-in... field, click on the Insert Word Field drop-down list on the Mail Merge toolbar.

This brings up the Insert Word Field: Fill-in dialog box:

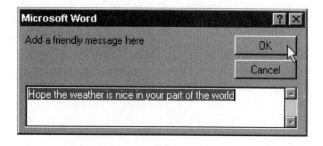

Type a prompt in the Prompt box (such as "Add a friendly message here") and then, if you want, type a suitable example sentence in the Default Fill-in Text box (such as "Hope the weather is nice in your part of the world"). If you'll want to be prompted only once so that your answer is printed in all the merged documents, check the Ask Once box. Otherwise, you'll be able to personalize each and every merged document. Then click OK.

Word will show you the prompt as it will appear when you merge the document:

Click OK. Word will insert a field code into your main document (field codes are explained in Chapter 32). It will appear as your default text unless you choose to view field codes in the Option dialog box (Tools ➤ Options, View tab). Then it will look something like this:

```
{ FILLIN "Add a friendly message here" \d "Hope the weather
is nice in your part of the world" }
```

When you merge the document, you'll be prompted for a personalized message.

Merge Record # and Merge Sequence

Merge Record # inserts the merge record number in the merge document. You might use it for keeping track of the records you print—for example, for invoice numbers.

Merge Sequence # inserts the merge-sequence number in the merge document. This can differ from the merge-record number if only some of the records in the data source are used for a merge. For example, if you used only data records 157 to 300 for a merge, the Merge Record # for the first one would be 157, but the Merge Sequence # would be 1.

Insert these fields from the Insert Word Field drop-down list on the Mail Merge toolbar.

Next Record and Next Record If...

Next Record merges the next record into the current merge document rather than into a new merge document. Next Record If... does the same if the comparison between two expressions is true. Insert these fields from the Insert Word Field drop-down list on the Mail Merge toolbar.

Skip Record If...

Skip Record If... skips the current document and moves to the next record if the comparison between two expressions is true. Insert a Skip Record If... field from the Insert Word Field drop-down list on the Mail Merge toolbar.

Try It

Try applying some of these tricks and fields on a few practice merge documents of your own. The best way to learn how the fields work is to play around with them.

Using the Mail Merge Toolbar

As I mentioned before, the Mail Merge Helper can feel like a straitjacket at first—it may seem to be pushing you all over the place, opening up this document and that, with little rhyme or reason. As you get used to it though, you'll probably find that it offers more flexibility than it at first appears to.

But if you don't get along with the Mail Merge Helper, put together your mail merge using the Mail Merge toolbar. We've looked at it briefly along the way, but here it is in all its glory:

Here's what the buttons on the Mail Merge toolbar do:

Icon	Name	Function
Insert Merge Field	Insert Merge Field	Inserts a merge field at the insertion point
Insert Word Field	Insert Word Field	Inserts a Word field (e.g., Ask...) at the insertion point
« »ABC	View Merged Data	Toggles between viewing merge fields and the data that will appear in them
⏮	First Record	Displays the first record in the data source
◀	Previous Record	Displays the previous record in the data source

Icon	Name	Function
`1`	Go to Record	Enter the number of the record you want to go to in this box
▶	Next Record	Displays the next record in the data source
▶❙	Last Record	Displays the last record in the data source
	Mail Merge Helper	Displays the Mail Merge Helper
	Check for Errors	Displays the Check for Errors dialog box
	Merge to New Document	Merges the main document and the data source to a new document
	Merge to Printer	Merges the main document and the data source to a printer
	Mail Merge	Displays the Merge dialog box
	Find Record	Displays the Find Record dialog box
	Edit Data Source	Displays the Data Form dialog box

Merge-Printing Labels and Envelopes

You can also use Word's Mail Merge Helper to merge labels of various kinds and envelopes. Because the procedures for merging labels and envelopes are very similar to those for form letters, we'll discuss them only briefly here.

Printing Labels on Laser Printers

The Mail Merge Helper makes merging labels on a laser printer dead simple. You use the Mail Merge Helper to create a main document containing a table with fixed-size cells and cell spacing that match the size and position of your blank labels. Then insert merge instructions in each table cell. Here's how to do it:

1. Select <u>T</u>ools ➤ Mail Me<u>r</u>ge to fire up the Mail Merge Helper.

2. Click the <u>C</u>reate button to drop down a list of options.

3. Select <u>M</u>ailing Labels from the drop-down list.

4. Arrange your data source as usual. Word will then invite you to set up your main document. In the Label Options dialog box that appears (Figure 28.13), make the appropriate choices for your printer and labels:

   - In the Printer Information box, select <u>L</u>aser or Dot <u>M</u>atrix as appropriate. If necessary, click the arrow to drop down the <u>T</u>ray list and select a different tray.

> **TIP** Consider selecting a different Tray option when printing labels on a network. That way, you might be able to avoid having someone else print a 90-page report on your precious disk labels.

Figure 28.13   **In the Label Options dialog box you select the type of printer and labels you're using.**

- In the Label Products box, select the brand of labels you want: Avery Standard, Avery Pan European, or Other. (Other includes brands such as Inmac and RAJA.)

- From the Product Number list, select the number for the labels you're using. If you don't know the number (for Avery products it appears on the box), consult the Label Information area to find out the size of the label selected in the Product Number list. If you're still no wiser, measure your labels carefully and choose the closest match.

- For precise layout information on the labels, choose the Details button. In the dialog box that appears, make any necessary adjustments in the labels' margin, pitch, dimensions, and layout, then click OK.

5. When you've chosen the labels to use, choose OK to close the dialog box.

6. The Create Labels dialog box will appear (see Figure 28.14). Enter the fields here by pulling down the Insert Merge Field list and selecting them in turn. Remember to include any necessary spaces and punctuation.

Figure 28.14   **Add the fields for your labels in the Create Labels dialog box.**

- To include a postal bar code, click the Insert Postal Bar Code button. In the Insert Postal Bar Code dialog box (shown below), enter the Merge Field with ZIP Code and Merge Field with Street Address in the appropriate boxes, then click OK.

Click OK when you're finished making choices in the Create Labels dialog box. Word will then enter your label fields into the main document, as shown in Figure 28.15.

Figure 28.15 *The labels merged into the main document.*

NOTE The NEXT and NEXTIF fields are ones you probably won't use very often, but here's what they do: NEXT instructs Word to merge the next records data without starting a new document. NEXTIF does the same thing, but you can enter criteria that must be met before NEXTIF will merge the next record's data without starting a new document.

7. Make any necessary adjustments to your main document (for example, adding Ask or Fill-In fields).

8. Open the Mail Merge Helper dialog box and choose the Merge button to merge your data source with the main document. Choose whether to merge to a new document or to the printer. (You can also use the Merge to New Document and Merge to Printer buttons on the Mail Merge toolbar here.)

9. Save your documents with meaningful names.

Making Custom Mailing Labels

If you can't find a mailing label format in the Label Options dialog box that match the labels you have, you can always create your own. To do so,

1. In the Label Options dialog box, find a label format that's close to the dimensions that you need and select it.

2. Click the Details button. This brings up an Address Information dialog box, such as this one:

Either type in new dimensions to match your mailing labels or play with the little arrow buttons to zero in on the correct dimensions.

The diagram will change to reflect the information you enter. When you are satisfied, click OK three times and then continue with step 6 in the previous section.

Printing a Label for a Single Piece of Mail

Labels are great for mass mailings, but you may also want to use individual labels for single pieces of mail every now and again. With your main document on the screen, select Tools ➤ Envelopes and Labels. This brings up the Envelopes and Labels dialog box:

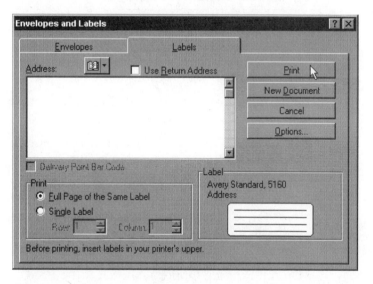

Correct the address, if necessary, use the Insert Address button to add an address from your personal Address Book, or check Use Return Address to print a return-address label. If you want to print a single label and not a full page of the same label over and over, check Single Label.

If the upper-left label is available on your label sheet, leave Row and Column set to 1. Otherwise, type in the Row and Column of the first available label.

When you are ready, click Print.

Part
5

Power Tools

Printing Addresses on Envelopes

Word offers the ability to print addresses on envelopes. This can be convenient for small numbers of envelopes; but as most laser printers require you to feed envelopes in by hand, printing large numbers of envelopes can be a slow business. Take a quick reality check before you arrange to print a whole slew of envelopes and consider using mailing labels on the envelopes instead.

TIP Before starting to prepare envelopes, make sure your return address is correct. Choose **T**ools ➤ **O**ptions to display the Options dialog box. Click on the User Info tab to view (and if necessary change) the name and mailing address. Click OK when you're finished.

1. Select **T**ools ➤ Mail Me**r**ge to fire up the Mail Merge Helper.

2. Click the **C**reate button to drop down a list of options.

3. Select **E**nvelopes from the drop-down list.

4. Arrange your data source as usual. Word will invite you to edit your main document.

5. In the Envelope Options dialog box that appears (Figure 28.16), make the appropriate choices for your envelopes:

   • On the Envelope Options tab, click the **F**ont button in the Delivery Address box or the F**o**nt button in the Return Address box to change the font in which the addresses appear. If necessary, adjust the position of the delivery address or return address by entering From **T**op and From **L**eft measurements in their boxes.

   • On the Printing Options tab, select the Feed **M**ethod and the tray to **F**eed From. Note that the default Feed From option is manual. For large numbers of envelopes, you'll be spending half the afternoon *chez* the printer.

NOTE Word displays the name of your currently selected printer in the Printing Options tab of the Envelope Options dialog box. If need be, change the printer by using **F**ile ➤ **P**rint, clicking Options, and then clicking the arrow to drop down the Default **T**ray list to select a different tray.

Figure 28.16 **Choose your envelopes in the Envelope Options dialog box.**

6. When you've chosen the envelope options and printing options, choose OK to close the dialog box.

7. The Envelope Address dialog box will appear (see Figure 28.17). Enter the fields here by pulling down the Insert Merge Field list and selecting them in turn. Remember to include any necessary spaces and punctuation.

   • To include a postal bar code, click the Insert Postal Bar Code button. In the Insert Postal Bar Code dialog box, enter the Merge Field with ZIP Code and Merge Field with Street Address in the appropriate boxes, then click OK.

   Click OK when you're finished making your choices in the Envelope Address dialog box. Word will then enter your label fields into the main document, as shown in Figure 28.18.

8. Make any necessary adjustments to your main document.

9. Open the Mail Merge Helper dialog box and choose the Merge button to merge your data source with the main document. Choose whether to merge to a new document or to the printer. (You can also use the Merge to New Document and Merge to Printer buttons on the Mail Merge toolbar.)

Figure 28.17   Enter fields for mailing labels in the Envelope Address dialog box.

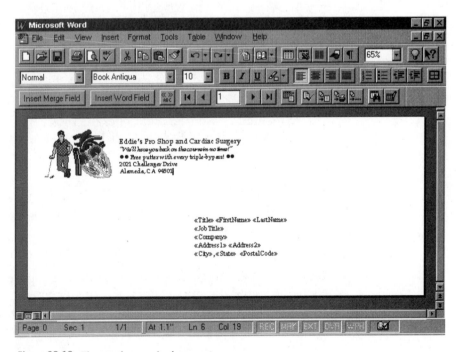

Figure 28.18   The envelope main document.

10. Save your documents with meaningful names.

 TIP   See Chapter 15 for more information on envelopes.

Creating Catalogs with Mail Merge

If you need to create a document with variations on the same information repeated throughout, you can use the Catalog option with Mail Merge. When you designate your main document as a catalog instead of as a form letter, each record from the data source is merged into a single document. (With form letters, each record creates a distinct resulting document.)

This enables you to create a document with a series of similar entries by only typing the basic information once. Then, as you merge the records from the data source into the catalog file, the contents of the main document will be repeated once for each record without any automatic section or page breaks between entries.

To perform a catalog merge, start with a fresh document. Select Tools ➤ Mail Merge. This brings up the Mail Merge Helper dialog box. Click the Create button and select Catalog. Click the Active Window button to use the new document as the main document.

Now click the Edit button and select Catalog. This will drop you into the main document with the Mail Merge toolbar across the top of the screen. Type into this document any information you want to repeat for each record and include merge fields as explained earlier in this chapter.

You can use any normal data source with a catalog document.

Tips, Techniques, and Troubleshooting

Here are some tips for working with Word's mail-merge feature:

▶ To change the appearance of merged characters—to make them bold or italic, or a larger point size—format their merge instructions in the main document. Merged characters take on the formatting of their merge instructions.

▶ If you move your data-source files, Word will ask you to relocate them before you can merge.

Part 5

Power Tools

▶ To print selected items from a longer data file, sort them and print just the range containing the desired records (from 10 to 30, for instance).

Shortcut Key
Combinations for Merging Documents

The following shortcut key combinations are available when merging documents using the Tools ➤ Mail Merge command:

Key Combination	Effect
Alt+Shift+K	Preview a mail merge
Alt+Shift+M	Merge a document
Alt+Shift+N	Print the merged documents
Alt+Shift+E	Edit a mail-merge data source
Alt+Shift+Q	Sort and filter records

Restoring a Mail-Merge
Document to a Normal Word Document

You can restore a mail-merge main document to a normal Word document when you've finished merging with it. This removes the association between the main document and its data source and header source (if it has one); that way, you can attach it to a different data source. The text of the main document, including merge fields and instructions, does not change.

To restore a main document to a normal Word document, follow these steps:

1. Open the Mail Merge Helper dialog box by selecting Tools ➤ Mail Merge.

2. In the Main Document section, choose the Create button to display the list of options.

3. Choose the Restore to Normal Word Document option.

4. In the Restore to Normal Word Document dialog box that appears, choose Yes. The association between the main document and its data sources will be removed.

Chapter 29

Using Charts and Graphs

FAST TRACK

Microsoft Graph is a supplementary application included with Word that you can use to create, import, and edit charts and graphs. These charts and graphs are *embedded* objects; not only can you insert them into any application that supports Object Linking and Embedding (more on this in the next chapter), but you can simply double-click them to open them (and Microsoft Graph) for editing.

You can create the following using Microsoft Graph:

- Area charts
- Bar charts
- Column charts
- Line charts
- Pie charts
- Scatter charts
- Combination charts
- 3-D variations on many of the above

To give you some idea of the possibilities Microsoft Graph offers, Figure 29.1 shows a chart created with Microsoft Graph and then inserted into a Word document.

Making Sure Graph Is Installed

First, make sure that whoever installed Word on your PC included Graph in the installation. A Typical installation of Word includes Graph, a Minimum installation doesn't include Graph, and a Custom installation lets you choose whether to install Graph.

If Graph isn't installed on your PC, dig out those Word installation disks and install it. Run the Setup program by choosing Programs ➤ Microsoft Word ➤ Setup from the Start menu in Windows. If you are running Microsoft Office, your option will be Programs ➤ Microsoft Office ➤ Setup from the Start menu. When Setup appears, choose the Custom option and follow the instructions for installing Graph.

NOTE For more information on installing Word on your PC, turn to Appendix A.

Figure 29.1 **A chart created with Microsoft Graph and inserted into a Word document.**

Getting Started with Word Graphs

The general steps for creating a graph are so simple that you can be up and running in a flash.

1. Open a Word document and place the insertion point where you want the new graph to appear.

2. Choose Insert ➤ Object and be sure the Create New tab is foremost; then double-click Microsoft Graph in the Object Type list.

3. Graph will open with its own toolbar, displaying a *datasheet window* that looks like a small spreadsheet, together with a *chart window* (aka a *graph window*—take your pick). Enter your data and labels into the datasheet window.

4. Notice that even though Graph has the same menus as Word, many of the menu commands are different. We'll look at how to use these

commands in the following sections. For now, just browse through them to familiarize yourself with the kinds of commands you'll be seeing.

5. Use Microsoft Graph's commands to embellish the graph with text, arrows, different typefaces and type sizes, and so on. Resize the graph by dragging the size box in the lower-right corner of its window.

6. When you're ready to insert the graph into your Word document, just click anywhere outside the graph. Your Word document will reappear, now containing the graph.

7. Caption, resize, reposition, frame, apply a border, and otherwise embellish the chart and its surrounding area using the same methods as with any other graphic object.

8. To make changes to the content and appearance of the chart itself, double-click on it in your Word document to launch Microsoft Graph and make the necessary changes.

9. Save your Word file when you've finished editing the graph.

 NOTE   If all you see in your Word document is { EMBED MSGraph Chart.5\s} you are looking at a field code; that is, you've got field codes turned on. To turn them off, select <u>T</u>ools ➤ <u>O</u>ptions, click on the View tab, and uncheck the Field Codes check box.

Parts of a Graph Project

There are three parts to any Graph project—the datasheet window, the chart, and the Graph object that you embed in your Word document. In the following sections, we'll look at each separately. Note that the chart no longer appears in its own window.

Figure 29.2 shows the datasheet window and the chart.

 TIP   If the Datasheet window appears in an awkward position—for example, if it's blocking your view of the chart—grab the window by clicking in its title bar and drag it to somewhere more convenient.

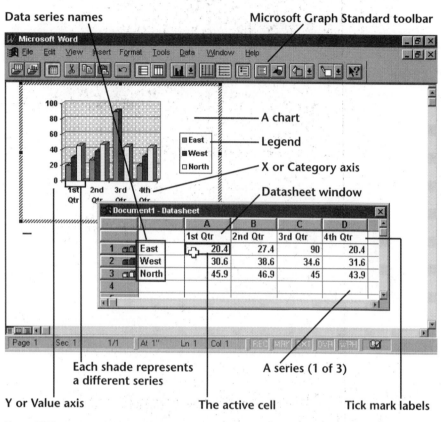

Figure 29.2   Microsoft Graph's Datasheet window and its graph.

The Datasheet Window

The datasheet window, which works much like any other window, is where you enter all the numbers and much of the text that you want to graph. As you can see in Figure 29.2, it's similar to a spreadsheet. When you start Microsoft Graph, you'll see a datasheet complete with sample data.

The following sections describe the parts of the datasheet window:

Cells

The individual rectangles containing numbers and text are called *cells*, just as they are in a spreadsheet. You can type and edit in cells as you'd expect. Enter each data item for your graph in a separate cell.

The Active Cell

To work in a cell, you must first make it active by clicking in it or moving to it with the arrow keys. The active cell is indicated by a dark border. In Figure 29.2, the active cell contains the number 20.4. Any data that you enter will appear in the active cell.

Rows and Columns

Cells are arranged in horizontal rows and vertical columns. A datasheet can contain a maximum of 1,024,000 cells (4000 cells by 256 columns). You can select a row or column by clicking its heading.

Row and Column Headings

Those gray boxes at the top and along the left of the datasheet in Figure 29.2 are row and column headings. When the data in a row or column is gray (dimmed), it will not appear in your graph. Double-click a heading to toggle its data on and off.

Data Points

Each cell containing a value is a *data point*. The datasheet in Figure 29.2 has 12 data points.

Data Series and Double Lines

A collection of related cells is called a *data series*. In Figure 29.2 there are three series—East, West, and North. Each series contains four data points.

A data series plots one line or piece of pie or one set of columns or bars in the chart.

Series Names

Series names are in the leftmost cells when a data series is plotted in horizontal rows. Series names are at the top of vertical columns when your graph will be plotted in columns. (In Figure 29.2, the series names are East, West, and North.)

Tick-Mark Labels

Tick-mark labels are the names that appear along the horizontal axes of area, column, and line charts, or along a bar chart's vertical axis. In Figure 29.2, the tick-mark labels are 1st Qtr, 2nd Qtr, and so on.

The Chart

The chart object has its own terminology. Here are the basics. Everything inside the borders surrounding the chart is considered to be part of the chart. This includes the legend, bars, pie slices, labels, arrows, and so on.

Data Markers

Data markers come in various shapes, depending upon the graph type. For example, the data markers are bars in bar charts, lines in line charts, pie slices in pie charts, and dots or symbols in line or scatter charts. Each marker represents the value of a single data point or value.

Data Series

Just as a data series in the datasheet represents a group of data points, so does a data series in the chart window. Figure 29.2 has three data series represented by three different shades of data markers.

Axis

An *axis* is a line along which data are plotted. Two-dimensional graphs like line and bar graphs usually have a horizontal axis (or X-axis) and a vertical axis (or Y-axis). 3-D charts have a third axis, called the Z-axis.

Tick Marks

Tick marks are the intersections of X and Y axes. They are usually labeled with tick-mark labels.

Gridlines

Gridlines are optional vertical and horizontal lines that make it easier to judge values on a graph. Gridlines begin at tick marks and continue through the chart either horizontally or vertically.

Chart Text

Chart text comes in two flavors—*attached text*, used for things like data and axes markers; and *unattached text*, which you can add by typing it. Use unattached text to point things out and annotate your chart. You type unattached text directly into the chart, and you can move it or size it.

NOTE   The terms *attached* and *unattached* with respect to chart text don't have anything to do with whether they're dating or not. Attached text is text that is associated with a particular element (such as an axis or a series), and as such is somewhat limited in terms of where it can go, while unattached text is free-floating text that can go anywhere.

Legends

Legends are little reference boxes that tell you which shades (or colors) are used to represent each data series. You can hide legends if they are unnecessary or get in the way. Look back to Figure 29.1 to see how useful legends can be in making things clear.

Graph Objects in Word Documents

When you click anywhere outside your graph's borders, it is automatically embedded in your Word document. You can resize objects, crop or frame them, add borders to them, and so on. Treat graph objects as you would any other embedded object. See Chapter 30 for more information on object linking and embedding (OLE).

Getting Online Help

You can get online help by pressing F1 at any point (the easy way) or by choosing either <u>H</u>elp ➤ <u>C</u>ontents or <u>H</u>elp ➤ <u>S</u>earch for Help On. Figure 29.3 shows what you get by pressing F1 at the beginning of a graph project and searching around a bit.

Click a topic of interest to read about it. Often, you'll have to go through several levels of the help system to reach your topic. Use the <u>C</u>ontents, <u>S</u>earch, and <u>B</u>ack buttons to navigate. Notice that you can print out help topics if you wish.

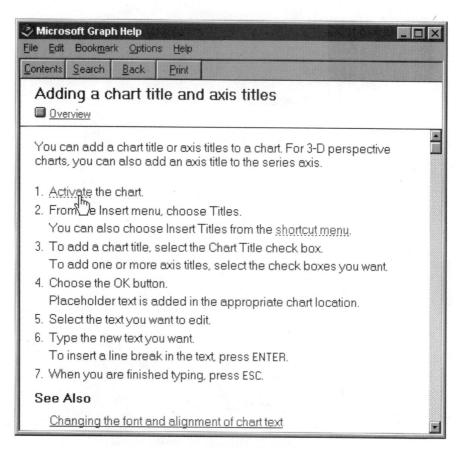

Figure 29.3   *Press F1 to get help while working on your graph.*

 TIP   Some key words and phrases, like the one the cursor is pointing to in Figure 29.3, lead to other topics or provide further information. Those with a solid underline contain hypertext jumps that will take you to a new help screen. Those with a dotted underline will pop up a box on the same screen explaining the word or phrase you clicked.

Inserting Excel
Worksheets in Word Documents

 If you have Excel, you can now insert a live Excel worksheet directly into a Word document without having to open Excel. Follow these steps:

1. Open a new document or place the cursor where you want the worksheet to go. Be sure the Formatting toolbar is showing.

2. Click the Insert Microsoft Excel Worksheet button on the Formatting toolbar. A grid will drop down that looks much like the one you see when you click the Insert Table button. It works exactly the same way.

3. Click and drag the cursor to indicate how many rows and columns you want in your worksheet (you can easily change this later).

4. When you release the mouse button, Word will insert an Excel worksheet with the specified number of rows and columns, as shown in Figure 29.4. Notice that the Standard and Formatting toolbars for Excel appear. Very slick!

Figure 29.4   *You can insert an Excel worksheet into your document without having to open Excel.*

5. Then you just go about your business with the worksheet as if you were using Excel. You can use most Excel formatting and data features. Consult an Excel manual for details.

6. When you are finished editing the data, click anywhere outside the worksheet and you'll return to your Word document with its regular Word toolbars.

 TIP If you want to move your worksheet around, frame it by selecting it and choosing Insert ➤ Frame. Then, in Page Layout view, you can move it to wherever you like, even having text flow around it.

If you want to modify the worksheet in some way, just double-click within it to return to editing mode. You can then make all kinds of changes. For instance, changing the number of rows and columns is very simple. Just select the worksheet and grab one of the black selection handles. Then drag the handle to add rows or columns. Notice that as you drag, the size of the grid is displayed in the Cell Location status area:

 WARNING To change the size of the worksheet, you must be in the Word document. Click anywhere outside the worksheet to return to your document. Then select the worksheet and drag the resizing handles (the black boxes).

Working in the Datasheet Window

Use the datasheet window to enter data. It behaves so much like a Word table that we won't go into exhaustive detail here. The next section offers some pointers.

Entering and Editing Cell Data

Here are some tips for entering and editing data:

▶ Click in the datasheet window to activate it; then click in a cell to edit its contents.

Part 5

Power Tools

▶ Always type data-series labels in the first column of a datasheet and category names in the first row.

▶ Changes to datasheet cell formatting (fonts, sizes, bold, etc.) are not reflected in the graph. (See *Formatting Chart Text* later in this chapter.) You apply formatting to all the cells in the datasheet at the same time.

▶ You can use the Edit ➤ Clear command in datasheets to clear the data, cell formatting, or both. Just choose the appropriate option from the Edit ➤ Clear submenu:

Importing Data

If you select a table in your Word document before inserting your chart, Microsoft Graph will import your selection into the datasheet when it opens.

NOTE If you throw Microsoft Graph a curveball by asking it to import something it can't, it'll tell you it "Cannot read this file." Try opening the application that created the file and using the Clipboard to transfer the data (we'll discuss this in a minute).

You can import data from other places using Graph's Edit ➤ Import Data command. In the Import Data dialog box (Figure 29.5), select the file you want to import.

WARNING If you import data when you already have data in the datasheet, Microsoft Graph will warn you that you're about to lose your data and formatting. Be sure you want to do this before clicking OK.

You can also use the Clipboard to import text. Bear in mind that incoming data must be comma-separated or tab-separated text and must not exceed the 4000-row by 256-column maximum.

Figure 29.5   Select the file from which you want to import data in the Import Data dialog box.

Part
5

NOTE   Remember that to include data in a graph, the data heading above or to the left of the data must be black (not gray). Click these headings to toggle them.

Navigating in Datasheets

Navigating in datasheets is so easy that you'll hardly have to read through this section. The usual navigational tricks work:

▶   Use →, ←, ↑, and ↓ to move from cell to cell.

▶   Press Tab to move from cell to cell; press Shift+Tab to move backwards from cell to cell. This is one way to move around, though clicking in the target cell is quicker.

Power Tools

▶ Home takes you to the first cell in the row; End takes you to the last cell in the row.

▶ Ctrl+Home takes you to the first cell containing a data point in your datasheet; Ctrl+End takes you to the last cell containing a data point.

▶ Dragging or Shift-clicking selects multiple cells, as does holding down Shift and pressing →, ←, ↑, or ↓.

▶ Clicking at the left edge of a row or the top of a column (in the gray cells) selects the entire row or column.

▶ To speed up data entry, select multiple cells before entering data; then tab from one to the next to move left to right or ↵ to move up and down. The active cell will never leave the selected area. For example, select a three-by-four block of cells. Make your entry in the first cell and press ↵. Graph will make the next cell down the active cell. When you reach the bottom of the block, Graph will take you to the first highlighted cell in the next column. (With Tab, you move sideways and go down a row when you reach the rightmost selected cell.)

▶ Minimize, maximize, and restore your datasheet window by using the familiar Windows buttons. Or click and drag the borders of the window to resize it.

▶ Scroll up and down your datasheet as you would in any window.

Number Formats in the Datasheet

Microsoft Graph allows you to format numbers in a variety of commonly accepted ways:

▶ Numbers too long to be displayed in cells will be stored as you typed them but displayed in scientific notation. For example, 1234567890 would be displayed as 1.235E+09.

▶ You can apply predefined number formats by selecting Format▶ Number, choosing Number in the Category area of the Number Format dialog box, and then double-clicking the Format Code you want. (see Figure 29.6). If you don't like any of the predefined formats, select one as a victim and edit it in the Code box. When you're done, click OK.

▶ Inspect the sample formats or read online help for assistance. Excel users will find the process and formats familiar. For instance, use dollar signs ($), pound signs (#), commas, decimal points (.), percent signs, parentheses,

Figure 29.6 Choose a number format that tickles your fancy in the Number Format dialog box. If you don't like any of them, you can create your own.

and colors to specify custom formats. Thus, **$#,###.;[Red]($#,###.)** would display and print dollars with commas and no pennies. Negative dollar amounts would be shown in parentheses and red. The custom format **0.0%** would display percentages to one decimal place.

Column Widths

Columns can be up to 255 characters wide, but 9 characters is the standard column width. You can change a column's width by dragging its right edge or use Format ➤ Column Width to specify column widths in characters.

Inserting and Deleting Rows and Columns

Inserting rows works much as it does in Word tables. Select the row beneath the point where you want to see a new one and choose Insert ➤ Cells. If you first select multiple rows, you'll insert a like number of new ones.

Part
5

Power Tools

To insert a column, select the column to the right of the place where you want to see a new one, and choose Edit ➤ Cells. If you first select multiple columns, you'll insert a like number of new ones.

> **NOTE** If you select a cell rather than a row or column, you'll get the Insert mini–dialog box. Select Insert Entire Row or Insert Entire Column, depending upon what you want.

To delete rows and columns, select them and choose Edit ➤ Delete.

> **TIP** You can insert and delete rows and columns even more quickly by using the keyboard shortcuts. To insert rows or columns, press Ctrl++ (that's Ctrl and +); to delete rows and columns, press Ctrl+– (Ctrl and –). Again, you can first select the number of rows or columns to delete.

Working with Charts

You no longer work with charts in a separate window. They cannot be edited directly in a Word document, though. Instead, you must double-click a chart to go into "chart edit" mode, where you can specify the appearance and size of the chart object you want to insert into your Word document.

The next few sections offer some tips for working with charts.

Pick the Right Chart Type

Use the Format ➤ AutoFormat command to pick the desired chart type for your projects. The right chart can convey information clearly and powerfully; the wrong chart can smother it. Below are descriptions of the types of charts available and their uses.

Area

Area charts show changes in relative values of multiple series over time. Use area charts to emphasize differences and amount of change (for example, changes in various presidents' approval ratings at different stages of their terms). Figure 29.7 shows some of the available area formats.

Figure 29.7 *Some area chart formats.*

Bar

Bar charts organize categories vertically and show comparisons between items (speeds of various disk drives, for instance). Figure 29.8 shows some of the available bar formats.

Figure 29.8 *Some bar chart formats.*

Column

Column charts organize the same types of information as bar charts, but they display it with vertical bars (columns). Figure 29.9 shows some of the available column formats.

Figure 29.9 **Some column chart formats.**

Line

Line charts emphasize time and rate of change—such as sales growth over a twelve-month period. Figure 29.10 shows some of the available line formats.

Pie

Pie charts show the relationships of parts to the whole—each department's contribution to the firm's total expense budget, for instance, or the number of arguments each member of the household causes. You can include only one data series in a pie chart, so it's not suited to a wide variety of uses. Figure 29.11 shows some of the available pie formats.

Doughnut

Like pie charts, doughnut charts are also use for showing the relationships of parts to the whole. Figure 29.12 shows some of the available doughnut formats.

Figure 29.10 **Some line chart formats.**

Figure 29.11 **Some pie chart formats.**

Radar

Radar charts are like area charts in that they are can be used to emphasize differences and amounts of change. Figure 29.13 shows some of the available radar formats.

Figure 29.12   *Some doughnut chart formats.*

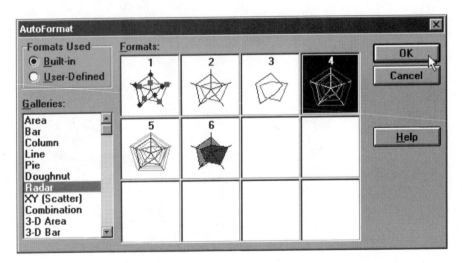

Figure 29.13   *Some radar chart formats.*

X-Y (Scatter)

Scatter charts are useful for demonstrating trends and patterns. They can show dependencies or relationships between variables. Figure 29.14 shows some of the available scatter formats.

Figure 29.14 *Some scatter chart formats.*

Combination

Microsoft Graph's combination charts can contain up to four axes representing data in different formats (lines and columns for instance). They offer a great way to overlay actual versus projected data or loosely related items like temperature and humidity. Figure 29.15 shows some of the available combination formats.

Figure 29.15 *Some combination chart formats.*

Part
5

Power Tools

3-D

Microsoft Graph's 3-D variations give perspective to data representations. As discussed later in this chapter, 3-D graphs can be rotated to change the bird's-eye view (this can sometimes emphasize or even distort relationships of related data—an effect I'll leave you to work out however you can). Figure 29.16 shows just a few of the many, many 3-D variations.

Figure 29.16   *Some 3-D Line chart formats.*

Changing the Default Chart Type

You can change the default chart type, so that a chart other than the column chart greets you when you open Microsoft Graph. This can be useful when you regularly work with one type of chart. Here's how to do it:

1. Create a chart of the desired appearance (chart type, formats, and so on).

2. Choose Tools ➤ Options and click the Chart tab to bring it forward.

3. Choose the Use the Current Chart button in the Default Chart Format drop-down. Your Custom Default will remain available in this box, should you want to change it again. Graph only allows one custom default format, but this format can be changed whenever it strikes your fancy.

4. Click OK.

Changing the Chart Size

Dragging a chart window's size box (in its lower-right corner) changes the size of the chart. Text and chart parts are automatically resized to fit the new window size. This new size will be reflected in your Word document when you click outside the chart to return to your Word document. (Don't confuse this feature with changing your Window size, described next.)

> **TIP**   Remember that you can change the size of a chart in Word if you embed the chart at an unsuitable size. Simply click and drag the sizing handles or select F<u>o</u>rmat ➤ Pict<u>u</u>re and change the size in the Picture dialog box.

Viewing Graphs in Different Sizes

If you wish to change the size of a chart on screens without affecting its size in your Word document, select <u>V</u>iew ➤ <u>Z</u>oom and choose a view percentage or type one in. You can also choose a zooming percentage with the Zoom Control drop-down list in the Standard toolbar. Zooming in or out changes the screen view but not the actual chart size and is useful for working on small chart elements or stepping back to get the big picture.

> **NOTE**   You cannot change the screen viewing size when you are in chart-editing mode. You must click outside your chart to adjust the zoom percentage from the Standard toolbar.

Editing Parts of a Chart

You can select various chart parts and then edit, move, and embellish them. In chart-edit mode, click to select a single item; Shift-click to select multiple items. Selected items are surrounded by handles. Solid black handles indicate that the selected item can be formatted with commands and moved or resized with your mouse. White handles mean you must use commands to make changes. (See Figure 29.17.)

For example, you can select the legend box or chart title and drag them to new locations. You can format selected text (change fonts, apply italics, etc.). Conversely, you can't move selected axes with a mouse, but you can modify them using menu commands.

Part
5

Power Tools

Figure 29.17   Black handles indicate that a selected object can be moved and resized with the mouse. White handles indicate that the selected object can be changed only by using commands.

The following items can be selected and altered:

▶ 3-D floor

▶ 3-D walls

▶ Arrows

▶ Axes

▶ Charts

▶ Data series (any)

▶ Drop lines

▶ Gridlines

▶ Hi-lo lines

▶ Legends

▶ Plot areas

▶ Series lines

▶ Text

▶ Up/Down bars

TIP Here's a hot tip. Frequently, double-clicking on an object in the chart window brings up a dialog box containing the available formatting options. For instance, double-clicking on an axis brings up the Axis Patterns dialog box. Double-clicking a pie wedge brings up the Area Patterns dialog box, and so on. Explore!

Dragging to Change Data

On some kinds of two-dimensional charts you can drag data points and thereby change the appearance of a chart *and* the underlying numbers in the datasheet! Yep. Read it again. For example, you can drag a column up or down and see the changes visually in the chart and numerically in the datasheet.

Try it. Click bars and columns, the selection boxes on lines, etc., twice. That is, for once you want two separate clicks, not a double-click. This will produce selection handles around the object and black handles at the draggable extremity. Drag these handles in the appropriate direction, as illustrated in Figure 29.18.

NOTE You can't drag to change data in some chart types. In others you can click until the cows come home, but you won't get a draggable black handle. Don't expect *too* much.

Typing Attached Title Chart Text

Here's how to type or edit attached text (titles):

1. Choose Insert ➤ Titles to display the Title dialog box.

2. In the Title dialog box, choose the object to which you want to attach the titles (the chart, an axis, etc.), then click OK:

Figure 29.18   Changing data is easy in charts. Just hold down Ctrl and drag the black handle to change values both in the chart and in the datasheet.

3.   Graph opens a tiny text object, surrounded by a gray border with selection handles, within easy commuting distance of the object you chose:

4.   Begin typing. Press ↵ to force new lines without ending the entry.

5.   Pick a new font, style, and so on; you can move the text around wherever you would like to.

Typing Unattached Chart Text

If you want to add to your chart unattached text notes that you can easily move, follow these steps:

1. Simply start typing in the active chart window. The text first appears in the center of your chart window. Press ↵ to force new lines without ending the entry.

2. When you've completed the entry, press Esc. A frame with handles will appear around the entry.

3. Pick a new font, style, and so on.

4. Position the text by clicking on it and dragging it to its new location.

Figure 29.19 shows a chart with a title and text added.

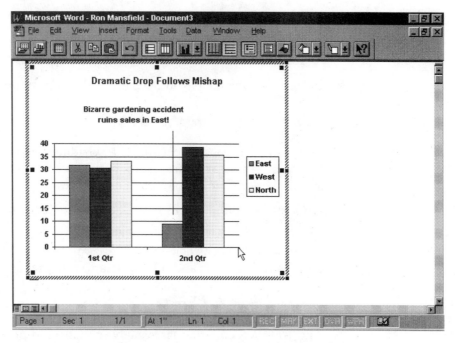

Figure 29.19   **A chart with a title and text and other embellishments added.**

Editing Chart Text

To edit chart text, first click to select it. Move the pointer into the text so that it changes to an I-beam; then click and use the I-beam cursor to select and edit the desired text.

Formatting Chart Text

To format chart text, click it so that it is surrounded by handles. Then use the Format ➤ Font command to change the appearance of the text. This displays the Format Object dialog box, which has the following tabs:

▶ Font, which offers you a choice of typefaces and sizes.

▶ Patterns, which allows you to specify borders and fill colors.

▶ Alignment, which offers you the following options:

> **Horizontal text alignment:** Left, Center, Right, and Justify
>
> **Vertical text alignment:** Top, Center, Bottom, and Justify
>
> **Text orientation:** horizontal, vertical, upwards, and downwards

▶ Properties, which lets you determine object positioning.

Gridlines on Charts

To specify gridlines, select Insert ➤ Gridlines and specify the gridlines you want in the Gridlines dialog box. You can choose Major Gridlines and/or Minor Gridlines for each of the axes.

Double-click on gridlines to pick different line patterns for them from the Line Patterns dialog box.

Alternately, you can click on the Horizontal or Vertical Gridlines toolbar buttons to toggle on and off the default gridline formatting.

Rotating 3-D Charts

The 3-D View command is available on Chart's Format menu when you are working with a 3-D chart. It reveals the Format 3-D View dialog box (see Figure 29.20).

Figure 29.20   *You can control the orientation of 3-D charts with the Format 3-D View dialog box.*

You can control elevation, perspective, rotation, axes orientation, and height by clicking on boxes that demonstrate these functions. The Right Angle Axes option forces right angles. Auto Scaling sometimes helps with the conversion of 2-D charts to 3-D charts.

WARNING   Use caution when changing a 3-D graph's orientation, particularly perspective. You can give misleading impressions of the relative size or importance of data this way. Of course, if you're doing it deliberately…

Saving Charts and Their Data

The only way to save charts and chart data is to embed them into a Word document, which is done automatically when you click anywhere outside the graph. You must then save the Word document to preserve the chart and data. Thereafter, choosing Save on the File menu, even in graph edit mode, saves the whole Word document, including the graph.

TIP   To embed a Microsoft Graph chart in an Excel spreadsheet, select Edit ➤ Copy Chart while you're in Graph and then paste the chart into the target spreadsheet.

Positioning Graphs in Word Documents

You can use normal paragraph-formatting techniques to position embedded graphs. For instance, to center a graph:

1. Select the embedded graph in your Word document by clicking on it.

2. Remove first-line indenting (if there is any) from the paragraph containing the graph.

3. Use the Center button on the Formatting toolbar or choose Format ➤ Paragraph and choose Center in the Alignment box on the Indents and Spacing tab of the Paragraph dialog box.

Resizing and Cropping Graphs

To resize and crop graphs, follow these steps:

1. Select the embedded graph in your Word document by clicking on it. Small handles appear around the edges and in the bottom-left corner.

2. Move the mouse pointer over one of the corner handles so that it changes into a double-headed arrow, click, and drag the corner handle to resize the graph. If you want to crop (cover up) portions of the graph, hold down the Shift key when you do this; the mouse pointer changes shape to overlapping L-shapes to indicate that you're cropping.

TIP   For more precise resizing and cropping of graphs, choose Format ➤ Picture and enter exact measurements or scaling percentages in its boxes. To leave white space around your graph—for example, between the graph and its border or the surrounding text—enter negative numbers in the Crop From boxes.

Editing and Updating

To update a graph, follow the steps below:

1. Double-click on the graph in your Word document or right-click on the graph and select Edit Chart from the shortcut menu. Word will enter chart-editing mode.

2. Make the desired changes in the graph.

3. Click anywhere outside the graph.

4. You will be returned to Word, and the updated graph will be in position.

5. Save your Word document to save the changes.

Other Ways to Incorporate Graphs in Your Word Documents

You can create graphs with other programs (Excel, for instance) and either copy and paste them via your Clipboard or link them to your Word document using Object Linking and Embedding. Read more about these techniques in Chapter 30.

Chapter 30

Linking and Embedding to Keep Things Current

FAST TRACK

With Word's Object Linking and Embedding (OLE), you can include in your Word documents information created in other applications. For example, you could create a picture in a drawing program like CorelDRAW or Micrografx Designer and then insert it into your Word document. You could include in a Word document a table from a spreadsheet in Microsoft Excel or data from a Microsoft Access report. In each case, you could choose to have the information updated automatically whenever the source was changed, updated only when you wanted it updated, or left forever as it was when you inserted it.

Big deal, I hear you say, but what does this mean to *me*? So you're a financial hotshot; you could insert in your annual report figures linked to your profit-and-loss statement in a spreadsheet or database, and then have Word update the report automatically whenever the spreadsheet or database changes. So you're a design whiz; you could keep your brochure up to date with your latest designs. As a crude example of this, Figure 30.1 shows a CorelDRAW drawing paste-linked into a Word document with

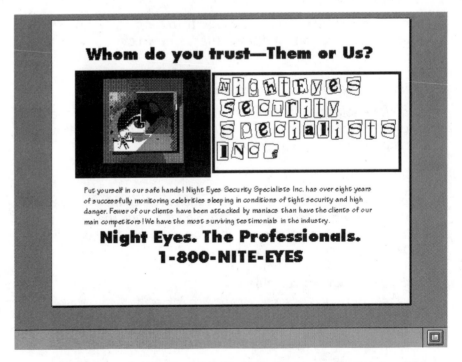

Figure 30.1 *This CorelDRAW drawing is linked to the Word document where it appears. Whenever the drawing is changed in CorelDRAW, it will also change in the Word document.*

automatic updating on. Every time I change the drawing in CorelDRAW, it'll be updated in the Word document.

Before Object Linking and Embedding, I would have had to reopen the source application, change the source data, and then copy and paste it into my Word document to bring it up to date. Believe me, this gets tedious fast.

Word implements several OLE features that are sure to interest you:

▶ You can display an embedded or linked object as an icon instead of at its full size. Because the icon takes less memory to display than the full object, scrolling in your document is faster.

▶ You can convert an embedded or linked object to a different application. For example, say I need to update the document in Figure 30.1 on a computer that doesn't have CorelDRAW installed: I can convert the linked object to a similar format and then update it. Clearly this offers welcome flexibility.

After a quick peek at the technical requirements for linking information between applications, we'll look at exactly what linking and embedding mean. Then we'll consider what each is for. Finally, we'll discuss how to link and embed.

Technical Requirements for Linking Information

To be able to link an object created in another application to a Word file, you need to be running both applications in Windows 95. Both applications must support either Object Linking and Embedding (OLE) or Dynamic Data Exchange (DDE). If your setup doesn't match these requirements, you won't be able to use Linking.

What Is Linking?

Linking is one way of attaching information from another application to a Word document. When you link an object to a Word document, the Word document stores the location of the object and its source application in a *field* in the document (see Chapter 32 for more on fields). The linked object in the Word document can then be updated at your convenience—you can choose to update it automatically whenever the source changes or manually just when you want to update it. You can lock the links when the document and the object it contains are finalized, and you can break the links so that objects cannot be updated any further.

If that isn't enough, you can also reconnect a lost link or change the source of a link—for example, if you update a different file in the source application.

What Is Embedding?

Embedding is an alternative way to attach information from another application to a Word document. When you embed information, it becomes part of the Word document and is stored in it. You can double-click the information in Word to open the source application with the information displayed ready for editing.

> **NOTE** Having a touch of *déjà* viewed? As discussed in the last chapter, graphs created with Microsoft Graph are embedded in your document. When you double-click one of them, Microsoft Graph opens with the chart and datasheet ready for editing.

You've no doubt worked out the corollary to this—embedding an object in a Word file increases the size of that file. Considerably. If you embed a whole bunch of big objects (TIFF true-gray files, for example), your Word files will grow to Brobdingnagian proportions. Time to dust off your wallet and buy a fistful more RAM. But seriously, don't embed too many objects in a file and expect your computer to run like Ricky Watters.

If you can't get around embedding masses of objects in your file (e.g., if you have to give other people your files), you can do a few things to improve matters. See the section *Converting an Embedded Object to a Graphic*, later in this chapter.

Why Link or Embed?

If you've read the above paragraphs, the reasons to link or embed should be pretty obvious. If you link objects in documents to their sources, you can update the objects either whenever the source objects change or whenever suits you. When your document is finalized, or ready for distribution, you can lock or break the links and freeze it in that state.

Another advantage of linking is that it keeps your documents from getting too large. No matter how large the linked information is, you only have to store it once: in the original file. The link itself increases the size of the document by only a few characters. Also, you can have one source for multiple target files.

One major disadvantage of linking is that when you give someone else your Word document that's linked to other files, that user must also have the source files and the applications those other files were created in to maintain the links. Another disadvantage is that making changes to linked data requires opening up the source file in the original application and changing the information there, then manually updating the links.

If you embed objects in documents, you can enjoy the quality of the originals in Word documents and the convenience of being able to edit them in the original application by double-clicking on them. No need to remember which object came from which source application—Word keeps track of that information for you.

The major disadvantage of embedding is that it can make your documents enormous when they contain embedded data from bulky sources, such as graphics files. If you don't need an active link and you're concerned about the size of your document, consider simply pasting in the data or image instead of embedding it. This will require less storage space.

Another disadvantage of embedding is that it does not allow you to change a series of linked documents by changing just the information in a single source to which all the other documents are linked. Changing the original source of embedded information has no effect on the document with the embedding.

The Risks of Automation

If you've decided to link all the information you've imported into Word with its sources and have it updated automatically, do me a favor and pause for a minute to consider the dangers of automatic updating.

For example, suppose you're writing the report that's going to send your career into the stratosphere. The report's in Word, and it contains figures drawn from your company's financial database in Microsoft Access. To keep the figures in the report up to date, you link the Access object in the Word document to its source. All well and good; next stop, the head office across from Le Parc. Time for the Accounting department to chuck a wrench in the works. The day before you present your report, some fool over there runs a test program on the database to track down a ten-cent overpayment on a shipment of widgets. Like a faithful dog, Word fixes up an instant update on your figures, your report is way off target, and you find yourself reporting to the branch office in Alpha Centauri instead.

Even if you're not connected to a network, and nobody but you can change your data, I'd recommend thinking carefully before using automatic updating. If you decide to go for it, keep a backup file with manual links just to humor me.

Link or Embed?

To link or to embed, that is the sixty-four-million–dollar question, as Rosenstern or Guildencrantz once said. Which is it going to be, and why?

You'll remember from the previous sections that embedded information becomes part of the Word document (and is stored in it), while linked information is stored in the source file in the source application. When you link, Word records the location of the information in the source file and displays a picture of the information in the Word document.

Here's the bottom line: *Link* when you will need to share information with another file. *Embed* when you know you will not need to share information with another file.

Keep a couple of other considerations in mind:

▶ Linking is a complicated operation. Even if your computer's a thundering, screaming P-6 workstation with twin overhead symmetrical multiprocessors, updating large linked files will take a while. If you have a slow computer, plan a few coffee breaks.

▶ Linking creates a number of temp files (you know, the ones that look like they've been named by dogs—~wrf0001f.tmp and so on). Plan to have a little space available for these; more importantly, check your computer every now and then for stray temp files and erase them (see the note below about this). You're most likely to have them if your computer crashes while working with linked files.

TIP Temp files (~dft064f.tmp and the like) are files created by Windows applications for temporary storage. They're supposed to be deleted automatically when you exit the application that produced then or when you quit Windows (depending on what produced them). Every now and then, check your disk for stray temp files *after* loading Windows and *before* running any Windows applications—i.e., before your applications get a chance to create new temp files—by selecting Find ➤ Files and Folders from the Start menu and specifying ~*.tmp. This will round up the usual suspects ready for deletion at dawn.

How to Link

Now that you've decided to link (brave soul!), how do you go about it? You can link an object using either the Edit ➤ Paste Special command or the Insert ➤ Object command. Edit ➤ Paste Special is a little easier, but with Insert ➤ Object you don't need to open up the source application. I'd recommend starting off by learning to link the easy way, then graduating to the more sophisticated way if need be.

Establishing a Link the Easy Way

With Edit ➤ Paste Special, you can choose either to link an existing object or to create a new object and then link it.

The simplest way to link an object to a Word file is as follows:

1. Fire up the source application for the object you want to link.

2. Create or open the file containing the object.

3. Select the object and copy it to the Clipboard (select Edit ➤ Copy, hit Ctrl+C or Ctrl+Ins, or click any Copy button the application offers).

4. Switch back to Word by pressing Alt+Tab or by clicking in the Task bar at the bottom of your screen and selecting Microsoft Word.

5. Put the insertion point at a suitable place in your Word document and select Edit ➤ Paste Special to open the Paste Special dialog box (see Figure 30.2).

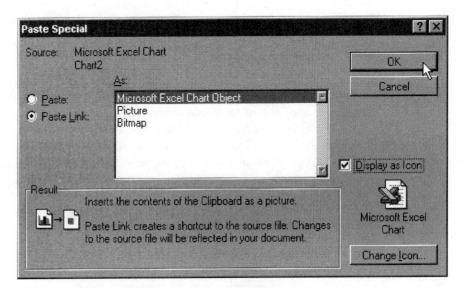

Figure 30.2   **Select the form in which you want the linked object to appear in the Paste Special dialog box.**

6. In the Paste Special dialog box, select the Paste Link option button to link the object to your Word file. The Paste Link option will be dimmed if it's not available—i.e., if the object copied to the Clipboard is in an application that doesn't support OLE.

7. In the As: box, select the form in which you want the linked object to appear. The Result box explains the effect of the option selected in the As: box. In this example, I have copied a chart from Excel.

8. Check the Display as Icon check box if you want to display the object as an icon in your Word document.

9. Click OK. The object will be paste-linked into your Word document.

NOTE When you paste your linked object into its destination document, you might see something like {LINK Excel.Chart.5 "C:\\WINDOWS\\Favorites\Chart, 1998 \a \p} or something equally incomprehensible. There is nothing wrong; this is a field code and links are inserted as fields. To see your object, choose Tools ➤ Options, click the View tab, and uncheck the Field Codes option.

Linking for the More Sophisticated

In case you're interested, the Insert ➤ Object command offers a slightly more complicated way of linking an object to your Word document.

Linking an existing object and creating a new object to link take you down different avenues of Word, so let's look at them separately to keep the dialog boxes straight.

To Link an Existing Object with Insert ➤ Object

Here's how to use Insert ➤ Object to link an existing object to a document:

1. In your Word document, put the insertion point where you want to insert the linked object.

2. Choose <u>I</u>nsert ➤ <u>O</u>bject. The Object dialog box will appear.

3. You're linking an existing object, so choose the Create from File tab (see Figure 30.3).

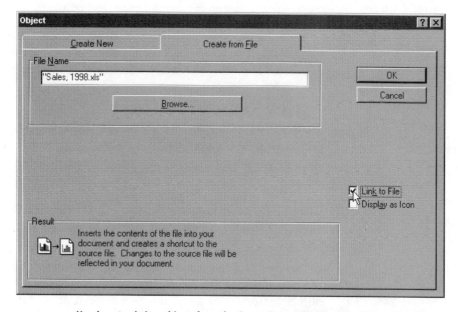

Figure 30.3   *You insert existing objects from the Create From File tab of the Object dialog box.*

4. Enter the name of the file from which you want to insert a linked object, or click Browse to select the file from an Open-like dialog box. When you find the file you want, click OK. In this example, the file is an Excel worksheet.

5. If you want to display the linked object as an icon in Word, check the Display as Icon check box. The standard icon for the application you chose will appear below the check box with a Change Icon button.

   - If you want to display a more exciting icon for your object—heck, you see the same boring old icon *all the time* in the Program Manager—select the Change Icon button. In the Change Icon dialog box, either select one of the icons the application offers, or click the Browse button to check out the icons from different applications. When you're done browsing, click OK to return to the Change Icon dialog box, and OK again to accept the icon you've chosen. It'll now appear in the Object dialog box.

6. Check the Link to File check box and click OK. The selected object will be inserted and linked to your Word file.

NOTE As mentioned earlier, with Insert ➤ Object you don't need to open up the source application for the object. However, the whole business *can* be so slow that you hardly save any time over opening the source application yourself and fixing things up manually. Watch this space for further news.

Create a New Object and Link It

To create a new object and link it to your Word document with Insert ➤ Object, follow these steps:

1. In your Word document, put the insertion point where you want to insert the linked object.

2. Choose Insert ➤ Object. The Object dialog box will appear. The Create New tab should be displayed by default (see Figure 30.4). If it isn't, select it.

3. In the Object Type box, select the application in which you want to create the new object. Check the Display as Icon check box if you want the new object to appear as an icon in your Word document. Change the icon if need be (see *To Link an Existing Object*, above, for details). In Figure 30.4, I've chosen to insert a Microsoft Graph 5.0 object.

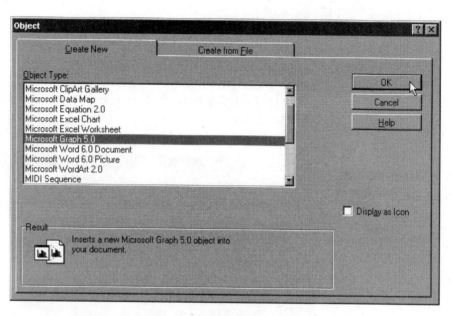

Figure 30.4   **The Create New tab of the Object dialog box.**

4. Choose OK. The application you chose will open.

5. Create the object you want; then click anywhere outside the object to return to Word. For some applications, you will have to select File ➤ Exit and Return to return to Word. The object will be inserted and linked to your document.

When Are Linked Documents Updated?

You can choose to have links updated in any of three ways:

▶ *Automatically.* This is the default. Links are created with automatic updating, so you'll have to change this option if you want something else.

▶ *Manually.* You update any or all links whenever you want to.

▶ *On printing.* Whenever you print the document, all links will be updated.

See the following sections for details on these three options.

Part 5

Power Tools

Choosing How to Update a Link

Updating a link is straightforward and intuitive:

1. Select Edit ➤ Links.

2. In the Links dialog box (see Figure 30.5), select the link or links that you want to update.

Figure 30.5   *You select the links to update, lock, or break in the Links dialog box.*

TIP   To update several links, hold down Ctrl while you click on each link, or hold down Shift and click on the first and last links of the desired range to select all the links between the two.

---

3. Choose how you want the selected links to be updated:

   • Choose the Automatic option button to update linked information every time the source file is changed.

   • Choose the Manual option button to update links only when you choose to do so.

4. Choose OK to close the Links dialog box and accept the changes you've made.

To Update a Link Manually

Update your links manually to retain the most control over your document and its linked objects. Here's how:

1. Select Edit ➤ Links.

2. In the Links dialog box, select the link or links that you want to update.

3. Choose the Update Now button to update the links.

 TIP To update links quickly, select the links you want to update and press F9.

To Update Links Every Time You Print

To make sure your documents are up to date whenever you print them, arrange for their links to be updated whenever you print. Here's how:

1. Select Tools ➤ Options.

2. In the Options dialog box, select the Print tab by clicking on it or by pressing **P**.

3. In the Printing Options area, check the Update Links check box (see Figure 30.6).

4. Click the OK button to close the dialog box. Links in your documents will now be updated whenever you print.

Editing Linked Information

You'll find you're best off editing linked information in its source file so that your changes are reflected in both the source file and the destination documents.

To edit linked information:

1. Select the linked information to edit. For example, click the linked object in your Word document.

2. Select Edit ➤ Object (this menu item will vary depending on what kind of object you have selected—e.g., Picture Link) and choose Edit from the mini-menu that appears. Word will open the source application with the selected information displayed.

3. Make the edits you want in the source file.

Figure 30.6   Check the Update Links check box in the Print tab of the Options dialog box to have links updated whenever you print documents.

4. Select File ➤ Exit to get back to your Word document, which will now reflect the edits you made in the source file.

    Saving your Word file at this point will also save the changes in the source file.

 TIP   You can often double-click an object to bring up its parent application, where you can then edit away to your heart's content. Some objects, though, such as sound and video clips, you must edit using the menu commands.

Breaking Links

If you want to prevent linked information from being updated ever again, you can break a link. Once you've broken a link, though, you cannot reconnect it other than by using Undo *pronto*. If you want to *temporarily* prevent linked information from being updated, you can *lock* a link—see the next section for details.

Here's how to break a link:

1. Select Edit ➤ Links.

2. In the Link dialog box, select the link or links that you want to break.

3. Choose the Break Link button. Word will display a dialog box asking if you are sure:

4. Choose Yes. The link or links will be broken.

TIP To break a link quickly using the keyboard, press Ctrl+Shift+F9.

Locking and Unlocking Links

You can *lock* links to temporarily prevent linked information from being updated. For example, suppose you're working on a technical manual with a number of screen illustrations. You've autoreferenced the figures in your text, and you've shot them and saved them to disk, using file names based on the figure numbers. If you need to add or delete any, updating the autoreference fields automatically is going to make your life miserable when you try to figure out which figure is which on disk. When you want to be able to update them again, you unlock the links. Here's how to both lock and unlock links:

1. Select Edit ➤ Links.

2. In the Link dialog box, select the link or links that you want to lock or unlock.

3. To lock a link or links, check the Locked check box. To unlock a link or links, uncheck the Locked check box.

Part 5

Power Tools

4. Choose OK to leave the Link dialog box and save your changes.

> **TIP** To lock links quickly using the keyboard, select the links and press Ctrl+F11. To unlock links, press Ctrl+Shift+F11. Use caution, though, because these shortcut commands lock and unlock *all* fields in your document, not just the links.

Reconnecting Lost Links

If you lose links in a document, blame yourself rather than the dog (sorry), but don't despair—you *can* reconnect lost links if there's another file you can use as the source.

How would you lose links? Well, you might delete the source file, forgetting that information in it was linked to a Word file. Someone else might even do this for you.

Here's how to reconnect lost links:

1. Choose Edit ➤ Links.

2. In the Links dialog box, choose the link you want to reconnect.

3. Choose the Change Source button.

4. In the File Name box of the Change Source dialog box, select the file to which you want to reconnect the link; then click OK.

   • If your document contains other links to the same source file, Word will ask you whether you want to change all links from the previous source file to the new source file. Choose Yes or No.

Word now has the uncanny ability to track linked documents that you rename or move. Even if you change the source document's name, Word will still be able to find it. Now if you delete the file altogether, well, that's another story.

So how will you know if your links have become lost? Well, the next time you update the links in your file, any lost links will generate an error message:

```
Error! Not a valid Filename.
```

If you no longer have the original source file, you can delete the linked data. If you've got a new source file, simply create a new link to the new source.

You could also lock the link to preserve the most recent data and the information in the link. Then, if you can locate or replace the source file, you can unlock the link and reconnect it to the source. (Locking and unlocking links are explained in the previous section.)

Another stopgap solution would be to break the link (as described in *Breaking Links*, earlier in this chapter). This would preserve the information but sever the faulty link.

Eliminating Graphical Representations of Links to Save Space

As I explained at the beginning of this chapter, a link takes up a lot less "space" than embedded data does because it stores information about where to find the data but it does not import all the data itself into the Word document. However, links do include graphical representations of the data or image linked, and these graphics take up some space. With enough of them, you can bog down your document almost as badly as you could with embedded data or images. (Either way, you'll eventually have to sit through the loading of the graphical images into your document.)

To store links without their graphical images:

1. Select Edit ➤ Links.

2. Select a link to be stored without its image.

3. Uncheck Save Picture in Document.

4. Click OK.

How to Embed

You can choose either to embed an existing object or to create an object and then embed it.

There's a dead simple way to embed objects, and then there's a more formal and more complicated way. Which would you like to learn first? Right. Here we go.

Embedding the Easy Way

Here's the easy way to embed objects in your documents:

1. Crank up the source application for the object you want to embed.

2. Create or open the file containing your victim object.

3. Select the object and copy it to the Clipboard (select Edit ➤ Copy, hit Ctrl+C or Ctrl+Ins, or click any Copy button the application offers).

4. Switch back to Word by pressing Alt+Tab or using the Task bar.

5. Put the insertion point at a suitable place in your Word document and paste in the object from the Clipboard by selecting Edit ➤ Paste Special. Word will embed the object in your document.

> **TIP**   If you want Word to do any of its fancy OLE tricks on your object, follow the above procedure through step 4 and then switch to step 5 in the following section, *Embedding an Existing Object*.

Embedding the Formal Way

If the way to embed described in the previous section is too easy for you, or you want to get a little more sophisticated with your object than simply pasting it in, use this method instead. Or combine the two.

Embedding an existing object and creating a new object to embed are a little different. Let's look at embedding an existing object first.

> **NOTE**   When you paste your embedded object into its destination document, you might see something like {EMBED Excel.Sheet.5} or some such. There is nothing wrong; this is a field code and embedded objects are inserted as fields. To see your object, choose Tools ➤ Options, click the View tab, and uncheck the Field Codes option.

Embedding an Existing Object

Here's how to embed an existing object in a document:

1. In your Word document, put the insertion point where you want to embed the object.

2. Choose Insert ➤ Object. The Object dialog box will appear.

3. As you're inserting an existing object, choose the Create from File tab.

4. Enter the name of the file from which you want to embed an object.

5. If you want to display the embedded object as an icon in Word, check the Display as Icon check box. The standard icon for the application you chose will appear below the check box with a Change Icon button.

6. Choose OK. The selected object will be embedded in your Word file.

Creating a New Object and Embedding It

To create a new object and embed it in your Word document, follow these steps:

1. In your Word document, put the insertion point where you want to embed the object.

2. Choose Insert ➤ Object. The Object dialog box will appear. The Create New tab should be displayed by default. (If it isn't, select it.)

3. In the Object Type box, select the application in which you want to create the new object. Check the Display As Icon check box if you want the new object to appear as an icon in your Word document. Change the icon if need be (see *To Embed an Existing Object*, above, for details).

4. Choose OK. The application you chose will open.

5. Create the object you want, then either click outside your object or select File ➤ Exit to return to Word. The object will be embedded in your document.

Editing Embedded Objects

You edit embedded objects just as you learned to edit graphs in Chapter 29:

1. Click the object to select it. Selection handles and a frame will appear around it, and "Double-click to Edit" will appear in the status area.

Part 5

Power Tools

2. You guessed it. Double-click the object. Your computer will chug and whir for a while (quite a while if your object is something complicated, like a Corel drawing—go get a jar of java or bug your office mate for a minute). Then the application in which the object was created will open with the object ready for editing.

3. Edit the object.

4. Click outside the object or select File ➤ Exit to quit the source application and return to Word. Word will reappear with the object updated to reflect your changes, as shown in Figure 30.7.

   You can use a shortcut menu to carry out common commands such as Cut, Copy, and Paste on an embedded object. Right-click on the offending object and select the command from the shortcut menu. The shortcut menu will vary depending on the source application for the embedded object.

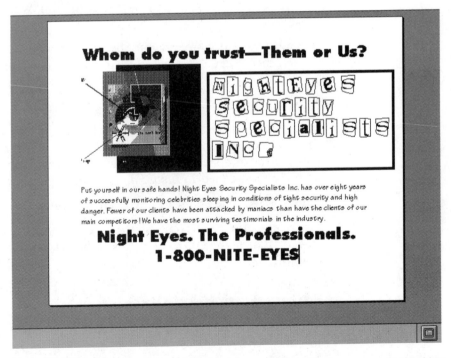

Figure 30.7 *When you select File ➤ Exit in the source application, Word reappears with the object updated to reflect your changes.*

NOTE   If the application temporarily trashes some of the Word menus and toolbars, click anywhere in the Word document to restore them. Bear in mind that embedding is even more puzzling for your computer than it is for you.

Editing Sound and Video Clips

If you've been using sound and video clips, you'll have spotted the fallacy in the preceding section. If you double-click a sound or video clip, you'll run it. These objects object to being edited this way. They just wanna play instead.

In such cases (and in others, if you like), you must edit embedded objects using the Object command:

1. Select the object you want to edit.

2. Select <u>E</u>dit ➤ <u>O</u>bject, choose the name of the object you want to edit, and choose Edit.

NOTE   If Word offers you the choice of Edit or Open, choose Edit to edit the object in the Word window or choose Open to open the application to which the object belongs and edit it there.

3. When you're finished editing the object, select <u>F</u>ile ➤ E<u>x</u>it and Return to get back to Word. Word will reappear with the edited object in place.

Converting an Embedded Object to a Different Format

If necessary, you can convert an embedded object to a different format. You might want to do this if you receive a file containing an embedded object created in an application you do not have or if you take a file created on your computer and containing embedded objects to a colleague's computer that does not have the relevant application.

To change an embedded object's source application:

1. Select the object to change.

2. Select <u>E</u>dit ➤ <u>O</u>bject, choose the object you want to convert, and select Convert from the extension menu.

Part 5

Power Tools

3. In the Convert dialog box, specify the application to which you want to convert the file.

   - Select the Convert To button to convert the embedded object permanently to the format you specify.

   - Select the Activate As button to convert the embedded object temporarily to the format you specify. You can then edit the object in that format, but when you save it, it will be saved in its original format.

4. Click OK.

When Are Documents Containing Embedded Objects Updated?

Trick question. Answer: When you choose to update them.

Remember that when you update embedded objects, you need to have the application or applications that created them loaded on the computer you're using.

Converting an Embedded Object to a Graphic

If you've been embedding objects like a maniac and your file is doing a Charles Atlas and splitting its shirt, you can reduce the file's size by converting the objects to graphics.

Before you do this, there's one little disadvantage you must know about: *You can't convert the graphic back to an embedded object.* And as you'll see, it's also likely that the resolution and overall quality of the graphic will suffer. Still want to do it? Here's how:

1. Select the object you want to convert.

2. Select Edit ➤ Object.

3. Choose Convert.

4. In the Object Type area of the Convert dialog box, select Picture. Click OK. The object will be displayed as a picture.

NOTE If you have field codes displayed, you will see the field {Embed Word Drawing}.

Removing Embedded Objects

Removing an embedded object is easier than winking. Select it and hit Delete. Alternatively, you can select it and choose Edit ➤ Cut if you want to place it somewhere else.

Editing Embedded Objects on Other People's Computers

As noted above, you cannot edit embedded objects on a computer that does not have the source applications installed. For instance, you might create a Word document with a linked Excel spreadsheet on your computer and take it in to show it to your boss. All goes well until you double-click the Excel object, only to find that your boss doesn't have Excel on her computer—she has Quattro Pro instead. *Bzzzzzzz!* Word won't like this.

WARNING When you take a file containing embedded objects to someone else's computer, make sure that the computer has all the necessary applications available before attempting to edit the embedded objects.

If you installed all the converters that come with Word, then you can edit an embedded object without having the source application available. If you did not install the converters, you can still run Microsoft Word Setup, do a partial installation, and install the relevant converters from the original disks.

To convert an embedded object to a different file format so that you can use it on a computer without the source application loaded, see *Converting an Embedded Object to a Different Format* earlier in this chapter.

Chapter 31

E-Mail and Other Network Features

FAST TRACK

To revise and return a document mailed to you

retrieve the document from your mail program and open it in Word, revise the document using annotations or revisions (depending on how the sender protected the document), and choose File ➤ Send to send the document on its way.

To merge revisions and annotations

into your original document, open the document containing the revisions you want to merge, select Tools ➤ Revisions, and click the Merge Revisions button. Select the original file in the Merge Revisions dialog box and click OK. Repeat the process for other revised copies of your document.

When using Word on a network

take precautions: Protect your documents from changes, save and back up your documents frequently, and be careful about who has access to your documents (if necessary, make them read-only).

If you're sharing documents a lot

remember a few basic points: Don't use templates that the other people in the group don't have; don't redefine built-in key combinations in shared templates; don't use fonts that the other people in the group don't have; and never, never, never lose your file-protection password.

Chances are that your place of work has a network. If it does, you'll know that networks add exciting new dimensions to working with computers: Not only can *you* screw up your documents, but someone else can access them from another workstation and screw them up for you. If you guard against that, the network can strike back by crashing while you're in the middle of a project and trashing all of your unsaved work.

The benefits of networks include access to files and applications that you haven't got on your workstation—other people's work, applications that simply won't fit on your PC, etc.—and instant communications with others on the network. (You can also install Word on a network rather than on an individual workstation, but that's beyond the scope of this book.) In this chapter, we'll look at Word's features for sending and sharing files on a network.

When you are on a network and your organization uses Microsoft Mail or a compatible mail program for in-house electronic communications, you can use the File ➤ Add Routing Slip and File ➤ Send commands to send and return copies of your Word documents to others.

You and your recipients must have Word and Microsoft Mail (or a compatible mail program) installed on your computers in order to use these features. Oh, and your network has to be running, but you'd probably guessed that already.

Sending Word Documents via E-Mail

WARNING Before we get into how easily you can propagate your Word documents all over the place, remember the importance of protecting them. You'll remember that we discussed this a bit in Chapter 7; we'll look at it again briefly later in this chapter in the *Network Considerations* section.

Sending Word documents via electronic mail is pretty simple:

1. Open the document you want to send.

NOTE If the document's already open because you've just created or altered it, make sure it's saved.

2. Select File ➤ Add Routing Slip. The Routing Slip dialog box will appear, as shown in Figure 31.1.

3. Click the Address button. In the Address Book dialog box (see Figure 31.2), select the names of the people you want to send the document to and click the To button. You might have to choose a different address book from the Show Names From The drop-down list.

TIP To route the document to one recipient after another (we'll get into this in a minute), arrange the names in the appropriate order by using the Move up- and down-arrow buttons.

Figure 31.1   The Routing Slip dialog box.

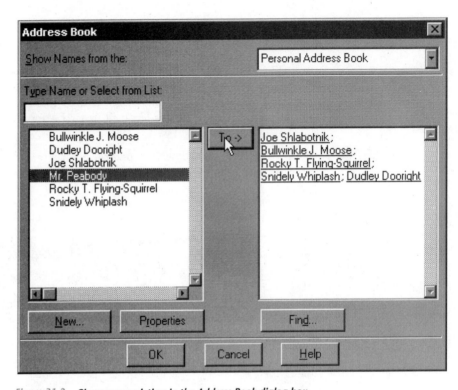

Figure 31.2   *Choose your victims in the Address Book dialog box.*

4. Click OK to return to the Routing Slip dialog box. The names you entered will appear in the To box.

> TIP If the To box shows that you've added someone you shouldn't have, click the Remove button to remove them from the list. Click OK again to get back to the Routing Slip dialog box.

5. Type the subject of your communiqué in the Subject box and any message in the Message Text box. Each recipient will get the same subject and message, so don't get too personal.

> TIP Word will automatically add to your message instructions that tell the recipients to select File ➤ Send when they are finished with the document you send them, so you don't need to write that in your message.

6. In the Route to Recipients area, choose whether you want the document to be sent to the recipients One After Another or All at Once.

 TIP If you send a document to the recipients One After Another, each successive recipient will see his or her predecessors' comments. This way, you may be able to avoid duplicate comments. If you send multiple copies to All At Once, everyone's comments will be between them and you (until you put them in the ultimate document and attribute them to their maker!). You'll probably also get quicker answers this way.

7. If you're ready to send your document, choose the Route button. The document will be sent to your chosen recipients as an attached Word file.

 TIP To further edit your document before you send it, click the Add Slip button, do your editing, and then select File ➤ Send to send the document. Click Yes in the confirmation dialog box.

Let's look quickly at three further options in the Routing Slip dialog box: Return When Done, Track Status, and Protect For.

Return When Done	Check the Return When Done box to have the document sent back to you when the last recipient finishes with the document and chooses File ➤ Send.
Track Status	Check the Track Status box to keep track of where your document has been routed. Word will send you a message each time the document is sent on to the next person in the To list.
Protect For	Select protection for your document from the drop-down list: **Annotations** allows recipients to add only annotations to the document; **Revisions** allows them to make changes (forcibly marked with revision marks) and add annotations; and **Forms** lets recipients enter information only in form fields (see Chapter 33 for more on forms).

Part 5

Power Tools

Revising and Returning a Mailed Document

If you're the target of an e-mailed Word document, here's how you do your bit:

1. Retrieve the document from your mail program in the usual way for that program and open the document in Word.

2. Revise the document depending on how the sender has protected it:

   - If the document allows annotations only, select Insert ➤ Annotation, type your annotation into the annotation pane, and click Close when you're done. (See *Inserting Annotations* in Chapter 24 for more details.)

   - If the document allows both revisions as well as annotations, just go ahead and make your revisions. Friendly Word will mark the revisions for you using revision marks (look back to Chapter 24 to refresh your memory if need be)—in fact, you won't be able to turn them off.

   - If the document is protected as a form, you're wearing a straitjacket. Fill in the fields (*all* the fields; be good) and don't try to do anything else.

3. Choose File ➤ Send. The Send dialog box will appear (see below), asking if you want to use the routing slip or send the document without using the routing slip. To wing the document on its merry way, choose the Route Document option and click OK.

   - If the original sender chose to route the document to recipients All At Once, this will return the document to the sender.

- If the original sender chose to route the document to recipients One After Another, this will pass the document on to its next victim—unless you're the last, in which case the document will be returned to the sender.

- If the original sender checked Track Status, Word will let the sender know when you send the document on to its next recipient. Yup, Big Brother is e-mailing about you.

> **NOTE** If you choose the Send Copy of Document Without Using the Routing Slip option, all protection the original sender chose remains in effect.

There, that was painless, wasn't it?

The Fun Part—
Merging Annotations and Revisions

So you sent out—all at once—seven copies of your latest marketing proposal for industrial-strength deodorant, *Hang-Gliding off Power Pylons,* and everyone got back to you with helpful comments. Well, sort of helpful. Most of them, anyway. Bunch of cynics, the lot of them. Now you need to merge the annotations and revisions into one copy so that you can pick out the best and trash the rest.

> **WARNING** You can't merge annotations and revisions back into the original document unless they're marked. Makes sense if you think about it. This is another good reason for protecting your document for revisions or annotations before sending it out. If you forget to protect your document, try using the Tools ➤ Revisions ➤ Compare Versions feature.

To merge all those pesky revision marks and annotations:

1. Retrieve your returned document from your mail program. Word will automatically ask you if you want to merge revisions with the original document.

2. Click OK. The Merge Revisions dialog box will appear, as shown in Figure 31.3.

3. Select the original file and click Open. The original document will open and the revisions will be merged into it.

4. Repeat as necessary with the other six copies of the report.

5. Now you have all the revisions in one place, and you can work your way through the document reviewing (accepting or rejecting) them; use Tools ➤ Revisions as discussed in Chapter 24.

NOTE When you merge revisions or annotations from multiple documents into the original, Word will use a different color for each reviewer (up to eight; after that, Word will cycle through the colors again).

Figure 31.3   Select the original file in the Merge Revisions dialog box. You can change drives and folders just as you would in any open dialog box.

For Additional Help with Mail

Mail and network connections can be confusing, particularly on the complex networks that have been proliferating recently. Consult your friendly network administrator or hallway guru.

Network Considerations

As I hinted at the beginning of this chapter, networks can be a source of grief as well as of joy to the Word user. While there's no way that you can absolutely safeguard all your work (short of sealing yourself and it in a lead-lined room), remember to take the following obvious precautions:

▶ Protect your documents from changes (see Chapter 7).

▶ Save your documents frequently and back them up to a safe medium as often as you're prepared to lose them—that should be pretty frequently.

▶ If you store your documents on a network drive, be careful about whom you give access to them. If necessary, make your documents read-only.

If you're sharing documents a lot, here are a few things to think about first:

▶ Don't use templates that the other people in the group don't have.

▶ If you share templates, keep them clean. Don't redefine built-in key combinations—you may confuse your co-workers, or worse.

▶ Don't use fonts that the other people in the group don't have. (But remember that you can embed TrueType fonts in shared documents so that other users who don't have the fonts installed can see the fonts and print them. Select Tools ➤ Options, click the Save tab in the Options dialog box, and check the Embed TrueType Fonts check box. See Chapter 9 for more information about this kind of thing.)

▶ Don't lose your file-protection password(s).

Chapter 32

Creating and Using Fields

FAST TRACK

Ummm...Fields. There. Now I've said it. If you're one of the people who runs screaming into the next jurisdiction whenever anybody mentions the word "field"—and if you're still reading this—take heart. You don't actually have to use fields. Not now, not ever. You could go through your whole life without using a single Word field. It might be tough, but you *could* do it.

On the other hand, if you *do* use fields, you can save yourself a tremendous amount of work. You can keep your documents up to date more easily, include material from different sources with the stab of a finger, and automate your life to a large extent. As you'll see shortly, you've probably already used fields—perhaps without even knowing it.

First, let's take a squint at what fields are. Then we'll look at what you might want to use them for. Finally, we'll get into examples and check out the new fields in Word.

What Are Fields?

Fields are special codes you use to tell Word to insert information into your documents. You can insert codes to add and automatically update text, graphics, and so on. For example, you could use codes like these:

```
{ AUTHOR \* MERGEFORMAT } {DATE \* MERGEFORMAT } {TIME \*
MERGEFORMAT } {TITLE \* MERGEFORMAT } Page {PAGE \* MERGE-
FORMAT } of {NUMPAGES \* MERGEFORMAT }
```

to create a footer that looks like this:

Janice Horsefly   04/01/96 8:33 AM   The Impact of Ultraviolet Lasers on the Cerebral Cortex   Page 291 of 316

Author, date and time, title, and the page number out of the total number of pages—not bad for a few seconds' work with half a dozen codes. If you formatted the codes, the result would look even better. But the best thing is that you can have these fields updated instantly at any time, either automatically or at the punch of a key. (Yes, the page-number and number-of-pages codes update themselves automatically, adjusting for each page of your document.)

If you don't want fields to be updated, you can lock them and then unlock them again when you need to update them.

As in the preceding example, Word usually displays the *result* of the field—the text or graphics the field will produce when printed. To indicate which text in your document is actually a field, you can have field results displayed shaded. You might want to do this if you find yourself hosing field codes accidentally. (See *Viewing Fields and Their Contents* later in the chapter.)

Where Do the Fields Get Their Information?

At this point, you might well be wondering where these fields get their information from. Out of thin air? By psychic transmission?

Unfortunately, it ain't quite so, Joanna. And we're not talking Newtons and radio PC-to-PC communications here, either. Your copy of Word already knows a lot about you. Whatever you entered for the user name and address when you first installed Word is stored for use in your documents; you can access it by selecting Tools ➤ Options and clicking the User Info tab in the Options dialog box. Word uses the Name field there for the Author name in the Summary tab of the Properties dialog box, the Initials for use in annotations, and the Mailing Address for the return address in any envelopes you print. Sure, you can change all of these, but remember, Word is storing information about you.

When you save a file and fill in the Summary tab of the Properties dialog box, Word stores that information for retrieval in fields. The Author information Janice Horsefly used in her footer came from this dialog box, as did the Title information. The Date and Time information comes from the system clock that you set in Windows or DOS. The page-information fields—the page number and the number of pages—Word itself generates from your document.

There isn't space here to go into all the different fields and where they get their information, but I think you get the idea: Some fields draw on permanent or semipermanent information (such as the user name), some draw on information you enter for any given document (title, keywords), and others are generated by Word (number of characters in a document, etc.).

Typical Uses of Fields

You can use fields in Word to

▶ Insert text, graphics, and other information in your documents

▶ Keep information updated as it changes

▶ Perform calculations

Most people's introduction to fields in Word comes when they put dates, times, and page numbers in their documents. Clicking the buttons for these fields on the Header and Footer toolbar is a pretty intuitive way of inserting fields. In fact, you might not even know they are fields unless you turn field codes on.

As you saw in Chapter 28, Word's mail-merge features make extensive use of fields. As you learned in Chapter 29, embedding charts from Microsoft Graph in Word documents also involves fields—as does Object Linking and Embedding, which we discussed in Chapter 30. Boy, you can hardly get away from the little buggers! In case you're wondering, the next chapter, *Creating and Using Forms*, will feature further fields. They've got you surrounded. You might as well make the best of it.

That said, let's look at how you insert fields in your documents to produce these wonderful results.

The Different Types of Fields

There are three types of fields—result fields, action fields, and marker fields.

▶ **Result fields** are the most common. They display information, which can come from within the document, from Word, from other documents, or from Windows.

▶ **Action fields** prompt the user to do something and then perform some action in response. There are only four: ASK, FILLIN, GOTOBUTTON, and MACROBUTTON.

▶ **Marker fields** simply mark a location without displaying anything in the document or "doing" anything.

The Basic Parts of a Field

Unless you specifically choose to see field codes, you will only see the images or information that the result fields display, the prompts from the action fields, and no sign at all of the marker fields. If you display fields (by visiting the View tab of the Tools ➤ Options dialog box and checking Fields), however, you will see neither results nor prompts. Instead you'll see the field *code*.

Field codes consist of three elements:

▶ Fields always begin and end with { and }, but these are not the simple curly-brace characters { and } that you can type in from the keyboard. They are called *field characters*.

▶ The first part of a field after the opening field character is the *field name* (for example, AUTHOR or TITLE, both of which refer to entries in the Summary tab of the Properties dialog box). The field name identifies the field and the result, action, or marking it performs.

▶ One or more optional *field instructions* (such as * MERGEFORMAT) modify the basic field result or action in some way, supplying default text, selecting an option among several choices in a Word command, giving the file name of a linked file, and so on. (MERGEFORMAT causes the field to retain its formatting when updated, but that's getting a little ahead of ourselves.)

Field instructions come in several flavors:

▶ *Bookmarks*, as elsewhere, refer to locations or selections in documents. Fields with bookmark instructions can make use of the contents of the bookmark as well as its page number.

▶ *Expressions* are instructions used with the = field. They are all mathematical or logical operations, values, or references to values stored or inherent in the document.

▶ *Text*: Enclosed in quotation marks (though this is not necessary for single words) or passed to the field as variables, text instructions simply supply text to a dialog box, prompt, or default box entry. (References to graphics are also considered text instructions, ironically enough.)

► *Switches* are instructions that further modify the result or action of a field. They all begin with the \ (backslash) character. They can take further instructions. There are four general switches:

* (format)

\# (numeric picture—that is, numeric format)

\@ (date-time picture—or format)

\! (lock result)

and myriad field-specific switches. A field can have a maximum of ten general switches and ten field-specific switches, though let's hope you never feel limited by this cap!

 NOTE   General field code switches are explained in nauseating detail later in this chapter under *Adding Switches to Fields.*

All of these types of field instructions can be represented by variables as well as by their literal names.

Inserting Fields

Some Word processes insert fields automatically. The Word commands for creating tables of contents and indices, the Page Number command on the Insert menu, many of the Mail Merge commands—all insert codes automatically.

There are two ways to insert fields manually. The easiest is to use the Field command on the Insert menu, but it is also possible to type field codes directly into the document (and there are a number of keyboard shortcuts for some of the most useful fields).

Inserting Fields with Insert ➤ Field

To insert a field in a document:

1. Put the insertion point where you want the field to appear.

2. Select Insert ➤ Field. The Field dialog box will appear (see Figure 32.1).

3. In the Categories list, select the field category you want.

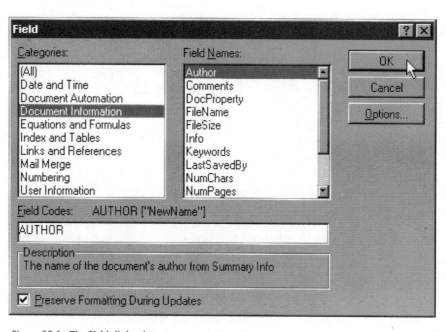

Figure 32.1 *The Field dialog box.*

 TIP Select [All] to see all the fields in alphabetical order.

---

4. Select the field you want.

5. Choose the Options button to add switches or formatting to the field you selected. In the Field Options dialog box (shown in Figure 32.2), select the switch or formatting you want in the box (its name varies depending on the options available for the selected field), and hit the Add to Field button. When you're finished adding formatting and switches, choose OK to return to the Field dialog box.

 TIP To remove switches or formatting from the field, select the Undo Add button (great use of English) in the Field Options dialog box.

---

6. Back in the Field dialog box, click OK to insert the selected field in your document.

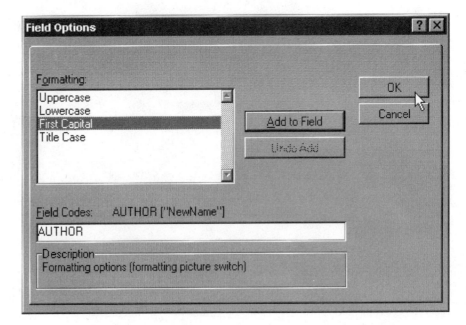

Figure 32.2   Select switches or formatting for your fields in the Field Options dialog box.

Inserting Field Codes Directly

If you know what you're doing, you can type field codes directly from the keyboard. Here's how:

1. Put the insertion point where you want to insert the new field.

2. Press Ctrl+F9. This inserts the field characters, like so—{   }—and leaves the insertion point in the middle, between the two field characters.

3. Type the field name followed by a space.

4. Type the field instructions you want, if any.

5. Press F9 to update the field immediately.

> **NOTE**   The above procedure works just as well if you do steps 3 and 4 before step 2 (that is, type the field name and instructions, select them and then press Ctrl+F9).

If you have mistyped, the field will display an error message, such as:

```
Error! Unknown switch argument.
```

If this happens, press Shift+F9 to display the field code again and correct your error.

Viewing Fields and Their Contents

You can view codes either as field results or as field codes. As discussed earlier, field results consist of the text or graphics that will be printed; field codes are the instructions to Word that will produce those text or graphics.

By default, Word displays field results, so you can see how your document will appear when printed. But when you are working with fields, you can display field codes instead of field results. You can display codes for a single field or for all fields at once.

To Display Field Codes for a Single Field

You display the field codes for a single field like this:

1. Place the insertion point in the field.

2. Click the right mouse button to display the pop-up shortcut menu.

3. Choose Toggle Field Display from the shortcut menu to turn on the codes for the field.

    To turn the codes off again, repeat the procedure. The toggle will return the codes to their result display.

To Display Field Codes for All Fields

When inserting or adapting field codes, you may want to display all the codes in a document so you can better see them. Here's how:

1. Select Tools ➤ Options.

2. In the Options dialog box, choose the View tab.

3. Check the Field Codes check box, and then click OK.

Part
5

Power Tools

Your fields will now appear as codes—{TITLE * MERGEFORMAT} and so on. To return them to text, repeat steps 1 through 3 but uncheck the Field Codes box.

> **WARNING**   Some field codes—the RD (Referenced Document), TA (Table of Authorities), TC (Table of Contents), and XE (Index Entry) fields—do not appear when other field codes are displayed; these field codes are formatted as hidden text. To reveal them, select <u>T</u>ools ➤ <u>O</u>ptions, select the View tab, and check the Hidden Text check box. To hide them again, uncheck the Hidden Text box.

To View Field Codes and Results at the Same Time

Sometimes you may find it helpful to view both field codes and their results at the same time—this lets you see what effect changing the field codes has on their results. To do so, split the document window into panes (by dragging the Split bar down from the top of the vertical scroll bar or by selecting Window ➤ Split and dragging the Split bar to an appropriate place) and set different view options for each pane.

To Display Field Results Shaded

You can choose to have field results displayed shaded so that you don't delete or alter them by mistake. Here's how:

1. Select <u>T</u>ools ➤ <u>O</u>ptions.

2. In the Options dialog box, choose the View tab.

> **NOTE**   You can choose When Selected in the Field Shading drop-down list to have fields shaded when they are selected or choose Never (the default) to avoid having any shading at all.

3. Pull down the Field Shading list (see Figure 32.3) and choose Always; then click OK.

> **NOTE**   Field shading is only a convenience for working on-screen; it is never printed.

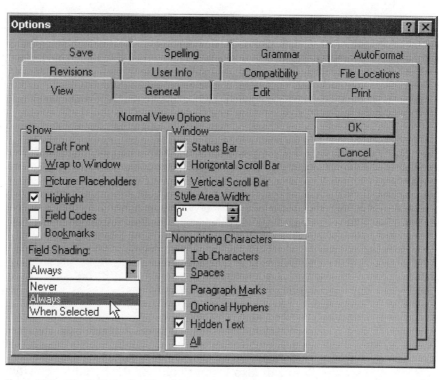

Figure 32.3   **The Field Shading list of the Options ➤ View tab.**

Printing Field Codes

Regardless of whether fields are shown as results (and prompts) or as field codes, they will not print as field codes unless you specifically request that they do when you print your document. It's often a good idea to print out a document with its field codes showing for reference. To do so:

1. Select File ➤ Print.

2. In the Print dialog box, click the Options button. You'll see the Print tab.

3. Check Field Codes in the Include with Document box.

4. Click OK. This returns you to the Print dialog box.

5. Click OK again to print your document.

   That's all there is to it.

Part
5

Power Tools

TIP   Field Codes will stay selected in the Print tab of the Options dialog box until you uncheck the box, so be sure to do that before printing again (unless you want field codes to print again next time).

Formatting Fields

Fields are simple to format: You can format either the field result itself or the field code, so with its field codes looking like *this:*

{ AUTHOR * MERGEFORMAT } {DATE * MERGEFORMAT } {TIME * MERGEFORMAT } *{TITLE \ * MERGEFORMAT}* Page {PAGE * MERGEFORMAT } of {NUMPAGES * MERGEFORMAT }

the example header from the beginning of the chapter could look like *this:*

Janice Horsefly   04/01/94 8:33 AM   *The Impact of Ultraviolet Lasers on the Cerebral Cortex*   Page 291 of 316

Yes, I know that's hideous. I was just trying to make the point. OK? Good.

You can also format field results by adding switches to the field codes. This is a little esoteric and is mainly useful for very sophisticated projects. We'll take a quick look at adding switches to field codes in the next section, but I suggest you format your field results the easy ways outlined earlier unless you've got a compelling reason to use switches instead. Save this for making minor adjustments to field codes you formatted slightly incorrectly.

Adding Switches to Fields

By adding *switches* to fields, you can customize the format of a field's result or lock the result. There are four general switches for fields, each of which has a plethora of permutations.

Here are the general switches:

Switch	Effect
Format(*)	Arabic or roman numerals. Adds formatting (for example, capitalization) to the field's result.
Numeric Picture (\#)	Controls the number of decimal places, literal characters, and so on for a numeric result.
Date-Time Picture (\@)	Formats a date or time (or both) result— to produce *April 1, 1996* or *11:59 PM*, for instance.
Lock Result (\!)	Prevents fields included in the result of a BOOKMARK, INCLUDE-TEXT or REF field from being updated.

NOTE Formatting created by switches takes precedence over manual formatting of the type demonstrated in the previous section.

Again, many field codes also have field-specific switches available in addition to the general switches. When you insert a field code with the Insert ➤ Field command, click the Options button to see the field-specific switches available for that field code, if any.

If you want to enter field-specific switches manually, you'll have to consult Appendix C.

Switches That Preserve Manual Formatting

If you can stand to learn a thing or two about switches, you can actually make it easier on yourself to format fields and keep them from reverting to other formats when updated. There are two switches that preserve the manual formatting of a field after updating. They are:

    * MERGEFORMAT

and

    * CHARFORMAT

Part
5

Power Tools

The * MERGEFORMAT switch preserves whatever manual formatting was applied to the *field result*, including both character formatting (such as boldface) and paragraph formatting (such as line spacing), and * CHARFORMAT applies whatever character formatting there is on the first character of the *field name* to the entire field result.

> **WARNING**   The * MERGEFORMAT switch applies the formatting of the previous field result word by word to the updated field result. If the formatting is complicated and the new field result has a different number of words, the formatting may "slip" and get screwed up. If this happens, reformat the field result manually.

* MERGEFORMAT also preserves picture formatting such as scaling and cropping dimensions.

Specific Format Switches

There are two other types of * format switches—those used for case conversion and those used for numeric conversion.

Case-Conversion Switches

The case-conversion options are as follows:

Switch	What It Does
* caps	Capitalizes the initial letter of *each* word in the result
* firstcap	Capitalizes the initial letter of the *first* word in the result
* lower	Makes all the letters in the result lowercase
* upper	Capitalizes all the letters in the result

Here are some examples:

Field	Result
{ AUTHOR * caps }	Ron Person
{ AUTHOR * lower }	ron person

Field	Result
{ AUTHOR * upper }	RON PERSON
{ *A*UTHOR * lower * firstcap * CHARFORMAT }	*Ron person*

Numeric Switches

And the numeric-conversion options are the following:

Switch	What It Does
* alphabetic	Converts the resulting number to the corresponding lowercase letter of the alphabet—10 becomes j, 27 becomes aa.
* Alphabetic	Converts the resulting number to the capitalized corresponding letter of the alphabet—10 becomes J, 27 becomes AA.
* arabic	Converts the resulting number to arabic (standard) form, which is the default anyway, but it overrides any manual change to the numeric form (such as a different option in the Page Number Format dialog box).
* cardtext	Spells out the resulting number (*card text* stands for *card*inal number—such as "one," as opposed to the ordinal "first"—*text* form) in lowercase letters.
* dollartext	Spells out the resulting number with initial letters capitalized, adds "and," and then displays the first two decimal places of the number (rounded off, if necessary) as an arabic numerator over 100, suitable for payroll checks.
* hex	Converts the resulting number to hexadecimal form.

Part
5

Power Tools

Switch	What It Does
* ordinal	Converts the resulting number to arabic ordinal form (1st, 2nd, 10th, etc.).
* ordtext	Spells out the resulting number in ordinal form (first, second, tenth, etc.).
* roman	Converts the resulting number to lowercase roman numerals.
* Roman	Converts the resulting number to uppercase roman numerals.

Here are some examples:

Field	Result
{ =2+2 * cardtext }	four
{ =7*5 * cardtext * caps }	Thirty-Five
{ =99/2 * dollartext * firstcap }	Forty-nine and 50/100
{ PAGE * ordinal * CHAR-FORMAT }	*2nd*
{ PAGE * ordtext }	second
{ PAGE * roman }	ii

Specific Numeric Picture Switches

Numeric picture switches control the appearance of the number displayed by the field code by using dummy characters to demonstrate the "picture" or pattern that the number's display should follow. Numeric picture switches can add characters such as $ or % to the number. They can also control the number of digits displayed, the way negative numbers are displayed, whether commas are used to separate digits in the thousands place, and so on.

The numeric-picture-switch instructions (they can be combined in many ways) are as follows:

Switch Instruction	What It Does
any character	Includes that character in the number display
'multiple words'	Includes the words between apostrophes in the number display
"several numeric picture instructions"	Combines the instructions between the quotation marks and preserves spacing
#	Optional digit placeholder; displays as a space if no digit is required
0	Required digit placeholder; displays as a zero if no digit is required
x	Truncating digit placeholder, eliminates any digits to the left unless placed after a decimal point, in which case it eliminates any digits to the right
. (period)	Decimal point, holds the place of the decimal point in relation to digit placeholders
, (comma)	Thousands separator, used to group numbers by thousands to make them easier to read (compare 100000 to 100,000)
–	Uses minus sign as indicator for negative numbers
+	Uses plus sign for positive numbers *and* minus sign for negatives (and a space for zero)

Switch Instruction	What It Does
; (semi-colon)	Separates custom positive and negative numeric pictures, or positive, negative, and zero numeric pictures

Here are some examples:

Field	Result
{ =10 \# $##.00 }	$10.00
{ =10 \# "## 'dollars'" }	10 dollars
{ =(1/2)*100 \# ##% }	50%
{ =10^5 \# #,### }	100,000
{ =10 \# -## }	10
{ =-10 \# -## }	-10
{ =3255.5-10000 \# $##,###.00;($##,###.00) }	($ 6,744.50)

Specific Date-Time Picture Switches

Date-time picture switches control the appearance of the date or time displayed by the field code by demonstrating the "picture" or pattern that the date or time's display should follow using instructions that are simple abbreviations for the parts of a time or date (h for hours, m for minutes, M for month, d for day, etc.).

The date-time–picture-switch instructions (they can be combined in many ways) are as follows:

Switch Instruction	What It Does
any character	Includes that character in the date display
'multiple words'	Includes the words between apostrophes in the number display (put quotation marks around the entire instruction)

Switch Instruction	What It Does
"several date-time picture instructions"	Combines the instructions between the quotation marks and preserves spacing
h	Hours of the twelve-hour clock without a leading zero for single-digit hours
hh	Hours of the twelve-hour clock with a leading zero for single-digit hours
H	Hours of the twenty-four–hour clock without a leading zero for single-digit hours
HH	Hours of the twenty-four–hour clock with a leading zero for single-digit hours
m	Minutes without a leading zero for single-digit minutes
mm	Minutes with a leading zero for single-digit minutes
s	Seconds without a leading zero for single-digit seconds
ss	Seconds with a leading zero for single-digit seconds
AM/PM	AM or PM as appropriate
am/pm	am or pm as appropriate
A/P	A or P as appropriate
a/p	a or p as appropriate
M	Month number without a leading zero for single-digit months
MM	Month number with a leading zero for single-digit months
MMM	Three-letter abbreviation for the month

Part
5

Power Tools

Switch Instruction	What It Does
MMMM	Full name of the month
d	Day of the month without a leading zero for single-digit days
dd	Day of the month with a leading zero for single-digit days
ddd	Day of the week as a three-letter abbreviation
dddd	Full name of the day of the week
yy	Year as a two-digit number with a leading zero for years ending in 01 through 09
yyyy	Year as a four-digit number

Here are some examples:

Field	Result
{ DATE \@ "dddd, MMMM d, yyyy" }	Thursday, September 1, 1998
{ DATE \@ dd/MM/yy }	01/09/98
{ DATE \@ d-M-yy }	1-9-98
{ TIME \@ h:mm:ss am/pm }	10:02:15 am

 TIP Don't forget that the month instruction is a capital M and the minute instruction is a lowercase m.

Using Bookmarks in Fields

Bookmarks that only indicate a location in the document can still return a page number or other information about that location. Bookmarks that refer to selections can supply the contents of the selection (text or numerical) to another field code instruction, switch, or mathematical expression. In expressions, bookmarks play the role of variables.

To include a bookmark in a field, simply type its name. A field may consist of only a bookmark.

You can also use the SET field to store a value in a bookmark, such as:

```
{ SET Title "Sales Coordinator" }
```

Changing the Contents of Fields

You can change field codes so they produce the results you're looking for. For example, you might have an =(Formula) that multiplies the bookmark TaxThemAll by 31 percent:

```
{=TaxThemAll*31%}
```

But if you find that 31 percent isn't giving you the revenue you need, you need to up it to 46 percent. Here's how:

1. Put the insertion point in the field.

2. If the field is showing its result, display the field codes by pressing Shift+F9 or by right-clicking the field and choosing Toggle Field Display from the shortcut menu.

3. Edit the field. Change 31 to **46**:

   ```
   {=TaxThemAll*46%}
   ```

4. Display the field result again by pressing Shift+F9 or by right-clicking the field and choosing Toggle Field Display from the shortcut menu.

5. Update the field by pressing F9 or by right-clicking the field and choosing Update Field from the shortcut menu.

Nesting One Field inside Another

In addition to text, switches, and other instructions, field codes may also contain other fields. It's easier to nest a field inside a field than you may think. To do so:

1. Insert the first field, either with the Insert Field command (in which case, press Shift+F9 afterward to display the field code) or by pressing Ctrl+F9 and entering the code manually.

2. Move the insertion point inside the field code to where you want the nested code to appear.

Part 5

Power Tools

3. Insert the nested field, again either with the Insert Field command or by pressing Ctrl+F9 and entering the code manually.

4. Press F9 to display the field result or prompt.

So, for example, if you want to prompt someone for their title and store that text as a bookmark called JobTitle, you could press Ctrl+F9, type **SET JobTitle** and a space, press Ctrl+F9 again, type **FILLIN "Enter your title"**, and press F9. This would display the following dialog box:

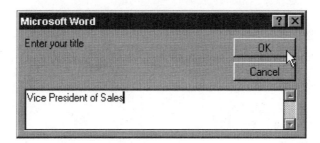

If you enter a title and click OK, the title you typed will be stored as the bookmark JobTitle. If you then make the following field code:

```
{ JobTitle }
```

and press F9, you will see the title you entered.

Updating Fields

As you'll have gathered by now, the whole point of inserting fields in your document rather than inserting straight information is that the fields are easy to update.

You can choose to update all fields at once or update them one at a time. Further, you can choose to update all fields whenever you print a document to ensure up-to-date information for your printouts.

Updating Fields One at a Time

To update fields one at a time, place the mouse pointer in the field in question and click the right mouse button to pop up the shortcut menu.

From the shortcut menu, choose Update Field. The field will be updated and will show its most recent result.

Updating All Fields Simultaneously

To update all fields in a document at once, choose Edit ➤ Select All and then click the right mouse button to pop up the shortcut menu. From the shortcut menu, choose Update Field. All the fields in the document will be updated to show their most recent results.

NOTE If a document has field codes only in its headers/footers, you need to have the Header/Footer pane displayed before choosing Select All or the shortcut menu will not have the Update Field option.

Updating Fields When You Print

Update fields when you print to make sure your documents, forms, and reports contain the most up-to-date information available. Here's how:

1. Select Tools ➤ Options.
2. In the Options dialog box, select the Print tab.
3. In the Printing Options area, check the Update Fields check box, then click OK.

   All the fields in your documents will now be updated each time the documents are printed. To stop this updating, repeat steps 1, 2, and 3, but uncheck the Update Fields check box.

WARNING Like other options in the Options dialog box, Update Fields is sticky—its setting will stay the same until you change it again.

Undoing or Halting Updates

If you've just updated fields and want to undo it, simply select Edit ➤ Undo Update Fields (or press Ctrl+Z). If you start updating a document and then realize that you don't want to update the whole thing or wait for it to finish, press Esc to cancel the process.

Part
5

Power Tools

Locking the Contents of Fields

When you want to keep the result of a field from being updated and changed, you can either *lock* the field or *unlink* it. Locking a field prevents the field from being updated until the field is unlocked, while unlinking a field permanently replaces the field with its current result.

To Lock a Field

To lock a field to prevent it from being updated:

1. Place the cursor in the field you want to lock.
2. Press Ctrl+F11 or Ctrl+3 to lock the field.

To Unlock a Field

To unlock a field so it can once again be updated:

1. Place the cursor in the field you want to unlock.
2. Press Ctrl+Shift+F11 to unlock the field.

To Unlink a Field

To unlink a field so it can never again be updated:

 WARNING   If you unlink fields and then later change your mind, you may not be able to undo your actions, so give it some thought beforehand.

1. Place the cursor in the field you want to unlink.
2. Press Ctrl+Shift+F9 or Ctrl+6 to unlink the field.

 NOTE   You can use Undo to restore fields you just unlinked, but only until *Unlink Fields* drops off the bottom of the Undo button's drop-down list.

Examples of Fields at Work

The more you use Word, the more chances you'll get to use fields to enhance your documents and minimize your work. Word uses fields for many of its specialized functions, and chances are you'll find yourself using fields without having consciously made the decision to do so. For example, in Chapter 29 you learned how to insert graphs into Word documents using Microsoft Graph, and in Chapter 30 you learned how to link and embed objects in Word documents. In either case, select Tools ➤ Options, visit the View tab, and check the Field Codes check box, and you'll find that you've been using field codes—your graph turns into a field code that reads { EMBED MS Graph }, and your link to a different application turns into something a little more esoteric. The mail-merge documents you learned about in Chapter 28 use all sorts of fields—some defined by Word and some by you, the user—to produce the form letters.

Chapter 33 further illustrates the many uses of fields in Word.

Moving Quickly between Fields

You can move quickly between fields by using Edit ➤ Goto and selecting Field in the Go to What area of the Go To dialog box. You can choose to move between particular fields, between any fields, or simply search for the previous or next field. Here's how:

 TIP To pop up the Go To dialog box quickly, press F5 or double-click some blank space in the left side of the status area.

1. Select Edit ➤ Go To.
2. In the Go to What box (see Figure 32.4), select Field.

Figure 32.4 **You can use the Go To dialog box to move rapidly between fields.**

Part 5

Power Tools

3. In the Enter Field Name box, select the name of the field or accept Any Field.

4. Choose the Next button to find the next occurrence of the chosen field or the Previous button to find the previous occurrence.

5. Click the Close button when you get where you want.

TIP   To go to the next field, press F11; to go to the previous field, press Shift+F11.

Shortcut Keys for Working with Fields

Word offers many shortcut keys for working with fields. Some we've touched on in this chapter; some we've met (or will meet) in other chapters. Here they all are, for your reference:

Key Combination	Effect
Alt+Shift+D	Insert a date field
Alt+Shift+P	Insert a page field
Alt+Shift+T	Insert a time field
Ctrl+F9	Insert a blank field
Ctrl+Shift+F7	Update linked information in the source document
F9	Update selected fields
Ctrl+Shift+F9	Unlink a field
Shift+F9	Toggle between field codes and results
Alt+F9	View field codes
Alt+Shift+F9	Perform the action in the field when the insertion point is positioned in the field
F11	Go to the next field
Shift+F11	Go to the previous field
Ctrl+F11	Lock a field
Ctrl+Shift+F11	Unlock a field

Using Fields
to Assign and Display Bookmarks

As you've already seen in this chapter, field codes can use bookmarks as variables, as ways to store and transmit information. In addition to the field codes that can take bookmarks as instructions, there are a couple that are specifically designed to store and display bookmark contents. They are SET and REF.

Storing Bookmark Contents with SET

The SET field code is used to assign a value to a bookmark. SET fields take the following form:

```
{ SET bookmark "text" }
```

The field assigns the text inside the quotation marks to the bookmark. You can also nest another field inside the SET field to prompt for the text to assign to the bookmark. Such a field would look something like this:

```
{ SET Zodiac { FILLIN "What is your sign?" \* MERGEFORMAT } }
```

This field displays a prompt on the screen asking the user to type in a sign of the zodiac. The text entered is assigned to the bookmark called Zodiac.

NOTE   The ASK field, described later in this chapter, can also be used to assign a value to a bookmark.

Displaying Bookmark Contents with REF

The REF field code is used to display the value contained in a bookmark. REF fields take the following form:

```
{ REF bookmark \optional switches }
```

The field displays the text associated with *bookmark*.

Part
5

Power Tools

The field-specific switches for REF are:

\f	Includes a footnote, endnote, or annotation number, incremented if necessary
\n	Inserts paragraph numbering (if any) from the paragraph marked by the bookmark

Working with Action Fields

In this section, you'll learn how to use the four action fields—ASK fields, FILLIN fields, GOTOBUTTON fields, and MACROBUTTON fields.

ASK Fields

ASK fields take the following form:

```
{ ASK bookmark "prompt text" \optional switches }
```

The field displays a dialog box that includes the prompt text and a text box. Whatever is entered into the text box is assigned to the bookmark.

The field-specific switches for ASK are:

\d *"default text"*	Supplies default text (highlighted) in the text box
\o	Prompts only once during a mail merge (instead of once for each resulting document)

FILLIN Fields

FILLIN fields take the following form:

```
{ FILLIN "optional prompt text" \optional switches }
```

The field displays a dialog box that can show a prompt. Whatever text you enter into it is inserted at the insertion point (as the field result, not as regular text).

The field-specific switches for FILLIN are:

\d *"default text"*	Supplies default text (highlighted) in the text box
\o	Prompts only once during a mail merge (instead of once for each resulting document)

GOTOBUTTON Fields

GOTOBUTTON fields take the following form:

```
{ GOTOBUTTON destination display-text }
```

The field shows the display text on the screen as a clickable field result or button (you can also insert a graphic into this field to have the button display as a graphic). Consider placing a border around the display text to make it look more like a button. Double-clicking the button jumps the reader to the destination, which can be any acceptable Go To destination (Go To is explained in Chapter 3) such as a bookmark, page number, table, and so on.

NOTE With many of these field codes, you won't be able to do much with them unless you have field codes visible. To turn them on, Choose Tools ➤ Options and, on the View tab, click to view Field Codes.

MACROBUTTON Fields

MACROBUTTON fields take the following form:

```
{ MACROBUTTON macro display-text }
```

The field shows the display text on the screen as a clickable field result or button (you can also insert a graphic into this field to have the button display as a graphic). Double-clicking the button executes the macro.

You can format the display text and add the * MERGEFORMAT switch to preserve the formatting through subsequent updates.

TIP If you insert the MACROBUTTON field with the Insert ➤ Field command, you can click the Options button to see a list of available macros to choose from.

Part 5

Power Tools

The field { MACROBUTTON FileSave **Double-Click Here to Save the File** } would display this text:

```
Double-Click Here to Save the File
```

Double-clicking there would be equivalent to selecting File ➤ Save.

Getting Field Code Help

Word has extensive online help for each field code with complete syntax and switches. To see this help for a specific field code, select Help ➤ Microsoft Word Help topics and click the Index tab to bring it to the front, click the letter button for the first letter of the field, and then click the index entry for complete information.

You can also get context-sensitive help directly when the insertion point is on a field code name. Just press F1 to jump directly to the help entry for that field.

NOTE　See also Appendix C for complete field and switch information.

Chapter 33

Creating and Using Forms

FAST TRACK

You can use the features of Word that you've learned about in the preceding chapters of this book to create your own business forms. You can create forms that you print to be filled in by hand or forms to be filled in online, saved as a file, and then printed.

For online forms, Word lets you protect areas against being filled in or changed; for example, you might have some *form fields* (areas of a form) that should not be filled in by an employee, and you almost certainly don't want anyone who is filling in the form to change its basic structure. You can specify that certain form fields have specific data types, formatting, or default text, and you can create check boxes and drop-down lists to help the user fill in the form. You can add macros that run automatically to a form and attach help messages to fields to further assist the users.

You may be thinking that protecting a form is an extreme measure, but the way Word arranges forms, you need to protect them to be able to fill them in properly. Until you protect a form, the fancy features like drop-down lists and help text attached to fields are set up to be edited rather than to be used.

You can add AutoText entries to a form you save as a template. You can also add macros, customized toolbars, customized menus, and the other features associated with templates.

Designing most forms involves using Word's table features (discussed in Chapter 11) to lay out the form and then applying character, paragraph, and table formatting to give the form a satisfactory appearance.

 TIP   When you create a form, save it as a *template* (discussed in Chapter 16) rather than as a document so you can open any number of copies based on it without altering its contents and then save them as documents. If you protect the template, that protection will also apply to all new documents based on that template. (When you need to change the form, you can edit the template directly.)

Designing and Creating Forms

When designing a form, you'll probably want to start with a rough draft or sketch of what you're trying to produce. While you *can* just type into your computer everything you think you'll need to include in the form and then hack it into shape, you may wind up with a beautifully designed form lacking just one crucial component.

If you can't be bothered to make a sketch, get a similar form from somewhere and scrawl your main items in its boxes. That'll give you a head start.

Figure 33.1 shows a job log I created for Unincorporated Inc., a deconstruction firm that deals with special projects. The job log illustrates some of the main features of forms in Word. In the coming sections, we'll look at how to insert these elements, using the job log as an example.

Starting a Form

To start a form, first open a new document to work in. The job log is to be an online form, so select the Template option button rather than the Document option button in the New dialog box.

Using normal keyboard procedures, enter your new template text that doesn't need to be in a table—for example, the main headings.

Displaying the Forms Toolbar

When working on forms, you can use either menu commands or the buttons on the Forms toolbar, shown in Figure 33.2. We'll discuss how to use both throughout this chapter.

If you want to use the Forms toolbar, display it: Either select View ➤ Toolbars, select Forms, and click OK or choose Insert ➤ Form Field and click the Show Toolbar button in the Form Field dialog box. If you do the former, the Forms toolbar will appear at the top of the screen; if you do the latter, it will appear where you last positioned it.

Adding a Table to the Form

Much of the Job Log form consists of tables, the cells of which contain the form fields and their descriptions. Here's how to insert a table in which to enter text or a form field:

1. Place the insertion point where you want the table to start.

Unincorporated Inc

J O B   L O G

Name:	Billy Bedlam
Date and Time Started:	
Date and Time Finished:	

Brief Details of Task:

Special Equipment Required:

☐ Bulldozer
☐ Shovel
☐ Thermos
☐ Stepladder
☐ Incendiaries
☐ Industrial Bribes

NOTES
All special equipment must be strictly accounted for in accordance with the company's Statutes Governing All Full-Time and Part-Time Employees—or else!

Report (60 words or fewer)

Employee's Signature   Supervisor's Signature

Figure 33.1   Unincorporated Inc.'s Job Log form.

Text Form Field button

Check Box Form Field button

Drop-Down Form Field button

Form Field Options button

Protect Form button

Form Field Shading button

Insert Frame button

Insert Table button

Figure 33.2 Drag the Forms toolbar wherever you want it or double-click on it to display it at the top of the screen.

 2. Click the Insert Table button on either the Standard toolbar or the Forms toolbar to display the table-insertion grid:

> **TIP**   You can also select T<u>a</u>ble ➤ <u>I</u>nsert Table and specify the number of rows and columns in the Insert Table dialog box.

3. Click the square that shows the number of rows (counting from the top) and columns (counting from the left) that you want in the table. Word will insert the table in your document.

4. Size the table by dragging its gridlines or by selecting T<u>a</u>ble ➤ Cell Height and <u>W</u>idth and specifying measurements in the Cell Height and Width dialog box.

> **NOTE**   By default, Word inserts tables as wide as your page with all cells the same width.

Type text into the table cells as usual (look back to Chapter 11 for information on working in tables) and format it in the normal ways.

Adding Borders and Shading to the Form

To add borders to a table, as in the Job Log form, select the table or the cells to which you want to add the border or shading; then select F<u>o</u>rmat ➤ <u>B</u>orders and Shading and specify borders and shading in the Paragraph Borders and Shading dialog box.

Inserting Form Fields into Your Form

There are three types of form fields you can insert into your form automatically. They are check boxes, text boxes, and drop-down list boxes. The Unincorporated, Inc. form contains all three types. The following sections detail how to insert each type of box.

Adding a Check Box to the Form

Word gives you the option of adding check boxes to your forms, like those for the "Special Equipment" in Figure 33.1. Here's how to do it:

1. Place the insertion point where you want the check box to appear.

2. Select <u>I</u>nsert ➤ For<u>m</u> Field to display the Form Field dialog box (see Figure 33.3).

Figure 33.3   **The Form Field dialog box.**

3. Select Check Box.

4. Select the Options button to specify more details about the check box. The Check Box Form Field Options dialog box will appear (see Figure 33.4).

Figure 33.4   **The Check Box Form Field Options dialog box.**

5. The following options are available:

   Check Box Size: Use Exactly to specify a fixed point size for the check box.

   Default Value: Choose Not Checked or Checked as the default value for the check box—that is, whether it should be checked or unchecked when the user opens the form.

   Run Macro On: To run a macro when the user enters or exits the form field, specify the macro in the Entry or Exit box.

   Bookmark: Type a bookmark name to be associated with the field. Macros reference bookmark names.

   Check Box Enabled: Clear this check box to make the form field read-only for users.

   Add Help Text: Click this button to display the Form Field Help Text dialog box so you can enter help messages.

6. When you've chosen your options, click OK to close the Check Box Form Field Options dialog box and insert the selected field into your document.

Adding a Text Box to the Form

A *text box* is a form field in which the user enters text. You can limit the text entry to a certain number of characters, and you can provide default text to show the user the type of text (or indeed the answer!) that you are expecting.

Here's how to insert a text box:

1. Place the insertion point where you want the text box to appear.

2. Select <u>I</u>nsert ➤ For<u>m</u> Field to display the Form Field dialog box.

3. Select Text Box.

4. Select the Options button to specify more details about the check box. The Text Form Field Options dialog box will appear (see Figure 33.5).

5. The following options are available:

   Type: Select the type of text form field you want—Regular Text, Number, Date, Current Date, Current Time, or Calculation.

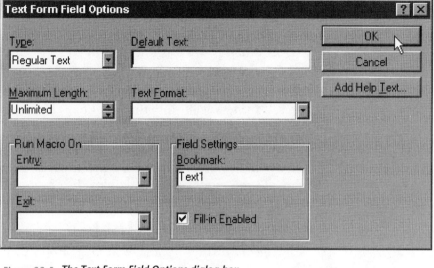

Figure 33.5 **The Text Form Field Options dialog box.**

Default Text: Enter any text you want to be displayed by default when the user opens the form. (This field changes to Expression when you choose Calculation in the Type box.)

Maximum Length: Enter the number of characters you want the form field to accept.

Text Format: Select the format for the data in the form field.

Run Macro On: To run a macro when the user enters or exits the form field, specify the macro in the Entry or Exit box.

Bookmark: Type a bookmark name to be associated with the field. Macros reference bookmark names.

Fill-in Enabled: Clear this to make the form field read-only for users. For example, Billy's supervisor might want to fill in the task description for each job and then disable the field before passing the form on to him.

Add Help Text: Click this button to display the Form Field Help Text dialog box so you can enter help messages.

6. When you've chosen your options, click OK to close the Check Box Form Field Options dialog box and insert the selected field into your document.

Part
5

Power Tools

For the Type box, choose *Regular Text* when any type of text entry will be acceptable (when you don't need to limit the type of text entry in any way).

Choose *Number* when you want only numeric entries in that particular text box. Choose *Date* when you want only date entries in that text box.

Choose *Current Date* or *Current Time* to have the current date or time entered automatically into that text box. The user will be unable to enter any text there.

Choose *Calculation* to add a column or row of numbers or to perform a more complex calculation. Like the Current Date and Current Time types of text boxes, a Calculation text box cannot be altered by the user.

Adding a Drop-Down List to a Form

Word gives you the option of adding drop-down lists to your forms, which can greatly help users and speed their input. Drop-down lists can also help you by restricting the information users can enter in the fields.

The Unincorporated Inc. job log contains a drop-down list of employee names:

To add a drop-down list to your form:

1. Place the insertion point where you want the drop-down list to appear.

2. Select Insert ➤ Form Field to display the Form Field dialog box.

3. Select the Drop-Down option.

4. Select the Options button to specify more details about the drop-down list. The Drop-Down Form Field Options dialog box will appear (see Figure 33.6).

5. In the Drop-Down Item text box, add items for the drop-down list to its right.

   - Click the Add button to add each new item to the list.

   - To remove an item from the drop-down list, select it in the Items in Drop-Down List box and click the Remove button.

   - To rearrange the items in the drop-down list, highlight the item to move and use the Move arrows to move it up or down.

6. Choose options in the dialog box:

   Run Macro On: To run a macro when the user enters or exits the form field, specify the macro in the Entry or Exit box.

   Bookmark: Type a bookmark name to be associated with the field. Macros reference bookmark names.

   Drop-Down Enabled: Clear this check box to make the form field read-only for users. For example, to prevent Billy Bedlam from falsely

Figure 33.6 *The Drop-Down Form Field Options dialog box.*

Part
5

Power Tools

attributing a dubious job report to Bullwinkle J. Moose, the supervisor might select Billy's name, lock the field, and forward the form to him.

Add Help Text: Click this button to display the Form Field Help Text dialog box so you can enter help messages.

7. When you've chosen your options, click OK to close the Check Box Form Field Options dialog and insert the selected field into your document.

Naming Form Fields

When you insert a form field, a bookmark is automatically created that names the form field and refers to it. By default, Word will choose sequential names for your form fields—Text1, Text2, Text3; Check1, Check2; Dropdown1, Dropdown2; etc. You can override this default, though, and give your form fields any names (any bookmarks) you want. Why would you want to do this? To make them easier to keep track of, especially if you are referring to your bookmarks with field codes or macros.

You can name a form field as you're inserting it or at any later time. To name the form field while inserting it, click the Options button on the Form Field dialog box (shown earlier in Figure 33.3), then enter a name in the Bookmark text box in the Field Settings area of the Options dialog box that appears. Proceed as usual.

To name a form field after you've already inserted it,

1. Unprotect the document if it's protected already.

2. Position the mouse pointer over the form field and click the right mouse button. A dialog box will drop down:

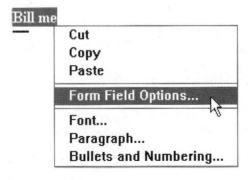

3. Select Form Field Options. This will bring up the appropriate Options dialog box (see Figures 33.4, 5, and 6).

4. Type a name in the Bookmark box in the Field Settings area and click OK.

> **NOTE** You can also just double-click an unprotected form field to bring up the appropriate Options dialog box.

Finding a Form Field

Suppose you need to fill in or modify a single field or a few fields in a large form. To find a form field, you must know its name (the bookmark that refers to it). If you know the name, there are two ways to find (and go to) the form field. Here's the first way:

1. Unprotect the document if it's already protected.

2. Select Edit ➤ Bookmark. This brings up the Bookmark dialog box:

3. Select the bookmark (form field) you want to go to.

4. Click the Go To button.

   Here's the second way:

1. Unprotect the document if it's already protected.

2. Select Edit ➤ Go To (Ctrl+G). This brings up the Go To dialog box:

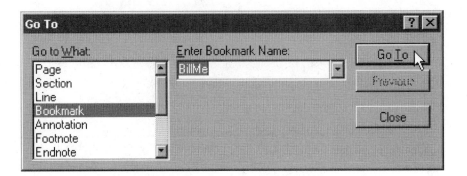

3. Select Bookmark in the Go to What list box.

4. Choose the bookmark (form field) you want from the Enter Bookmark Name drop-down list box.

5. Click the Go To button.

Take your pick.

Formatting Form Fields

If you want the text entered or selected in a form field to be formatted, you have to format the fields yourself before protecting the document. Users will not be able to format the text they enter or select.

The best time to format a field is right after inserting it. You have all the usual methods available to you for character and paragraph formatting. You can:

▶ Pull down the Format menu, select a formatting choice, and choose the type of formatting you want (for example, Format ➤ Font, Bold, OK).

▶ Click the field with the right mouse button, select a formatting choice from the drop-down menu that pops up, and choose the type of formatting you want (for example, right mouse click, Font, Bold, OK).

▶ Click a formatting icon on the Formatting toolbar (for example, click the Bold button).

▶ Press a keyboard shortcut (for example, Ctrl+B).

Adding Help Text to a Form

As mentioned in the previous sections, you can add help text to your form fields to assist the user in filling them in. Here's how to do it:

1. Double-click the form field in question to display the Form Field Options dialog box. (Exactly *which* form field options dialog box will appear depends on the type of form field you select.)

2. Click the Add Help Text button. The Form Field Help Text dialog box will appear.

   • To add a status bar entry, select the Status Bar tab.

   • To add a help key entry, select the Help key tab.

   Figure 33.7 shows the Form Field Help Text dialog box with the Status Bar tab selected. This is perhaps the more useful option for short entries because the help text will appear in the status bar when the user encounters the field. (With Help Key entries, the user must press F1 to display the help, which appears in a message box.)

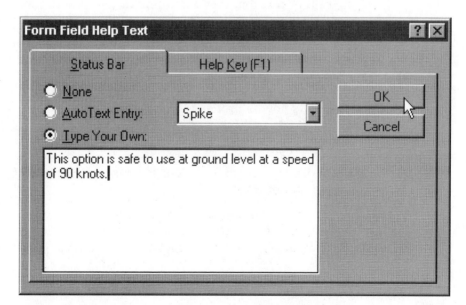

Figure 33.7 **Decide whether you want to display help in the status bar or when the user presses F1 here in the Form Field Help Text dialog box.**

Part
5

Power Tools

3. Choose the entry you want:

   None: Turns off the help text.

   AutoText Entry: Lets you choose an existing AutoText entry from the drop-down list.

   Type Your Own: Lets you do just that, up to 255 characters.

4. Select OK to close the Form Field Help Text dialog box and then click OK in the Form Field Options dialog box.

Protecting a Form

Having unprotected forms these days can be a risk, given the high incidence of networks and file sharing. You'll probably want to protect or lock your templates to make sure nobody else can modify them accidentally or otherwise. When a template is protected, documents based on it will be protected too, and users will only be able to fill in form fields and unprotected areas. Users benefit too because pressing Tab will take them from form field to form field without stopping in table cells or text that they cannot modify.

 WARNING As mentioned at the beginning of this chapter, you need to protect a form before the check boxes, text boxes, drop-down lists, and help features will work.

Here's how to protect a form from changes:

1. With the form open and in the current window, select Tools ➤ Protect Document.

2. In the Protect Document dialog box (see Figure 33.8), select the Forms option button.

3. To protect some sections of the form but not others, select the Sections button (which will be dimmed if unavailable—for example, if your document doesn't have sections) and, in the Section Protection dialog

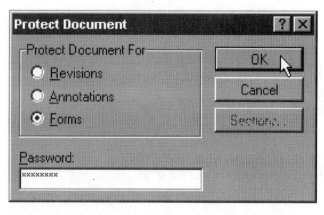

Figure 33.8 *Choose the Forms option button in the Protect Document dialog box to protect your form. Enter a password if you like.*

box that appears (see below), check the check boxes for the sections you want to protect.

4. To assign a password to the form, type one into the Password box. Word will display asterisks (for the benefit of anyone reading over your shoulder) for each character you type, and when you select OK, Word will ask you to reenter the password in the Confirm Password dialog box.

WARNING Passwords can be up to 15 characters long and can contain letters, numbers, symbols, and spaces. They're case-sensitive—you must type upper- or lowercase letters correctly in the password each time.

To unprotect your form, select <u>T</u>ools ➤ Un<u>p</u>rotect Document. If you entered a password when protecting the document, Word will pop up an Unprotect Document dialog box in which you have to enter the password. (If you get the password wrong, Word will pop up a dialog box telling you that this password is incorrect, whereupon you can try again. But don't worry—Word's not like one of those ATMs that retain your card "for your security" after you miskey your PIN three times. You can keep trying to get the password right until the cows come home.)

Disabling Specific Form Fields

In addition to the document protection, which you must turn on to activate your form fields, you may also want to disable certain form fields to prevent the user from altering them. To disable a form field:

1. Unprotect the document if it's already protected.

2. Double-click the form field to bring up its Options dialog box (or click the right mouse button and choose Form Field Options).

3. Uncheck the Enabled (Check Box Enabled, Fill-in Enabled, Drop-Down Enabled) option in the Field Settings area.

4. Click OK.

Filling In an Online Form

When you've finished creating and editing your form, set protection as described in the earlier section *Protecting a Form*, and save it as a template rather than as a document. You (or someone else) can then open copies of the form on any computer that can access the template and fill them in online.

With protection set, Word will prevent the user from accessing anything but the form fields; the user can move from one form field to the next by pressing Tab.

Printing a Form's
Data without Printing the Form Itself

Word lets you print the data in a form without printing the form itself. You might want to do this to fill in a preexisting paper form, such as a government form. You would set up your form template in Word to match exactly the target form and print only the data in the form. (Needless to say, this would take a *lot* of careful measuring and might not be worth the headache.) The data would then be printed in the correct areas of the target form.

To print a form's data without printing the form itself:

1. Select <u>T</u>ools ➤ <u>O</u>ptions to display the Options dialog box.
2. Select the Print tab by clicking it or by pressing **P**.
3. Check the Print Data Only for Forms check box in the Options for This Document Only area; then click OK.

Printing a Form Along with Its Data

To print the entire form, both its structure and contents, simply print the finished document the normal way. You can:

▶ Click the Print button on the Standard toolbar.
▶ Select File ➤ Print (Ctrl+P) and click OK.

Printing a Blank Form

If you want to print out an empty form to keep a printed version of the blank form handy, simply open a new copy of the form from the template:

1. Select File ➤ New or press Ctrl+N, but don't click the New File button on the Standard toolbar.
2. Select your form from the list in the Template dialog box that appears.
3. Click OK.
4. Click the Print button on the Standard toolbar or select File ➤ Print (Ctrl+P) and click OK.

Saving a Form's Data without Saving the Form Itself

Similarly, you can save the data in a form without saving the form itself. This is useful for saving form data as a single record to use in a database. Here's how:

1. Select <u>T</u>ools ➤ <u>O</u>ptions to display the Options dialog box.

2. Select the Save tab by clicking it or by pressing **S**. (If the Save tab is already displayed, pressing **S** again will display the Spelling tab.)

3. Check the Save Data Only for Forms check box, then click OK.

> **NOTE** Of course, to save the form with the entered data, simply save the form as you would any Word document: Click the Save button on the Standard toolbar or select File ➤ Save (Ctrl+S).

Attaching Macros to a Form

As mentioned earlier in this chapter, you can attach both AutoText and macros to a form by making the original file a template rather than a document. We'll get into macros in the next chapter, but I should just mention here that forms are a classic place to use some of Word's autoexecuting macros:

Macro Name	Effect and Use
AutoNew	Runs whenever you open a new document based on the template to which it is attached
AutoOpen	Runs whenever you open an existing document based on the template to which it is attached
AutoClose	Runs whenever you close a document based on the template to which it is attached

You might set up an AutoNew macro to arrange the form for filling in—you could display on the screen toolbars the user might need and remove ones not needed, maximize the screen display, automatically update selected fields or the information available for them, or display a help message. You could write an AutoOpen macro that would advise users when the form was last updated and advise them to save a backup copy under a different name before they destroy your precious data. Finally, an AutoClose macro could back up the changes to the form to a different folder or drive, restore general screen preferences, display a message box advising the user to update other connected forms, and so on. You get the idea.

Creating a Form with Fill-In Dialog Boxes

If you are creating a form that will reuse the same information in several different places, then you might want to use field codes to enter, store, and reuse text so that the text entered in one form field can be reused in all the other form fields that require the same information, including fields in other, related, forms. Entries such as names and addresses are especially suited to this approach.

A FILLIN field displays a dialog box prompting the user for an entry. After the user types an entry and clicks OK, the FILLIN field passes the entry to a bookmark.

If you combine the FILLIN field with a SET field and some REF fields, you can assign the text entered in response to the FILLIN field to a bookmark, and then refer to that bookmark (and thereby its contents) in other places in your form.

To do this, you'll need to nest a FILLIN field inside a SET field, like so:

```
{ SET CustAdd { FILLIN "Type the customer's address" } }
```

TIP   Fields in general, the FILLIN field, and nesting fields are all covered in much greater depth in Chapter 32.

Then you can reuse the bookmark value throughout the form with the REF field, like so:

```
{ REF CustAdd }
```

Part
5

Power Tools

Inserting the Field Codes

There are two ways to insert a field code. You can do it with Insert ➤ Field, or you can enter the field manually. Let's try it both ways with the nested field. To insert the SET field manually,

1. Press Ctrl+F9. This inserts the field characters { } and leaves the insertion point between the two field characters.

2. Type **SET** and a space.

3. Type the name of the bookmark you want to assign.

4. Normally, here you would type the value to be assigned to the bookmark. Instead, you can now insert the FILLIN field.

To insert a FILLIN field automatically,

1. Select Insert ➤ Field. This brings up the Field dialog box:

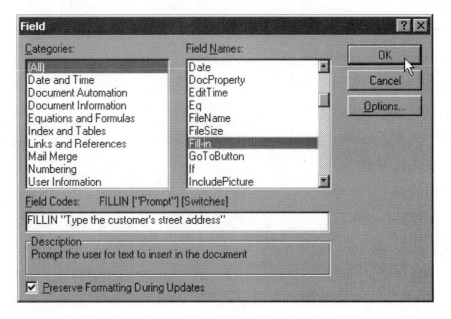

2. Select [All] in the Categories box if it's not already selected.

3. Select Fill-in in the Field Names box.

4. Type a space and then a prompt between quotation marks in the Field Codes box.

5. If you want default text, type a space, then **\d**, another space, then the default text you want between quotation marks.

6. Click OK.

   Now, wherever you want to reuse that bookmark value, insert the REF field as described above.

Testing the Fill-In Form by Updating the Fields

Once you have created (all or part of) your form, you can test your fill-in fields by updating them. First, of course, you have to save the template containing the form and then start a new document based on that template.

1. Select Edit ➤ Select All to select the whole document, all fields included.

2. Press F9 to update all selected fields.

3. One field at a time, enter the information requested and click OK.

> **WARNING** When entering fields by hand and especially when nesting them, it is easy to make typographical errors that render the fields unworkable. While testing your form this way, you may therefore see an error message displayed in the place of a field, rather than a prompt or updated value. If this happens, select the field and press Shift+F9. Then check the field carefully for spelling and syntax.

Setting Up an AutoNew Macro to Start the Updating Automatically

Because any time anyone opens a new document based on your form template they'll expect to fill in the fields in the form, you might as well attach an AutoNew macro to the form that starts the updating process. This way, as soon as the user opens the new document, the first prompt will appear, and the user will be taken field by field through the form automatically.

To do this,

1. Select Tools ➤ Macro. This brings up the Macro dialog box:

2. Type **AutoNew** in the Macro Name box.

3. Click the Record button. This brings up the Record Macro dialog box.

4. Click the Make Macro Available To drop-down list box and select the option Documents Based On *your-template*.

5. Click OK. The macro starts recording.

6. Press Ctrl+A (to select the whole document).

7. Press F9 to start the updating process. The first fill-in prompt will appear on the screen.

8. Press Esc repeatedly until all the prompts have come and gone.

9. Click the Stop Recorder button in the little floating Macro Record toolbar.

10. Press Ctrl+S or click the Save button on the Standard toolbar to save the template with the new macro.

To test your AutoNew macro, select File ➤ New to start a new document, choose the form template, and click OK.

Chapter 34

Creating and Using Macros

FAST TRACK

To record a macro 778

start the macro recorder, enter a name for the macro in the Record Macro Name box, enter a description, and decide where to assign the macro. Click OK to get rid of the Record Macro dialog box; then perform the actions you want to record. To stop recording the macro, double-click REC in the status area or click the Stop button on the Macro Record toolbar.

To suspend and resume recording a macro 782

click the Pause button on the Macro Record toolbar to pause recording; click it again to restart recording.

To run a macro 783

choose the toolbar button, menu option, or key combination to which you assigned it or choose Tools ➤ Macro, select its name in the Macro dialog box, and click the Run button.

To edit a macro 786

select Tools ➤ Macro, select the macro you want to edit, then click the Edit button. Make your edits, then close the file and save changes.

To copy a macro from one template to another 788

select File ➤ Templates and click the Organizer button in the Templates and Add-Ins dialog box. In the Organizer dialog box, choose the Macros tab, select the macro you want to copy, then choose the Copy button.

To rename a macro 789

select Tools ➤ Macro and click the Organizer button. In the left list box, choose the macro to rename and then click the Rename button. Enter the new name in the Rename dialog box and click OK.

To delete a macro 789

select Tools ➤ Macro, highlight the macro to delete in the Macro dialog box, and click the Delete button.

Most people are afraid of macros, which is a shame. Macros aren't nearly as bad as people make them out to be, and they can simplify your life considerably. All right, your work life. Macros are much more fun than having your teeth drilled. Once you get them working, they're even quicker.

First, we'll discuss what macros are and what they can do for you. Second, we'll look at Word's tools for creating, recording, editing, and running macros. Third, we'll discuss five automatic macros that every Word user should consider trying.

 TIP Macros don't have to be fancy. You can write macros that simply automate repetitive keystrokes and mouse clicks. This reduces the risk of repetitive stress disorders.

What Are Macros?

A macro is a series of Word commands grouped together as a single command to make everyday tasks easier. You can assign a macro to a toolbar, menu, or shortcut keys (see Chapter 36 for more on this) and run it by simply clicking a button, selecting a menu choice, or pressing a key combination.

Macros are recorded as instructions in Word's macro language, Word-Basic, so-called because it uses words and it's basic. Well, more like because it's the Basic language used by Word. Don't let WordBasic worry you; you can create macros without understanding a single word of it.

You can create a macro in two ways:

▶ Record a series of actions using the keyboard and mouse. This is the easiest way.

▶ Type a macro directly into a macro-editing window. This way you have more flexibility and can include WordBasic instructions that you can't record using the keyboard and mouse.

If you record a macro using the keyboard and mouse, you can then open it in the macro-editing window and edit it. Often the best way to create a macro is to record as much of it as possible using the keyboard and mouse, then edit it and add further WordBasic instructions in the macro-editing window.

How You Might Use Macros

So what would you actually *use* a macro for? Well, several things: to perform routine editing and formatting tasks faster; to combine several commands that you always have to perform in sequence; to instantly adjust an option in a remote dialog box (for example, to change printers and set printer options with one keystroke); or to automate a complex series of tasks.

For example, say you write your reports with the body text in double-spaced Courier 12-point with 1″ margins all the way around your paper. You print out drafts like that—nice and easy to read, and you don't care how typewriterish it looks—but when you print out your final report, it needs to look completely different, single-spaced 10-point Times Roman for the body text, three levels of headings in different sizes of a display font like Braggadocio, $1\frac{1}{2}″$ margins. Oh, and you always forget to run a spelling and grammar check before you print it. You could write a macro to:

▶ Change the body text to 10-point Times Roman.

▶ Apply the three heading styles to the relevant paragraphs.

▶ Adjust the margins and line spacing.

▶ Force you to check the spelling and grammar.

You gotta admit that beats dentistry any day.

Things You Can Do without Using Macros

Of course, macros are hardly the only form of automated convenience that Word offers. Before delving into the challenging process of recording a custom macro to create a shortcut, consider first whether you can achieve the effect you want with Styles, the Style Gallery, AutoFormat, AutoCorrect, AutoText, the Spike, Bookmarks, Field Codes, Form Fields, or even Find and Replace. Some of these tools can also be used in combination with macros.

▶ Styles help automate the formatting process, allowing you to apply multiple character and paragraph formats to separate text elements in a

Part
5

Power Tools

single step. They also allow you to change formatting consistently throughout your document. Styles are covered in Chapter 14.

▶ AutoFormat takes a lot of the formatting decisions out of your hands but gives you a lot of control over accepting or rejecting its suggestions. AutoFormat is covered in Chapter 14.

▶ AutoCorrect is designed to fix your typos as you make them, but you can also add abbreviations to it that are automatically expanded into their full references as soon as you type them. AutoCorrect is covered in Chapter 17.

▶ AutoText is an even more sophisticated way to create abbreviations and store boilerplate text for reuse. AutoText is covered in Chapter 17.

▶ The Spike enables you to skim through a document and pull out specific pieces of it and then deposit them all in another location. The Spike is covered in Chapter 17.

▶ Bookmarks make it easier for you to navigate through your documents and can also play the role of variables with field codes and macros. Bookmarks are covered in Chapter 25.

▶ Field codes produce a result or start a macro somewhere in the document. They can interact with the user, taking and storing input or even producing varying results depending on the user's entry. Field codes are covered in Chapter 32 and Appendix C.

▶ Form Fields can automate the process of creating a document or filling out a form. They can also be combined with field codes to take user input and reuse it throughout a document. Form Fields are covered in Chapters 32, 33, and Appendix C.

▶ Find and Replace can automate some of your editing, particularly when you need to make identical or similar changes throughout a document. With advanced Replace features, you can carefully fine-tune what gets changed and what does not. Find and Replace are covered in Chapter 20.

The Macro Toolbar

The Macro toolbar appears whenever you start the Macro Recorder. It contains twelve buttons and a name box, as shown in Figure 34.1.

Figure 34.1 *The Macro toolbar.*

Here's what the different parts of the Macro toolbar do. Don't worry about them too much at the moment but be prepared to come back to this section for reference when working on your macros.

Toolbar Item	What It Does
Macro name box	Lists the name of the macro
Record	Turns recording a macro on or off
Record Next Command	Records the next command executed
Start	Starts running the current macro
Trace	Highlights each statement as the active macro executes it
Pause/Continue	Pauses or continues running the macro
Stop	Stops running the macro
Step	Runs the active macro one step at a time
Step Subs	Runs the active macro one step at a time, considering subroutines one step
Show Variables	Lists the active macro's variables

Part 5

Power Tools

Toolbar Item	What It Does
Add/Remove REM	Adds or removes a REM (remark) at the beginning of each selected line in the active macro
Macro	Runs, creates, deletes, or revises a macro
Dialog Editor	Launches the macro Dialog Editor, a mini-application that you can use to design dialog boxes

Recording Your Own Macros

To record your own macros, you start the Word macro recorder and record a sequence of actions. You then stop the recorder and edit the macro if need be. Then you can run the macro whenever you need to perform the same sequence of actions.

Things to Do before Recording a Macro

Before you actually start recording your macro, make sure that the Word workspace is in roughly the same shape it will be in whenever you run the macro. If you end up doing some "housecleaning" while recording the macro, all of those steps will be included in the macro as well and often won't make sense.

NOTE   On the other hand, you can save some tasks—like going to the top of the document—for the beginning of the macro, if they're going to be necessary every time the macro runs.

It's good to think about what position your documents will be in when you run your new macro on them. It helps clarify the steps that will be needed when you start recording the macro.

1. Make sure you've got open the kind of document you'll use your macro in. (Open a document from the Normal template if you'll want your macro available to all documents.)

2. Run through the procedure without recording it to notice all the steps (it's easy to forget the details!).

3. If the macro involves selecting something, decide if you want to make the selection before the recording (in which case the macro will work properly only after you've selected something), or after.

4. Think up a good name for the macro.

5. Decide if you'll want a keyboard shortcut for it (and think of one easy to remember), if you'll want it on a toolbar, or if you'll want to slap it on a menu. You can do all three if you wish.

Thinking through the Steps to Record Ahead of Time

Here's an example. Let's take a look at creating a simple macro to maximize the space available to you on the screen. We need to do the following:

▶ Maximize Word for Windows.

▶ Maximize the document window.

▶ Hide the horizontal ruler, the toolbars, the scroll bars, and the status bar.

To do this with the mouse or keyboard would involve a series of simple actions staggeringly tedious to repeat, so this is a great candidate for a macro.

Starting the Macro Recorder

There are three ways to start the macro recorder:

▶ Double-click REC on the status bar. This is the quick and easy way.

▶ Select Tools ➤ Macro; then click the Record button in the Macro dialog box (see Figure 34.2). Easy but slower. You may want to save this for when you type in a macro rather than recording it.

▶ Click the Record button on the Macro toolbar. This involves having the Macro toolbar displayed (it'll be displayed when you start recording a macro).

Part
5

Power Tools

Figure 34.2   **The Macro dialog box.**

Record the Macro

Let's look at the steps for recording a macro, and then record the one proposed above.

1. Start the macro recorder by double-clicking REC on the status bar. The Record Macro dialog box will appear (see Figure 34.3).

2. Enter a name for the macro in the Record Macro Name box.

    - If you don't give your macro a name, Word will name it Macro1, Macro2, and so on. This is all fine and convenient for the time being, but unless you rename your macros, the default names will be most uninformative after a while.

    - No spaces, commas, or periods allowed in the name.

3. Enter a description of what the macro does in the Description box. This is optional but strongly recommended, even if it's only *Second try at infernal maneuver, 4/1/95. Delete tomorrow.* This description will appear

Figure 34.3 *In the Record Macro dialog box, give your macro a name (and optional description) and assign it to a toolbar, a menu, or a keyboard shortcut.*

on the status line for a macro you assign to a menu item or toolbar button. You've got up to 255 characters, so get typing.

4. To assign the macro to a toolbar, a menu, or a keyboard shortcut, click the Toolbars, Menus, or Keyboard button. This will fire up the Customize dialog box with the appropriate tab selected, as shown in Figure 34.4, where I've chosen to assign the FixUpMyScreen macro to the Help menu. Click Add to add the macro to the menu. See Chapter 36 for details on assigning macros to the toolbars and the keyboard (or just follow your instincts).

5. If your current document is attached to a template other than Normal, drop down the Save Changes In list and select either that template or Normal.

NOTE If the current document is attached to Normal, Word will automatically store the macro there. As you can see, that's the case here.

6. Click OK. Now you can finally start recording your macro.

Part
5

Power Tools

Figure 34.4   I'm assigning the FixUpMyScreen macro to the Help menu in the Customize dialog box.

The Macro Recorder toolbar will appear on the screen:

It has two buttons—from left to right, a stop button and a pause button (sort of like a tape recorder, right? so where's the fast forward?). The little mini–control menu in the upper-left corner of the Macro Recorder toolbar just closes the toolbar without stopping recording. If you click it by mistake, you'll need to select Tools ➤ Macro to pause or stop the recording.

 TIP   A handy trick to know is that if you accidentally close the Macro Record toolbar, you can end the macro by double-clicking the REC button in the status area again.

Notice also that the mouse pointer gets a little cassette tape icon attached to it, to remind you that you're recording.

Notice also the REC box in the status bar becomes highlighted. This is also supposed to remind you that you're recording.

Actually, Finally, Recording the Macro

Now, perform the actions you want to record. If you stopped the macro recorder, start it up again! Here are the steps for recording the FixUp-MyScreen macro:

1. Click Word's maximize button to maximize Word.

2. Click the document window's maximize button to maximize the document window.

3. Select View ➤ Ruler to turn off the ruler. (If that turns the ruler on rather than off, don't worry—we'll fix the problem when we edit the macro.)

4. Select Tools ➤ Options to display the Options dialog box; then choose the View tab. Uncheck the check boxes for Horizontal Scroll Bar, Vertical Scroll Bar, and Status Bar, and click OK.

5. Select View ➤ Toolbars to display the Toolbars dialog box, then uncheck the Standard and Formatting check boxes.

6. To stop recording the macro, click the Stop button on the Macro Record toolbar (or double-click the word REC in the status bar). The Macro Recorder toolbar will disappear.

   There, one macro recorded! No pain, lots of gain, and no Novocain. We'll open the macro up in a moment. But first, a brief intermission.

What Gets Recorded and What Doesn't

Technically, the macro recorder does not record *actions* that you perform. It records the *commands*, the results of your actions. When you change something about your document while recording the macro, the macro remembers what you changed it to, not what it used to be.

> **WARNING**   Some Word commands simply toggle between two possibilities, such as Show/Hide. For commands of that sort, the macro recorder will only record that the status was changed. When played back, the macro will change the status without regard to which toggle position it starts in.

For commands chosen from a dialog box, you must click OK for the result to be recorded. And clicking OK in a dialog box records the selected state, including all defaults, of every option *in that tab* of the dialog box. To record commands in another tab of the same dialog box, you must open the dialog box again, switch to the other tab, make your selections, and click OK again.

The macro recorder generally does not record mouse motions. Well, that's not exactly right. You choose commands by pulling down menus and clicking toolbar icons with the mouse, and those results will be recorded, but you can't select (and therefore also can't drag and drop, of course) text or other elements of your document with the mouse.

> **NOTE**   You can, of course, select text, copy it, paste it, cut it, and move it with the keyboard shortcuts. Select text by holding down Shift and pressing the arrow keys and other movement keys (or by using the Extend command—F8—and the arrow and movement keys). Use Ctrl+C to copy, Ctrl+V to paste, and Ctrl+X to cut. Use cut and paste together to move.

Because the macro recorder records results, not literal keystrokes, when you play back your macro, you won't see menus being pulled down and ghost mouse clicks like a player piano. You'll just see Word clinically and surgically executing your commands.

Taking a Break from Recording the Macro

Word allows you to suspend and resume recording a macro as you like. If you reach some impasse in the procedure that you don't want to record for posterity, or just want to record isolated actions here and there as the fancy strikes you, here's what to do:

1. Click the Pause button on the Macro Record toolbar to pause recording.

2. Perform the actions you don't want to record.

3. Click the Pause button again to restart recording (just like a tape recorder!).

Solving Problems Recording a Macro

If you make a mistake while recording a macro, you can pause the macro as explained in the previous section and put the document back to the way it should be before continuing, or you can stop recording the macro and then start over from the beginning. The latter may be easier if you are near the beginning of the recording process.

NOTE If you pause the macro recording and fool around with the document, then you'll still need to edit the macro when you're done to eliminate the mistake from the recording. Editing macros is covered later in this chapter.

If you choose some incorrect settings in a dialog box and can't remember what the original choices were, you can simply click the Cancel button or press Esc to close the dialog box without recording your incorrect selections. (Remember, the macro recorder will only record your actions in a dialog box if you click OK when you are done.)

Another thing you can do is select Edit ➤ Undo, press Ctrl+Z, or even click the Undo drop-down menu button on the Standard toolbar to undo your mistake. However, you must still check and edit the macro when you are finished, because the macro recorder will record both the incorrect action and the Undo. Not only is this confusing to anyone looking at the macro listing later (or watching it work), it may also give the wrong result, as the Undo may only undo the last result of your previous action, if, as with some Ruler, toolbar, or dialog box commands, there is more than one result.

Running a Macro

Once you have recorded a macro, there are a number of ways to play it back. You should test your macro out on a saved document right away to make sure it's working correctly. If it isn't, either edit it, as explained in the next section, or record it again from scratch.

Here are the different ways to run a macro:

▶ Select Tools ➤ Macro, choose the macro, and click the Run button.

▶ Click a MACROBUTTON field code in a document (as explained in Chapter 32).

▶ Run another macro that itself runs this macro.

▶ Click the macro's toolbar icon.

▶ Select the macro's menu command.

▶ Press the macro's keyboard shortcut.

TIP If you can't find a macro later when you try to run it, chances are you assigned the macro to a specific template and now have a different template open.

Assigning a Macro to a Toolbar, Menu, or Keyboard Shortcut After the Fact

Of course the last three options above will only be available to you if, when you first started the recording process, you assigned the macro to a toolbar, menu, or keyboard shortcut. If you did not do it then and wish you had, things get a little trickier.

1. Select Tools ➤ Customize. This brings up the Customize dialog box:

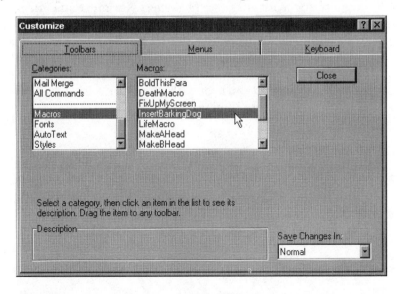

2. Click the appropriate tab (Toolbars, Menus, or Keyboard).

3. Select Macros in the Category box.

4. Choose the macro you want to assign.

5. Then drag the macro you want to a toolbar, select a menu and position, or enter a keystroke combination.

6. For menus, click Add. For keystrokes, click Assign.

Macros that Start Themselves

AutoNew, AutoOpen, AutoClose, and AutoExec macros (they are all explained later in this chapter) run automatically when certain events occur. As you might imagine, they behave as follows:

▶ AutoNew macros start when you start a new document based on the template the macro is stored in;

▶ AutoOpen macros start when you open a document containing them;

▶ AutoClose macros start when you close a document containing them;

▶ AutoExec macros start whenever you run Word.

You can also run Auto macros in all the other ways that you run normal macros.

Running a Macro from the Macro Dialog Box

Whether or not you've assigned your macro to a menu, toolbar, or keyboard shortcut, you may always run any macro from the Macro dialog box.

1. Select Tools ➤ Macro. This brings up the Macro dialog box (see Figure 34.2).

2. Select the macro you want to run. (If you don't see the macro you're looking for, change the selection in the Macros Available In box to the template containing the macro.)

3. Click the Run button.

Part
5

Power Tools

Editing Macros

Once you've recorded a macro, you can edit and run it. Often, you'll want to edit macros before running them, either to remove flaws recorded in the macro or to enhance the macro with WordBasic commands that you cannot record.

Here's how to edit a macro:

1. Select Tools ➤ Macro. The Macro dialog box will appear.

2. Select the list of macros to choose from by dropping down the Macros Available In box.

3. Choose the macro you want to edit; then click the Edit button. The macro-editing window will appear, displaying the text of the macro you chose. Figure 34.5 shows the text of the FixUpMyScreen macro.

4. Edit the macro.

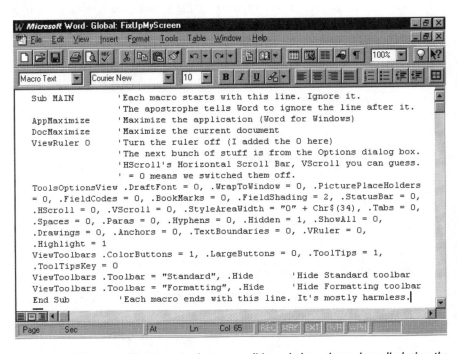

Figure 34.5 You can edit macros in the macro-editing window, shown here displaying the FixUpMyScreen macro with added comments.

NOTE If your ViewRuler line toggled the ruler on rather than switching it off, change it to ViewRuler 0 to make sure the macro switches the ruler off.

5. Close the file and choose Yes when Word invites you to save changes.

 NOTE You'll notice that the macro appears in a window much like any normal Word document. For your purposes, it *is* a Word document, and you can edit it as you would any document.

As you look over the listing of a macro, notice what was recorded and what wasn't. Again, the macro is not so much a recording of everything you did as a recording of the *results* of everything you did. If you made a mistake and then selected Undo, there will be at least one command line for the mistaken command and then an additional line for the Undo command. (You can delete both the mistake and the Undo line.)

Also, if you made selections from a dialog box, look at the commands that were recorded (for example, look at the ToolsOptionsView command in Figure 34.5). You'll see that every element of the dialog box registered some setting, whether you changed the default or not. When editing a macro, you can remove the extra parts of commands (the arguments) that are irrelevant to your purposes. It's not necessary to do that, but it does make the macro easier to read and interpret if you need to edit it again or see what it does later.

 TIP While editing a macro, be sure to save it every now and again. Select File ➤ Save All to save any open documents, including macros. (Word will automatically prompt you to save your macros—as changes to the templates they're in—when you quit, but it's safer to save them yourself while you're still working on them.)

Organizing Your Macros

Word's Organizer dialog box simplifies managing your macros. You can use it to move, copy, or rename a macro. By default, macros are stored in the Global Template in Normal and so are available for use with every Word document. However, you can store them in other templates if you wish. For example, if you have a macro that's only useful for annual reports, you might include it in your Annual Report template.

Copying Macros from One Template to Another

Word lets you easily copy macros from one template to another. So, you can record or write a macro in the Normal template, then decide you only need it in your I'm Clever template, and transfer it across.

Here's how to copy a macro from one template to another:

1. Select File ➤ Templates. The Templates and Add-Ins dialog box will appear.

2. Click the Organizer button to display the Organizer dialog box (see Figure 34.6).

3. Choose the Macros tab.

4. If necessary, close the open file, select the Open File button, and open the template or document containing the macro.

5. Select the macro you want to copy, then choose the Copy button.

> **TIP**   To select a range of items, hold down Shift and click the first and last items. To select several individual items, hold down Ctrl and click each one.

Figure 34.6   The Organizer dialog box lets you manage your macros with minimal effort.

6. Click the Close button when you've finished copying macros.

 TIP You can also get to the Organizer dialog box by selecting <u>T</u>ools ➤ <u>M</u>acro and clicking the Organizer button in the Macro dialog box.

Renaming a Macro

If you give several macros in different templates the same name, or if you record your macros as Macro1, Macro2, Macro3, and so on, you may want to rename macros at some point. Here's how to do it:

1. Select <u>T</u>ools ➤ <u>M</u>acro. The Macro dialog box will appear.

2. Click the Organizer button. The Organizer dialog box will appear with the Macros tab selected.

3. In the left list box, choose the macro to rename. If necessary, choose a different template in the Macros Available In list box.

4. Click the Rename button. The Rename dialog box will appear.

5. Enter the new name for the macro and click OK. The macro will be renamed.

Deleting a Macro

Getting rid of a macro you no longer need is easy and intuitive:

1. Select <u>T</u>ools ➤ <u>M</u>acro. The Macro dialog box will appear.

2. Highlight the macro to delete.

3. Click the Delete button.

4. Click the Close button to return to your document.

Part 5

Power Tools

Using the Sample Macros That Come with Word

Word supplies a bunch of sample macros that are built into sample templates stored in the Templates subfolder. One way to learn more about macros and get some practice editing them is to check out these sample macros.

As described in the previous section, you can copy any of these macros from the templates they are associated with to a new template using the Organizer. Once you've done that, you can run the macros, open them up for editing, and change them, if you want, without harming the originals stored in the sample templates.

Word's Automatic Macros

Even if you never get deeply into writing and using macros, you should look briefly at Word's five autoexecuting macros. With only a little effort, you can use these to set and restore screen preferences, open a bunch of documents, and generally make life a little more pleasant for you.

The five automatic macros are:

Macro Name	What It Does
AutoExec	Runs when you start Word
AutoNew	Runs when you open a new file
AutoOpen	Runs when you open a file you created before
AutoClose	Runs when you close a file (new or created before)
AutoExit	Runs when you exit Word

You can create automatic macros just as you do any other macros—by typing the commands into the macro-editing window (reached by selecting the Edit or Create button in the Macro dialog box), by recording a series of actions, or by a judicious mixture of the two. The sections below suggest a few uses for these automatic macros; no doubt you'll quickly come up with your own uses.

Uses for an AutoExec Macro

If you don't like having Word automatically create a new document based on the Normal template whenever you start Word, you could write a brief AutoExec macro to specify a new document based on a different template, such as Special for You.

```
Sub MAIN
     FileNew .Template = "Special for You"
End Sub
```

Or you could arrange to have Word open the same file—for example, a journal—whenever you start Word and go to either your last edit or the end:

```
Sub MAIN
     FileOpen "C:\Winword7\Journal\April 4, 1997"
If MsgBox("Click OK to go to the scene of the last crime;
click Cancel to start a new entry at the end of the jour-
nal.", "OK, So Whaddaya Wanna Do Widdya Journal?", 1 + 32)
Then GoBack Else Goto NewStuffLokiSaveUs
Goto Bye
NewStuffLokiSaveUs:
     EndOfDocument
Bye:
End Sub
```

Get your imagination to work on a good AutoExec macro—it can improve your life.

Uses for an AutoOpen Macro

While you can have only one AutoExec macro for your copy of Word, you can have a different AutoOpen macro for each template. As a result, you may want to use AutoOpen macros to customize the screen for templates, to display a message box to greet the user, or both:

```
Sub MAIN
Print "Hang on a tick while yer favorite template custom-
izes yer screen..."
     ViewToolbars .ColorButtons = 1, .LargeButtons = 1,
.ToolTips = 1
```

Part
5

Power Tools

```
                    ViewToolbars .Toolbar = "Standard", .Show
                    ViewToolbars .Toolbar = "Formatting", .Show
                    ViewRuler
            MsgBox "Screen customized to your satisfaction—well, mine
            anyway.", "Thank you! You are free to proceed!", 0 +48"
            End Sub
```

Uses for an AutoNew Macro

You can use an AutoNew macro in similar ways to an AutoOpen macro to set up the screen and options for a given template. But you might also want to ensure that the user saves the file immediately to prevent lost data and gives it the necessary summary information for you to keep track of things:

```
Sub MAIN
Dim SaveNow As FileSaveAs
Dialog(SaveNow)
Dim SumItAllUp As FileSummaryInfo
Dialog(SumItAllUp)
End Sub
```

Here (in the custom SaveNow dialog box that would be displayed by the `Dialog (SaveNow)` command) the user is automatically asked to save the document. Other possibilities include setting up the screen to suit the user or document.

Uses for an AutoClose Macro

The AutoClose macro is the perfect choice for either restoring screen preferences for documents using other templates or, as in the example below, backing up the file being closed to a file server or backup drive:

```
Sub MAIN
    ClosingFile$ = FileName$()
    FileClose 1
    Copyfile ClosingFile$, "f:\ronstuff\worddocs\backup"
    MsgBox "Backed up your file successfully!", "Backup",
    0 + 64
End Sub
```

NOTE As with the AutoOpen and AutoNew macros, you can have an AutoClose macro for each different template. This gives you great flexibility.

Uses for an AutoExit Macro

An AutoExit macro runs whenever you quit Word. You might want to use it to reset any environment options that your other macros and templates are liable to change. That way, when you restart Word, all the settings will be as you like them.

Here's how you might turn off the toolbars that the AutoOpen macro earlier turned on:

```
Sub MAIN
        ViewToolbars .Toolbar = "Standard", .Hide
        ViewToolbars .Toolbar = "Formatting", .Hide
MsgBox "Thank you for using your own copy of Word for Win-
dows. Please have a good day.", "Drive Safely and Be Nice
to Your Spouse", 0 +48
End Sub
```

Debugging Your Macros

If your macro is not working properly, you can use the Step button on the Macro toolbar to debug it. *Debugging* is a programming term for finding the errors in a program. As the macro executes, you can step through it one command at a time and figure out exactly when it goes wrong. (After a macro fails, the offending command is highlighted in red, so that should help, too.)

If necessary, you may have to include special commands at various places in your macro to display the current contents of variables (see *Macros That Talk Back* later in this chapter).

Advanced Macros and WordBasic

To get any fancier with macros, you have to bite the bullet and learn a little bit about WordBasic. Look, it's not as bad as it sounds. Remember how to edit a macro you've already recorded? Those commands shown

Part 5

Power Tools

in the Figure 34.5 macro listing are WordBasic commands. So you've been dealing with WordBasic already even if you didn't realize it.

Word macros consist entirely of WordBasic commands. (Actually, the same is true of all Word commands. When you pull down the File menu and select Open, that action is equivalent to running the FileOpen command macro.)

This is not a book for programmers, so I don't expect you to have a background in "writing code," and I'm not going to try to turn you into a software engineer. The rest of this chapter, however, will cover some of the more straightforward uses of WordBasic.

The Structure of WordBasic Commands

WordBasic is itself based on a programming language called BASIC that was developed to teach beginners programming. BASIC requires less "housekeeping" on the part of the programmer (you don't have to declare variables, reserve memory, or anything like that) and is fairly easy to learn and use. BASIC commands are as close to plain English as is possible.

WordBasic is a tailored version of BASIC with all sorts of built-in commands relating to word processing and Windows standards (such as the format of dialog boxes, which is the same from program to program in Windows). It also contains the necessary commands for more complicated structures, such as subroutines, conditionals, and loops.

Subroutines are miniature programs that branch off from a main program. *Conditionals* are statements that execute actions only if some other condition is true. *Loops* are sets of statements that start over from the beginning and execute repeatedly until or unless some other condition occurs. (*Infinite loops* are poorly structured loops that continue repeating forever unless interrupted, such as "Lather, rinse, repeat.")

The elements of any WordBasic command are its statements, functions, variables, constants, and arguments.

▶ *Statements* perform actions.

▶ *Functions* return (produce) results.

▶ *Variables* carry values that can be assigned and changed.

▶ *Constants* are values that don't change.

▶ *Arguments* modify statements and functions.

The FixUpMyScreen macro shown in Figure 34.5 consists entirely of statements and arguments. The macro comprises a series of actions performed on the Word screen. The ViewRuler command includes an argument (0) to specify exactly what it should do (not just toggle the Ruler from its previous position, but actually turn it off no matter what). Actually, in a sense, the 0s and 1s used to switch various statements or arguments on and off are technically constants.

Variables can contain text (in which case they are called string variables) or numbers (numeric variables). String variables always ends in the symbol $ (which is, by association, pronounced *string*).

Both string and numeric variables can be manipulated. There are functions to pluck out specific parts of a string or concatenate two strings together. There are also basic mathematical operators (the familiar +, −, *, /, and so on) as well as mathematical functions that perform more complicated operations on numeric variables.

Getting Advanced Macro Help

In Word 95 you seek WordBasic advanced help a little differently than you did in earlier Word versions, partly because of an apparent indexing bug. Select Help ➤ Microsoft Word ➤ Microsoft Word Help Topics. This brings up the Help window. Click the Find tab if necessary to bring it foremost (see Figure 34.7).

Type a WordBasic-related term like **statement** or **macro** and click Search. Then choose one of the resulting topics and click Display to bring up the Help window (see Figure 34.8).

Note: Early versions of Word 95 appear to have a WordBasic-related help bug in the help index. Usually you can click the Cancel and OK buttons a dozen or more times when you get the empty alert boxes and numerous other notices of trouble. Eventually, you'll get to the desired help screen.

Or, you can sometimes just type the word **statement** in the Find tab, or type the name of the specific statement of interest and work without the index.

Figure 34.7 **Use the Find tab to search for WordBasic help on the specific topic of interest. I've typed "statement" here.**

If you're looking for information on a specific command, you can either type the words **Statements and Functions by Category** to zero in on it, or type **Statements and Functions Index** to look for it alphabetically. (They both lead eventually to the same information.) Figure 34.9 shows the WordBasic Statements and Functions Index. Again, users of early Word versions might have trouble reaching this index.

Click the letter button for the first letter of the command (statement or function) that you're looking for. Then click the entry itself to go to an informative Help entry. Figure 34.10 shows the entry for the Edit-Replace command.

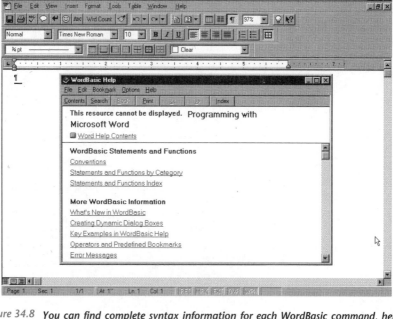

Figure 34.8 You can find complete syntax information for each WordBasic command, help in making dialog boxes, and all kinds of examples and helpful explanations.

Figure 34.9 The WordBasic Statements and Functions Index.

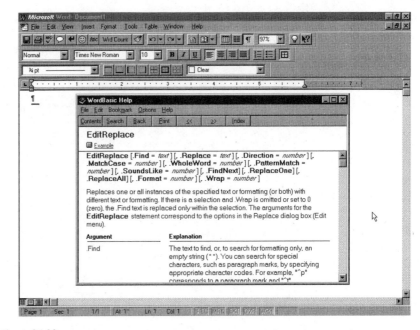

Figure 34.10   *The EditReplace entry with complete syntax information on each argument, some tips, and links to related entries.*

Not-Too-Hard WordBasic Programming

If you start creating more ambitious macros (go ahead, you can call 'em WordBasic programs!), you'll soon want to know how to prompt the user for input, how to display results, how to deal with multiple possibilities, and how to create subroutines or loops. In the next few sections, I'll give you a start in all of those areas.

Hello in There!—Talking to Macros

As your macros get more sophisticated, you're going to want to make them more responsive and flexible. One way to do this is to have them prompt the user for input and then do different things depending on what gets "put in." The flip side of this is that you'll want your macros to report on what they're doing—that's the output side of the coin. Recorded macros are taciturn. They do their work and disappear. But you can set up your macros to both "listen" and "talk."

Getting User Input

An interactive macro has to be able to accept input from the user (and store the value of the input as a variable). There are several ways to do this. The simplest is to put a prompt in the status bar.

Simple Input on the Status Bar

To prompt the user on the status bar, use the Input command. With Input, you can prompt for the value of a string or numeric variable. Input statements have the syntax

```
Input [Prompt$,] Variable[$]
```

So the statement:

```
Input "What is your title", Job$
```

will display the prompt in quotation marks on the status bar and store the user's input in a string variable called Job$:

```
What is your title?
```

Notice that WordBasic adds the question mark to your prompt.

 TIP You can prompt for numeric input just as easily.

To respond to this type of prompt, type an answer and press Enter.

User Input in a Box

For a more elaborate (and harder to miss) form of input, you can use the InputBox$ command to put a dialog box up on the screen. The InputBox$ statement has the syntax

```
Variable$ = InputBox$(Prompt$ [,Title$] [,Default$])
```

So the statement:

```
Job$ = InputBox$("What is your title?","Personnel")
```

will display the prompt in a dialog box with the title specified and no default answer in the text box, and store the response in a variable called Job$:

Notice that WordBasic does not automatically supply a question mark for the InputBox$ prompt. To respond to this sort of prompt, type an answer and click OK.

Just Yes or No, Please

If all you need from the user is a Yes or No answer, then you can use the MsgBox() command. The MsgBox() command has the following syntax:

```
Variable = MsgBox(Message$ [,Title$] [,Type])
```

where *Type* can be any number from 0 to 5 and indicates the type of response buttons available:

0	OK
1	OK, Cancel
2	Abort, Retry, Ignore
3	Yes, No, Cancel
4	Yes, No
5	Retry, Cancel

If you don't specify a type, the default is 0. The statement

```
Answer = MsgBox("Do you have any additional comments?","Com-
ments",4)
```

will display the prompt in a dialog box headed with the title string and containing Yes and No buttons.

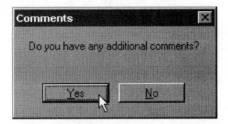

The response is stored in the variable Answer. With MsgBox(), if the first button is clicked, the value returned is −1. For the second button, it's 0, and if there are 3 buttons, the third returns 1.

NOTE   The button responses, such as Yes, No, and Cancel, don't do anything by themselves. Your WordBasic program must take the value returned and do something with it, depending on what it is. See *If Statements* later in this chapter for more on conditionals.

Macros That Talk Back

So now you know a couple of different ways to pass information to your macros. You'll also need to know how your macros can report information back to you. As with input, there's a simple way to do it that displays information on the status bar and another fairly easy way that displays a dialog box.

On the Status Bar

To display text on the status bar, use the Print command. Print statements have the syntax

```
Print Variable[$]
```

So the statement:

```
Print "Vice President of Marketing"
```

or

```
Print Job$
```

will display the string named:

Vice President of Marketing

TIP You can print numeric values just as well.

In a Message Box

If you want your macro to really announce the information it has, you can use the MsgBox. The MsgBox statement has the syntax

```
MsgBox Message$ [,Title$] [,Type])
```

So the statement:

```
MsgBox "Your title is "+Title$, "Personnel"
```

will display the message in a dialog box with the title specified and an OK button:

NOTE The type options for MsgBox are the same as for the MsgBox() input command explained earlier.

Creating Dialog Boxes

You've already seen how to display simple dialog boxes and use them to get input or display output, but those dialog boxes are still fairly limited in what they can do. If you understand a little more about how dialog boxes work, you can modify existing dialog boxes or even create your own.

Understanding Dialog Boxes

Word commands that call up dialog boxes translate into WordBasic macro commands with many parameters. You saw in the sample macro FixUpMyScreen earlier in this chapter how recording the selection of the View tab of the Options dialog box translated into a WordBasic ToolsOptionsView command with every option in that tab recorded as a parameter set to some value (see Figure 34.5).

This set of parameters recorded from the dialog box is known as an array. If you want to create a dialog box or modify an existing one, you have to first plan out the array that the dialog box command will use.

In recording that macro, I selected Tools ➤ Options, then turned off the horizontal and vertical scroll bars and the status bar, and clicked OK. That action was recorded as:

```
ToolsOptionsView .DraftFont = 0, .WrapToWindow = 0, .Pic-
turePlaceHolders = 0, .FieldCodes = 0, .BookMarks = 0,
.FieldShading = 2, .StatusBar = 0, .HScroll = 0, .VScroll =
0, .StyleAreaWidth = "0" + Chr$(34), .Tabs = 0, .Spaces =
0, .Paras = 0, .Hyphens = 0, .Hidden = 0, .ShowAll = 0,
.Drawings = 0, .Anchors = 0, .TextBoundaries = 0, .VRuler = 0
```

Those parameters listed after the ToolsOptionView command are all *fields* in the command's array. Figure 34.11 shows the View tab of the Options dialog box.

So each element of the dialog box (tab) corresponds to a field in the WordBasic command's array.

Creating Your Own Dialog Boxes

Whether you realized it or not, Word came with another program called the Dialog Editor. You use the Dialog Editor to lay out your dialog box. You then copy and paste it into your macro, and it produces the skeletal WordBasic commands you'll need to display the dialog box. After that, you still have to add the instructions that use the information the dialog box can gather and store.

This process can become rather involved, and although there's fairly good support in the WordBasic section of Word Help, you really need the *Microsoft Word Developer's Kit*, available from Microsoft, if you plan

Part
5

Power Tools

Figure 34.11 *Notice how in the View tab of the Options dialog box the different check boxes, text boxes, and drop-down lists correspond to parameters in the ToolsOptionsView command.*

to get serious about this level of WordBasic. Just to give you an idea, though, I'll take you through a simple example.

1. Select Tools ➤ Macro to bring up the Macro dialog box.

2. Type **Questionnaire.**

3. Click the Create button. This will open a new blank macro-editing window and put the Macro toolbar on the screen.

4. Now click the Dialog Editor button.

   This starts the Dialog Editor program with a generic dialog box in the middle of the screen (see Figure 34.12).

   That dialog box in the middle of the screen is only a dummy, a picture. Think of it as a drawing board.

5. Select Item ➤ Text.

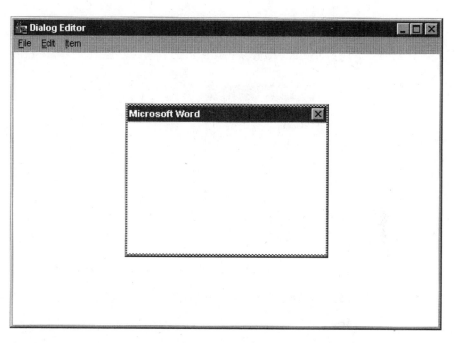

Figure 34.12 **The Dialog Editor program makes assembling a dialog box a snap. Making it do**
something is a little trickier.

6. Type **My name is**.

7. Select Item ➤ Text Box.

8. Select Item ➤ Text and type **My quest is**.

9. Select Item ➤ Text Box.

10. Select Item ➤ Text and type **My favorite color is**.

11. Select Item ➤ List Box. This brings up the New List Box dialog box:

12. Click Drop-Down and then click the OK button.

13. Select Item ➤ Button. The New Button dialog box will appear:

14. Click Check Box and then click the OK button.

15. Type **I like ice cream**.

16. Select Item ➤ Button. Make sure the OK option is selected and then click the OK button.

17. Select the OK button and move it to the lower-right corner of the dialog box, as shown:

18. Double-click the title bar of the dummy dialog box. This brings up the Dialog Information dialog box.

19. Select the words *Microsoft Word* in the Text$ dialog box and type **Personnel Questionnaire**.

20. Click OK.

TIP To edit the text or variable names associated with any part of the dialog box you're working on, simply double-click the element or select it and then select Edit ➤ Info.

21. With the dialog box dummy still selected, press Ctrl+C (or select Edit ➤ Copy).

22. Select File ➤ Exit. This should put you back in the macro-editing window.

23. Press Ctrl+V (or select Edit ➤ Paste).

Word pastes into your macro listing the command equivalents of all the dialog box elements you selected:

```
Begin Dialog UserDialog 320, 144, "Personnel Questionnaire"
    Text 10, 6, 85, 13, "My name is", .Text1
    TextBox 10, 22, 160, 18, .TextBox1
    Text 10, 46, 87, 13, "My quest is", .Text2
    TextBox 10, 62, 160, 18, .TextBox2
    Text 10, 86, 145, 13, "My favorite color is", .Text3
    DropListBox 10, 107, 160, 108, DropListBox1$(),
.DropListBox1
    CheckBox 10, 126, 145, 16, "I like ice cream", .CheckBox1
    OKButton 209, 110, 88, 21
End Dialog
```

Now, as I mentioned, there's more to using dialog boxes than creating their shells in the dialog box editor. If you added the commands for displaying a dialog box and ran your macro now, it would look pretty, displaying the dialog box you created, but it would not be "wired up" to anything inside.

To make your macro good for something, you might start by giving the variables descriptive names that you can understand later (though that's not necessary from Word's point of view—it will work just as well with the generic variables it supplied). Replace .TextBox1 with .Name, .TextBox2 with .Job, DropListBox1$() with Colors$(), .DropListBox1 with .Color, and .CheckBox1 with .IceCream. (You can get rid of the fields .Text1, .Text2, and .Text3.)

Next, you'd have to create an array variable for the drop-down list box choices by inserting something like this before the Begin Dialog command:

```
Dim Colors$(3)
Colors$(0) = "Blue"
Colors$(1) = "Red"
Colors$(2) = "Yellow"
Colors$(3) = "None of the above"
```

NOTE You're dealing with computers here now, and they like to start counting at zero.

Now the generic dialog box is not going to be big enough for the drop-down list you've built into it, so you'll have to change the height dimensions. Experiment with different sizes and positions for the dialog box, drop-down list box, check box, and OK button by changing their coordinate values in the WordBasic statements. The four numbers listed for each screen element are *X, Y* pairs. The first number is the horizontal coordinate of the upper-left corner, and the second number is the vertical coordinate; the third and fourth numbers define the lower-right corner in the same way.

You'll have to do something with the values that are stored—both the text entered in the text boxes and the results of the drop-down list and check-box responses (which are returned as numbers—0 or 1 for unchecked or checked, 0 through 3 for the drop-down list box choices). If your macro has *control structures*, things that make decisions based on conditions, then you need to pass the variables on to those structures.

Finally, you'll have to include the command to set up an array to hold the field variables of the dialog box:

```
Dim dlg As UserDialog
```

and then you need to include a command that will display the dialog box:

```
Dialog dlg
```

or

```
Variable = Dialog(dlg)
```

Basic Programming Structures

For fully functioning WordBasic programs, you need *control structures* so that the macro can decide what to do in various situations. This means the macro needs to be able to recognize different conditions and respond differently to them, and to repeat certain processes under certain conditions.

If Statements

The basic conditional command is the If statement. A simple If statement has the syntax

```
If Condition Then Instruction [Else Instruction]
```

So the statement:

```
If Job$ = "Vice President of Marketing" Then Goto Marketing
Else Goto End
```

will compare the value of Job$ to the text in quotes and then send the macro interpreter to one section of the macro if the variable matches the text or to another section if it does not.

TIP   Goto is explained a little farther ahead.

You can turn a recorded command into an If statement easily by preceding what the macro recorded with the If command and following it with a Then statement.

Loops

Most advanced macros require certain actions to be repeated until some condition is met. This is known in programming as *looping*. There are several different ways to create loops.

Goto

The simplest loop uses the Goto command. Goto is fairly straightforward. It sends the macro interpreter to the section named in the command. Its syntax is

```
Goto Label
```

Part
5

Power Tools

For it to work, you must label a part of the macro. Simply add a line before that section with the label name followed by a colon.

> **WARNING** If you use Goto by itself and the label it goes to precedes the Goto command, you'll create an infinite loop, with no alternative for the macro but to repeat the loop forever (until you stop it).

To be effective as a control structure, the Goto command must be combined with a conditional command, such as an If statement.

For ... Next

For ... Next statements give you more control over the looping. Their syntax is

```
For Counter = Start To End [Step Increment]
...
Next [Counter]
```

So the commands

```
For Decade = 10 To 100 Step 10
Print Decade
Next
```

would print 10, 20, 30, etc., up to 100 on the status bar (so quickly that if you try it you'll probably only see the 100).

You need to specify the counter variable name in the Next statement only if you have more than one For ... Next loop going at once.

While ... Wend

While ... Wend loops are a little more subtle. They allow you to have a loop running while some condition obtains. Their syntax is

```
While Condition
...
Wend
```

While ... Wend loops are flexible, as the conditions that govern how often they will repeat can change during the execution of the loop.

Chapter 35

Using Word and Word Documents with Other Applications

FAST TRACK

W ord makes it easy to work with documents created in other applications. So if you used WordPerfect for all your documents before switching to Word for Windows, you'll still be able to open and work with your old documents. If you've just upgraded from Word 6.0*x* to Word for Windows 95, you'll have no problem at all, because Word 95 saves files in Word 6 format... or so it claims.

Exactly which files created in other applications your copy of Word can open depends on the converters you installed with your copy of Word. See the *Make Sure You've Got the Right Filters Installed* section at the end of this chapter if you know that you don't have some necessary converters installed or if Word won't open documents you suspect it should be able to.

Opening a Document Created in Another Application

With Word, you can easily open documents created in many other applications.

1. Select File ➤ Open or click the Open button on the Standard toolbar. The Open dialog box will appear (see Figure 35.1).

Figure 35.1 **Pop up the Files of Type list in the Open dialog box to display files other than those in Word format.**

2. In the Look In box, select the drive and folder of the target document. (Hey, Ron, this is real easy! Didn't we do this in Chapter 2? Yes. Read on, MacDuff.)

> **WARNING**   Windows 95's new long file names coupled with the default setting that *hides* file extensions opens up a huge can of worms here. Since you can no longer see the file extensions (if they are turned off), you will not be able to tell what is what in the Open dialog box. You might think that Word now compensates for this by simply finding all Word documents. But life is never that simple. If a document has an extension other than *.doc*, hidden or not, Word will not consider it a Word document, even if it is one.

3. If your file is not a Word document, pull down the Files of Type list and select the appropriate option. If your target document was created in an application other than Word, you'll probably want All Files.

> **TIP**   If you know the extension of the file you want, type it into the File Name box and press ⌐ for a finer sort—for example, **.sam* for Ami Pro documents or **.xls* for Excel spreadsheets (or **.sam; *.xls* to see both). That way, you can get the type of file you want without having to sift through all the other junk that may be cluttering up the folder.

4. Select the file you want to open and click OK. Word will open the file for you, with the following exceptions.

   - If Word doesn't recognize the contents of the file, it will try to use the converters suggested by the file's extension. If that doesn't work, Word will ask you to choose a converter, as shown in Figure 35.2. Choose the converter you think corresponds to the contents of the file and click OK.

   - If you choose the wrong filter, Word will tell you so in no uncertain terms:

Part 5

Power Tools

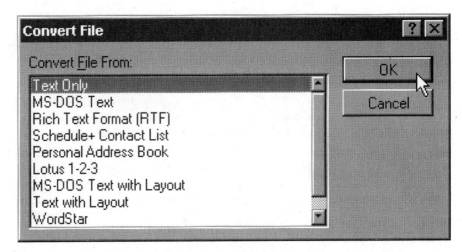

Figure 35.2   *Word will pop open the Convert File dialog box if you ask it to open a file whose format it doesn't recognize.*

- Click OK to get out of this dialog box and try again with another format. (Click Help to get a complicated online explanation of what I'm about to tell you.)

NOTE   Remember that a file's extension may not correspond to its contents: You could take a TIFF file called Oddfaces.tif and rename it Oddfaces.doc or Whatsup.doc, but it would still be a TIFF file, not a Word document. Similarly, Idiots.ws could be a WordPerfect 6 or XyWrite file rather than the WordStar file its extension suggests. It could even be CorelDRAW! Here's a quick, free tip: Save your files with the extensions that are the default for that type of file; most applications do this automatically. If you do this, life will be friendlier.

To make Word automatically display the Convert File dialog box when you open a file with a different format, check the Confirm Conversion at Open check box on the General tab of the Options dialog box.

If a document isn't converted correctly, your best bet is to close it without saving changes and try converting it again using a different converter.

If Word Refuses to Recognize the File

If Word can't get a handle on what format the file is, you have little choice but to accept the Text Only option it will offer you in the Convert File dialog box. Word will then display the file as if its contents had been text-only. This conversion may mangle a file beyond all recognition. Figure 35.3 shows a five-slide presentation in PowerPoint, a format that Word resolutely refuses to acknowledge (professional jealousy, no doubt), and what Word pretends to think the document contains.

In cases like this, try saving the file in Word for Windows format in the source application and then opening it in Word. Failing that, you may have to resort to saving it as a .txt file in the source application and then opening it as a (true!) text-only file in Word. This way, you'll get your text ungarbled, but you'll lose all the formatting.

Part 5

Power Tools

Figure 35.3 *In the left corner, a five-slide PowerPoint presentation, and in the right corner, Word's brave attempt to translate it. If you look at Word's status bar, you'll see that it has converted the hapless file into 254 pages of gibberish—quite impressive for five PowerPoint slides.*

Saving the Converted Document

The file you converted is now stored in your computer's memory. To keep it as a Word for Windows document, you need to save it as a Word file. If you select File ➤ Save, Word will display the Save Format dialog box asking if you want to save the file in Word format or in its original format. Here's the Save Format dialog box you'll see if the file in question is a Word 2.x for Windows document:

Note the warning in the Save Format dialog box that you may lose some formatting if you don't save the file in Word format.

To save the file in Word format and thus avoid this message, choose File ➤ Save As, select Word Document in the Save as Type drop-down list, and (optionally) give the file a new name in the Save As dialog box.

NOTE The Save as Type box will automatically show the format of the original document.

Saving a Word Document in Another Format

What if you need to use a Word file in another application or in an earlier version of Word? Simply save the file in the other application's file format:

1. Select File ➤ Save As. The Save As dialog box appears.

2. Display the Save as Type list and choose the format you want. (There's quite a list to scroll through, and it's not in alphabetical order.)

3. Enter a new name for the file in the File Name box, and choose OK.

WARNING Don't count on a Word file's summary information (reached by selecting File ➤ Properties) being carried to any format except Word and Rich Text Format (RTF).

Saving Time by Converting Several Files at Once

To convert a whole bunch of documents at a time, either to or from Word format, run the BatchConverter macro located in Convert7.dot.

First make sure Convert7.dot is loaded as a global template:

1. Choose File ➤ Templates. The Templates and Add-ins dialog box will appear (see Figure 35.4).

2. If Convert7.dot is shown in the Global Templates and Add-ins box, go to step 5. If Convert7.dot isn't shown, click the Add button. The Add Template dialog box will appear (see Figure 35.5).

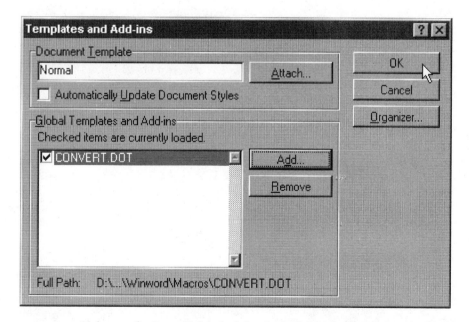

Figure 35.4 *Make sure the Convert7.dot check box is checked in the Templates and Add-ins dialog box.*

Part
5

Power Tools

Figure 35.5 *Select Convert7 from the Winword\Macros subfolder in the Add Template dialog box.*

3. In the Add Template dialog box, change the folder to Winword\Macros, select Convert7, and click the OK button. Convert7.dot will appear in the Global Templates and Add-ins box.

4. Make sure the Convert7.dot check box is checked (see Figure 35.4), and then click OK to close the Templates and Add-ins dialog box.

Now run the BatchConverter macro in Convert7.dot:

1. Select Tools ➤ Macro, choose BatchConverter from the list of macro names, and click the Run button.

2. In the Batch File Converter dialog box that appears (see Figure 35.6), choose "From another format to Word for Windows" or "To another format from Word for Windows"; then click the Next> button.

3. In the next Batch File Converter dialog box that appears, choose the format in the Convert From box and click the Next> button.

4. Choose the drive and folder where the files to convert are located, and then click the Next> button.

5. Choose the drive and folder in which to place the converted files, and then click the (you guessed it) Next> button.

Figure 35.6 *Select the type of conversion you want in the Batch File Converter dialog box and hit the Next> button.*

6. Choose the files to be converted by double-clicking them one at a time or by choosing the Select All button to convert all.

TIP **To remove a file, double-click it in the Files to Convert List box.**

7. Click the Next> button. The Batch File Converter will convert your files and display a message of congratulations when it's done.

8. Click the Next> button to repeat the conversion with more files or click Finish to close the Converter. (Click Cancel if you didn't convert anything.)

Exchanging Information with Applications for which Word Has No Converter

If you need to use a Word file in an application for which Word has no converters, save the file as a plain-text file:

1. Select File ➤ Save As. The Save As dialog box will appear.

2. Pull down the Save as Type list and choose one of the text formats:

   • You'll get very similar effects with the two *text* (Text Only and MS-DOS Text) and the two *text with line breaks* options unless you're

Part
5

Power Tools

doing something very sophisticated: Your text will be saved without formatting, and all line-break characters, section breaks, and page breaks will be converted to paragraph marks.

• Rich Text Format saves all formatting, converting formatting to text instructions that other applications can read. You'll know if you want to use RTF.

3. Give your file a different name. Word will add the appropriate extension (.TXT or whatever).

4. Open the file in the other application and work on it there.

> **NOTE**   Many companies offer third-party conversion programs. For example, check out Design Software's Word for Word.

Customizing Word's Conversions

If you don't always get the results you want when you convert a document created in another application into a Word file, you can customize Word's conversions to improve compatibility with the other application. For example, differences in fonts or printer drivers in the other application might cause lines and pages to break in unsuitable places.

To customize Word's conversions, run the EditConversionsOptions macro in Convert.dot:

1. First, make sure Convert.dot is loaded and active. (See the section *Saving Time by Converting Several Files at Once* earlier in this chapter for details on how to do this.)

2. Select Tools ➤ Macro. The Macro dialog box will appear.

3. Select the EditConversionsOptions macro and click the Run button. The Edit Conversions Options dialog box will appear, as shown in Figure 35.7.

4. Pull down the Conversion list and select the conversion you want—in the figure, I've selected Word for MS-DOS 3.0–6.0, which has a decent list of conversion options.

Figure 35.7 **Select the conversion you want and highlight the conversion option in the Edit Conversions Options dialog box (watch the area at the bottom of the dialog box for information on options).**

5. In the list of conversion options, highlight the one you're interested in (scroll if necessary). The area at the bottom of the dialog box will display information on that option.

6. Select Yes or No for each option you're interested in (or enter a setting in the Setting box and then click Set), then click OK to carry out your changes.

Part
5

Power Tools

Improving Word's Compatibility with Other Applications

Word includes many options for improving its compatibility with the following word processors: WordPerfect, Word for Windows 1.0 and 2.0, Word for the Macintosh 5.*x*, and Word for MS-DOS. There's also a Custom choice for working with other word processors.

> **NOTE** Microsoft claims that Word 95 saves files in Word 6 format, so theoretically, there shouldn't be any difference between Word 6 and Word 95 files, and the latter should run just fine with Word 6. But what about formatting attributes such as highlighting, which didn't exist in Word 6? Even Dan Quayle (remember him?) could figure out what happens to such cases. Watch this space for further details.

Word saves compatibility options with the document when you convert it. You can turn these compatibility options on or off at any time. These options affect only how the document behaves while you work with it in Word; it will still behave the same way in the other word processor if you convert it back to its original format.

To turn the compatibility options on or off:

1. Select Tools ➤ Options. The Options dialog box will appear.

2. Click the Compatibility tab to bring the compatibility options to the front (see Figure 35.8).

3. Drop down the Recommended Options For list and choose the file format you want.

4. In the Options box, check or uncheck boxes to turn the options on or off.

5. To use the compatibility options you're now setting for all new documents you create using Word, choose the Default button. Word will ask whether this is really what you want to do:

Figure 35.8   *The Options dialog box with the Compatibility tab foremost.*

6.   Click Yes if it is what you want; click No if it isn't.

7.   If the document contains any fonts that aren't available on your computer, Word will substitute some default font that may not be what you want. To apply a different substitute font, click the Font Substitution button in the Options dialog box. In the resulting Font Substitution dialog box, the Missing Document Font box lists the fonts that could not be matched. Choose a font whose substitution you want to change and then drop down the Substituted Font list and choose a suitable font. To convert fonts permanently, hit the Convert Permanently button and choose Yes in the confirmation dialog box. When you're finished assigning substitute fonts, choose OK.

8.   Click OK to accept your choices and close the Options dialog box.

Make Sure You've Got the Right Filters Installed

As discussed earlier in this chapter, Word uses programs called converters or filters to convert documents from one file format (for example, WordPerfect, Works) to another (for example, Word itself). The converters available to you depend on which ones you installed on your computer when you installed Word.

If you chose a Complete installation of Word, all its converters and graphics filters should be available to you. But if you chose a Laptop installation, a Typical installation, or a Custom installation, you may not have all the filters you need.

To install the filters, run the Microsoft Word Setup program again by choosing Word Setup from the Start submenu. If you can't find this command, select <u>R</u>un from the Start menu, browse to find Setup.exe (usually in Winword\Setup), and follow the instructions to install converters and filters. Bear in mind that each converter or filter you install takes up extra space on your hard drive, so if you're pressed for space, you may want to select only the converters and filters you know you'll need. You can install other converters and filters by running Setup again at any point.

TIP　If you're having a hard time finding Setup.exe on your hard disk, try using the Find command on the Start menu.

Chapter 36

Personalizing Word

FAST TRACK

This chapter discusses how to customize Word. You'll learn how to change Word's standard menu settings, toolbars, and keyboard shortcuts. You'll learn how to add, delete, and rename menus. While reading this chapter, you might also want to refer to Appendix B, which contains a complete list of each Word command, a description of its function, some tips on use, and associated keyboard shortcuts.

A Caution

Imagine living in a community where everyone made their own laws. One driver could decide that red traffic lights mean go and green lights mean speed (I know, some do this already). Your neighbor could decide to build a toxic-waste dump in his or her backyard (yes, likewise). Similarly, changing Word's look, feel, and functions carries risks and responsibilities.

Adding a couple of extra commands like PrevWindow and NextWindow (which take you to the previous window and next window, respectively, without your having to specify which number window you'd like) to the File or View menu won't usually harm anyone. Deleting menu items that you never use might also seem reasonable—if you never use tables, you could get rid of most of the Table menu and put something more useful in its place. But what if you substitute a tricky command like ExitWindows, which closes Word *without even giving you a chance to save changes* and then quits Windows, for File ➤ Exit? You could even give it the same hot key. Anybody who didn't know your machine wouldn't stand a chance and would probably lose unsaved work when they tried to exit Word.

Moving things from menu to menu or from toolbar to toolbar (or from menu to toolbar to key combination—here's that flexibility we were talking about) may make life easier and more logical for you, but it may make life difficult for others who need to use your machine. Imagine being a temporary worker trying to figure out a completely reorganized set of Word menus, or even a copy of Word with no visible menus and most of the screen obscured by toolbars that are not easy to remove (the menus have gone, remember). The training of new hires can be slowed by undocumented, department-wide changes to menus as well.

If you work in a large organization, your systems manager may have strong feelings about your changing Word's menus, toolbars, and shortcuts. Check first. With that out of the way, let's look at ways to personalize Word.

> **NOTE**   What? Before we get on, you want to know what that ExitWindows command is for? When I asked that same question, I was told, "Don't ask." Perhaps if you were racing to the DOS prompt. Just watch out for someone putting an AutoExec macro (see Chapter 34 for more details) containing the command ExitWindows in your copy of Word!

Default Settings

Word's original settings are referred to as the *defaults*. Microsoft's designers have chosen settings they feel will work for the majority of people doing general typing and correspondence. For instance, they assume you will use standard letter-size ($8\frac{1}{2}'' \times 11''$) paper and have specified right, left, bottom, and top margins that should accommodate most binding, header, and footer needs. They have turned on popular Word features and turned off more esoteric ones that annoy some people. They have organized the menus for you and held back many potential menu choices.

Many of these defaults will not suit you perfectly. For instance, you probably won't want to type all your documents in Times New Roman 10 point, as Word's designers apparently would have you do. Maybe you want to use legal-size paper or print out all your documents on postcards. This is all quite natural and perfectly harmless. But rather than having to change one particular feature the same way every time you start a document, you'll probably want to change Word's default settings and save yourself time and temper.

Understanding and Changing Word's Options

Word gives you a great deal of control over its various features. For example, you can dictate default view settings, menu appearance, default font settings, and much more. Many of these choices are made using the <u>T</u>ools ➤ <u>O</u>ptions command and the tabs in the Options dialog box. These choices apply to all your Word templates.

Choices made using the <u>T</u>ools ➤ <u>C</u>ustomize command and the tabs in the Customize dialog box are template-specific—they apply only to the template in which you arrange them. This means you could have Normal.dot and all documents based on it display the default Word menus, toolbars, and so on, but have your Clever Me and Special for You templates and their documents display customized menus and toolbars. This way, both you and your default temp can be happy.

> **TIP** For some of Word's default settings, you don't use the Options or Customize dialog boxes. To change the default font, for example, you would visit the Format ➤ Fonts dialog box, change your settings, and then click the Defaults button. Similarly, the File ➤ Page Setup dialog box has a Defaults button for its settings.

View

The View tab (see Figure 36.1) lets you control what you see by default in your document. For instance, if you want to see hidden text, check the Hidden Text check box. If you want a 3″ style area, here's where you set it up. The following sections discuss these different options in more detail.

These are the default settings for the options on the View tab:

Feature	Default Setting
Show	
Draft Font	Off
Wrap to Window	Off
Picture Placeholders	Off
Highlight	On
Field Codes	Off
Bookmarks	Off
Field Shading	When Selected
Window	
Status Bar	On
Horizontal Scroll Bar	On

Figure 36.1   *You decide what you want to see in your documents in the View tab of the Options dialog box. I've decided to hide the horizontal scroll bar and display hidden text.*

Feature	Default Setting
Vertical Scroll Bar	On
Style Area Width	0"
Nonprinting Characters	
Tab Characters	Off
Spaces	Off
Paragraph Marks	Off
Optional Hyphens	Off
Hidden Text	Off
All	Off

Draft Font

The Draft Font choice is for Outline and Normal views and determines whether Word displays your prose in the fonts you've chosen or in its draft font. The draft font is the font used in menus, the message boxes saying that your system is about to crash, and so on. It's faster to use than your fancy fonts; it's also uglier. Use this option when you're hacking the text in large documents on a small-brained computer and you're not worried about how things look on-screen.

Draft font displays any character formatting as underlined and bold. All for speed.

NOTE   When you're in Page Layout view, you'll get three different options: Draft Font will change to Drawings. Again, this speeds up scrolling the document. You'll also get an Object Anchors option, which displays the anchor connecting an anchored object to a paragraph as a little anchor symbol. Text Boundaries displays dotted lines around page margins, text columns, objects, and formats.

Wrap to Window

Wrap to Window wraps the text from one line to the next within the document window. Use this when you need to work with several windows visible on your desktop at the same time and you don't want your text to be wider than the window.

Picture Placeholders

On slower PCs, Word can slow to a crawl if your document contains large graphics. To speed up work in such documents, mark the Picture Placeholders check box to display graphics as empty boxes.

Highlight

It's a good idea to leave this on as it allows you to highlight text on-screen (and on printouts, if you have a color printer). Unchecking this box might speed up slower machines.

Field Codes

You'll probably want to view field codes rather than field results when you're inserting and editing fields. Simply check the check box. As you learned in Chapter 32, fields look like this:

```
{ EDITTIME \* MERGEFORMAT }
```

Bookmarks

Check the Bookmarks check box to display the bookmarks and links your document contains. Bookmarks appear in square gray brackets.

Field Shading

When you're working with a document that contains fields, you can choose to have their results shaded so you can avoid changing them by mistake—remember, the results may look like regular text. Choose from When Selected (when the insertion point is in the field), Always, and Never.

Status Bar

If you find the information on the status bar confusing, or if you simply need more space on your screen for displaying your immortal words in huge point sizes, uncheck this box to remove the status bar.

Horizontal Scroll Bar

If you never use the horizontal scroll bar—and why should you, if your documents fit in the width of the screen and you don't need the three buttons to flip between views—you can remove it by unchecking the check box. That'll give you a little more space on the screen.

Vertical Scroll Bar

If you always use the keyboard for moving through your documents, you may want to remove the vertical scroll bar from your screen to give yourself a bit more space. Simply uncheck the box, and it'll be gone.

Style Area Width

You'll recall that the style area is the area to the left of the text that shows the applied style names. By default, the style area width is 0″, so you don't see it. To display it, enter a positive decimal measurement, such as 0.5″ (which should be enough for most of the predefined style names; if you define styles with long names, enter a larger measurement). To rid the display of the style area, enter 0 (that's an actual zero, not a capital O).

Tab Characters

Check the Tab Characters check box to display tabs as right-pointing arrows. You may want to do this if you're aligning things and can't be bothered to use tables, or if you handle a lot of documents formatted by less skillful Word users and want to distinguish tabs from first-line indents. Tabs are also displayed or hidden by the Show/Hide ¶ toolbar button.

Spaces

Check the Spaces check box to display spaces entered with the spacebar as dots about halfway up the height of the line. This helps you find double or triple spaces in proportional fonts. Spaces are also displayed or hidden by the Show/Hide ¶ toolbar button.

Paragraph Marks

Check the Paragraph Marks check box to display hard returns entered with ↵ as ¶. This can be especially useful when you're editing a document that uses styles and deleting the wrong paragraph mark inadvertently will apply the wrong style to your text. Paragraph marks are also displayed or hidden by the Show/Hide ¶ toolbar button.

Optional Hyphens

Optional hyphens—the ones you insert to indicate where to break a word if it falls at the end of a line—are normally not displayed. To display them, check the Optional Hyphens check box.

Hidden Text

To view hidden text, check the Hidden Text check box. It will appear as text with a dotted underline. Bear in mind that while viewing hidden text will change the line breaks and pagination of your document, hidden text will not print unless you've selected Tools ➤ Options ➤ Print tab ➤ Hidden Text.

All

Check this check box to display all the nonprinting characters—tabs, spaces, paragraph marks, optional hyphens, and hidden text. You can still toggle them off with the Show/Hide ¶ button, but this *unchecks* All. A little confusing until you think of them as two different ways to do the same thing.

> **TIP** If you don't always want nonprinting characters displayed but like to know what's there every now and then, you can get the same effect more easily by clicking the Show/Hide ¶ button on the Standard toolbar.

General Options

The options on the General tab (see Figure 36.2) modify Word settings such as the default units of measurement and the display of three-dimensional effects. You can also choose how many of your last-opened

Options ☐ ? ☐ ✕

Save	Spelling	Grammar	AutoFormat
Revisions	User Info	Compatibility	File Locations
View	General	Edit	Print

General Options

- ☑ Background Repagination
- ☐ Help for WordPerfect Users
- ☐ Navigation Keys for WordPerfect Users
- ☐ Blue Background, White Text
- ☑ Beep on Error Actions
- ☐ Confirm Conversion at Open
- ☑ Update Automatic Links at Open
- ☑ Mail as Attachment
- ☑ Recently Used File List: `9` Entries
- ☑ TipWizard Active

Measurement Units: `Inches`

[OK] [Close]

Part 5

Power Tools

Figure 36.2 *You decide how many of your last-opened files Word tacks onto the bottom of the File menu in the General tab of the Options dialog box. I've gone for the max—nine.*

files Word tacks onto the bottom of the File menu, whether Word repaginates your document in the background as you work, and whether Word beeps at you when you screw up. This is a good tab to mess around with.

In the following sections we'll look briefly at each of the settings on the General tab. But first, here's a quick summary of the default settings:

Feature	Default Setting
Background Repagination	On
Help for WordPerfect Users	(User prompt at installation)
Navigation Keys for WordPerfect Users	Off
Blue Background, White Text	Off
Beep on Error Actions	On
Confirm Conversion at Open	Off
Update Automatic Links at Open	On
Mail as Attachment	On
Recently Used File List	On; 4 Entries
TipWizard Active	On
Measurement Unit	Inches

Background Repagination

With the Background Repagination check box checked, as it is by default, Word automatically repaginates your documents as you work, computing new lines and page endings whenever you are not typing. There's not much wrong with that except it takes a bit of your computer's memory, so unless you're running an immensely complex project on a very slow computer or you're typing like an infinite number of monkeys, I suggest you leave this checked. If you uncheck the box, Word will not repaginate until you turn it back on or print. (Background repagination is always on in Page Layout view and Print Preview. Think about it.)

Help for WordPerfect Users

The Help for WordPerfect Users check box will be selected if you agreed to have it active when you installed Word. With this option selected, Word displays information or demonstrates a command when you press a WordPerfect for DOS key combination in Word. This disables many of Word's own key combinations, so you'll have to make up your mind about which to use.

Navigation Keys for WordPerfect Users

Check the Navigation Keys for WordPerfect Users check box to change the functions of the Page Up, Page Down, Home, End, and Esc keys to their WordPerfect equivalents. Bear in mind that this disables those keys' regular functions for Word.

Blue Background, White Text

I guess this is a techno-nerdy takeoff on that book *Blue Water, White Death*, but this command has nothing to do with sharks. Check the check box to display the text as white characters on a blue background. Don't ask how this is supposed to help you.

Beep on Error Actions

Here's a good one. When the Beep on Error Actions check box is checked, as it is by default, Word will give you a subtle auditory admonition whenever you screw up. If this bugs you, uncheck the check box to get the sounds of silence. It's cheaper than bashing in your monitor with a brickbat.

Confirm Conversion at Open

 With this option enabled, Word will always bring up the Convert File dialog box when you try to open a non-Word document. This can be handy if you want to specify exactly how Word should convert the file and you suspect it is going to botch the job.

Update Automatic Links at Open

The Update Automatic Links at Open check box is one you might seriously consider unchecking. When it's checked, any information in a document that's linked to other files is updated every time you open the document. If you're linked to something fancy, like a drawing-application figure or six, you'll be subjected to a few minutes of your hard disk grinding before you can use the document. Then again, keeping it checked will keep your documents up-to-date. Forcibly.

Mail as Attachment

Check the Mail as Attachment check box to attach documents to a mail message. You need to have an e-mail program installed on your computer to use this option.

Recently Used File List

The Recently Used File List box controls the number of your last-used files that appear at the bottom of the File menu. Choose between 0 and 9. Most people find this feature useful, but some consider it a threat to security. (The boss can find out about all those love letters you were writing while ostensibly working on your report.) You decide. If you add any commands to the File menu and choose 9 for this list, the menu may not fit on your screen. Life's tough.

TipWizard Active

This option keeps the TipWizard in memory. If you turn this off, you will not retain the "paper trail" TipWizard keeps of its advice, meaning that when you turn it on, you will see tips only for the current command.

Measurement Units

Pull down the Measurement Units list and choose Inches, Centimeters, Points, or Picas as the default measurement unit for Word. You may want to choose Points or Picas if you're typesetting things.

Edit Options

The Edit tab (see Figure 36.3) is where you control a whole bunch of important options that affect the way you work. This is where you control whether what you type will replace a selection or bump it along, how Word handles drag-and-drop editing, and whether Word worries about extra spaces when you use cut and paste.

Figure 36.3 **The Edit tab of the Options dialog box.**

In the following sections, we'll look at each of the options on the Edit tab. But first, here are their default settings:

Feature	Default Setting
Typing Replaces Selection	On
Drag-and-Drop Text Editing	On
Automatic Word Selection	On
Use the INS Key for Paste	Off
Overtype Mode	Off
Use Smart Cut and Paste	On
Allow Accented Uppercase	Off
Picture Editor	Microsoft Word

Part
5

Power Tools

Typing Replaces Selection

With the Typing Replaces Selection check box checked, any text you've selected gets deleted as soon as you start typing. This saves you the step of deleting a selection when you want to replace it, but if your mind doesn't work that way and you find this option awkward, uncheck the check box. Then selected text will be bumped along to the right when you type something.

Drag-and-Drop Text Editing

Drag-and-drop, as you'll recall from Chapter 2, lets you move or copy selected text without pasting it to the Clipboard. If you never use it, turn it off by unchecking the Drag-and-Drop Text Editing check box.

Automatic Word Selection

When the Automatic Word Selection check box is checked, Word selects the entire word (*including any trailing space at the end*) when you select any part of it by dragging the mouse pointer from the previous word. If this bugs you (it does me), uncheck the check box.

Use the Ins Key for Paste

Check the Use the INS Key for Paste check box if you get tired of pressing Shift+Ins to insert the contents of the Clipboard into your document. Needless to say, this stops you from using the Ins key to toggle between Insert and Overtype modes.

Overtype Mode

Check the Overtype Mode check box to have Overtype mode turned on by default when you use Word for Windows. Few people want this.

Use Smart Cut and Paste

Check the Use Smart Cut and Paste check box to have Word automatically remove extra spaces when you delete text or add spaces when you insert text. This isn't one hundred percent perfect, but it's pretty cool.

Allow Accented Uppercase

Check the Allow Accented Uppercase check box if you're working with text formatted as French and you want to allow the spelling and grammar checkers to suggest that Word add an accent mark to an uppercase letter. If you're not working in French, leave this check box unchecked, as it is by default.

Picture Editor

Select the application you want to use as a picture editor from the drop-down list. Your choices will depend on what's loaded on your machine.

Printing Options

The Print tab (see Figure 36.4) allows you to make some vital settings, so listen up for a minute. You can decide to print backwards (à la Merlin), you can make sure fields and links get updated before you print, and you can print stuff like annotations and hidden text with your document.

Figure 36.4   The Print tab of the Options dialog box.

In the following sections we'll look at each option in turn. Before that, let's take a quick glance at their default settings:

Feature	Default Setting
Printing Options	
Draft Output	Off
Reverse Print Order	Off
Update Fields	Off
Update Links	Off
Background Printing	On
Include with Document	
Summary Info	Off
Field Codes	Off
Annotations	Off
Hidden Text	Off
Drawing Objects	On
Options for Current Document Only	
Print Data Only for Forms	Off
Default Tray	From Print Manager

NOTE   What options you have will depend upon your printer.

Draft Output

Check the Draft Output check box to print your documents with minimal formatting. The amount of formatting that will be printed depends on the printer. As its name implies, this option is intended for fast printing of drafts of documents.

Reverse Print Order

Check the Reverse Print Order check box to print your documents starting at the last page. You might want to use this if you've got one of those weird copiers that reverses the order of collated copies. Don't use it when printing envelopes.

Update Fields

Make sure the Update Fields check box is checked if you want all fields in your document (for example, date fields and page numbers) to be updated whenever you print. If you're aiming for special effects, uncheck this check box.

Update Links

Check the Update Links check box to have all links in your document updated every time you print. If the sources for your links are apt to change or be unavailable, leave this check box unchecked.

Background Printing

Check the Background Printing check box if you want to be able to continue working in Word while you print a document. Bear in mind that background printing takes up memory and is liable to slow down both your work and your printing, thus vexing you mightily. I'd recommend unchecking this check box.

Summary Info

Check the Summary Info check box to have Word print file-summary information on a separate page after printing the document.

Field Codes

Check the Field Codes check box to have Word print the field codes rather than the field results in the document.

Annotations

Check the Annotations check box to have Word print out a document's annotations on a separate page at the end of the document.

Hidden Text

Check the Hidden Text check box to have Word print out any hidden text the document contains. Hidden text will look like normal text when printed; Word doesn't print the dotted underline you see for hidden text on the screen. Bear in mind that printing hidden text will affect line and page breaks in your document; if that matters to you, view hidden text on-screen before printing it and do any necessary fiddling with line and page breaks.

Drawing Objects

Check the Drawing Objects check box to have Word print drawing objects (for example, charts, graphics, and equations) created in Word with the document.

Print Data Only on Forms

Check the Print Data Only on Forms check box to print only the information entered in form fields in a form—not the form itself. You might want to use this for filling in preprinted forms. Note that this option applies only to the current document, not to all documents.

Default Tray

Choose a default paper tray from the drop-down list. The default setting is From Print Manager, as that's where you'll probably set printing options for all your Windows applications. If you want to use different paper sources for different sections of documents (for example, if you're printing an envelope and a letter), use File ➤ Page Setup.

Options for Revision Marks

Word lets different reviewers on the same document use different-colored revision marks. Choose Tools ➤ Options and select the Revisions tab of the Options dialog box (see Figure 36.5) to specify the revision options you want.

In the following sections we'll discuss each option in turn, but here are the default settings for the Revisions tab:

Feature	Default Setting
Inserted Text	
Mark	Underline
Color	By Author
Deleted Text	
Mark	Strikethrough
Color	By Author

Figure 36.5   *The Revisions tab of the Options dialog box.*

Feature	Default Setting
Revised Lines	
Mark	Outside Border
Color	Auto
Highlight Color	Yellow

Inserted Text

Drop down the list for the Mark option and select the format with which you want to mark new text. Choose from none, Bold, Italic, Underline, and Double Underline.

Color for Inserted Text

Drop down the list for the Color for New Text option and select the color with which you want to mark new text. Choose By Author for automatic choice of colors by Word for the first eight people to revise the document (after that, Word starts over with the colors), or choose one of the colors manually.

Mark Deleted Text

Use the Mark drop-down list to select how you want to display text you are deleting from the document. Choose Hidden or Strikethrough.

Color for Deleted Text

Drop down the Color list and select the color with which you want to mark deleted text. Choose By Author for automatic choice of colors by Word for the first eight people to revise the document (after that, Word starts over with the colors), or choose one of the colors manually.

Mark Revised Lines

Drop down the Mark list and select how to mark revised lines. Choose from None, Left Border, Right Border, or Outside Border (the default).

Color for Revised Lines

Drop down the list and select the color with which to mark revised lines. Choose By Author for automatic choice of colors by Word for the first eight people to revise the document (after that, Word starts over with the colors), or choose one of the colors manually. Consider using a different color for each group of authors when working on large projects with more than eight authors.

Highlight Color

You can specify the default color for Word's new Highlight feature. This behaves much like a regular hand highlighter pen, and as such you have a choice of eight colors: black, blue, cyan, green, magenta, red, yellow, and white. The latter, I can only surmise, is for those times you've enabled Blue Background, White Text in the View tab. You can also set it to No Highlight, which removes any highlighting.

User Info

The User Info tab (see Figure 36.6) specifies information about the primary user of the copy of Word for Windows you are using: the

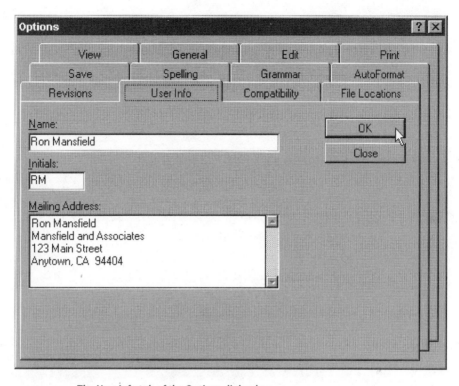

Figure 36.6 **The User Info tab of the Options dialog box.**

name, the return address for envelopes, and the initials to be used for annotations.

For a little change of pace, the User Info tab doesn't have default options worth listing. It takes its information from what you entered when installing Word.

Name

Type the name for Word to use as the author in the Summary tab of the Properties dialog box (File ➤ Properties) for documents you create. The default setting is the name entered when installing.

Initials

Enter the initials you want Word to use for annotation marks. The default setting is the initials entered for the name when installing Word.

Part
5

Power Tools

Mailing Address

The Mailing Address area displays the return address used on envelopes once you've used the Create Envelope command. Until then, the default setting is the address entered when installing Word. Any address you enter here will be displayed as the return address in the Envelopes and Labels dialog box.

Compatibility Options

The options on the Compatibility tab determine how Word displays documents created either in earlier versions of Word or in other word processing programs. Use these settings to make such documents in Word more closely match their originals.

Figure 36.7 shows the Compatibility tab of the Options dialog box.

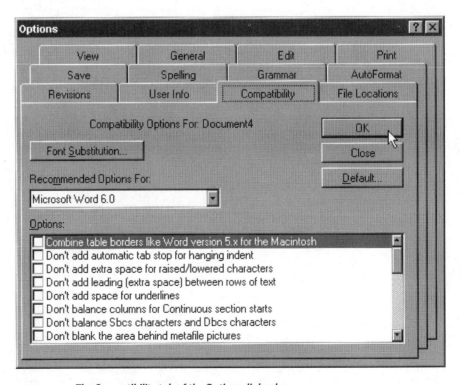

Figure 36.7   **The Compatibility tab of the Options dialog box.**

Font Substitution

If the active document has fonts that are not available on your computer, select the Font Substitution button to choose substitute fonts.

Recommended Options For

Pull down the Recommended Options For drop-down list and select the word-processing application for which to set options. Select Custom to specify options for an unlisted application. In the list of Options, check the options you want to use.

File Locations

The File Locations tab (see Figure 36.8) of the Options dialog box lets you define where your documents, templates, and other items are stored by default.

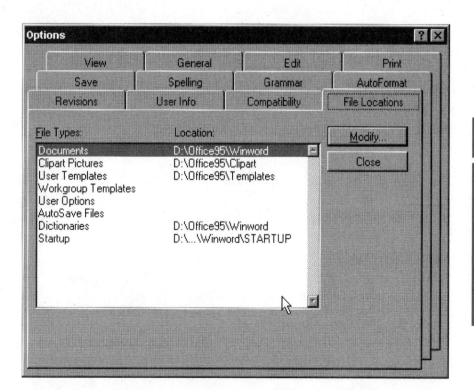

Part
5

Power Tools

Figure 36.8 *You can define where your documents, templates, and other items are stored by default in the File Locations tab of the Options dialog box.*

As you can see, I'm actually running Word in Microsoft Office, meaning that all my files are nested down one level farther (in the Office95 folder) than they would be otherwise. Here are the default settings for options on the File Locations tab if you are running Word by itself:

File Type	Default Location
Documents	C:\WINWORD
Clipart Pictures	C:\WINWORD\CLIPART
User Templates	C:\WINWORD\TEMPLATE
Workgroup Templates	(Depends on workgroup selections)
User Options	C:\WINWORD
AutoSave Files	(Depends on system settings)
Dictionaries	C:\WINWORD
Startup	C:\WINWORD\STARTUP

To set a new default location for an item, select the item and choose the Modify button. In the Modify Location dialog box, select the drive and folder for the item, and then click OK. You can create a new subfolder by clicking the Create New Folder button.

TIP Define a new default location for documents to keep them apart from your Word program files.

Save Options

The settings on the Save tab in the Options dialog box (see Figure 36.9) let you customize how and when you save your documents and choose protection for file sharing for the current document. (See Chapter 7 for more about saving.)

In the following sections we'll look at each of the options. But first, here's a sneak preview of their settings:

Feature	Default
Save Options	
Always Create Backup Copy	Off
Allow Fast Saves	On

Figure 36.9   You can decide how and when you save your documents in the Save tab of the Options dialog box. I've chosen to always create a backup copy and not use the fast save option.

Feature	Default
Prompt for Document Properties	Off
Prompt to Save Normal Template	Off
Save Native Picture Formats Only	Off
Embed TrueType Fonts	Off
Save Data Only for Forms	Off
Automatic Save Every:	On; 10 Minutes
File Sharing Options	
Protection Password	Off
Write Reservation Password	Off
Read-Only Recommended	Off

Always Create Backup Copy

Check the Always Create Backup Copy check box to have Word make automatic backups for you. Each time you save a document, Word saves a duplicate with a .BAK extension. This is a useful option if you tend to bastardize your documents by mistake, but bear in mind that it doubles your disk-space requirements, and takes a little more housekeeping attention.

Allow Fast Saves

Check the Allow Fast Saves check box to speed up saving. Word then records only the changes to the document when you save it (rather than resaving the whole file).

> **NOTE** Fast saves take up more space than regular saves. This option can also cause problems for some third-party conversion programs. If you're strapped for space, consider switching off fast saves.

Prompt for Document Properties

Back in the days of the horse and buggy, this used to be called the Prompt for Summary Info option. Now, in the sleek, shiny, metallic present, the summary information that used to occupy its own dialog box is found as a tab in the highly informative but mostly pedestrian Properties dialog box. Check the box to have Word display said Properties dialog box automatically whenever you save a new document. If you use the Summary tab to set up headers or footers in your document, you'll probably want to enable this option.

Prompt to Save Normal Template

Meet the new option, same as the old option. Yes, this one's just been renamed. Check the Prompt to Save Normal Template check box if you want Word to consult you when you exit before saving changes you made to the default settings in your Word session. This box is unchecked by default, so Word automatically saves changes to Normal when you exit.

Save Native Picture Formats Only

Check the Save Native Picture Formats Only check box if you want to save only the Windows version of imported graphics. If you bring graphics into Word from another platform (for example, from the Macintosh), you can reduce the size of the Word document by storing only the version of the graphics that is native to Word.

Embed TrueType Fonts

Check the Embed TrueType Fonts check box if you want others who read the document on PCs that do not have the fonts used in it to be able to view it with the right fonts. If you're not sharing documents, leave this box unchecked, since it's a real hard drive space hog.

Save Data Only for Forms

Check the Save Data Only for Forms check box to save the data in a form as a record you can use in a database. To save the data with the form, leave this box unchecked.

Automatic Save Every nn Minutes

Check the Automatic Save Every *nn* Minutes check box to have Word provide a safety net for you in the event of a power failure or computer crash. When you restart Word after a power failure or a crash, Word will open all documents open at the time of the crash and display (Recovered) in the title.

Set the number of minutes between 1 and 120. While Word autosaves your document, you'll have to stop working for a few seconds.

Protection Password

Enter a password (up to 15 characters: letters, spaces, symbols, and numbers are all okay) in the Protection Password text box to prevent other users from opening the current document.

Write Reservation Password

Enter a password (up to 15 characters: letters, spaces, symbols, and numbers all okay) in the Write Reservation Password text box to prevent other users from saving changes to the current document. Reenter the password in the confirmation dialog box. You'll then need to enter the password to open the document normally, but you can open the document as read-only by choosing the Read-Only button in the Password dialog box.

Part
5

Power Tools

Read-Only Recommended

Check the Read-Only Recommended check box to recommend that others open the current document as read-only. (It's only a recommendation—they can disregard it.)

Spelling Options

The Spelling tab has been revamped. The settings on the Spelling tab in the Options dialog box let you control the behavior of Word's spelling checker (covered in Chapter 19). You can instruct the spelling checker to ignore certain words, use up to ten dictionaries, and use a specific language. Figure 36.10 shows the Spelling tab of the Options dialog box.

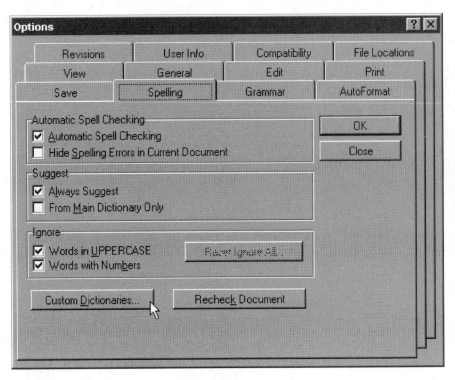

Figure 36.10   **The Spelling tab of the Options dialog box.**

In the following sections, we'll look at each of the options. But first, here's a preview of their default settings:

Feature	Default Setting
Automatic Spell Checking	
Automatic Spell Checking	On
Hide Spelling Errors in Current Document	Off
Suggest	
Always Suggest	On
From Main Dictionary Only	On
Ignore	
Words in UPPERCASE	Off
Words with Numbers	Off

Automatic Spell Checking

This option is enabled by default, and it instructs Word to do background spell checking. This can be a real boon, because Word flags all unfamiliar words with a squiggly red underline, pointing out potential spelling problems. Uncheck the box if you don't want to take advantage of Word's tireless efforts to make you look good.

Hide Spelling Errors in Current Document

On the other hand, automatic spell checking can be a pain in the neck if you've got a lot of technical information or perhaps computer code. Check this option to have Word restrain itself on the particular document you're working on. It is better to use this option than to uncheck the Automatic Spell Checking option if you want to effect the change just for your current document, because you might forget to turn auto-spelling back on...

Always Suggest

Check the Always Suggest check box to have Word display suggested spellings for misspelled words it finds during a spelling check.

From Main Dictionary Only

Check the From Main Dictionary Only check box to have Word display suggested correct spellings from the main dictionary but not from any open custom dictionaries.

Words in UPPERCASE

Check the Words in UPPERCASE check box to have Word's spelling checker ignore words in which every character is uppercase. This is useful for working with technical terms, abbreviations, and so on.

Words with Numbers

Check the Words with Numbers check box to have Word's spell checker ignore any word that contains a number. This too is useful for working with technical terms and the like.

Reset Ignore All

Click the Reset Ignore All button to stop Word from ignoring the words you marked with Ignore All during the current Word session. This button isn't available until you've told Word to ignore all instances of a word.

Custom Dictionaries

Click this button to bring up the Custom Dictionaries dialog box. Here is where you specify which dictionaries are to be loaded. Don't forget that dictionaries must be loaded in order for Word to use them in spell checks.

Recheck Document

Clicking this button instructs Word to recheck the spelling in your document.

Grammar

Here's where you get to choose which rules Word's grammar checker (covered in Chapter 19) uses when critiquing your documents. Figure 36.11 shows the Grammar tab of the Options dialog box.

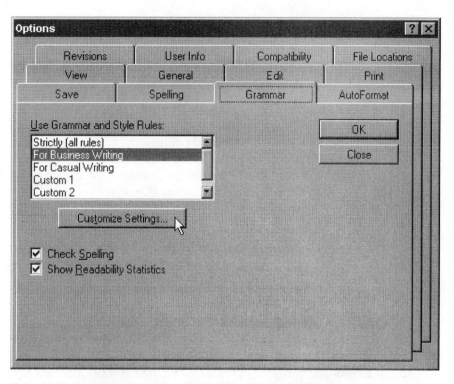

Figure 36.11 *Choose the rules you want Word to apply to your documents in the Grammar tab of the Options dialog box.*

Here are the default settings for the options on the Grammar tab:

Feature	Default Setting
Use Grammar and Style Rules	For Business Writing
Check Spelling	On
Show Readability Statistics	On

Use Grammar and Style Rules

Choose from Strictly (All Rules), For Business Writing, and For Casual Writing to define which rules Word uses when grammar-checking your documents. Choose Custom 1, Custom 2, or Custom 3 to set up your own rules without disturbing Word's preset offerings.

Customize Settings

Click the Customize Settings button to produce the Customize Grammar Settings dialog box, in which you can choose which rules to apply by default to your documents.

Check Spelling

Uncheck the Check Spelling check box (checked by default) if you don't want to check spelling in your documents while checking the grammar—for example, if you've been auto-spellchecking and don't want to have to click the Ignore button fifty times.

Show Readability Statistics

Uncheck the Show Readability Statistics check box (checked by default) if you don't want to see the Readability Statistics dialog box after each completed grammar check.

AutoFormat Options

This tab has changed quite a bit. The options on the AutoFormat tab (see Figure 36.12) let you set rules for Word to follow when it automatically formats text with the built-in styles (Chapter 14). For example, you can instruct Word to replace straight quotes with smart quotes.

Here are the default settings for the options on the AutoFormat tab:

Feature	Default Setting
Show Options For	
AutoFormat/AutoFormat As You Type	AutoFormat As You Type
Apply As You Type	
Headings	Off
Borders	On
Automatic Bulleted Lists	On
Automatic Numbered Lists	On

Figure 36.12   The AutoFormat tab of the Options dialog box.

Feature	Default Setting
Replace As You Type	
Straight Quotes with "Smart Quotes"	On
Ordinals (1st) with Superscript	On
Fractions (1/2) with Fraction Character ($^1/_2$)	On
Symbol Characters with Symbols	On

Show Options for AutoFormat/AutoFormat As You Type

 These radio buttons toggle between the AutoFormat and AutoFormat As You Type modes of the AutoFormat dialog box. The former sets general AutoFormatting settings, while the latter actually enforces them; in other words, you can get your settings just right and then toggle them on and off. If AutoFormat is selected, there will be an additional option—Styles—in an area called Preserve. Checking this prevents Word from changing the styles in your document; it is off by default.

Headings

Check the Headings check box if you want Word to automatically apply Heading 1 through Heading 9 styles to headings.

Borders

 Enabling this option instructs Word to do automatic bordering. This is really quite simple: if you type either three hyphens (-) in a row or three equal signs (=) and then hit ↵, Word will make a single or double border across the page.

Automatic Bulleted Lists

 Check the Automatic Bulleted Lists check box if you want Word to automatically apply list and bullet styles to bulleted lists. Bear in mind that Word will automatically remove any manually inserted bullets in the process.

Automatic Numbered Lists

 Check the Automatic Numbered Lists check box if you want Word to automatically apply list and number styles to numbered lists. Bear in mind that Word will automatically remove any manually inserted numbers in the process.

Straight Quotes with Smart Quotes

Check the Straight Quotes with Smart Quotes check box if you want Word to replace "" with "" and " with " when it formats your document.

Ordinals (1st) with Superscript

The automatic ordinals feature makes things like *1st* into things like 1st. Word does this lovely little bit of typesetting without your having to lift a finger or mess around with superscripting if you enable this option.

Fractions (1/2) with Fraction Character ($^1/_2$)

This feature takes fractions like 1/2 and turns them into genuine typeset fractions: $^1/_2$. Isn't that nice?

Symbol Characters with Symbols

Check the Symbol Characters with Symbols check box if you want Word to replace characters used in place of symbols with symbols—for example, (TM) with ™, (R) with ®, and (C) with ©.

Customizing Word's Toolbars

You can customize Word's toolbars to simplify the way you work. You can add and remove commands, macros, AutoText entries, and styles and move buttons from one toolbar to another. You can even create custom toolbars. You can move toolbars to different positions on the screen or have them float freely above the document. You can move and resize a floating toolbar as if it were a window. In the following sections we'll look at the different things you can do with toolbars.

Figure 36.13 shows how zany you can get with toolbars by illustrating the "text porthole" concept.

Displaying Toolbars

To display toolbars, select View ➤ Toolbars. In the Toolbars dialog box (see Figure 36.14), check the check boxes for the toolbars you want to see, and click OK.

NOTE You can't display the Mail Merge toolbar unless you're running a mail merge. (Select Tools ➤ Mail Merge to fire up the Mail Merge Helper.)

To remove a toolbar from the screen, select View ➤ Toolbars and uncheck the check box of the guilty party.

Part
5

Power Tools

Figure 36.13   *I've arranged my toolbars for easy access.*

Figure 36.14   *Check the check boxes for the toolbars you want to see in the Toolbars dialog box.*

TIP To display and remove toolbars using the mouse, right-click on a displayed toolbar to display a shortcut menu and click to display an unchecked toolbar or to hide a checked toolbar. Click Toolbars or Customize to display the Toolbars or Customize dialog box.

Moving and Resizing Toolbars

You can place toolbars anywhere on your screen and resize them to a number of shapes.

To move a toolbar displayed at the top of the screen, click in the blank space and drag it to where you want it. It'll change shape as soon as you drag it out of the toolbar area at the top of the screen. Alternatively, double-click in the blank space to display it in its last floating position on the screen.

To return a toolbar to the top of the screen, click in the blank space and drag it to the top of the screen, where it'll revert to its long and wide shape. Alternatively, double-click in the blank space to flip it back up there.

To resize a floating toolbar, move the mouse pointer over one of its borders so that a double-headed arrow appears, then click and drag the border to the shape you want. Toolbar shapes adjust in jumps, not smoothly, so that they're the right size and shape for their buttons.

Changing the Predefined Toolbars

If you want, you can change Word's predefined toolbars. You might want to remove buttons that you never use or change the command that an existing button runs. Here's how:

1. Display the toolbar you want to change.
2. Choose Tools ➤ Customize. The Customize dialog box will appear.
3. Select the Toolbars tab (see Figure 36.15).
4. To add a button, select the correct category in the Categories box, then drag the button or item to where you want it on the toolbar.
5. To delete a button, drag the button off the toolbar and drop it in the dialog box (or anywhere else where no toolbar is).
6. When you're done, click the Close button.

Part
5

Power Tools

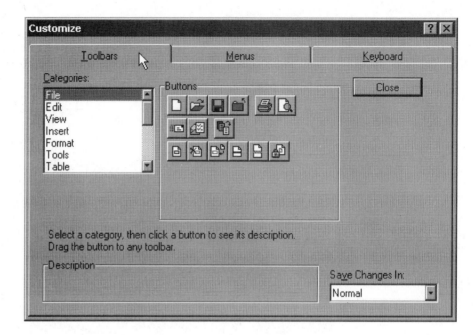

Figure 36.15   The Toolbars tab of the Customize dialog box.

 WARNING When you delete a built-in toolbar button, it'll still be available in the Customize dialog box. But when you delete a custom toolbar button, it's gone for good. Consider creating a storage toolbar for keeping unused buttons rather than deleting them permanently.

Moving or Copying a Toolbar Button

Here's how to move or copy buttons from one toolbar to another:

1. Select Tools ➤ Customize. The Customize dialog box will appear.

2. Select the Toolbars tab.

 TIP To move a toolbar button quickly, without opening the Customize dialog box, hold down Alt and drag the button to where you want it. To copy a button, hold down Ctrl+Alt and drag the button to where you want it.

3. To move a button, drag it to where you want it on the same toolbar or on another toolbar.

4. To copy a button, hold down Ctrl and drag the button to where you want it on the same toolbar or on another toolbar. Word will automatically close the gap left (when you move a button) and shift the buttons along in the new location. So if you want fifteen smiley FoxPro faces on your Microsoft toolbar, go right ahead.

5. Click the Close button.

> **NOTE** To add space before a button, go to the Toolbar tab in the Customize dialog box and drag a button a little way to its right. When you're done, close the dialog box. This is a good way to regroup buttons on custom toolbars as the ways you use those toolbars evolve.

Resetting a Built-In Toolbar

If you modify a built-in toolbar and then regret it, here's how to restore it to its original settings:

1. Select <u>V</u>iew ➤ <u>T</u>oolbars. The Toolbars dialog box will appear.

2. Highlight the toolbar you want to restore, and then click the Reset button.

3. In the Reset Toolbar dialog box (see Figure 36.16), select the template in which to make the change, and then choose OK.

4. Click OK to close the Toolbars dialog box.

Figure 36.16   *The Reset Toolbar dialog box.*

Part
5

Power Tools

Creating a Custom Toolbar

If you find yourself using buttons on half a dozen different toolbars in the course of the day's work, you may want to create a custom toolbar with only the buttons you need on it. Here's how:

1. Select View ➤ Toolbars. The Toolbars dialog box will appear.

2. Click the New button. The New Toolbar dialog box will appear:

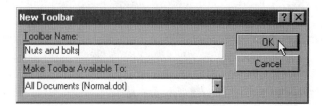

3. Type a name for the new toolbar in the Toolbar Name box.

4. Select the template in which to store the toolbar in the Make Toolbar Available To: box, and then click OK. Word will display the Customize dialog box with the Toolbars tab selected and a new toolbar without buttons in its own toolbar window.

5. In the Categories box, select the category containing the first button to add to the new toolbar.

6. Drag the appropriate button to the new toolbar (see Figure 36.17).

7. Add further buttons as appropriate.

8. When you finish building your new toolbar, click the Close button.

   Your new toolbar will appear in the Toolbars dialog box and in the shortcut menu produced by right-clicking a displayed toolbar.

Deleting a Custom Toolbar

When you get sick of your custom toolbars, you can easily delete them:

1. Select View ➤ Toolbars to display the Toolbars dialog box.

2. Highlight the custom toolbar you want to delete and click the Delete button.

3. Click Yes in the confirmation dialog box.

Figure 36.17   Dragging a button to the new toolbar.

NOTE   Word won't let you delete the toolbars it provides, only your custom toolbars.

Renaming a Custom Toolbar

You can rename a custom toolbar at any point:

1. Select File ➤ Templates. The Templates and Add-Ins dialog box will appear.

2. Click the Organizer button. The Organizer dialog box will appear.

3. Select the Toolbars tab (see Figure 36.18).

4. In the left or right box, highlight the toolbar to rename, then click the Rename button.

Part
5

Power Tools

Figure 36.18 Select the toolbar you want to rename in the Toolbars tab of the Organizer dialog box.

5. In the Rename dialog box (shown below), enter a new name and click OK.

6. Click Close to close the Organizer dialog box.

Copying a Toolbar from One Template to Another

If you create a toolbar in one template and you'd like to make it available in another, it's easy:

1. Select File ➤ Templates. The Templates and Add-Ins dialog box will appear.

2. Click the Organizer button. The Organizer dialog box will appear.

3. Select the Toolbars tab.

4. Click the Close File button on the left side of the Organizer dialog box. It turns into an Open File button.

5. Click the Open File button. An Open dialog box appears. Find and select the template you want to copy the toolbar *from*. Then click OK.

6. Click the Close File button on the right.

7. Click the Open File button that appears in its place. In the Open dialog box that appears, select the template you want to copy the toolbar *to* (see Figure 36.19).

8. Highlight the toolbar or toolbars to copy, then click the Copy >> button.

9. Click Close to close the Organizer dialog box.

The toolbar (or toolbars) you selected will be copied to the other template.

Figure 36.19 *The Toolbars tab of the Organizer dialog box, ready to copy toolbars from one open template to another.*

Part
5

Power Tools

Assigning an Item to a Toolbar Button

You can assign toolbar buttons to run commands, macros, fonts, AutoText entries, or styles. You can attach toolbars to specific templates, which gives you great flexibility.

To assign an item to a toolbar button:

1. Open a document based on the template containing the item you want to assign—or open the template itself. ·

2. Display the toolbar you want to change.

3. Select Tools ➤ Customize. The Customize dialog box will appear.

4. Choose the Toolbars tab (see Figure 36.20).

5. In the Save Changes In box, select the template containing the item you want to assign to the toolbar.

6. In the Categories box, select the category containing the command to add.

Figure 36.20   *The Toolbars tab of the Customize dialog box.*

7. Drag the item name from the box to the right of the Categories box to the toolbar.

> **NOTE** When you choose an item without a built-in button, you'll get a blank button on the toolbar, and Word will open the Custom Button dialog box. (See the section *Creating a Custom Button*, coming up in a moment.)

8. Select a button, then click the Assign button, and then click Close.

Creating a Custom Button

If you're assigning a toolbar button to an item for which Word does not have a built-in button image, step 7 of the *Assigning an Item* procedure above brings you to the Custom Button dialog box. At this point you have three options:

▶ Use the Clipboard to paste in an image from a graphics application.

▶ Visit the Button Editor dialog box and modify an existing button to suit your needs.

▶ In the Custom Button dialog box, create a text label for the button.

Pasting a Button Image from a Graphics Application

If you've got a good graphics program, you can have some fun creating your own image; then paste it onto a button via the Clipboard:

1. In the Custom Button dialog box, click Cancel to return to the Toolbars tab of the Customize dialog box.

2. Switch to your graphics application. Create the image and copy it to the Clipboard, preferably in bitmap or picture format.

3. Switch back to Word, where your target toolbar should still be displayed, along with the Toolbars tab.

4. Right-click the blank toolbar button that will receive the image.

5. Choose Paste Button Image from the shortcut menu.

6. Click the Close button.

Part
5

Power Tools

Creating or Modifying a Button Image in the Button Editor

If you don't have a graphics program, you can use the Button Editor to create or modify a button image for the item you've just assigned:

1. In the Custom Button dialog box, either select a button from the palette and then click Edit to modify it, or simply click Edit to start from scratch.

2. The Button Editor will appear (see Figure 36.21), displaying the image you selected (if any) or a blank bitmap grid.

3. Change the button image to your liking.

4. Click the Close button.

 TIP You can use the Button Editor to modify any button at any time, if you feel creative. Just display the toolbar whose button you want to modify, select Tools ▸ Customize and click the Toolbars tab, and then right-click the button. From the shortcut menu that appears, choose Edit Button Image and you'll see the Button Editor.

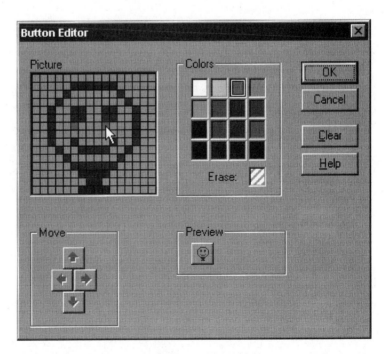

Figure 36.21 *Change or design your button in the Button Editor.*

Creating a Text Label for a Button

Labeling a toolbar button with text may seem a little boring to the graphically inclined, but for many of us it's the quickest and clearest way of identifying what a button does. For example, the single letter H might identify a button for a macro that generates headers.

1. In the Custom Button dialog box, the item name appears in the Text Button Name text box, already selected. Type whatever replacement label you want.

2. Click the Assign button to close the dialog box.

Restoring a Built-In Toolbar Button's Image

If you don't like the changes you made to the image on a button, you can easily restore it:

1. Display the toolbar whose button you want to change.

2. Select Tools ➤ Customize. The Customize dialog box will appear.

3. Select the Toolbars tab.

4. Right-click the button you want to restore.

5. Choose Reset Button Image from the shortcut menu.

6. Choose Close.

Enlarging Toolbar Buttons

If you're tired of peering at Word's toolbar buttons, unable to make out one button from another, you may want to enlarge the toolbar buttons. The only problem with doing this is that fewer buttons will fit across the width of the screen; you may want to remove unnecessary commands from the toolbars so the necessary ones fit.

To display large toolbar buttons:

1. Select View ➤ Toolbars to display the Toolbars dialog box.

2. Check the Large Buttons check box, then click OK. Your toolbars will appear with large buttons, as illustrated in Figure 36.22.

To restore toolbar buttons to their normal size, select View ➤ Toolbars and uncheck the Large Buttons check box.

Part
5

Power Tools

Figure 36.22 *The difference between toolbars with large buttons (top) and regular buttons (bottom).*

Customizing Word's Menus

Word lets you control the appearance and arrangement of its menus. You can add, delete, and reposition menu items. You can also change the keyboard shortcuts for most menu items. You can use this flexibility to make your copy of Word extremely easy to use or to deliberately restrict someone's options. For example, you could prevent a temp worker from applying any formatting to your precious documents.

Adding Menu Items

Here's how to customize Word's menus to contain the commands, macros, fonts, AutoText entries, and styles you need most often:

1. Open a document based on the template containing the item you want to assign—or open the template itself.

2. Select <u>T</u>ools ➤ <u>C</u>ustomize. The Customize dialog box will appear.

3. Click the Menus tab (see Figure 36.23).

4. In the Save Changes In box, select the template in which the item is stored.

5. In the Categories box, select the category to which the item belongs.

6. Select the item you want to assign in the Commands box to the right of the Categories box.

7. Choose the menu you want in the Change What Menu box.

Figure 36.23 **The Menus tab of the Customize dialog box.**

8. In the Position On Menu box, select (Auto) to let Word automatically position similar menu items together, select (At Top) or (At Bottom) to position the item at the top or bottom of the menu, or select the item below which to position the item if you want to position it within the menu list.

9. In the Name on Menu box, either accept the default name or type the name you want to appear. Put an ampersand (&) in front of the hot key letter.

10. Click the Add button or Add Below button. (Word will offer you one or t'other.)

11. To close the Customize dialog box, click the Close button.

NOTE To add a menu-item separator bar, choose (Separator) in the Commands area of the Customize dialog box, position it as described above, and click the Add or Add Below button.

Removing Menu Items

Here's the quick way to remove items you don't need from menus:

1. Press Ctrl+Alt+– (that's Ctrl+Alt+minus). The mouse pointer will change to a heavy horizontal line:

 NOTE If you change your mind, press Esc to return the mouse pointer to normal.

2. Click the menu item you want to remove. It'll disappear.

   This method is much more fun than using the Tools ➤ Customize dialog box, selecting the command to remove, and then clicking the Remove button, but that way works, too.

 NOTE To remove a menu-item separator bar, choose (Separator) in the Commands area of the Customize dialog box and click the Remove button.

Restoring Built-In Menus to Their Original Settings

To quickly restore all built-in Word menus to their original state:

1. Select Tools ➤ Customize. The Customize dialog box will appear.
2. Choose the Menus tab.
3. Select the template to restore in the Save Changes In box.
4. Click the Reset All button.

5. Click Yes in the confirmation dialog box.

6. Click the Close button.

 WARNING Think twice before restoring all menus, especially if you've made any significant changes. Consider backing up any superb pieces of customization so you can't trash them in an instant with the Reset All button.

Adding New Menus

Word lets you add your own menus—a real boon to wonks! You can add as many menus as you want, but they might not all fit on your screen.

To add a new menu:

1. Select Tools ➤ Customize. The Customize dialog box will appear.

2. Choose the Menus tab.

3. Select the template for the new menu in the Save Changes In box.

4. Select the Menu Bar button. The Menu Bar dialog box will appear:

5. Enter the name for the menu in the Name on Menu Bar box. Use an ampersand (&) in front of a letter to designate a hot key.

6. Position the new menu using the Position on Menu Bar box:

   • To position it first, select First.

   • To position it last, select Last.

- To position the menu after another menu, select the menu for it to appear after.

7. Click the Add or Add After button (Word will offer you one or the other, depending on your choice in step 6) to add the menu.

8. Choose the Close button to close the Menu Bar dialog box, add menu as described before, and choose the Close button again to close the Customize dialog box.

Renaming Menus

You can rename a menu so it suits your purposes better. Perhaps Fail would be more appropriate than File, or Fools than Tools? Here's how:

1. Select Tools ➤ Customize. The Customize dialog box will appear.

2. Choose the Menus tab.

3. Select the template containing the menu you want to rename in the Save Changes In box.

4. Select the Menu Bar button. The Menu Bar dialog box will appear.

5. Select the menu to rename in the Position on Menu Bar box.

6. Type the new name in the Name on Menu Bar box.

7. Click the Rename button.

8. Click the Close button to close the Menu Bar dialog box and then click the Close button on the Customize dialog box to close that, too.

Customizing Word's Keyboard Shortcuts

You can get the most use from your keyboard by customizing Word's keyboard shortcuts. You can assign shortcut keys to commands, macros, fonts, AutoText entries, styles, and special characters. You want Ctrl+A to change selected text to 40-point Kidnap? *No problemo*. You need Ctrl+Shift+T to type: "I was quite ecstatic to see you last night, darling!"? Read on!

Changing Keyboard Shortcuts

Here's how to see what your current keyboard shortcuts are and change them:

1. Select Tools ➤ Customize. The Customize dialog box will appear.

2. Select the Keyboard tab (see Figure 36.24).

3. In the Categories box, select the category containing the items you want.

4. In the Commands box, select the command whose shortcut you want to view. The shortcut will appear in the Current Keys box.

5. Move to the Press New Shortcut Key box and press the keyboard shortcut you want to assign. Word will display the current assignation of that keyboard shortcut.

6. Click the Assign button to assign the shortcut key to the item.

7. Click the Close button to close the Customize dialog box.

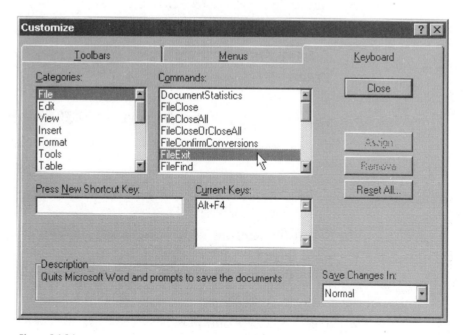

Figure 36.24 The Keyboard tab of the Customize dialog box.

Part
5

Power Tools

> TIP   Here's a shortcut: Press **Ctrl+Alt++** (that's **Ctrl+Alt+plus**). The mouse pointer changes to a command symbol. Choose a menu command or click a toolbar button. Word will display the Customize dialog box showing the command you select. Follow steps 5–7 of the preceding list.

Deleting Shortcuts

By deleting shortcuts, you can prevent yourself or another user of your computer from performing unwanted actions. Here's how:

1. Select Tools ➤ Customize. The Customize dialog box will appear.
2. Choose the Keyboard tab.
3. Select the template containing the item whose shortcut you want to remove in the Save Changes In box.
4. In the Categories box, select the category containing the item.
5. In the Commands box, select the item.
6. Select the shortcut key to delete in the Current Keys box.
7. Click the Remove button.
8. Choose the Close button to close the Customize dialog box.

Reverting to Default Keyboard Shortcuts

Here's how to restore all shortcut key assignments to their original settings:

1. Select Tools ➤ Customize. The Customize dialog box will appear.
2. Choose the Keyboard tab.
3. Select the template containing the shortcut key assignments you want to restore in the Save Changes In box.
4. Click the Reset All button.
5. Choose Yes in the confirmation dialog box that Word throws at you.
6. Click the Close button to close the Customize dialog box.

Like resetting the toolbars, this is a quick way of undoing many hours of work; so be sure you really want to abandon your custom key combinations.

Features for Physically Challenged Users

Word includes a number of features to assist physically challenged users. These are discussed in the following sections.

Microsoft's Access Pack

For people with motion or hearing disabilities, Microsoft's Access Pack provides better access to computers running Windows. With the Access Pack, you can:

▶ Type Shift+, Ctrl+, and Alt+key combinations with one finger.

▶ Instruct applications to ignore accidental keystrokes.

▶ Adjust the repeat rate (the rate at which a key registers multiple presses when held down) or turn off character repeating.

▶ Use the keyboard to control the mouse cursor.

▶ Use an alternate input device to control the keyboard and mouse.

▶ Display visually when the computer beeps or makes sounds.

Getting Access Pack

You'll find Access Pack in the file Access.exe in the Microsoft Windows Driver Library. You can also download the Microsoft Windows Driver Library from network services—CompuServe, GEnie, Microsoft On-line, and Microsoft Download Service (MSDL). MSDL's number is (206) 936-MSDL (that's 936-6735).

If you don't have a modem, you can order the Access Pack by calling Microsoft Product Support Services at (206) 637-7098 or (206) 635-4948 (text telephone).

Single-Handed Keyboard Layouts

If you have difficulty using the standard QWERTY keyboard, you can get from Microsoft Dvorak keyboard layouts that make the most frequently typed characters on a keyboard more accessible.

There are three Dvorak keyboard layouts:

▶ Two-handed

▶ Left hand only

▶ Right hand only

The left-handed and right-handed layouts can be used by people who type with a single finger or with a wand. You don't need any special equipment to use them.

Low Vision Aids

Users with impaired vision can customize the Word display to make it easier to see. In Chapter 3, we discussed how to zoom in and out to improve your view of Word, and in the *Enlarging Toolbar Buttons* section earlier in this chapter, we looked at how to display Word's large toolbar buttons. It's also possible to choose a large font size in the Format ➤ Font dialog box and set it as the default.

Further products available include screen-enlargement utilities and screen readers that provide output by synthesized voice or refreshable Braille displays.

Audio Documentation

You can get Microsoft software documentation on audio cassettes and floppy disks. Contact Recording for the Blind, Inc., at this address:

Recording for the Blind, Inc.
20 Roszel Road
Princeton, NJ 08540
Phone: (800) 221-4792
Phone outside the U.S.: (609) 452-0606
Fax: (609) 987-8116

TDD Product Support

Microsoft provides a text telephone (TT/TDD) service to give people who are hard of hearing access to product and support services.

Microsoft Sales and Service and Microsoft Product Support Services are open 6 A.M. to 6 P.M. Pacific time. Here are the numbers for the text telephones:

Microsoft Sales and Service: (800) 426-9400

Microsoft Product Support Services: (206) 635-4948

Microsoft will charge you for their support services. You have been warned.

For More Assistance and Information

For more information on Microsoft products and services for people with disabilities, contact Microsoft Sales and Service at (800) 426-9400 (voice) or (800) 892-5234 (text telephone).

For general information on how computers can help you, consult a trained evaluator. To find one, contact the National Information System, Center for Developmental Disabilities, Benson Building, University of South Carolina, Columbia, SC 29208. Here are its numbers:

Voice/text telephone outside South Carolina: (800) 922-9234, ext. 301

Voice/text telephone in South Carolina: (800) 922-1107

Voice/text telephone outside the United States: (803) 777-6222

You can also get the *Trace ResourceBook* from the Trace R&D Center at the University of Wisconsin-Madison. The *Trace ResourceBook* describes and illustrates about 2000 products to help people with disabilities use computers. Here is the address for the Trace R&D Center:

Trace R&D Center
S-151 Waisman Center
1500 Highland Avenue
Madison, WI 53705-2280
Voice telephone: (608) 263-2309
Text telephone: (608) 263-5408
Fax: (608) 262-8848

Appendices

Appendix A
Installing Word

I n the good old days, we just showed you how to install Word for Windows from floppies, and that was it. Today, however, life is more complicated, because there are more options designed to make things simpler! Funny that...

Nowadays, many people are installing from CD-ROMs, which makes a lot of sense, given the size of Word and other applications. Furthermore, Microsoft is making it very tempting for people to go ahead and spring the extra money, over what it would cost to buy Word by itself, to purchase the whole office suite. You can get MS Office (which includes Word, Excel, PowerPoint, and Schedule+) for an incredible cost of roughly half-again the cost of Word.

This appendix shows how to install Word using the MS Office Setup software. We also assume you will be installing from a CD-ROM (although additional steps are included for those of you who like to spend all afternoon installing a mountain of floppies). If you are *not* installing Word as part of Office, don't worry; your installation will look virtually identical. You just won't have as many choices.

System Requirements

You can install Word for Windows 95 on any machine that runs Windows 95 (including an 80386) that has a minimum of 8 MB of RAM. Note that you probably can't realistically run Word 95 on a 386. Best to just pony up for that 486! You cannot use Word 95 with a system earlier than Windows 95. You'll need an EGA or better display. You really should have a mouse or trackball, though it is not a requirement. Disk-space estimates vary with your needs.

A *Minimum* installation requires 5 to 6 MB of disk space. You'll get just the bare bones—the program, Spelling checker, and Word's Readme Help file (*not* online help). Travelers, listen up. You are gonna wish you had the online help at midnight in some hotel room. Read on.

If you are installing on a laptop, Word will automatically detect this and ask if you would like a *Laptop* installation. While this installation puts more stuff on your computer and makes certain allowances for the limitations of laptops, just think how frustrating it would be to be on the road and realize that you can't install the feature you *need* to use, because your installation disk is 6000 miles away.

A *Typical* installation requires 18 MB or more. It includes the program, Spelling checker, new online help (well worth the disk space!), and supplementary programs like WordArt and Graph.

A full installation requires 25 to 30 MB. If you have the room, do a full install; then go back later to remove things you never use, like the Grammar checker and Equation Editor. But at least try them and the many other tools provided in a full installation. After all, you paid for them, didn't you?

> **TIP** Because Word 95 can use your old custom dictionaries, glossaries, styles, and templates, the installer doesn't throw out these files when it deletes Word version 6. But just to be safe, you might want to make backup copies of these things before you run Setup. Also, back up your system files before installing the software.

Network users can choose a "Workstation" installation, which requires around 4 MB of local hard-disk real estate. Read more about network installations later in this appendix.

Word's installer will check to see if you have enough space, but you can save some time by making sure there is room beforehand.

Running Setup from a CD-ROM or Floppies

The files on the installation disk, whether you are installing from a CD-ROM or from floppies, cannot simply be dragged onto your hard disk. You need to run the Setup program, which will walk you through the simple installation steps:

1. Start Windows.

2. Insert the first Setup disk in a floppy drive if you are installing from floppies.

3. Choose Run from the Start menu.

4. If you are installing from floppies, type in the disk-drive name (A: or B:) and **Setup**, as shown here:

If you are installing from a CD-ROM, when you insert the disk it will display a splash screen offering you the option of installing or upgrading your software.

5. Click the Install (or perhaps Upgrade) icon.

6. In a moment, you will see a Setup dialog box similar, but probably not identical, to this one:

7.   The choices you will be given will vary with your situation. Read each choice carefully before clicking the Continue button.

8.   When asked if you want a Typical, Minimum, Laptop, Complete or Custom installation, opt for Complete if you have the required disk space. You can always remove unwanted elements after you've had a chance to explore them.

9.   If you are installing Office, you may have to click the Change Options button to get to the Word installation options (see *Custom Installation and Removing the Unwanted*, below).

10.   If you are installing from a CD-ROM, that's pretty much it. Word (or all of MS Office) will be installed straight from the CD-ROM without requiring your intervention. If you haven't invested in a CD-ROM drive yet and are using floppies, though, go get yourself some lunch or a good book, 'cause you're going to be disk-swapping for about an hour and half. Word will tell you what floppies it needs when. All you have to do is take the old floppy out, put the correct one in, and click OK or press Enter. Fun, isn't it?

11.   When the installation is finished, Setup will ask you to restart your computer. It is not wise to defy the will of Setup, so just click Restart.

12.   Your computer will restart and you will be ready to dazzle the free and other worlds with your bold and innovative faxes!

Running Setup from a Server

If your company has a network and is licensed to do so, you may be able to install Word from the server (over the network) without the need for floppy shuffling. Contact your network administrator for details.

Custom Installation and Removing the Unwanted

If you choose not to do a complete installation, you can tell Setup which items you want to install. And you can revisit the Setup program later to remove items you don't use. This is helpful if you have limited disk space or if one of your nonessential floppies is damaged.

In either case, you'll see a series of dialog boxes, each with lists of items that can be added or removed. Most of the dialog boxes also contain Change Options buttons that give you more detailed control. For example, the first dialog box lets you add or delete all Online Help, while the next level down lets you pick and choose from options like Help for WordPerfect Users, WordBasic Help, and Help for Microsoft Word. As you add or remove checks in the various option boxes, Word revises its estimation of the required disk space and displays the statistics at the bottom of the dialog boxes.

The "top-level" dialog box looks like this:

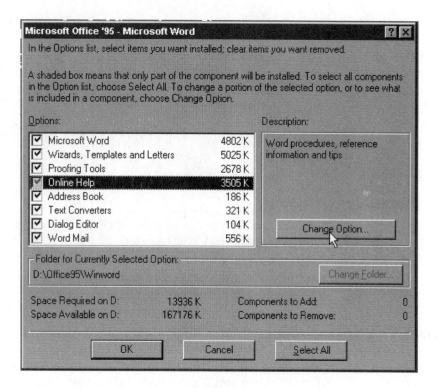

To reach the detailed choices, click the Change Option button:

 TIP   It's a good idea to install the templates and sample documents, as they contain helpful files and examples. If you choose not to install certain features, they will either not appear on your Word menus or will always be dimmed. You can always return to Setup later and install just the items you left off when you last did a custom installation.

Using Old Word Files

If you have old Word documents, custom dictionaries, and templates from Word version 6 scattered around your hard disk, you will be able to use them with Word 95. Word will convert them when you open them, and you can either save them as Word 95 files or save them as earlier version files. You can even use your old custom menu, Toolbar, and keyboard settings, although you may be better off personalizing the Word 95 tools from scratch.

If you have modified Word's Standard styles in earlier versions, Setup tries to preserve these changes. Macros should work as well.

It goes without saying that you should explore the effects of Setup's "automatic" conversions and accommodations before you start any large rush projects that depend upon them.

Appendix B

Word Commands and Their Shortcuts

Following is a list of Word's most commonly used commands and their shortcuts. The expression (Num) denotes that you must press the indicated key on the numeric keypad, and that NumLock must be turned on. Also note that some commands require text or objects to be selected; others work either with or without a current selection.

Command	Shortcut
Align center	Ctrl+E
Align justify	Ctrl+R
Align left	Ctrl+L
All caps (toggle)	Ctrl+Shift+A
Apply Heading 1	Ctrl+Alt+1
Apply Heading 2	Ctrl+Alt+2
Apply Heading 3	Ctrl+Alt+3
Apply list bullet	Ctrl+Shift+L
AutoFormat	Ctrl+K
AutoText	F3, Ctrl+Alt+V
Bold	Ctrl+B, Ctrl+Shift+B
Bookmark	Ctrl+Shift+F5
Change case	Shift+F3
Citation	Alt+Shift+I
Clear	Delete
Close current pane	Alt+Shift+C
Collapse outline	Alt+_, Alt+Shift+- (Num)
Copy	Ctrl+C, Ctrl+Ins
Copy format	Ctrl+Shift+C
Copy text	Shift+F2
Customize keyboard settings	Ctrl+Alt++ (Num)
Cut	Ctrl+X, Shift+Del
Delete previous word	Ctrl+Backspace
Demote to body text	Ctrl+Shift+N

Command	Shortcut
Document close	Ctrl+W, Ctrl+F4
Document maximize	Ctrl+F10
Document move	Ctrl+F7
Document restore	Ctrl+F5
Document size	Ctrl+F8
Document split	Ctrl+Alt+S
Edit mail merge data source	Alt+Shift+E
Exit	Alt+F4
Extend down one line	Shift+↓
Extend left	Shift+←
Extend one screen down	Shift+Page Down
Extend one screen up	Shift+Page Up
Extend paragraph up	Ctrl+Shift+↑
Extend right	Shift+→
Extend selection	F8
Extend to end of document	Ctrl+Shift+End
Extend to end of line	Shift+End
Extend to end of window	Ctrl+Shift+Page Down
Extend to start of document	Ctrl+Shift+Home
Extend to start of line	Shift+Home
Extend to start of window	Ctrl+Shift+Page Up
Extend up one line	Shift+↑
Extend word left	Ctrl+Shift+←
Extend word right	Ctrl+Shift+→
Field click	Alt+Shift+F9
Find	Ctrl+F

Command	Shortcut
Font	Ctrl+D or Ctrl+Shift+P (twice)
Font size	Ctrl+Shift+P
Go back	Shift+F5, Ctrl+Alt+Z
Go to	Ctrl+G, F5
Go to annotation	Alt+F11
Go to end of column	Alt+Page Down, Alt+Shift+Page Down
Go to end of document	Ctrl+End
Go to end of line	End
Go to end of row	Alt+End, Alt+Shift+End
Go to end of window	Ctrl+Page Down
Go to previous page	Ctrl+Alt+Page Up
Go to start of document	Ctrl+Home
Go to start of line	Home
Go to start of row	Alt+Home, Alt+Shift+Home
Go to start of window	Ctrl+Page Up
Hanging indent	Ctrl+T
Help	F1
Help tool	Shift+F1
Hidden	Ctrl+Shift+H
Increase font 1 point	Ctrl+]
Increase font size	Ctrl+>
Indent	Ctrl+M
Insert annotation	Ctrl+Alt+A
Insert column break	Ctrl+Shift+Enter
Insert date field	Alt+Shift+D
Insert endnote	Alt+Ctrl+E
Insert field	Ctrl+F9

Command	Shortcut
Insert footnote	Ctrl+Alt+F
Insert merge field	Alt+Shift+F
Insert page break	Ctrl+Enter
Insert page field	Alt+Shift+P
Insert spike	Ctrl+Shift+F3
Insert time	Alt+Shift+T
Italic	Ctrl+I, Ctrl+Shift+I
Justify	Ctrl+J
Left justify	Ctrl+L
Lock fields	Ctrl+3, Ctrl+F11
Mail merge check	Alt+Shift+K
Mark index entry	Alt+Shift+X
Mark TOC entry	Alt+Shift+O
Menu add	Ctrl+Alt+=
Menu bar	F10
Merge to a document	Alt+Shift+N
Merge to the printer	Alt+Shift+M
Move left	←
Move right	→
Move text	F2
New	Ctrl+N
Next field	F11, Alt+F1
Next window	Ctrl+F6
Normal style	Ctrl+Shift+N, Alt+Shift+5 (Num)
Open	Ctrl+O, Ctrl+F12, Ctrl+Alt+F2
Open or close up paragraph	Ctrl+Shift+O
Other pane	F6, Shift+F6

Command	Shortcut
Outline demote	Alt+Shift+→
Outline expand	Alt+Shift++
Outline move down	Alt+Shift+↓
Outline move up	Alt+Shift+↑
Outline promote	Alt+Shift+←
Outline show first line	Alt+Shift+L
Overtype	Ins
Paste	Ctrl+V, Shift+Ins
Previous field	Shift+F11, Alt+Shift+F1
Print	Ctrl+P, Ctrl+Shift+F12
Print preview	Ctrl+F2, Ctrl+Alt+I
Redo	Alt+Shift+Backspace
Redo or repeat	Ctrl+Y, F4, Alt+Enter
Remove menu	Ctrl+Alt+–
Repeat find	Shift+F4, Ctrl+Alt+Y
Replace	Ctrl+H
Reset character formatting	Ctrl+spacebar, Ctrl+Shift+Z
Reset paragraph formatting	Ctrl+Q
Restore	Ctrl+F5
Right justify	Ctrl+R
Save	Shift+F12, Ctrl+S, Alt+Shift+F2
Save as	F12
Select all	Ctrl+A, Ctrl+5 (Num)
Select block	Ctrl+Shift+F8
Select table	Alt+5 (Num)
Show all headings	Alt+Shift+A
Show Heading 1	Alt+!

Command	Shortcut
Show Heading 2	Alt+@
Show Heading 3	Alt+#
Show Heading 4	Alt+$
Show Heading 5	Alt+%
Show Heading 6	Alt+^
Show Heading 7	Alt+&
Show Heading 8	Alt+*
Show Heading 9	Alt+(
Shrink font	Ctrl+<
Shrink font 1 point	Ctrl+[
Shrink selection	Shift+F8
Small caps	Ctrl+Shift+K
Space $1\frac{1}{2}$ line	Ctrl+5
Space double space	Ctrl+2
Space single space	Ctrl+1
Spellcheck	F7
Spike	Ctrl+F3
Style list	Ctrl+Shift+S
Subscript	Ctrl+=
Superscript	Ctrl+plus sign
Symbol font	Ctrl+Shift+Q
System info	Ctrl+Alt+F1
Thesaurus	Shift+F7
Toggle field display	Shift+F9
Underline	Ctrl+U
Underline double	Ctrl+Shift+D
Undo	Ctrl+Z, Alt+Backspace
Unhang	Ctrl+Shift+T
Unindent	Ctrl+Shift+M

Command	Shortcut
Unlink fields	Ctrl+6, Ctrl+Shift+F9
Unlock fields	Ctrl+4, Ctrl+Shift+F11
Update fields	F9, Alt+Shift+U
Update source	Ctrl+Shift+F7
Update table autoformat	Ctrl+Alt+U
View fields codes	Alt+F9
View normal	Ctrl+Alt+N
View outline	Ctrl+Alt+O
View page	Ctrl+Alt+P
Word underline	Ctrl+Shift+W

Appendix C

Field Codes
and Their Switches

General Switches

All field codes can include general switches, which are mostly used for formatting purposes. The four types of general switches are

Switch Type	Used for
*	Text formatting
\#	Numeric formatting
\@	Date and time formatting
\!	Locking the result

General switches are explained in depth in Chapter 32. The rest of this appendix will explain each individual field code and the *field-specific* switches that pertain to each.

Field Codes and Field-Specific Switches

For each field code in Word, I'll give the syntax (that is, the form of the field code), an explanation of the field, and a list of the field-specific switches you can use with the field.

As a matter of convention, the name of the field code will appear in all caps, anything optional will appear between square brackets, and any variable (anything that can be different every time) will be italicized.

= (Formula)

The = field is also called the Formula field. It takes this form:

```
{ =expression or formula }
```

It always consists of the = sign and then either a mathematical expression (using the normal mathematical operators—+, –, /, *, and so on—as well as logical operators) or a formula. Formulas can include bookmarks; references to table cells, rows, or columns; and so on.

Advance

Advance fields take this form:

```
{ ADVANCE [\switches] }
```

The Advance field moves the insertion point relative to its current location or to the left or top margin.

The switches control the direction and distance that the insertion point moves. They are as follows:

Switch	Moves the insertion point
\l n	Moves the insertion point n points to the left
\r n	Moves the insertion point n points to the right
\u n	Moves the insertion point n points up
\d n	Moves the insertion point n points down
\x n	Places the insertion point n points to the right of the left margin
\y n	Places the insertion point n points below the top margin

NOTE   A point is almost exactly equal to 1/72 inch.

Ask

Ask fields take this form:

```
{ ASK bookmark "prompt text" [\switches] }
```

The field displays a dialog box that includes the prompt text and a text box. Whatever is entered into the text box is assigned to the bookmark.

The field-specific switches for Ask are

\d "*default text*"	Used to supply default text (highlighted) in the text box.
\o	Prompts only once during a mail merge (instead of once for each resulting document).

Author

The Author field takes this form:

```
{ AUTHOR ["New Name"] }
```

By itself, the { AUTHOR } field code displays the name of the author of the document (from the User Info tab of the Options dialog box—Tools ➤ Options). With a new name in quotation marks, as a variable, or input with a prompt, the field stores the new author name.

AutoNum

The AutoNum field takes this form:

```
{ AUTONUM }
```

This field is used to number paragraphs. Placed at the beginning of a paragraph, it displays a number. It counts all the preceding paragraphs that also start with the AutoNum field and have the same paragraph style (Normal if nothing else), and displays the next number in that sequence. If you rearrange, copy, or insert paragraphs with AutoNum, the numbers will always reflect the current order.

AutoNumLgl

The AutoNumLgl field takes this form:

```
{ AUTONUMLGL }
```

This field is used to number paragraphs in traditional legal format. Placed at the beginning of a paragraph, it displays a number. It counts all the preceding paragraphs that also start with the AutoNumLgl field and have the same paragraph style (Normal if nothing else), and it displays the next number in that sequence. If you rearrange, copy, or insert paragraphs with AutoNumLgl, the numbers will always reflect the current order.

If you use AutoNumLgl field codes with more than one paragraph style, then each style gets its own sequence, starting with 1., 2., 3.; followed by 1.1, 1.2, 1.3; and then 1.1.1, 1.1.2, and so on. The precedence of the styles is determined first by their heading levels if they are numbered, and otherwise strictly by the order in which they appear.

AutoNumOut

The AutoNumOut field takes this form:

```
{ AUTONUMOUT }
```

Appendices

This field is used to number paragraphs in traditional outline format. Placed at the beginning of a paragraph, it displays a number. It counts all the preceding paragraphs that also start with the AutoNumOut field and have the same paragraph style (Normal if nothing else), and it displays the next number in that sequence. If you rearrange, copy, or insert paragraphs with AutoNumOut, the numbers will always reflect the current order.

If you use AutoNumOut field codes with more than one paragraph style, then each style gets its own sequence, starting with I., II., III.; followed by A., B., C.; and then 1., 2., and so on. The precedence of the styles is determined first by their heading levels if they are numbered, and otherwise strictly by the order in which they appear.

AutoText

The AutoText field takes this form:

```
{ AUTOTEXT entry }
```

This field displays the contents of the AutoText *entry*.

BarCode

The BarCode field takes this form:

```
{ BARCODE "text" [\switches] }
```

This field inserts a postal bar code based on the literal *text* enclosed in quotation marks.

The field-specific switches for BarCode are

bookmark \b	Creates a postal bar code based on the text contained in *bookmark*.
\f "*letter*"	Inserts a Facing Identification Mark (FIM). If "*letter*" is "A", it inserts a courtesy reply mark. If "*letter*" is "C", it inserts a business reply mark.
\u	Identifies the bar code as a US postal address.

Bookmark

The Bookmark field takes this form:

```
{ bookmark [\switches] }
```

You don't literally type the word "bookmark." Instead, you type the bookmark name. This field displays the contents of the named *bookmark*. This is the same as the Ref field.

The field-specific switches for *bookmark* are

\f   Includes and increments footnote, endnote, or annotation numbers.

\n   Inserts paragraph numbering (if any) from the marked paragraph.

Comments

The Comments field takes this form:

```
{ COMMENTS ["new comments"] }
```

By itself, the **{ COMMENTS }** field code displays the comments in the Summary Info dialog box. With new comments in quotation marks, as a variable, or input with a prompt, the field stores the new comments.

Compare

The Compare field takes this form:

```
{ COMPARE expression1 comparison expression2 }
```

It compares *firstexpression* with *secondexpression* using the *comparison* operator. If the comparison is true, Compare returns a value of 1. If the comparison is false, it returns 0. The expressions can be bookmarks, strings, numbers, or other fields that return values or mathematical formulas. For string expressions of more than one word, enclose the string in quotation marks. Valid *comparison* operators are

=   is equal to

<   is less than

<=   is less than or equal to

>   is greater than

>=   is greater than or equal to

<>   is not equal to

For the = and <> operators, the second expression can include the wild-card characters ? and *; use ? for any single character to match or * for any number of characters.

CreateDate

The CreateDate field takes this form:

```
{ CREATEDATE }
```

It displays the creation date of the document it's in.

You can, of course, add the \@ general field switch for date and time "picture" formatting to control the appearance of the date. The \@ options are explained in Chapter 32.

Database

The Database field takes this form:

```
{ DATABASE [\switches] }
```

It displays the result of a database query. Usually inserted with the Insert ➤ Database command, this field is a difficult one to construct by hand.

The field-specific switches for Database are

\c *instructions*	The instructions that ODBC uses to make the connection to the database.
\d *"path\ filename"*	The path and file name of the database.
\s *instructions*	The SQL instructions that query the database.
\f *number*	Inserts data into the Word document starting from the data record *number*.

\t *number*	Inserts data into the Word document ending with the data record *number*.
\l "*number*"	Applies a format from the Table AutoFormat dialog box.
\b *number*	Specifies which attributes of the format set by the \l switch apply to the table:

0	None
1	Borders
2	Shading
4	Font
8	Color
16	AutoFit
32	Heading rows
64	Last Row
128	First Column
256	Last Column

You can add the numbers together to specify more than one attribute. If you leave out the number, the switch defaults to 16, AutoFit.

Date

The Date field takes this form:

```
{ DATE [\l] }
```

It displays the current date. The only field-specific switch is \l. It specifies that the date be displayed with the last format chosen for a date (via Insert ➤ Date and Time).

You can, of course, add the \@ general field switch for date and time "picture" formatting to control the appearance of the date. The \@ options are explained in Chapter 32.

DDE

The DDE field takes this form:

```
{ DDE application document [place-reference] }
```

It creates a dynamic data exchange (DDE) link with another Windows application. When DDE is updated, it displays current information from the source document.

The *application* instruction is the name of the Windows application. The *document* instruction is the file name of the source document. The optional *place-reference* switch varies in format from application to application. For example, if the source document is a spreadsheet, the *place-reference* would generally be a range named or specified from cell to cell.

DDEAuto

The DDEAuto field takes this form:

```
{ DDEAUTO application document [place-reference] }
```

It creates a dynamic data exchange (DDE) link with another Windows application that updates itself automatically whenever you open the document the field is in.

The *application* instruction is the name of the Windows application. The *document* instruction is the file name of the source document. The optional *place-reference* switch varies in format from application to application. For example, if the source document is a spreadsheet, the *place-reference* would generally be a range named or specified from cell to cell.

EditTime

The EditTime field takes this form:

```
{ EDITTIME }
```

It displays the editing time, in minutes, since the document's creation. Editing time is defined as the time the document is open.

Embed

The Embed field takes this form:

{ EMBED *application* [*switches*] }

Inserts an object created in another application, using OLE. You can't insert the Embed field by hand (Insert ➤ Object and Edit ➤ Paste Special can insert the field automatically), but you can edit an existing Embed field code.

You can't change the *application*. The only field-specific switch is \s, which returns the object to its original scale and cropping when it is updated. (The general * mergeformat switch has the opposite effect, keeping the current scale and cropping when the field is updated.)

EQ (Equation)

The EQ (Equation) field takes this form:

{ EQ [*switches*] }

EQ produces a mathematical equation assembled from the switches and their contents. Field-specific switches for EQ are

\a(*element1, element2, etc.*)	Draws a two-dimensional array using any number of elements. The following options can come between the \a switch and the elements in parentheses:

\al	Align left within columns
\ac	Align center within columns
\ar	Align right within columns
\co*n*	*n* columns (default is 1)
\vs*n*	*n* points of vertical spacing between lines
\hs*n*	*n* points of horizontal spacing between columns

\b(*element*)

Brackets a single element in a size appropriate to the element. The default brackets are parentheses. The following options can come between the \b switch and the element in parentheses:

\lc\c   Draws the left-bracket character using the character specified for *c*. If you specify {, [, (, or <, then Word uses the corresponding closing character as the right bracket. If you specify any other character, Word uses that character for both.

\rc\c   Draws the right-bracket character using the character specified for *c*.

\bc\c   Draws both bracket characters using the character specified for *c*.

\d( )

Specifies precisely where the next character is drawn. The following options can come between the \d switch and the empty parentheses:

\fo*n*   Forward *n* points

\ba*n*   Back *n* points

\li   Draws a line from the end of the displaced character to the beginning of the next character.

\f(*numerator, denominator*)

Creates a fraction with *numerator* and *denominator* centered above and below the division line.

\i(*lower-limit, upper-limit, integrand*)	Creates an integral. The following options can come between the \i switch and the elements in parentheses:

\su	Changes the symbol to a capital sigma (Σ) and creates a summation.
\pr	Changes the symbol to a capital pi (Π) and creates a product.
\in	Creates an in-line format with the limits displayed to the right of the symbol instead of above and below.
\fc\c	Substitutes a fixed-height character specified by *c* for the symbol.
\vc\c	Substitutes a variable-height character specified by *c* for the symbol. The symbol matches the height of the third element.

\l(*element1, element2, etc.*)	Creates a list of values separated by commas or semicolons.
\o(*element1, element2, etc.*)	The \o switch overstrikes each successive element on top of the previous ones. Any number of elements is permitted. Each character is printed within an invisible character box. The following options can come between the \o switch and the elements in parentheses:

\al	Aligns the left edges of the characters' boxes.

\ac	Aligns the centers of the characters' boxes. This is the default.
\ar	Aligns the right edges of the characters' boxes.
\r(*element* [,*root*])	Draws a radical (√), using one or two elements. A single element appears as a square root. With two elements, the first element—the exponent—is drawn above the radical, and the second element is drawn inside.
\s(*element1*) [(*element2*) (*etc.*)]	Positions elements as superscripts or subscripts. Each \s code can have one or more elements. If more than one element is specified, the elements are stacked and left-aligned. The following options can come before any parenthetical elements:
\ai*n*()	Adds space above a line in a paragraph by the number of points specified by *n*.
\up*n*()	Moves a single element up the number of points specified by *n*. The default is 2.
\di*n*()	Adds space below a line in a paragraph by the number of points specified by *n*.
\do*n*()	Moves a single element down the number of points specified by *n*. The default is 2.

\x(*element*)   Creates a border for an element. When used without options, this code draws a box around the element. The following options can come between the \x switch and the element in parentheses:

\to   Top border

\bo   Bottom border

\le   Left border

\ri   Right border

FileName

The FileName field takes this form:

```
{ FILENAME [\p] }
```

It displays the file name of the document. The option \p switch causes it to display the entire path as well as the file name.

FileSize

The FileSize field takes this form:

```
{ FILESIZE [\switches] }
```

It displays the size of the document in bytes. Field-specific switches are

k   Displays the result in kilobytes, rounded to the nearest whole number.

\m   Display the results in megabytes, rounded to the nearest whole number.

Fillin

The Fillin field takes this form:

```
{ FILLIN ["prompt"] [\switches] }
```

It displays a dialog box prompting for the text to appear in the place of the field. The field-specific switches for Fillin are

\d *"default"*	Specifies a default result in the dialog box.
\o	Prompts only once during a mail merge.

FormCheckbox

The FormCheckbox field takes this form:

```
{ FORMCHECKBOX }
```

It inserts a check box in a form. You cannot insert this field manually, nor can you modify it.

FormDropdown

The FormDropdown field takes this form:

```
{ FORMDROPDOWN }
```

It inserts a drop-down list in a form. You cannot insert this field manually, nor can you modify it.

Formula (=)

See the = field entry at the beginning of this appendix.

FormText

The FormText field takes this form:

```
{ FORMTEXT }
```

It inserts a text box in a form. You cannot insert this field manually, nor can you modify it.

GotoButton

The GotoButton field takes this form:

```
{ GOTOBUTTON destination display text }
```

It shows the display text on the screen as a clickable field result or button (you can also insert a graphic into this field to have the button display as a graphic). Double-clicking the button jumps the reader to the destination, which can be any acceptable Go To destination (Go To is explained in Chapter 3) such as a bookmark, page number, table, and so on.

If

The If field takes this form:

```
{ IF expression1 comparison expression2 "true text" "false
text" }
```

It compares *expression1* with *expression2* using the *comparison* operator. If the comparison is true, it displays the *true text*. If the comparison is false, it displays the *false text*. The expressions can be bookmarks, strings, numbers, or other fields that return values or mathematical formulas. For string expressions of more than one word, enclose the string in quotation marks. Valid *comparison* operators are

=	is equal to
<	is less than
<=	is less than or equal to
>	is greater than
>=	is greater than or equal to
<>	is not equal to

For the = and <> operators, the second expression can include the wild-card characters ? and *; ? for any single character to match or * for any number of characters.

IncludePicture

The IncludePicture field takes this form:

```
{ INCLUDEPICTURE filename [\switches] }
```

It inserts the named graphic file. If you include the path with the file name, you must type each backslash twice; for example, c:\\art\\picture.bmp. Field-specific switches are

\c *converter*	Specifies the file name of the graphics filter to use.
\d	Specifies that graphic information not be stored in the document.

IncludeText

The IncludeText field takes this form:

{ INCLUDETEXT *filename* [*bookmark*] [*switches*] }

It inserts the named source document or the contents of *bookmark* in the named document. If you include the path with the file name, you must type each backslash twice; for example, c:\\work\\report.doc. The only field-specific switch is

\c *converter*	Specifies the file name of the converter to use.

Index

The Index field takes this form:

{ INDEX [*switches*] }

It builds and inserts an index based on entries marked with the XE field. Field-specific switches are

\b *bookmark*	Builds an index for the section of the document marked by *bookmark*.
\c *n*	Creates an index with *n* columns.
\d "*c*"	Defines the separator character (*c*) for sequences defined by the \s switch (default is "-").
\e "*c*"	Defines the separator character between an index entry and its page number (default is ", ").

\f "*entry type*"	Creates an index using only the specified entry type (using only XE fields with the same "*entry type*" text).
\g "*c*"	Defines the separator character (*c*) used in a page range (default is "–").
\h "*heading text*"	Inserts a heading between groups in the index (include A in the heading text string to have the sequential letter of the alphabet in each heading).
\l "*c*"	Defines the separator character (*c*) used between page numbers (default is ", ").
\p *letter1-letter2*	Limits the index to entries beginning with letters between *letter1* and *letter2*, inclusive. Use ! for *letter1* to include all symbols at the beginning.
\r	Runs index subentries on the same line as the main entry.
\s *sequence-name*	When there are Seq fields in the document, includes the sequence number before the page number, joined by whatever character is specified with the \d switch.

Info

The Info field takes this form:

```
{ [INFO] info-type ["new value"]  }
```

Displays the current value of *info-type* or assigns "*new value*" to it. *info-type* may be any of the following:

AUTHOR

COMMENTS

CREATEDATE

EDITTIME

FILENAME

FILESIZE

KEYWORDS

LASTSAVEDBY

NUMCHARS

NUMPAGES

NUMWORDS

PRINTDATE

REVNUM

SAVEDATE

SUBJECT

TEMPLATE

TITLE

The Info field for any of the above info types is the same as the field by the same name (all of which are listed in this Appendix).

Keywords

The Keywords field takes this form:

```
{ KEYWORDS "new keywords" }
```

By itself, it displays the keywords from the Summary Info dialog box. With new keywords in quotation marks, as a variable, or input with a prompt, the field stores the keywords.

LastSavedBy

The LastSavedBy field takes this form:

```
{ LASTSAVEDBY }
```

It displays the name, taken from the Summary Info dialog box, of the last person who saved the document.

Link

The Link field takes this form:

```
{ LINK application filename [place-reference] [\switches] }
```

It inserts a link in the document to the named file or to the referenced place in the file. Field-specific switches are

\a	Link updates automatically.
\b	Inserts the linked object as a bitmap.
\d	Does not store graphic data in the document.
\p	Inserts the linked object as a graphic.
\r	Inserts the linked object in RTF (rich text format).
\t	Inserts the linked object in text-only format.

MacroButton

The MacroButton field takes this form:

```
{ MACROBUTTON macroname display text }
```

It shows the display text on the screen as a clickable field result or button (you can also insert a graphic into this field to have the button display as a graphic). Double-clicking the button runs the named macro.

MergeField

The MergeField field takes this form:

```
{ MERGEFIELD fieldname }
```

It merges the data from the data source into the main document during a mail merge.

MergeRec

The MergeRec field takes this form:

```
{ MERGEREC }
```

It inserts the number of the current data record during a mail merge.

MergeSeq

The MergeSeq field takes this form:

```
{ MERGESEQ }
```

It inserts the number of the current data record during a mail merge, counting only records included in the merge.

Next

The Next field takes this form:

```
{ NEXT }
```

It inserts the next record during a mail merge into the current document. Place it before the second set of MergeField fields and thereafter.

NextIf

The NextIf field takes this form:

```
{ NEXTIF expression1 comparison expression2 }
```

It compares *firstexpression* with *secondexpression* using the *comparison* operator. If the comparison is true, it merges the next data record into the current document during a mail merge. If false, it merges the next data record into a new document. The expressions can be bookmarks, strings, numbers, other fields that return values, or mathematical formulas. For string expressions of more than one word, enclose the string in quotation marks. Valid *comparison* operators are

=	is equal to
<	is less than
<=	is less than or equal to
>	is greater than
>=	is greater than or equal to
<>	is not equal to

For the = and <> operators, the second expression can include the wild-card characters ? and *; ? for any single character to match or * for any number of characters.

NoteRef

The NoteRef field takes this form:

```
{ NOTEREF bookmark [\f] }
```

It displays the reference mark of the footnote or endnote marked by *bookmark*. Include the \f switch to retain the formatting of the mark.

NumChars

The NumChars field takes this form:

```
{ NUMCHARS }
```

It displays the number of characters in the document, taken from the Summary Info dialog box.

NumPages

The NumPages field takes this form:

```
{ NUMPAGES }
```

It displays the number of pages in the document, taken from the Summary Info dialog box.

NumWords

The NumWords field takes this form:

```
{ NUMWORDS }
```

It displays the number of words in the document, taken from the Summary Info dialog box.

Page

The Page field takes this form:

```
{ PAGE }
```

It displays the current page.

Appendices

PageRef

The PageRef field takes this form:

```
{ PAGEREF bookmark }
```

It displays the page number of a bookmark.

Print

The Print field takes this form:

```
{ PRINT "printer codes" }
```

It sends printer codes to the printer.

PrintDate

The PrintDate field takes this form:

```
{ PRINTDATE }
```

It displays the date the document was last printed. You can, of course, add the \@ general field switch for date and time "picture" formatting to control the appearance of the date. The \@ options are explained in Chapter 32.

Private

The Private field takes this form:

```
{ PRIVATE }
```

It stores data for a document converted from other file formats in case the document ever needs to be converted back.

Quote

The Quote field takes this form:

```
{ QUOTE "text" }
```

It inserts the specified text into the document.

RD (Referenced Document)

The RD (Referenced Document) field takes this form:

```
{ RD filename }
```

It identifies a file to be included in a table of contents, table of authorities, or index. The field is automatically formatted as hidden text.

Ref

The Ref field takes this form:

```
{ REF bookmark }
```

It displays the contents of *bookmark*. It's equivalent to the Bookmark field, also listed in this Appendix.

The field-specific switches for Ref are

\f   Includes and increments footnote, endnote, or annotation numbers.

\n   Inserts paragraph numbering (if any) from the marked paragraph.

RevNum

The RevNum field takes this form:

```
{ REVNUM }
```

It displays the number of document revisions, using statistics from the Summary Info dialog box.

SaveDate

The SaveDate field takes this form:

```
{ SAVEDATE }
```

It inserts the date and time the document was last saved, using statistics from the Summary Info dialog box. You can, of course, add the \@ general field switch for date and time "picture" formatting to control the appearance of the date. The \@ options are explained in Chapter 32.

Section

The Section field takes this form:

    { SECTION }

It displays the number of the current section.

SectionPages

The SectionPages field takes this form:

    { SECTIONPAGES }

It displays the total number of pages in the current section.

Seq (Sequence)

The Seq (Sequence) field takes this form:

    { SEQ *identifier bookmark* [*switches*] }

It displays a sequential number, counting all the previous Seq fields with the same *identifier*. The identifier word can be anything. Include a bookmark to cross-reference the contents of the bookmark. Field-specific switches are

\c	Inserts the most recent sequence number.
\h	Hides the field result.
\n	Inserts the next sequence number (this is the default).
\r *n*	Resets the sequence number to *n*.

Set

The Set field takes this form:

    { SET *bookmark* "*text*" }

It defines the contents of *bookmark*.

SkipIf

The SkipIf field takes this form:

{ SKIPIF *expression1 comparison expression2* }

It compares *firstexpression* with *secondexpression* using the *comparison* operator. If the comparison is true, it skips the next data record into the current document during a mail merge. If false, it does not. The expressions can be bookmarks, strings, numbers, or other fields that return values or mathematical formulas. For string expressions of more than one word, enclose the string in quotation marks. Valid *comparison* operators are

=	is equal to
<	is less than
<=	is less than or equal to
>	is greater than
>=	is greater than or equal to
<>	is not equal to

For the = and <> operators, the second expression can include the wild-card characters ? and *; ? for any single character to match or * for any number of characters.

StyleRef

The StyleRef field takes this form:

{ STYLEREF "*style-name*" [*switches*] }

It displays text from the nearest paragraph with the named style. Field-specific switches are

\l	Tells Word to search from the bottom of the page instead of the top.
\n	Inserts any paragraph numbering from the referenced paragraph.

Subject

The Subject field takes this form:

```
{ SUBJECT ["new subject"] }
```

By itself, the { SUBJECT } field code displays the subject of the document (from the User Info tab of the Options dialog box—Tools ➤ Options). With a new subject in quotation marks, as a variable, or input with a prompt, the field stores the new subject.

Symbol

The Symbol field takes this form:

```
{ SYMBOL character-number [\switches] }
```

Displays the character that corresponds to the specified character-number in the ANSI character set. Field-specific switches are

\f "*font name*"	Specifies the font.
\h	Inserts the symbol without affecting the line spacing.
\s *n*	Specifies the font size as *n* points.

TA (Table of Authorities Entry)

The TA (Table of Authorities Entry) field takes this form:

```
{ TA [\switches] }
```

It defines the text and page number for a table of authorities entry. The field is formatted as hidden text. Field-specific switches are

\b	Boldfaces the page number in the entry.
\c *n*	Defines the category number as *n*.
\i	Italicizes the page number in the entry.
\l "*long citation text*"	Defines the long citation for the entry.
\r *bookmark*	Includes the range of pages marked by *bookmark*.
\s "*short citation text*"	Defines the short citation for the entry.

TC (Table of Contents Entry)

The TC (Table of Contents Entry) field takes this form:

```
{ TC "text" [\switches] }
```

It defines the text and page number for a table of contents entry. The field is formatted as hidden text. The field-specific switches are

\f *entry-identifier*	Identifies the entry as a certain type, using a one-letter *entry-identifier*, for use in tables of just those entry types.
\l *level-identifier*	Identifies the level of the entry using a one-letter *level-identifier*.
\n	Suppresses the page number for the entry.

Template

The Template field takes this form:

```
{ TEMPLATE [\p] }
```

It displays the file name of the document's template from the Summary Info dialog box. The \p switch adds the path to the file name.

Time

The Time field takes this form:

```
{ TIME }
```

It displays the current time. You can, of course, add the \@ general field switch for date and time "picture" formatting to control the appearance of the date. The \@ options are explained in Chapter 32.

Title

The Title field takes this form:

```
{ TITLE ["New Title"] }
```

By itself, the { TITLE } field code displays the name of the title of the document (from the Summary Info dialog box). With a new title in quotation marks, as a variable, or input with a prompt, the field stores the new title.

TOA (Table of Authorities)

The TOA (Table of Authorities) field takes this form:

```
{ TOA \c category [\other switches] }
```

It builds and inserts a table of authorities based on entries marked with the TA field. Field-specific switches are

\b *bookmark*	Builds a table of authorities for the section of the document marked by *bookmark*.
\c *n*	Builds a table of authorities only with entries with category number *n*.
\d "*c*"	Defines the separator character (*c*) between a sequence number and a page number for sequences defined by the \s switch (default is "-").
\e "*c*"	Defines the separator character (*c*) between a table-of-authorities entry and its page number (default is a tab with dot leaders).
\f	Removes the formatting applied to the entries.
\g "*c*"	Defines the separator character (*c*) used in a page range (default is "–").
\h	Includes the category heading for the entries in a table of authorities.
\l "*c*"	Defines the separator character (*c*) used between page numbers (default is ",").
\p	Replaces five or more page references for the same authority with "passim."

\s *sequence-name*	When there are Seq fields in the document, includes the sequence number before the page number, joined by whatever character is specified with the \d switch.

TOC (Table of Contents)

The TOC (Table of Contents) field takes this form:

```
{ TOC [\switches] }
```

It builds and inserts a table of contents based on entries marked with the TC field. Field-specific switches are

\a	Builds a table of figures with neither labels nor numbers.
\b *bookmark*	Builds a table of contents for the section of the document marked by *bookmark*.
\c *n*	Builds a table of authorities only with entries with category number *n*.
\d "*c*"	Defines the separator character (*c*) between a sequence number and a page number for sequences defined by the \s switch (default is "-").
\f *entry-identifier*	Builds a table of contents using only TC fields with the same single-character *entry-identifier*. (The default *entry-identifier* is c. Including no identifier is equivalent to specifying c as the identifier.)
\l *identifier1– identifier2*	Builds a table of contents using only a range of entry levels specified by the \l switch in the TC fields.
\n	Builds a table of contents without page numbers.

\o "*headingNo–headingNo*"	Builds a table of contents using paragraphs formatted with built-in heading styles numbered in the specified range.
\p	Specifies the separator character used between a table entry and its page number (default is a tab with dot leaders).
\s *sequence-name*	When there are Seq fields in the document, includes the sequence number before the page number, joined by whatever character is specified with the \d switch.
\t "*style1, style2, etc.*"	Builds a table of contents using paragraphs formatted with the styles listed in quotation marks.

UserAddress

The UserAddress field takes this form:

    { USERADDRESS "[New Address]" }

By itself, the { USERADDRESS } field code displays the name of the user address (from the User Info tab of the Options dialog box). With a new address in quotation marks, as a variable, or input with a prompt, the field stores the new user address.

UserInitials

The UserInitials field takes this form:

    { USERINITIALS ["New Initials"] }

By itself, the { USERINITIALS } field code displays the user initials (from the User Info tab of the Options dialog box). With new initials in quotation marks, as a variable, or input with a prompt, the field stores the new user initials.

UserName

The UserName field takes this form:

{ USERNAME ["*New UserName*"] }

By itself, the { USERNAME } field code displays the user name (from the User Info tab of the Options dialog box). With a new name in quotation marks, as a variable, or input with a prompt, the field stores the new user name.

XE (Index Entry)

The XE (Index Entry) field takes this form:

{ XE "*text*" [*switches*] }

It defines the text and page number for an index entry. The field is formatted as hidden text. To indicate a subentry, include the main entry text, then a semicolon, and then the subentry. The field-specific switches are

\b	Boldfaces the page number for the index entry.
\f *entry-identifier*	Identifies the entry as a certain type, using a one-letter *entry-identifier*, for use in indexes of just those entry types.
\i	Italicizes the page number for the index entry.
\r *bookmark*	Includes the range of pages marked by *bookmark* in the page number for the entry.
\t "*text*"	Inserts the text in quotation marks instead of a page number (such as in "See" entries).

Glossary of Word's Menu Commands

Word for Windows 95 comes with a wealth of features reached with a variety of menu commands. Sure, many of your old friends are still there (such as File ➤ New and Tools ➤ Customize), but some of the shortcuts have changed. Hence this alphabetized list of menu commands, created especially for you by taking the program disks and banging a few nails into them.

> **NOTE** This list is alphabetical, meaning the commands do *not* appear in the same order here as they do on the menus, nor are the menus in the same order as they appear on your screen.

For each entry, the command is listed first, followed by the shortcut (if there is one) in parentheses, and then a brief description of what the command does. If a command appears only under particular circumstances, I'll point that out.

> **TIP** You can change any of Word's predefined shortcuts in the Customize dialog box (reached with Tools ➤ Customize).

Edit ➤ *AutoText*   Use to instruct Word to insert text automatically.

Edit ➤ *Bookmark*   (Ctrl+Shift+F5) Use to mark places in your document that you want to visit frequently.

Edit ➤ *Clear*   (Delete) Removes any text from highlighted cells.

Edit ➤ *Copy*   (Ctrl+C) Places a copy of the highlighted material in the Clipboard, leaving the original alone.

Edit ➤ *Cut*   (Ctrl+X) Removes the highlighted material, placing it in the Clipboard.

Edit ➤ *Find*   (Ctrl+F) Use to locate specific text strings, formatting, styles, or special characters.

Edit ➤ *Go To*   (Ctrl+G) Use to go to specific pages, sections, bookmarks, etc.

Edit ➤ *Links*   Use to make adjustments to the settings that link documents to one another.

Edit ➤ *Object*   Use to make adjustments to objects you have embedded in your Word document.

Edit ➤ *Paste*   (Ctrl+V) Places a copy of whatever material is contained in the Clipboard at the insertion point.

Edit ➤ *Paste Special*   Works the same as Edit ➤ Paste, but brings up a dialog box with a variety of Paste options (for instance, allows you to paste Excel spreadsheets or to paste the material without any formatting).

Edit ➤ *Repeat*   (Ctrl+Y) Instructs Word to perform the most recent command again. This has various functions, depending upon what you have just done.

Edit ➤ *Replace*   (Ctrl+H) Use to locate specific text strings (words, phrases, or other sequences of characters), formatting, styles, or special characters and replace them with other text strings, formatting, styles, or special characters (you can even replace material with the Clipboard contents).

Edit ➤ *Select All*   (Ctrl+A) Selects all text in your document.

Edit ➤ *Undo*   (Ctrl+Z) Undoes your most recent action. Like Edit ➤ Repeat, the precise function of this command will vary depending upon what you have just done.

File ➤ *Add Routing Slip*   Sends a document to reviewers to revise. After each reviewer makes comments, the document is sent on to the next individual on the routing list, eventually finding its way back to you.

File ➤ *Close*   (Ctrl+W) Closes the active document pane.

File ➤ *Exit*   (Alt+F4) Exits Word for Windows entirely.

File ➤ *New*   (Ctrl+N) Begins a new, untitled document.

File ➤ *Open*   (Ctrl+O) Opens a saved document from disk.

File ➤ *Page Setup*   Use to specify all aspects of your page's appearance, with respect to the printer (that is, margins, page orientation, page size, etc.).

File ➤ *Print*   (Ctrl+P) Use to print documents.

File ➤ *Print Preview*   (Ctrl+F2) Use to see how your documents will look before you actually print them.

File ➤ *Save*   (Ctrl+S) Saves your document to disk.

File ➤ *Save All*   Saves all open documents to disk.

File ➤ *Save As*   Allows you to save your document under a different name, format, etc.

File ➤ *Send*   Sends a message with an attached document.

File ➤ *Properties*   Use to learn, fill in, or change basic information about the document, such as the author's name. This information can be valuable when used with File ➤ Find File.

File ➤ *Templates*   Use to choose templates or add-ins.

Format ➤ *AutoFormat*   (Ctrl+K) Examines your document, looking for ways to improve the appearance of it. Will make certain formatting changes automatically.

Format ➤ *Borders and Shading*   Use to assign borders and shading to paragraph elements.

Format ➤ *Bullets and Numbering*   Use to create numbered or bulleted lists.

Format ➤ *Change Case*   (Shift+F3) Use to change the casing in the selected text (e.g., from ALL CAPS to Sentence casing, and so on).

Format ➤ *Columns*   Use to specify how many columns you wish and to fine-tune the amount of white space, among other things.

Format ➤ Drawing Object   Use to edit drawn objects you have inserted in your document.

Format ➤ Drop Cap   Use to automatically create drop caps.

Format ➤ Font   (Ctrl+D) Use to change the font, size, or letter style of the selected text.

Format ➤ Frame   Use to edit frames in your document.

Format ➤ Heading Numbering   Automates the number of headings for different parts of a document.

Format ➤ Paragraph   Use to apply formatting to paragraphs, including indents, tabs, space between paragraphs, and more.

Format ➤ Picture   Use to crop, size, and stylize pictures you have imported into your document.

Format ➤ Style   (Ctrl+Shift+S) Use to apply existing styles to text or to create new styles.

Format ➤ Style Gallery   Use to browse through the existing styles in Word's various templates and sample documents.

Format ➤ Tabs   Use to determine where tabs will go and what kind they will be. You can also assign tab leaders from here.

Help ➤ About Microsoft Word   Gives information about the version of Word you are using as well as bringing up information that will explain to you how to get technical support from Microsoft.

Help ➤ Answer Wizard   Allows you to search for help on specific topics. You can type in key words, and this command will help you find them.

Help ➤ The Microsoft Network   Assists you in connecting to forums on the Microsoft Network, where you can get help on specific topics that perhaps aren't covered in the depth you need in the Online Help.

Help ➤ *Microsoft Word Help Topics* (F1 or Shift+F1) Brings up a list of help topics, including What's New. You can also reach the help index with this command so you can quickly find the topic you are looking for.

Help ➤ *WordPerfect Help* Tells WordPerfect users how to do something in Word that they were used to doing differently in WordPerfect.

Insert ➤ *Annotation* (Alt+Ctrl+A) Use to place annotations in your documents.

Insert ➤ *Break* Use to insert various kinds of breaks (section, page, column, and so on).

Insert ➤ *Caption* Use to place a caption in your document.

Insert ➤ *Cross-reference* Use to place a cross-reference mark in your document, linking two or more parts. These are handy because they update automatically when you shift information about.

Insert ➤ *Database* Inserts information from a database into your document as a table.

Insert ➤ *Date and Time* (Alt+Shift+D, Alt+Shift+T) Use to place formatted date and time fields in your document. Using fields that update automatically can be a surefire way of keeping track of latest drafts and such.

Insert ➤ *Field* Use to place any of Word's hundreds of different types of fields. A field is not text itself, rather it is a code to Word to insert a specific kind of text or specific information.

Insert ➤ *File* Use to place an entire file within another file.

Insert ➤ *Footnote* (Alt+Ctrl+F: Footnote; Alt+Ctrl+E: Endnote) Use to place a footnote (or endnote) mark in your text. Word will automatically update the number sequence if you add or delete footnotes (or endnotes).

Insert ➤ *Form Field* Use to put fields (check boxes, etc.) in forms that you are creating.

Insert ➤ *Frame*   Use to place a frame in your document, where you can place text, graphics, etc., that you want to move around easily on the page. You also use this command to frame existing material.

Insert ➤ *Index and Tables*   (Alt+Shift+X: Mark Index Entry; Alt+Shift+O: Mark Table of Contents Entry) Use to mark material so Word knows to include it in the Table of Contents or Index.

Insert ➤ *Object*   Use to insert one of a large variety of objects (such as drawings, spreadsheets, or text files) in your document.

Insert ➤ *Page Numbers*   Use to specify exactly how your page numbers should look and where they should appear. You can also use this command to start page numbering anew in new sections.

Insert ➤ *Picture*   Use to place pictures *not* created in Word at the insert point.

Insert ➤ *Symbol*   Use to insert a variety of special characters (such as ☺, •, and so forth).

Last Four Files List (File Menu)   If this time-saving option is enabled (in the View tab of the Options dialog box), your last four files will appear at the bottom of the File menu. All you have to do to open one is choose its name.

Open Documents List (Window Menu)   This list shows all open documents. To make a different document active, select its name from the list.

Table ➤ *Cell Height and Width*   Use to adjust the height and width of individual cells in a table.

Table ➤ *Convert Text to Table*   Use to take regular text in your document and turn it into table form.

Table ➤ *Delete Cells*   Use to delete cells in a table.

Table ➤ *Formula*   Use to insert special formulas into tables (for example, formulas that will sum the values of specific cells).

Table* ➤ *Headings   Use to automate the creation of headings for the columns of the table.

Table* ➤ *Gridlines   Turns on and off the nonprinting lines that show on-screen.

Table* ➤ *Insert Cells* (*Table* ➤ *Insert Table*)   Use to insert rows or columns into a table. (Use to insert a new table.)

Table* ➤ *Merge Cells   Use to combine several cells into one.

Table* ➤ *Select Column   Use to select entire columns in tables.

Table* ➤ *Select Row   Use to select entire rows in tables.

Table* ➤ *Select Table   (Alt+5 on the keypad) Use to select an entire table.

Table* ➤ *Sort Text   Use to sort items in a table (alphanumerically).

Table* ➤ *Split Cells   Use to separate one cell into two or more cells.

Table* ➤ *Split Table   Breaks a table into more than one table.

Table* ➤ *Table AutoFormat   Gives a list of predefined formats and lets you preview the appearance of the table.

Tools* ➤ *AutoCorrect   Use this feature to instruct Word to always correct certain mistakes *as you go*. Use with caution, though, as this can be a double-edged sword!

Tools* ➤ *Customize   Allows you to personalize dozens of different aspects of Word's functionality. You can enable or disable features, determine what appears on-screen, and specify how or where files are to be saved, among many others. Mostly lets you change the contents of toolbars and menus (including keyboard shortcuts).

Tools* ➤ *Envelopes and Labels   Use to help automate the process of addressing envelopes or printing out sheets of labels.

Tools ➤ *Grammar*   Use to reach the Grammar checker, which can help you correct improper grammar and style in your documents.

Tools ➤ *Hyphenation*   Use to automate the hyphenation of your documents.

Tools ➤ *Language*   Use to specify which language defaults Word should use in its various document-polishing tools (the Grammar check, the Spelling checker, and so on).

Tools ➤ *Macro*   Use to access and create macros. Macros are automated series of commands. This feature is fairly advanced, but it can save you a lot of time.

Tools ➤ *Mail Merge*   Use to automate the process of creating lists of addresses for mass mailings.

Tools ➤ *Options*   Similar to Tools ➤ Customize, allows you to specify dozens of different aspects of Word's functionality. A collection of options for viewing, spelling, editing, printing, etc.

Tools ➤ *Protect Document*   Use to protect documents from being changed or even viewed. Several levels of protection are offered, including passwords.

Tools ➤ *Revisions*   Use to indicate where you've made changes on drafts of material.

Tools ➤ *Spelling*   (F7) Use the Spelling checker to ensure that you are using standard spelling in your documents.

Tools ➤ *Thesaurus*   (Shift+F7) Use Word's thesaurus to spice up your prose by finding alternative ways of saying the same thing.

Tools ➤ *Word Count*   Use to get an exact character, word, page, line, or paragraph count for your document.

View ➤ *Annotations*   Shows you all annotations in a document.

View ➤ *Footnotes*   Shows you all footnotes in a document.

View ➤ *Full Screen*   Removes all toolbars, rulers, and scroll bars, leaving just your text.

View ➤ *Header and Footer*   Shows you any headers or footers you have created in your document or allows you to create new ones.

View ➤ *Master Document*   Used when creating large documents, consisting of multiple subdocuments. Facilitates cross-referencing and the creation of an index and TOC.

View ➤ *Normal*   (Ctrl+Alt+N) Shows you your document in Normal view. This is the most simple view, showing formatting and special characters but not footers or headers, nor where items will print on the page.

View ➤ *Outline*   (Ctrl+Alt+O) Shows you your document in Outline view. This view is ideal for organizing large documents, as it allows you to quickly move around large blocks of text.

View ➤ *Page Layout*   (Ctrl+Alt+P) Shows you your document in Page Layout view. This is the most robust view, showing items exactly where they will print on the page, including margins and side-by-side columns. It is very slow, however.

View ➤ *Ruler*   Shows the rulers.

View ➤ *Toolbars*   Allows you to show or remove any of Word's eight toolbars on-screen.

View ➤ *Zoom*   Allows you to enlarge or shrink the document on-screen for better viewing. This will not change the actual printed *size* of the document.

Window ➤ *Arrange All*   Shows all open document windows so you can see them simultaneously.

Window ➤ *New Window*   Opens a new pane (windows) for the active document.

Window ➤ *Split*   (Ctrl+Alt+S) Divides the main window of the current document in two so you can scroll in separate parts of the document simultaneously or view different parts in different views.

Index

Note to the Reader: Main entries are in **bold**. **Boldfaced** numbers indicate pages where you will find the principal discussion of a topic or the definition of a term. *Italic* numbers indicate pages where topics are illustrated in figures.

COMPLETE AND EASY, FOR BEGINNERS AND UPGRADERS

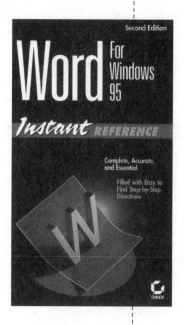

Here's the industry's most comprehensive instant reference guide to the latest version of Word. You'll find thorough, no-nonsense coverage of virtually every feature and function, presented in an easy-to-use alphabetical format. An excellent value for new and upgrading Word users alike.

352 pages
ISBN: 1766-X

SYBEX

COMPREHENSIVE, ORGANIZED, AND COMPLETE

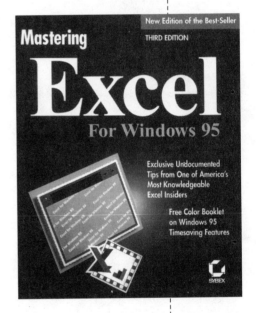

This completely revised edition reveals new and overlooked ways to reduce work, improve performance, and achieve better results. You'll find highlighted coverage of new features; new chapters on charting, pivot tables, and macros; loads of insider information; and a comprehensive function reference. Includes a pull-out color guide on Windows 95, revealing all the new time-saving features.

1,050 pages
ISBN: 1785-6

YOUR KEY
TO ACCESS DATABASES

Here's the updated, expanded new third edition of database guru Alan Simpson's best-selling guide to Access. Learn to use improved Form and Report Wizards, the integrated development environment, new menus and toolbars, Windows 95 Briefcase, drag and drop capabilities, and more. Includes a pull-out color guide on Windows 95, revealing all the new time-saving features. CD includes database examples described in the book.

1,200 pages
ISBN: 1764-3

FOR EVERY COMPUTER QUESTION,
THERE IS A SYBEX BOOK THAT HAS THE ANSWER

Each computer user learns in a different way. Some need thorough, methodical explanations, while others are too busy for details. At Sybex we bring nearly 20 years of experience to developing the book that's right for you. Whatever your needs, we can help you get the most from your software and hardware, at a pace that's comfortable for you.

We start beginners out right. You will learn by seeing and doing with our **Quick & Easy** series: friendly, colorful guidebooks with screen-by-screen illustrations. For hardware novices, the **Your First** series offers valuable purchasing advice and installation support.

Often recognized for excellence in national book reviews, our **Mastering** titles are designed for the intermediate to advanced user, without leaving the beginner behind. A **Mastering** book provides the most detailed reference available. Add our pocket-sized **Instant Reference** titles for a complete guidance system. Programmers will find that the new **Developer's Handbook** series provides a more advanced perspective on developing innovative and original code.

With the breathtaking advances common in computing today comes an ever increasing demand to remain technologically up-to-date. In many of our books, we provide the added value of software, on disks or CDs. Sybex remains your source for information on software development, operating systems, networking, and every kind of desktop application. We even have books for kids. Sybex can help smooth your travels on the **Internet** and provide **Strategies and Secrets** to your favorite computer games.

As you read this book, take note of its quality. Sybex publishes books written by experts—authors chosen for their extensive topical knowledge. In fact, many are professionals working in the computer soft-ware field. In addition, each manuscript is thoroughly reviewed by our technical, editorial, and production personnel for accuracy and ease-of-use before you ever see it—our guarantee that you'll buy a quality Sybex book every time.

To manage your hardware headaches and optimize your software potential, ask for a Sybex book.

FOR MORE INFORMATION, PLEASE CONTACT:

Sybex Inc.
2021 Challenger Drive
Alameda, CA 94501
Tel: (510) 523-8233 • (800) 227-2346
Fax: (510) 523-2373

SYBEX

Sybex is committed to using natural resources wisely to preserve and improve our environment. As a leader in the computer books publishing industry, we are aware that over 40% of America's solid waste is paper. This is why we have been printing our books on recycled paper since 1982.

This year our use of recycled paper will result in the saving of more than 153,000 trees. We will lower air pollution effluents by 54,000 pounds, save 6,300,000 gallons of water, and reduce landfill by 27,000 cubic yards.

In choosing a Sybex book you are not only making a choice for the best in skills and information, you are also choosing to enhance the quality of life for all of us.

[1767-8] Mastering Word for Windows 95

GET A FREE CATALOG JUST FOR EXPRESSING YOUR OPINION.

Help us improve our books and get a **FREE** full-color catalog in the bargain. Please complete this form, pull out this page and send it in today. The address is on the reverse side.

Name _____ **Company** _____

Address _____ **City** _____ **State** ___ **Zip** _____

Phone (   ) _____

1. How would you rate the overall quality of this book?

❑ Excellent
❑ Very Good
❑ Good
❑ Fair
❑ Below Average
❑ Poor

2. What were the things you liked most about the book? (Check all that apply)

❑ Pace
❑ Format
❑ Writing Style
❑ Examples
❑ Table of Contents
❑ Index
❑ Price
❑ Illustrations
❑ Type Style
❑ Cover
❑ Depth of Coverage
❑ Fast Track Notes

3. What were the things you liked *least* about the book? (Check all that apply)

❑ Pace
❑ Format
❑ Writing Style
❑ Examples
❑ Table of Contents
❑ Index
❑ Price
❑ Illustrations
❑ Type Style
❑ Cover
❑ Depth of Coverage
❑ Fast Track Notes

4. Where did you buy this book?

❑ Bookstore chain
❑ Small independent bookstore
❑ Computer store
❑ Wholesale club
❑ College bookstore
❑ Technical bookstore
❑ Other _____

5. How did you decide to buy this particular book?

❑ Recommended by friend
❑ Recommended by store personnel
❑ Author's reputation
❑ Sybex's reputation
❑ Read book review in _____
❑ Other _____

6. How did you pay for this book?

❑ Used own funds
❑ Reimbursed by company
❑ Received book as a gift

7. What is your level of experience with the subject covered in this book?

❑ Beginner
❑ Intermediate
❑ Advanced

8. How long have you been using a computer?

years _____
months _____

9. Where do you most often use your computer?

❑ Home
❑ Work

❑ Both
❑ Other _____

10. What kind of computer equipment do you have? (Check all that apply)

❑ PC Compatible Desktop Computer
❑ PC Compatible Laptop Computer
❑ Apple/Mac Computer
❑ Apple/Mac Laptop Computer
❑ CD ROM
❑ Fax Modem
❑ Data Modem
❑ Scanner
❑ Sound Card
❑ Other _____

11. What other kinds of software packages do you ordinarily use?

❑ Accounting
❑ Databases
❑ Networks
❑ Apple/Mac
❑ Desktop Publishing
❑ Spreadsheets
❑ CAD
❑ Games
❑ Word Processing
❑ Communications
❑ Money Management
❑ Other _____

12. What operating systems do you ordinarily use?

❑ DOS
❑ OS/2
❑ Windows
❑ Apple/Mac
❑ Windows NT
❑ Other _____

13. On what computer-related subject(s) would you like to see more books?

_____

_____

_____

_____

14. Do you have any other comments about this book? (Please feel free to use a separate piece of paper if you need more room)

_____

_____

_____

_____

- - - - - - - - - - - - - PLEASE FOLD, SEAL, AND MAIL TO SYBEX - - - - - - - - - - - -

SYBEX INC.
Department M
2021 Challenger Drive
Alameda, CA
94501

Double-Clicking on Word's Hotspots

Opens Page Setup dialog box

Opens Indent and Spacing tab in Paragraph dialog box

Opens headers or footers

Allows you to edit drawings

Toggles split window

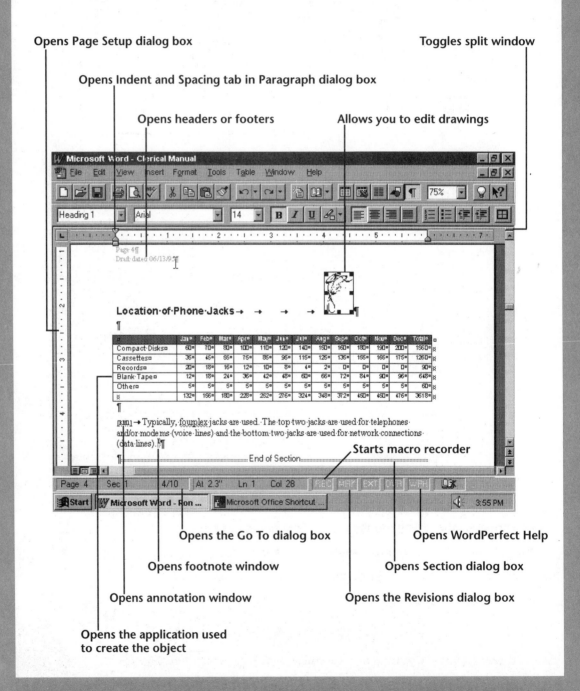

Starts macro recorder

Opens the Go To dialog box

Opens WordPerfect Help

Opens footnote window

Opens Section dialog box

Opens annotation window

Opens the Revisions dialog box

Opens the application used to create the object